■ Debating Christian Th

Debating
Christian Theism

EDITED BY

J. P. Moreland,
Chad Meister,

AND

Khaldoun A. Sweis

OXFORD
UNIVERSITY PRESS

OXFORD
UNIVERSITY PRESS

Oxford University Press is a department of the University of Oxford.
It furthers the University's objective of excellence in research, scholarship,
and education by publishing worldwide.

Oxford   New York
Auckland   Cape Town   Dar es Salaam   Hong Kong   Karachi
Kuala Lumpur   Madrid   Melbourne   Mexico City   Nairobi
New Delhi   Shanghai   Taipei   Toronto

With offices in
Argentina   Austria   Brazil   Chile   Czech Republic   France   Greece
Guatemala   Hungary   Italy   Japan   Poland   Portugal   Singapore
South Korea   Switzerland   Thailand   Turkey   Ukraine   Vietnam

Oxford is a registered trademark of Oxford University Press in the UK and certain other
countries.

Published in the United States of America by
Oxford University Press
198 Madison Avenue, New York, NY 10016

Library of Congress Cataloging-in-Publication Data
Debating Christian theism / edited by J.P Moreland, Chad Meister, and Khaldoun Sweis.
    pages cm
Includes index.
    ISBN 978–0–19–975543–1 (pbk. : alk. paper) — ISBN 978–0–19–975544–8 (alk. paper) —
ISBN 978–0–19–998143–4 (ebook)   1. Theology, Doctrinal.   2. Apologetics.   3. Theism.
4. God—Proof.   I. Moreland, James Porter, 1948 – editor of compilation.
    BT75.3.D43 2013
    230—dc23
    2013003700

CONTENTS

Louise Antony is professor of philosophy at the University of Massachusetts Amherst. She is the author of many articles on topics in epistemology, philosophy of the mind, philosophy of language, philosophy of religion, and feminist theory. She is the editor of and a contributor to *Philosophers Without Gods: Meditations on Atheism and the Secular Life*. She is the coeditor (with Charlotte Witt) of *A Mind of One's Own: Feminist Essays on Reason and Objectivity* and (with Norbert Hornstein) of *Chomsky and His Critics*.

Julian Baggini is the author of several books, including *Welcome to Everytown: A Journey into the English Mind*; *Complaint*; *Atheism: A Very Short Introduction*; and *The Ego Trick*. His PhD was awarded by University College London for his thesis on personal identity. He is the cofounder of *The Philosophers' Magazine* (http://www.philosophersmag.com). He has also appeared as a cameo character in two Alexander McCall-Smith novels. His website is http://www.julianbaggini.com.

Marcus Borg is Canon Theologian at Trinity Episcopal Cathedral in Portland, Oregon; Hundere Chair of Religion and Culture Emeritus at Oregon State University; past president of the Anglican Association of Biblical Scholars; and author of twenty books, including the best-sellers *Meeting Jesus Again for the First Time*, *The Heart of Christianity*, *Reading the Bible Again for the First Time*, *Speaking Christian*, and most recently *The Evolution of the Word* (a chronological New New Testament). His books have been translated into eleven languages.

Joseph Bulbulia teaches in the Religious Studies Programme at Victoria University of Wellington, New Zealand. He is president elect of the International Association for the Cognitive Science of Religion (http://www.iacsr.com). He is a Distinguished International Fellow of the Religion Cognition and Culture Unit at Aarhus University in Denmark (http://teo.au.dk/en/research/current/cognition/), and is a principle investigator at LEVYNA, the world's first experimental laboratory in the study of religion (http://www.levyna.cz). He has authored or coauthored more than fifty peer-reviewed publications on the evolutionary study of religion.

Robin Collins is distinguished research professor of philosophy and chair of the Department of Philosophy at Messiah College in Mechanicsburg, Pennsylvania. He has written more than thirty-five articles and book chapters on a wide range of topics in philosophy of physics, philosophy of religion, and philosophy of mind. He has become most well-known for the argument for theism based on the fine-tuning of the cosmos for life. He is currently finishing two books on the topic: one that carefully explicates the physics and cosmology behind claims of cosmic fine-tuning and one that carefully works through the potential philosophical and theological implications of the fine-tuning evidence.

Paul Copan is Pledger Family Chair of Philosophy and Ethics at Palm Beach Atlantic University. He has authored and edited more than twenty books, including (with Paul K. Moser) *The Rationality of Theism*, (with Chad Meister) *Philosophy of Religion: Classic and Contemporary Issues*, and (with Mark Linville) *The Moral Argument*. He has coauthored (with William Lane Craig) *Creation Out of Nothing: A Biblical, Philosophical, and Scientific Exploration*, and he has contributed essays to a number of edited books and professional journals.

Kevin Corcoran is professor of philosophy at Calvin College in Grand Rapids, Michigan. Named by *Princeton Review* as one of "the best 300 professors," he has authored or edited *Soul, Body and Survival*; *Rethinking Human Nature*; and *Church in the Present Tense*, in addition to authoring many articles for scholarly journals and edited volumes.

William Lane Craig is a research professor of philosophy at Talbot School of Theology in La Mirada, California. He has authored or edited more than thirty books, including *The Kalam Cosmological Argument*; *Divine Foreknowledge and Human Freedom*; *Theism, Atheism, and Big Bang Cosmology*; and *God, Time, and Eternity*, as well as more than a hundred articles in professional journals of philosophy and theology, including *The Journal of Philosophy, American Philosophical Quarterly, Philosophical Studies, Philosophy,* and *British Journal for Philosophy of Science*.

James Crossley is professor of Bible, culture and politics at the University of Sheffield. He is author of numerous books and articles on Christian origins and the reception of biblical texts in contemporary culture. His recent publications include *Jesus in an Age of Terror* (2008), *New Testament and Jewish Law: Guide for the Perplexed* (2010), and *Jesus in an Age of Neoliberalism: Quests, Scholarship and Ideology* (2012). He is currently working on ways of redirecting the quest for the historical Jesus.

Stephen T. Davis is Russell K. Pitzer Professor of Philosophy at Claremont McKenna College in Claremont, California. He has written more than seventy academic articles and written or edited some fifteen books, including *God, Reason, and Theistic Proofs* (1997), *Encountering Evil: Live Options in Theodicy* (2001), *Christian Philosophical Theology* (2006), and *Disputed Issues: Contending for Christian Faith in Today's Academic Setting* (2009).

Craig A. Evans is Payzant Distinguished Professor of the New Testament at Acadia University in Wolfville, Nova Scotia, Canada. He has authored and edited more than sixty books, including *Jesus and His Contemporaries, Ancient Texts for*

New Testament Studies, and *Jesus and His World: The Archaeological Evidence*. He coauthored with Tom Wright *Jesus, the Final Days*. He has contributed many essays to scholarly journals and books and for many years served as editor of the *Bulletin for Biblical Research*.

Nicholas Everitt is currently a Senior Honorary Fellow at the University of East Anglia, having retired as a senior lecturer in philosophy. He is the author of *The Non-Existence of God* and (with Alec Fisher) *Modern Epistemology*. He has published a number of articles in *Mind, Analysis, Kant-Studien, Faith and Philosophy, Religious Studies*, and *Philosophical Quarterly*, covering topics in the philosophy of religion, philosophy of the mind, epistemology, and moral philosophy.

Evan Fales is associate professor of philosophy at the University of Iowa in Iowa City, Iowa. His most recent book is *Divine Intervention: Metaphysical and Epistemological Puzzles*. In the area of philosophy of religion, he has published on such topics as science and religion, mystical experience as evidence, reformed epistemology, God and free will, and divine command ethics. He has also contributed essays to anthologies on a variety of topics in the philosophy of religion.

Richard M. Gale is professor emeritus of philosophy at the University of Pittsburgh. He is the author of *The Language of Time, Problems of Negation and Nonbeing, On the Nature and Existence of God, The Divided Self of William James, God and Metaphysics*, and *John Dewey's Quest for Unity*.

Jerome Gellman is professor emeritus of philosophy, Ben-Gurion University, Beersheva, Israel. He has published more than 100 articles in philosophy and Jewish thought. He has published five books, the latest of which is *For God's Love Has Overwhelmed Us—A Theology of the Jews as the Chosen People for the Twenty-First Century*. He edits a series *Philosophy of Religion – World Religions*.

Stewart Goetz is the Ross Frederick Wicks Distinguished Professor in Philosophy and Religion at Ursinus College in Collegeville, Pennsylvania. He has written extensively on the freedom of choice and the nature of the self. His books include *Naturalism* (coauthored with Charles Taliaferro, 2008); *Freedom, Teleology, and Evil* (2008); *The Soul Hypothesis* (coedited with Mark Baker, 2011); *A Brief History of the Soul* (coauthored with Charles Taliaferro, 2011); *The Purpose of Life: A Theistic Perspective* (2012); and *The Routledge Companion to Theism* (coedited with Charles Taliaferro and Victoria Harrison, 2012).

Patrick Grim is distinguished teaching professor of philosophy at the State University of New York at Stony Brook. He has published numerous articles and books, including *The Incomplete Universe: Totality, Knowledge, and Truth; The Philosophical Computer: Exploratory Essays in Philosophical Computer Modeling;* and *Mind and Consciousness: 5 Questions*. He is the founder and coeditor of twenty-five volumes of *The Philosopher's Annual*.

Gary Habermas is distinguished research professor and chair of the Department of Philosophy at Liberty University in Lynchburg, Virginia. He has published almost forty books, eighteen on the subject of Jesus' resurrection. Other topics include near-death experiences, religious doubt, and personal suffering. He has also contributed more than sixty-five chapters or articles to other books, plus more than 100 articles and reviews to journals and other publications. He has been a visiting or adjunct professor at fifteen different graduate schools and seminaries in the United States and abroad.

John Hick was emeritus professor of both University of Birmingham (UK) and the Claremont Graduate University, Claremont, California. He was a fellow of the Institute for Advanced Research in Arts and Social Sciences, University of Birmingham, and a vice president of the British Society for the Philosophy of Religion and of the World Congress of Faiths. He has published more than twenty books, including *The Myth of God Incarnate*, *The Metaphor of God Incarnate*, *The Myth of Christian Uniqueness*, *An Interpretation of Religion: Human Responses to the Transcendent*, and *Evil and the God of Love*.

Paul F. Knitter is the Paul Tillich Professor of Theology, World Religions, and Culture at Union Theological Seminary in New York City. Most of his publications have dealt with understanding and engaging religious diversity. Among the most notable are *No Other Name? A Critical Survey of Christian Attitudes Toward World Religion*, *The Myth of Christian Uniqueness: Toward a Pluralistic Theology of Religions* (edited with John Hick), *Jesus and the Other Names: Christian Mission and Global Responsibility*, *Introducing Theologies of Religions*, *The Myth of Religious Superiority: A Multifaith Exploration* (edited with John Hick), and *Without Buddha I Could Not Be a Christian*.

E. J. Lowe is professor of philosophy at Durham University (UK). He specializes in metaphysics, the philosophy of logic and language, the philosophy of the mind and action, and early modern philosophy. His books include *Kinds of Being: A Study of Individuation, Identity, and the Logic of Sortal Terms*; *Subjects of Experience*; *The Possibility of Metaphysics: Substance, Identity, and Time*; *A Survey of Metaphysics*; *Personal Agency: The Metaphysics of Mind and Action*; *More Kinds of Being: A Further Study of Individuation, Identity, and the Logic of Sortal Terms*; and *Forms of Thought: A Study in Philosophical Logic*.

Michael Martin received a PhD from Harvard University and presently is professor of philosophy emeritus at Boston University. His books include *Atheism: A Philosophical Justification*; *The Case Against Christianity*; *Atheism, Morality and Meaning*; *The Cambridge Companion to Atheism*; *The Impossibility of God* (with Ricki Monnier); and *The Improbability of God* (with Ricki Monnier).

Chad Meister is professor of philosophy at Bethel College in Mishawaka, Indiana. His publications include *Evil: A Guide for the Perplexed*; *Introducing Philosophy* *of Religion, God and Evil* (with James K. Dew); *The Oxford Handbook of Religious Diversity*; and (with Charles Taliaferro) *The Cambridge Companion to Christian Philosophical Theology*. He is general coeditor (with Paul Moser) of *Cambridge Studies in Religion, Philosophy, and Society* and (with Charles Taliaferro) of the forthcoming six-volume set, *The History of Evil*.

J. P. Moreland is distinguished professor of philosophy at Biola University in La Mirada, California. He has authored, edited, or contributed to thirty-five books, including *Does God Exist?*, *Philosophy of Religion: Selected Readings*, *Naturalism: A Critical Analysis*, *Universals*, and *Consciousness and the Existence of God*. He has also published more than eighty articles in professional journals, including *American Philosophical Quarterly*, *Australasian Journal of Philosophy*, *MetaPhilosophy*, *Philosophy and Phenomenological Research*, *Religious Studies*, and *Faith and Philosophy*.

Wes Morriston is professor of philosophy at the University of Colorado Boulder, where he has taught since 1972. During that period he has received several teaching prizes and has authored numerous scholarly articles in the philosophy of religion.

Paul K. Moser is professor of philosophy at Loyola University, in Chicago, Illinois. He is the author of *The Severity of God: Religion & Philosophy Reconceived*, *The Evidence for God: Religious Knowledge Reexamined*, and *The Elusive God: Reorienting Religious Epistemology*. He is also editor of *Jesus and Philosophy*, general editor of the book series *Oxford Handbooks of Philosophy*, editor of the journal *American Philosophical Quarterly*, and coeditor (with Chad Meister) of *Cambridge Studies in Religion, Philosophy, and Society*.

Michael Murray is a senior visiting scholar in philosophy at Franklin and Marshall College in Lancaster, Pennsylvania. In addition to a variety of articles in the history of philosophy and the philosophy of religion, he has recently authored or edited *Philosophy of Religion* (with Michael Rea); *Nature Red in Tooth and Claw: Theism and the Problem of Animal Suffering*; *The Believing Primate: Scientific, Philosophical, and Theological Reflections on the Origin of Religion* (with Jeffrey Schloss); and *On Predestination and Election* and *Divine Evil?* (with Michael Rea and Michael Bergmann).

Harold Netland is professor of philosophy of religion and intercultural studies at Trinity Evangelical Divinity School in Deerfield, Illinois. Among his publications are *Dissonant Voices: Religious Pluralism and the Question of Truth*; *Encountering Religious Pluralism*; and (with Keith Yandell) *Buddhism: A Christian Exploration and Appraisal*.

Graham Oppy is professor of philosophy and head of the School of Philosophical, Historical and International Studies at Monash University in Melbourne,

Australia. He is the author of *Ontological Arguments and Belief in God* (1996), *Arguing about Gods* (2006), *Philosophical Perspectives on Infinity* (2006), and (with Michael Scott) *Reading Philosophy of Religion* (2009). He is also editor (with Nick Trakakis) of *The History of Western Philosophy of Religion* (2008, 5 vols.), *A Companion to Philosophy in Australia and New Zealand* (2009), and *The Antipodean Philosopher* (2010 and 2011, 2 vols.).

Keith M. Parsons is professor of philosophy at the University of Houston–Clear Lake, in Houston, Texas, where he has won awards both for research and for teaching. He has published in the fields of the philosophy of science, the history of science, and the philosophy of religion. His books include *Drawing Out Leviathan: Dinosaurs and the Science Wars, Copernican Questions: A Concise Invitation to the Philosophy of Science,* and *God and the Burden of Proof.* He was the founding editor of the philosophical journal *Philo* and has participated in numerous scholarly forums, workshops, and debates.

Stephen J. Patterson is the George W. Atkinson Professor of Religious and Ethical Studies at Willamette University in Salem, Oregon. He is the author of several books, including *The God of Jesus: The Historical Jesus and the Search for Meaning* and *Beyond the Passion: Rethinking the Death and Life of Jesus.*

Katherin Rogers is professor of philosophy in the Philosophy Department at the University of Delaware in Newark, Delaware. Her books include *Perfect Being Theology* and *Anselm on Freedom.* She has published articles in collections and in professional journals including *Faith and Philosophy* and *Religious Studies.*

Jeffrey Schloss is professor of philosophy at Westmont College in Santa Barbara, California. He has published numerous articles and books, the latter including *The Believing Primate: Scientific, Philosophical, and Theological Perspectives on the Origin of Religion* (with Michael Murray); *Evolution and Ethics: Human Morality in Biological and Religious Perspective*; and *Altruism and Altruistic Love: Science, Philosophy, and Religion in Dialogue.*

Thomas D. Senor is professor of philosophy and chair of the Philosophy Department at the University of Arkansas in Fayetteville, Arkansas. He is the editor of *The Rationality of Belief and the Plurality of Faith,* and has published articles on epistemology, philosophy of religion, political philosophy, and philosophy of mind. He has served on the executive committee of the Society of Christian Philosophers and on the editorial boards of *Religious Studies* and *European Journal for Philosophy of Religion.*

Victor J. Stenger is adjunct professor of philosophy at the University of Colorado and emeritus professor of physics at the University of Hawaii. His is a retired elementary particle physicist and author of eleven books, including *God: The Failed Hypothesis: How Science Shows That God Does Not Exist, The Fallacy* *of Fine-Tuning: Why the Universe Is Not Designed for Us,* and *God and the Folly of Faith: The Fundamental Incompatibility of Science and Religion.*

Richard Swinburne is emeritus professor of the philosophy of religion at the University of Oxford and a fellow of the British Academy. He is the author of some fifteen books on philosophy of religion and various other areas of philosophy. He is best known for his defense of arguments of natural theology from the general features of the universe to the existence of God, especially in his book *The Existence of God* (2nd ed., 2004) and the shorter version *Is there a God?* (rev. ed., 2010). His new book *Mind, Brain, and Free Will* will be published early in 2013.

Charles Taliaferro is professor of philosophy at St. Olaf College in Northfield, Minnesota. He is the author, coauthor, editor, or coeditor of twenty books, most recently *The Image in Mind: Theism, Naturalism and the Imagination,* coauthored with Jil Evans. With Stewart Goetz he is the coauthor of *A Brief History of the Soul* and coeditor of *The Routledge Companion to Theism.* He has been a visiting scholar at Oxford, Princeton, New York University, and Columbia, and he is the philosophy of religion area editor for *Blackwell's Philosophy Compass* and the book review editor for *Faith and Philosophy.*

Jerry L. Walls is professor of philosophy at Houston Baptist University in Houston, Texas. Among his books is a recently completed trilogy on the afterlife: *Hell: The Logic of Damnation* (1992); *Heaven: The Logic of Eternal Joy* (2002); and *Purgatory: The Logic of Total Transformation* (2012). He is also the editor of *The Oxford Handbook of Eschatology* (2008) and the coauthor, with David Baggett, of *Good God: The Theistic Foundations of Morality* (2011).

Keith Ward is a professorial research fellow at Heythrop College, London, and Regius Professor Emeritus of Divinity at the University of Oxford. He is a fellow of the British Academy and author of a number of books, including a five-volume comparative and systematic theology, and several books on science and religion, Christian theology, and philosophy of religion.

Tim Winter is university lecturer in Islamic Studies in the Faculty of Divinity, University of Cambridge, and dean of the Cambridge Muslim College. In addition to articles on Ottoman religion and Muslim–Christian relations, he has published translations of medieval Arabic texts and is editor of the *Cambridge Companion to Classical Islamic Theology.*

■ Debating Christian Theism

Introduction

Since the arid days of Logical Positivism from the 1920s to the 1950s, philosophy has given rise to a rich and fertile landscape of traditional topics in the discipline, including the restoration of metaphysics to central philosophical prominence. And since the late 1970s, there has been a renewed interest in philosophy of religion, with a growing number of scholars defending historical Christian ideas. Around the same time, many in the field of biblical studies took a decidedly conservative turn, with more and more researchers taking the New Testament documents, for example, as historically serious sources about the life, teachings, deeds, and resurrection of Jesus of Nazareth and the early Christian movement that followed. The result of these trends is that an intellectually robust articulation and defense of historic Christianity has returned to the academy. This return has been noticed by those who are not sanguine about it. In a recent article in the journal *Philo* (an academic journal that examines philosophical issues from an explicitly naturalist perspective), Quentin Smith laments what he calls "the desecularization of academia that evolved in philosophy departments since the late 1960s." He bemoans,

> Naturalists passively watched as realist versions of theism ... began to sweep through the philosophical community, until today perhaps one-quarter or one-third of philosophy professors are theists, with most being orthodox Christians ... in philosophy, it became, almost overnight, "academically respectable" to argue for theism, making philosophy a favored field of entry for the most intelligent and talented theists entering academia today.[1]

Smith then concludes, "God is not 'dead' in academia; he returned to life in the late 1960s and is now alive and well in his last academic stronghold, philosophy departments."[2] Smith's point could be made with equal weight with regard to New Testament studies.

Critics of Christianity have not sat by idly while all this was occurring. In fact, from popular writings to more scholarly treatments, a new wave of objections has been raised against Christianity. For example, in recent years, a small but vocal and growing number of intellectual atheists have spawned a movement dubbed the "New Atheism." These atheists promulgate protracted and polemical responses to theism, and they are not modest in their agenda or approach. Richard Dawkins, for example, boldly proclaims: "I am attacking God, all gods, anything and everything supernatural, wherever and whenever they have been or will be invented."[3] In a similar vein, French atheist philosopher Michel Onfray claims that atheism is facing a "final battle" against "theological hocus-pocus" and must organize and rally its troops.[4] Their vehemence may* perhaps best be explained as an exasperated reaction to the theistic revival. Nevertheless, Christian theism is proving to be exceedingly resilient.

Unfortunately, until now the debate about the pros and cons of historic Christianity has been scattered throughout professional journals and technical monographs. In our view, this situation needed correcting, so in this book we have gathered an internationally respected team of thinkers to dialogue about twenty key topics at the center of the debate. These topics were selected after much consultation with scholars throughout the relevant fields, and we have invited the best representatives we could find to address each topic. Our method of approach was to select each topic, secure experts for and against a Christian view of the issue, and commission a pro and con essay on the subject. The contributors were free to write on whatever they thought was important. More specifically, each contributor wrote his or her chapter without having access to the contribution of his or her interlocutor. So, even though each writer did not respond directly to the opposing chapter, there is usually some interaction with the previously proffered treatments of a topic by one's dialogue partner. The advantage of this approach is that, while interaction does take place, each topic has two contributions—one positive, one negative—that are fresh, independent, and up to date. Each writer was invited to say whatever she or he thought needed to be said about the subject at hand.

We, the editors, offer you, then, a high-level, fair, and balanced treatment of twenty topics of central importance to the truth and rationality of historic Christianity. Our hope is that you will find this work helpful and stimulating, and we also hope it will serve to foster even more dialogue about the important topics within the book's purview.

■ NOTES

1. Quentin Smith, "The Metaphilosophy of Naturalism," *Philo* 4, no. 2 (2001): 3–4. A sign of the times—*Philo* itself, unable to succeed as a secular organ, has now become a journal for general philosophy of religion.

2. Smith, "The Metaphilosophy of Naturalism," 4.

3. Richard Dawkins, *The God Delusion* (New York: Houghton Mifflin, 2006), 36.

4. *Wall Street Journal*, "As Religious Strife Grows, Europe's Atheists Seize Pulpit," April 12, 2007.

PART I

Debates About God's Existence

A Cosmological Argument

1 The Kalam Argument

■ WILLIAM LANE CRAIG

The *kalam* cosmological argument for a Creator of the universe traces its roots to the efforts of early Christian theologians to rebut the Aristotelian doctrine of the eternity of the universe. In light of the substantive contribution made by its medieval Muslim proponents, I use the word *kalam* (the Arabic word used to designate medieval Islamic theology) to denominate this version of the cosmological argument.

The argument has enjoyed a resurgence of interest in recent decades. Noting the widespread debate over the argument today, Quentin Smith observes, "The fact that theists and atheists alike 'cannot leave [the] Kalam argument alone' suggests that it may be an argument of unusual philosophical interest or else has an attractive core of plausibility that keeps philosophers turning back to it and examining it once again."[1]

Taking the existence of the universe (where "universe" refers to contiguous space–time and its contents) as given, we ask three consecutive questions, which present us with mutually exclusive and exhaustive alternatives.

1. FIRST QUESTION

First, did the universe begin to exist?

Universe

↙ ↘

beginning   beginningless

There are intriguing reasons, both philosophical and scientific, for thinking that the universe did, in fact, have a beginning.

1.1 First philosophical argument

One argument for the finitude of the past is based upon the impossibility of the existence of an actually infinite number of things. It may be formulated as follows:

1. An actual infinite cannot exist.
2. An infinite temporal regress of events is an actual infinite.
3. Therefore an infinite temporal regress of events cannot exist.

In order to assess this argument, we need to have a clear understanding of its key terms. First and foremost among these is "actual infinite." Aristotle argued that no actually infinite magnitude can exist (*Physics* 3.5.204b1–206a8). The only legitimate sense in which one can speak of the infinite is in terms of potentiality: something may be infinitely divisible or susceptible to infinite addition, but this type of infinity is potential only and can never be fully actualized (*Physics* 8.8. 263a4–263b3). The concept of a potential infinite is a dynamic notion, and so we must say that the potential infinite is an indefinite collection that is at any particular time finite. The nineteenth-century German mathematician Georg Cantor called the potential infinite a "variable finite" and attached the sign ∞ (called a lemniscate) to it; this signified that it was an "improper infinite." The actual infinite he pronounced the "true infinite" and assigned the symbol $\aleph_0$ (aleph zero) to it. This represented the number of all the numbers in the series $1, 2, 3 \ldots$ and was the first infinite or transfinite number, coming after all the finite numbers.

Modern set theory, as a legacy of Cantor, is exclusively concerned with the actual as opposed to the potential infinite. An infinite set in Zermelo–Fraenkel axiomatic set theory is defined as any set R that has a proper subset that is equivalent to R.[2] The crucial difference between an infinite set and an indefinite collection is that the former is conceived as a determinate whole actually possessing an infinite number of members, while the latter never actually attains infinity, though it increases perpetually.

Second, by the word *exist* I mean "be instantiated in the mind-independent world." We are inquiring whether there are extratheoretical correlates to the terms used in our mathematical theories. I thereby hope to differentiate the sense in which existence is denied to the actual infinite from what is often called "mathematical existence." Kasner and Newman strongly distinguish the two when they assert, "'Existence' in the mathematical sense is wholly different from the existence of objects in the physical world."[3] "Mathematical existence" is frequently understood as roughly synonymous with "mathematical legitimacy." Now a commitment to the mathematical legitimacy of some notion does not entail a commitment to the existence of the relevant entity in the nonmathematical sense. When Kasner and Newman say, "the infinite certainly does not exist in the same sense that we say, 'there are fish in the sea,'"[4] *that* is the sense of existence that is at issue here.

Third, the above remarks also make clear that when it is alleged that an actual infinite "cannot" exist, the modality at issue is not strict logical possibility. Otherwise the presumed strict logical consistency of axiomatic set theory would be enough to guarantee that the existence of an actual infinite is possible. Rather, what is at issue here is so-called metaphysical possibility, which has to do with something's being actualizable.

Finally, by an "event" I mean any change. Since any change takes time, there are no instantaneous events so defined. Neither could there be an infinitely slow event, since such an "event" would in reality be a changeless state. Therefore any event will have a finite, nonzero duration. In order that all the events comprised by the temporal regress of past events be of equal duration, one arbitrarily stipulates some event as our standard and, taking as our point of departure the present standard event, we consider any consecutive series of such standard events ordered according to the relation *earlier than*. The question is whether this series of events comprises an actually infinite number of events or not. If not, then since the universe cannot ever have existed in an absolutely quiescent state, the universe must have had a beginning. It is therefore not relevant whether the temporal series had a beginning *point* (a first temporal instant). The question is whether there was in the past an event occupying a nonzero, finite temporal interval that was absolutely first, that is, not preceded by any equal interval.

Premise 1 asserts that an actual infinite cannot exist in the real world. It is frequently alleged that this sort of claim has been falsified by Cantor's work on the actual infinite and by subsequent developments in set theory, which provide a convincing demonstration of the existence of actual infinites. But this allegation is far too hasty. It not only begs the question against (i) denials of the mathematical legitimacy of the actual infinite on the part of certain mathematicians (such as intuitionists), but, more seriously, it begs the question against (ii) antirealist views of mathematical objects. Most antirealists would not go to the intuitionistic extreme of denying mathematical legitimacy to the actual infinite; rather, they would simply insist that acceptance of the mathematical legitimacy of certain notions does not imply an ontological commitment to the reality of various objects. Cantor's system and axiomatized set theory may be taken to be simply a universe of discourse, a mathematical system based on certain adopted axioms and conventions, which carries no ontological commitments. In view of the plethora of alternatives to realism (e.g., fictionalism, conceptualism, modal structuralism, constructibilism, logical neutralism, etc.), one cannot justifiably simply assume that the language of mathematics commits us ontologically to mind-independent entities, especially to such obscure objects as sets. The realist, then, if he is to maintain that mathematical objects furnish a decisive counterexample to premise 1, must provide some overriding argument for the reality of mathematical objects, as well as rebutting defeaters of all the alternatives consistent with classical mathematics—a task whose prospects for success are dim, indeed. One may hold that while the actual infinite is a fruitful and consistent concept within the postulated universe of discourse, it cannot be transposed into the real world.

The best way to support premise 1 is by way of thought experiments that illustrate the various absurdities that would result if an actual infinite were to be instantiated in the real world. Benardete, who is especially creative and effective at concocting such thought experiments, puts it well: "Viewed *in abstracto*, there is no logical contradiction involved in any of these enormities; but we have only to confront them *in concreto* for their outrageous absurdity to strike us full in the face."[5]

Let us look at just one example: David Hilbert's famous brainchild "Hilbert's Hotel."[6] Hilbert invites us imagine a hotel with an infinite number of rooms and to suppose that *all the rooms are occupied.* There is not a single vacant room throughout the entire infinite hotel. Now suppose a new guest shows up, asking for a room. "But of course!" says the proprietor, and he immediately shifts the person in room 1 into room 2, the person in room 2 into room 3, the person in room 3 into room 4, and so on, out to infinity. As a result, room 1 now becomes vacant, and the new guest gratefully checks in. But remember, before he arrived, all the rooms were already occupied!

But the situation becomes even stranger. For suppose an infinity of new guests shows up at the desk, each asking for a room. "Of course, of course!" says the proprietor, and he proceeds to shift the person in room 1 into room 2, the person in room 2 into room 4, the person in room 3 into room 6, and so on out to infinity, always putting each former occupant into the room with a number twice his own. Because any natural number multiplied by two always equals an even number, all the guests wind up in even-numbered rooms. As a result, all the odd-numbered rooms become vacant, and the infinity of new guests is easily accommodated. And yet, before they came, all the rooms were already occupied! In fact, the proprietor could repeat this process *infinitely many times* and could always accommodate new guests.

But Hilbert's Hotel is even stranger than the great mathematician made it out to be. For suppose some of the guests start to check out. Suppose the guests in rooms 1, 3, 5,... check out. In this case an infinite number of people have left the hotel, but there are no fewer people in the hotel. In fact, we could have every other guest check out of the hotel and repeat this process infinitely many times, and yet there would never be any fewer people in the hotel.

But now suppose instead that the persons in rooms 4, 5, 6,... check out. At a single stroke the hotel would be virtually emptied, the guest register reduced to three names, and the infinite converted to finitude. And yet it would remain true that the same number of guests checked out this time as when the guests in rooms 1, 3, 5,... checked out. Can anyone believe that such a hotel could exist in reality? Hilbert's Hotel is absurd. Since nothing hangs on the illustration's involving a hotel, the metaphysical absurdity is plausibly attributed to the actual infinite as such.

About the only thing the detractor of the argument can do at this point is, in Graham Oppy's words, simply "embrace the conclusion of one's opponent's *reductio ad absurdum* argument."[7] For, Oppy explains, "these allegedly absurd situations are just what one ought to expect if there were... physical infinities." Oppy's suggested response, however, falls short: it does nothing to prove that the envisioned situations are not absurd, but only serves to reiterate, in effect, that *if* an actual infinite could exist in reality, then there could be a Hilbert's Hotel, which is not in dispute. The problem cases would, after all, not be problematic if the alleged consequences would not ensue. Rather, the question is whether these consequences really are metaphysically possible. He who finds such scenarios metaphysically intolerable cannot be gainsaid simply by the skeptic's willingness to embrace the absurd.

Premise 2 states that an infinite temporal regress of events is an actual infinite. The point seems obvious enough, for if there has been a sequence composed of an infinite number of events stretching back into the past, then the set of all events in the series would be an actually infinite set. The regress of past events, in contrast to the progress of events toward the future, cannot be merely potentially infinite, for then it would have to be finite but growing in the *earlier than* direction, which is absurd.

It follows that an infinite temporal regress of events cannot exist. Therefore the universe began to exist.

1.2 Second philosophical argument

A second, independent philosophical argument in support of the premise that the universe began to exist is based on the impossibility of the formation of an actual infinite by successive addition. The argument may be simply formulated:

4. A collection formed by successive addition cannot be an actual infinite.
5. The temporal series of past events is a collection formed by successive addition.
6. Therefore the temporal series of past events cannot be an actual infinite.

By "successive addition" one means the accrual of one new element at a (later) time. The temporality of the process of accrual is critical here. For while it is true that $1 + 1 + 1 + \cdots$ equals $\aleph_0$, the operation of addition signified by "+" is not applied successively, but simultaneously, or better, timelessly. Mathematical equations do not take any time to be true. In contrast, we are concerned here with a temporal process of successive addition of one element after another.

The impossibility of the formation of an actual infinite by successive addition seems obvious in the case of beginning at some point and trying to reach infinity. For, given any finite number n, $n + 1$ equals a finite number. Hence $\aleph_0$ has no immediate predecessor; it is not the terminus of the natural number series, but stands, as it were, outside it and is the number of all the members in the series. One sometimes therefore speaks of the impossibility of counting to infinity, for no matter how many numbers one counts, one can always count one more number before arriving at infinity.

The question then arises whether, as a result of time's asymmetry, an actually infinite collection, though incapable of being formed by successive addition by beginning at a point and adding members, nevertheless could be formed by successive addition by never beginning but ending, at a point; that is to say, ending at a point after having added one member after another from eternity.

Although the problems will be different, the formation of an actually infinite collection by never beginning and ending at some point seems scarcely less difficult than the formation of such a collection by beginning at some point and never ending. If one cannot count *to* infinity, how can one count down *from* infinity? In order for us to have "arrived" at today, temporal existence has, so to speak, traversed an infinite number of prior events. But before the present event could occur, the event immediately prior to it would have to occur, and before that event could occur, the event immediately prior to it would have to occur, and so on ad infinitum. One gets driven back and back into the infinite past, making it impossible for any event to occur. Thus, if the series of past events were beginningless, the present event could not have occurred, which is absurd.

It is unavailing to say that an infinite series of past events cannot be formed only in a finite time but that such formation is possible given infinite time, for that riposte only pushes the question back a notch: how can an actually infinite series of equal temporal intervals successively elapse? Tenseless correlations are irrelevant here. Granted that the series of past events, if infinite, can be mapped 1–1 onto an equally infinite series of past temporal intervals, the question remains how such a temporal series of intervals can be lived through so as to arrive at the present.

Wholly apart from these Zeno-inspired arguments, the notion that the series of past events could be actually infinite is notoriously difficult. Consider, for example, a thought experiment proposed by al-Ghazali involving two beginningless series of coordinated events. He envisions our solar system's existing from eternity past, the orbital periods of the planets being so coordinated that for every 1 orbit that Saturn completes, Jupiter completes 2.5 times as many. If they have been orbiting from eternity, which planet has completed the most orbits? The correct mathematical answer is that they have completed precisely the same number of orbits. But this seems absurd, for the longer they revolve, the greater becomes the disparity between them, so that they progressively approach a limit at which Saturn has fallen infinitely far behind Jupiter. Yet, being now actually infinite, their respective completed orbits are somehow magically identical. Indeed, they will have "attained" infinity from eternity past: the number of completed orbits is always the same. So Jupiter and Saturn have each completed the same number of orbits, and that number has remained equal and unchanged from all eternity, despite their ongoing revolutions and the growing disparity between them over any finite interval of time.

Or consider the case of a man who claims to have been counting down from infinity and who is now finishing:..., −3, −2, −1, 0. We could ask, why did he not finish counting yesterday or the day before? By then an infinite time had already elapsed, so that he has had ample time to finish. Thus at no point in the infinite past should we ever find the man finishing his countdown, for by that point he should already be done. In fact, no matter how far back into the past we go, we can never find the man counting at all, for at any point we reach he will already have finished. But if at no point in the past do we find him counting, this contradicts the hypothesis that he has been counting from eternity. This shows again that the formation of an actual infinite by never beginning but reaching an end is as impossible as beginning at a point and trying to reach infinity.

Premise 5 may seem rather obvious. It is, in fact, a matter of great controversy. It presupposes a tensed theory of time, according to which the collection of all past events prior to any given event is a collection that is instantiated sequentially or successively in time, one event coming to pass on the heels of another. Since temporal becoming is an objective feature of the physical world, the series of past events is not, as on a tenseless theory of time, a tenselessly existing manifold, all of whose members are equally real. Rather, the members of the series come to be and pass away one after another.

Space does not permit a review of the arguments for and against the tensed and tenseless theories of time respectively. But on the basis of a case such as I have elsewhere presented,[8] I take us to be justified in affirming the objective reality of temporal becoming and hence the formation of the series of temporal events by successive addition.

It follows from premises 4 and 5 that the temporal series of events cannot be actually infinite, and therefore the universe began to exist.

1.3 Scientific confirmation

Apart from these philosophical arguments, there has emerged during the course of the twentieth century provocative empirical evidence that the universe is not past eternal. The standard big bang model describes a universe that is not eternal in the past, but which came into being a finite time ago. Moreover—and this deserves underscoring—the origin it posits is an absolute origin ex nihilo. For not only all matter and energy, but space and time themselves come into being at the initial cosmological singularity. As Barrow and Tipler emphasize, "At this singularity, space and time came into existence; literally nothing existed before the singularity, so, if the Universe originated at such a singularity, we would truly have a creation *ex nihilo.*"[9] On such a model the universe originates ex nihilo in the sense that at the initial singularity it is true that *there is no earlier space–time point* or it is false that *something existed prior to the singularity.*

So the salient question becomes, is the standard model correct, or, more precisely, is it correct in predicting an absolute beginning of the universe? Although there is a good deal of evidence in favor of the expansion of the universe, the standard big bang model will need to be modified in various ways. The model is based on Einstein's General Theory of Relativity (GR), but Einstein's theory breaks down prior to the Planck time (10^{-43} seconds after the big bang). One will need to introduce quantum physics to describe that era, but no one is sure how GR and quantum physics are to be integrated into a quantum theory of gravitation.

Still, uncertainty concerning the physical description of the universe prior to the Planck time need not affect the fundamental prediction of an absolute beginning of the universe. For the relevant question is not whether some quantum theory of gravity will enable physicists to resolve the initial singularity into a well-defined physical state, but whether that state or its predecessors can be successfully extrapolated to past infinity, so as to achieve a beginningless universe. The well-known quantum gravity model proposed by James Hartle and Stephen Hawking, for example, resolves the initial singularity but preserves an absolute beginning of the universe. In their recent, popular *The Grand Design*, Hawking and Mlodinow explain,

> Suppose the beginning of the universe was like the South Pole of the earth, with degrees of latitude playing the role of time. As one moves north, the circles of constant latitude, representing the size of the universe, would expand. The universe would start as a point at the South Pole, but the South Pole is much like any other point. To ask what happened before the beginning of the universe would become a meaningless question, because there is nothing south of the South Pole.[10]

On this interpretation their "no boundary" model has no singular past boundary point, but nonetheless is characterized by a beginning of both time and the universe.

To date, all attempts to push the past back to infinity have encountered barriers that in principle block any such extrapolation. To put it more positively: the only viable nonstandard models are those that involve an absolute beginning to the universe.

The history of twentieth-century cosmogony has, in one sense, been a series of failed attempts to craft acceptable nonstandard models of the expanding universe in such a way as to avert the absolute beginning predicted by the standard model. This parade of failures can be confusing to the layman, leading him to mistakenly infer that the field of cosmology is in constant flux, as new theories of the universe's origin continually come and go, with no assured results. In fact, the standard model's prediction of an absolute beginning has persisted through a century of astonishing progress in theoretical and observational cosmology and survived an onslaught of alternative theories. With each successive failure of alternative cosmogonic theories to avoid the absolute beginning of the universe predicted by the standard model, that prediction has been corroborated.

Indeed, a watershed of sorts appears to have been reached in 2003 with Arvind Borde, Alan Guth, and Alexander Vilenkin's formulation of a theorem establishing that any universe that has on average over its past history been in a state of cosmic expansion cannot be eternal in the past but must have a space–time boundary. Theorists intent on avoiding the absolute beginning of the universe could previously take refuge in the period prior to Planck time, an era so poorly understood that one commentator has compared it with the regions on the maps of ancient cartographers marked "Here there be dragons!"—it could be filled with all sorts of chimeras. But the Borde–Guth–Vilenkin theorem is independent of any physical description of the universe prior to Planck time, being based instead on deceptively simple physical reasoning that will hold regardless of our uncertainty concerning that era. It single-handedly sweeps away the most important attempts to avoid the absolute beginning of the universe, in particular the hypothesis of an eternal inflationary multiverse and higher-dimensional brane cosmologies. Vilenkin pulls no punches: "It is said that an argument is what convinces reasonable men and a proof is what it takes to convince even an unreasonable man. With the proof now in place, cosmologists can no longer hide behind the possibility of a past-eternal universe. There is no escape, they have to face the problem of a cosmic beginning."[11]

The Borde–Guth–Vilenkin theorem is now widely accepted by cosmologists. As a result, theorists who would avert the beginning of the universe are forced to deny the single assumption of that theorem: that the universe's history has been on average one of cosmic expansion. Any universe that meets this condition cannot be extrapolated into the infinite past. Although speculative models of the universe have been crafted on the assumption that that condition is not met, such models encounter daunting difficulties, both observationally and theoretically.[12] Thus we appear to have strong empirical confirmation of the conclusion to which philosophical argument led us: the universe began to exist.

∎ 2. SECOND QUESTION

This brings us to our second question: was the beginning of the universe caused or uncaused?

Universe
beginning   beginningless
caused   uncaused

I take it to be obvious that it is far more plausible that the beginning of the universe was caused rather than uncaused. First and foremost, such an answer is rooted in the metaphysical intuition that something cannot come into being from nothing. To suggest that things could just pop into being uncaused out of nothing is to quit doing serious metaphysics and to resort to magic. Second, if things really could come into being uncaused out of nothing, then it becomes inexplicable why just anything or everything does not come into existence uncaused from nothing. Why do bicycles and Beethoven and root beer not pop into being from nothing? Why is it only universes that can come into being from nothing? What makes nothingness so discriminatory? There cannot be anything about nothingness that favors universes, for nothingness does not have any properties. Third, the principle that "out of nothing nothing comes" plays an indispensable role in our scientific knowledge of the world. Philosopher of science Bernulf Kanitscheider observes, "the most successful ontological commitment that was a guiding line of research since Epicurus and Lucretius" is the principle *out of nothing nothing comes*, which Kanitscheider calls "a metaphysical hypothesis that has proved so fruitful in every corner of science that we are surely well advised to try as hard as we can to eschew processes of absolute origin."[13] Rightly so.

■ 3. THIRD QUESTION

Our third question concerns what sort of cause the universe must have: personal or impersonal?

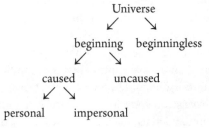

Conceptual analysis of what it is to be a cause of the universe enables us to recover a number of striking properties that this ultramundane cause must possess and that are of theological significance. For example, the cause must be uncaused, since an infinite regress of causes is impossible. This first cause must also be changeless, since, once more, an infinite temporal regress of changes cannot exist.[14] From the changelessness of the first cause, its immateriality follows. For whatever is material involves incessant change on at least the molecular and atomic levels, but the uncaused first cause exists in a state of absolute changelessness. Given some relational theory of time, the uncaused cause must therefore also be timeless, at least sans the universe, since in the utter absence of events time would not exist. Hence the uncaused first cause must transcend both time and space and be the cause of their origination. Moreover, such a being must be enormously powerful, since it brought the entirety of physical reality, including all matter and energy and space–time itself, into being without any material cause.

Finally, and most remarkably, such a transcendent cause is plausibly taken to be personal. I shall give two arguments for this conclusion. First, the person-hood of the first cause is already powerfully suggested by the properties that have been deduced by means of our conceptual analysis. For there appear to be only two candidates that can be described as immaterial, beginningless, uncaused, timeless, and spaceless beings: either abstract objects or an unembodied mind. Abstract objects like numbers, sets, propositions, and properties are very typically construed by philosophers who include such things in their ontology as being precisely the sort of entities that exist necessarily, timelessly, and spacelessly. Similarly, philosophers who hold to the possibility of a disembodied mind would describe such mental substances as immaterial and spaceless, and there seems no reason to think that a cosmic mind might not also be beginningless and uncaused. No other candidates that could be suitably described as immaterial, beginningless, uncaused, timeless, and spaceless beings come to mind. But no sort of abstract object can be the cause of the origin of the universe, for abstract objects are not involved in causal relations. Thus the cause of the universe must be an unembodied mind.

Second, this same conclusion is also implied by the fact that only personal, free agency can account for the origin of a first temporal effect from a changeless cause. We have concluded that the first cause exists timelessly and changelessly without the universe, and a finite time ago it brought the universe into existence. Now this is exceedingly odd. The cause is in some sense eternal, and yet the effect that it produced is not eternal but began to exist a finite time ago. How can this be? If the necessary and sufficient conditions for the production of the effect are eternal, then why is not the effect eternal? How can all the causal conditions sufficient for the production of the effect be changelessly existent and yet the effect not also be existent along with the cause? How can the cause exist without the effect?

The best way out of this dilemma is agent causation, whereby the agent freely brings about some event in the absence of prior determining conditions. Because the agent is endowed with freedom of the will, he can spontaneously initiate new effects by freely bringing about conditions that were not previously present. For example, a man sitting changelessly from eternity could freely will to stand up; thus a temporal effect arises from an eternally existing agent. Similarly, a finite time ago a Creator endowed with free will could have freely brought the world into being at that moment. In this way, the Creator could exist changelessly and timelessly sans creation but choose to create the world in time. By "choose" one need not mean that the Creator changes his mind about the decision to create, but that he freely and eternally intends to create a world with a beginning. By exercising his causal power, he therefore brings about that a world with a beginning comes to exist.[15] So the cause is eternal, but the effect is not. In this way, then, it is possible for the temporal universe to have come to exist from an eternal cause: through the free will of a personal Creator.

A conceptual analysis of what properties must be possessed by an ultramundane first cause thus enables us to recover a striking number of the traditional divine attributes. If the universe has a cause, then an uncaused, personal Creator of the universe exists, who sans the universe is beginningless, changeless, immaterial, timeless, spaceless, and enormously powerful. And this, as Thomas Aquinas was wont to remark, is what everybody means by "God."

NOTES

1. Quentin Smith, "Kalam Cosmological Arguments for Atheism," in *The Cambridge Companion to Atheism*, ed. M. Martin, 183 (Cambridge: Cambridge University Press, 2007).

2. A proper subset is a subset that does not exhaust all the members of the original set, that is to say, at least one member of the original set is not also a member of the subset. Two sets are said to be equivalent if the members of one set can be related to the members of the other set in a one-to-one correspondence, that is, so related that a single member of the one set corresponds to a single member of the other set and vice versa. Equivalent sets are regarded as having the same number of members. An infinite set, then, is one that is such that the whole set has the same number of members as a proper subset.

3. Edward Kasner and James Newman, *Mathematics and the Imagination* (New York: Simon & Schuster, 1940), 61.

4. Ibid.

5. José Benardete, *Infinity: An Essay in Metaphysics* (Oxford: Clarendon Press, 1964), 238.

6. The story of Hilbert's Hotel is related in George Gamow, *One, Two, Three, Infinity* (London: Macmillan, 1946), 17.

7. Graham Oppy, *Arguing about Gods* (Cambridge: Cambridge University Press, 2006), 48.

8. William Lane Craig, *The Tensed Theory of Time: A Critical Examination* (Dordrecht: Kluwer Academic Publishers, 2000); William Lane Craig, *The Tenseless Theory of Time: A Critical Examination* (Dordrecht: Kluwer Academic Publishers, 2000).

9. John Barrow and Frank Tipler, *The Anthropic Cosmological Principle* (Oxford: Clarendon Press, 1985), 442.

10. Stephen Hawking and Leonard Mlodinow, *The Grand Design* (New York: Bantam Books, 2010), 134–135.

11. Alex Vilenkin, *Many Worlds in One: The Search for Other Universes* (New York: Hill and Wang, 2006), 176.

12. See William Lane Craig and James Sinclair, "The *Kalam* Cosmological Argument," in *Blackwell Companion to Natural Theology*, ed. William L. Craig and J. P. Moreland (Oxford: Wiley-Blackwell, 2009), 101–201; see further William Lane Craig and James Sinclair, "On Non-Singular Spacetimes and the Beginning of the Universe," in *Scientific Approaches to Classical Issues in Philosophy of Religion*, ed. Yujin Nagasawa (London: Macmillan, 2012), 95–142.

13. Bernulf Kanitscheider, "Does Physical Cosmology Transcend the Limits of Naturalistic Reasoning?," in *Studies on Mario Bunge's "Treatise,"* ed. P. Weingartner and G. J. W. Dorn (Amsterdam: Rodopi, 1990), 344.

14. We should not be warranted, however, in inferring the immutability of the first cause, since immutability is a modal property, and from the cause's changelessness we cannot infer that it is incapable of change. But we can know that the first cause is changeless, at least insofar as it exists sans the universe.

15. And, I should say, thereby enters time Himself. So the Creator is timeless sans creation but temporal since creation.

▨ FOR FURTHER READING

Craig, W. L. "Graham Oppy on the Kalam Cosmological Argument." *International Philosophical Quarterly*, Volume 51, Issue 3, September 2011, 303–30.

Moore, A. W. *The Infinite*. London: Routledge, 1990.

Moreland, J. P. "Libertarian Agency and the Craig/Grünbaum Debate about Theistic Explanation of the Initial Singularity." *American Catholic Philosophical Quarterly* 71 (1998): 539–554.

Oppy, G. *Philosophical Perspectives on Infinity*. Cambridge: Cambridge University Press, 2006.

2 Doubts About the Kalam Argument

■ WES MORRISTON

For more than thirty years, William Lane Craig has vigorously championed the kalam cosmological argument. The argument begins with two familiar premises:

1. Whatever begins to exist has a cause.
2. The universe came into existence.

From premises 1 and 2 it follows that the universe has a cause. Further reflection is then supposed to show that this cause must have been a nontemporal, unchanging, immaterial, and unimaginably powerful person who created the universe out of nothing.

In the present essay I shall explore and evaluate the case for accepting the two main premises of the kalam argument. Before proceeding further, however, I want to make sure that the word "universe" is understood in a sense strong enough to enable the friends of the kalam argument to reach the conclusion they are aiming for—that the universe was created out of nothing by a person having the impressive features mentioned at the end of the previous paragraph. In order, for example, to show that the cause of the universe is a timeless, unchanging, and immaterial being who created it out of nothing, we need to know that it is the cause—not just of the space, time, and matter of *our* universe, but of the space, time, and matter of *any* universe that might ever have existed. So the claim we need to investigate is whether the whole of physical reality must have a beginning and a cause. With this understood, let us turn our attention to the case for premise 2.

■ 1. SCIENTIFIC ARGUMENTS FOR PREMISE 2

Two scientific considerations—one based on the expansion of the universe, the other on its thermodynamic properties—are offered in support of premise 2. In my opinion, neither of these arguments settles the matter, but my principal interest lies elsewhere and my treatment will have to be brief.

1.1 Expansion and the big bang

It is a commonplace that the history of the universe can be traced back to a big bang that (according to current estimates) occurred about 13.7 billion years ago. Unfortunately matters are not that simple. At best, the extrapolated Hubble expansion takes us back to a time when the universe was in a state of extremely high energy and density. At 10^{-12} seconds after the big bang, it is thought to have been about 100 billion electron volts (100 GeV); at 10^{-35} seconds, it rises to 10^{14} GeV.[1] When energy levels are that high, quantum effects are extremely significant, physics is entirely speculative, and just about everything is up for grabs. In such an extreme situation it isn't clear what physical laws apply, and—although the implications of this are often missed—the physics of the early universe are far too unsettled to enable us to extrapolate all the way back to a "time zero."[2] Indeed, to speak of the "early universe" at all is a bit of a misnomer; what we're really talking about here is just the universe as far back in time as we can "see," given currently well-established physical theory.[3]

There is yet another reason for skepticism about this source of evidence for premise 2. Even if we could extrapolate all the way back to a time zero, this would establish merely that the space-time of our universe has a beginning. It would give us no reason to conclude that there is nothing on the other side of that beginning (an earlier universe operating in accordance with quite different physical laws, perhaps?), and no reason therefore to think that the whole order of nature (physical reality as a whole) has an absolute beginning.[4]

There is, to be sure, an ongoing riot of speculation about these matters. But for the present, there is no telling which, if any, of the hypotheses currently being explored and tested will win out. Until the physicists have sorted things out on empirical grounds, I do not think we should rush to judgment.[5]

1.2 The thermodynamic properties of the universe

Craig also stresses a second scientific consideration. Given the second law of thermodynamics, the universe must, in a finite amount of time, arrive at a state of equilibrium and suffer "heat death." So if the history of the universe did not have a beginning, heat death would always already have taken place. Since that has not happened, we are invited to conclude that the universe has not always existed and that there must have been an absolute beginning.

The problem with this argument is (once again) that we don't know enough about the so-called "early" universe to say just how far back the second law reaches. Consequently we are unable to say how long the universe might have been in that mysterious "early" state. The most we are therefore entitled to conclude is that the history of entropy has a beginning.

2. PHILOSOPHICAL ARGUMENTS FOR AN ABSOLUTE BEGINNING

There are, however, two purely philosophical arguments for premise 2. Both seek to show that a beginningless series of discrete events is impossible. If this could be established (and if we could assume that the history of the universe consists of a series of discrete events), then we would not have to wait for the physicists to sort things out to conclude that the universe has a beginning—at least in the sense that there must have been a very first event in its history.[6]

2.1 First philosophical argument: the impossibility of an actual infinite

The first of these arguments employs the concept of an *actual infinite*, which Craig defines as "a collection of definite and discrete members whose number is greater than any natural number 0, 1, 2, 3, ... "[7] A beginningless series of discrete events could be placed in one-to-one correlation with the natural numbers. The number of events in such a series would therefore be $\aleph_0$ (the first transfinite cardinal), so it would be an actual infinite in the sense just defined. If it could be established that an actual infinite could not exist in the real world, then it would follow that a beginningless series of discrete events is impossible and we would have the absolute beginning we are looking for.

Craig has tried to show just this. Actually infinite collections, he believes, have absurd properties that make them impossible. By way of illustration and argument, he asks us to consider the case of "Hilbert's Hotel" (Craig 2008, 108ff). This imaginary hotel has infinitely many rooms, each of which accommodates a single person. So what's the problem? Well, even if the hotel were full, space could still be found for more guests without kicking anyone out or making anyone double up or building any new rooms. All we'd have to do to make space for a single new guest would be to move each current guest to the next room. To make infinitely many rooms available, we could have each current guest move to the room with double his or her old room number. This feature of a Hilbert's Hotel is alleged to be absurd, and the absurdity is blamed entirely on the fact that the hotel is infinite.

Craig also stresses another implication—this one having to do with inverse arithmetical operations. If the guests in rooms other than, say, the first three checked out, the hotel would be virtually emptied—only three guests would remain. But if the guests in every other room checked out, infinitely many guests would remain. And yet precisely the same number ($\aleph_0$) of guests would have checked out. This, Craig thinks, is obviously absurd.

Arithmetic avoids these implications by leaving subtraction undefined for infinity. But while that may keep things working smoothly in the strange world of mathematics, Craig points out that in the real world there is nothing to prevent guests from checking out of a hotel. From this, he once again draws the conclusion that there could be no such thing as an infinite hotel.

The lesson, of course, is supposed to be completely general. A true actual infinite, Craig says, is metaphysically impossible across the board. If, for example, numbers existed in reality, they would constitute an actual infinite; so Craig thinks we should adopt an antirealist view of mathematical objects.[8] The same of course goes for an infinite (because beginningless) series of discrete events.

What are we to make of these claims? Some friends of the actual infinite respond by saying that the properties of the infinite are simply different from those of the finite. Of course *we* can't build an infinite hotel. But a God who could create the whole of physical reality out of nothing could make a universe as large as he liked—even an infinitely large one. And if he did, he could certainly put an infinite hotel into it. A hotel like that would indeed have the weird properties highlighted above. But so what?

Although I have a good deal of sympathy for this reaction, I want to press a subtler objection. The supposed absurdities of a Hilbert's Hotel do not follow merely from its infinity, but rather from what happens when infinity is combined with other features of this imaginary hotel. If the guests could not be moved, they could not be moved to other rooms in such a way as to make room for new guests. Nor would we have to worry about how many guests would remain when different actual infinities of guests have left the hotel.

It is not at all clear, then, that Craig is entitled to conclude that no actual infinite whatever is possible. To see this, notice that mathematical objects (if there are such) are not "movable." So the allegedly absurd implications of a Hilbert's Hotel do not afflict infinite collections of them. More importantly for our purposes, past events are not movable. Unlike the guests in a hotel, who can leave their rooms, past events are absolutely inseparable from their respective temporal locations. Once an event has occurred at a particular time, it can't be "moved" to some other time. The signing of the Declaration of Independence, for instance, cannot be "moved" out of July 4, 1776. Of course, time continued to pass, and new events were (and continue to be) added to those that had already occurred when the signing of the Declaration had been completed. But that is no more absurd than making space for new guests by building new rooms.

It may be thought that I have taken the infinite hotel example too literally. Even if (*per impossibile*) the guests could not be moved, we would still have the following absurd implication. Hilbert's Hotel could have accommodated the same guests in its even-numbered rooms, and infinitely many additional guests in its odd-numbered rooms. This won't help to refute realism about mathematical objects, since there is no interesting sense in which they could have occupied different "locations." But it might be thought that it does demonstrate the absurdity of a beginningless series of discrete events. How so? Well, if we distinguish between the beginningless series of events and the beginningless series of temporal locations at which they occur, then it might seem that the same events could have been spread out in time in such a way as to make "room" for infinitely many more events.[9]

Whether this is genuinely possible depends, I think, on our view of time. In a relational view, the series of events and the series of temporal locations are inseparable and it makes no sense to suppose that the same events could have been distributed across the same temporal locations in a totally different way. But suppose we waive that point and (at least for the sake of argument) adopt an absolute view of the nature of time. Have we (at last) arrived at a genuine absurdity? At something that makes it clear that a beginningless series of events is impossible? I won't address this question directly. What I will do instead is to argue that such a conclusion would come at a heavy price, since it would force us to conclude that an endless series of future events is no less impossible than a beginningless one.

A favorite verse of a much loved hymn comes to mind:

> When we've been there ten thousand years,
> Bright shining as the sun,
> We've no less days to sing God's praise,
> Than when we first begun.

Of course, we shall never arrive at a time at which we have already said infinitely many heavenly praises. At each stage in the imagined future series of praises, we'll have said only finitely many. But that makes no difference to the point I am about to make. If you ask "How many distinct praises *will* be said?" the only sensible answer is *infinitely many*.

I anticipate the following objection. The series of future praises is a merely *potential* infinite. It is, in Craig's words, "a collection that is increasing toward infinity as a limit but never gets there." Such a collection, Craig says, is "really indefinite, not infinite."[10] This objection is badly confused. The salient points are these.

In the first place, the series of praises, each of which *will* be said, is not growing since each of its members has yet to occur. Even when the first of those praises is said, the series of *future* praises will still not be growing. Instead (if the passage of time is real), it is the series of praises that *have* been said that will begin having members added to it.

In the second place, there need be nothing "indefinite" about a series of future events. To see this, suppose that God has exercised his supreme power in such a way as to determine that a single angel—Gabriel, say—will speak certain words of praise at regular intervals forever. Suppose further that God has left none of the details open, and that each of Gabriel's future praises is both predetermined and completely determinate—specified down to the smallest detail.

Under these circumstances, there is a one-to-one correspondence between Gabriel's future praises and the natural numbers. So his future praises must count as "a collection of definite and discrete members whose number is greater than any natural number." They are therefore an actual infinite, and whatever paradoxes may be implied by the hypothesis of a beginningless series of past events must also be implied by this endless series of predetermined (and determinate) future events.

In response to this worry, Craig distinguishes between two questions: (1) How many praises will be said? and (2) What is the number of praises that will be said? The answer to the first question, he says, is "potentially infinitely many." But the answer to the second question is "none": there simply is no number such that it is the number of praises that will be said.[11]

I have already given my reasons for thinking that a series of future praises such as the one I have imagined does not satisfy Craig's own definition of a "potential infinite." But what of his answer to the second question? Why does he think that "none" is the right answer to the question about the number of praises in my imagined series of future praises? The answer might appear to be that Craig is a "presentist" who thinks that there is no number of future events because future events don't exist.

Now most philosophers could not give this answer, since they are "eternalists." According to them, temporal becoming is illusory and there is no difference in ontological status between present events and future ones. But what if Craig were right in supposing that only present events exist? Would that help his case? It might seem not, since it would oblige him to say that there is no number of past events either. But Craig is ready with an explanation. Even though past events do not exist, he says, "they are still part of the actual world in a way that future events are not, since the actual world comprises everything that has happened."[12]

What's going on here? Well, Craig appears to be drawing a distinction between saying that something *exists* and saying that it is *actual*. Past events don't exist, but they are actual because they have become so. Future events, by contrast, neither exist nor are they actual. Unlike past events, they have yet to become actual.

What should we make of this distinction? Is it the case that something that *will* occur (especially if it has already been *determined* to occur) is less a part of "actuality" than something that *has* occurred? That seems like a stretch to me. But even if it were true, it would not help Craig's case, since the items in a collection do not have to be "actual" in his special sense in order to be numerable. To see this, suppose that instead of predetermining each member of an *endless* series of praise events, God merely predetermines each member of a *finite* series. For definiteness, suppose that he creates a perfectly functioning timer, sets it to ten minutes, and fixes things up in such a way that Gabriel cannot help saying certain words of praise whenever the timer registers that an additional minute has passed. Does the fact that Gabriel's future praises have not yet been "actualized" entail that they are numberless? Not at all. The number of praises, each of which will occur, is obviously ten.[13]

Let us return, then, to the case of an endless series of praise events. Unlike a series of ten, there will never be a time at which all the events in an endless series of future events have been actualized. Does this imply that "none" is the correct answer to the question about the number of future praise events? It does not. As long as each of those future events is definite and discrete and determined to happen, they can be placed in one-to-one correspondence with the natural numbers, and their number must be $\aleph_0$ (the first transfinite cardinal number). Their ontological status (whatever it turns out to be) provides no more reason for saying that the correct answer to the question about their number is "none" than it does in the case of a finite series of future events.

Even on a presentist view, then, there is no relevant difference between a beginningless series of past events and an endless series of events each of which is determined to occur in the future. The absurdities that supposedly attend a series that can be placed in one-to-one correlation with the natural numbers will afflict an endless series just as much as a beginningless one. To this simple point, the passage of time makes not a particle of difference.

At this juncture, a committed finitist might want to bite the bullet and concede that an endless series of future events is (also) impossible. This seems implausible to me, but I cannot prove that it is mistaken. However, I doubt that many advocates of the kalam cosmological argument will be happy with this implication, since most of them believe both in divine omnipotence and in life everlasting. Given life everlasting, the future must be endless, and given divine omnipotence, it must be possible for God to cause it to be the case that each of an endless series of praises will be said.

2.2 Second philosophical argument: successive addition and the actual infinite

Let us turn next to Craig's "successive addition" argument for premise 2. According to this argument, any series of (discrete) events in time must be formed by successive addition. As each event occurs, it is "added" to those that have already occurred. That goes for a beginningless series of events as much as for any other. However, a beginningless series would be an actual or completed infinite. Since no infinite series can be formed by successive addition, it follows that a beginningless series of events in time has contradictory properties. It must be formed by successive addition (since it is a series of events in time), but it can't be (since it is an actual infinite). A beginningless series of events is therefore absolutely impossible.

One obvious worry about this argument concerns the claim that an actual infinite cannot be completed by successive addition. We cannot, of course, begin with a first event and successively add more events until infinitely many have been added. But in a beginningless series (if such were possible) there would be no first event. At each stage of the series, infinitely many would already have been added. At each stage, therefore, a different infinite series would already have been completed. Why could a beginningless series of past events not have been "formed" in this way? Craig explains:

> Before the present event could occur, the event immediately prior to it would have to occur; and before that event could occur, the event immediately prior to it would have to occur; and so on ad infinitum. So one gets driven back and back into the infinite past, making it impossible for any event to occur. Thus, if the series of past events were beginningless, the present event could not have occurred, which is absurd.[14]

Well, yes, before the present event occurred, the event immediately prior to it must have occurred; and before it occurred, the one immediately prior to it must have occurred. If, then, a series of events has no beginning, then before any given event in that series occurs, infinitely many previous ones must have occurred. That's all perfectly correct. But it's hard to see what the problem is supposed to be, since on the hypothesis of a beginningless past each of those infinitely many events *has* occurred. When the present arrives, all of its (infinitely many) predecessors are past.

So what does Craig mean when he says that "one gets driven back and back into the infinite past?" And why does he think this would make it "impossible for any event to occur?" I suppose one would be "driven back and back" into the beginningless past if one were (foolishly) looking for the starting point of a series that has no starting point. One would also be "driven back and back" if one were (again foolishly) trying to enumerate all the events in a series that has no first member. Neither of these projects can succeed. But so what? From the fact that we cannot—beginning now—complete the task of enumerating all the events in a beginningless series, it does not follow that the present event cannot arrive or that a beginningless series of events that have already arrived is impossible. To suppose otherwise would be to confuse the items to be enumerated with the enumerating of them—it would be like arguing that there must be finitely many natural numbers because we can't finish counting them.

There is admittedly one way in which the possibility of a beginningless series of past events entails the possibility of an infinite count. Instead of imagining someone who is "driven back and back" ad infinitum, we must imagine someone who has always already counted out the previous item in a beginningless series. As you might expect, Craig argues that this too is impossible:

> To say that the infinite past could have been formed by successive addition is like saying that someone has just succeeded in writing down all the negative numbers, ending at 0. We could ask, why didn't he finish counting yesterday or the day before or the year before? By then an infinite time had already elapsed, so that he should already have finished. Thus at no point in the infinite past could we ever find the man finishing his countdown, for by that point he should already be done! In fact, no matter how far back into the past we go, we can never find the man counting at

all, for at any point we reach he will already have finished. But if at no point in the past do we find him counting, this contradicts the hypothesis that he has been counting from eternity. This shows again that the formation of an actual infinite by never beginning but reaching an end is as impossible as beginning at a point and trying to reach infinity.[15]

This is much too quick for me. Given beginningless time, our man has indeed always already had enough time to complete his count of all the negative numbers, but it does not follow that he must have done so. It's true that we have been given no reason why he is reaching zero just now rather than at some earlier time. I'm not sure we couldn't build a reason into our story, but that is a side issue. The important point is this: from the fact that we know of no reason *why* something is so, it does not follow that it is impossible for it to *be* so.

■ 3. MUST WHATEVER BEGINS TO EXIST HAVE A CAUSE?

Let us turn, finally, to premise 1. Why should we believe that everything—even the whole of physical reality—must have a cause if it begins to exist? Craig claims that this principle is "rooted in the metaphysical intuition that something cannot come into being from nothing." If things could just "pop into being uncaused out of nothing," he says, then it would be "inexplicable why just anything and everything do not come into existence uncaused from nothing."[16] By way of illustration and argument, he asks, "Does anyone in his right mind really believe that, say, a raging tiger could suddenly come into existence uncaused, out of nothing, in this room right now?" Assuming a negative answer to this question, Craig jumps to the conclusion that the same goes for the universe. If, "prior to the existence of the universe," he asks, "there was absolutely nothing—no God, no space, no time—how could the universe possibly have come to exist?"[17]

Quite a lot has gone wrong here. For one thing, we are invited to characterize the negation of premise 1 in a potentially misleading way. To the philosophically unsophisticated reader, it sounds rather as if Craig is equating the denial of premise 1 with the suggestion that once upon a time ("prior to the existence of the universe") there was a situation in which nothing at all (not even time) existed—and then, "out of" that black hole of nothingness, the universe "popped into existence." This is, to be sure, utter nonsense. There is no "time at which there is no time," and if there were nothing at all, there would (of course) be nothing at all—not even a "popping into existence." But such absurdities are not entailed by the simple denial of the proposition that the beginning of the universe has a cause.

In my view, then, advocates of the kalam argument would do well to avoid talking about the impossibility of something coming into existence out of sheer nothingness. It is a source of potential confusion, and it adds nothing to the case for premise 1. Charitably interpreted, the claim that something can't come from nothing is the claim that nothing can come into existence uncaused.

Here is another, more substantive, worry about the way in which Craig defends premise 1. I quite agree that a tiger couldn't spring into existence uncaused. But we have been given no reason to think that what's true of a tiger applies to physical reality as a whole. Remember that we're talking about the origin of the whole natural order here. A tiger comes into existence within the natural order, and within that order it is indeed impossible for things like tigers to just pop into existence. But as far as I can see, there is no comparable context for the origin of physical reality as a whole, and no analogous reason for thinking that it could not have begun to exist uncaused.

However, Craig insists that his causal principle is not "a merely physical law like the law of gravity or the laws of thermodynamics, which are valid for things within the universe." Instead, he says, it is "a metaphysical principle: being cannot come from non-being; something cannot come into existence uncaused from nothing. The principle therefore applies to all of reality, and it is thus metaphysically absurd that the universe should pop into being uncaused out of nothing."[18]

Well, yes, that is what Craig claims. Stripped of all the vivid but confusing talk about "popping into being uncaused out of nothing," Craig is saying two things: first, that premise 1 is true, and second, that it is a *metaphysically necessary* truth—true, I suppose one might say, in all possible worlds. At this point, I believe that Craig has simply lost the thread of the argument. Recall that he began by arguing that this metaphysical principle must be true on the ground that it is required to explain "why just anything and everything do not come into existence uncaused from nothing." In response, I have pointed out that the premise of this argument is patently false. Within the natural order, it is quite easy to explain where tigers come from and why they can't just pop into existence. We don't need a general metaphysical principle in order to provide the desired explanation. It is not dialectically apt merely to repeat that the metaphysical principle in question is true.

Interestingly, Craig also defends premise 1 on empirical grounds. He says that it is "constantly confirmed in our experience," and from this he concludes that even "atheists who are scientific naturalists...have the strongest of motivations to accept it."[19] This is surely a bit quick. It's true that we often discover causes, but not always. One wonders what Craig thinks *dis*confirmation of his principle would look like. But leaving this point aside, one wonders what exactly it is that a "scientific naturalist" has been given such a strong reason to accept. Is it Craig's all-embracing metaphysical principle, or is it the comparatively modest claim that within the natural order things don't begin to exist without (natural) causes? As far as I can see, Craig has given no reason for preferring the first of these answers.

It is also worthy of note that the empirical route is quite a dangerous one for the friends of the kalam argument to take if they want to conclude that the universe was created out of nothing by the will of a timeless and immaterial person a long time ago. Here are some other well-attested empirical generalizations, each of which is incompatible with that hypothesis about the origin of the universe:

1. Material things come from material things.
2. Nothing is ever created out of nothing.
3. Nothing is ever caused by anything that is not itself in time.
4. The mental lives of all persons have temporal duration.
5. All persons are embodied.

It might of course be said that while these generalizations apply within the natural order, they do not apply to the natural order as a whole or to its cause. But then, of course, one could reasonably ask why the same should not be said of the claim that whatever begins to exist has a cause.

It is also worth pointing out that prima facie, at least, quite a number of these generalizations have as much claim to be metaphysical truths as Craig's premise 1. One might be left with the impression that the friends of the kalam argument are picking and choosing metaphysical principles to suit the needs of the argument they want to make.[20]

▪ 4. CONCLUDING REMARKS

This concludes what I have to say about the twin pillars of the kalam argument. I do not claim to have shown that either premise is false—merely that they are not adequately supported by the arguments I have discussed. This is, to be sure, a somewhat disappointing conclusion. But (in the spirit of Socrates) I have long thought it important to know when we don't know.

▪ NOTES

1. See Bradley Monton, "Prolegomena to any Future Physics-based Metaphysics," *Oxford Studies in Philosophy of Religion Volume III* (Oxford: Oxford University Press, 2011), 142–165.

2. One scientist I consulted (Michael Shull, professor of astrophysical and planetary sciences and College Professor of Distinction at the University of Colorado in Boulder) put the matter succinctly in correspondence: "I find it surprising that someone would claim . . . that the extrapolated Hubble expansion, back to "time zero" (13.7 billion years ago) was the start of everything. We know so little about the laws of physics at these times, small lengths, enormous energies, even the nature of space and the vacuum."

3. Philosopher of physics Bradley Monton offers an extraordinarily clear, careful, and well-informed presentation of the general line of argument briefly developed here (Monton, "Prolegomena to any Future Physics-based Metaphysics").

4. A layperson might wonder whether it makes any sense to talk about what happened before the beginning of space-time. It's quite clear, however, that it can make sense. To borrow an illustration from Craig (William Lane Craig, "The Origin and Creation of the Universe: A Response to Adolf Grünbaum," *British Journal for the Philosophy of Science* 43, no. 2 (1992): 238–239), one can imagine an immaterial Creator doing a sort of "countdown" to creation: "5, 4, 3, 2, 1, fiat lux!" Here we have a temporal sequence whose members occur prior to the beginning of our space-time. Craig himself calls this a "knockdown argument" for the conclusion that "time as it plays a role in physics is at best a measure of time rather than constitutive or definitive of time" (William Lane Craig, "Design and the Cosmological Argument," in *Mere Creation: Science, Faith and Intelligent Design*, ed. W. A. Dembski (Downers Grove, IL: Intervarsity Press, 1998), 350–351).

5. Craig and Sinclair have done a remarkable job of summarizing and critically evaluating the theories currently offered (William Lane Craig, "The Kalam Cosmological Argument," in *The Blackwell Companion to Natural Theology*, ed. W. L. Craig and J. P. Moreland (Chichester: John Wiley & Sons, 2009), 101–201). I have neither the expertise nor the space to contribute to this fascinating debate. But there is no getting around the fact that there is as yet nothing even remotely approaching a true scientific consensus about these matters.

6. Neither argument establishes that the earliest *event* has a beginning "edge," but I shall be making nothing of this qualification here. For some helpful remarks on this topic, see Craig, The Kalam Cosmological Argument, 184–185).

7. William Lane Craig, *Reasonable Faith: Christian Truth and Apologetics*, 3rd ed. (Wheaton, IL: Crossway Books, 2008), 116.

8. Craig, *Reasonable Faith*, 117.

9. For a helpful development of this point, see J. P. Moreland, "A Response to a Platonistic and to a Set-Theoretic Objection to the Kalam Cosmological Argument," *Religious Studies* 39, no. 4 (2003): 381–382.

10. Craig, *Reasonable Faith*, 116–117.

11. William Lane Craig, "Taking Tense Seriously in Differentiating Past and Future: A Response to Morriston," *Faith and Philosophy* 27, no. 4 (2010): 454–455.

12. Craig, "Taking Tense Seriously," 456.

13. Notice that I did not say that the number of praises that will *have* occurred is ten. That's true too, but it is important to distinguish between the following questions:

(i) How many will have occurred when all have been said?

(ii) How many are such that each will be said?

The answer to (ii) is the same as the answer to (i) for any finite series of future events, but not for an infinite one.

14. Craig, *Reasonable Faith*, 122.

15. Craig, *Reasonable Faith*, 124.

16. Craig, *Reasonable Faith*, 111.

17. Craig, *Reasonable Faith*, 113.

18. Craig, *Reasonable Faith*, 133–134; see also Craig, "The Kalam Cosmological Argument," 186–187.

19. Craig, *Reasonable Faith*, 111–112.

20. However, Craig does provide an interesting discussion of 2 and 3 ("The Kalam Cosmological Argument," 188–189). For my take on this, see Wes Morriston, "Causes and Beginnings in the Kalam Argument: Reply to Craig," *Faith and Philosophy* 19, no. 2 (2002): 238–241.

■ FOR FURTHER READING

Draper, P. "A Critique of the Kalam Cosmological Argument." In *Philosophy of Religion: An Anthology*, 6th ed., ed. Louis P. Pojman and Michael Rea, 172–177. Boston, MA: Wadsworth, 2011.

Morriston, W. "Must Metaphysical Time Have a Beginning?" *Faith and Philosophy* 20, no. 3 (2003): 288–306.

Nagasawa, Y. "The Big Bang, Infinity, and the Meaning of Life." In *The Existence of God* (New York: Routledge, 2011), 102–152.

Oppy, G. "Craig and the Kalam Arguments." In *Arguing About Gods* (Cambridge: Cambridge University Press, 2006), 137–153.

A Teleological Argument

3   The Fine-Tuning Evidence is Convincing

■ ROBIN COLLINS

In this essay I will argue that the evidence is convincing that in multiple ways the structure of the universe must be precisely set—that is, "fine-tuned"—for the existence of embodied conscious agents (ECAs) of comparable intelligence to humans, not merely for the existence of any form of life as Stenger often assumes.[1] Many prominent cosmologists and physicists concur—for example, Sir Martin Rees, former Astronomer Royal of Great Britain.[2] In response, Victor Stenger, my interlocutor, often argues that a satisfactory "scientific" explanation can be given of the fine-tuning, and hence there is no need to invoke God or multiverses. This objection will only work if the explanation does not merely transfer the fine-tuning up one level to the newly postulated laws, principles, and parameters. As astrophysicists Bernard Carr and Martin Rees note, "even if all apparently anthropic coincidences could be explained [in terms of some deeper theory], it would still be remarkable that the relationships dictated by physical theory happened also to be those propitious for life."[3] To explain away the fine-tuning, therefore, one must show that one's deeper explanation is itself not very special, a requirement Stenger largely ignores.

Elsewhere I have developed the fine-tuning argument in substantial detail,[4] but can only summarize the basics here. In brief, I first consider the claim that there is no God and that there is only one universe—what I call the naturalistic single-universe hypothesis. I then argue that given this hypothesis and the extreme fine-tuning required for ECAs, it is very surprising—in technical language, very epistemically improbable—that a universe exists with ECAs. I then argue that we can glimpse a good reason for God to create a universe containing ECAs that are vulnerable to each other and to the environment: specifically, such vulnerable ECAs can affect each other for good or ill in deep ways. Besides being an intrinsic good, I argue that this ability to affect one another's welfare allows for the possibility of eternal bonds of appreciation, contribution, and intimacy, which elsewhere I argue are of great value.[5] Since moral evil and suffering will inevitably exist in a universe with such ECAs, I conclude that the existence of the combination of an ECA-structured universe and the type of evils we find in the world is not surprising under theism. Thus, by the likelihood principle of confirmation theory (in which a body of evidence confirms the hypothesis under which it is least surprising), the existence of such an ECA-structured universe, even when combined with the existence of evil, confirms theism over the naturalistic single-universe hypothesis. Finally, I argue that the existence of multiple universes does not adequately account for many cases of fine-tuning: one reason is that the laws governing whatever generates the many universes would have to itself be fine-tuned to produce even one life-permitting universe; another is that the universe is not fine-tuned for mere observers—which is the only kind of fine-tuning the multiverse hypothesis can explain—but rather for ECAs that can significantly interact with each other.[6]

In this essay I will focus on the fine-tuning evidence, considering three different kinds of fine-tuning: the fine-tuning of the laws/principles of physics, the fine-tuning of the initial distribution of mass-energy in the universe, and the fine-tuning of the fundamental parameters/constants of physics. Because of limitations of space, I will only elaborate on a few of the most accessible cases of fine-tuning and respond to Stenger's objections to them. Also, I agree with Stenger that some popularly cited cases of fine-tuning do not hold up to careful scrutiny. This is why it is critical to carefully develop and evaluate each purported case. I did this for a limited number of cases elsewhere,[7] and am currently finishing a comprehensive treatment of the fine-tuning evidence; physicist Luke Barnes has also presented an extensive list of cases of fine-tuning along with an extensive critique of Stenger.[8]

■ 1. LAWS OF NATURE

As an example of the fine-tuning of the laws and principles of physics, consider the requirements of constructing atoms, the building blocks of life. As a thought experiment, suppose that one were given the law of energy and momentum conservation, the second law of thermodynamics, and three fundamental particles with masses corresponding to that of the electron, proton, and neutron. Further suppose that one were asked to decide the properties these particles must have and the laws they must obey to obtain workable building blocks for life. First, one would need some principle to prevent the particles from decaying, since by the second law of thermodynamics particles will decay to particles with less mass-energy if they can. For electrons, protons, and neutrons in our universe, this is prevented by the *conservation of electric charge* and the *conservation of baryon number*. Since there are no electrically charged particles lighter than an electron, the conservation of electric charge prevents electrons from decaying into lighter particles—such as less massive neutrinos and photons. (If an electron did decay, there would be one less negatively charged particle in the universe, and thus the sum of the negative plus positive charges in the universe would have changed in violation of this conservation law.) Similarly, protons and neutrons belong to a class of particles called baryons. Since there are no baryons lighter than these, baryon conservation prevents a proton from decaying into anything else, and allows neutrons to decay only into the lighter proton (plus an electron and neutrino).

Next, there must be forces to hold the particles together into structures that can engage in complex interactions. In our universe, this is accomplished by two radically different forces. The first force, the *electric force*, holds electrons in orbit around the nucleus; if this, or a relevantly similar force, did not exist, no atoms could exist. Another force, however, is needed to hold protons and neutrons together. The force that serves this function in our universe is called the *strong nuclear force*, and it must have at least two special characteristics. First, it must be stronger than the repulsive electric force between the positively charged protons. Second, it must be very short range—which means its strength must fall off much, much more rapidly than the inverse square law $(1/r^2)$ characteristic of the electric force and gravity. Otherwise, because of the great strength it must have—around 10^{40} times stronger than the gravitational attraction between protons and neutrons—all protons and neutrons in any solid body would be almost instantly sucked together, eliminating the building blocks necessary for life.

Finally, at least two more laws/principles are needed. First, without an additional law/principle, classical electromagnetic theory predicts that an electron orbiting a nucleus will radiate away its energy, rapidly falling into the nucleus. This problem was resolved in 1913 by Niels Bohr's introduction of the quantization hypothesis, which says that electrons can occupy only certain discrete orbital energy states in an atom. Second, to have complex chemistry, something must prevent all electrons from falling into the lowest orbital. This is accomplished by the Pauli exclusion principle, which dictates that no two electrons can occupy the same quantum state—which in turn implies that each atomic orbital can contain at most two electrons. This principle also serves another crucial role, that of guaranteeing the stability of matter, as originally proved by Freeman Dyson and Andrew Lenard in 1967.[9]

The above examples show that building blocks for highly complex, self-replicating structures require the right set of laws and principles. If, for instance, one of the above laws/principles were removed (while keeping the others in place), ECAs would be impossible. This is not all, though. For those building blocks—such as carbon and oxygen—to be synthesized (as happens in stars), and then for an adequate habitat to exist for ECAs to evolve (such as a planet orbiting a stable star of the right temperature), requires even more of the right laws. For example, a law is needed to tell masses to attract each other to form stars and planets—that is, a law of "gravity."

In various places Stenger has argued that the laws/principles of physics do not need fine-tuning because they are based on a combination of symmetry and the random breaking of it.[10] Symmetries reflect some property being the same under a specified transformation—one's face is symmetrical if it looks the same in a mirror—which transforms the part of the face that is left of center to right of center and vice versa. Since symmetries are about sameness, and since one would expect things to remain the same without an outside agent, Stenger concludes that symmetries are the natural state of affairs and therefore do not need further explanation. One cannot explain the laws of nature by merely appealing to symmetry, however: if the universe were completely symmetrical, it would remain the same under all possible interchanges of elements, and therefore would comprise one undifferentiated whole. Consequently, as the famous scientist Pierre Curie pointed out, "dissymmetry is what creates the phenomena." [11] Stenger attempts to attribute this necessary dissymmetry to *randomly* broken symmetry.[12] But why would randomly broken symmetry give rise to precisely the right set of laws required for life instead of the vast range of other possibilities? Stenger never tells us and thus evades the real issue.

■ 2. FINE-TUNING OF INITIAL CONDITIONS

The initial distribution of mass-energy must fall within an exceedingly narrow range for life to occur. According to Roger Penrose, one of Britain's leading theoretical physicists, "In order to produce a universe resembling the one in which we live, the Creator would have to aim for an absurdly tiny volume of the phase space of possible universes."[13] How tiny is this volume? According to Penrose, this volume is one part in $10^{10^{123}}$ of the entire volume.[14] (10^{123} is 1 followed by 123 zeroes, with 10 raised to this power being enormously larger.) This is vastly smaller than the ratio of the volume of a proton ($\sim 10^{-45}$ m^3) to the entire volume of the visible universe ($\sim 10^{84}$ m^3); the precision required to "hit" the right volume by chance is thus enormously greater than would be required to hit an individual proton if the entire visible universe were a dartboard!

Since in standard applications of statistical mechanics, the volume of phase space corresponds to the probability of the system being in that state, it turns out that the configuration of mass-energy necessary to generate a life-sustaining universe such as ours was enormously improbable—one part in $10^{10^{123}}$. Since entropy is the logarithm of the volume of phase space, another way of stating the specialness of the initial state is to say that to support life like ours, the universe must have been in an exceedingly low entropy state relative to its maximum possible value.

Two of the most popular attempted scientific explanations of this low entropy are (1) to combine inflationary cosmology with a multiverse hypothesis, or (2) to invoke some special law that requires a uniform gravitational field, and hence maximally low entropy, at the universe's beginning. Both of these "explanations" are very controversial, with Penrose arguing on theoretical grounds that inflationary cosmology could not possibly explain the low entropy and others arguing that Penrose's solution—in which there is a special law—simply reinstantiates the problem elsewhere.[15]

I do not have space to review all the proposals here. I merely note that even if a solution is found, it will likely involve postulating a highly special theoretical framework (such as an inflationary multiverse), and will therefore involve a new fine-tuning of the laws of nature. To argue for this, I will begin by looking at Stenger's purported scientific solution to the low entropy problem, one that does not appear to require any special theoretical framework or law—namely, the claim that it is the result of the fact that the universe started out very small in size. Stenger claims that because the very early universe was equivalent to a black hole, it had the highest possible entropy for an object that size, and thus was in the most probable (and hence least special) state. Yet, he claims, this was a much lower entropy state than that of the current universe:

> I seem to be saying that the entropy of the universe was maximal when the universe began, yet it has been increasing ever since. Indeed, that's exactly what I am saying. When the universe began, its entropy was as high as it could be for an object that size because the universe was equivalent to a black hole from which no information can be extracted.[16]

Stenger's claims are completely backwards. The standard Bekenstein–Hawking formula for the entropy of a black hole shows that if the matter in the universe were compressed into a black hole, its entropy would be *far larger* than that of the current universe. As California Institute of Technology cosmologist Sean Carroll notes,

> The total entropy within the space corresponding to our early universe turns out to be about 10^{88} at early times ... If we took all of the matter in the observable universe and collected it into a single black hole, it would have an entropy of 10^{120}. That can be thought of as the maximum possible entropy obtainable by re-arranging the matter in the universe, and that's the direction in which we're evolving.[17]

Thus if, as Stenger claims, the universe began as a black hole, its entropy would have been far larger than it is now, contradicting the second law of thermodynamics, which requires that entropy always increase. As Carroll notes, the challenge is to explain why the "early entropy, 10^{88}, [was] so much lower than the maximum possible entropy, 10^{120}."[18] Stenger not only has failed to address this problem, he has failed to understand the problem itself.

Apart from the above calculation, there are many fatal objections to the claim that the low entropy of the early universe was due to the universe's small size, objections that have been widely known for more than thirty years but of which Stenger seems unaware. Penrose, for instance, notes that if the universe were eventually to collapse back in on itself, the second law of thermodynamics implies that entropy will increase even though the universe would be getting smaller in size.[19] Further, it is highly implausible to postulate that the second law would be violated: if entropy were to decrease with time, then photons of light would return to burnt-out stars and cause the nuclear fuel in the stars to undergo a reverse process of fusion; buildings that had fallen into ruin would come back together; and the like. This is clearly something we would not expect.

Summarizing the current consensus, philosopher of physics Huw Price states that "the smooth early universe turns out to have been incredibly 'special', even by the standards prevailing at the time. Its low entropy doesn't depend on the fact that there were fewer possibilities available."[20]

I am not saying here that some more fundamental theory will not be found that "explains" the initial (and current) low entropy of the universe, only that the theory would almost certainly have to involve some set of special mechanisms to yield such a low entropic initial state; otherwise physicists would almost surely have found it by now.

▩ 3. FUNDAMENTAL CONSTANTS/PARAMETERS OF PHYSICS

Besides laws and initial conditions, ECAs require that the so-called fundamental constants of physics have the right values. Although there are around seven that need fine-tuning, I will only consider two of these: the constant governing the strength of gravity and the cosmological constant. (Other constants that need fine-tuning are the weak force strength, the strong force strength, the strength of electromagnetism, the strength of the primordial density fluctuations, and the neutron–proton mass difference.)

The gravitational constant G appears in Newton's law of gravity, $F = Gm_1m_2/r^2$, along with Einstein's law of gravity. (Here F is the force between two masses, m_1 and m_2, separated by a distance r.) The value of G depends on the units one uses: for example, in the Standard International (SI) units of meters, kilograms, seconds, its value is $6.674 \times 10^{-11} \, \mathrm{m^3/kg/s^2}$, whereas in Planck (or so-called natural) units its value is stipulated to be 1. To avoid this dependence on units, physicists often use a unitless measure of the strength of gravity, α_G, commonly defined as $\alpha_G \equiv G(m_p)^2/\hbar c$, where m_p is the mass of the proton, $\hbar$ is the reduced Planck's constant (i.e., $h/2\pi$), and c is the speed of light.[21] Since the units of G, m_p, $\hbar$, and c all cancel out, α_G is a pure number ($\sim 5.9 \times 10^{-39}$) that does not depend on the choice of units, such as those for length, mass, and time. In the Internet preprint (November 2010) of his essay in this volume and elsewhere,[22] Stenger has fallaciously claimed that since the strength of gravity could be defined in terms of the mass, m_x, of any elementary particle (i.e., $\alpha_G \equiv G(m_x)^2/\hbar c$), there can be no fine-tuning of α_G. The freedom to define α_G in terms of other elementary particles, however, clearly does not affect the fine-tuning of $G(m_p)^2/\hbar c$, only whether one calls it the "strength of gravity." Thus Stenger's claims are irrelevant to whether $G(m_p)^2/\hbar c$ is fine-tuned.

Next, I define a constant as being fine-tuned for ECAs if and only if the range of its values that allow for ECAs is small compared to the range of values for which we can determine whether the value is ECA permitting, a range I call the "comparison range." For the purposes of this essay, I will take the comparison range to be the range of values for which a parameter is defined within the current models of physics. For many physical constants, such as the two presented here, this range is given by the Planck scale, which is determined by the corresponding Planck units for mass, length, and time. As Cambridge University mathematical physicist John Barrow notes, Planck units define the limits of our current models in physics:

> Planck's units mark the boundary of applicability of our current theories. To understand [for example] what the world is like on a scale smaller than the Planck length, we have to understand fully how quantum uncertainty becomes entangled with gravity.[23]

Barrow goes on to state that in order to move beyond the boundary set by Planck units, physicists would need a theory that combines quantum mechanics and gravity; all current models treat them separately. Consequently all fine-tuning arguments are relative to the current models of physics. This does not mean that the arguments must assume that these models correspond to reality, only that the variety of cases of fine-tuning in our current models strongly suggests that fine-tuning is a fundamental feature of our universe, whatever the correct models might be.

Since Planck units are defined by requiring G, c, and $\hbar$ to be 1, the above definition of α_G implies that $\alpha_G = m_p^2$. Thus, in Planck units, α_G is determined by the mass of the proton. Now, the Planck scale is reached when the particles of ordinary matter exceed the Planck mass. For the proton, this is about 10^{19} of its current mass, corresponding to a 10^{38} increase in α_G (since $\alpha_G = m_p^2$ in Planck units), making it very close to the strength of the strong nuclear force. This yields a theoretically possible range for α_G of 0 to $10^{38} \alpha_{G0}$, where α_{G0} represents the value of α_G in our universe.

One type of fine-tuning of α_G results from planetary constraints, as illustrated by considering the effect of making α_G a billion-fold larger in our universe, still very small compared to the Planck scale. In that case, no ECAs could exist on Earth since they would all be crushed. Suppose, however, that one both increased α_G and reduced Earth's size. Would that solve the problem? No, for three reasons. First, since ECAs seem to require a minimal brain size, if Earth were too small, there would not be a large enough ecosystem for ECAs to evolve. Second, smaller planets cannot produce enough internal heat from radioactive decay to sustain plate tectonics. It is estimated that a planet with less than 0.23 the mass of the Earth, or less than about one-half Earth's radius, could not sustain plate tectonics for enough time for ECAs to evolve.[24] Plate tectonics, however, is generally regarded as essential to both stabilizing the atmosphere (by recycling carbon dioxide [CO_2]) and keeping mountains from being eroded to sea level;[25] thus without it, terrestrial ECAs would be impossible. Because the force F of gravity on a planet's surface is proportional to its radius R when the density

D is kept constant ($F \propto \alpha_G DR$),[26] this means that any planet in our universe on which ECAs evolved would have a surface gravitational force at least one-half that of Earth's (assuming a similar composition). This gives a twofold leeway in increasing α_G before the surface force on any ECA-containing planet would have to be proportionally greater. If, for instance, α_G were increased by 100-fold, the surface force on any planet with terrestrial ECAs would be at least fifty times as large. Even if terrestrial ECAs could exist on such a planet, it would be far less optimal for them to develop civilization, especially advanced scientific civilization (think of the difficulty of building houses or forging metals with the surface force of gravity fifty times larger). Thus α_G appears to be not only fine-tuned for the existence of ECAs, but also fine-tuned for civilization. Using the theoretically possible range for α_G, this consideration yields a degree of fine-tuning of at least $100/10^{38}$—that is, 1 part in 10^{36}.[27]

Third, to retain an atmosphere, the average kinetic energy of the molecules in the atmosphere must be considerably less than the energy required for a molecule to escape the planet's gravitational pull—called the molecule's "gravitational binding energy," E_G. For a life-permitting planet, this energy is fixed by the temperature required for liquid water—between 0°C and 100°C. In our universe, it is estimated that a planet with a mass of less than 0.07 that of Earth, or a radius of two-fifths that of Earth, would lose its atmosphere by 4.5 billion years.[28]

Now $E_G \propto \alpha_G R^2$, whereas $F \propto \alpha_G R$, as noted above.[29] This means, for instance, that if α_G were increased by a factor of 100 and the radius of Earth were decreased by the same factor, the force on the surface would remain the same, but E_G would have decreased by a factor of $1/100$ (i.e., $100 \times (1/100)^2$). This would be a far greater decrease in E_G than the factor of $(2/5)^2 \sim 1/5$ allowable decrease calculated using the lower radius limit above. Increasing α_G therefore can only be partially compensated for by decreasing planetary size if the planet is to remain life-permitting. In fact, simple calculations reveal that even with the maximal compensatory shrinking of the planet, the force must increase as the square root of the increase α_G after the factor $2/5$ leeway mentioned above is taken into account.[30] If, for example, one increased α_G by 10,000, the minimal gravitational force on the surface of any ECA-permitting planet would increase by a factor of 40 (i.e., $\sqrt{10{,}000} \times [2/5]$). In addition to these two reasons, there are several other stringent constraints on α_G for the existence of life-sustaining stars.[31] So the constraints on gravity are significantly overdetermined.

In his Internet preprint of the accompanying chapter, Stenger claims that α_G's fine-tuning has a natural scientific explanation that involves no surprise. Says Stenger, "The reason gravity is so weak in atoms is the small masses of elementary particles. This can be understood to be a consequence of the standard model of elementary particles in which the bare particles all have zero masses and pick up small corrections by their interactions with other particles."[32] Although correct, Stenger's claim does not explain the fine-tuning, but merely transfers it elsewhere.

The new issue is why the corrections are so small compared to the Planck scale. Such small corrections seem to require an enormous degree of fine-tuning, which is a general and much discussed problem within the standard model. As particle physicist John Donoghue notes, for the various particles in the standard model, "their 'bare' values plus their quantum corrections need to be highly fine-tuned in order to obtain their observed values [such as the relatively small mass of the proton and neutron]."[33] Stenger's attempt to explain away this apparent fine-tuning is like someone saying protons and neutrons are made of quarks and gluons, and since the latter masses are small, this explains the smallness of the former masses. Such an explanation would merely relocate the fine-tuning.

Next, I turn to the most widely discussed case of fine-tuning in the physics literature, that of the cosmological constant, or more generally, the "dark energy" density of the universe. This fine-tuning has been discussed for more than thirty years and is still unresolved, as can be seen by searching the physics archive at http://arxiv.org/find. Dark energy is any energy existing in space that, if positive, would of itself cause the universe's expansion to accelerate; in contrast, normal matter and energy (such as photons of light) cause it to decelerate. If the dark energy density, ρ_d, is too large, this expansion will accelerate so fast that no galaxies or stars can form, and hence no complex life.[34] The degree of fine-tuning of ρ_d is given by the ratio of its life-permitting range to the range of possible values allowed within our models. Assuming ρ_d is positive, it can have a value from zero to the Planck energy density, which is approximately 10^{120} times the standardly estimated maximum life-permitting value, ρ_{dlife}, of the dark energy density. Hence the commonly cited value of this fine-tuning is 1 part in 10^{120} ($\rho_{dlife}/10^{120}\rho_{dlife}$). This fine-tuning problem is given added force by the fact that a central part of the framework of current particle physics and cosmology invokes various fields that contribute anywhere from $10^{53}\rho_{dlife}$ to $10^{120}\rho_{dlife}$ to ρ_d. This seems to require the postulation of unknown fields with extremely fine-tuned energy densities that exactly, or almost exactly, cancel the energy densities of the fields in question to make ρ_d less than ρ_{dlife}.

Could this fine-tuning be circumvented by postulating a new symmetry or principle that requires that the dark energy be zero? This proposal faces severe problems. First, inflationary cosmology—the widely accepted, though highly speculative, framework in cosmology—requires that the dark energy density be enormously larger than ρ_{dlife} in the very early universe. Thus one would have to postulate that this symmetry or principle only began to apply after some very early epoch was reached—a postulate that in turn involves a "fine-tuning" of some combination of the laws, principles, or fundamental parameters of physics. Second, in the late 1990s it was discovered that the expansion of the universe is accelerating, which is widely taken as strong evidence for a small positive value of ρ_d. A positive value of ρ_d, however, is incompatible with any principle or symmetry requiring that it be zero. Perhaps, as Stenger often suggests, some set of laws or principles requires that it have a very small nonzero value. Even if this is correct, the fine-tuning is likely to be transferred to why the universe has the right set of laws/principles to make ρ_d fall into the small life-permitting range $(0$ to $\rho_{dlife})$ instead of somewhere else in the much, much larger range of conceivable possibilities $(0$ to $10^{120}\,\rho_{dlife})$. Stenger never addresses this issue, seemingly oblivious to this transference problem.[35]

■ 4. CONCLUSION

The above cases of fine-tuning alone should be sufficient to show that, apart from a multiverse hypothesis, the issue of fine-tuning is not likely to be resolved by future physics. Even if physicists found a theory that entailed that initial conditions of the universe and the constants of physics fall into the ECA-permitting range, that would still involve an extreme fine-tuning at the level of the form of the laws themselves. Finally, note that the cases of fine-tuning are multiple and diverse, so even if one cannot be certain of any given case, together they provide a compelling case for an extraordinarily fine-tuned universe.

■ NOTES

1. I would like to thank Nathan Van Wyck, Øystein Nødtvedt, David Schenk, and physicists Luke Barnes, Daniel Darg, Stephen Barr, and Don Page for helpful comments on the penultimate version of this chapter. Finally, I would especially like to thank the John Templeton Foundation and Messiah College for supporting the research that undergirds this chapter. This essay was written before Stenger published his recent book (*The Fallacy of Fine-Tuning: Why the Universe Is Not Designed for Us* (Amherst, NY: Prometheus Books, 2011)) and so mostly references his previous work on fine-tuning.

2. Martin Rees, *Just Six Numbers: The Deep Forces That Shape the Universe* (New York: Basic Books, 2000).

3. Bernard Carr and Martin Rees, "The Anthropic Principle and the Structure of the Physical World," *Nature* 278 (1979): 612.

4. See, Robin Collins, "The Teleological Argument: An Exploration of the Fine-Tuning of the Universe," in *The Blackwell Companion to Natural Theology*, ed. William Lane Craig and J. P. Moreland (Chichester: John Wiley & Sons, 2009), 202–281.

5. See Robin Collins, "The Connection Building Theodicy," in *The Companion to the Problem of Evil*, ed. Dan Howard-Snyder and Justin McBrayer (Malden, MA: Wiley-Blackwell, forthcoming).

6. For this last argument, see Robin Collins, "The Anthropic Principle: A Fresh Look at its Implications," in *A Companion to Science and Christianity*, ed. James Stump and Alan Padgett (Malden, MA: Wiley-Blackwell, 2012).

7. Robin Collins, "Evidence for Fine-Tuning," in *God and Design: The Teleological Argument and Modern Science*, ed. Neil A. Manson (London: Routledge, 2003), 178–199.

8. Luke A. Barnes, "The Fine-Tuning of the Universe for Intelligent Life," http://arxiv.org/abs/1112.4647. My manuscript is tentatively entitled *Cosmic Fine-Tuning: The Scientific Evidence*.

9. Elliott Lieb, "The Stability of Matter," *Reviews of Modern Physics* 48, no. 4 (1976): 553–569.

10. For example, see Victor J. Stenger, "Natural Explanations for the Anthropic Coincidences," *Philo* 3, no. 2 (2000): 50–67.

11. Quoted in Elena Castellani, "On the Meaning of Symmetry Breaking," in *Symmetries in Physics: Philosophical Reflections*, ed. Katherine Brading and Elena Castellani (Cambridge: Cambridge University Press, 2003), 324.

12. Stenger, "Natural Explanations."

13. Roger Penrose, *The Emperor's New Mind: Concerning Computers, Minds, and the Laws of Physics* (New York: Oxford University Press, 1989), 343.

14. Ibid.

15. See Roger Penrose, *The Road to Reality: A Complete Guide to the Laws of the Universe* (New York: Alfred A. Knopf, 2004), 753–757. Also see Collins, "Teleological Argument," Section 6.3, 262–272.

16. Victor J. Stenger, *God: The Failed Hypothesis: How Science Shows That God Does Not Exist* (Amherst, NY: Prometheus Books, 2007), 120.

17. Sean Carroll, *From Eternity to Here: The Quest for the Ultimate Theory of Time* (New York: Dutton, 2010), 62.

18. Ibid., 63.

19. Penrose, *The Emperors' New Mind*, 329.

20. Huw Price, *Time's Arrow and Archimedes' Point: New Directions for the Physics of Time* (Oxford: Oxford University Press, 1996), 81–82.

21. One could also define α_G relative to other elementary particles, but the mass of the proton or neutron is the usual choice in these contexts because they constitute almost the entire mass of normal atomic matter.

22. Victor J. Stenger, "The Universe Shows No Evidence for Design," http://www.colorado.edu/philosophy/vstenger/Fallacy/NoDesign.pdf (accessed January 10, 2011); and Stenger, *The Fallacy of Fine-Tuning*, 151–152.

23. John Barrow, *The Constants of Nature: The Numbers That Encode the Deepest Secrets of the Universe* (New York: Vintage Books, 2004), 43.

24. Darren M. Williams, James F. Kasting, and Richard A. Wade, "Habitable Moons Around Extrasolar Giant Planets," *Nature* 385 (January 16, 1997): 235.

25. Ibid.

26. By Newton's law of gravity, $F \propto \alpha_G M/R^2 \propto \alpha_G DR^3/R^2 = \alpha_G DR$, where M is the mass of the planet for the variation of surface force considered here. The density is largely independent of the size of the planet.

27. Equivalently, in Planck units m_p must be fine-tuned to 1 part in 10^{18}.

28. Williams et al., "Habitable Moons," 235.

29. $E_G \propto \alpha_G M/R \propto \alpha_G DR^3/R = \alpha_G DR^2$.

30. Since $E_G \propto \alpha_G R^2$, to hold E_G constant (and thus retain an atmosphere), R can only decrease by the square root of the increase in α_G. Hence, since $F \propto \alpha_G R$, F must increase by the square root of the increase in α_G.

31. See Collins, "Evidence for Fine-Tuning," 192–194, and Bernard Carr, "The Anthropic Principle Revisited," in *Universe or Multiverse?*, ed. Bernard Carr (Cambridge: Cambridge University Press, 2007), 79.

32. Stenger, "Universe Shows No Evidence."

33. John F. Donoghue, "The Fine-Tuning Problems of Particle Physics and Anthropic Mechanisms," in *Universe or Multiverse?*, ed. Bernard Carr (Cambridge: Cambridge University Press, 2007), 231.

34. ρ_d could also be negative. If ρ_d is too large in the negative direction ($-\rho_d < -\rho_{d\text{life}}$), the universe would collapse too soon for life to develop.

35. Even if the acceleration is due to something else, such as a small correction term in Einstein's general theory of relativity, the fine-tuning would merely be transferred elsewhere—e.g., to why the correction term is so small compared to the Planck scale.

■ FOR FURTHER READING

Barrow, J., and F. Tipler. *The Anthropic Cosmological Principle*. Oxford, UK: Oxford University, 1986.

Collins, R., P. Draper, and Q. Smith. "Section Three: Science and the Cosmos." In *God or Blind Nature? Philosophers Debate the Evidence* (2007–2008). http://www.infidels.org/library/modern/debates/great-debate.html.

Davies, P. *The Accidental Universe*. Cambridge: Cambridge University Press, 1982.

Leslie, J. *Universes*. New York: Routledge, 1989.

Manson, N., ed. *God and Design: The Teleological Argument and Modern Science*. New York: Routledge, 2003.

4 The Universe Shows No Evidence for Design

■ VICTOR J. STENGER

▒ 1. THE FINE-TUNING ARGUMENT

In recent years many theologians and Christian apologists have convinced themselves that they have a convincing argument for the existence of God. They claim that the parameters of physics are so finely tuned that if any one of them were just slightly different in value, life would not have been possible anywhere in the universe. Assuming, on no basis whatsoever, that those parameters are independent and could have taken on any value over a wide range, they conclude that the probability of a universe with the particular set of parameters as ours is infinitesimally small. Further assuming, on no basis whatsoever, that the probability of a divine creator is not equally infinitesimally small, they conclude that such a creator existed who fine-tuned the universe for life, particularly human life. Note that there is also no basis whatsoever to assume that this creator was the personal God worshipped by Christians, Muslims, and Jews. A deist creator works equally well.

Leading Christian apologist William Lane Craig summarized the argument this way in his 1998 debate with philosopher/biologist Massimo Pigliucci (and in other debates):[1]

> During the last 30 years, scientists have discovered that the existence of intelligent life depends upon a complex and delicate balance of initial conditions given in the Big Bang itself. We now know that life-*prohibiting* universes are vastly more probable than any life-*permitting* universe like ours. How much more probable?
>
> The answer is that the chances that the universe should be life-permitting are so infinitesimal as to be incomprehensible and incalculable. For example, Stephen Hawking has estimated that if the rate of the universe's expansion one second after the Big Bang had been smaller by even one part in a hundred thousand million million, the universe would have re-collapsed into a hot fireball.[2] P. C. W. Davies has calculated that the odds against the initial conditions being suitable for later star formation (without which planets could not exist) is one followed by a thousand billion billion zeroes, at least.[3]
>
> John Barrow and Frank Tipler estimate that a change in the strength of gravity or of the weak force by only one part in 10^{100} would have prevented a life-permitting universe.[4] There are around 50 such quantities and constants present in the Big Bang which must be fine-tuned in this way if the universe is to permit life. And it's not just

each quantity that must be exquisitely fine-tuned; their *ratios* to one another must be also finely-tuned. So improbability is multiplied by improbability by improbability until our minds are reeling in incomprehensible numbers.

Cosmologists have proposed a very simple, purely natural solution to the fine-tuning problem. Their current models strongly suggest that ours is not the only universe, but part of a *multiverse* containing an unlimited number of individual universes extending an unlimited distance in all directions and for an unlimited time in the past and future. If that's the case, we just happen to live in that universe which is suited for our kind of life. The universe is not fine-tuned to us; we are fine-tuned to our particular universe.

Now, theists and many nonbelieving scientists object to this solution as being "nonscientific" because we have no way of observing a universe outside our own. In fact, a multiverse is more scientific and parsimonious than hypothesizing an unobservable creating spirit and a single universe. I would argue that the multiverse is a legitimate scientific hypothesis, since it agrees with our best knowledge.

Although I believe the multiverse explanation is adequate to refute fine-tuning, it remains an untested hypothesis. In this essay I will make a case against fine-tuning that will not rely on speculations beyond well-established physics or on the existence of multiple universes. I will show that fine-tuning is a fallacy based on our knowledge of this universe alone.

▪ 2. LAWS AND MODELS

Before I get to the parameters that are supposedly fine-tuned, let me say a word about my basic, underlying assumptions. First, I assume that the models of physics are human inventions, and so it follows that the quantities, parameters, and "laws" that appear in these models are likewise. These elements must agree with observations, and so they must have something to do with whatever objective reality is out there. They are not arbitrary. But we have no way of knowing if the ingredients of the models, such as space, time, mass, and elementary particles exist in close correspondence to that reality.

And so, the parameters that are supposedly fine-tuned by a deity are just those physicists use in their models and need not have any specific ontological significance. The claim of fine-tuning of the parameters of physics is equivalent to a claim that our languages have been fine-tuned so they have grammatical rules that are highly unlikely to have occurred naturally.

Second, physicists in the twentieth century discovered that there is a set of principles or "metalaws" that must be present in all physics models. In order to describe the universe objectively, physicists must formulate their models so that they describe observations in ways that are independent of the point of view of particular observers. This gives the model builders no choice but to include the great conservation principles of energy, linear momentum, angular momentum, and electric charge and all of classical physics including Maxwell's equations of electromagnetism and Einstein's theory of special relativity. Much of quantum mechanics, including the Heisenberg uncertainty principle, also must be included.[5]

Thus, when I argue below that some parameter is in a range consistent with known physics, the apologist cannot come back with "Where did the physics come from?" The physics came from physicists formulating models that must include the metalaws. And, as we will see, the values of the parameters in the models that successfully describe all observations in our universe are within the ranges expected from these metalaws.

▪ 3. THE PARAMETERS

While many authors have written on fine-tuning and given examples, I will rely on the most complete list assembled by microbiologist Rich Deem on his *God and Science* Web site.[6] Deem also lists, without details, estimates of the precision at which each parameter had to be tuned to produce our kind of life. These are the numbers that make Craig's mind reel.

Deem's main reference is physicist and Christian apologist Hugh Ross and his popular book *The Creator and the Cosmos*, first published in 1993.[7] Ross is the founder of Reasons to Believe, which describes itself as an "international and interdenominational science-faith think tank."[8] A list of twenty-six claimed "design evidences" can be found in the book.[9] Ross has further developed his arguments in a chapter called "Big Bang Model Refined by Fire" in the anthology *Mere Creation: Science, Faith & Intelligent Design.*[10]

Two of the parameters that appear in most lists of fine-tuned quantities are

- the speed of light in a vacuum c and
- Planck's constant h.

As basic as these parameters are to physics, their values are arbitrary. The fundamental unit of time in physics is the second. The units for all other variables are defined relative to the second. The value of c is then chosen to define what units will be used to measure distance. To measure distance in meters you choose $c = 3 \times 10^8$. To measure distance in light-years you choose $c = 1$.

Note that the speed of light in a medium can be different from c.

The value of Planck's constant h is chosen to define what units you will be using to measure energy. To measure energy in joules you use $h = 6.626 \times 10^{-34}$. To measure energy in electron-volts you use $h = 4.136 \times 10^{-15}$. Physicists like to work in what they call "natural units," where $\hbar = h/2\pi = c = 1$.

TABLE 4.1. *Fine-Tuning of Five Physical Parameters*

Parameter	Maximum deviation
Ratio of electrons to protons	$1/10^{37}$
Ratio of electromagnetic force to gravity	$1/10^{40}$
Expansion rate of universe	$1/10^{55}$
Mass density of universe	$1/10^{59}$
Cosmological constant	$1/10^{120}$

Conclusion: No fine tuning; units are chosen for convenience and have no fundamental significance.

I will move next to the five parameters that Deem lists as being so finely tuned that no form of life could exist in a universe in which any of the values differed by an infinitesimal amount from their existing values in our universe. These are given in Table 4.1, along with the maximum allowed deviation according to Deem.

3.1 Ratio of electrons to protons

Ross asserts that if this ratio were larger, there would be insufficient chemical binding. If smaller, electromagnetism would dominate gravity, preventing galaxy, star, and planet formation.

The fact that the ratio is one can be easily explained. The number of electrons in the universe should exactly equal the number of protons from charge conservation, on the reasonable assumption that the total electric charge of the universe is zero—as it should be if the universe came from "nothing" and charge is conserved.

Conclusion: No fine-tuning; the parameter is fixed by established physics and cosmology.

3.2 Ratio of electromagnetic force to gravity

Ross says that if this ratio were larger, there would be no stars less than 1.4 solar masses and hence short and uneven stellar burning. If it were smaller, there would be no stars more than 0.8 solar masses and hence no heavy element production.

The ratio of the forces is calculated for a proton and electron and depends on their charges and masses. If the masses were much larger, the forces would be closer in value. Despite the statement often heard in most physics classrooms that gravity is much weaker than electromagnetism, there is no way one can state absolutely the relative strengths of gravity and any other force.

The reason gravity is so weak in atoms is the small masses of elementary particles. This can be understood to be a consequence of the standard model of elementary particles in which the bare particles all have zero masses and pick up small corrections by their interactions with other particles.

Conclusion: No fine-tuning; the parameter is fixed by established physics and cosmology.

3.3 Expansion rate of the universe

Ross claims that if it were larger there would be no galaxy formation; if smaller the universe would collapse prior to star formation.

This is also the parameter that apologists William Lane Craig[11] and Dinesh D'Souza[12] referred to when they lifted out of context a quotation from Stephen Hawking's bestseller *A Brief History of Time*, which also bears repeating:

> If the rate of expansion one second after the Big Bang had been smaller by even one part in a hundred thousand million million, the universe would have collapsed before it ever reached its present size.[13]

Craig and D'Souza both ignored the explanation Hawking gave seven pages later for why no fine-tuning was needed:

> The rate of expansion of the universe would automatically become very close to the critical rate determined by the energy density of the universe. This could then explain why the rate of expansion is still so close to the critical rate, without having to assume that the initial rate of expansion of the universe was very carefully chosen.[14]

Conclusion: No fine-tuning; the parameter is fixed by established physics and cosmology.

The expansion rate and mean mass/energy density of the universe go hand in hand, so let me bring in the next of Deem's critical parameters.

3.4 Mass density of the universe

While Deem lists this as the "mass of the universe," I am sure he meant mass density. This is what Ross lists. Ross tells us that if it were larger, there would be too much deuterium from the big bang and stars would burn too rapidly. If it were smaller, there would be insufficient helium from the big bang and too few heavy elements would form.

According to inflationary cosmology, during the tiny fraction of a second after the universe appeared, it expanded exponentially by many orders of magnitude so that it became spatially flat like the surface of a huge balloon. This implies that the mass/energy density of the universe is now very close to its critical value in which the total kinetic energy of all its bodies is exactly balanced by their negative gravitational potential energy. In fact, this was a prediction of inflation that was not an established fact when the model was first proposed. If it had not turned out the way it did, inflation would have been falsified. The success of this prediction is one of several reasons cosmologists consider inflationary cosmology to now be a well-established part of the standard model of cosmology.

The critical density depends on the Hubble parameter, which is the rate of expansion. The "one part in a hundred thousand million million" that Hawking and the apologists refer to is the precise relation between the density and the Hubble parameter that follows to at least that precision from the inflationary model.

Conclusion: No fine-tuning; the parameter is fixed by established physics and cosmology.

3.5 The cosmological constant

Deem gives $1/10^{120}$ as the maximum deviation for the cosmological constant, which is a parameter in Einstein's general theory of relativity. Apparently he obtained this number from the result of the calculation of the total zero-point energy density of boson (integer spin) fields in the universe. Elementary particles are identified as the "quanta" of these fields. The zero-point energy is the energy left over when all the quanta of a field are removed. This calculation comes out 120 orders of magnitude higher than the observed upper limit on the vacuum energy density of the universe.[15] A principle called *supersymmetry* that is predicted to exist at high energy but is not yet verified, pending results from the Large Hadron Collider, reduces the energy density to "only" 10^{50} times the observed value, still a long way from agreement.

The energy density associated with the cosmological constant is the favorite candidate for the dark energy that is presumed to be responsible for the acceleration of the universe's expansion. Dark energy constitutes almost three-quarters of the total mass/energy of the universe. Since the universe has an average density equal to the critical density, the dark energy density is almost as big, though still many orders of magnitude below its calculated value. Any calculation that disagrees with the data by fifty or more orders of magnitude has to be wrong and cannot be taken seriously.

Now, physicists still have not reached a consensus on the cosmological question. Some prominent figures such as Steven Weinberg, Stephen Hawking, and Leonard Susskind think the answer lies in multiple universes.

However, one idea that is currently getting much attention is the *holographic universe*. This is a speculation based on established physics, and so is not simply off the wall.

In calculating the zero-point energy density, we sum over all the states in a volume equal to the instantaneous volume of the visible universe. The holographic principle says that the maximum information that can be stored in a region of space is proportional to the surface area of that region. Thus, to get the zero-point energy density, we should have summed over just the states on the surface rather than the full volume. When we do that we obtain an energy density equal to the critical density, just the value it appears to have.

Conclusion: The standard calculation of this parameter is grossly wrong and should be ignored. Viable possibilities exist for explaining its value, and until these are all ruled out, no fine-tuning can be claimed.

This takes care of the five parameters that are claimed to be fine-tuned to such precision that even a tiny deviation would make life of any kind impossible. Next let us move to those parameters for which proponents of fine-tuning can only claim that life would be very unlikely if the values of the parameters were different.

3.6 The Hoyle prediction

We begin our discussion of the less critical parameters by relating how, in 1951, astronomer Fred Hoyle argued that the carbon nucleus had to have an excited state at 7.7 MeV above its ground state in order for enough carbon to be produced in stars to make life in the universe possible. This story is of great historical interest because it is the only case where anthropic reasoning has led to a successful prediction.

However, recent calculations have demonstrated that the same carbon would have been produced if the excited state were anyplace between 7.716 MeV and 7.596 MeV. Furthermore, sufficient carbon for life would have occurred for an excited state anywhere from just above the ground state to 7.933 MeV. A state somewhere in such a large range is expected from standard nuclear theory. Furthermore, carbon may not be the only element upon which life could be based.

Conclusion: No fine-tuning; the parameter is within the range allowed by established physics and cosmology.

3.7 Relative masses of the elementary particles

The masses of elementary particles affect many features of the universe and a number of fine-tuning claims refer to their values. Let me begin with the mass difference between the neutron and proton. If the difference in masses between the neutron and proton were less than the sum of the masses of the electron and neutrino (the neutrino mass in our universe is negligible for this purpose, but may not be in some other universe), there would be no neutron decay. In the early universe, electrons and protons would combine to form neutrons and few, if any, protons would remain. If the mass difference were greater than the binding energies of nuclei, neutrons inside nuclei would decay, leaving no nuclei behind.

There is a range of 10 MeV or so for the mass difference to still be in the allowed region for the full periodic table to be formed. The actual mass difference is 1.29 MeV, so there is plenty of room for it to be larger. Since the neutron and proton masses are equal to a first approximation, and the difference results from a small electromagnetic correction, it is unlikely to be as high as 10 MeV.

Next let us bring in the mass of the electron, which also affects the neutron decay story. A lower electron mass gives more room in parameter space for neutron decay, while a higher mass leaves less. It can have any value from 0 to 1.29 MeV in our universe and from 0 to around 4 MeV in any universe and we would still have neutron decay.

Conclusion: No fine-tuning; the parameter is within the range allowed by established physics and cosmology.

The ratio of the electron and proton masses helps determine the region of parameter space for which chemistry is unchanged from our universe, which we can show is quite substantial. No fine-tuning is evident here either.

3.8 Relative strengths of the forces and other physics parameters

The dimensionless relative force strengths are the next set of physical parameters whose fine-tuning is claimed for reasons I find wanting. The gravitational strength parameter a_G is based on an arbitrary choice of units of mass, so it is arbitrary. Thus a_G cannot be fine-tuned. There is nothing to tune.

Next let us consider the strength of the weak interaction a_W. Ross claims it is fine-tuned to give the right amount of helium and heavy element production in the big bang and in stars. The key is the ratio of neutrons to protons in the early universe when, as the universe cools, their production reactions drop out of equilibrium. A range of parameters is allowed.

The electromagnetic strength represented by the dimensionless parameter a, historically known as the fine-structure constant and having the famous value 1/137 at low energies. Ross tells us that there would be insufficient chemical bonding if it were different. But the many-electron Schrödinger equation, which governs most of chemistry, scales with a and the mass of the electron. Again, a wide range allows for the chemistry of life.

There are many places where the value of a relative to other parameters comes in. We saw that the weakness of gravity relative to electromagnetism in matter was due to the natural low masses of elementary particles. This can also be achieved with a higher value of a, but it's not likely to be orders of magnitude higher.

The relative values of a and the strong force parameter a_S also are important in several cases. When the two are allowed to vary, no fine-tuning is necessary to allow for both nuclear stability and the existence of free protons.

There are two other facts that most proponents of fine-tuning ignore: (1) the force parameters a, a_S, and a_W are not constant, but vary with energy; (2) they are not independent. The force parameters are expected to be equal at some unification energy. Furthermore, the three are connected in the current standard model and are likely to remain connected in any model that succeeds it.

Conclusion: No fine-tuning; the parameters are in the range expected from established physics.

Other parameters such as the decay rate of protons and the baryon excess in the early universe have quite a bit of room to vary before they result in excess radiation.

3.9 Cosmic parameters

We have already disposed of the cosmic parameters that seem so crucial in making any livable universe possible. The mass density of the universe, the expansion rate, and the ratio of the number of protons and electrons are not only not fine-tuned, they are fixed by conventional physics and cosmology.

The deuterium abundance needed for life is small and a wide range of two orders of magnitude is allowed.

Martin Rees and others have claimed that the lumpiness of matter, represented by a quantity Q, in the universe had to be fine-tuned within an order of magnitude to allow for galaxy formation. An order of magnitude is hardly the kind of fine-tuning the theists are claiming. What's more, varying the nucleon mass along with Q allows, again, for more parameter space for life.

More detailed calculations using the standard concordance model of cosmology indicate that five parameters contribute to the density fluctuations that provide for galaxy formation. So it is a gross simplification to just talk about varying the single parameter Q. And, when an alternative, the cold big bang model, is used, an even wider range of parameters becomes possible.

3.10 Simulating universes

The gross properties of the universe are determined by just three parameters: the electromagnetic strength a and the masses of the proton and electron, m_p and m_e. From these we can estimate quantities such as the maximum lifetime of stars, the minimum and maximum masses of planets, the minimum length of a planetary day, and the maximum length of a year for a habitable planet. Generating 10,000 universes in which the parameters are varied randomly on a logarithmic scale over a range of 10 orders of magnitude, I find that 61 percent of the universes have stellar lifetimes of more than 10 billion years, sufficient for some kind of life to evolve.

Christian philosopher Robin Collins, my opponent in this debate, objected to my preliminary, twenty-year-old conclusion that long stellar lifetimes are not fine-tuned.[16] He argues that not all these universes are livable, that I have not accounted for life-inhibiting features. He refers to Barrow and Tipler, who estimated that $a \leq 11.8a_s$ for carbon to be stable.[17]

Since in this study I was varying all the parameters by ten orders of magnitude, I would not expect such a tight criterion to be satisfied very often. Nevertheless,

I have checked and found the Barrow–Tipler limit to be satisfied 59 percent of the time. As we will see below, I have also studied what happens when the parameters are varied by just two orders of magnitude. Then 91 percent of the time we have $a \leq 11.8a_s$.

Applying rather tight limits to all three parameters, 13 percent of all universes are capable of supporting some kind of life not too different from ours. Varying by two orders of magnitude, which is more realistic since the parameters are not independent but related, I find that 92 percent of the universes have stellar lifetimes of more than 10 billion years and 37 percent are capable of supporting some kind of life not too different from ours. Life very different from ours remains possible in a large fraction of the remaining universes, judging from the large stellar lifetimes for most.

■ 4. A FINAL CONCLUSION

The proponents of fine-tuning make serious errors in physics, cosmology, probability theory, and data analysis. While not every proponent makes every error, there is a remarkable similarity to the arguments you find in the theist literature. Let me list the errors of fine-tuning proponents that I have uncovered in my research:

1. They make fine-tuning claims based on the parameters of our universe and our form of life, ignoring the possibility of other life forms.
2. They claim fine-tuning for physics constants such a c and h whose values are arbitrary.
3. They assert fine-tuning for quantities such as the ratio of electrons to protons, the expansion rate of the universe, and the mass density of the universe, whose values are precisely determined by physical theory.
4. They assert that the relative strengths of the electromagnetic and gravitational forces are fine-tuned, when in fact this quantity cannot be universally defined.
5. They assert that an excited state of the carbon nucleus had to be fine-tuned for stars to produce the carbon needed for life, when calculations show a wide range of values for the energy level of that state that will produce enough carbon.
6. They claim fine-tuning for the masses of elementary particles when the ranges of these masses are set by well-established physics and sufficiently constrained to give some form of life.
7. They assume the strengths of the various forces are constants that can independently change from universe to universe. In fact, they vary with energy and their relative values and energy dependences are close to being pinned down by theory, in ranges that make some kind of life possible.

8. They make a serious analytical mistake in always taking all the parameters in the universe to be fixed and varying only one at a time. This fails to account for the fact that a change in one parameter can be compensated for by a change in another, opening up more parameter space for a viable universe.

9. They misunderstand and misuse probability theory.

10. They claim many parameters of Earth and the solar system are fine-tuned for life, failing to consider that with 100 billion to a trillion planets in the visible universe, and the countless number beyond our horizon, a planet with the properties needed for life is likely to occur many times.

I also assert that some fine-tuners are wrong when they reject the multiverse solution as "unscientific." I will not call that an error, since the issue is arguable, whereas the ten examples above are not. But I do not think it is unscientific to speculate about invisible, unconfirmed phenomena that are predicted by existing models that, so far, agree with all the data. The neutrino was predicted to exist in 1930 based on the well-established principle of energy conservation and was not detected until 1956, and even then indirectly. If the physics community used the fine-tuners' criterion, my late colleague Fred Reines and his collaborator Clyde Cowen would not have been able to get the money and support to engage in their search.

As my discussion illustrates, the explanations for apparent fine-tuning are technical and require adequate training to understand. A proper analysis finds there is no evidence that the universe is fine-tuned for us.[18]

■ NOTES

1. William Lane Craig, "The Craig-Pigliucci Debate: Does God Exist?," http://www.leaderu.com/offices/billcraig/docs/craig-pigliucci2.html (accessed February 13, 2010).

2. Stephen W. Hawking, *A Brief History of Time: From the Big Bang to Black Holes* (New York: Bantam, 1988), 121–122.

3. P. C. W. Davies, *Other Worlds* (London: Dent, 1980), 6.

4. John D. Barrow and Frank J. Tipler, *The Anthropic Cosmological Principle* (Oxford: Oxford University Press, 1986).

5. Victor J. Stenger, *The Comprehensible Cosmos: Where Do the Laws of Physics Come From?* (Amherst, NY: Prometheus Books, 2006).

6. Rich Deem "Evidence for the Fine Tuning of the Universe," *God and Science*, http://www.godandscience.org/apologetics/designun.html (accessed November 27, 2008).

7. Hugh Ross, *The Creator and the Cosmos: How the Greatest Scientific Discoveries of the Century Reveal God* (Colorado Springs: NavPress, 1995).

8. "Reasons to Believe," http://www.reasons.org/ (accessed December 20, 2008).

9. "Evidence for Design," http://www.reasons.org/resources/apologetics/index.shtml#design_in_the_universe (accessed December 20, 2008).

10. Hugh Ross, "Big Bang Model Refined By Fire," in *Mere Creation: Science, Faith & Intelligent Design*, ed. William A. Dembski (Downers Grove, IL: Intervarsity Press, 1988), 363–383.

11. William Lane Craig, "The Craig-Pigliucci Debate: Does God Exist?," http://www. leaderu.com/offices/billcraig/docs/craig-pigliucci1.html (accessed February 13, 2010).

12. Dinesh D'Souza, *Life After Death: The Evidence* (Washington, DC: Regnery Publishing, 2009), 84.

13. Hawking, *A Brief History of Time*, 121–122.

14. Ibid., 128.

15. Stenger, *The Comprehensible Cosmos*, 308–309.

16. Robin Collins, "The Teleological Argument: An Exploration of the Fine-Tuning of the Universe," in *The Blackwell Companion to Natural Theology*, ed. William Lane Craig and James Porter Moreland (Chichester: Wiley-Blackwell, 2009).

17. Barrow and Tipler, *The Anthropic Cosmological Principle*, 326.

18. This article is based on the author's book, *The Fallacy of Fine-Tuning: How the Universe Is Not Designed for Us* (Amherst, NY: Prometheus Books, 2011).

■ FOR FURTHER READING

Hawking, S. W. *A Brief History of Time: From the Big Bang to Black Holes.* Toronto: Bantam Books, 1988.

Stenger, Victor J. *The Fallacy of Fine-Tuning: How the Universe is Not Designed for Us.* Amherst, NY: Prometheus Books, 2011.

———. *Has Science Found God?: The Latest Results in the Search for Purpose in the Universe.* Amherst, NY: Prometheus Books, 2003.

Susskind, L. *Cosmic Landscape: String Theory and the Illusion of Intelligent Design.* New York: Little, Brown and Co., 2005.

An Ontological Argument

5   A Modal Version of the Ontological Argument

■ E. J. LOWE

The original version of the ontological argument for the existence of God is due to St. Anselm.[1] He argued that God is, by definition, a being than which none greater can be conceived; that such a being exists at least in the mind of the conceiver, that is, in conception; that it is greater to exist in reality than to exist merely in conception; and hence that such a being does exist in reality. This argument speaks explicitly only of God's *existence*, not of his *necessary* existence. Modal versions of the ontological argument speak of the latter. Typically they run roughly as follows. God is, by definition, a *necessary* being—one that *necessarily* exists; but, given that such a being is *possible*, it exists at least in *some* possible world, *w*. However, since it is thus true in *w* that this necessary being exists, it is true in *w* that this being exists in *every* possible world, including the actual world, hence this being exists also in actuality.[2] There are many objections that can be and have been raised against both modal and nonmodal versions of the ontological argument. Rather than try to rebut those objections or refine existing versions of the argument,[3] what I shall do in this chapter is to develop a new kind of modal ontological argument for the existence of God—or, more precisely and somewhat less ambitiously, for the existence of a *necessary concrete being*. I shall explain in due course why, although this kind of argument differs from more familiar variants of the modal ontological argument, it does still unquestionably qualify as a modal ontological argument. Above all, it is an a priori argument that focuses on *necessary* existence, not just existence.

▨ 1. THE NEW ARGUMENT

First, I need to present some definitions. For the argument to proceed, I need to define both what is meant by a *necessary* being and what is meant by a *concrete* being. My definition of the former is as follows:

(D1) x is a necessary being $=_{df} x$ exists in every possible world.

In contrast to a necessary being, we have *contingent* beings, defined thus:

(D2) x is a contingent being $=_{df} x$ exists in some but not every possible world.

Next, I define a *concrete* being as follows:[4]

(D3) x is a concrete being $=_{df} x$ exists in space and time, or at least in time.

In contrast to a concrete being, we have *abstract* beings, defined thus:

(D4) x is an abstract being $=_{df} x$ does not exist in space or time.

Observe that, according to these definitions, a being cannot be both concrete and abstract: being concrete and being abstract are *mutually exclusive* properties of beings. Also, all beings are either concrete or abstract, at least on the plausible assumption that a being cannot exist in space without also existing in time: the abstract/concrete distinction is *exhaustive*. Consequently, a being is concrete if and only if it is not abstract. (And, in fact, it is only this *consequence* of (D3) and (D4) that is crucial for the argument that follows, so that any other pair of definitions with the same consequence would serve its purposes just as well.) However, there is no logical restriction on combinations of the properties involved in the concrete/abstract and the necessary/contingent distinctions. In principle, then, we can have *contingent concrete* beings, *contingent abstract* beings, *necessary concrete* beings, and *necessary abstract* beings. An example of a contingent concrete being would be a particular horse or a particular mountain. An example of a necessary abstract being would be a particular number or a particular geometrical form. An example of a contingent abstract being would be a set all of whose members are contingent beings, such as the set of all existing horses. An example of a necessary concrete being would be God, if indeed such a being exists. I concede that it is somewhat controversial to say that God, if he exists, exists *in time*, although many theologians have maintained that he does. One reason, however, why I take God, if he exists, to be a concrete being in this sense is that it is difficult to see how an *abstract* being could have any *causal powers*, including the power of creating contingent concrete beings, which God is supposed to have. To say that God exists in time is not to imply that he must change over time: he may still be eternal and immutable. Although I am not in a position to prove that there can be *only one* necessary concrete being, I think it is very plausible to suppose this. Of course, the traditional God of the philosophers is more than just a unique necessary being with creative powers, but is also omniscient, omnipotent, and perfectly good. Again, I am not in a position to prove that the necessary concrete being whose existence I hope to establish must have these further properties. However, since most objectors to any version of the ontological argument think that it fails at a much earlier hurdle than this, I shall still consider myself to have achieved something of no little significance if I can at least demonstrate the existence of a necessary concrete being.

The first two premises of my argument are these:

(P1) God is, by definition, a necessary concrete being.

(P2) Some necessary abstract beings exist.

As noted earlier, examples of necessary abstract beings include numbers—for instance, the natural numbers, 0, 1, 2, 3, and so on ad infinitum. Why should we suppose that these numbers exist? Simply because there are mathematical truths concerning them—such as the truth that 2 + 3 = 5—and these truths are *necessary* truths, that is, true *in every possible world*. The natural numbers are the *truthmakers* of such truths—the entities in virtue of whose existence those truths obtain—and hence those numbers must exist *in every possible world*, in order to make those truths obtain in every possible world.[5]

The third premise of my argument is this:

(P3) All abstract beings are dependent beings.

By a dependent being, in this context, I mean a being that depends for its existence on some other being or beings. This kind of dependence can be called *existential dependence* and may be defined (at least to a first approximation) as follows:[6]

(D5) *x* depends for its existence on *y* =$_{df}$ necessarily, *x* exists only if *y* exists.

(D5), however, only defines the existential dependence of one *particular* entity on another. We need also to speak of the existential dependence of one kind of entity on another, which we may define (again to a first approximation) as follows, where *F*s and *G*s are entities of different kinds (for instance, abstract beings and concrete beings):

(D6) *F*s depend for their existence on *G*s =$_{df}$ necessarily, *F*s exist only if *G*s exist.

Now, if (P3) is true, it seems reasonable to draw the following conclusion:

(C1) All abstract beings depend for their existence on concrete beings.

Of course, it might be suggested that, contrary to (C1), at least some and possibly all abstract beings depend only on other abstract beings for their existence. But this would seem to be problematic, because it would imply that, where abstract beings are concerned, there can be either *circles* of existential dependence or *infinite descending chains* of existential dependence, with the consequence that the existence of some or all abstract entities is not properly grounded. Let us then rule this out explicitly by invoking another premise, namely:[7]

(P4) All dependent beings depend for their existence on independent beings.

This still allows that a dependent being may depend for its existence on another dependent being, provided that, via some finite chain of dependence, it ultimately depends for its existence on one or more independent beings. We need to bear in mind here that the relation of existential dependence is a transitive relation: if x depends for its existence on y and y depends for its existence on z, then x depends for its existence on z.

Alternatively, however, (P3) might be challenged, with the contention that at least some abstract beings are independent beings. Let me briefly consider this possibility here, though I shall return to the matter at the end of this chapter, since it is connected with other issues of theological significance. According to one position in the philosophy of mathematics, numbers are to be understood as being set-theoretical entities. For instance, it may be proposed that the number 0 is identical with the so-called empty set, $\varnothing$, that the number 1 is identical with the unit set of the empty set, $\{\varnothing\}$, that the number 2 is identical with the unit set of the unit set of the empty set, $\{\{\varnothing\}\}$, and so on ad infinitum. Now, in this view, it seems clear that each number except for the number 0 depends for its existence on all of the preceding numbers in the series of natural numbers, simply because any set depends for its existence on its members. But it may be contended that the number 0, here taken to be the *empty set*, does not depend for its existence on anything else at all. However, I think we ought to be skeptical about the very existence of the so-called empty set: I believe that it is a mere mathematical fiction.[8] After all, how could there really be any such thing as a set with no members, when what a set is, according to our common understanding, is something that "collects together" certain other things, these things being its members. How could something "collect together" nothing?

Anyway, although there is plenty of room for further discussion about these matters, I am going to take it that (P3) and (P4) are both true and hence that (C1), which follows from them, is also true. Sufficiently many good metaphysicians would agree with me for these to qualify as relatively safe assumptions, for the purposes of the present argument.[9] Note that from (P3), together with definitions (D3) and (D4), we can also infer:

(C2) The only independent beings are concrete beings.

Now, from (C1) we can infer the following:

(C3) There is no possible world in which only abstract beings exist.

And from (P2) we can infer this:

(C4) There is no possible world in which no abstract beings exist.

But (C3) and (C4) together imply the following:

(C5) In every possible world there exist concrete beings.

What (C5) means is that there is no "empty world"—a world devoid of anything existing in space and time, or at least in time.[10] However, there are two different reasons for which (C5) could be true. One possibility is that (C5) is true because there is a necessary concrete being—a concrete being that exists in every possible world. This, of course, is what I should like to prove to be the case. And, indeed, it is because (C5) is true that we have at least a prima facie reason to believe that the following is true (or, at least, not to reject it out of hand as false):

(C6) A necessary concrete being is possible.

But another possibility is that (C5) is true just because in every possible world there exist contingent concrete beings—different ones in different worlds. This may very well be the case, but it is obviously not sufficient to prove what I want to prove.

Fortunately, though, I think it can be compellingly argued that only if there is a necessary concrete being can the truth of (P2) be adequately explained. This is because I consider the following further premise to be very plausibly true:

(P5) No contingent being can explain the existence of a necessary being.

The reason why (P5) is so plausible is this. A necessary being is, by definition (D1), a being that exists in every possible world, whereas a contingent being is, by definition (D2), a being that exists in some but not every possible world. Suppose, then, that N is a certain necessary being (e.g., the number 7) and that C is a certain contingent being (e.g., Mount Everest). How could C explain N's existence? After all, N exists in possible worlds in which C does *not* exist—so C evidently cannot explain N's existence in those possible worlds. But how, then, can C explain N's existence even in worlds in which C does exist? For what C would have to explain is why N, a necessary being, exists in those worlds, that is, a being that exists in every possible world. It would, apparently, thereby have to explain why N exists also in worlds in which C does not exist, which we have already ruled out as impossible. Someone might try to reply that different contingent beings could explain the existence of the same necessary being in different possible worlds: that Mount Everest, say, explains the existence of the number 7 in this, the actual world, while the Golden Mountain, say, explains the existence of the number 7 in some other possible world. But that seems absurd. Surely a contingent being, such as Mount Everest—even an abstract contingent being, such as the set whose members are the Seven Hills of Rome—simply doesn't have the power to explain the existence of a necessary being, such as the number 7. Again, the problem is that what it would purportedly be explaining the existence of is something that exists in every possible world and hence something whose existence far transcends its own. Furthermore, to contend that the existence of a necessary being, N, is explained in different possible worlds by different contingent beings in those worlds threatens to undermine the very necessity of

N's existence. For then it appears to be a mere cosmic accident that every possible world happens to contain something that is, allegedly, able to explain the existence of *N* in that world.

Here it might be objected that, even if (P5) is true, we are not entitled to assume that, where necessary beings are concerned, their existence needs to be explained at all. However, while I agree that there may be no need to explain the existence of a necessary being that is an independent being, I think that the existence of dependent beings does always call for explanation:

(P6) The existence of any dependent being needs to be explained.

And recall that we have already agreed, by endorsing (P2), that some necessary abstract beings—such as the numbers—exist and that, by (P3), these are all dependent beings. So, with the additional help of (P6), we may now infer:

(C7) The existence of necessary abstract beings needs to be explained.

Observe, next, that the fact that an entity *x* depends for its existence on an entity *y* does not imply that *y* explains the existence of *x*. Similarly, the fact that *F*s depend for their existence on *G*s does not imply that *G*s explain the existence of *F*s. Existence-explanation is not simply the inverse of existential dependence. If *x* depends for its existence on *y*, this only means that *x* cannot exist without *y* existing. This is not at all the same as saying that *x* exists because *y* exists, or that *x* exists in virtue of the fact that *y* exists. So the mere fact that, by (C5), necessary abstract beings cannot exist without concrete beings existing doesn't imply that concrete beings of just any kind, necessary or contingent, can explain the existence of necessary abstract beings. Indeed, we have already seen good reason to uphold (P5), that no contingent being can explain the existence of a necessary being. At the same time, it is clear that only concrete beings of some kind can explain the existence of necessary abstract beings since the latter, being one and all dependent beings, cannot explain their own existence:

(P7) Dependent beings of any kind cannot explain their own existence.

Furthermore, it seems clear:

(P8) The existence of dependent beings can only be explained by beings on which they depend for their existence.

From (P7), (P8), and (P3), together with (C1), we may now conclude:

(C8) The existence of necessary abstract beings can only be explained by concrete beings.

And from (C7), (C8), and (P5) we may conclude:

(C9) The existence of necessary abstract beings is explained by one or more necessary concrete beings.

From (C9) we may finally infer our desired conclusion:

(C10) A necessary concrete being exists.

2. THE STATUS OF THE ARGUMENT

To draw the whole argument together, I shall now set it out in a concise and con-solidated form in which we can ignore some of the subsidiary conclusions that we drew along the way. The key premises are as follows:

(P2) Some necessary abstract beings exist.
(P3) All abstract beings are dependent beings.
(P4) All dependent beings depend for their existence on independent beings.
(P5) No contingent being can explain the existence of a necessary being.
(P6) The existence of any dependent being needs to be explained.
(P7) Dependent beings of any kind cannot explain their own existence.
(P8) The existence of dependent beings can only be explained by beings on which they depend for their existence.

From (P3) and (P4), together with definitions (D3) and (D4), we may conclude:

(C1) All abstract beings depend for their existence on concrete beings.

From (P2), (P3), and (P6) we may conclude:

(C7) The existence of necessary abstract beings needs to be explained.

From (C1), (P3), (P7), and (P8) we can conclude:

(C8) The existence of necessary abstract beings can only be explained by concrete beings.

From (C7), (C8), and (P5) we may conclude:

(C9) The existence of necessary abstract beings is explained by one or more neces-sary concrete beings.

And from (C9) we may conclude:

(C10) A necessary concrete being exists.

Setting aside, for the moment, any further doubts that this argument might pro-voke, I need at this point to address the question of whether it really qualifies as a version of a *modal ontological argument*. It is observed that the argument does not appeal to claim (C6)—that a necessary concrete being is possible—although, of course, if our final conclusion (C10) is true then so too, a fortiori, is (C6), since whatever is actually the case is thereby also possibly the case.

Standard versions of the modal ontological argument do appeal to something like (C6), from which it is then concluded that something like (C10) is true, on the grounds that whatever is possibly necessarily the case is thereby actually necessarily the case. However, arguing for the truth of (C6) without appealing to (C10) is notoriously difficult, and moreover, the principle of modal logic whereby "whatever is possibly necessarily the case is thereby actually necessarily the case" is also controversial. The fact that our new argument does not appeal either to (C6) or to this principle is therefore to its advantage, but it may also lead some to object that it consequently doesn't really qualify as a type of modal ontological argument.

In response to such an objection, I would reply that the new argument is, in line with modal ontological arguments quite generally, (1) a wholly a priori argument and (2) an argument that focuses on the notion of necessary existence rather than just on that of actual existence. By (1) I mean that all of the argument's premises are advanced as being a priori truths and that its conclusion follows from these by valid deductive reasoning—in short, that it is an a priori proof of the existence of a necessary concrete being. As for (2), this should be clear from the fact that the argument purports to establish the existence of a necessary being, that is, a being that necessarily exists, not just one that actually exists. Of course, in establishing this, it also assumes the existence of other necessary beings, by adopting premise (P2). But these are not necessary beings of the same kind as that whose existence the argument attempts to prove, being only abstract rather than concrete beings. Hence the argument cannot fairly be accused of being circular or of begging the question. That necessary abstract beings exist, such as numbers, is certainly not entirely uncontroversial, but it is far less controversial than that a necessary concrete being exists. Indeed, I would urge that all of the premises of the new argument are individually considerably less controversial than its conclusion. They are also clearly mutually consistent. And this, really, is the most that one can generally hope to achieve in a philosophical argument: that its premises nontrivially entail its conclusion and that every one of those premises has considerable plausibility and is considerably less controversial than its conclusion. For an argument with these features has the merit of providing us with a persuasive reason to endorse an interesting conclusion that, considered merely on its own, might appear to be implausible. In general, the more mutually independent premises such an argument has, the more persuasive it is, because this enables each premise to be individually more plausible despite the initial implausibility of the conclusion. So it is actually an advantage of our new argument that it has no fewer than seven premises. Of course, as we have seen, not all of these premises are simply asserted without any attempt at justification. Indeed, for almost all of them, and certainly for all of the more controversial ones, some justification has been offered.

Despite this response, some philosophers might suspect that what I have really offered is some version of the cosmological argument for the existence of God or of a God-like being. In response to such an objection I would reply that I have nowhere appealed to the existence of the cosmos as something that needs to be explained by something "external" to it, where by "the cosmos" I mean the sum total of existing concrete beings. The only beings whose existence I have assumed, and whose existence I seek to explain, are necessary abstract beings. Moreover, I have nowhere appealed to causal considerations in my argument. When I talk about existence-explanation, I do not mean causal explanation, but only metaphysical explanation. This should be evident from the fact that I talk about explaining the existence of abstract beings, which, as I have made clear, I do not regard as being capable of standing in causal relations to anything, since they do not exist in space or time. Consequently, even if my argument looks rather different from standard versions of the modal ontological argument, I believe that if it is to be classified as belonging to any traditional form of argument for a "supreme being" at all, it can only be said to be a version of the modal ontological argument.

▓ 3. FURTHER THEOLOGICAL IMPLICATIONS OF THE ARGUMENT

Now I want to return, as promised earlier, to the question of whether all abstract beings are indeed dependent beings, since it is crucial to my argument that at least all necessary abstract beings have this status. A clue here, however, is provided by the very expression "abstract." An abstract being, it would seem, is one which, by its very nature, is in some sense abstracted from—literally, "drawn out of, or away from"—something else. To that extent, then, any such being may reasonably be supposed to depend for its existence on that from which it is "abstracted." All of the most plausible examples of abstract beings are, interestingly enough, entities that are, in a broad sense, objects of reason—such entities as numbers, sets, and propositions. They are all objects that stand in rational relations to one another, such as mathematical and logical relations. Very arguably, however, it does not make sense to think of such entities as existing and standing in such relations independent of some actual or possible mind that could contemplate and understand them. But then we have a very good candidate for the sort of being "from" which such entities may be supposed to be somehow "abstracted": namely, a mind of some kind, upon which they would thereby depend for their existence. But if the main argument of this chapter is correct, then in the case of necessary abstract beings like these, the being upon which they depend for their existence and which explains their existence must be a necessary concrete being. Putting these two thoughts together—(1) that necessary abstract beings, insofar as they are objects of reason, are "mind-dependent" beings, and (2) that they are dependent for their existence on a necessary concrete being—we are led to the conclusion that the being in question must be a rational being with a mind and, indeed, with a mind so powerful that it can comprehend all of mathematics and logic. Thus, despite my earlier warning that the argument of this chapter does not directly establish the existence of a being with all of the traditional "divine attributes," it does in fact go considerably further in this direction than might initially be supposed. It does, in short, speak strongly in favor of the existence of a necessary concrete being possessed of a rational and infinite mind—something very much like the traditional "God of the philosophers." Seen in this light, my "new" modal ontological argument even has a close affinity with St. Anselm's original argument. For, clearly, if it were to be suggested that the "necessary concrete rational being" whose existence I claim to have established is itself merely an object of reason, not something existing in concrete reality, then it may be replied that this would reduce that being to something that is just another necessary abstract being, and thus to something once more requiring the existence of an infinitely "greater" being, in the shape of the necessary concrete rational being whose existence my argument is designed to prove.

■ NOTES

1. See M. J. Charlesworth, St Anselm's Proslogion (Oxford: Clarendon Press, 1965).

2. See A. Plantinga, The Nature of Necessity (Oxford: Clarendon Press, 1974), chap. 10.

3. I try to do both in "The Ontological Argument," in The Routledge Companion to Philosophy of Religion, ed. C. Meister and P. Copan, 331–340 (London: Routledge, 2007), where I also say more about the history of the ontological argument.

4. For further discussion and defense of this and the following definition, see E. J. Lowe, "The Metaphysics of Abstract Objects," Journal of Philosophy 92 (1995): 509–524. I want to allow that immaterial souls, if they exist and lack all spatial properties, may nonetheless be accounted as concrete beings, by virtue of existing at least in time if not also in space. Note, however, that—as I shall soon explain—my argument does not require me to adopt precisely these definitions.

5. For more on truth and truthmakers, see E. J. Lowe and A. Rami, eds., Truth and Truth-Making (Stocksfield, UK: Acumen, 2009), in which an essay of my own on the subject is included.

6. For further discussion and some refinements, see E. J. Lowe, "Ontological Dependence," in The Stanford Encyclopedia of Philosophy (Spring 2010 ed.), ed. E. N. Zalta, http://plato.stanford.edu/archives/spr2010/entries/dependence-ontological/. Note, however, that the two definitions (D5) and (D6) presented below are not in fact formally called upon in the version of the ontological argument that I am now developing, so that in the remainder of this chapter the notion of existential dependence may, for all intents and purposes, be taken as primitive. There is an advantage in this, inasmuch as finding a perfectly apt definition of existential dependence is no easy task, as I explain in "Ontological Dependence." In particular, for the purposes of the present chapter, existential dependence really needs to be understood as an asymmetrical relation, and neither (D5) nor (D6) secures this.

7. Elsewhere I call such a principle an "axiom of foundation," by analogy with a similar principle in set theory: see E. J. Lowe, *The Possibility of Metaphysics: Substance, Identity, and Time* (Oxford: Clarendon Press, 1998), 158.

8. Cf. Lowe, *The Possibility of Metaphysics*, 254.

9. I do concede, however, that both assumptions have been challenged by good philosophers too. For a challenge to (P4), see J. Schaffer, "Is There a Fundamental Level?" *Noûs* 37 (2003): 498–517.

10. Lowe, *The Possibility of Metaphysics*, 252–255.

▨ FOR FURTHER READING

Hartshorne, C. *Anselm's Discovery: A Re-Examination of the Ontological Argument for God's Existence*. La Salle, IL: Open Court, 1965.

Malcolm, N. "Anselm's Ontological Arguments." *Philosophical Review* 69 (1960): 41–62.

Oppy, G. 2011. "Ontological Arguments." In *The Stanford Encyclopedia of Philosophy* (Fall 2011 ed.), ed. E. N. Zalta. http://plato.stanford.edu/archives/fall2011/entries/ontological-arguments.

Tooley, M. "Plantinga's Defence of the Ontological Argument." *Mind* 90 (1981): 422–427.

van Inwagen, P. "Ontological Arguments." *Noûs* 11 (1977): 375–395.

6

Lowe on "The Ontological Argument"

■ GRAHAM OPPY

I am a naturalist: I hold that natural reality exhausts causal reality. Since I am a naturalist, I am committed to the claim that there are no successful arguments against naturalism.

Theists claim that God is the cause—creator, ground, source, origin—of natural reality. Thus theists are committed to the denial of naturalism, and naturalists are committed to the denial of theism. In particular, given that I am committed to the claim that there are no successful arguments against naturalism, I am committed to the claim that there are no successful arguments for the existence of God. Hence I am committed to the claim that there are no successful ontological arguments for the existence of God.

I do not claim that it is *certain* that naturalism is true. Rather, I give very high credence to the claim that naturalism is true. But, given that I assign very high credence to the claim that naturalism is true, I give very low credence to the claim that there are successful arguments against naturalism. In consequence, I give very low credence to the claim that there are successful arguments for the existence of God, and, a fortiori, I give very low credence to the claim that there are successful ontological arguments for the existence of God.

How do we determine whether arguments are successful? In the context of evaluation of the relative merits of naturalism and theism, we imagine a dialogue between proponents of the two views. (Perhaps we can think of these proponents as embodiments or personifications of the two views.) The overall aim of the dialogue is to try to reach consensus about which of the two views scores best across the full range of theoretical virtues: simplicity, scope, coherence, evidential fit, predictive power, and so forth. While there are many different aspects to the dialogue—sharing information, clarifying points of detail, and so forth—we are here primarily interested in the role that might be played by the introduction of arguments. That is, we are interested in parts of the dialogue that involve moves with the following form:

Proponent: "$P_1, \ldots, P_n$, therefore C."

Since those who put forward ontological arguments intend to put forward arguments in which the conclusion is a logical consequence of the premises, we can here confine our attention to those kinds of arguments.

What is the purpose of making a move like this in the dialogue? The proponent of an argument (of which that proponent supposes that the conclusion is a logical consequence of the premises) is implicitly claiming that there is a logical contradiction in the view held by the other party in the dialogue, and is explicitly claiming that that logical contradiction is due to the other party's acceptance of the premises and lack of acceptance of the conclusion of the given argument. (Recall that C is a logical consequence of $P_1, \ldots, P_n$, just in case $\{P_1, \ldots, P_n, \sim C\}$ is inconsistent.) Thus minimum conditions on success for an argument of this kind—apart from the requirement that the conclusion is indeed a logical consequence of the premises—are (1) that the premises are all accepted by the other party to the argument, and (2) that the conclusion of the argument is not accepted by the other party to the argument.

If an argument is not now successful because the other party to the argument does not accept one or more of the premises, it remains open that the argument could become successful in the future (if the other party were to change their mind about the relevant premises). Hence, in particular, if the proponent of the argument is able to find successful arguments for the relevant premises, then those new arguments could be "put together" with the currently unsuccessful argument to yield a successful argument. However, one should not make the mistake of confusing potential success with success: an argument that has premises that are not accepted by the other party to the debate is just an unsuccessful argument.[1]

Given the way that I have characterized arguments—as collections of premises and conclusions—it should come as no surprise to learn that I do not believe that there is any such thing as "the ontological argument." Rather, there are many ontological arguments—that is, many arguments that roughly fit the following characterization: they have as their conclusion the claim that God exists, or something that is (perhaps incorrectly) supposed by proponents to entail that God exist, and their premises include only claims that are (perhaps incorrectly) supposed by proponents to be both necessary and knowable a priori. In *Ontological Arguments and Belief in God*[2] I provided a taxonomy of six major families of ontological arguments; in *Arguing about Gods*[3] I noted that there are further families that went unnoticed in that original taxonomy.

I claim that detailed examination of all the ontological arguments that have hitherto been produced bears out the claim that no one has yet produced a successful ontological argument: that is, no one has produced an ontological argument that succeeds in establishing that naturalism is logically inconsistent. I claim, further, that the ontological arguments that have been produced to date fail in a wide variety of different ways. (There are many different ways in which conclusions can fail to be logical consequences of their premises. There are many different claims that have been premises in ontological arguments that have been produced to date, and there are many different reasons why naturalists reject one or another of those claims.) Finally—although I have not always held this view—I claim that there is no successful naturalist argument for the conclusion that the claim that someone will produce a successful ontological argument in the future should be given zero credence. Of course, given that naturalists suppose that naturalism has very high credence, naturalists suppose that theism has very low credence (and thus, a fortiori, naturalists suppose that the claim that someone will produce a successful ontological argument in the future has even lower credence)—but I see no reason why naturalists need to suppose that they have successful arguments for the claim that there will never be successful ontological arguments.

In this chapter I am going to examine the discussion of "the ontological argument" in "The Ontological Argument".[4] I have not taken up Lowe's discussion elsewhere. I propose to argue that "the argument" that Lowe looks favorably upon is not successful.

■ 1.

In the course of his discussion, Lowe gives a number of different arguments which he takes to be trivial reformulations of one another. While I think that there are significant differences between the arguments that Lowe examines, I propose to focus initial attention on what I take to be the "core" argument that Lowe endorses:

1. It is possible that there is an absolutely independent being (premise).
2. Necessarily, if there is an absolutely independent being, then it is necessary that there is an absolutely independent being (premise).
3. (Hence) There is an absolutely independent being (from 1 and 2, by modal logic).
4. (Hence) God exists (from 3, by definition of "God").

First, let us consider this argument from the standpoint of theism, that is, from the standpoint of the proponent of the argument in our dialogue. Suppose that theism says that there is just one necessarily existent and essentially absolutely independent causal agent upon which the existence of all else necessarily depends. If theism says this, then, by the lights of theism, the argument from 1 through 3 is sound: the premises are true, and the conclusion follows logically from the premises. As Lowe notes, there is a question about the inference of 4 from 3; as things stand, there is nothing in the premises that entails that there is just one absolutely independent being. Perhaps, though, this is not hard to fix:

1. It is possible that there is exactly one absolutely independent being (premise).
2. Necessarily, if there is exactly one absolutely independent being, then it is necessary that there is exactly *that* one absolutely independent being (premise).

3. (Hence) There is exactly one absolutely independent being (from 1 and 2).
4. (Hence) God exists (from 3, by definition of "God").

With this revision, the argument from 1 through 4 will be judged sound by theists who suppose that God is the one necessarily existent and essentially absolutely independent causal agent. (Of course, not all theists accept this conception of God. But we can suppose that the theist in our dialogue does.)

It is worth noting that our theist accepts the following claim about metaphysical possibility: all metaphysically possible worlds have the same origin—each metaphysically possible world issues from the same initial, essentially absolutely independent source. Moreover, plausibly, our theist is further committed to the claim that differences between worlds emerge either as a result of brute contingent initial[5] differences—the essentially absolutely independent source has different initial properties in different worlds—or else as a result of the outworking of objective chance.[6]

Second, we turn to consider the argument from the standpoint of naturalism, that is, from the standpoint of the other participant in our dialogue. From the outset, we can suppose that our naturalist accepts the same kind of view about metaphysical possibility that is accepted by our theist: either all metaphysically possible worlds "overlap" with an initial segment of the actual world, or else all metaphysically possible worlds share an initial "source," which has brute contingent properties. Moreover, from the outset, we can also suppose that our naturalist accepts that differences between worlds emerge either as a result of those brute contingent initial differences, or else as a result of the outworking of objective chance.[7]

Any naturalist who supposes that it is impossible for there to be an infinite regress and who accepts the above account of metaphysical possibility will suppose that the initial state of natural reality constitutes an essentially absolutely independent source for natural reality.[8] That is, any naturalist who supposes that it is impossible for there to be an infinite regress, and who accepts that all metaphysically possible worlds have the same origin as the actual world will accept that the origin of natural reality is an absolutely independent being. But, of course, a naturalist who supposes that every metaphysically possible world originates in the same natural state as the actual world does not thereby suppose that God exists. A key difference between naturalism and theism is that naturalists suppose that agency and consciousness are late and local features of reality, whereas theists suppose that agency and consciousness are initial features of reality. If agency and consciousness do not figure in our definition of "God," we risk applying the name to something that does not deserve to bear it.

I take it that our naturalist need not be committed to the existence of exactly one absolutely independent being. Our naturalist will suppose that, if there is an infinite regress, then there is no absolutely independent being—and, a fortiori, that it is not possible that there is exactly one absolutely independent being. If our naturalist is undecided between "infinite regress" and "necessary initial state," then our naturalist will be undecided whether there is exactly one absolutely independent being. But our naturalist will also note that the argument that the theist is propounding provides no assistance at all in the resolution of that indecision.

Some naturalists might also be undecided about, or opposed to, the theory of metaphysical possibility that I have attributed to my naturalist. Those naturalists will reject the second premise of the argument; they will suppose that reality might have a purely contingent origin, if, indeed, it has an origin at all. Such an origin would be "absolutely independent" in the sense that it would not depend upon anything else, but it would not be "absolutely independent" in the sense of being "noncontingent." Again, a naturalist who took this line would be able to note that the argument that our theist propounds provides no assistance at all in the choice between "infinite regress," "necessary origin with no contingent features," "necessary origin with contingent features," and "contingent origin."⁹

In short, the ontological argument that I formulated at the beginning of this section is plainly not a successful argument. While it is true that (some) theists will suppose that the argument is sound, it seems to me that naturalists can reasonably say that they are prepared to grant both of the premises of the argument if and only if they further suppose that natural reality has an origin that is an absolutely independent *natural* being.

▪ 2.

After setting out "the ontological argument," Lowe provides responses to "well-known objections" (p. 334). In particular, Lowe argues that "the ontological argument" is not properly criticizable on the grounds that it simply defines God into existence (p. 337), nor on the grounds that existence is not a real predicate (p. 335), nor on the grounds that it is vulnerable to Gaunilo's "perfect island" objection (p. 334).

I am happy to grant to Lowe that the particular ontological argument that is set out in the first section of this essay is not vulnerable to any of these three objections. However, I deny that the same is true of some of the other arguments that Lowe sets out in his essay—arguments that, as I noted above, Lowe claims are "versions" of "the ontological argument." Consider, for example, the following "version" of Lowe's reconstruction of St. Anselm's *Proslogion II* argument:

1. A being than which no greater (being) can be conceived exists at least in the mind (premise).
2. It is greater to exist in reality than to exist only in the mind (premise).
3. (Therefore) A being than which no greater (being) can be conceived exists not only in the mind but also in reality (from 1 and 2).
4. (Therefore) God exists (from 3, by definition of "God").

Against this argument it seems to me that we should join with Gaunilo in asking proponents to explain why the following argument is not equally cogent:

1. An island than which no greater island can be conceived exists at least in the mind (premise).
2. It is greater to exist in reality than to exist only in the mind (premise).
3. (Therefore) An island than which no greater island can be conceived exists not only in the mind but also in reality (from 1 and 2).
4. (Therefore) The blessed isle exists (from 3, by definition of "the blessed isle").

Surely our naturalist can quite correctly observe that (1) the argument attributed to St. Anselm is valid just in case the argument attributed to Gaunilo is valid; and (2) that, at least by the lights of naturalists, there is nothing that speaks more heavily in favor of the first premise of the argument attributed to St. Anselm than in favor of the first premises of the argument attributed to Gaunilo. But, if that's right, then surely we can conclude that, on the supposition that the argument that is attributed to Gaunilo is not successful, the argument attributed to St. Anselm is also not successful. And who would wish to say that the argument attributed to Gaunilo is successful?

It is surely right to say—as Lowe insists—that an island than which no greater can be conceived would not be—and, indeed, could not be—an absolutely independent being, whereas a being than which no greater can be conceived would be an absolutely independent being. But a naturalist who wishes to endorse Gaunilo's objection to St. Anselm's *Proslogion II* argument can accept this point with equanimity. For—as is evident to inspection—the claim that a being than which no greater can be conceived would be an absolutely independent being plays no role at all in St. Anselm's *Proslogion II* argument. A naturalist can insist that existence is great-making for *beings* just in case existence is great-making for *islands* while also accepting that only beings other than islands can be absolutely independent.

It is no less evidently right to say that a naturalist could not sensibly think to make the same claim about the ontological argument discussed in section 1 above. The argument

1. It is possible that there is exactly one absolutely independent island (premise).
2. Necessarily, if there is exactly one absolutely independent island, then it is necessary that there is exactly *that* one absolutely independent island (premise).
3. (Hence) There is exactly one absolutely independent island (from 1 and 2).

is manifestly less cogent than the argument that we discussed in the first section, because the first premise in the parallel argument is obviously less plausible than the first premise in the original argument. But there is no surprise in this: there are very different things to say about different arguments.[10]

A better "parallel" for the revised version of the argument presented in the first section of this chapter might be thought to be something like the following:

1. It is possible that there is exactly one absolutely independent being (premise).
2. Necessarily, if there is exactly one absolutely independent being, then it is necessary that there is exactly *that* one absolutely independent being (premise).
3. (Hence) There is exactly one absolutely independent being (from 1 and 2).
4. (Hence) There is exactly one absolutely independent natural being (from 3, assuming naturalism).

However, it seems to me even better to say that there is no reason to look for "parallels" to the argument discussed in the first section of this chapter, since there is no reason to suppose that naturalists need to object to the central part of that argument. Gaunilo's strategy is attractive only in cases where its deployment plausibly shows that something is wrong with a target argument in circumstances in which it is hard to pinpoint the precise fault in that target argument. The argument discussed in the first section of this chapter is not an instance of that kind of argument.

▪ 3 .

No doubt some who read this chapter will think that it is incredible to suppose that naturalists could accept that there is an absolutely independent being. Lowe himself provides an argument that might be taken to establish this point:

> Even within the most fundamental category of substance, there are degrees of being, because there are degrees of existential dependence. Consider, for instance, something such as a pile or heap of rocks...The pile evidently depends for its existence on the individual rocks that make it up—whereas they do not, conversely, depend for their existence on it. In that sense, the pile is a more dependent being than is any of the rocks that compose it. However, the rocks in turn depend for their existence on other things, most obviously the various mineral particles of which they themselves are composed.
>
> It would seem that all material substances are, very plausibly, dependent beings in this sense, even if some turn out to be simple substances, not composed of anything further. For it seems that they are all *contingent* beings, where a contingent being is one that does not exist of necessity. Consider, for example, a single elementary particle of physics, such as a certain individual electron, e, which is, according to the current physical theory, not composed of anything more fundamental. Surely,

e might not have existed at all. But could e have been the only thing to exist? We might think that we can imagine a world in which all that exists is this single electron e. But, in fact, modern physics would repudiate this idea as nonsensical. Electrons are not really to be thought of as being "particles" in a commonsense way, but are, rather, best thought of as quantized states of a space-permeating field; and according to this way of thinking of them, it really makes no sense to envisage one of them as having an existence that is wholly independent of anything else.

However, even though it makes no sense to think of an electron, or indeed any "material substance", as having such a wholly independent existence, we clearly can make sense of the idea of a being that does have such an existence: a being that depends for its existence, in any sense whatsoever, on absolutely nothing other than itself (p. 332, italics in original).

Consider natural reality. It is plausible naturalistic metaphysical speculation that *it* could not have failed to exist. Suppose that natural reality has an origin—that is, suppose that there is not an infinite regress of states of natural reality. There are two simple hypotheses that we might frame about that origin.[11] On the one hand, that origin might involve a single, simple substance. On the other hand, that origin might involve a single substance that is composed of other substances. In this latter case, on the assumption that there is no infinite regress, the single substance is ultimately composed of many simple substances.

If the origin involves a single, simple substance, then we have a being that is in every sense absolutely independent: it exists of necessity, it has no parts, it does not depend for its identity on anything else,[12] and so forth. If, on the other hand, the origin involves a single substance that is composed of other substances, then matters are more complicated. Perhaps there are many beings that are in every sense absolutely independent: they exist of necessity, have no parts, do not depend for their identity on anything else, and so forth; or perhaps there are some beings among them that are not quite absolutely independent in every sense, because they depend for their identity upon the others. Moreover, perhaps the "largest" being is one that is not quite absolutely independent because, even though it exists of necessity, and does not depend for its identity upon anything else, it does have parts; or perhaps the "largest" being is one that is even further from being absolutely independent because, even though it exists of necessity, it both has parts and depends for its identity upon those parts; and so on.[13]

More carefully, then, our naturalist can say the following: If natural reality has an origin, then that origin—the initial state of natural reality—*might* exist of necessity, have no parts, and not depend for its identity upon anything else.[14] If natural reality has an origin with all three of these properties, then, plausibly, natural reality has an origin that is absolutely independent in every sense. Of course, even if natural reality has an origin that exists of necessity and that does not depend upon anything else for its identity, it is highly speculative to suppose that that origin has no parts. But, from the naturalist point of view, it doesn't really matter whether, if there is an origin, that origin has parts: the more important aspects of ontological independence are necessity of existence and identity independence. Moreover, even if natural reality has an origin that exists of necessity, it is also speculative to suppose that the identity of that origin does not depend upon the parts of that origin. But, again, from the naturalist point of view, it doesn't really matter whether, if there is an origin, the identity of that origin is independent of the parts of that origin: the most important aspect of ontological independence is necessity of existence. And, of course, as noted before, the naturalist will in any case hold that it is speculative to suppose that natural reality has an origin, and not less speculative to suppose that, if natural reality has an origin, then it has a necessarily existent origin. However—these recent considerations notwithstanding—the important point upon which the naturalist insists is that, if the naturalist were to grant the various assumptions that are needed in order to justify the claim that there is an absolutely independent being, then the naturalist would also justifiably insist that that absolutely independent being is the initial natural part of natural reality.

Despite the foregoing remarks, I don't dispute everything that Lowe says in the above quotation. Thus, for example, I think that naturalists can—and should—agree that the range of contingency for material objects may be very extensive even if natural reality has a necessarily existent origin. In particular, as I have argued elsewhere,[15] I think that naturalists should accept that all noninitial states have causes, and that all noninitial objects have causes of their existence. However, if objective chance is widespread, then the dependence of many—or most, or nearly all, or perhaps even all—noninitial states and objects on an original state and whatever objects it involves would not be a matter of metaphysical necessitation. But clearly, even if all of this is accepted, it remains open to naturalists to insist that not all material substances are contingent beings—and, in particular, that the initial part of natural reality is not a contingent being.

■ 4.

On the basis of the preceding discussion, I conclude that Lowe's ontological arguments are unsuccessful. Moreover, as I noted initially, there are no more successful ontological arguments that have been produced to date. And there is no reason to suppose that there are hitherto undiscovered successful ontological arguments: if anything, what evidence there is points in the other direction. (If there is a successful ontological argument, why is it still undiscovered, given the huge amount of time and effort that have been invested in devising arguments of this kind?) However, as I also noted earlier, there is no particularly strong reason to suppose that it is certain that we shall never have a successful ontological argument—and nor is there any reason to suppose that our just-noted historical point can be parlayed into a successful argument for the conclusion that there are no successful ontological arguments.

Elsewhere I have argued that what goes for ontological arguments also goes for other arguments about the existence of God: there are no successful arguments on either side of the dispute between naturalists and theists.[16] That's not to say that I deny that there are local areas where one view has a clear advantage over the other: for example, I hold that when it comes to the question of why there is something rather than nothing, naturalism has a clear advantage over theism.[17] But naturalism and theism—when fully elaborated—are comprehensive theories; in consequence, comparison of their virtues is a more or less intractable task. A successful deductive argument would clearly suffice to break the deadlock, and, in part, this may help to explain why there are still some who persist in constructing and offering purported ontological proofs for the existence of God (and others who persist in constructing and offering logical arguments from evil that would be proofs of the nonexistence of God). However, if I am right, those people could all find more profitable ways to spend their time.

▓ NOTES

1. Perhaps it might be said that someone failing to accept a premise hardly suffices to show that it is rationally permissible for them to fail to accept that premise. Of course, this is true. But we should be skeptical of the claim that it is rationally impermissible for someone to fail to accept a given premise unless we can give that person a successful argument that has the premise in question as its conclusion. (Part of the point of entering into debate is to move beyond the position of labeling people "irrational" with no justification beyond the fact of disagreement.)

2. Graham Oppy, *Ontological Arguments and Belief in God* (Cambridge: Cambridge University Press, 1996).

3. Graham Oppy, *Arguing about Gods* (Cambridge: Cambridge University Press, 2006), especially chap. 2, "Ontological Arguments," 49–96.

4. E. J. Lowe, "The Ontological Argument," in *The Routledge Companion to Philosophy of Religion,* ed. C. Meister and P. Copan (Oxford: Routledge, 2007), 332–340.

5. "Initial"? Initial in the order of dependency! I take it that naturalists suppose that the order of dependency is the causal order. Perhaps theists also make this supposition. If not, no matter, the supposition plays no role in the subsequent discussion.

6. I assume that if there are libertarian free actions, then those are objectively chancy. Those who disagree with me about this will wish to list at least one further way in which differences between possible worlds can emerge.

7. Like his theistic opponent, our naturalist supposes that many ordinary judgments about "possibility" are actually judgments about "epistemic" or "doxastic" possibility. In particular, on this account of metaphysical possibility, it often turns out that judgments about conceivability are only good guides to "epistemic" or "doxastic" possibility.

8. In section 3 of this chapter I shall give a reasonably detailed consideration of the senses in which a naturalist can suppose that the initial state of natural reality involves an absolutely independent being.

9. Of course, there are also naturalists who eschew—or abhor—the kind of metaphysics implicit in the foregoing discussion. Naturalists who are undecided about, or opposed to, metaphysical understandings of causation, modality, dependence, and so forth can still take away something from this discussion. For them, the lesson is that they could reconsider their indecision about—or opposition to—metaphysical understandings of causation, modality, dependence, and so forth without thereby incurring a commitment to reconsider their rejection of theism.

10. Should we go on to say that St. Anselm's *Proslogion II* argument goes wrong because it supposes that existence is a great-making property (and that, in turn, this is wrong because existence is not a real predicate)? I don't think so; however, here is not the place to try to develop an argument in support of this contention.

11. For the purposes of this discussion, I ignore more complex hypotheses that one might frame about the origin of natural reality.

12. For the notion of identity-dependence—and for very useful clarification of different conceptions of ontological dependence—see E. J. Lowe, "Ontological Dependence," *Stanford Encyclopedia of Philosophy*, 2009, http://plato.stanford.edu/entries/dependence-ontological/.

13. It is probably worth pointing out that if there is an initial state of natural reality, that initial state will not contain electrons (nor any other "elementary particles"). In well-established models of our universe, electrons are not present in the very earliest stages of our universe—and, in many current cosmological models, there are parts of natural reality that are antecedent to our universe.

14. Of course, the "might" in this sentence is epistemic or doxastic, it is not metaphysical.

15. See Graham Oppy, "Uncaused Beginnings," *Faith and Philosophy* 27, no. 1 (2010): 61–71.

16. See Oppy, *Arguing about Gods*.

17. See Graham Oppy, "God," in *Continuum Companion to Metaphysics*, ed. B. Barnard and N. Manson, 245–267 (London: Continuum, 2012) for details.

■ FOR FURTHER READING

Leftow, B. "The Ontological Argument." In *The Oxford Handbook of Philosophy of Religion*, ed. W. Wainwright, 80–115. Oxford: Oxford University Press, 2005.

Matthews, G. "The Ontological Argument." In *The Blackwell Guide to the Philosophy of Religion*, ed. W. Mann, 81–102. Malden, MA: Blackwell, 2005.

Maydole, R. (2009) "The Ontological Argument." In *The Blackwell Companion to Natural Theology*, ed. W. Craig and J. Moreland, 552–592. Malden, MA: Wiley-Blackwell, 2009.

Oppy, G. "Anselm and the Ontological Argument." In *Philosophy of Religion: The Key Thinkers*, ed. J. Jordan, 22–43. London: Continuum, 2011.

———. "The Ontological Argument." In *Philosophy of Religion: Classic and Contemporary Issues*, ed. P. Copan and C. Meister, 112–126. Malden, MA: Blackwell, 2008.

A Moral Argument

7 Ethics Needs God

■ PAUL COPAN

Let me briefly clarify what I do and do not defend in this chapter. My argument will not advance the following points:

- *Objective moral values exist.* Both sides here represented assume this.[1]
- *Belief in God is required for recognizing moral truths.* Properly functioning naturalists, Buddhists, Confucians, and theists know the right thing to do.
- *Atheists/nontheists cannot live decently or be kind to others.* Indeed, some may exhibit greater moral virtue than some professing theists.
- *Atheists/nontheists cannot formulate ethical systems that overlap or mesh with theologically oriented ones.*
- *Certain Old Testament practices, actions, or regulations are historically and contextually confined and should not be taken as normative and universal.* Frequently critiques of theism include inferior moral practices, laws, and actions in the Old Testament—and fall prey to many misunderstandings and misrepresentations. I thoroughly address this topic elsewhere.[2]

What I *am* arguing is this:

- *Theism offers a far more likely context than naturalism/nontheism for affirming objective moral values and duties.* Naturalism does not lead us to expect the emergence of human rights and universal benevolence—a point equally applicable to other nontheistic worldviews.
- *Many naturalists themselves observe that naturalism's context simply cannot lead us to human rights/dignity and moral duties.*
- *Theism offers a more plausible context than atheism/nontheism for affirming a cluster of features related to human dignity and moral duties.*
- *The convergence of contingent human dignity and worth and necessary moral truths makes much more sense in theism than in naturalism.*
- *Euthyphro objections leave theism unscathed and raise their own problems for the naturalistic/nontheistic moral realists.*

In general, I shall argue that moral epistemology must be anchored in the metaphysical resources of theism to provide the most plausible context to account for objective moral values.[3]

■ 1. PRELIMINARIES ON NATURALISTIC MORAL REALISM

My sparring partner in this volume, Louise Antony, repudiates as mercenary all ethical actions and attitudes motivated by fear of judgment or reward from God. God is morally superfluous. Antony's moral atheism is the "perfect piety."[4]

In like manner, naturalist Erik Wielenberg claims that objective morality's ontological and epistemological foundation consists of certain brute ethical facts: they "have no explanation outside of themselves; no further facts make them true" (ontological), and we can know these brute ethical facts immediately without inferring them from other known facts (epistemological).[5] Necessary moral truths didn't evolve with humanity but are "part of the furniture of the universe." They "constitute the ethical background of every possible universe," creating the framework for assessing the actions of any moral agent (whether human or divine). On Wielenberg's *nontheistic nonnatural moral realism*, morality cannot be called "natural" since, like beauty, it supervenes on certain natural properties under certain conditions, though it is not reducible to these natural properties.[6]

■ 2. THEISM: THE MORE NATURAL SETTING FOR OBJECTIVE MORAL VALUES

Finding atheists who think God and objective morality stand or fall together is quite easy, and naturalistic moral realists should take note. Here's a sampling:

- Jean-Paul Sartre: "It [is] very distressing that God does not exist, because all possibility of finding values in a heaven of ideas disappears along with Him."[7]
- Friedrich Nietzsche: "*There are altogether no moral facts*"; indeed, morality "has truth only if God is the truth—it stands or falls with faith in God."[8]
- Bertrand Russell rejected moral realism and retained the depressing view that humanity with all its achievements is nothing "but the outcome of accidental collocations of atoms"; so we must safely build our lives on "the firm foundation of unyielding despair."[9]
- J. L. Mackie: "Moral properties constitute so odd a cluster of properties and relations that they are most unlikely to have arisen in the ordinary course of events without an all-powerful god to create them."[10]
- Richard Dawkins concludes that a universe of "just electrons and selfish genes" would mean "there is, at bottom, no design, no purpose, no evil and no good, nothing but blind pitiless indifference."[11]

Moral values such as human dignity and worth make more sense on theism than naturalism. Why think that value would emerge from valuelessness? Wielenberg claims the "no value from valuelessness" maxim is question-begging on the theist's part. (He favors the maxim, "From valuelessness, value sometimes comes.")[12] Yet Wielenberg's maxim is itself terribly question-begging.[13] Just ask: *what should we expect if naturalism is true?* Russell, Nietzsche, Sartre, Mackie, and Dawkins are just a few fish in the larger naturalistic pond who recognize naturalism's inability to generate objective values such as universal benevolence and human rights. Theism has no such problem.

As we shall see, the same applies to consciousness, rationality, and free will/personal responsibility. Naturalism itself leads us to question similar question-begging maxims such as "from non-conscious matter, consciousness sometimes comes," "from deterministic processes, free will sometimes comes," and "from non-rational matter, rationality sometimes comes." (In the spirit of Wielenberg, we could add yet another question-begging naturalistic maxim: "From nothing, something may sometimes come." Due to space limitations, however, I cannot elaborate here.)[14]

The worldview favoring a robust moral world is theism, in which a good, rational, supremely aware Creator makes human beings in his image. God's existence secures the existence of genuine value and rights in the contingent world, easily accounting for human dignity, rights, moral responsibility (which includes rationality and free will), and duties. On naturalism, however, why think that morally responsible, valuable beings would be the product of mindless, nonrational, physical, valueless, nonconscious processes? Unlike theism, naturalism's context can't anticipate the emergence of value.[15]

A *personal* Creator, who makes human *persons* in the Creator's image, serves as the ontological basis for the existence of objective moral values, moral obligation, human dignity, and rights. Consider: (1) Without the existence of a personal God, no persons would exist *at all.* God is the sufficient reason for the existence of anything (rather than nothing) at all. And (2) if no persons would exist, then no moral properties would be instantiated or realized in our world. Without this personal God and Creator of other persons, why think moral properties would be instantiated? Moral values—the instantiation of moral properties—and personhood are intertwined: moral properties are instantiated through personhood, which is ontologically rooted in God's personhood. Again, if naturalism is true and the universe is inherently meaningless, we simply should not expect human dignity and rights to emerge. Surely intellectual honesty forces us to admit that human rights and universal benevolence *more naturally or fittingly flow* from a theistic universe than a naturalistic one.[16]

■ 3. THEISM'S NATURALNESS VERSUS NATURALISM'S SHOCKING COSMIC COINCIDENCES

Even if such naturalists reject that humans are nothing more than accidental collocations of atoms or molecules in motion, the context problem still persists. Consider the following reasons.

First, a theistic context for human dignity and rights is far more natural and expected than a nontheistic one of valueless molecules producing value. To say that value "sometimes" may emerge from valuelessness" (Wielenberg) reflects an ungrounded metaphysical optimism.

Second, the naturalistic moral scenario is indeed a shocking coincidence, unlike the natural connection between a personal, good God's existence and that of morally valuable creatures. Let's assume that moral facts are necessarily part of the universe's furniture and that the beings luckily evolved via a torturous, profoundly contingent series of unguided physical events to be morally constituted and thus obligated to those preexisting facts. It is strange in excelsis and staggeringly coincidental that these moral facts should (a) "just exist" and (b) perfectly correspond to intrinsically valuable beings that happen to emerge so late on the cosmic scene. These moral facts were, somehow, anticipating moral creatures that would evolve and be duty-bound to them! Theism, by contrast, does not lean on such a weak metaphysical reed; rather, it brings together unproblematically two otherwise unconnected features—moral facts (rooted in a divine necessary being's personhood) and moral creatures in whose image they have been made.

Third, objective moral values supervening upon naturalistically evolved, neurologically sophisticated organisms present a problem for the naturalist: why think that our moral awareness/development reflects those preexistent moral facts? After all, we could have developed a contrary morality that would have enhanced survival and reproduction. Michael Ruse offers this counterfactual: instead of evolving from "savannah-dwelling primates," we, like termites, could have evolved needing "to dwell in darkness, eat each other's faeces, and cannibalise the dead." If the latter were the case, we would "extol such acts as beautiful and moral" and "find it morally disgusting to live in the open air, dispose of body waste and bury the dead."[17]

Michael Shermer affirms that our remote ancestors have genetically passed on to us our sense of moral obligation within, and this is (epigenetically) reinforced by group pressure. Ultimately, to ask "Why should we be moral?" is like asking "Why should we be hungry or horny?"[18] Yet C. S. Lewis earlier observed that, on naturalism, moral impulses are no more true (or false) "than a vomit or a yawn."[19] Thinking "I ought" is on the same level of "I itch." Indeed, "my impulse to serve posterity is just the same sort of thing as my fondness for cheese" or preferring mild or bitter beer.[20] Naturalism's inability to get beyond descriptions of human behavior and psychology ("is") does not inspire confidence for grounding moral obligation ("ought"). At best, the atheist/naturalist should remain tentative about it—though Antony and Wielenberg somehow confidently push past such moral tentativity.

Atheistic moral realists naively think they can escape Ruse's point that our "sense of right and wrong and a feeling of obligation to be thus governed" is of "biological worth," serves as "an aid to survival," and "has no being beyond this."[21]

What if our belief in moral duties is a "corporate illusion fobbed off on us by our genes to get us to cooperate"?[22] The philosopher Elliot Sober rejects the purported claim that ethical beliefs can't be true if they're the product of naturalistic evolution, which commits both the genetic and naturalistic fallacies.[23] That is, it's possible that even if one's beliefs are produced by nonrational mechanisms, this doesn't entail their falsity. Sober misses the bigger point: if our beliefs are *accidentally true*, being pumped into us by physical and social forces beyond our control, they still do not qualify as "knowledge" (warranted true belief). And we may hold many *false* beliefs that help us as a species to survive—for example, the belief in intrinsic human rights when we don't in fact possess them.

So naturalism's context doesn't inspire confidence in (a) the emergence of objective moral values; (b) the actual existence of human dignity, duty, and rights (however strongly we are wired to believe in their existence); or (c) in the trustworthiness of our belief-forming structures since naturalistic evolution is interested in survival, not truth (more below).

■ 4. THEISM AND THE REQUISITE FEATURES FOR MORAL BEINGS

Naturalistic moral realists will acknowledge that humans are "accidental, evolved, mortal, and relatively short-lived,"[24] but they claim that this, by itself, does not present the total (moral) picture. (This, incidentally, is precisely the point I've just made—namely, the emergence of human rights and moral values is non-question-beggingly anticipated by theism, *not* naturalism). Such naturalistic thinkers commonly point to three key features or subvening properties on which human dignity and rights supervene: (1) freedom/free will,[25] (2) the ability to reason and discern between right and wrong, and (3) and the capacity of self-awareness or self-consciousness.[26]

A major criticism of naturalistic moral realists is the insouciant and gratuitous assumption that moral values just emerge via supervenience on natural nonmoral properties (such as a sufficiently developed brain and nervous system). The result? Morally valuable, duty-bound, rights-bearing human beings. Note atheist David Brink's parallel: "Assuming materialism is true, mental states supervene on physical states, yet few think that mental states are metaphysically queer."[27] So if the mental supervenience on the physical is such a naturalistic "slam dunk," why not objective moral values? Many nontheists simply fail to take seriously just how gratuitous such assumptions are: Why think matter and energy—which lack inherent meaning and purpose—could come close to producing rights-bearing, valuable beings? Theism has no such troubles—just the opposite, as we continue to note below.

Below we discuss a remarkable irony: these aforementioned naturalistic moral realists claim that one (or perhaps some combination) is sufficient to ground the three requisite features of human dignity and worth—the capacity for self-awareness/self-consciousness, reason, and free will. Yet other naturalists quite convincingly argue that naturalism cannot account for these very features on which the naturalistic moral realist hangs her hopes.

1. *Self-awareness/-consciousness*: Moral beings have the capacity of self-awareness, rising above genetics and environment to consider intentions, varying motivations, and prospective choices. Yet naturalistic philosophers of mind acknowledge that the emergence of (self-)consciousness from nonconscious matter is a huge problem:
    - Colin McGinn: "We know that brains are the *de facto* causal basis of consciousness, but we have, it seems, no understanding of how this can be so. It strikes us as miraculous, eerie, even faintly comic."[28]
    - Geoffrey Madell: "The emergence of consciousness, then is a mystery, and one to which materialism signally fails to provide an answer."[29]
    - David Papineau: As to why consciousness emerges in certain cases, "to this question physicalists 'theories of consciousness' seem to provide no answer."[30]

In contrast to theism (which affirms a supremely self-aware being), naturalism's resources have no predictable room for (self-)consciousness.[31] Strike one!

2. *Reason*: Moral beings have the capacity to take and reflect on alternative moral paths and make moral judgments. Now while the emergence of creaturely rationality in the context of a rational God makes sense, naturalistic evolution, in contrast, is interested in survival, not truth. That is, we may form many *false* survival-enhancing beliefs such as "humans are morally responsible" or "humans have dignity and rights"—a phenomenon that naturalists commonly acknowledge:
    - Patricia Churchland: "Boiled down to its essentials, a nervous system enables the organism to succeed in the four F's: feeding, fleeing, fighting, and reproducing... Truth, whatever that is, definitely takes the hindmost."[32]
    - Richard Rorty: Truth is "un-Darwinian."[33]
    - Michael Ruse: Morality is a "corporate" illusion that has been "fobbed off on us by our genes to get us to cooperate."[34] That is, "we think it has an objective status."[35]
    - James Rachels: "Man is a moral (altruistic) being, not because he intuits the rightness of loving his neighbor, or because he responds to some noble ideal, but because his behavior is comprised of tendencies which natural selection has favoured."[36]

We are left wondering, "Why trust our minds, whose thoughts are the result of mindless molecules affecting other mindless molecules?" How has Ruse escaped this corporate illusionism to which all the rest of us are subject? As we have noted, Ruse's belief turns out to be accidental true belief (which does not qualify as knowledge)—not warranted true belief (which does). The same problem plagues the naturalistic moral realist as well.

The theist does not have to resort to such mental and moral gymnastics. If a trustworthy God has created our noetic structure (not to mention an ordered, biofriendly universe that our minds can study and understand), then we have all the more reason for generally trusting these faculties or capacities rather than constantly doubting their reliability—even if, here and there, we may get things wrong. Indeed, we have been designed to trust our faculties (moral, rational, perceptual), and constantly failing to trust them is a sign of cognitive malfunction. It would be wrong-headed to abandon them.[37]

When it comes to naturalism, we should ask: Why should Wielenberg and Antony adopt human dignity and rights over against the views of Ruse and Rorty, whose naturalistic evolutionism entails truth being incidental to survival? Naturalism doesn't inspire confidence here either. Strike two.[38]

3. *The capacity of free will:* Naturalistic moral realists commonly claim that humans possess moral responsibility/free will, having "risen above" the genetic determinism of our evolutionary predecessors. Again, this intuition of free will, however strong, is an illusion according to other naturalists:

- William Provine: "Free will as traditionally conceived—the freedom to make uncoerced and unpredictable choices among alternative courses of action—simply does not exist. There is no way the evolutionary process as currently conceived can produce a being that is truly free to make choices."[39]
- Francis Crick: Our sense of identity and free will is "nothing more than the behavior of a vast assembly of nerve cells and their associated molecules."[40]
- Thomas Nagel: "There is no room for agency in a world of neural impulses, chemical reactions, and bone and muscle movements." Given naturalism, it's hard not to conclude that we're "helpless" and "not responsible" for our actions.[41]
- John Searle: We believe "we could have done something else" and that human freedom is "just a fact of experience." However, "the scientific" approach to reality undermines the notion of a self that could potentially interfere with "the causal order of nature."[42]
- John Bishop: Our scientific understanding of human behavior seems to be in tension with a presupposition of the ethical stance we adopt toward it."[43]

So, the necessary metaphysical requirements for moral beings—(self-) consciousness, rationality, and free will/moral responsibility—are undermined by a naturalistic context of nonconscious matter directed by nonrational and

deterministic processes. Value cannot emerge because self-consciousness, rationality, and free will cannot emerge in a naturalistic universe.

What's more, our natural history from the big bang to the bacterium is
one without value and with no predictable hope for giving rise to valuable,
rights-bearing beings. A universe of electrons and selfish genes has no metaphysical wherewithal to produce beings possessing intrinsic dignity and worth (and
thus certain inviolable rights). Naturalistic moral realists Antony, Wielenberg,
and Sinnott-Armstrong—wishful thinkers all—latch on to a theistically
grounded human dignity and moral freedom, which is certainly understandable;
after all, these atheists too have been made in the image of the God they deny.
Yet their context leaves us with no metaphysical shred of confidence that value
will or could be produced.

According to Ron Bontekoe, naturalism's morally bleak metaphysic undermines human dignity: "Human beings cannot be deserving of a special measure
of respect by virtue of their having been created 'in God's image' when they have
not been *created* at all (and there is no God). Thus the traditional conception of
human dignity is also undermined in the wake of Darwin."[44] In contrast, a good
personal Creator proves to be the more robust, metaphysically rich, lesssurpris-
ing, and less ad hoc context for the emergence of intrinsic dignity and rights.

■ 5. THE EUTHYPHRO QUESTION

Plato's *Euthyphro* dialogue raises the question: "Is what is holy holy because
the gods approve it, or do they approve it because it is holy?" (10a). In theistic terms, either God's commands are *arbitrary* (something is good *because* God
commands it—and he could have commanded the opposite), or there must be
some *autonomous moral standard* (which God consults in order to command).
Given the abundance of literature rebutting such a notion,[45] it is no mild shock
that Antony takes this as an "explicit and vivid" dilemma from which there is no
escape.[46]

The theist easily evades this false dilemma; there is a third way: goodness is
nonarbitrarily rooted in God's necessarily good personhood (or character), not
in divine commands. Antony's mistaken assumption that "good = commanded
by God" and therefore God could issue entirely opposite commands is strange
in excelsis. Unlike humans, God does not have duties to follow, nor does he need
them. Rather, God naturally does what is good because his character is good,
loving, and just. Thus it would be strange that God would have duties or be obligated to his own divine commands—particularly when God's personhood is the
very source of goodness. Antony incorrectly assumes that William of Ockham's
version of the divine command theory is the only game of its kind in town—
that God *could* command, say, torturing babies for fun, and this would become
obligatory. Yet to say that there is no good or bad except what God commands

(as Antony does) is a gross distortion. While God's commands are relevant to ethics, they do not define or constitute goodness. For instance, God may give commands (say, kosher or planting laws for national Israel) that are not permanently binding, nor is there any reason to think these are inherently good.

What's more, we've seen above that the horns of the Euthyphro "dilemma" are not exhaustive; moreover, instead of God's commanding something because it is good (or vice versa), we can speak of God's commanding *because he loves us* and *because he is concerned about maximizing our ultimate well-being.*[47] Moreover, for God to command something like torture or rape goes against the very foundation of ethics—namely, God's necessarily good character. To ask, "What if God were to command rape or baby torture?" that would be like saying, "What if one could make a square circle or be a married bachelor?"

True, our moral intuitions are not infallible, even if we get the basics right; they may stand in need of correction. And a wise, all-good God may on rare occasions or in dire conditions command something jarring (e.g., for Abraham to offer up Isaac), which means he will have morally sufficient reasons for doing so (e.g., to test Abraham's faith that God will show himself trustworthy to fulfill his promise, even if it means raising Isaac from the dead). That being said, we do have certain unshakable intuitions that it is always wrong to rape or torture babies for fun, so it would be self-contradictory that a necessarily good God would command such things.

Strangely, Antony's writings do not address what seems a most obvious response to the Euthyphro. All human beings have been endowed with value by God (ontology) and thus have the capacity to know what is good (epistemology). God's commands—far from being arbitrary—are in accordance with God's necessarily good personhood. And when God acts, he simply does what is right. And we humans would not *know* goodness (epistemology) without God's granting us a moral *constitution*, including rights, reason, and free will (ontology).

More can be said about the Euthyphro here:

- If the naturalistic (or nontheistic) moral realist is correct about needing to have some standard external to God, then she herself cannot escape a similar dilemma, mutatis mutandis. We ask naturalistic moral realists like Antony: "Are these moral facts good simply because they are good, or is there an independent standard of goodness to which they conform?" Their argument offers them no actual advantage over theism. If two entities are sufficient to establish a relation (here, between God's personhood and human personhood), inserting yet a third entity—some moral standard independent of God to assess the connection between them—becomes superfluous. The skeptic's demand is unwarranted.

  For instance, atheist Michael Martin thinks that an ideal observer theory (IOT) renders a theistic grounding obsolete. ("Good" is what "an ideal observer would approve under ideal conditions.")[48] Not so fast. For one thing, Roderick Firth, the IOT's founding father, was a theist who claimed that "an ideal observer will be a partial description of God, if God is conceived to be an infallible moral judge."[49] Contra Martin, the theist can easily appropriate the IOT!

Second, despite Martin's use of the Euthyphro against theists, he is hoisted with his own petard, exposing just how innocuous the Euthyphro objection really is: if torturing babies for fun is wrong because an ideal observer says so, then is torturing babies for fun wrong because the ideal observer says so, or does the ideal observer say so because torturing babies for fun is wrong? If we use Martin's (and Antony's) logic, we would still have a moral standard independent of the ideal observer—an IIOT!

- The naturalist's query becomes pointless: we must eventually arrive at some self-sufficient, self-explanatory stopping point beyond which the discussion cannot go. Why is this "independent moral standard" any less arbitrary a stopping point than God's own intrinsically good personhood? Why must we bow to the naturalist's insistence on some independent moral standard when God's moral goodness would suffice? Naturalist Wielenberg's invoking a nonnaturalistic realm (which resembles Platonism) is already taking a transcendental step toward theism, conceding that something more than naturalism is required to ground moral realism.

- The necessity of moral truths does not diminish their need for grounding in a necessary personal God, who exists in all possible worlds.[50] God, who necessarily exists in all possible worlds, is the source of all necessary moral truths that stand in asymmetrical relation to God's necessity. This can be compared to the necessary truth "consciousness necessarily exists"; this is precisely because God—a supremely self-aware being—exists in all possible worlds. God's existence also means that objective moral values are necessary—that is, they exist in all possible worlds precisely because a supremely good God exists all possible worlds. That is, God's existence is explanatorily prior to these moral values. The same can be said about logical or mathematical truths as well.[51]

- God, who is essentially perfect, does not have obligations to some external moral standard; God simply acts, and, naturally, it is good. An intrinsically good God is not duty-bound; rather than having moral obligations, he simply expresses the goodness of his personhood in his acts and commands. As H. O. Mounce suggests, "God cannot hold anything good unless he *already* values it. But then his valuing cannot *depend* on its being good."[52] If the creator were evil, then we would not be obligated to obey or worship such a being since such a being would not be maximally excellent and thus worthy of worship ("worth-ship").

- Though God's personhood grounds his commands, they still play an important role. Divine commands may partially serve as guidance in particular instances where there would otherwise be no moral obligation (e.g., certain food, planting, or clothing laws to distinguish Old Testament Israel from surrounding nations). Furthermore, divine commands may strengthen or reinforce moral motivation. For example, sometimes we know what to do intellectually, but the gentle prodding or even strong rebuke of a caring friend may be just what we need to spur us into action. Beyond this, we know that commands often add greater weight or seriousness to moral obligations of which we are aware. We may be familiar with general ethical principles, but the command of a genuine moral authority often assists in our taking our duties more seriously than if we merely had a theoretical knowledge of general moral principles.[53]
- The acceptance of objective values assumes a kind of ultimate goal or design plan for human beings. This would make little sense given naturalism (since we are the products of mindless, unguided processes), but it makes much sense given theism, which presumes a design plan or ideal standard for human beings.
- Even if there were some moral standard independent of God, it still would fail to account for how humans, given their valueless, unguided, deterministic, materialistic origins, came to be morally valuable, rights-bearing, morally responsible beings. What's more, this transcendent moral standard assumed by Antony and Wielenberg still can't account for the human moral freedom required to submit to such a standard given a materialistic, deterministic world.
- The Euthyphro dilemma fails to distinguish between moral good (an axiological category) and moral right (a deontic category, denoting obligation/duty). For example, giving all one's possessions to the poor may be good, but this doesn't entail a universal obligation. This good–right distinction enables us to determine what good (supererogatory) actions rise above the obligatory. Again, what is good is not identical to what God commands, but what God commands will ultimately be good. And, as we've seen, God is necessarily good; so if he on rare occasion commands something jarring or morally difficult, he will do so with morally sufficient reason.[54]

Not only does the Euthyphro dilemma pose no threat to a theistically rooted ethic, but a similarly configured argument (as in the first bullet point above) can be launched against the naturalistic moral realist who is convinced of the Euthyphro's efficacy.

One final point: The naturalistically explicable impulse of self-sacrifice for one's own offspring or even species makes no rational sense—a sharp contrast to the theistic worldview. On naturalism, why should a person surrender his momentary existence—all the existence he will *ever* have—so that his offspring may survive? Or why endure lifelong imprisonment in a Communist jail for refusing to reveal the whereabouts of an innocent who is an "enemy of the state"? Accounting for self-sacrificial acts or virtuous acts that bring lifelong hardship and anguish or even death is problematic for naturalistic moral realists.

On the other hand, theism assures us that God does not demand of us more than we can bear and that God will guarantee that a morally virtuous life and even self-sacrifice are not in vain if one's trust is in God. In this case, God's existence guarantees that a moral life and happiness will ultimately come together.[55] Naturalists must concede that, in their view, virtue will frequently go unrewarded and that the unjust and wicked will frequently "get away with murder." In contrast, the true believer is motivated by dedication to a personal being, not to mere abstract facts and duties. Ultimate happiness is not found in some crass material or hedonistic reward, as critics commonly charge, but in the enjoyment of the company of the God whom the believer has served and in whose personhood is the very standard of goodness. Thus the believer can and should be good for goodness' sake. That is, to pursue virtue for its own sake since God's personhood itself is the fount of goodness and God is also the guarantor that a life rightly lived will not, in the final day, be ignored. Atheism is not perfect piety.

■ NOTES

1. For a defense of objective moral values, see Paul Copan, "God, Naturalism, and the Foundations of Morality," in *The Future of Atheism: Alister McGrath and Daniel Dennett in Dialogue*, ed. Robert Stewart (Minneapolis: Fortress Press, 2008).

2. Paul Copan, *Is God a Moral Monster? Understanding the Old Testament God* (Grand Rapids, MI: Baker, 2011); also, idem, "Are Old Testament Laws Evil?" in *God Is Great, God Is Good: Facing New Challenges to Belief in God*, ed. Chad Meister and William Lane Craig (Downers Grove, IL: InterVarsity Press, 2009).

3. On some troubles with a naturalistic moral epistemology, see chapter 6 in Thomas Nagel, *The Last Word* (New York: Oxford, 1997).

4. See Louise Antony, "Atheism as Perfect Piety," in *Is Goodness Without God Good Enough? A Debate on Faith, Secularism, and Ethics*, ed. Robert K. Garcia and Nathan L. King (Lanham, MD: Rowman & Littlefield, 2009).

5. Erik J. Wielenberg, "Objective Morality and the Nature of Reality," *American Theological Inquiry* 13, no. 2 (2010): 79. Walter Sinnott-Armstrong takes a similar view regarding the evolution of moral values, but moral facts are like the laws of physics ($e = mc^2$) and mathematics ($2 + 2 = 4$). Walter Sinnott-Armstrong, *Morality Without God?* (Oxford: Oxford University Press, 2009), 92–93.

6. Erik J. Wielenberg, *Value and Virtue in a Godless Universe* (New York: Cambridge University Press, 2005), 52. I grant Wielenberg's "nonnaturalistic" label; ultimately his naturalistic worldview is the target of my critique.

7. Jean Paul Sartre, *Existentialism and Human Emotions* (New York: Philosophical Library, 1957), 22.

8. Friedrich Nietzsche, *Twilight of the Idols and the Anti-Christ* (New York. Penguin Books, 1968), 55, 70.

9. Bertrand Russell, "A Free Man's Worship," in *Mysticism and Logic and Other Essays* (London: Allen & Unwin, 1963), 41. Antony and Wielenberg nobly attempt to salvage Russell as a moral realist, yet Russell abandoned his moral realism early on, thanks to George Santayana. By 1927, Russell wrote, "I no longer regard good and evil as objective entities wholly independent of human desires." Bertrand Russell, *An Outline of Philosophy* (London: George Allen & Unwin, 1927), 238. See Mark D. Linville's documentation of Russell's descent into moral subjectivism in *Philosophy and the Christian Worldview: Analysis, Assessment and Development*, ed. David Werther and Mark D. Linville (New York: Continuum, 2012). On this, see Antony's debate with William Lane Craig on God and morality, http://videorow. blogspot.com/2010/03/william-lane-craig-discusses-morality.html (accessed April 15, 2010); see also Wielenberg, *Value and Virtue*.

10. J. L. Mackie, *The Miracle of Theism* (Oxford: Clarendon Press, 1982), 115. Note: the issue of power to create moral values is not quite the way to state the matter, but let that pass.

11. Richard Dawkins, *River Out of Eden: A Darwinian View of Life* (New York: Basic Books/Harper Collins, 1995), 132–133.

12. Erik J. Wielenberg, "In Defense of Non-Natural, Non-Theistic Moral Realism," *Faith and Philosophy* 26, no. 1 (January 2009): 40n.

13. Oddly, atheist Graham Oppy challenges the weakest (straw man) theistic "arguments from morality," yet he ignores the solid ones, including those pointing to theism's metaphysical basis for intrinsic human dignity and rights. Graham Oppy, *Arguing for Gods* (Cambridge: Cambridge University Press, 2006), 352–376.

14. Incidentally, naturalists help themselves to another metaphysical free lunch—namely, the beginning of the universe from nothing. Indeed, the big bang cosmological model's resembling the biblical doctrine of creation out of nothing has not escaped the notice of naturalistic astrophysicists. For instance, John D. Barrow and Joseph Silk acknowledge: "Our new picture is more akin to the traditional metaphysical picture of creation out of nothing, for it predicts a definite beginning to events in time, indeed a definite beginning to time itself." They ask: "what preceded the event called the 'big bang'? . . . the answer to our question is simple: nothing." John D. Barrow and Joseph Silk, *The Left Hand of Creation*, 2nd ed. (New York: Oxford University Press, 1993), 38, 209.

However, if, as Paul Davies points out, the universe was either caused or uncaused (a metaphysical impossibility), then some nonnaturalistic entity independent of the natural world brought it into being.

Likewise, Paul Davies concludes: "'What caused the big bang?' . . . One might consider some supernatural force, some agency beyond space and time as being responsible for the big bang, or one might prefer to regard the big bang as an event without a cause. It seems to me that we don't have too much choice. Either . . . something outside of the physical world . . . or . . . an event without a cause." Paul Davies, "The Birth of the Cosmos," in *God, Cosmos, Nature and Creativity*, ed. Jill Gready (Edinburgh: Scottish Academic Press, 1995), 8–9.

The universe's being ontologically haunted undermines naturalism since nature itself sprang into being from something outside itself. Though the universe's cause may be dismissed as a "brute fact," we're dealing with something exceedingly powerful—and an entity more fundamental than the universe itself. Not all brute facts are equal; some are explanatorily deeper ("more brute"!) than others.

15. On the problems with naturalistic accounts of supervenience, see Alvin Plantinga, "Naturalism, Theism, Obligation, and Supervenience," *Faith and Philosophy* 27 (2010): 247–272.

16. Christian Smith, "Does Naturalism Warrant a Moral Belief in Universal Benevolence and Human Rights?," in *The Believing Primate: Scientific, Philosophical, and Theological Reflections on the Origin of Religion*, ed. Jeffrey Schloss and Michael J. Murray (Oxford: Oxford University Press, 2009), 294.

17. Ibid., 311. This example can be found in Ruse's "Evolutionary Ethics: A Phoenix Arisen," 241–242, where he humorously refers to the termites' "rather strange foodstuffs"!

18. Michael Shermer, *The Science of Good and Evil* (New York: Henry Holt and Company, 2004), 56–77.

19. C. S. Lewis, *Miracles* (New York: Macmillan, 1960), 37.

20. Ibid., 38, 37.

21. Michael Ruse, *The Darwinian Paradigm* (London: Routledge, 1989), 262, 268.

22. Michael Ruse and E. O. Wilson, "The Evolution of Ethics," in *Religion and the Natural Sciences*, ed. J. E. Huchingson (Orlando: Harcourt Brace, 1993), 310–311.

23. Elliott Sober, *Philosophy of Biology* (Boulder, CO: Westview, 1993), 202–208. The genetic fallacy is the ascription of truth or falsity to a belief based solely on its origin. The naturalistic fallacy makes the sneaky move from "is" to "ought"—from factual description to moral prescription.

24. Wielenberg, "In Defense of Non-Natural, Non-Theistic Moral Realism," 35.

25. Walter Sinnott-Armstrong affirms humans have freedom and free will, which gives them dignity; *Morality Without God*, 69–70. Michael Shermer emphasizes that humans have "risen above" our genetically determined evolutionary predecessors into moral freedom; *The Science of Good and Evil*, 19–22.

26. Humans "can reason, suffer, fall in love, set goals for themselves" and "experience happiness and tell the difference between right and wrong." Wielenberg, "In Defense of Non-Natural, Non-Theistic Moral Realism," 40.

27. David O. Brink, "Moral Realism and the Sceptical Arguments from Disagreement and Queerness," *Australasian Journal of Philosophy* 62 (1984): 120. See also Brink's *Moral Realism and the Foundation of Ethics* (Cambridge: Cambridge University Press, 1989) and his "The Autonomy of Ethics," in *The Cambridge Companion to Atheism*, ed. Michael Martin (Cambridge: Cambridge University Press, 2006).

28. Colin McGinn, *The Problem of Consciousness* (Oxford: Basil Blackwell, 1990), 10–11.

29. Geoffrey Madell, *Mind and Materialism* (Edinburgh: Edinburgh University Press, 1988), 141.

30. David Papineau, *Philosophical Naturalism* (Oxford: Blackwell, 1993), 119.

31. The issue of nonhuman animal consciousness is beside the point; *any* consciousness cannot be accounted for, given naturalism's context.

32. Patricia Churchland, "Epistemology in the Age of Neuroscience," *Journal of Philosophy* 84 (October 1987): 548–549.

33. Richard Rorty, "Untruth and Consequences," *New Republic* (31 July 1995): 32–36.

34. Michael Ruse and E. O. Wilson, "The Evolution of Ethics," in *Religion and the Natural Sciences*, ed. J. E. Huchingson (Orlando: Harcourt Brace, 1993), 310–311.

35. Michael Ruse, "Evolutionary Ethics: A Phoenix Arisen," in *Issues in Evolutionary Ethics*, ed. Paul Thompson (Albany, NY: SUNY Press, 1995), 236.

36. James Rachels, *Created From Animals: The Moral Implications of Darwinism* (Oxford: Oxford University Press, 1990), 77.

37. Alvin Plantinga, *Warranted Christian Belief* (New York: Oxford University Press, 2000), 185.

38. Moreover, does Aristotle have more worth than Joe the Plumber because the former has greater rational powers?

39. William Provine, "Evolution and the Foundation of Ethics," *Marine Biological Laboratory Science* 3 (1988): 27–28.

40. Francis Crick, *The Astonishing Hypothesis: The Scientific Search for the Soul* (New York: Charles Scribner's Sons, 1994), 3.

41. Thomas Nagel, *The View from Nowhere* (New York: Oxford University Press, 1986), 111, 113.

42. John Searle, *Minds, Brains, and Science* (Cambridge, MA: Harvard University Press, 1986 reprint) 87, 88, 92.

43. John Bishop, *Natural Agency* (Cambridge: Cambridge University Press, 1989), 1.

44. Ron Bontekoe, *The Nature of Dignity* (Lanham, MD: Rowman & Littlefield, 2008), 15–16.

45. For example, William P. Alston, "Some Suggestions for Divine Command Theorists," in *Christian Theism and the Problems of Philosophy*, ed. Michael D. Beaty (Notre Dame, IN: University of Notre Dame Press, 1990); Thomas V. Morris, "Duty and Divine Goodness" and "The Necessity of God's Goodness," in *Anselmian Explorations* (Notre Dame, IN: University of Notre Dame Press, 1987); Thomas V. Morris, *Our Idea of God* (Downers Grove, IL: InterVarsity Press, 1991); Paul Copan, "The Moral Argument," in *The Rationality of Theism*, ed. Paul Copan and Paul K. Moser (London: Routledge, 2003); William J. Wainwright, *Religion and Morality* (Burlington, VT: Ashgate, 2005).

46. Antony, "Atheism as Perfect Piety," 70.

47. David Baggett and Jerry L. Walls, *Good God: The Theistic Foundations of Morality* (New York: Oxford University Press, 2011), 46.

48. See chap. 3 in Michael Martin, *Atheism, Morality and Meaning* (Amherst, NY: Prometheus Press, 2002).

49. Roderick Firth, "Ethical Absolutism and the Ideal Observer," *Philosophy and Phenomenological Research* 12 (1952): 333.

50. Even some theists incorrectly argue that necessary moral truths exist independently of God—that is, "murder is wrong" would hold true even if God does not exist. Richard Swinburne, *The Coherence of Theism* (Oxford: Oxford University Press, 1977), 204; Keith Yandell, "Theism, Atheism, and Cosmology," in *Does God Exist?: The Craig–Flew Debate*, ed. Stan W. Wallace (Aldershot, UK: Ashgate, 2003), 96. However, their odd view that God is not necessarily existent in all possible worlds is the culprit here; if that is granted, then the intrinsic connection between necessary moral facts and this necessarily good being becomes clear.

51. William Lane Craig, "The Most Gruesome of Guests," in *Is Goodness Without God Good Enough?*, ed. Nathan King and Robert Garcia (Lanham, MD: Rowman & Littlefield, 2009), 169–171.

52. H. O. Mounce, "Morality and Religion," in *Philosophy of Religion*, ed. Brian Davies (Washington, DC: Georgetown University Press, 1998), 278.

53. See Linda Zagzebski, *Divine Motivation Theory* (Cambridge: Cambridge University Press, 2004); Richard Swinburne, "What Difference Does God Make to

Morality?," in *Is Goodness Without God Good Enough?: A Debate on Faith, Secularism, and Ethics*, ed. Robert K. Garcia and Nathan L. King (Lanham, MD: Rowman & Littlefield, 2009), 151–165.

54. Baggett and Walls, *Good God*, 47.

55. Peter Singer and John E. Hare, "Moral Mammals: Does Atheism or Theism Provide the Best Foundation for Human Worth and Morality?," in *A Place for Truth*, ed. Dallas Willard (Downers Grove, IL: InterVarsity Press, 2010), 190.

■ FOR FURTHER READING

Baggett, D., and J. L. Walls. *Good God: The Theistic Foundations of Morality*. New York: Oxford University Press, 2011.

Copan, P. "God, Naturalism, and the Foundations of Morality." In *The Future of Atheism: Alister McGrath and Daniel Dennett in Dialogue*, edited by R. Stewart, 141–162. Minneapolis: Fortress Press, 2008.

Hare, J. M. *God and Morality: A Philosophical History*. Oxford: Blackwell, 2007.

Linville, M. R. "The Moral Argument," in *The Blackwell Companion to Natural Theology*, edited by W. L. Craig and J. P. Moreland, 391–448. Oxford: Blackwell, 2009.

Smith, C. "Does Naturalism Warrant a Moral Belief in Universal Benevolence and Human Rights?," in *The Believing Primate: Scientific, Philosophical, and Theological Reflections on the Origin of Religion*, edited by J. Schloss and M. J. Murray, 292–316. Oxford: Oxford University Press, 2009.

8   The Failure of Moral Arguments

■ LOUISE ANTONY

Many people, including many philosophers, believe that morality constitutes a problem for atheists. Some philosophers take the strong position that the very existence of moral value depends upon the existence of God, and thus that atheists must, in the end, be nihilists. Others take the position that atheists cannot provide an adequate account of moral value. Call the first position *incompatibility* and the second *inadequacy*. Each thesis has served as a major premise in one or another version of what is called the "moral argument" for the existence of God.

It should not be thought that incompatibility divides theists from atheists. It is open to an atheist to endorse incompatibility, provided he or she is prepared to accept the consequences. An atheist who wishes to avoid nihilism, however, must deny incompatibility. Such an atheist—call her a "moral atheist"—will concede that incompatibility, if true, would provide a compelling reason to believe in God. But while the moral atheist must deny incompatibility, she need not refute it. On the face of it, there is no inconsistency between believing in morality and disbelieving in God, and so the onus is on the proponent of incompatibility to show that, appearances to the contrary notwithstanding, the moral atheist's position harbors some deep contradiction. In section 1 of this chapter I will examine three of the most well-known arguments for incompatibility, and demonstrate that none provides a sound inference from atheism to nihilism.

It might seem that the situation is different with inadequacy, that here the burden is on the moral atheist to show that there is a nontheistic metaethic that meets the explanatory demands laid down by the theist. But in fact, the moral atheist can shift the burden here as well. It's not enough for proponents of inadequacy to point to shortcomings in secular metaethical theories, they have to show that their theist metaethics can do what the secular theories cannot. In section 2 I will argue that positing God gives the theist no advantage over the atheist in addressing puzzling issues about the metaphysics, etiology, and epistemology of moral value. Indeed, I'll argue, the God hypothesis raises more metaethical questions than it answers.

▓ 1. INCOMPATIBILITY

Let *atheism* be the doctrine that it is not the case that there is a unique, necessary, eternal, immaterial, personal being who created the universe and who possesses all perfections—specifically omniscience, omnipotence, and benevolence. Let *nihilism* be the doctrine that no moral property is instantiated. Let *morality* refer to the denial of nihilism. The term *moral atheism* will designate the conjunction of atheism and morality.

Since, obviously, one can consistently affirm atheism while denying nihilism, any derivation from the former thesis to the latter will require additional premises. Proponents of incompatibility claim to find such premises in one of two places: either within the atheist's presumed "worldview" or within the concept of morality itself. In section 1.1 I'll look at two representative arguments of the first type. In section 1.2 I'll examine one widely cited argument of the second type, William Lane Craig's "accountability" argument.

1.1 Materialism, naturalism, and atheism

Atheism, as I've defined it, is a very narrow doctrine. But to many people the term "atheism" evokes a broad stereotype, and many popular objections to atheism are really objections to elements of this stereotype. So, too, are several familiar versions of the moral argument, including two versions found in the works of William Lane Craig and Paul Copan.[1] Although Craig claims that these arguments demonstrate that atheism is incompatible with morality, they can at best show the incompatibility of morality with what Craig refers to as "the atheistic view," specifically, with the doctrines of *materialism* and *naturalism*. Arguments directed at these doctrines, even if sound, cannot show that morality depends upon God. If all that these proponents can show in the end is that morality is incompatible with materialism or naturalism, then they leave a vast space for the moral atheist to occupy. That being said, I acknowledge that many atheists are in fact committed to the doctrines of materialism and naturalism—as indeed I am—so it is still important to look critically at arguments that purport to derive nihilism from either of these doctrines.

It will not be possible for me to discuss all such arguments, so I will focus on two of the most popular: the nothing-but argument, and the naturalist's dilemma.[2]

1.1.2 *The nothing-but argument*

Moral arguments against atheism are often presented enthymematically in terms of a "nothing-but" claim: if atheism is true, human beings are "nothing but" brute animals, or "nothing but" swarms of molecules. Here's a representative example from William Lane Craig:

> On the atheistic view, there's nothing special about human beings. They are just accidental byproducts of nature that have evolved relatively recently on an infinitesimal speck of dust called the planet Earth.

Or again:

> On the atheistic view, human beings are just animals, and animals have no moral obligations to each other.[3]

But why must an atheist accept either of these nothing-but claims? According to Craig, these claims follow from materialism, an element of the "atheistic view." Materialism denies the existence of souls. From this, says Craig, it follows that "there's nothing special about animal beings," and thus that human beings have no moral value.

> Naturalists are typically materialists or physicalists, who regard man [sic] as a purely animal organism. But if man has no immaterial aspect to his being (call it soul or mind or what have you), then we're not qualitatively different from other animal species. On a materialistic anthropology there's no reason to think that human beings are objectively more valuable than rats. When a terrorist bomb rips through a market in Baghdad, all that happens is a rearrangement of the molecules that used to be a little girl.[4]

Is this a good argument against materialism? No.

So far, the argument looks like this:

1. If materialism is true, then human beings are nothing but animals [accidental byproducts/collection of molecules].
2. Animals [accidental byproducts/collections of molecules] are devoid of moral value.

The conclusion, we know, is supposed to be this:

3. Therefore, if materialism is true, then human beings are devoid of moral value.

To be valid, the argument needs an additional premise. Here's one possibility, suggested by Craig in the last quoted passage:

4. If Qs are nothing but Ps, then Qs are not qualitatively different from Ps.

Premise (4) will do the trick, but only if there is no equivocation between premise (1) and premise (4); "nothing but" has to mean the same thing in both contexts. But there's the rub. In any sense that would make premise (1) acceptable to the materialist, premise (4) will come out false.

A materialist may use a nothing-but claim to say something about composition. In that sense, the claim that "human beings are nothing but collections of molecules" would mean "human beings are made entirely out of molecules." But when we plug that sense of "nothing but" into premise (4), we get the following:

> 4′. If human beings are made entirely out of molecules, then they are not qualitatively different from other collections of molecules.

But no materialist need accept this. Different collections of molecules have vastly different sets of properties. Animals, plants, rocks, cotton candy, and Michelangelo's *David* are all "nothing but" (in the sense we're considering) collections of molecules, but they differ qualitatively from each other in many ways. What determines a thing's kind is not what it is composed of ultimately—ultimately we are all composed of the same stuff—but rather the way the stuff is put together, the way it is organized.

Another possible interpretation: nothing-but claims are sometimes used to draw contrasts. To say of a despised politician, "so-and-so is nothing but a shill for the insurance industry," would be to draw a contrast with some more charitable view of the politician—so-and-so is a shill for the insurance industry *as opposed to* a sincere but naive political neophyte, or *as opposed to* a principled opponent. In this contrastive sense, materialists will all agree that human beings are nothing but animals as opposed to spirits, or that they are nothing but swarms of molecules as opposed to units of immaterial substance. But once again, we get a non sequitur when we substitute into premise 4 this contrastive sense of "nothing but":

4″. If human beings are animals as opposed to immaterial spirits, then they are not qualitatively different from other animals.

The truth of premise 4 depends on taking "nothing but" in a very different way—as a *deflationary* or *eliminativist* claim. To say that that a thing of type Q is nothing but P in this sense is to disparage the kind or property of being Q, to say that being Q amounts to nothing more than being P, or even that there is no such thing as being P: "magicians are nothing but clever tricksters;" "flying saucers are nothing but swamp gas;" or, as Richard Dawkins might say, "morality is nothing but disguised self-interest." Understood in this deflationary or eliminativist sense, to say that human beings are nothing but animals is to say that the things we call "human beings" have no properties other than the ones they share with nonhuman animals, with nonhuman swarms of molecules, or with nonhuman accidental byproducts. Obviously a materialist can deny any of these claims.

There's yet another problem. Premise 2, "animals are devoid of moral value," begs the question against the moral materialist. The materialist who thinks both that human beings are animals and that human beings have moral value is hardly going to accept the claim that animals are devoid of moral value. If the moral materialist is right, then there are some animals that possess moral value, that is to say, human beings. The same point holds, *mutatis mutandis*, for the other versions of premise 2.

In short, nothing-but arguments are either invalid or question-begging, or both. No materialist is required to deny that human beings have distinctive properties, properties that are not found elsewhere in nature, and properties that ground moral properties. All a materialist is obliged to deny is that such distinctive properties depend upon a human being's having an immaterial soul.

1.1.3 The naturalist's dilemma

Another popular argument, found, for example, in the work of Paul Copan, charges that naturalism undermines ethics. (Again, I note for the record that not all atheists are naturalists, so this argument, even if successful, cannot establish theism.) Naturalism, for our purposes, can be taken to be the view that all entities, processes, and events are governed by *natural* law; there are no *supernatural* forces.

This argument claims that naturalists face a dilemma about the status of our ethical commitments. If naturalism is true, then either human ethical beliefs and dispositions are the product of natural law operating on chance circumstances or they are the product of natural selection. But each of these etiologies gives us some reason to doubt our ethical commitments. If the first horn is true, then it's arbitrary that our beliefs have the particular content they have, and we therefore have no reason to think that they are true. If the second story is true, then the contents are not arbitrary, but they turn out not to be ethical. In short, if naturalism is correct, then either we don't know what's right, or we don't even know what "right" is. Call the first horn the *argument from arbitrariness* and the second the *screening-off argument*.

Let's start with the argument from arbitrariness. It begins with a premise the naturalist will accept: if naturalism is true, then all states of affairs throughout the universe, including the contents of human minds and the character of human behavior, are shaped by natural law operating on chance circumstances. But, the argument continues, the laws of nature are insensitive to ethical or normative facts. Such facts can therefore have played no role in shaping the particular ethical beliefs and behavioral dispositions that we happen to possess. It is thus arbitrary, from an ethical point of view, what the content of our ethical beliefs came to be. Since our ethical beliefs could have had any content whatsoever, there is no reason to think that the particular contents our ethical beliefs happen to have are correct.

It's important to see that this argument is not committing the genetic fallacy—it does not argue that beliefs with naturalistic origins must be false. The issue, as Paul Copan rightly notes, is justification, not truth. Even if our ethical beliefs *are* true, he writes, "it is by accident rather than through some epistemic virtue."[5] But if that's the case, then it would suffice to answer the argument from arbitrariness to show that, within a purely natural world, there is a way that human beliefs could have been shaped by ethically significant factors. This can be done.

Let me return to the point I made in connection with nothing-but arguments. The world may be homogeneous at the micro level—nothing but quarks, perhaps—but the varying arrangements of the microparticles give rise to great variety at the macro level. The phenomena that "emerge" when we abstract from the microphysical details fall into regularities of their own—these regularities form the domains of chemistry, biology, geology, and the other "special sciences." The first point, then, is that there is nothing in the naturalist picture that precludes there being lawlike regularities at higher levels than physics.

Human beings fall into a particularly special class of macrophenomena. The particles that constitute us are arranged so that we have brains and nervous systems that support a *psychology*. To have a psychology is to have the capacity to form mental representations, and to use those representations in guiding interactions with the environment. Creatures with psychologies can integrate representations of the way the world is (*beliefs*) with representations of the way they'd like the world to be (*desires*) and choose a course of action that makes sense, given those beliefs and desires. They can also use representations to *reason*—to generate new beliefs and to find novel solutions to problems. Finally, at least some creatures with representational capacities can make themselves sensitive to a certain class of properties—what we might call (somewhat misleadingly) *theoretical* properties. These are properties, roughly, that a creature can only know about by inference from properties available to the senses. Thus any visually sensate creature can detect the size, shape, and color of a hammer, but only a creature that can infer or remember the purpose of such an object can see *that* it is a hammer. Psychological properties are themselves, in this sense, theoretical properties. It takes a metarepresentational capacity to be able to recognize other beings as representers, as creatures with beliefs, desires, intentions, or emotions.

Ethical properties, too, are theoretical properties involving, crucially, the capacity to see other creatures as psychological beings. It can be seen that one creature is colliding with another, but it takes psychological inference to classify the event as a case of one creature's *attacking* another, and a further inference to conclude that the attack is a case of aggression. It can be seen that one creature has five apples and another only one, but it takes iterated inferences to see that distribution as unfair.[6] Human beings can and do perform such inferences. Because of our representational capacities, we are sensitive to the factors that (as I'll argue in the next section) provide the naturalistic grounding of normative facts: for example, that there are other sensate creatures capable of experiencing pain and other cognitive creatures with desires and plans they wish to fulfill.

Psychology thus offers a naturalistically sound supplement to natural selection as a way of explaining the emergence of certain kinds of order in the world. Creatures who are able to think can generate regularities that otherwise would not exist, specifically, regularities that involve rational, rather than merely causal factors. Ask a hundred schoolchildren to add two and two, and you'll get "four" (close to) a hundred times. The explanation is not that there is a brute causal regularity between utterances of the question and utterances of the answer; it is, rather, that the children are sensitive to the *content* of the question, and that they *know* the right answer. There is a rational relation—a relation of making sense—between the naturalistic factors that are ethically significant and the contents of the ethical beliefs that we form in response, and so we have a naturalistically sound way of explaining how our ethical beliefs could have been shaped by normatively significant factors. There is no reason whatsoever to think that the contents of our ethical beliefs are arbitrary.

Let's turn to the screening-off argument. This argument is concessive: it allows that there may be a shaping force in nature after all, namely natural selection, and also that it may have shaped human beliefs and dispositions in a way that gives them the appearance of ethical commitments. However, the argument continues, even if natural selection did shape human cognition and affection, it shaped them not on the basis of what is *morally* good, but rather on the basis of what is *prudentially* good—whatever will promote the survival of the organism. Natural selection, in other words, cannot select for sound ethical values; at best it can select beliefs and dispositions that happen to coincide with the requirements of ethics. Ethical considerations, even if they existed, would be *screened off* by effects of self- (or species-) interest. Thus naturalism gives us reason to doubt that our putatively ethical commitments are actually ethical.

This argument commits a fallacy common to many discussions (atheist as well as theist) of natural selection: it confuses the question of what is selected *for* with the question what is selected.[7] Traits that have adaptive value can come bundled with traits that don't. Thus the fact that the first trait but not the second was selected for is no argument that the second trait is not present. The ability to play the flute was probably not selected for, but it came bundled along with digital dexterity, which (plausibly) was. Perhaps natural selection could not select for the ethical rightness of a set of attitudes; this does not show that attitudes with the property of ethical rightness could not have been selected. Consider parental love. The screening-off argument claims that if it was adaptive for human parents to experience the state we call "love," the state would not really be *love*. Fallacy! If parental love—a psychological state with a particular content—leads parents to invest energy in the care of their offspring, then parental love will get selected, even if it's the caring behavior rather than the love itself that is selected for. Evolution is indifferent to the explanation why the parental energy is invested; it only cares that it is invested. It's true that the "nurturing" behavior of some species is illusory—that the parent organisms in such species are simply triggered, biologically, to engage in behavior that happens to increase their offspring's chances for survival. But that doesn't mean that human parental investment is secured by the same mechanism. We have excellent evidence that psychological states—loving one's children, recognizing one's duty—play a role in good parenting among humans, and the theory of natural selection gives us no reason to think otherwise. Evolution is as happy with psychological mechanisms as with biologically rigid instincts, if they get the job done. And if the mechanisms are allowed to be psychological, evolution can tell us nothing about the likely contents of our beliefs and desires. The only way, in fact, to find out what actually motivates human beings, is to directly study what motivates human beings. When we do that, we discover (what most of us actually knew already) that human beings do act, at least some of the time, on the basis of ethical reasons.

1.2 Accountability

Another way to defend incompatibility is to find some feature that ostensibly characterizes moral value and show that this feature could not be realized in a world without God. William Lane Craig makes these claims for a feature he calls *accountability*. While Craig has here made at least a prima facie case for a specifically theistic metaethics, it is ultimately unsuccessful. Accountability in Craig's sense is not necessary for morality. It is, moreover, in any case, insufficient—a point I'll take up in section 2.

What exactly is "accountability"? Craig seems to have in mind two different ideas. The first idea is that, in order for a given system of proscriptions and prescriptions to be genuinely moral, it must be the case that, at least ultimately, the commission of proscribed actions will have negative consequences and the commission of prescribed actions will have positive consequences. Or, more straightforwardly, what's required is that "evil and wrong will be punished; righteousness will be vindicated. Despite the inequities of this life, in the end the scales of God's justice will be balanced."[8] What could ensure the satisfaction of such a condition? According to Craig, only a personal God, who doles out the appropriate consequences in order to hold human beings morally accountable.

The second idea is that accountability is part of the constitutive conditions for a principle to be *binding*, for it to be generative of obligation. Here I see Craig imagining God as a Hobbesian sovereign; it is the certainty of the sovereign's sanctions in cases of transgressions that makes it the case that the law must be obeyed. Without the existence of such a system of sanctions, it makes no sense to speak of the law binding anyone. And without that idea, the notion of obligation becomes empty. Humanly contrived systems of sanctions are fallible: violations may go unnoticed, or noticed but unpunished, and virtue, too frequently, must serve as its own reward. Hence, without a transcendent law-enforcer, there could be no sense of obligation that transcends the realm of human conventions, and the power of human enforcement.

Surely "accountability" in the first sense can be dispatched pretty quickly. The suggestion that there would be no moral value unless virtue was certain to be rewarded and vice punished is tantamount to a reduction of moral value to prudential value. Craig implicitly grants the psychological egoist her central claim when he asserts that, absent accountability, no one would have any rational motive for behaving morally.

> Even if there were objective moral values and duties under naturalism, they are irrelevant because there is no moral accountability. If life ends at the grave, it makes no difference whether one lives as a Stalin or as a saint.[9]

"Makes no difference" here must mean "makes no difference *to me*," since making a moral difference ought to count as something significant to anyone who believes in morality. Thus according to Craig, if there is no guarantee that it will somehow someday accrue to one's benefit, "sacrifice for another person is just stupid."[10] I assume that "stupid" here means "irrational." But rationality is a matter of appropriately matching actions to ends, of choosing to do that which maximizes the likelihood of achieving one's ends without sacrificing more important ends. In that case, sacrifice would be "stupid" only if there were no possible end that a person could possess that would rationalize incurring a cost to herself. The only reason to think that persons could not possess such ends is if one thought, with the egoist, that all ends are ultimately self-regarding.

In contrast, it seems to me to be part of a mature sense of morality to understand that moral obligation and self-interest can conflict. It also seems to me that proper moral motivation requires acting on the basis of what is right, regardless of what is good *for me*. I see absolutely no reason to doubt that people do sometimes act on the basis of genuinely moral motives, and without any expectation of ultimate reward. Here's an email message from Rachel Corrie, a 23-year-old peace activist, sent to her mother a month before Corrie was crushed to death by an Israeli bulldozer during a protest of Palestinian home demolitions:

> I'm witnessing this chronic, insidious genocide and I'm really scared, and questioning my fundamental belief in the goodness of human nature. This has to stop. I think it is a good idea for us all to drop everything and devote our lives to making this stop. I don't think it's an extremist thing to do anymore. I still really want to dance around to Pat Benatar and have boyfriends and make comics for my coworkers. But I also want this to stop.[11]

To dismiss Corrie's sacrifice as "stupid" is for Craig to deny that Corrie knows her own motives, or else to impugn her honesty.

"Accountability" in the second sense is the idea that a system of sanctions is constitutively necessary for moral obligation to exist. If that is correct, the argument goes, then without God to establish and impose transcendental sanctions, there could be no universally binding moral code.

Now the idea that prescriptions can only be "binding" if there are negative consequences attaching to violations of the prescriptions has some plausibility in the case of human civil law; a civil law that is wantonly violated is a law in name only. But there can be a binding law, even in the human realm, if the people under its jurisdiction treat it as a law. It is sufficient for this that persons take the lawfulness of some principle as a reason to do or to refrain from doing some particular action. Taking lawfulness as a reason is not at all the same thing as weighing the costs and benefits of performing a certain action. If Tony Soprano[12] tells me to hire his nephew, then I have a reason to do it, even if I think Tony has no right to make such a demand. I may hire his nephew, but if so, I do it not because I believe I ought to, but because I believe that if I don't I will probably get whacked.

The making of laws in the human case is, after all, ultimately a matter of social convention. What is important about the conventions that constitute lawmaking is that they involve the recognition of authority. To recognize the authority of a person or group to create law is to accept the standing obligation to treat as law the determinations of that person or group. What this shows is that it is not the system of sanctions that makes a law morally binding, but rather the recognition of the lawmaker's right to make law. It is not, in other words, the power of the lawmaker to enforce his or her will that generates obligation, it is the authority of the lawmaker that makes it so. "Authority" is a normative notion. Even if God were the source of the particular rules we regard as moral imperatives, it would have to be his antecedent moral authority, not his powers of enforcement, that makes the rules morally binding.

What all this means is that if "accountability" is indeed a necessary condition for the existence of moral obligation (and I've given some reason to think it is not), it is not sufficient. There is more that a theistic metaethics must say, and that is, what it is that makes God *good*. The theist, in other words, is going to have to confront the *Euthyphro* argument, to which I now turn.

■ 2. INADEQUACY

The second, possibly more popular form of moral argument for the existence of God is based on the claim that a nontheistic metaethical view cannot adequately explain various features of moral value or account for its presence in our world. I've labeled this view *inadequacy*. Arguments from inadequacy are abductive in form; they argue that a certain hypothesis—that God exists—provides a better explanation of morality than does any nontheistic alternative. Defeating inadequacy does not require demonstrating that some nontheistic metaethics does meet the explanatory demands laid out; it's enough to show that positing God doesn't help.

I'll focus on the related charges that moral atheists cannot explain the *objectivity* of moral value, and that they cannot explain how morality is *grounded*.[13] I take it that theists and atheists will agree about what it means to say that morality is objective: first, whether something is right or wrong does not depend on any human being's attitudes toward it, and second, moral facts are independent of human will. But what is "grounding"? It must be said here, first of all, that there is no philosophical consensus whatsoever about what kind of relation grounding is, nor even about whether there is a single relation picked out univocally by all uses of the term within philosophical discourse. Among those philosophers who agree that there is some important metaphysical relation that is properly called grounding, there is no agreement about how to characterize the relationship. But perhaps we can work well enough with some examples.

One might hold that, in general, properties are grounded in or by their instances. In that case, God would ground moral goodness by instantiating it. But so would any morally good being. To this it might be replied that human (and other finite) moral agents are only sporadically good, and that (if they are purely material beings) they exist for only a finite amount of time. In that case, the argument would continue, morality would not be fully grounded, since there would be times and possible worlds in which moral goodness is uninstantiated. This would be, in effect, to impose a further constraint on the grounding relation—for a property to be grounded, it must be the case that it is instantiated in every possible world. Such a requirement would make an awful lot of properties ungrounded; we'd need to know why goodness has to meet a condition that so many others fail.

Another possible way of conceiving grounding is as a truth-making relation. If grounding is conceived in this way, then the claim that moral value is grounded in God's nature seems to give wrong results. It seems much more natural—and plausible—to say that the truth makers for claims about moral value are facts about the capacities that moral agents have in virtue of which they are subject to moral concern. On the theist account that we are considering, the truth maker for my duty to refrain from causing you gratuitous pain is that God has the nature he has. On the naturalistic account, the truth makers are the facts that (1) you have the capacity to feel pain, and (2) I have the cognitive and affective capacities to realize that. To say that God's nature is independent of the facts about your and my capacities, what makes it the case that I have this duty toward you, is to say that those capacities are morally irrelevant. Without a being with God's nature in the picture, it would be neither true nor false that I ought to refrain from hurting you, irrespective of the fact that you are a being capable of feeling pain, and of the fact that I know this full well.

Sticking with the truth-making construal for the moment, let's think about the moral value of interpersonal relationships. Familial relationships, romantic relationships, and friendships all have a moral dimension. They are all, at their best, cemented by mutual and morally laudable concern for the well-being of another person, a concern that recognizes and is shaped by the moral status of the other person. It seems to me to make perfect sense to say that the moral value of interpersonal relationships is grounded in the personhood of the individuals involved—to say that your status as a being of a certain sort, with certain capacities, is what makes it appropriate for me to enter into, for example, a friendship with you and to take your well-being as a prima facie end when I consider how to act. To say instead that your status as a morally appropriate target of my affection and my concern depends instead on God seems to me to run counter to all moral intuition, not to mention human psychology. It entails that my concern for my husband, my children, and my friends is misguided to the extent that I think it is they who matter; their actual value lies in the external fact that they matter to someone else.

That is just a sketch of how the moral atheist might answer the demand to provide a grounding for morality. But the proponent of inadequacy will reject any such account, no matter how detailed; she thinks she has an in-principle argument against the possible adequacy of a naturalistic grounding for moral facts. Natural facts are all nonnormative, she'll say, and no set of nonnormative facts entail any normative fact. Since the moral atheist has only the natural facts at her disposal, she will never be able to give a thorough grounding for morality. The theist, however, has an additional resource: God. As a supernatural being, God can ground the normative facts by approving or commanding them.

I will concede immediately that there is a puzzle here. I agree that normative facts cannot be derived from nonnormative facts, that given any set of nonnormative facts, it is, as G. E. Moore put it, an "open question" whether a given normative fact obtains. But my contention is that Moore's challenge is just as pressing for the theist. No nonnormative set of facts about God will entail that God is good, but without the premise that God is good, the proffered grounding will always be incomplete: God may have commanded it, but is it *good*? We have already seen how the open question arises in the case of Craig's explanation of "accountability"—we get accountability only if it is stipulated antecedently that God is *authorized* to dole out punishments and rewards. But since authorization is a normative notion, we end up back at our starting place. To understand why the commands of a morally good being are "binding" on us in a way that the edicts of a dictator are not just is to understand why morality is objectively binding in the first place.

This is the *Euthyphro* challenge, updated: is that which is morally good, morally good because God approves it, or does God approve what's morally good because it's morally good? The theist needs to make the first horn of the dilemma true, or she has no account of grounding—or rather, no account different from any available to the atheist. But the first horn fails to explain why "moral goodness" is morally good. If we take seriously the claim that morally good actions are morally good in virtue of God's approving them, then the claim that God approves all and only the morally good is stripped of content. Or, to be more precise, it makes the claim into a kind of definitional truth, a mere stipulation.

Let's consider an analogy: a judge issuing a verdict. "I find the defendant guilty," says the judge. Does such a finding, and such a pronouncement, *make* the defendant guilty? In one sense it does. "Guilty" can and sometimes does serve to mark out the condition of having been duly tried and convicted of a crime. In this sense, finding a person guilty is, in J. L. Austin's sense, an *illocutionary act*, and the defendant's "guilt" is an *illocutionary effect* of the judge's ruling. Illocutionary effects are constitutively grounded in the conventions that transform certain linguistic acts into actions of a different type. The defendant's guilt in this sense is grounded in the legal conventions governing criminal proceedings, and in the judge's satisfaction of the conditions conventionally determined to constitute a legal ruling. In the other sense of "guilty," the judge's ruling is irrelevant to the defendant's status. The defendant is guilty in this sense if and only if she has committed the crime with which she is charged; if she is guilty, that fact is grounded in what she did and not in what the judge did. Let's call the first sense "judicial guilt" and the second "objective guilt."

Now, of course, we want it to be the case that judicial guilt and objective guilt go hand in hand. The legal conventions and procedures that constitute the judicial system are therefore designed (or are supposed to be designed) in such a way as to maximize the chances that the two conditions coincide. Ideally a judge will issue a finding that renders the defendant judicially guilty when and only when, the defendant is objectively guilty, and only because the defendant is guilty. If there were no such thing as objective guilt, the legal system would be pointless or worse. "Judicial guilt" could still exist; it would be, as before, the condition of having been the object of a certain illocutionary act, to which consequences of various weights might or might not be attached. But there could be no question of a judge being a good or a bad judge, since there would be no objective condition to which the judge's rulings had to answer. But such a system of trial and punishment, untethered to the objective facts about guilt and innocence, would be Kafkaesque.[14]

The lesson will be clear. To say that moral goodness is grounded in God's approval is to say that there is nothing but (as we might call it) "divine-judicial goodness." There is only that condition or property that is conferred upon an action by God's (as it were) illocutionary act of approving. To say, alternatively, that God's approvals are independent of, and explained by, the moral goodness of the acts he approves is to say that God is a perfect judge: he issues approvals when and only when the conditions for objective goodness are satisfied.

In a way, it's puzzling why, of all God's attributes, moral goodness is the one held to be constituted merely by God's possessing it. God is omniscient, but what's true is not held to be true in virtue of God's believing it; God is omnipotent, but something is not a possible power because God possesses it. In both these cases, we allow that something external to God delineates the domain, and the perfection of God's nature lies in the perfection of the matchup between the two. To say that God approves the good because it is good is not to say that God is "bound by" an external standard any more than saying that God believes only what's true limits his powers of cognition. A God who approves all and only what is objectively good would be a morally perfect being, just as a God who believes all and only truths would be an epistemically perfect being.

■ 3. CONCLUSION

There may be many good reasons to believe in God, but I hope that I've shown that the existence of morality is not one of them. Neither materialism nor naturalism entails nihilism, and "accountability" is a red herring. Finally, even if one is a theist, one should affirm the independence of moral value from the existence of God. Not only is that the philosophically sounder position to take; it may also be the more pious one.

■ NOTES

1. For example, see William Lane Craig, "The Indispensability of Theological Meta-Ethical Foundations for Morality," http://www.reasonablefaith.org/site/News2?page=NewsArticle&id=5175; and Paul Copan, "God, Naturalism, and the Foundations of Morality," in *The Future of Atheism: Alister McGrath and Daniel Dennett in Dialogue*, ed. Robert Stewart (Minneapolis: Fortress Press, 2008). Available at http://www.paulcopan.com/articles/.

2. For a comprehensive survey and critique of theistic arguments against materialism and naturalism, see Michael Martin, *Atheism, Morality, and Meaning* (Amherst, NY: Prometheus Books, 2002).

3. William Lane Craig, *Is Goodness Without God Good Enough?*, ed. Robert K. Garcia and Nathan L. King (Lanham, MD: Rowman & Littlefield, 2009), 67–84.

4. William Lane Craig–Louise Antony debate, *Is God Necessary for Morality*, "Opening Statement."

5. Copan, "God, Naturalism, and the Foundations of Morality," 154.

6. Interestingly, there is evidence that our close primate cousins also are sensitive to fairness. See the work by Sarah Brosnan, http://www2.gsu.edu/~wwwcbs/inequity.html.

7. See Elliot Sober, *Nature of Selection* (Cambridge, MA: MIT Press, 1984), especially p. 99.

8. Craig, *Is Goodness Without God Good Enough?*, 31.

9. Craig, "Theological Foundations," http://www.reasonablefaith.org/site/News2?page=NewsArticle&id=5175.

10. Craig, "Theological Foundations."

11. "Rachel's Letters," http://www.ifamericansknew.org/cur_sit/rachelsletters.html.

12. Tony Soprano is the powerful capo of a fictional mafia family in the wildly popular HBO series *The Sopranos*.

13. It is worth mentioning that the assumption that morality is objective is substantive and subject to dispute. There are many defenders of expressivism and other forms of noncognitivism, and their arguments deserve a response.

14. See Franz Kafka, *Der Process* (*The Trial*) 1914–5, first published in 1925. Available through Project Gutenberg: http://www.gutenberg.org/ebooks/7849

▨ FOR FURTHER READING

Anderson, E. "If God is Dead, Is Everything Permitted?" In *Philosophers Without Gods*, edited by L. Antony, 215–230. Oxford: Oxford University Press, 2007.

Antony, L. "Atheism as Perfect Piety." In *Is Goodness Without God Good Enough?* edited by R. K. Garcia and N. L. King, 67–84. Lanham, MD: Rowman & Littlefield, 2009.

Hubin, D. C. "Empty and Ultimately Meaningless Gestures?" In *Is Goodness Without God Good Enough?*, edited by R. K. Garcia and N. L. King, 133–50. Lanham, MD: Rowman & Littlefield, 2009.

Martin, M. *Atheism, Morality, and Meaning.* Amherst, NY: Prometheus Books, 2002.

Sinnott-Armstrong, W. *Morality Without God?* Oxford: Oxford University Press, 2009.

An Argument from Consciousness

9 The Argument from Consciousness

■ J. P. MORELAND

Consciousness is among the most mystifying features of the cosmos. Colin McGinn claims that its arrival borders on sheer magic because there seems to be no naturalistic explanation for it: "How can mere matter originate consciousness? How did evolution convert the water of biological tissue into the wine of consciousness? Consciousness seems like a radical novelty in the universe, not prefigured by the after-effects of the Big Bang; so how did it contrive to spring into being from what preceded it?"[1] Accordingly, some argue that, while finite mental entities may be inexplicable on an atheistic, naturalist worldview, they may be best explained by theism, thereby furnishing evidence for God's existence. This chapter shall clarify the argument for God's existence from finite consciousness (hereafter, AC) and evaluate three alternatives to it.

At this point, a preliminary assumption should be made explicit. Causal explanations in the natural sciences should exhibit a kind of causal necessity—physical causal explanations must show why an effect must follow given the relevant causal conditions. At least five reasons have been proffered for this assumption:

1. Causal necessitation unpacks the deepest, core realist notion of causation, namely, causal production according to which a cause "brings about" or "produces" its effect.
2. Causal necessitation fits the paradigm cases of causal explanation (e.g., macrosolidity/impenetrability in terms of microlattice structures, repulsive forces; mass proportions in chemical reactions in terms of atomic models of atoms/molecules, bonding orbitals, energy stability, charge distribution) central to the core theories (e.g., the atomic theory of matter) that constitute a naturalist worldview and in terms of which it is purported to have explanatory superiority to rival worldviews.
3. Causal necessitation provides a way of distinguishing accidental generalizations (e.g., plants grow when exposed to the sun's heat) from true causal laws (plants grow when exposed to the sun's light).
4. Causal necessitation supports the derivation of counterfactuals (if that chunk of gold had been placed in aqua regia, then it would have dissolved) from causal laws (gold must dissolve in aqua regia).
5. Causal necessitation clarifies the direction of causality and rules out the attempt to explain a cause by its effect.

■ 1. THE ARGUMENT

AC may be expressed in inductive or deductive form. As an inductive argument, AC may be construed as claiming that given theism and naturalism as the live options fixed by our background beliefs, theism provides a better explanation of consciousness than naturalism and thus receives some confirmation from the existence of consciousness.

AC may also be expressed in deductive form. Here is one deductive version of AC:

1. Genuinely nonphysical mental states exist.
2. There is an explanation for the existence of mental states.
3. Personal explanation is different from natural scientific explanation.
4. The explanation for the existence of mental states is either a personal or natural scientific explanation.
5. The explanation is not a natural scientific one.
6. Therefore the explanation is a personal one.
7. If the explanation is personal, then it is theistic.
8. Therefore the explanation is theistic.

Theists such as Robert Adams[2] and Richard Swinburne[3] have advanced a slightly different version of AC that focuses on mental/physical correlations and not merely on the existence of mental states. Either way, AC may be construed as a deductive argument.

Graham Oppy suggests that the atheist could reject premise (1) in favor of some form of strict physicalism.[4] However, premise (1) expresses a highly plausible, commonsense understanding of conscious states such as sensations, thoughts, beliefs, desires, volitions. So understood, mental states are in no sense physical since they possess five features not owned by physical states:

(i) there is a raw qualitative feel or a "what it is like" to have a mental state such as a pain;

(ii) many mental states have intentionality—*ofness* or *aboutness*—directed toward an object (e.g., a thought is *about* the moon);

(iii) mental states are inner, private, and immediate to the subject having them;

(iv) mental states fail to have crucial features (e.g., spatial extension, location) that characterize physical states and in general cannot be described using physical language;

(v) mental states are constituted by qualitatively simple properties (e.g., being a pain or a sensation of red), but physical states are constituted by quantitative, structural properties (e.g., being a C-fiber firing).

Premises (2), (4), and (5) are the ones most likely to come under attack.

(3) turns on the fact that personal explanation differs from event causal covering law explanations employed in natural science. Associated with event causation is a covering law model of explanation according to which some event (the *explanandum*) is explained by giving a correct deductive or inductive argument for that event. Such an argument contains two features in its *explanans*: a (universal or statistical) law of nature and initial causal conditions. Such explanations are underwritten by a physical model (e.g., ideal gas theory) that shows how the causal law operates as it does. In contrast, a personal explanation (divine or otherwise) of some state of affairs brought about intentionally by a person will employ notions such as the intention of the agent, the relevant power of the agent that was exercised in causing the state of affairs, and the means used to accomplish the intention.

Advocates of AC employ the difference between these two modes of explanation to justify premise (2). Briefly, the argument is that given a defense of premises (4) and (5), there is no natural scientific explanation of mental entities. Thus the phenomena cited in premise (1) may not be taken as unique facts that can be explained naturalistically. Moreover, the appearance of mental entities and their regular correlation with physical entities are puzzling phenomena that cry out for explanation. Since personal explanation is something people use all the time, this distinctive form of explanation is available, and its employment regarding the phenomena cited in premise (1) removes our legitimate puzzlement regarding them.

Premise (7) seems fairly uncontroversial.[5] To be sure, Humean-style arguments about the type and number of deities involved could be raised at this point, but these issues would be intramural theistic problems of small comfort to naturalists. That is, if the explanation for finite conscious minds is supernatural, then naturalism is false. Premise

(4) will be examined in conjunction with two alternatives to AC that reject it: Colin McGinn's position and panpsychism.

That leaves premise (5). At least five reasons have been offered for why there is no natural scientific explanation for the existence of mental states (or their regular correlation with physical states):

(i) *The uniformity of nature.* Prior to the emergence of consciousness, the universe contained nothing but aggregates of particles/waves standing in fields of forces relative to each other. The story of the development of the cosmos is told in terms of the rearrangement of microparts into increasingly more complex structures according to natural law. On a naturalist depiction of matter, it is brute mechanical, physical stuff. The emergence of consciousness seems to be a case of getting something from nothing. In general, physicochemical reactions do not generate consciousness, but they do in the brain, yet brains seem similar to other parts of organisms bodies (e.g., both are collections of cells totally describable in physical terms). How can like causes produce radically different effects? The appearance of mind is utterly unpredictable and inexplicable. This radical discontinuity seems like an inhomogeneous rupture in the natural world. Similarly, physical states have spatial extension and location but mental states seem to lack spatial features. Space and consciousness sit oddly together. How did spatially arranged matter conspire to produce nonspatial mental states? From a naturalist point of view, this seems utterly inexplicable.

(ii) *Contingency of the mind/body correlation.* The regular correlation between types of mental states and physical states seems radically contingent. Why do pains instead of itches, thoughts, or feelings of love get correlated with specific brain states? Based on strong conceivability, zombie worlds (worlds physically like ours in which creatures' bodies move like ours do but in which there is no consciousness) and inverted qualia worlds (worlds where people discriminate red objects from other objects and use the word "red" while pointing to them, but do so on the basis of having a sensation of blue while looking at red objects and who have a sensation of red while looking at blue objects) are possible. No amount of knowledge of the brain state will help to answer this question. Given the requirement of causal necessitation for naturalistic causal explanations, there is *in principle* no naturalistic explanation for either the existence of mental states or their regular correlation with physical states. For the naturalist, the regularity of mind/body correlations must be taken as contingent brute facts. But these facts are inexplicable from a naturalistic standpoint, and they are radically unique compared to all other entities in the naturalist ontology. Thus it begs the question simply to announce that mental states and their regular correlations with certain brain states is a natural fact.

(iii) *Epiphenomenalism and causal closure.* Most naturalists believe that their worldview requires that all entities whatever are either physical or depend on the physical for their existence and behavior. One implication of this belief is commitment to the causal closure of the physical. On this principle, when one is tracing the causal antecedents of any physical event that has a cause, one will never have to leave the level of the physical. Physical effects have only physical causes. Rejection of the causal closure principle would imply a rejection of the possibility of a complete and comprehensive physical theory of all physical phenomena—something that no naturalist should reject. Thus, if mental phenomena are genuinely nonphysical, then they must be epiphenomena— effects caused by the physical that do not themselves have causal powers. But epiphenomenalism is false. Mental causation seems undeniable. The admission of epiphenomenal nonphysical mental entities may be taken as a refutation of naturalism.

(iv) *The inadequacy of evolutionary explanations.* Graham Oppy suggests that there may be an adequate evolutionary explanation for consciousness.[6] But this suggestion fails to capture adequately the nature and limitations of evolutionary explanation. Naturalists are committed to the view that, in principle, evolutionary explanations can be proffered for the appearance of all organisms and their parts. It is not hard to see how an evolutionary account could be given for new and increasingly complex physical structures that constitute different organisms. However, organisms are black boxes as far as evolution is concerned. As long as an organism, when receiving certain inputs, generates the correct behavioral outputs under the demands of fighting, fleeing, reproducing, and feeding, the organism will survive. What goes on inside the organism is irrelevant and only becomes significant for the processes of evolution when an output is produced. Strictly speaking, it is the output, not what caused it, that bears on the struggle for reproductive advantage. Moreover, the functions organisms carry out consciously could just as well have been done unconsciously. Finally, evolutionary processes merely involve the rearrangement of purely physical parts, and it's hard to see how this could cause something entirely different (consciousness) to come into being. Thus the sheer existence of conscious states, the precise mental content that constitutes them, and their regular correlation with types of physical states are outside the pale of evolutionary explanation.

(v) *The inadequacy of using the label "emergence."* Simply labeling mental properties as emergent is not a solution to their instantiation, rather it is just a name for the problem to be solved. In fact, the emergence of mental properties is more like the emergence of normative (e.g., moral) properties than the supervenience of structural properties such as the properties of solidity or digestion. Even the atheist J. L. Mackie admitted that the emergence of moral properties provided evidence for a moral argument for God's existence analogous to AC: "Moral properties constitute so odd a cluster of properties and relations that they are most unlikely to have arisen in the ordinary course of events without an all-powerful god to create them."[7] Mackie is right on this point. Given theism, if a naturalist were simply to claim that the emergence of moral properties was a basic naturalistic fact, this would be an ad hoc, question-begging ploy of assuming a point not congruent with a naturalistic worldview, but quite at home in a theistic one. A naturalist's "explanation" of consciousness is guilty of the same charge.

We have looked at five reasons why many scholars, including many naturalists, hold that naturalism requires the rejection of consciousness construed along dualist lines.

■ 2. THE ATHEISTIC NATURALISTIC WORLDVIEW

At this point it may be wise to look briefly at the nature of naturalism as a worldview to gain further insight into why consciousness is such a problem for naturalists. Currently naturalism is the most plausible form of atheism, so it is the alternative to AC that I shall examine. Naturalism usually includes

- different aspects of a naturalist epistemic attitude (e.g., a rejection of so-called first philosophy: there is no philosophical knowledge or justified beliefs that are independent of and more basic than scientific knowledge) along with an acceptance of either strong or weak scientism (either science provides justified beliefs or science is vastly better than other disciplines in providing justified beliefs);
- a grand story, which amounts to a causal account of how all entities have come to be, told in terms of an event causal story described in natural scientific terms with a central role given to the atomic theory of matter and evolutionary biology; and
- a general ontology in which the only entities allowed are those that either (a) bear a relevant similarity to those thought to characterize a completed form of physics or (b) can be explained according to the causal necessitation requirement in terms of the grand story and the naturalist epistemic attitude.

For our purposes, it is important to say a bit more about naturalist ontological commitments. A good place to start is with what Frank Jackson calls the location problem.[8] According to Jackson, given that naturalists are committed to a fairly widely accepted physical story about how things came to be and what they are, the location problem is the task of locating or finding a place for some entity (e.g., semantic contents, mind, agency) in that story. As an illustration, Jackson shows how the solidity of macro-objects can be located within a naturalist worldview. If solidity is taken as impenetrability, then given the lattice structure of atoms composing, say, a table and chair, it becomes obvious why they cannot penetrate each other. Given the naturalist microstory, the macroworld could not have been different: the table could not penetrate the chair. Location requires showing how the troublesome entity had to arise given the grand story.

There are three constraints for developing a naturalist ontology and locating entities within it:

- Entities should be knowable by empirical, scientific means.
- The origin of those entities should be necessitated by physical entities and processes according to the grand story.
- Entities should bear a relevant similarity to those found in chemistry and physics or be shown to depend necessarily on entities in chemistry and physics.

Given theism and naturalism as rivals, theists who employ the argument from consciousness seek to capitalize on the naturalistic failure to come to terms with consciousness by offering a rival explanation for its appearance. That failure is why most prominent naturalists[9] reject premise (1) of AC ("Genuinely non-physical mental states exist") and either eliminate or, in one way or another, identify conscious states with physical ones.

Unfortunately for naturalists, consciousness has stubbornly resisted treatment in physical terms. Consciousness has been recalcitrant for naturalists and premise (1) is hard to dismiss. Aware of this problem, various alternatives to theism and AC have been provided that accept premise (1). In the next section we shall look at three representative options.

▪ 3. THREE ALTERNATIVES TO AC

3.1 Alternative 1: John Searle's biological naturalism

John Searle has developed a naturalistic account of consciousness that would, if successful, provide justification for rejecting premise (5) of AC.[10] According to Searle, for fifty years philosophy of the mind has been dominated by strict physicalism because it was seen as a crucial implication of taking the naturalistic turn. For these naturalists, if one abandons strict physicalism, one has rejected a scientific naturalist approach to the mind/body problem and opened oneself up to the intrusion of religious concepts and arguments about the mental.

In contrast, Searle's own solution to the mind/body problem is biological naturalism: while mental states are exactly what dualists describe them to be, nevertheless they are merely emergent biological states and processes that causally supervene upon a suitably structured, functioning brain. Brain processes cause mental processes, which are not ontologically reducible to the former. Consciousness is just an ordinary (i.e., physical) feature of the brain and, as such, is merely an ordinary feature of the natural world.

Given that he characterizes consciousness as dualists do, why does Searle claim that biological naturalism does not represent a rejection of scientific naturalism, which in turn opens the door for religious concepts about and explanations for the mental? Searle's answer to this question is developed in three steps.

In step 1, he cites several examples of emergence (liquidity, solidity, features of digestion) that he takes to be unproblematic for naturalists and claims that emergent consciousness is analogous to the unproblematic cases.

In step 2, he formulates two reasons why consciousness is not a problem for naturalists: (i) The emergence of consciousness is not a problem if we stop trying to picture or image consciousness. (ii) In standard cases (heat, color), an ontological reduction (e.g., identifying a specific color with a wavelength) is based on a causal reduction (e.g., claiming that a specific color is caused by a wavelength) because our pragmatic interests are in reality, not appearance.

In these cases we can distinguish the *appearance* of heat and color from the *reality*, place the former in consciousness, leave the latter in the objective world, and go on to define the phenomenon itself in terms of its causes. We can do this because our interests are in the reality and not the appearance. The ontological reduction of heat to its causes leaves the appearance of heat the same. Regarding consciousness, we are interested in the appearances, and thus the irreducibility of consciousness is merely due to pragmatic considerations, not to some deep metaphysical problem.

In step 3, Searle claims that an adequate scientific explanation of the emergence of consciousness consists of a detailed, lawlike set of correlations between mental and physical state tokens.

Several things may be said in response to Searle's position. Regarding steps 1 and 2, his cases of emergence (rigidity, fluidity) are not good analogies to consciousness since the former are easy to locate in the naturalist epistemology and ontology, but consciousness is not. Given a widely accepted physicalist description of atoms, molecules, lattice structure, and the like, the rigidity or fluidity of macro-objects follows necessarily. But there is no clear necessary connection between any physical state and any mental state. For example, given a specific brain state normally "associated" with the mental state of being appeared to redly, inverted qualia worlds (worlds with that physical state but radically different mental states "associated" with it), zombie worlds (worlds with that physical state and no mental states at all), and disembodied worlds (worlds with beings possessing mental states with no physical entities at all) are still metaphysically possible. It is easy to locate solidity in a naturalist framework, but the same cannot be said for consciousness.

Further, the emergence of genuinely new properties in macro-objects that are not part of the microworld (e.g., heat construed as warmth, color construed commonsensically as a quality) presents problems for naturalists in the same way consciousness does and, historically, that is why they were placed in consciousness. Contrary to Searle, they were not so placed because of the pragmatics of our interests. For example, historically the problem was that if so-called secondary qualities were kept in the mind-independent world, there was no naturalistic explanation for why they emerged on the occasion of a mere rearrangement in microparts exhaustively characterized in terms of primary qualities. Secondary qualities construed along commonsense lines are not among the primary qualities employed to characterize the microworld, and indeed seem contingently linked to the microworld. It is this straightforward ontological problem, not the pragmatics of reduction or the attempt to image consciousness, that presents difficulties for naturalism.

Regarding step 3, "explanations" in science that do not express the sort of necessity we have been discussing are better taken as descriptions, not explanations. For example, the ideal gas equation is a description of the behavior of gases. An explanation of that behavior is provided by the atomic theory of gas. Further, given theism and AC, it is question-begging and ad hoc for Searle to assert that mental entities and mental/physical correlations are basic, since such entities are natural in light of theism but unnatural given philosophical naturalism. As naturalist Jaegwon Kim notes, the correlations are not explanations.[11] They are the very things that need explaining and, given a proper understanding of the real questions, no naturalistic explanation seems to be forthcoming. By misconstruing the problem, Searle fails to address the real issue and, weighed against AC, his position is inadequate.

3.2 Alternative 2: Colin McGinn's agnostic "naturalism"

Naturalist Colin McGinn has offered a different solution.[12] Given the radical difference between mind and matter as it is depicted by current or even an ideal future physics, there is no naturalistic solution that stays within the widely accepted naturalist epistemology and ontology. Darwinian explanations fail as well because they cannot account for why consciousness appeared in the first place. What is needed is a radically different kind of solution to the origin of mind, one that must meet two conditions: it must be a naturalistic solution, and it must depict the emergence of consciousness and its regular correlation with matter as necessary and not contingent facts.

McGinn claims that there must be two kinds of unknowable natural properties that solve the problem. There must be some general properties of matter that enter into the production of consciousness when assembled into a brain. Thus all matter has the potentiality to underlie consciousness. Further, there must be some natural property of the brain, which he calls C^*, that unleashes these general properties.

The temptation to take the origin of consciousness as a mystery, indeed, a mystery that is best explained theistically, is due to our ignorance of these properties. However, given C^* and the general properties of matter, the unknowable link between mind and matter is ordinary, commonplace, and necessitates the emergence of consciousness. Unfortunately evolution did not give humans the faculties needed to know these properties and thus they are in principle beyond our grasp. We will forever be agnostic about their nature. However, they must be there since there must be some naturalistic explanation of mind, as all other solutions have failed.

McGinn offers two further descriptions of these unknowable yet ordinary properties that link matter and mind: they are not sense perceptible, and since matter is spatial and mind nonspatial, they are either in some sense prespatial or are spatial in a way that is itself unknowable to our faculties. In this way, these unknowable properties contain at least the potentiality for both ordinary spatial features of matter and the nonspatial features of consciousness as judged by our usual concept of space.

In sum, the mind/matter link is an unknowable mystery due to our cognitive limitations resulting from our evolution. And since the link is quite ordinary, we should not be puzzled by the origin of mind, and no theistic explanation is required.

Critics have offered at least three criticisms of McGinn's position. First, given McGinn's agnosticism about the properties that link mind and matter, how can he confidently assert some of their features? How does he know they are non-sensory, prespatial, or spatial in an unknowable way? How does he know some of these properties underlie all matter? Indeed, what possible justification can he give for their reality? The only one he suggests is that we must provide a naturalistic solution and all ordinary naturalistic ones either deny consciousness or fail to solve the problem. But given the presence of AC, McGinn's claims are simply question-begging. Indeed, his agnosticism seems to be a convenient way of hiding behind naturalism and avoiding a theistic explanation. Given that theism enjoys a positive degree of justification prior to the problem of consciousness, he should avail himself of the explanatory resources of theism.

Second, it is not clear that his solution is a version of naturalism, except in name only. In contrast to other entities in the naturalist ontology, McGinn's linking properties cannot be known scientifically, nor are they relevantly similar to the rest of the naturalist ontology. Thus it becomes vacuous to call these properties "naturalistic." McGinn's own speculations strike one as ad hoc in light of the inadequacies of naturalistic explanations. In fact, McGinn's solution is actually closer to an agnostic form of panpsychism (see below) than to naturalism. Given AC, McGinn's solution is an ad hoc readjustment of naturalism.

Third, McGinn does not solve the problem of consciousness, he merely relocates it. Rather than having two radically different entities, he offers us unknowable properties with two radically different aspects (e.g., his links contain the potentiality for ordinary spatiality and nonspatiality, for ordinary materiality and mentality). Moreover, these radically different aspects of the linking properties are just as contingently related as they seem to be without a linking intermediary. The contingency comes from the nature of mind and matter as naturalists conceive it. It does not remove the contingency to relocate it as two aspects of an unknowable third intermediary with both.

3.3 Alternative 3: Panpsychism

Currently there are few serious advocates of panpsychism, though it has been suggested by Graham Oppy,[13] Thomas Nagel,[14] and David Chalmers.[15] The main exception to this rule is panpsychist David Skrbina.[16] Roughly, panpsychism is the view that all matter has consciousness in it. Since each parcel of matter has its own consciousness, the brain is conscious since it is just a collection of those parcels. Consciousness is pervasive in nature so its apparent emergence in particular cases is not something that requires special explanation. One can distinguish two forms of panpsychism. According to the strong version, all matter has conscious states in it in the same sense that organisms such as dogs and humans do. According to the weak form, regular matter has consciousness in a degraded, attenuated way in the form of protomental states that, under the right circumstances, yield conscious mental states without themselves being conscious.

The strong form is quite implausible. For one thing, regular matter gives no evidence whatever of possessing consciousness. Further, if all matter has consciousness, why does it emerge in special ways only when certain configurations of matter are present? And if conscious human beings are in some sense merely combinations of little bits of consciousness, how are we to account for the unity of consciousness and why do people have no memory of the conscious careers of the bits of matter prior to their combination to form humans? There is no answer to these questions and few, if any, hold to strong panpsychism.

What about the weak version? Given the current intellectual climate, a personal theistic or a naturalistic explanation would exhaust at least the live—if not the logical—options. It is widely thought that weak panpsychism has serious problems in its own right, for example, explaining what an incipient or protomental entity is, how the type of unity that appears to characterize the self could emerge from a mere system of parts standing together in various causal and spatiotemporal relations, and why certain physical conditions are regularly correlated with the actualization of consciousness when the connection between consciousness and those conditions seems to be utterly contingent.

Moreover, panpsychism is arguably less reasonable than theism on other grounds. Given justification for this claim, theism enjoys greater positive epistemic justification than does panpsychism prior to consideration of the issue of consciousness, and all things being equal, the appeal to panpsychism to explain consciousness is undermotivated.

Finally, panpsychism is merely a label for and not an explanation of the phenomena to be explained. As Geoffrey Madell notes, "the sense that the mental and the physical are just inexplicably and gratuitously slapped together is hardly allayed by adopting...a pan-psychist...view of the mind, for [it does not] have an explanation to offer as to why or how mental properties cohere with physical."[17]

■ 4. CONCLUSION

Prominent naturalist Jaegwon Kim has observed that "if a whole system of phenomena that are prima facie not among basic physical phenomena resists physical explanation, and especially if we don't even know where or how to begin, it would be time to reexamine one's physicalist commitments."[18] For Kim, genuinely nonphysical mental entities are the paradigm case of such a system of phenomena. Kim's advice to fellow naturalists is that they must simply admit the irreality of the mental and recognize that naturalism exacts a steep price and cannot be had on the cheap. However, if feigning anesthesia—denying that consciousness construed along commonsense lines is real—is the price to be paid to retain naturalism, then the price is too high. Fortunately the theistic argument from consciousness reminds us that it is a price that does not need to be paid.

▪ NOTES

1. Colin McGinn, *The Mysterious Flame* (New York: Basic Books, 1999), 13–14.

2. Robert Adams, "Flavors, Colors and God," in *The Virtue of Faith*, ed. Robert Adams, 243–262 (Oxford: Oxford University Press, 1987); reprinted in *Contemporary Perspectives in Religious Epistemology*, ed. R. Douglas Geivett and Brendan Sweetman (New York: Oxford University Press, 1992), 225–240.

3. Richard Swinburne, *The Evolution of the Soul* (Oxford: Clarendon, 1997), 174–199, and *The Existence of God* (Oxford: Clarendon, 2004), 192–212; cf. J. P. Moreland, *Consciousness and the Existence of God* (New York: Routledge, 2008).

4. Graham Oppy, *Arguing About Gods* (Cambridge: Cambridge University Press, 2006), 396–397.

5. But see Oppy, *Arguing About Gods*, 400–401.

6. Oppy, *Arguing About Gods*, 396.

7. J. L. Mackie, *The Miracle of Theism* (Oxford: Clarendon, 1982), 115.

8. Frank Jackson, *From Metaphysics to Ethics* (Oxford: Clarendon, 1998), 1–5.

9. David Papineau, *Philosophical Naturalism* (Oxford: Blackwell, 1993).

10. John Searle. *The Rediscovery of the Mind* (Cambridge, MA: MIT Press, 1992).

11. Jaegwon Kim, *Philosophy of Mind* (Boulder, CO: Westview Press, 1996), 8.

12. McGinn, *The Mysterious Flame*.

13. Oppy, *Arguing About Gods*, 399.

14. Thomas Nagel, *The View from Nowhere* (New York: Oxford University Press, 1986).

15. David Chalmers, *The Conscious Mind* (New York: Oxford University Press, 1996).

16. David Skrbina, *Panpsychism in the West* (Notre Dame, IN: University of Notre Dame Press, 2006).

17. Geoffrey Madell, *Mind and Materialism* (Edinburgh: Edinburgh University Press, 1990), 3.

18. Jaegwon Kim, *Mind in a Physical World* (Cambridge, MA: MIT Press, 1998), 96.

▪ FOR FURTHER READING

Hasker, W. *The Emergent Self*. Ithaca, NY: Cornell University Press, 1999.

Kim, J. *Physicalism or Something Near Enough*. Princeton, NJ: Princeton University Press, 2005.

McGinn, C. *The Mysterious Flame*. New York: Basic Books, 1999.

Moreland, J. P. *Consciousness and the Existence of God*. New York: Routledge, 2008.

———. *The Recalcitrant Imago Dei*. London: SCM Press, 2009.

Oppy, G. *Arguing About Gods*. Cambridge: Cambridge University Press, 2006.

Searle, J. *The Rediscovery of the Mind*. Cambridge, MA: MIT Press, 1992.

Swinburne, R. *The Evolution of the Soul*. Oxford: Clarendon, 1997.

10 Consciousness, Theism, and Naturalism

■ GRAHAM OPPY

There has recently been a surge in publications espousing arguments from consciousness for the existence of God.[1] In particular, J. P. Moreland has produced a series of articles in which he promotes the virtues of the following argument:[2]

1. Mental events are genuine nonphysical mental entities that exist.
2. Specific mental and physical event types are regularly correlated.
3. There is an explanation for these correlations.
4. Personal explanation is different from natural scientific explanation.
5. The explanation for these correlations is either a personal or natural scientific explanation.
6. The explanation is not a natural scientific one.
7. Therefore the explanation is a personal one.
8. If the explanation is personal, then it is theistic.
9. Therefore the explanation is theistic.

In this chapter I propose to focus on Moreland's defense of arguments from consciousness.[3] In particular, I shall argue against his claim that considerations about consciousness favor theism over naturalism.

Moreland's argument that considerations about consciousness favor theism over naturalism depends crucially upon his account of naturalism, his account of theoretical virtues, and his method of assessing the relative merits of theism and naturalism. So I begin with some discussion of his treatment of each of these topics.

1. NATURALISM

On Moreland's account, "naturalism"—that is, the view that "the spatiotemporal universe of entities postulated by our best current (or ideal) theories in the physical sciences, particularly physics, is all there is"[4]—has three major constituents.

First, there is naturalistic epistemology: "the naturalist epistemic attitude." According to Moreland, naturalistic epistemology is scientistic: naturalists suppose either that "non-scientific fields are ... vastly inferior to science in their epistemic standing and do not merit full credence" or else that "unqualified cognitive value resides in science and in nothing else."[5] More exactly, according to Moreland, naturalistic epistemology is committed to the claim that "there is no such thing as first philosophy ... [but rather only] continuity between philosophy and natural science" and to the claim that "scientific theories...employ combinatorial modes of explanation."[6]

Second, there is the naturalistic creation account: "the naturalist Grand Story." According to Moreland, the naturalist grand story says:

> All of reality—space, time and matter—came from the Big Bang and various heavenly bodies developed as the universe expanded. On at least the Earth, some sort of pre-biotic soup scenario explains how living things came into being from non-living chemicals. And the processes of evolution, understood in either neo-Darwinian or punctuated equilibrium terms, gave rise to all of the life forms we see including human beings.[7]

Moreland goes on to note what he takes to be "three key features" of the naturalist grand story. These are (1) that "at its core are two theories that result from combinatorial modes of explanation: the atomic theory of matter and evolutionary theory," (2) that it "expresses a scientistic philosophical monism according to which everything that exists or happens in the world is susceptible to explanations by natural scientific methods," and (3) that it is "constituted by event causality and eschews both irreducible teleology and agent causation in which the first relatum of the causal relation is in the category of substance and not event."[8]

Third, there is general naturalistic ontology: "the naturalist ontology." According to Moreland, the naturalist ontology only includes entities that "bear a relevant similarity to those thought to characterize a completed form of physics."[9] More exactly, according to Moreland, naturalistic ontology involves commitments to (1) causal closure of the basic microphysical level, (2) ontological dependence of entities and their activities at supervenient levels on entities and their activities at the basic microphysical level, and (3) necessary spatial extension of both concrete particulars and property instances possessed by those concrete particulars.

Finally, according to Moreland, there is an ordering amongst these three components of naturalism: "the epistemic attitude justifies the aetiology, which together justify the ontological commitment."[10] On Moreland's view, the existence of this ordering justifies the further claim that naturalists ought to accept "the naturalist Grand Story" and "the naturalist ontology," and allows him to "identify a substantial burden of proof for alternative naturalist ontologies that bloat naturalist metaphysical commitments beyond what is justifiable within the constraints that follow from the other two aspects of a naturalist worldview."[11]

My conception of naturalism is very different from Moreland's. I take it that the core of naturalism is the claim that natural reality exhausts causal reality: there is no supernatural causation. That's it. In itself, naturalism has no commitment to the details of Moreland's "Grand Story." Most naturalists these days suppose that it is an open question whether all of reality came from the big bang; at least some suppose that there are many hitherto unanswered questions about the emergence of life on Earth. Moreover, in itself, naturalism has no commitment to Moreland's "naturalist epistemic attitude." Many naturalists—myself included—suppose that naturalism is to be preferred to theism on grounds of theoretical virtue, that is, on grounds that might properly be thought to belong to "first philosophy"; most naturalists take themselves to be committed to fundamental theories that employ noncombinatorial modes of explanation (e.g., thermodynamics). Again, in itself, naturalism has no commitment to Moreland's "naturalist ontology." To make the most obvious point: there are some naturalists who espouse "one-level" ontologies;[12] and, of course, there are many naturalists who deny that there are spatially extended tropes. Finally, in itself, naturalism is plainly not committed to the ordering that Moreland imposes on his components of naturalism. I think that very few naturalists would accept the suggestion that justified acceptance of a naturalistic "grand story" depends upon the prior adoption of a scientistic attitude: on the contrary, if a scientistic attitude comes, then it does so as a justified consequence of the acceptance of a naturalistic "grand story." Moreover, no naturalists should accept the details of the scientism that Moreland would foist upon them: there is nothing second-rate about the knowledge that I obtained when I watched my son play football yesterday, and yet that knowledge does not depend upon my knowledge of science.

Here's how I see the wider dispute. Theism is committed to the claim that natural reality has a supernatural personal cause. Naturalism is committed to the claim that there are none but natural causes. Theistic and naturalistic theories are all elaborations of these basic claims. When we compare particular theistic and naturalistic theories, we need to be careful not to overstate the conclusions that can be drawn from our comparisons. Our guiding ideal is perhaps something like this: we take the best fully elaborated theistic and naturalistic theories and compare them in the light of a complete account of theoretical virtues. But, in practice, we are confronted with a range of limitations: we do not have fully elaborated theories of either kind, and we do not have a complete account of theoretical virtues. So the best we can do is to proceed with caution: we should only compare theories that have been worked out to more or less the same degree of detail, and we should bear in mind a wide range of theoretical virtues when we carry out our theoretical comparisons.

■ 2. THEORETICAL VIRTUES

Moreland draws attention to four topics in what he calls "theory acceptance" (though I think it would be better called "theory choice" or "theory assessment").

The first issue is about what he calls "basicality." It involves "deciding whether it is appropriate to take some phenomenon as basic such that only a description and not an explanation for it is required, or whether that phenomenon should be understood as something to be explained in terms of more basic phenomena."[13]

The second issue is about what he calls "naturalness." About this, he says: "some entity e is natural for a theory T just in case either e is a central, core entity of T or e bears a relevant similarity to central, core entities in e's category within T." He goes on to add: "Given rivals R and S, the postulation of e in R is *ad hoc* and question-begging against advocates of S if e bears a relevant similarity to the appropriate entities in S, and in this sense is at home in S, but fails to bear this similarity to the appropriate entities in R."[14]

The third issue is about what he calls "epistemic values." After making a list of "normative properties that confer some degree of justification on theories that possess them"—simplicity, descriptive accuracy, predictive success, fruitfulness in guiding new research, capacity for solving internal and external conceptual problems, use of certain types of explanation, following of certain methodological rules—Moreland goes on to note that rival theorists can "rank the relative merits of epistemic values in different ways" and can even "give the same epistemic virtue a different meaning or application": "In arguing against B, it may be inappropriate for advocates of A to cite its superior comportment with an epistemic value when B's proponents do not weigh that value as heavily as they do a different one they take to be more central to B. For example, given rivals A and B, if A is simpler than B but B is more descriptively accurate than A, then it may be inappropriate—indeed, question-begging—for advocates of A to cite A's simplicity as grounds for judging it superior to B."[15]

The fourth issue is about what he calls "simplicity." Here, Moreland distinguishes between what he calls an "epistemic principle of simplicity"—entities must not be multiplied beyond necessity—and what he calls an "ontological principle of simplicity"—our ontology/preferred theory about the world should be simple. After suggesting that some naturalistic philosophers conflate these two principles, he goes on to argue that naturalists *should* adopt them both.[16]

My take on all of this is rather different from Moreland's. I agree with him that, when weighing the relative merits of competing theories, we should consider "simplicity," "basicality," "naturalness," and "appropriateness of fit to data." Other things being equal: (1) simpler theories are better than more complex theories; (2) theories with fewer ontological, ideological, and explanatory primitives are better than theories with more ontological, ideological, and explanatory primitives; (3) theories that involve fewer ad hoc assumptions are better than theories that involve more ad hoc assumptions; and (4) theories with "appropriate" fit to data are better than theories that do not have "appropriate" fit to data. I also agree with Moreland that it is not straightforward to weigh the relative merits of competing theories taking account of these (and other) theoretical desiderata: when two theories differ along all four of these dimensions (and more besides), there may be no clear answer to the question of which of the two theories is better. However, where I certainly part company from Moreland is in *not* supposing that a theory might be more theoretically virtuous if it includes a judgment of the relative importance of the various theoretical virtues. If A and B differ in both simplicity and "appropriateness" of fit with data, but all else is equal, then the better theory is the one that effects the best trade-off between simplicity and "appropriateness" of fit with data. If A is less ad hoc than B, and all else is equal, then A is better than B, even if A's postulation of e is ad hoc and B's postulation of e is not ad hoc. Moreover, considerations about "begging the question" are utterly irrelevant to these kinds of judgments.[17]

Of course, I do not accept that naturalists should suppose that their "ontology/preferred theory of the world" should be simple. Rather, what is true is that naturalists should suppose that their "ontology/preferred theory of the world" effects the best trade-off among all of the theoretical virtues. In particular, in the present context, naturalists suppose that their "ontology/preferred theory of the world" effects a better trade-off among all of the theoretical virtues than the trade-off among those virtues that is effected by theism.

▪ 3. MORELAND'S METHOD

How does Moreland argue for the superiority of theism over naturalism (when it comes to considerations about consciousness and other mental properties)? He begins with the thought that naturalism is committed to a sparse set of base "ingredients." Given this set of base "ingredients," the only other things to which naturalism is legitimately committed are things that can be "deduced" from the base "ingredients," or "structures" that are composed from the base "ingredients." Any other "ingredients" would be "contingent brute facts," and so "highly suspicious."[18] In particular, then, "naturalism" could have no legitimate truck with (1) sui generis, simple, epiphenomenal, intrinsically characterizable properties that are "new" relative to base; (2) sui generis, simple, intrinsically characterizable, properties—with causal powers construed as passive liabilities—that are "new" relative to base; (3) sui generis, simple, intrinsically characterizable, properties—with active causal powers—that are "new" relative to base; or (4) unified entities—with active causal powers—that are "new" relative to base. But, on Moreland's account, on any naturalist theory, mental properties—and, in particular, certain kinds of conscious mental properties—fall into categories (1)–(3) and minds fall into category (4).

As I noted in the previous section, I agree that, when we assess the relative merits of competing theories, one thing that we must consider is the comparative simplicity of the theories: their comparative ontological commitments, their comparative ideological commitments, and so forth. However, when we make this kind of assessment we have to make sure that there is no "double counting" of commitments: if a theory is committed to things that are appropriately "entailed by" or "composed from" other things to which a theory is committed, then those things that are "entailed by" or "composed" from other things to which the theory is committed do not count as additional commitments. Properly speaking, then, every theory should be taken to have a commitment to a sparse set of base "ingredients": any theory is committed to its base "ingredients" and gets for free anything that can be "deduced" from those base ingredients or that is "composed from" those base ingredients.

Given this much, it may seem clear that there are various ways in which mental properties and entities could figure in naturalist theories. First, it could be that mental properties and entities are "base ingredients": mental properties and mental entities count among the ontological and ideological commitments of naturalist theories. Second, it could be that mental properties and entities are "deducible from" or "composed of" base ingredients—and, in that case, they do not figure among the ontological and ideological commitments of naturalist theories. (Perhaps it could also be that some mental properties and entities count among the ontological and ideological commitments of naturalist theories and some do not, because some mental properties and entities are "deducible from" or "composed of" other mental properties and entities, or are "deducible from" or "composed of" a combination of other mental and nonmental properties and entities. (For ease of exposition, I shall simply ignore this consideration in what follows.)) Third, it could be that there are no mental properties and entities: in that case, mental properties and entities do not figure in naturalist theories, but naturalist who take this line deny that their theories are any the worse for having this feature.

We might call the three views distinguished in the preceding paragraph "eliminative naturalism," "reductive naturalism," and "nonreductive naturalism." Nonreductive naturalism is distinguished from eliminative naturalism and reductive naturalism by way of its commitment to "irreducible" mental properties and entities, that is, to mental properties and entities that are not "deducible from" or "composed of" nonmental properties and entities. However, exactly what these distinguished views amount to depends upon two further questions that we have not yet addressed: first, what exactly do we mean by "mental properties and entities"; and second, what exactly do we mean if we claim that some properties and entities are "deducible from" or "composed of" other properties and entities.

In the present context, we can perhaps afford to be somewhat stipulative about what we mean by "mental properties and entities." It is clear from Moreland's presentation that he supposes that there are certain kinds of "sui generis, simple, intrinsically characterizable properties"—and certain kinds of entities that are, in particular, bearers of these "sui generis, simple, intrinsically characterizable properties"—that are paradigmatically "mental," and that pose a particular threat to naturalism. In general philosophical usage, the term "mental" can be applied to a wide range of entities and properties: beliefs, desires, intentions, emotions, itches, tickles, pains, sensations, perceptions, intuitions, thoughts, acts of will, decisions, and so on.[19] However, it is not very controversial—and not much contested—that, in large part, these entities and properties are not properly thought of in terms of "sui generis, simple, intrinsically characterizable properties." If there are any sui generis, simple, intrinsically characterizable mental properties, then these will be what philosophers typically call *qualia*—phenomenal qualities associated with experiences, such as the tasting of Vegemite, or the feeling of gustatory pleasure, or the hearing of a Brahms lullaby, or the like. And many philosophers have supposed that, if there are qualia—that is, if, for example, the tasting of Vegemite (typically) involves a particular, sui generis, simple, intrinsically characterizable property—then there is good reason to suppose that qualia should figure among the "base ingredients" in an adequate total theory of the world.

Unfortunately the question of what we might mean if we claim that some properties and entities are "deducible from" or "composed of" other properties and entities is much less tractable than the question of how we should understand the term "mental" in the context of Moreland's argument from consciousness. A natural first thought is that we need some distinctions that Moreland fails to draw. On the one hand, we can make sense of the idea that one property is "deducible from" another. We can say what it is for one property to entail a second, or for a set of properties to entail a further property, and so forth. On the other hand, we can make sense of the idea that one entity is "composed of" other entities. We can say—at least roughly—what it is for some entities to jointly comprise a further entity, and we can also make some comments about the ways in which the properties of a constituted entity may—or may not—be related to the properties of the entities from which it is constituted. However, despite Moreland's fairly explicit claims to the contrary, I do not think that we can make sense of the idea that a property might be "composed of" such things as entities, relations, and events. Here is the sort of thing that Moreland says:

> Emergent supervenience is the view that the supervenient property is a simple, intrinsically characterisable, novel property different from and not composed of the parts, properties, relations, and events at the subvenient level ... A structural property is one that is constituted by the parts, properties, relations and events at the subvenient level.[20]

I think that there must be some kind of category mistake here; at the very least, I can make no sense of the idea that a higher-level *property* might have as constituents lower-level *objects* and *events*. (Suppose you think that chemical properties belong to a higher level than physical properties: molecules have chemical properties, whereas neutrons and protons only have physical properties. Surely you cannot sensibly propose that chemical properties have neutrons and protons as constituents; rather, you may and should say that it is the bearers of chemical properties—for example, molecules—that have neutrons and protons as constituents.)

▪ 4. QUALIA

There are two famous arguments for the claim that qualia should figure among the "base ingredients" in an adequate total theory of the world: Frank Jackson's knowledge argument[21] and David Chalmers' zombie argument.[22] Both arguments have been endlessly discussed; I shall only make very brief comments upon them here.

Chalmers' zombie argument relies crucially upon the assumption that there could be a world that is exactly like the world in which we live except that it does not contain any qualia. In that other possible world, people behave exactly as we do—right down to some among them claiming that they have qualia—but people in that world do not have access to the sui generis, simple, intrinsically characterizable phenomenal qualities that are associated with our experiences. I agree that, if it is possible that there is a world that is exactly like the world in which we live except that it does not contain any qualia, then qualia should figure among the "base ingredients" in an adequate total theory of our world. However, I think that it is highly implausible to suppose that it is possible that there is a world that is exactly like the world in which we live except that it does not contain any qualia (if it is indeed true that our world contains qualia). On the contrary, I think that, on the best theory of real possibility, it is not really possible that there could be a world that is exactly like the world in which we live except that it does not contain any qualia (if it is indeed true that our world contains qualia).[23]

Jackson's knowledge argument relies upon the assumption that someone who knew all of the physical (and natural) truths about our world might nonetheless lack knowledge about what it is like to have certain kinds of experiences (e.g., what it is like to taste Vegemite): such a person might fail to have knowledge of the sui generis, simple, intrinsically characterizable phenomenal qualities that are associated with our experiences. Here, I am tempted by a two-part response. On the one hand, it does not seem to me to be plausible to suppose that we can tell whether someone who knew *all* of the physical (and natural) truths might nonetheless lack knowledge about what it is like to have certain kinds of experiences. On the other hand, if someone who knows all of the physical (and natural) truths might nonetheless lack knowledge about what it is like to have certain kinds of experiences, then I take it that what is plausible to suppose that they might lack is an ability rather than an item of knowledge. (Perhaps such a person would not have the ability to identify Vegemite by its taste until they had first tasted Vegemite. But this gap in their abilities would not point to any gap in their propositional knowledge.)

Even if I am right that the arguments from Chalmers and Jackson are unpersuasive, it remains open that qualia should nonetheless figure among the "base ingredients" in an adequate total theory of the world. Since I do not have space here to consider other arguments that have been advanced in favor of qualia, I can do no more than record my views. Where Moreland is clearly sympathetic to the idea that qualia should figure among the "base ingredients" in an adequate total theory of the world, I am highly skeptical of the suggestion that there are any qualia—that is, I am highly skeptical of the claim that there are sui generis, simple, intrinsically characterizable phenomenal qualities associated with experiences. At least in broad outline, I am sympathetic to the kind of view about consciousness that is developed by Dennett.[24] However, I should add—contra Moreland—that I think that it is just a mistake to suppose that the kind of view that Dennett advocates somehow amounts to "feigning anaesthesia."[25] Thus, for example, I do not deny that we have experiences, but I do insist that our having of experiences is our undergoing of certain kinds of natural processes (most prominently, neural processes).

■ 5. MY VIEW

I regard physicalism—the view that the "base ingredients" of the world are all physical—as a plausible metaphysical hypothesis. I take this hypothesis to have at least two parts. First, that there are no things—no objects—that ultimately have anything other than physical constituents. Second, that there are no properties whose possession by objects is not entailed by the world's possession of the physical properties that it possesses. (I leave for some other occasion consideration of the question whether there are further parts to the hypothesis concerning states, or events, or processes, or laws, or the like.)

I regard naturalism—the view that the "base ingredients" of the world are all natural (as opposed to supernatural)—as a considerably more plausible metaphysical hypothesis than physicalism. I take the naturalistic hypothesis to have at least two parts. First, that there are no things—no objects—that ultimately have anything other than natural (as opposed to supernatural) constituents. Second, that there are no properties whose possession by objects is not entailed by the world's possession of the natural (as opposed to supernatural) properties that it possesses. (I leave for some other occasion consideration of the question of whether there are further parts to the hypothesis concerning states, or events, or processes, or laws, or the like.)

As a rough first pass, I take it that supernatural things—or supernatural objects—would be either (1) things—or objects—that do not have spatiotemporal locations but that nonetheless are causally responsible for and/or have causal effects on things—or objects—that do have spatiotemporal locations; or else (2) things—or objects—with spatiotemporal locations bring about causal effects at spatiotemporally remote locations in the absence of spatiotemporally continuous causal processes connecting their actions to those effects, unless somehow making use of quantum entanglement or the like. Given this account of supernatural things—or supernatural objects—I take it that supernatural properties would be properties that can be possessed only by supernatural things—or supernatural objects—or, if there are things that have both natural and supernatural parts, by things—or objects—that have at least some supernatural parts.

I am inclined to think that Moreland holds that, according to the above account of the supernatural, human minds are supernatural things—or supernatural objects—that is, he holds that human minds do not have spatiotemporal locations but they do, nonetheless, have causal effects on things—or objects—that have spatiotemporal locations (in particular, human bodies). But, of course, Moreland has further commitments to the supernatural: for instance, he supposes that there is a supernatural person who created natural reality ex nihilo, who is responsible for sustaining the existence of natural reality and who is directly causally responsible for events that occur in natural reality. When we come to ask about the bearing of consciousness and other mental properties on the choice between naturalism and theism, we need to bear these further considerations in mind.

Here's a choice setup. First, there is the naturalist picture that I prefer. Causal reality is exhausted by natural reality. Human beings are entirely natural creatures. The mental processes of human beings are nothing but natural processes (in particular, neural processes). Human beings act with compatibilist freedom—their actions are, for the most part, the products of their naturally acquired beliefs, desires, intentions, and so forth—but not with libertarian freedom—there is no such thing as "agent causation." Human beings have rich mental lives—they have desires, intentions, emotions, itches, tickles, pains, sensations, perceptions, intuitions, thoughts, acts of will, and so forth—but they do not have qualia, that is, sui generis, simple, intrinsically characterizable phenomenal qualities associated with experiences. Of course, this is not to deny that people are conscious, or that they have consciousness. Rather, it is just to deny one particular conception of what it is to be conscious and of what consciousness is.

Second, there is the naturalist picture that would be preferred by a naturalist who believes in both qualia and agent causation. Causal reality is exhausted by natural reality. Human beings are entirely natural creatures. The mental processes of human beings are nothing but natural processes (in particular, neural processes). Human beings have rich mental lives: they have desires, intentions, emotions, itches, tickles, pains, sensations, perceptions, intuitions, thoughts, acts of will, and so forth—and these things are often associated with qualia, that is, sui generis, simple, intrinsically characterizable phenomenal qualities associated with experiences. Different versions of this picture tell different stories about the nature of the connection between qualia and human mental states; merely for the sake of definiteness, we shall suppose here that it is a matter of metaphysical necessity. (Different versions of the story also tell different stories about freedom. We need not worry about that difference here.)

Third, there is the theistic picture that Moreland prefers. Causal reality outruns natural reality. In particular, supernatural reality contains God—a conscious supernatural agent—and it also contains conscious human minds. Human beings are partly natural, partly supernatural creatures. The mental processes of human beings are supernatural processes, but they are "correlated" with natural processes (in particular, neural processes). Sometimes human beings act with libertarian freedom; sometimes their actions issue from their supernatural part. Human beings have rich mental lives involving qualia, that is, sui generis, simple, intrinsically characterizable phenomenal qualities associated with experiences. The actions of human beings—and, indeed, everything else that involves natural reality—depends upon God's causal involvement (as necessary causal sustainer).

When we consider the theoretical virtues of these views, it seems to me that the first is better than the second, and that the second is much better than the third. Here, I will simply indicate reasons for supposing that the first is better than the third.

It is clear—and Moreland effectively concedes as much—that the first view does much better when it comes to simplicity (and to considerations of ontological and ideological commitment). On the naturalist view, there is one kind of reality, one kind of causation, and one kind of explanation, whereas on the theistic view there are two kinds of reality, two kinds of causation, two kinds of explanation, two "parts" of human beings, and so forth. Moreover, the theistic account requires interactions between the two kinds of reality, and between the two "parts" of human beings. And the theistic account is committed to things— for example, qualia and libertarian freedom—that are clearly philosophically problematic (whereas the naturalist view does not have these problematic commitments). All else being equal, then, there would be clear reason to prefer naturalism to theism.

If we are to prefer theism to naturalism, then, we must suppose that the enormous extra investment—the greater complexity, the addition of ontological and ideological commitments—yields advantages elsewhere. Where might those advantages be? Suppose, for example, that we think that there is a genuine difficulty in understanding how the undergoing of mental processes could be nothing more than the undergoing of natural (neural) processes. Do we have a better understanding of how mental processes could be nothing more than processes in a nonspatiotemporal supernatural realm that are somehow correlated with neural processes? While I am not prepared to concede that there are genuine difficulties involved in understanding how the undergoing of mental processes could be nothing more than the undergoing of natural (neural) processes, I do want to say that I cannot see any advance in understanding that is afforded by the theistic view—and I also want to add that I certainly cannot see an advance in understanding that repays the massive increase in ontology and ideology over the naturalistic view.

When we take all of the theoretical virtues into account—simplicity, descriptive accuracy, predictive success, fruitfulness in guiding new research, capacity for solving internal and external conceptual problems, use of certain types of explanation, following of certain methodological rules, and so forth—it seems to me that we should end up preferring the first picture to the third. However, it may be that the assessment of the two pictures against some of these theoretical virtues ends up depending very heavily upon prior views about the relative plausibility of fuller elaborations of these two theoretical pictures. One of the standard theoretical virtues is fit with other established views; someone who supposed that theism was otherwise well established might suppose that, even when it comes to consciousness, theism trumps naturalism on that account. But, of course, if that were the case, then a more sober assessment would be that while, in itself, considerations about consciousness do favor naturalism over theism, those considerations about consciousness are outweighed by considerations elsewhere. Said differently: if we just restrict our attention to the pictures of theism and naturalism sketched above, and ignore questions about the ways in which these pictures might be more fully elaborated, then, on grounds of theoretical virtue, we should prefer the naturalistic picture to the theistic picture.[26]

■ 6. CONCLUDING REMARKS

The conclusion of Moreland begins as follows:

> Strong naturalism/physicalism has been in a period of Kuhnian paradigm crisis for a long time, and physicalist epicycles have multiplied like rabbits in the past two decades. Moreover, the various versions of physicalism are in a stagnating period of stalemate. Increasingly, naturalists are turning to emergentist views of consciousness. The truth is that naturalism has no plausible way to explain the appearance of emergent mental properties in the cosmos.[27]

You have to admire his effrontery. I know how a more belligerent naturalist than I would respond: *Naturalism marks a new dawn after a long dark age of supernaturalism! If you really want epicycles, stagnation and stalemate, consider the history of theology!*, and so on. Whatever justice there might be in this more belligerent response, I shall here rest content with the claim that, to the extent that we can give an assessment of the relative theoretical virtue of naturalistic and theistic accounts of consciousness and the mental lives of human beings, that assessment seems to favor naturalism over theism.

■ NOTES

1. One indicator of just how recent this surge in publications has been: there is no entry on arguments from consciousness in P. Quinn and C. Taliaferro, eds., *A Companion to*

Philosophy of Religion, 1st ed. (Oxford: Blackwell, 1997), but there is an entry on this topic in C. Taliaferro, P. Draper, and P. Quinn, eds., *A Companion to Philosophy of Religion*, 2nd ed. (Oxford: Blackwell, 2010). There are sympathetic treatments of arguments from consciousness in R. Swinburne, *The Existence of God* (Oxford: Clarendon, 1979), especially 152–179; R. Adams, "Flavours, Colours and God," in *Contemporary Perspectives on Religious Epistemology*, ed. D. Geivett and B. Sweetman (New York: Oxford University Press, 1992), 225–240; C. Taliaferro, *Consciousness and the Mind of God* (Cambridge: Cambridge University Press, 1994), and "Naturalism and the Mind," in *Naturalism: A Critical Analysis*, ed. W. Craig and J. P. Moreland (London: Routledge, 2000), 67–108; W. Hasker, *The Emergent Self* (Ithaca, NY: Cornell University Press, 1999); J. Foster, *The Immaterial Self* (London: Routledge, 2001); J. P. Moreland, "The Argument from Consciousness," in *The Rationality of Theism, ed.* P. Copan and P. Moser (London: Routledge, 2003), 204–220, "The Argument from Consciousness" in *The Routledge Companion to Philosophy of Religion*, ed. C. Meister and P. Copan (London: Routledge, 2007), 373–384, *Consciousness and the Existence of God: A Theistic Argument* (London: Routledge, 2008), and "The Argument from Consciousness," in *The Blackwell Companion to Natural Theology*, ed. W. L. Craig and J. Moreland (Oxford: Blackwell, 2010), 282–342; Y. Nagasawa, *God and Phenomenal Consciousness: A Novel Approach to Knowledge Arguments* (Cambridge: Cambridge University Press, 2008); and S. Goetz, "Arguments from Consciousness and Free Will," in *A Companion to Philosophy of Religion*, 2nd ed., ed. C. Taliaferro, P. Draper, and P. Quinn (Oxford: Blackwell, 2010), 392–397; among others.

2. The argument given here is taken directly from Moreland, "The Argument from Consciousness" [2010], 296. Closely related arguments are presented in Moreland, "The Argument from Consciousness" [2003], 206, and Moreland, "The Argument from Consciousness" [2007], 374. In these related arguments, the second and third premises are replaced by a single premise that claims there is an explanation for the existence of mental events.

3. I discuss Swinburne's argument from consciousness at some length in G. Oppy, *Arguing About Gods* (Cambridge: Cambridge University Press, 2006). Discussion of further arguments from consciousness will need to wait for some other occasion.

4. Moreland, "The Argument from Consciousness" [2010], 284.

5. Moreland, "The Argument from Consciousness" [2010], 284.

6. Moreland, "The Argument from Consciousness" [2010], 284.

7. Moreland, "The Argument from Consciousness" [2010], 285.

8. Moreland, "The Argument from Consciousness" [2010], 285.

9. Moreland, "The Argument from Consciousness" [2010], 284.

10. Moreland, "The Argument from Consciousness" [2010], 284.

11. Moreland, "The Argument from Consciousness" [2010], 283.

12. For example, J. Heil, *From an Ontological Point of View* (Oxford: Clarendon, 2003).

13. Moreland, "The Argument from Consciousness" [2010], 294.

14. Moreland, "The Argument from Consciousness" [2010], 295.

15. Moreland, "The Argument from Consciousness" [2010], 295.

16. Moreland, "The Argument from Consciousness" [2010], 291–292.

17. It is a category mistake to say—as Moreland does—that one theory begs the question against another theory, or that proponents of one theory beg the question against proponents of another theory simply by espousing the theory that they in fact espouse. The proper targets for charges of "begging the question" are arguments, and proponents thereof.

18. Moreland, "The Argument from Consciousness" [2010], 290.

19. We can further distinguish, at least, between mental events and mental states, between what is occurrent and what is standing, between propositional and nonpropositional attitudes, and so forth.

20. Moreland, "The Argument from Consciousness" [2010], 288.

21. See F. Jackson, "Epiphenomenal Qualia," *Philosophical Quarterly* 32 (1982): 127–136. Jackson has since changed his mind: he no longer supposes that his knowledge argument provides a good reason to suppose that qualia are "base ingredients" of our world.

22. See D. Chalmers, *The Conscious Mind: In Search of a Fundamental Theory* (Oxford: Oxford University Press, 1996). In this book, Chalmers defends a kind of panpsychism in which "qualia" are ubiquitous "base ingredients" of our world. It is worth noting that Chalmers supposes that functionalism gives an adequate account of the rest of our mental lives: beliefs, desires, intentions, and so forth.

23. See D. Dennett, D. *Consciousness Explained* (London: Penguin, 1991), especially 405–406, for expression—and defense—of this view (or something very much like it).

24. Dennett, *Consciousness Explained*.

25. Dennett, *Consciousness Explained*, 340.

26. Moreland, "The Argument from Consciousness" [2010], note 1, says: "Oppy…rejects all-too-briefly cumulative case arguments…and thus in my view does not give them sufficient consideration." Two brief comments. First, the argument I have given in this chapter does not depend upon my skepticism about cumulative case arguments. Second, I have since defended my skepticism about cumulative case arguments at much greater length. See, e.g., G. Oppy, "Über die Aussichten erfolgreicher Beweise für Theismus oder Atheismus," in *Gottesbeweise von Anselm bis Gödel*, ed. J. Bromand and G. Kreis (Frankfurt am Main: Suhrkamp Verlag, 2011).

27. Moreland, "The Argument from Consciousness" [2010], 339.

▓ FOR FURTHER READING

McLaughlin, B. "Emergence and Supervenience." *Intellectica* 25, no. 2 (1997): 25–43.

Moreland, J. P. "The Argument from Consciousness." In *The Blackwell Companion to Natural Theology*, ed. W. Craig and J. P. Moreland, 282–342. Oxford: Wiley-Blackwell, 2009.

Oppy, G. "Review of J. P. Moreland's *Consciousness and the Existence of God: A Theistic Argument. European Journal for Philosophy of Religion* 3 (2011): 193–212.

Swinburne, R. *The Evolution of the Soul*, rev. ed. Oxford: Clarendon, 1997.

———. *The Existence of God*. Oxford: Clarendon, 1979, especially 152–179.

The Coherence of Theism: Part I

11 Problems with Omnipotence

■ NICHOLAS EVERITT

Many theists take omnipotence to be one of God's defining properties. In explaining what omnipotence is, they have tacitly accepted a number of constraints, of which I will mention three.

▨ 1. CONSTRAINTS ON OMNIPOTENCE

1. *Self-consistency constraint.* The concept of omnipotence is self-consistent, that is, it is possible for a being to be omnipotent. Taliaferro says of one definition that it faces a "forceful difficulty," namely, that the definition "would hinder any being whatsoever from being omnipotent."[1] This is a "difficulty" only if one presupposes that the concept is self-consistent. No one would regard it as a forceful difficulty in a definition of, for example, "highest prime number" if it had the consequence that there could be no such number.

2. *Coinstantiation constraint.* The property of omnipotence can be coinstantiated with the other properties that are traditionally thought to be essential properties of God, such as omniscience, moral perfection, etc. In abstraction from theism, there is no reason for thinking that it must be possible for an entity to have both omnipotence and such other properties. But in practice, theists would have little interest in a conception of omnipotence that, although self-consistent, entailed that nothing could be both omnipotent and omniscient, omnipotent and supremely good, etc.

3. *Intuitions constraint.* Any account of the concept must not stray far from our pretheoretical intuitions about what omnipotence might be.[2] Since most of us have no regular use (and perhaps no use at all) for the concept, it is unlikely that there will be a detailed and widely shared set of intuitions. But however we understand the concept, we might expect that (to put it at its vaguest), given the "omni" part of the word, there is some element of universality, and given the "potence" part, it is a matter of powers, and hence is to do with being all-powerful, with having the power to do anything.

In seeking to meet these constraints, increasingly complicated definitions of omnipotence have been propounded. A natural starting point is to define omnipotence as the power to perform any task. On such an account, an omnipotent being can create or destroy absolutely anything at will, and he can make absolutely anything happen. But several qualifications are nearly always made to this starting position.

The most widely accepted qualification is that omnipotence cannot include the power to do anything that it is logically impossible for anyone to do. Thus omnipotent beings do not have to be able to create round squares, make 2 + 2 − 5, etc.[3] One might at once conclude that the concept of omnipotence is self-contradictory, but the consensus is that since *no one* can do what is logically impossible, omnipotence cannot reasonably include the power to do the logically impossible. A tension between the self-consistency and intuitions constraints is thus resolved in favor of the former.

In practice, this consensus is misleading, since there is no appropriate account of logical possibility and impossibility. Some accounts are precise but too narrow to be serviceable here,[4] while other accounts avoid narrowness at the cost of imprecision.[5] A further complication is that some authors recognize the existence of other kinds of impossibility (such as metaphysical and conceptual) that are alleged also to be acceptable restrictions on definitions of omnipotence.

A further qualification, again widely accepted, is that an omnipotent being cannot change the past. It is uncontroversial that such a being could have prevented, for example, the Battle of Hastings (say by drowning the Norman army as it crossed the channel). But given that the battle occurred nearly 1000 years ago, not even an omnipotent being (it is said) can now bring it about that the battle never occurred. This is arguably ruled out by the previous exclusion of what is logically impossible, but it is often treated as a separate restriction. Again, a tension between the first two constraints is resolved in favor of insisting that the concept of omnipotence is self-consistent.

A third restriction, widely accepted by theists but more controversial, is that an omnipotent being cannot bring about the free actions of other agents. Many theists accept this because they also accept a libertarian account of free will, according to which a free action is one that is wholly uncaused by anything outside the agent. It is therefore logically impossible for it to be brought about even by an omnipotent being. But for those who accept a compatibilist account of free action, there is no reason to think that omnipotence does not include the power to bring about such free actions.

Another possible restriction arises from the much-discussed question of whether an omnipotent being could make a stone that he was unable to lift. We, it is said, are able to make weights that we are unable to lift, so the task is a logically possible one. If an omnipotent being cannot make the stone, then there is something that he cannot do, although we can, and hence he cannot be omnipotent. Alternatively, if he can make the stone, but he cannot lift it, again there is something that he cannot do, and he cannot be omnipotent.

The most common theistic response is that an omnipotent being cannot make such a stone, but that fact does not prove his lack of omnipotence. For making a stone that cannot be lifted by a being who can lift anything that it is logically possible to lift is not a logically possible task. It is therefore one that an omnipotent being need not be able to perform. This response thus appeals to the same thought as the one mentioned above, that omnipotence cannot require the power to do what is logically impossible.

However, it remains easy to specify other tasks that an omnipotent being could not perform. No being can have all powers, because having some powers rules out having some others. For example, humans have the power to write a book that is not written by an omnipotent being, and this is a power that could not be possessed by any omnipotent being.[6]

Partly because of the number of qualifications that are needed to ensure the consistency of the concept of omnipotence when it is understood in terms of "can do anything," many theists accept that, as two recent authors put it, such an approach is "fruitless."[7] More recent conceptions have differed in two respects. First, omnipotence as the power to perform tasks has been replaced by omnipotence as the power to actualize states of affairs. Second, the focus on the power to actualize *all* logically possible states of affairs has been replaced by a focus on the *maximum power* to actualize states of affairs—the implication being that the gap between "maximal possible" and "all possible" will allow the circumvention of problems arising from the "all" formulation. Hoffman and Rosenkrantz say: "This *comparative* sense of omnipotence as maximal power is the only sense which has a chance of being intelligible."[8]

However, "maximal power" conceptions, unless further qualified, remain open to some of the same objections. Two pairs of defenders of such conceptions both add explicit clauses to their definitions of maximal power to exclude the power to change the past or to cause the actions of free agents.[9] But problem cases, such as having the power to write a nonomnipotent-authored book, remain.

Swinburne tries to block such counterexamples as the latter by saying that an omnipotent being O can actualize "any logically contingent state of affairs after [time] t, the description of which does not entail that [O] did not bring it about at t."[10] This clause would exclude all putative counterexamples that are described as "not actualized by O," as in the book example above. But apart from being an arbitrary qualification whose only motivation is the consistency constraint, such a blocking maneuver has the unacceptable consequence that Plantinga's McEar is omnipotent. Plantinga famously imagined a character, later named "McEar," whose essential attribute is to be able to do nothing but scratch his ear.[11] Given that McEar's impotence in every non-ear-scratching respect is entailed by his essence, his impotence does not count against his omnipotence. Yet to class him as omnipotent would violate the intuitions constraint.

Flint and Freddoso explicitly seek to exclude McEar types of cases. After producing four "pedantically specific" conditions of adequacy for a definition, they add a further "refreshingly vague" clause, namely, that "to count as omnipotent a being should have the maximum amount of power consistent with our first four conditions."[12] If this requirement were defensible, it would exclude both the McEar and the book type of counterexamples. But in fact this fifth condition turns out to be distressingly rather than refreshingly vague. It is difficult to find any measure of power and hence any way of determining the maximum amount of power.

As an initial constraint on any general account of degree of power, the following looks plausible:

(1)   If A has all the powers that B has, but B does not have all the powers that A has, then A is more powerful than B.

But even here, questions arise over what it is for A to "have the same power" as B. In writing *The Long Wait*, was Mickey Spillane exercising the same power as Kant when he wrote *The Critique of Pure Reason*, the power of actualizing a possible book? Or would Spillane have had to write a philosophy text (perhaps a philosophical masterpiece?) to count as exercising the same power? If God and Satan can both actualize fear among nations, do they in that respect have the same power?

The problem is that each power that we might attribute to ourselves falls under many descriptions. Some of these descriptions will apply to both of two agents, A and B, and in that sense we might say that they have the same power; but some of these descriptions will apply to A but not to B, and in that sense we might say that A and B differ in their powers.

However, suppose that somehow we can tell for any state of affairs actualized by A and any state of affairs actualized by B whether A and B have exercised the same power. There arises a further question. Suppose

(2)   A has the power to actualize some but not all of the state of affairs that B can actualize, and B has the power to actualize some but not all of the states of affairs that A can actualize.

Who is more powerful then? Intuitively the answer will depend on how many more powers one has than the other has, and the scope of those powers. Suppose, for example, that

(3)   A can actualize nearly all the state of affairs that B can actualize, and a great number in addition, and B can actualize very few of the things that A can actualize, and very few things that A cannot actualize.

Intuitively we might think that A is more powerful than B. But suppose that the very many powers that A has but B lacks form a dense cluster of rather trivial powers for actualizing states of affairs (he can drum with his fingers 1 inch, or 2 inches, or 3 inches, etc., from the edge of the table), whereas the few powers that B has but A lacks are on a cosmic scale (the power to part the waters of the oceans, make planets wobble in their orbits, etc.). Then intuition suggests that B is more powerful than A. This means that there are two further sources of vagueness and uncertainty in any comparative account of omnipotence as maximal power: first, how can we measure the scope of a power? Second, if we can somehow measure the scope of the power, how are we to trade off the *numbers* of powers against the scope of the power? This is a problem that arises in (3), and it will arise equally in connection with the following:

(4) A lacks the power to actualize any of the states of affairs that B can actualize and B lacks the power to actualize any of the states of affairs that A can actualize.

In the absence of a principled way of settling these uncertainties, any version of theism that depends on the currently favored "maximal power" interpretation of omnipotence faces not so much refutation as an intolerable vagueness. Problems of this sort afflict not just older versions of the "maximal power" conception, but also more recent ones, such as that offered by Hoffman and Rosenkrantz.[13]

Further, even if any intuitively satisfactory explanation of maximal power will leave God much more powerful than humans, it is not so clear that the same will be true of God in relation to other supernatural forces. Although a literal belief in Satan, or Cartesian demons, or other supernatural forces is not part of classical theism, it is nonetheless true that many theists have also believed in the possibility and sometimes the actuality of other supernatural beings than God. Since God is thought to be *essentially* omnipotent, on the "maximal power" conception, he is the most powerful being not just in the actual world, but also in all possible worlds. So theism needs a method for quantifying powers that will allow comparisons between all actual beings, and all possible beings as well. Without such a method, any claim that a being is "essentially maximally powerful" is too vague to be serviceable; but no such method has so far been propounded.

Finally, there is an uncertainty in how an appeal to maximal power should be taken.

On the first interpretation, the reductionist, the concept of omnipotence is *analyzed as* maximal power, and since the latter is supposed to be logically acceptable, the former is too. Craig, for example, says that Flint and Freddoso, through a rigorous and painstaking analysis, formulated an adequate *explication of omnipotence* (a.k.a. "maximal power").[14]

On a second interpretation, which we can call the rejectionist, the appeal is conceding that the concept of omnipotence is logically flawed, and that there can be no omnipotent being, but that the different concept of maximal power will be an acceptable substitute. Thus Hoffman and Rosenkrantz say:

from what we have said about the restrictions that any coherent account of God's power must place on this power, *a better term for God's power than "omnipotence" would be "maxipotence."*[15]

In a much earlier article, Geach voiced the similar thought that there is no self-consistent concept of omnipotence and that theism should instead use the concept of the almighty.[16] As Metcalf observes,[17] we do not in general think that having *all* F is the same as having *maximal* F (being *all*-knowing is not the same as being *maximally* knowing), so why should we think that being maximally powerful is the same as being all-powerful?

Each interpretation presents problems for theism. Since many theists claim omnipotence as an essential attribute of God, the first interpretation, which accepts that nothing can be omnipotent, entails that God does not exist. The second interpretation violates the intuitions constraint, because there are so many types of states of affairs that it has to allow that a maximally powerful (and hence omnipotent) being cannot actualize.

Let us suppose, however, that all these problems can be overcome. It still remains unclear that the coinstantiation constraint can be satisfied. For example, omnipotence and omniscience are prima facie incompatible (because an omniscient being cannot learn anything),[18] and omnipotence and necessary existence are prima facie incompatible (because a necessarily existing being does not have the power to end its own existence). In what follows, I will focus in more detail on two other incompatibilities.

■ 2. PROBLEMS WITH OMNIPOTENCE AND IMMATERIALITY

I can run and jump, eat a sandwich, and drink a beer, and no immaterial being can perform any of these actions (or actualize states of affairs in which he performs these actions). So, omnipotence and immateriality are mutually inconsistent.

One possible response is that an omnipotent being, O, could always equip himself with a body, and using that body, perform the full range of actions that are open to human beings.[19] But this response raises some puzzling questions about the relation of persons to their bodies. If we are in some sense separable from our bodies, and merely use them as instruments during normal embodied life, then the response looks tenable. But if we are identical with our bodies, or necessarily supervenient on them, then the response will fail. For even if O could make a human being move in human-like ways, such as walking, it would not be O who was walking, but O making something or someone else walk, and body-dependent actions would remain impossible for O. (For Christian theists, the issue is complicated by a belief in the Incarnation, in which God is supposed to have taken on human form. Theists then face the problem of reconciling the three thoughts that in some sense Jesus was God, that Jesus was partly material, and that God is wholly immaterial.)

A second natural reply is that such problem cases can be excluded by saying that O is omnipotent if and only if O can realize any state of affairs where this is not made logically impossible by O's other essential attributes. Given that God is essentially immaterial, and being immaterial is logically incompatible with walking, etc., God's inability to walk, etc., would not show that he was not omnipotent. But this is in effect the same response as the Swinburne move mentioned earlier, and is open to the same McEar objection: if being able to do nothing but scratch his ear is McEar's one essential attribute, then the fact that he cannot walk across the room will not stop him being omnipotent since it is an action whose performance is incompatible with his essential attribute.

Rogers tries a different tack. She says that an omnipotent being "cannot perform any task for which limitation and weakness is required on the part of the performer,"[20] the implication being that "limitation and weakness" are required if one is to be able to run and jump, eat and drink, etc. One can half-see how this idea is meant to work in certain limited domains. For example, weak muscles in my legs limit my power to sprint or do well in the high jump. But it is clearly false to think that having any legs at all is a limit on my power of sprinting or jumping—as if I would run or jump better without them. Having legs are what makes it possible for me to run and jump. And why is having a body per se a form of "limitation and weakness"? True, it debars one from performing actions that one could (let us assume) perform without it, but equally, not having a body (if we can make sense of that idea) debars one from performing actions that one can perform only with a body.

3. IS OMNIPOTENCE COMPATIBLE WITH ESSENTIAL PERFECT GOODNESS?

A second conflict arises from the relations between omnipotence and essential perfect goodness. An essentially omnipotent being can act wrongly, but an essentially perfect being cannot sin, therefore no essentially omnipotent being can be essentially perfect.

Some theists have tried to exclude any possible conflict between God's omnipotence and his moral perfection (crystallized in the question "Can God sin?") by including a moral element in the definition of omnipotence. For example, the final clause in the definition of omnipotence offered by Stewart is that if O is omnipotent, "no being greater in overall power *and moral excellence* can be conceived."[21] This is to impose a twofold requirement:

(i) An omnipotent being is one such that no being greater in power can be conceived.

(ii) An omnipotent being is one such that no being greater in moral excellence can be conceived.

So, X cannot be an omnipotent being unless both conditions are met.

Stewart gives no reasons for thinking that moral excellence is an essential component of omnipotence (doesn't it violate the intuitions constraint?), but the implicit reasoning seems to be that it must be present in order to exclude the possibility of a being, X, who has all the powers that God has and also the further power of being able to act wrongly.

However, aside from this being a question-begging reason for introducing moral excellence (why not simply say that God, as morally excellent, cannot also be omnipotent?), the proposal faces the problem that there is no reason to think that the two descriptions must pick out the same being. Suppose that I think, on the face of it quite plausibly:

(iii) If X and Y differ in power only in that X can actualize some states of affairs that Y cannot actualize, then X is more powerful than Y.

It then follows that someone who is maximally powerful at bringing about states of affairs will be someone than whom someone more morally excellent *is* conceivable. In other words, the most powerful being conceivable, and the most excellent being conceivable, will be two different beings. So there cannot be an omnipotent being as defined by Stewart. Accepting (iii) means that there is a trade-off between power and excellence, such that no being can achieve both maximal possible power and maximal possible excellence.

Taliaferro is another author who argues that God's inability to sin does not mean that he cannot be maximally powerful. In support of this claim, he quotes with approval St. Anselm's remark that the power to do evil

> is not power but impotence. For, he who is capable of these things is capable of what is not for his own good... and the more capable of them he is, the more power have adversity and perversity against him; and the less has he himself against these.[22]

But St. Anselm's argument is here a bad one. Take first the claim that sinning is not for the good of the agent. If "good" here means "contributing to the moral stature of the agent," this is true, but it fails to support the conclusion that sinning is not the exercise of a power. If "good" means "benefit," then the claim is false (sometimes the wrong action does benefit the agent); and even if true, it would not support the conclusion. In general, there is no reason to think that sinning involves being *overcome* by "adversity and perversity"—the so-called adversity and perversity may be freely chosen.

Taliaferro also calls on St. Thomas Aquinas in support of his value-based understanding of divine power. Aquinas remarks that

> to sin is to fall short of a perfect action; hence to be able to sin is to be able to fall short in action, which is repugnant to omnipotence. Therefore it is that God cannot sin, because of his omnipotence.[23]

But Aquinas's argument is as bad as Anselm's. It depends on equivocation. The sense of "falling short" in which sinning might be said to fall short of a perfect action is "having less moral value." The sense in which falling short is repugnant to omnipotence is trying to do something and failing. The fact that sinning falls short in the first sense does not entail that it falls short in the second, and the claim that God's inability to sin does not undermine his supposed omnipotence collapses.

A different line is taken by Morris who claims that "there is no discrete power of sinning, no distinct power to sin, no power the exercise of which is, in itself, sufficient for doing evil or sinning."[24]

Morris's thought is that tokens of a given action type will count as sinning in one context and not in another. In one context, squeezing a trigger may constitute the sinful action of murder, while in another context an exactly similar action may be morally permissible. The same power, namely to pull a trigger, is, Morris urges, in play in both cases. So although there may be a power of trigger-pulling, there is no power of sinning; and if there is no power of sinning, it cannot be a power that God lacks.

This, too, is an ultimately unsuccessful defense of the compatibility of omnipotence and moral perfection. We can note first that if there is no power to sin, by parity of reasoning there will be no power to do good. Indeed, Morris goes on to claim that there is no power to rape, lie, steal, or murder, presumably since the actions whose performance in one context constitute raping, lying, stealing, and murdering will in another context be perfectly innocent.

But more seriously, the atheist will insist on a distinction between having a power and being able to exercise the power. Consider one of Morris's own examples, the power to squeeze the trigger of a gun.[25] Consider a context C in which exercising that power would constitute an act of murder. In C, humans can exercise that power, but in C, God, as essentially morally perfect, cannot. His exercise of the power in C is ruled out by his essential goodness. Although he can *in general* squeeze triggers, he cannot squeeze this trigger here and now, in the context in which doing so would constitute murder. There is thus a state of affairs (the squeezing of the trigger in C) that humans can bring about but God cannot.

All that Morris's argument shows is that the huge number of actions that a maximally powerful and morally excellent being would be unable to perform cannot all be ascribed to his lacking a power, since it is not a single power that is involved in the performance of all those actions.

■ 4. CONCLUSION

I have argued that there is no theistically acceptable concept of omnipotence. Taken at face value, the concept is inconsistent. When qualifications are added so that omnipotence does not require the power to change logical truths, to alter the past, or to cause the free actions of other agents, the intuitions constraint is violated and problem cases like that of McEar remain. To exclude these problems, theists have moved to maximal power. But this is either the tacit admission that omnipotence cannot apply to God, or it involves further violations of the intuitions constraint. Further problems arise with the alleged coinstantiation of omnipotence and other divine attributes such as immateriality and goodness. If, as the tradition maintains, omnipotence is essential to God, the conclusion must be that there can be no God.

■ NOTES

1. Charles Taliaferro, *Contemporary Philosophy of Religion* (Oxford: Blackwell, 1998), 64–65.

2. Cf. Thomas P. Flint and Alfred J. Freddoso, "Maximal Power," in *Philosophy of Religion: A Reader and a Guide,* edited by William Lane Craig (Edinburgh: Edinburgh University Press, 2002): "No being should be considered omnipotent if he lacks the kind of power which it is clear an omnipotent being ought to possess" (p. 278).

3. Descartes is famously thought to have denied that this qualification is needed, but few theists have followed him in this.

4. W. V. O. Quine, "Two Dogmas of Empiricism," reprinted with minor changes in *From a Logical Point of View* (Cambridge, MA: Harvard University Press, 1980), 20–46.

5. See Alvin Plantinga, *The Nature of Necessity* (Oxford: Clarendon Press, 1982), chap. 1.

6. As an analogy, consider the set of all possible legal moves in a game of chess. Knights can make one set of moves, rooks another, bishops another, and queens another. Queens can make all the moves that rooks and bishops can, but none of those of knights.

7. Joshua Hoffman and Gary Rosenkrantz, *The Divine Attributes* (Oxford: Blackwell, 2002), 167.

8. Joshua Hoffman and Gary Rosenkrantz, "Omnipotence," in *A Companion to Philosophy of Religion,* ed. Philip L. Quinn and Charles Taliaferro (Oxford: Blackwell, 1999), 230 (italics in original). Other authors who interpret omnipotence in terms of powers to actualize states of affairs include Flint and Freddoso, "Maximal Power," in *The Existence and Nature of God,* ed. Alfred J. Freddoso (Notre Dame: University of Notre Dame Press, 1983); Thomas Metcalf, "Omniscience and Maximal Power," *Religious Studies* 40 (2004): 289–306; Katherin Rogers, *Perfect Being Theology* (Edinburgh: Edinburgh University Press, 2000), 92–106; Melville Y. Stewart, *The Greater Good Defence: An Essay on the Rationality of Faith* (London: St. Martin's Press, 1993), 19–32; and Edward Wierenga, *The Nature of God: An Enquiry Into the Divine Attributes* (Ithaca, NY: Cornell University Press, 1989). A recent author who perseveres with the "task" conception of omnipotence is Jordan Howard Sobel, *Logic and Theism: Arguments For and Against Beliefs in God* (Cambridge: Cambridge University Press, 2004), 346–368. For a dissenting view about whether "states of affairs" terminology marks an improvement, see Metcalf, "Omniscience and Maximal Power," 2004.

9. Flint and Freddoso (1983); Hoffman and Rosenkrantz (1999).

10. Richard Swinburne, *The Coherence of Theism* (Oxford: Clarendon Press, 1986), 152.

11. Alvin Plantinga, *God and Other Minds* (Ithaca, NY: Cornell University Press, 1967), 170. Cf. Thomas Metcalf's McNothing in "Omniscience and Maximal Power," 294.

12. Flint and Freddoso (1983).

13. Hoffman and Rosenkrantz, *The Divine Attributes*; and "Omnipotence."

14. Craig (2002), 211 (italics added).

15. Hoffman and Rosenkrantz (1999), fn. 9 (italics added).

16. Peter Geach, "Omnipotence," *Philosophy* 48 (1973): 7.

17. Metcalf (2004).

18. See Metcalf "Omniscience and Maximal Power," or Michael Martin, "Divine Incoherence," *Sophia* 46, no. 1 (2007): 75–77, for a different argument to the same conclusion.

19. Nicholas Everitt, *The Non-existence of God* (London: Routledge, 2004), 262.

20. Rogers (2000), 97.

21. Stewart (1993), 31.

22. St. Anselm, quoted in Taliaferro, *Contemporary Philosophy of Religion,* 77; the same line of thought recurs in Taliaferro, *Evidence and Faith* (Cambridge: Cambridge University Press, 2005), 402.

23. St. Thomas Aquinas, *Summa Theologica* I 25 3, quoted in Taliaferro, *Contemporary Philosophy of Religion,* 77.

24. Thomas V. Morris, *Anselmian Explorations* (Notre Dame, IN: University of Notre Dame Press, 1989), 73.

25. I here overlook any problems in the thought that an immaterial being might pick up a gun and squeeze the trigger. If God could part the waters of the Red Sea, squeezing a trigger should present him with no difficulty.

■ FOR FURTHER READING

Grim, P. "Impossibility Arguments." In *The Cambridge Companion to Atheism*, ed. Michael Martin, 199–214. Cambridge: Cambridge University Press, 2007.

Hoffman, J. and Rosenkrantz, G. "Omnipotence" *Stanford Encyclopedia of Philosophy*, 2006. http://plato.stanford.edu/entries/omnipotence.

Metcalfe, T. "Omniscience and Maximal Power," 289–306. *Religious Studies* 40, 2004.

Rogers, K. *Perfect Being Theology*, 92–106. Edinburgh: Edinburgh University Press, 2000.

Sobell, J. H. *Logic and Theism: Arguments for and against beliefs in God*, 346–368. Cambridge: Cambridge University Press, 2004.

12 Coherence of Divine Power

■ CHARLES TALIAFERRO

Some philosophers focus on the coherence and nature of divine power in abstraction from living world religions. Discussions of whether a fictional character named McEar (a character who is only able to scratch his ear) exists or whether God can make an oatmeal dish so big that even God cannot eat it have no role in religious life, though they are the kinds of cases that are discussed in some philosophical treatments of omnipotence. When we do explore *religious* responses to the power of God in Judaism, Christianity, and Islam, however, we discover not abstract puzzles about pure power, but instead we discover that at the core of divine attributes is the central claim that *God is worthy of the highest praise or worship*. Divine power is not, then, an abstract or abstruse concept of *maximal brute power* (the power to do anything whatsoever), but a concept of praise-worthy power, the power of the best and the highest (*optimus maximus*). C. A. Campbell rightly sees theism as inextricably defined in terms of divine perfection.

> Theism in general proclaims that God is wholly perfect; and, as is entirely natural, it interprets this divine perfection in terms of the 'highest we know; in human experience; applying to God accordingly, such concepts as those of goodness, wisdom and power in their highest manifestation.[1]

Such a theistic vision is sometimes called perfect being or Anselmian theology.[2]

Some popular critics of theism seem to completely ignore the evident centrality of values in theistic religious tradition. For a flagrant example, consider Richard Dawkins's description of "the God Hypothesis": "There exists a superhuman, supernatural intelligence who deliberately designed and created the universe and everything in it."[3] Dawkins sees "goodness" as a mere "extra," rather than a core belief about God in theistic tradition. And yet, supreme, praise-worthy goodness is at the beginning and center of theistic religion, not a latent or ad hoc add-on.

I suggest that philosophical reflection on omnipotence in abstraction from its religious context of value and praise may be classified under the heading of the *philosophy of power* or *philosophy of God* as distinct from the philosophy of religion. In this chapter, my concern is the nature and coherence of omnipotence in the philosophy of religion.

Let's first clarify the nature of divine power in Anselmian theology, and then address some challenges it faces.

■ 1. PRELIMINARY OBSERVATIONS

Once we are clear about the religious setting for the belief that God is omnipotent, we can see through many of the so-called paradoxes of omnipotence, some of which seem to involve self-contradiction and conceptual incoherence. Is it problematic if the God of theism exists, but God cannot make a square circle (an enclosed figure that both has four right angles and lacks four right angles at the same time)? Or if God cannot make 2 + 2 = 5? These (ostensible?) states of affairs are not coherent; they make no sense as possible states of affairs under any possible condition. The equation 2 + 2 = 5 is intelligible and it has what philosophers call a truth value (namely it is impossible for 1 + 1 + 1 + 1 to equal 1 + 1 + 1 + 1 + 1), but it is in the same camp as obvious nonsense (dancing with the concept of justice or shaking hands with the year 1066 or the claim that the number 3 is more green than a smiling cat). In my view none of the cases like these that some philosophers have contrived to undermine omnipotence have any weight whatsoever. Once we are clear about frameworks, so-called obstacles to omnipotence may be seen through as idle. For example, given that time is necessarily one-directional (irreversible), of course an omnipotent being cannot reverse time; we've started off with the thesis that the past cannot be reversed by holding that time is necessarily one-directional. This "cannot," as in "God cannot reverse time," in relation to necessary truths is the strongest case of "cannot" imaginable. It is not "cannot" in the sense that I cannot travel faster than the speed of light. We can imagine the physical constants of the cosmos altering so that I might just do this; in fact, if we lived in a Newtonian cosmos (the world as Newton conceived of it, a world that seems coherent and self-consistent) there would be no barrier to an object traveling faster than the speed of light. And even in contemporary relativistic physics there is speculation that there are particles—tachyons—that travel faster than the speed of light; if coherent, this is further reason for thinking that while I cannot travel faster than the speed of light, the supposition that I might is not absolute nonsense like the claim that green ideas sleep furiously.

Religious tradition is full of claims that God can do what *for us* is impossible (create and sustain in existence indefinitely many worlds), but there is no claim I know of in concrete, living religious traditions that God can do what is *absolutely, logically impossible*, the equivalent of nonsense even beyond *Alice in Wonderland*. And some of the cases of so-called obstacles to divine omnipotence seem merely capricious or of only conceptual as opposed to real interest. Would it be a limitation on divine power if God cannot make something God cannot make? Or God cannot write a poem that God does not write? These are no more real limits than the idea that a square is somehow deficient if it has four right angles.

Further refinement of the concept of omnipotence in theistic tradition will depend on one's other philosophical commitments. If you are a nominalist (and deny there are Platonic objects often called *states of affairs*), you will not articulate God's power in terms of obtaining of states of affairs, but if (like me) you are a Platonist this will not be a problem. If you are what is called a compatibilist, who believes a person can be free and yet fully determined by an external power, you will believe it is possible for God to make free persons do whatever God wants. But if (again like me) you believe that freedom rules out determinism (to be truly free, a person's choices cannot be *necessitated* by antecedent and contemporary events plus laws of nature), no being whatsoever, including God, can make a free person's choice determined.

Some of the philosophical commitments that will inform our understanding of God's power in theism will depend on value judgments. In perfect being theology, we hold that God necessarily exists—God's nonexistence is impossible. Along with some (but not many) philosophers I have argued that if there are reasons for thinking it is even possible that God exists, then God exists in reality. This is called the ontological argument, a topic for another occasion.[4] But given that God exists necessarily, there is something I can do that God cannot, namely I can commit suicide. We have to then ask whether my power to kill myself is praiseworthy or a supreme excellence. Maybe, for finite imperfect creatures, suicide for the sake of honor is admirable, or perhaps it is not admirable and the fact that a person refuses to kill himself is admirable. But when we are contemplating a being of unsurpassable goodness, is the power of self-annihilation itself a good-making property? This seems highly doubtful. The Platonic, Anselmian strand in theism adopts precisely the opposite position: God is the source of irrepressible life and goodness. For the Anselmian (and Augustinian, as cited by Professor Everitt), the power to sin is not befitting or worthy of praise; it is simply not the meritorious great-making power that defines theistic tradition.

The Anselmian framework has received ample support from feminist philosophers of religion who lament male philosophical treatments of omnipotence as a valorization or praise of pure unalloyed power. Dorothee Soelle (rightly, in my view) is repelled by concepts of omnipotence that are shorn of values:

> As a woman I have to ask why it is that human beings honor a God whose most important attribute is power, whose prime need is to subjugate, whose greatest fear is equality...Why should we honor and love a being that does not transcend but only reaffirms the moral level of our present male dominated culture? Why should we honor and love this being...if his being is in fact no more than an outsized man?[5]

Soelle's view is in continuity with this assertion by one of the first philosophers who may be classified as a feminist in modern philosophy, Mary Wollstonecraft:

> Man, accustomed to bow down to power in his savage state, can seldom divest himself of this barbarous prejudice, even when civilization determines how much superior mental is to bodily strength; and his reason is clouded by these crude opinions, even

when he thinks of the Deity.—His omnipotence is made to swallow up, or preside over his other attributes, and those mortals are supposed to limit his power irreverently, who think that it must be regulated by his wisdom.[6]

Anslemians as well as feminists hold that maximal praise-worthy power does not include the power to molest and rape females, or anyone. Such "powers" are not divine or praise-worthy.

In the space remaining I take up two challenges to the coherence of omnipotence as understood in the philosophy of religion. Two troubling matters arise from reflection on divine power in religious tradition, the first one impacting only Christians. In Christian tradition, Jesus Christ is fully human and fully divine. If perfection (and thus being without sin) is divine, how is it that Jesus (according to tradition) was tempted to sin (e.g., Matthew 4)? The second challenge concerns the coherence of God as a powerful, yet incorporeal or nonphysical, purposive being or reality. Is such a concept coherent, or is there something unintelligible about a creative agent that is not physically embodied or a material being?

■ 2. REPLIES TO TWO OBJECTIONS: THE PROBLEMS OF INCARNATE TEMPTATION AND INCORPOREAL AGENCY

As for the problem of temptation, there are several alternatives. One would be to argue that in the Incarnation Jesus did not always know he was fully divine and thus did not know that sinning was inimical to his essential nature. In this schema, Jesus might be tempted to sin by doing an act he thought was a bona fide possibility.[7] To take a quirky but perhaps not unlikely case: imagine Pat is in a committed relationship and deeply faithful to her partner and so would not, on reflection, be able to commit adultery, but Pat is not always aware of this steadfast trait. In a state of self-forgetfulness and in a romantic setting, Pat might be genuinely tempted to have an affair even though when Pat steps back and weighs options, Pat would not be able to intend and carry out the affair. Would the bare fact of being tempted itself be a sin? Might it be that only an imperfect (not essentially good) being could be tempted? Didn't Pat fail when Pat was in a state of self-forgetfulness? This is not obvious. True, ancient philosophy commends the dictum "Know thyself," but arguably it may be a feature of normal, even healthy human life that we cannot always be in a state of heightened self-awareness. And some philosophers have argued that the inclination to do wrong (and thus the possibility and reality of temptation) may be an essential component of moral formation.[8] Perhaps if Pat was never self-forgetful, Pat would not be able to demonstrate her fidelity when it has been put to the test. One may even argue that some temptation to do genuinely wrong acts reflects goodness or excellence of character. Imagine that Mother Theresa believes (correctly) that she should not steal money from those with surplus wealth to aid the poor. Arguably we may regard her having a genuine temptation to steal to be a mark of goodness rather than a sin. So, one may plausibly argue that Christ could have been tempted to do wrong even if (ultimately) his divine nature would not allow him to actually do something evil or wrong.

Other moves are possible: Christians traditionally believe Christ to be wholly God (*totus deus*) but not the whole of God (*totum dei*). One may argue that in the Incarnation Jesus was not essentially but contingently good. This viewpoint is sometimes advanced as part of the idea that in the Incarnation the second person of the Trinity underwent a radical self-limitation or Kenosis—the Greek term for "emptied" that is used when, in the New Testament, it is claimed that Christ Jesus "emptied Himself, taking the form of a bond-servant" (Philippians 2:7). Today there are abundant concepts of the Trinity that allow for alternative formations of an incarnation.[9] While I suggest that Christian orthodoxy is committed to recognizing Jesus as essentially good, one could also adopt more liberal positions and, for example, treat the divine nature of Jesus as a revelatory property (e.g., Jesus is divine insofar as his life and teaching reveal the nature of God).

What about the idea that God is incorporeal or nonphysical? Some philosophers challenge the intelligibility of a person existing in a disembodied state. John Hospers, for example, questions thought experiments in which it appears a person persists but without his or her body:

> You see—with eyes?—no, you have no eyes, since you have no body. But let that pass for a moment; you have experiences similar to what you would have if you had eyes to see with. But how can you look toward the foot of the bed or toward the mirror? Isn't looking an activity that requires having a body? How can you look in one direction or another if you have no head to turn? And this isn't all; we said that you can't touch your body because there is no body there; how did you discover this?... Your body seems to be involved in every activity we try to describe even though we have tried to imagine existing without it.[10]

Michael Martin makes a similar point. He suggests that Biblical language about God speaking only makes sense given a very anthropomorphic concept of God in which God is thought of as embodied.

> If one interprets God as a nonspatial, nontemporal being without a body, what sense can one make of God's performing a speech act?... The existence of a voice issuing commands seems to presume some physical vocal apparatus; golden letters written in the sky would seem to presuppose some physical writing appendage. However, this understanding of God assumes anthropomorphism rejected by sophisticated theologians today.[11]

A full reply to such objections would take us deep into philosophical work on the nature of consciousness. Briefly, I suggest that objections like Hospers' and

Martin's carry weight so long as one adopts a radically materialist or behaviorist account of the mental. If it turns out that thinking, acting, and so on, are *necessarily* physiological processes, then the supposition that there can be a nonphysical thinking, acting being is nonsense. But the current state of play in the philosophy of mind is not firmly materialist. In our case, can speaking or seeing be identified as numerically the same thing as physiological-chemical processes? Michael Lockwood offers this contemporary overview of the problems facing materialism when it comes to the existence of consciousness:

> Let me begin by nailing my colours to the mast. I count myself a materialist, in the sense that I take consciousness to be a species of brain activity. Having said that, however, it seems to me evident that no description of brain activity of the relevant kind, couched in the currently available languages of physics, physiology, or functional or computational roles, is remotely capable of capturing what is distinctive about consciousness. So glaring, indeed, are the shortcomings of all the reductive programmes currently on offer, that I cannot believe that anyone with a philosophical training, looking dispassionately at these programmes, would take any of them seriously for a moment, were it not for a deep-seated conviction that current physical science has essentially got reality taped, and accordingly, *something* along the lines of what the reductionists are offering *must* be correct. To that extent, the very existence of consciousness seems to me to be a standing demonstration of the explanatory limitations of contemporary physical science. On the assumption that some form of materialism is nevertheless true, we have only to introspect in order to recognize that our present understanding of matter is itself radically deficient. Consciousness remains for us, at the dawn of the twenty-first century, what it was for Newton at the dawn of the eighteenth century: an occult power that lies beyond the pool of illumination that physical theory casts on the world we inhabit.[12]

Philosophers such as Thomas Nagel, Galen Strawson, William Hasker, and others have argued that consciousness itself is not identical with brain matter and bodily behavior. As Colin McGinn points out:

> The property of consciousness itself (or specific conscious states) is not an observable or perceptible property of the brain. You can stare into a living conscious brain, your own or someone else's, and see there a wide variety of instantiated properties—its shape, colour, texture, etc.—but you will not thereby see what the subject is experiencing, the conscious state itself.[13]

For us, seeing and speaking requires eyes or at least a visual cortex and mouths, vocal cords, and motor control, but we no longer seem under the spell of behaviorist models that assume such an external physiological analysis is sufficient to capture the consciousness involved in thinking and acting.

Hospers and Martin are correct, even obviously so, that *ordinary* perception and audition are physically embodied, but it is a considerable leap to think that all conceivable forms of consciousness must take such an embodied format. (As an aside, classical theistic philosophers and theologians have historically treated all anthropomorphic attributions to God as metaphors. Imagine trying to accept as literal truth 2nd Chronicles 16:9: "For the eyes of the Lord run to and fro throughout the whole earth" (Revised Standard Version).) I conclude that the case for materialism and behaviorism is weak, and thus cannot be used to argue that the theistic concept of a nonphysical, powerful, good, purposive being (God in theistic religious tradition) is incoherent.

■ 3. CONCLUSION

Using Hospers' and Martin's examples, if we want to understand the nature of seeing and speaking, we do well to investigate the actual context of such practices. By analogy, if we want to understand divine power or omnipotence, we do well to look at its historical context. When we do, we see that such divine power is understood to be worthy of awe and praise. It is not bare power, uninformed by goodness and value. And when we look more closely at the language used of God's power (God creates, loves, knows, becomes revealed or disclosed by sacred images and scripture) we see that even in our own case, such language as it is used to describe human power goes beyond the narrow confines of materialism and behaviorism. For further arguments backing up these claims, please see *Consciousness and the Mind of God* and the collection of essays in *The Soul Hypothesis*.[14]

■ NOTES

1. C. A. Campbell, *On Selfhood and Godhead* (London: Allen & Unwin, 1957), 307.
2. See T. V. Morris, *Our Idea of God* (Notre Dame, IN: University of Notre Dame Press, 1991); Morris 1998; D. J. Hill, *Divinity and Maximal Greatness* (London: Routledge, 2005).
3. R. Dawkins, *The God Delusion* (New York: Houghton Mifflin, 2006), 31.
4. See C. Taliaferro, *Philosophy of Religion: A Beginner's Guide* (Oxford: One World Press, 2009).
5. O. Soelle, *The Strength of the Weak* (Philadelphia: Westminster Press, 1984), 97.
6. M. Wollstonecraft, *A Vindication of the Rights of Women* (Mineola, NY: Dover, 1996), 45.
7. T. V. Morris, *The Logic of God Incarnate* (Ithaca, NY: Cornell University Press, 1986).
8. E. Stump, *Wandering in Darkness* (Oxford: Oxford University Press, 2010).
9. See T. McCall and M. Rea, eds., *Philosophical and Theological Essays on the Trinity* (Oxford: Oxford University Press, 2009).
10. John Hospers, "Is the Notion of Disembodied Existence Intelligible?," in *Immortality*, ed. Paul Edwards (Amherst, NY: Prometheus Books, 1997), 280.
11. M. Martin, *Atheism* (Philadelphia: Temple University Press, 1990), 11.
12. Michael Lockwood, "Consciousness and the Quantum World: Putting Qualia on the Map," in *Consciousness: New Philosophical Perspectives*, ed. Quentin Smith and Aleksander Jokic (Oxford: Oxford University Press, 2003), 447.
13. C. McGinn, *The Problems of Consciousness* (Oxford: Blackwell, 1990), 10–11.

14. C. Taliaferro, *Consciousness and the Mind of God* (Cambridge: Cambridge University Press, 1994); M. Baker and S. Goetz, *The Soul Hypothesis* (London: Continuum, 2011).

▦ FOR FURTHER READING

Geach, P. *Providence and Evil.* Cambridge: Cambridge University Press, 1977.

Goetz, S., and C. Taliaferro. *A Brief History of the Soul.* Oxford: Wiley-Blackwell, 2011.

Hoffman, J., and G. Rosenkrantz. "Omnipotence." In *A Companion to Philosophy of Religion,* ed. C. Taliaferro, P. Draper, and P. Quinn, 243–250. Oxford: Wiley Blackwell, 2010.

Kenny, A. *The God of the Philosophers.* Oxford: Clarendon Press, 1979.

Leftow, B. "Omnipotence." In *The Oxford Handbook of Philosophical Theology,* ed. T. Flint and M. Rea, 167–198. Oxford: Oxford University Press, 2009.

Morris, T. *Anselmian Explorations.* Notre Dame, IN: Notre Dame University Press, 1987.

Rowe, W. "Divine Power, Goodness, and Knowledge." In *The Oxford Handbook of Philosophy of Religion,* ed. W. Wainwright, 15–35. Oxford: Oxford University Press, 2005.

Taliaferro, C., and J. Evans. *The Image in Mind: Theism, Naturalism, and the Imagination.* London: Continuum, 2011.

———, eds. *Turning Images in Philosophy, Science, and Religion.* Oxford: Oxford University Press, 2011.

Taliaferro, C., V. Harrison, and S. Goetz, eds. *The Routledge Companion to Theism.* London: Routledge, 2012.

Taliaferro, C., and C. Meister. *The Cambridge Companion to Christian Philosophical Theology.* Cambridge: Cambridge University Press, 2009.

The Coherence of Theism: Part II

13 Problems with Omniscience

■ PATRICK GRIM

■ 1. INTRODUCTION: "GOD" AND "OMNISCIENCE"

Here are my ground rules:

- "God" is defined as a "a being necessarily existent, timeless, ubiquitous, omnipotent, omniscient, and morally perfect, the creator of the universe." That is the target. If no being fits the bill, there is no God.
- I am not interested in "God" used as a purported name for something-big-but-we-know-not-what, allowing claimants to change their claims regarding any or all purported properties. In my usage, we could not find out that God is very knowledgeable but not omniscient, that he is occasionally cruel, or that he is actually a fairly normal mortal selling insurance in the suburbs of Chicago. The properties of omnipotence, omniscience, and moral perfection do not merely characterize God contingently. They define the meaning of the term "God" on a central classical conception. That is the target. If no being fits the bill, there is no God.
- The standard properties listed face logical problems both singly and in combination. I will concentrate on just one of those properties, and in isolation: the notion of omniscience, or of being all knowing. I focus on the classical definition: a being is omniscient if it knows everything. More precisely, a being is omniscient if and only if it knows all truths—and, we have to add, believes no falsehoods.[1] The beliefs of an omniscient being would correspond precisely to a set of all and only truths.
- Here again let me emphasize the ground rules. Omniscience demands knowing everything. It is not satisfied by knowing all of some limited class of propositions. It is not satisfied by knowing everything that a being of some particular type might be able to know, for example. It is not satisfied by some we-know-not-what optimum of knowledge that falls short of knowing everything. If no being knows literally everything, no being is omniscient. If no being is omniscient, there is no God.

■ 2. THE DIVINE LIAR

Consider the following:

1. X does not believe that (1) is true.

For X we substitute any name or referring expression. For any such substitution we can ask whether (1) is true or false. If (1) is true, X does not believe it, and thus X cannot be said to know all truths. If X is false, it is false that X does not believe it. It must then be true that X believes it. X therefore believes a falsehood.

The trap is set. In light of (1), there is no X that can qualify as omniscient. For any candidate put forward, there will be a form of (1) that must be either true or false. But if true, the candidate cannot qualify as omniscient. If false, the candidate cannot qualify as omniscient. There can be no omniscient being, and thus can be no God.

■ 3. OMNISCIENCE AND THE KNOWER

It is clear that the problem above is constructed on the model of the liar. A second problem for omniscience follows the paradox of the knower.

Consider any formal system containing axioms adequate for arithmetic. Those axioms formalize statements as simple as the principle that every natural number has a successor, that zero is the successor of no natural number, and that addition and multiplication operate in the familiar way. We take such axioms to be true on their face. We take them to be true, moreover, because we take arithmetic to be true.

For any such system it is well known that we will be able to encode formulas recoverably as numbers. We will use $\bar{A}$ to refer to the numbered encoding for a formula A. It is well known that for any such system we will be able to define a derivability relation I such that $\vdash I(\bar{A}, \bar{B})$ just in case B) is derivable from A.

Let us introduce a symbol "∇" within such a system, applicable to numerical encodings $\dot{A}$ for formula A. We might introduce ∇ as a way of representing universal knowledge, for example—the knowledge of an omniscient being within at least the realm of this limited formal system. Given any such symbol with any such use we would clearly want to maintain each of the following:

If something is known by such a being, it is so: $\qquad \nabla(\bar{A}) \rightarrow A$

This fact is itself known by such a being: $\qquad \overline{\nabla(\nabla(\bar{A}) \rightarrow A)}$

If B is derivable from A in the system,

and A is known by such a being, then

B is known by such a being as well: $\qquad I(\bar{A}, \bar{B}) \rightarrow . \nabla(\bar{A}) \rightarrow \nabla(\bar{B})$.

The simple truth, however, well established as a logical theorem, is that no symbol can consistently mean what we have proposed ∇ to mean, even in a context as limited as formal systems of arithmetic.[2] The addition of these simple claims to any system containing basic truths of arithmetic would give us a contradiction.

Given the basic truths of arithmetic, omniscience is a contradictory concept. Because arithmetic is true, there is no omniscient being. Because arithmetic is necessarily true, no omniscient being is possible.

4. THE ESCAPE ROUTE OF HIERARCHY

Both of the problems raised to this point—both the knower and the divine liar—can be finessed by familiar hierarchical techniques. The proposal in Russell, in Tarski, in Kripke and in others is that truth and related predicates form a hierarchy of different levels, each of which applies only to statements (including statements involving truth) on lower levels.[3] On such an approach we can say that we know precisely what goes wrong with the divine liar and ∇: each attempts to apply a truth-related predicate beyond its hierarchically restricted reach. The formal charms of a hierarchical approach are many. But one thing such a route does not offer is any hope for the concept of omniscience. If truth forms a stratified hierarchy, there can be no notion that applies to truths on *all* levels. That is precisely the point of the appeal to hierarchy: were one to quantify over all levels, or to reinstitute a notion of "truth at any level," all the machinery would be in place to create the same logical problems in the same form. If hierarchy prohibits any notion of "truth on all levels," however, it also prohibits any notion of omniscience; knowledge of truth "on all levels" is precisely what the concept of omniscience would demand.

The appeal to hierarchy, though of logical interest and importance, offers no solution for the logical difficulties of omniscience.

5. THE CANTORIAN ARGUMENT

The beliefs of an omniscient being, we have said, would correspond precisely to a set of all and only true propositions. Because there can be no set of all and only true propositions, there cannot be what an omniscient being would have to know, and thus there can be no omniscient being.

The proof that there can be no set of all truths goes as follows. Consider any set of truths **T**:

$$\mathbf{T} = \{t_1, t_2, t_3, \ldots\}.[4]$$

And consider the elements of its power set PT, containing all subsets of T:

$\{\varnothing\}$
$\{t_1\}$
$\{t_2\}$
$\{t_3\}$

.
.
.

$\{t_1, t_2\}$
$\{t_1, t_3\}$

.
.
.

$\{t_1, t_2, t_3\}$

.
.
.

To each element of the power set there will correspond a unique truth—at least the truth that that element contains a particular truth t_1 as a member, for example, or that it does not contain t_1 as a member:

$$t_1 \in \{t_1, t_2, t_3\}$$
$$t_1 \notin \{t_2, t_3\}$$

By Cantor's theorem, we know that the power set of any set contains more members—it is larger, or has a greater cardinality—than the set itself. There will then be more truths than are contained in **T**. But **T** can be taken as *any* set of truths. For any set of truths, we can show that there are more truths than it contains. There can therefore be no set of *all* truths.

The Cantorian argument strikes at a crucial assumption essential to any notion of omniscience—that truth approaches some final totality or "all." That assumption is provably false. Truth explodes beyond any attempt to capture it as a totality, and that explosion takes the form of logical contradiction. There can therefore be no coherent notion of omniscience.

■ 6. THE CANTORIAN ARGUMENT EXTENDED

Is there no escape from the Cantorian argument? One might propose that truths form a "proper class" instead of a set, where important restrictions are placed on "classes." In a range of formal theories classes are introduced in such a way that we are prohibited from forming classes of classes in certain ways, thereby restricting the reach of the power set axiom.[5] But those maneuvers are widely recognized as both logically ad hoc and philosophically unsatisfying: some truth will undoubtedly hold regarding any bunch, cluster, or collection of truths, raising precisely the same problems as before.

A number of authors have suggested that the real target of the argument is not truths in their plurality, but the notion of truth as a "completed totality" in the singular. What if we think of truth as an inescapable "many" rather than a "one"? Richard Cartwright, D. A. Martin, Keith Simmons, and Alvin Plantinga have all made proposals along these lines.[6]

Although tempting, the appeal to truth as a "many" that cannot form a "one" turns out to be ineffective, because the core argument does not in any essential way depend on reference to a single set, class, or collection of all truths. It can be phrased directly in terms of a "many," entirely in the plural, and using only a notion of relations between things.[7]

For properties P_1 and P_2, the required formal properties of relations can be outlined as follows. Those things that are P_1 can be mapped one-to-one *into* those things that are P_2 just in case there is a relation R such that:

$$\forall x \forall y [P_1 x \wedge P_1 y \wedge \exists z(P_2 z \wedge Rxz \wedge Ryz) \rightarrow x = y]$$
$$\wedge \forall x [P_1 x \rightarrow \exists y \forall z(P_2 z \wedge Rxz \leftrightarrow z = y)].$$

Those things that are P_1 can be mapped one-to-one *onto* those things that are P_2 just in case (here we simply add a conjunct):

$$\forall x \forall y [P_1 x \wedge P_1 y \wedge \exists z(P_2 z \wedge Rxz \wedge Ryz) \rightarrow x = y] \wedge$$
$$\forall x [P_1 x \rightarrow \exists y \forall z(P_2 z \wedge Rxz \leftrightarrow z = y)]$$
$$\wedge \forall y [P_2 y \rightarrow \exists x(P_1 x \wedge Rxy)].$$

It will be true for some P_1 and P_2 that a mapping *into* is possible but a mapping *onto* is not; relative to the things that are P_1 there will be too many things that are P_2 to allow a full mapping of those things that are P_1 *onto* those things that are P_2.

Consider, then, any "many" truths you like—the truths that any particular being knows, for example. Consider also truths about one or more of those truths. Using the notions outlined above, phrased entirely in the plural, it is possible to show that the first truths can be mapped *into* but not *onto* the second truths. There are too many of the latter. No matter however many truths are at issue therefore, they cannot be *all* the truths. Appeal to a plural "many" rather than a single set—or class—like "one" offers no escape; it is still true that there can be no omniscient being.

7. THE OPTION OF NEW LOGICS

Given elementary logic, the inescapable conclusion is that omniscience is impossible. Any God would have to be omniscient. Given elementary logic, there can therefore be no God.

One way of phrasing the result is this: Within any logic we have, there can be no totality of truths. Within any logic we have, there can therefore be no omniscience. I think the qualifier "within any logic we have" deserves to be taken seriously. But it is not the simple escape route it might appear.

"Ah, within any logic we have...But perhaps within some new logic there *will* be a place for a totality of truths, and *will* be a place for omniscience." The problem with such a response is that it may be as empty as it is easy. In the face of *any* argument, however tight, in defense of *any* inconsistent concept, however clear the contradictions, one might *always* say, "Ah, within any logic we have...But perhaps within some new logic..." At this point in the discussion, therefore, such an appeal no more constitutes a genuine reply than does the same appeal in defense of square circles, married bachelors, or army intelligence. Within any logic we have, there can be no married bachelors. Within any logic we have, there can be no omniscient being.

What gives the invocation of new logics some greater bite in this case is that some initial steps have been taken in such a direction. In recent work, Nicholas Rescher and I have explored options for alternative logics regarding indeterminate collectivities.[8] Such collectivities would include semantically indeterminate collectivities such as "the world's foothills," indeterminate in membership because of the vagueness of the term "foothills." They would also include epistemically indeterminate collectivities such "people no-one knows ever existed." It is obvious that there are such people, but it is equally obvious we cannot specify them. Indeterminate collectivities will also include ontologically indeterminate collectivities such as the electrons in a particular lump of californium that will decay over the next minute. What is important for our purposes is the idea that indeterminate collectivities might include *logically* indeterminate collectivities as well.

Among logically indeterminate collectivities, we have proposed, might be "plena," envisaged explicitly as hypercardinal multiplicities with "number beyond number." The idea is to recognize plena as collectivities such that every subcollectivity s of a plenum P stands in unique correlation with some member of P itself. Using $\exists_s$ to stand for "exists in unique correlation with s," the definitional condition for plena P is then

$$(\forall s)(s \subset P \rightarrow (\exists_s x)\, x \in P).$$

So conceived, there would be a mapping of all subcollectivities of a plenum into its members, that is, a mapping m such that

$$(\forall s)(s \subset P \rightarrow (\exists x)(x \in P \,\&\, x = m(s) \wedge (\forall s')(s' \neq s \rightarrow m(s') \neq m(s)))).$$

If any sense is to be made of propositions, facts, or truths in full collective generality, it would have to be as plena. In full collective generality these would boast a characteristic that no set and no class can possibly satisfy—the condition of having as many elements as their power collectivities, precisely the definitional characterization of plena. For each subcollectivity of a plena of truths, for example, there will be a unique truth, and thus "more" elements of the plena than are evident at any point of comprehension. Plena would be precisely those multiplicities that refuse to cohere in some final totality, a completed "whole" or "all."

What "new logic" would be required to make room for plena and other indeterminate collectivities? There appear to be three possibilities.[9]

One alternative is to abandon the law of excluded middle, which plays a major role in all of the arguments above. One would have to recognize propositions that are neither true nor false, and would lose standard patterns of inference in consequence—the inference from the falsity of "X does not exist" to the truth of "X exists," for example. What is required is a *strong* abandonment of the law of excluded middle, not to be satisfied simply by the addition of a further "neutral" perhaps, for "neither true nor false." What is demanded is rather a logic in which there are semantic black holes: propositions with no semantic value at all, with the emphatic reminder that "having no semantic value" is not itself to be treated as a semantic value.

Within such a logic, it turns out, negation could no longer be exhaustive: one could not, for example, use "not P" to target *all* the cases in which P does not hold.

It is an indication of how drastic this first alternative is that a second alternative is no more drastic: the alternative of abandoning the law of contradiction instead.[10] On this second approach, there would be propositions that are *both* true and false. Proof of the truth of a proposition would therefore not entail that it might not be false as well. Proof of the truth of a theological claim would not guarantee that it might not be false nonetheless. In such a logic the notion of an exclusive negation would lose its grip: "not P" would no longer exclude P.

Those alternatives are each so drastic, it turns out, that a more comfortable logic may be one in which both the law of excluded middle and the law of contradiction fail to hold in full generality. In such a case there would be no univocal concept of negation, replaced instead with two negations—one exclusive but not exhaustive, the other exhaustive but not exclusive.

"Ah, within any logic we have omniscience proves impossible . . . but perhaps within some new logic . . ." As argued elsewhere, each of the deviant logics mentioned is worthy of further work, both formal and philosophical.[11] But even first steps make it clear that any such logic invokes a realm far stranger than might at first appear. The concept of omniscience, one might argue, is firmly embedded in a classical conception of the fabric of the universe that is woven using classical logic throughout. To try to save a concept of omniscience by abandoning the logic constitutive of its natural context would be far more destructive, entailing far more radical revisions even in theology, than to simply abandon the concept itself.

There is of course a further and far less drastic alternative. If truth and related predicates form a structured hierarchy, the Cantorian argument will lose traction much as did the knower and the divine liar. But structured hierarchy would come at the same cost here as before, essentially conceding the conclusion of the Cantorian argument. Given such a hierarchy, there will then be no concept that

applies to *all* truths, and correspondingly no coherent notion of omniscience.[12].
The problem of the essential indexical

Omniscience faces further logical difficulties, distinct from those above.
Primary among these is the problem of the essential indexical.

Consider a case borrowed from John Perry.[13] I follow a trail of spilled sugar
around and around a tall aisle in the supermarket in search of the shopper who
is making a mess. Suddenly I realize that the trail of sugar is spilling from a torn
sack in *my* cart and that *I* am the culprit—*I* am making a mess.

What I realize at that point is that

1. I am making a mess.
The interesting point is that this proposition is *not* the same as
2. Patrick Grim is making a mess,
nor can it be the same proposition as
3. *He* is making a mess,
where I am the "he" that is indicated.

We can easily construct cases in which I know (2) or (3) without knowing (1).
In an amnesia case I may know that Patrick Grim is making a mess without realizing that I am Patrick Grim, for example, and thus do not know (1). I may see
that *he* is making a mess—that oaf in the fish-eye mirror—without yet realizing
that oaf is *me*. What I know in knowing (2) or (3) therefore falls short of what I
know in knowing (1). The proposition expressed by (1) will not be adequately
captured by anything like (2) or (3).

Another clear indication that (2) and (3) express propositions different from
(1) is that (1) offers a complete explanation for things that (2) and (3) cannot.
When I stop myself short in the supermarket, gather up my broken sack, and
start to tidy up, my doing so may be quite fully explained by saying that I have
realized that I am making a mess. But it could not be fully explained by saying
that I realize either (2) or (3). In (1) "I" plays an essential indexical—essential
to what I know in knowing that I am making a mess. In order for (2) or (3) to
offer a full explanation for my behavior, I at least have to add the knowledge
that *I* am Patrick Grim, or that *I* am him—thereby reintroducing the essential
indexical "I."

The argument can be also be constructed for indexicals other than "I." What I
come to realize when I realize that the meeting is starting *now* is not simply what
others know when they know that the meeting starts at noon, expressed timelessly and without tense. The fact that I know the meeting is starting *now* fully
explains my hurry to gather up the required materials in my office. My knowing
that the meeting starts at noon would *not* explain that hurry…unless of course
we added that I also know that it is *now* noon, thereby reintroducing the temporal indexical. My knowing what I know now explains something that my knowing what others might know timelessly or at other times could not explain. The

two must therefore be different: what I know now is not merely what they know then. It follows that there are things known *now* that simply cannot be known timelessly.[14] We can run a similar argument using indexicals of place regarding my knowledge that the bomb is to fall *here*.

But let us return to the indexical "I." The closest others can come to knowing what I know in knowing (1) is knowing something like (2) or (3). But neither of these amounts to what I know in knowing (1). There are therefore things that I know—what I know when I know I am making a mess, for example—that no other being can know.

An omniscient being would know everything—certainly everything known by any being. But no being other than me can know some of the things that I know, and I am clearly not omniscient. There can therefore be no omniscient being.

9. INDEXICAL ESCAPE ROUTES

What options are open for the defender of omniscience in the face of the argument from essential indexicals? As indicated in the ground rules, I am not interested in any evasive or deflationary redefinition of "omniscience" as less than "omni," such that "knowing everything" could be satisfied by knowing significantly less.[15]

The only direct attack is to insist that another *could* know what I know in knowing that I am making a mess. There are indeed precedents for such a move in other work on indexicals. Consider, for example, the case in which I see the mess-maker in the fish-eye mirror at the end of the supermarket aisle and come to the conclusion that *he* is making the mess. My further realization a moment later that it is I who am making a mess, it has been proposed, involves not a new proposition, but a change of perspective. What differs, John Perry proposes, is not what is known, but simply the "belief state" in which it is known.[16]

On such an approach, omniscience might again seem possible. But what it would demand would ultimately be a notion of knowledge radically different than ours. When I suddenly realize that the man in the mirror is *me*, there is clearly something that I have learned. There is something that I didn't know before that I do know now. There is indeed a piece of crucial information that I have just acquired that I did not have before—the fact that it is *me* that is making a mess. All of these reflect our standard concept of knowledge. The simple fact that there *is* something that I learn, recognize, or come to realize in such a case is a fact to which no "belief state" account is capable of doing justice. On any such account it is emphatically not the case that there would be anything new to learn.

Similar comments apply to other indexicals. When it dawns on me not merely that the meeting starts at noon, but that it starts *now*, there is something that I come to realize for the first time. When I knew merely that the bomb was going to fall at a spot marked on the map, there was a crucial piece of information I lacked. What I didn't yet realize was that it was going to fall *here*.

We can also appeal to the fact that what I know carries over to other propositional attitudes. What I come to realize in the mess-making case is precisely the thing that I am then ashamed of—the fact that it is *me* that is making a mess. What I might not have believed before, what suddenly surprises me, and what I realize with a shock is that the meeting is starting *now*. What I come to know about the bomb's fall is precisely what I was afraid of—that it will fall *here*.

Given our concept of knowledge, and given the links of that concept with other propositional attitudes, it is not merely a "belief state" or a perspective that changes when I come to realize, for example, that it is *me* that is making a mess. At least part of what has changed is what I know. In the straightforward and familiar ontology of what is known, the argument from indexicals does show quite explicitly that no being can know what I know.

Omniscience is defined in terms of knowledge, taken in the standard and familiar sense. In that standard and familiar sense there can be no being that knows everything. There can be no omniscient being.

■ 10. AGAINST OMNISCIENCE

Logical problems regarding the concept of omniscience seem to me as close to a knock-down argument as one ever gets. Given our concept of knowledge and its objects, no being can know everything known; there can be no omniscient being. Within any logic we have, there can be no totality of truths. Omniscience is defined in terms of a totality of truths. There can thus be no omniscient being.

One might propose changing logics. One might propose changing concepts. But one might always attempt either of those evasive maneuvers in the face of *any* argument, however tight, for *any* conclusion, however solid. The logical problems facing omniscience seem to me as close to a knock-down argument as one ever gets.

There may be good reasons to explore alternative logics. But to abandon fundamental principles of classical logic in order to save a concept soaked through and through with the classical logic of classical theology would not seem to be among them. To change our concept of knowledge in order to save a concept of omniscience would seem futile; it would no longer be the standard concept of omniscience one would be saving.

■ NOTES

1. See Patrick Grim, "Some Neglected Problems of Omniscience," *American Philosophical Quarterly* 20 (1983): 265–277.

2. For details, see David Kaplan and Richard Montague, "A Paradox Regained," *Notre Dame Journal of Formal Logic* I (1960): 79–90; C. Anthony Anderson, "The Paradox of the Knower," *Journal of Philosophy* 80 (1983): 338–355; and Patrick Grim, "Truth, Omniscience, and the Knower," *Philosophical Studies* 54 (1988): 9–41. A further Gödelian argument against omniscience appears in Patrick Grim, *The Incomplete Universe: Totality, Knowledge, and Truth* (Cambridge, MA: MIT Press, 1991), chap. 3. Nor will it suffice to envisage an omniscience operator in place of an omniscience predicate. See Patrick Grim, "Operators in the Paradox of the Knower," *Synthese* 94 (1993): 409–428.

3. Bertrand Russell, "Mathematical Logic as Based on the Theory of Types," (1908), in Jean van Heijenoort, *From Frege to Gödel: A Source Book in Mathematical Logic* (Cambridge, MA: Harvard University Press, 1967); Alred Tarski, "The Concept of Truth in Formalized Languages" (1935), in *Logic, Semantics, and Mathematics*, ed. John Corcoran, trans. J. H. Woodger (Indianapolis, IN: Hackett, 1983), 152–278; Saul Kripke, "Outline of a Theory of Truth," *Journal of Philosophy* 72 (1975): 690–715.

4. Despite the standard linear progression, there is no suggestion here that any such set be denumerable. The argument is generalizable to a "set of all truths" of any size.

5. Gary Mar proposes Quine's New Foundations (NF) as a class theory in which Cantor's theorem, and thus the Cantorian argument, will not hold ("Why 'Cantorian' Arguments against the Existence of God Do Not Work," *International Philosophical Quarterly* 33 (1993): 429–499). But the technical disappointments of NF are well known (see, e.g., J. B. Rosser and Hao Wang, "Non-standard Models for Formal Logic," *Journal of Symbolic Logic* 15 (1950): 113–129). Of greater philosophical importance in the present context is the fact, detailed below, that the argument can be phrased entirely in terms of intuitive principles regarding truth, without sets or classes.

6. Richard Cartwright, "Speaking of Everything," *Noûs* 28 (1994): 1–20; D. A. Martin, "Sets versus Classes," quoted in Keith Simmons, "On an Argument Against Omniscience," *Noûs* 27 (1993): 22–33; Alvin Plantinga and Patrick Grim, "Truth, Omniscience, and Cantorian Arguments: An Exchange," *Philosophical Studies* 71 (1993): 267–306.

7. It is true that relations are often instantiated in set theory in terms of ordered sets. But we can clearly think in terms of properties and relations independently of set-theoretic extensions.

8. Nicholas Rescher and Patrick Grim, *Beyond Sets: Toward a Theory of Collectivities* (Frankfurt: Ontos/Verlag, 2010); Rescher and Grim, "Plenum Theory," *Noûs* 42 (2008): 422–459, reprinted in Nicholas Rescher, *Being and Value* (Frankfurt: Ontos/Verlag, 2008).

9. Here I cannot go into detail. The interested reader is referred to chap. 6 of Rescher and Grim, *Beyond Sets*.

10. In classical logic, of course, the two are equivalent: $\forall p(p \lor \sim p) \leftrightarrow \sim\exists p(p \land \sim p)$. In alternative logics that equivalence will not generally hold, but abandonment of either demands major logical sacrifice.

11. See Rescher and Grim, *Beyond Sets*, especially chap. 6.

12. Prospects for other forms of hierarchy, no less surprising and perhaps not entirely distinct from abandonment of the law of excluded middle or law of contradiction, are discussed in Rescher and Grim, *Beyond Sets*.

13. John Perry, "The Problem of the Essential Indexical," *Noûs* 13 (1979): 3–21. Perry's argument is anticipated in "Hector-Neri Castañeda, "'He': A Study of the Logic of Self-Consciousness," *Ratio* 8 (1966): 130–157. See also David Lewis, "Attitudes de dicto and de se," *Philosophical Review* 88 (1979): 513–543.

14. It follows that no timeless being can be omniscient. Because that is a combinatory problem for multiple attributes, I put it aside here.

15. Yujin Nagasawa attempts precisely this type of definitional evasion: "Even if Grim is right in saying that God cannot know what I know," he claims, "there is no reason to accept his conclusion that God cannot be omniscient." Nagasawa's strategy, following the tracks of a similar strategy regarding omnipotence, is to redefine the term such that a being that knows all that a being of that kind can essentially know would qualify as omniscient. I object a move toward redefinition at all. But it's also true that on such an approach "omniscience" would come dirt cheap. A stone is essentially incapable of knowing anything. Were omniscience to require of a being knowing merely all that a being of that type could essentially know, any stone would qualify as omniscient. On such a redefinition, therefore, there would literally be as many omniscient beings as there are grains of sand on the beach. See Yujin Nagasawa, "Divine Omniscience and Knowledge de se," *International Journal for Philosophy of Religion* 53 (2003): 73–82.

16. John Perry, "Frege on Demonstratives," *Philosophical Review* 86 (1977): 474–487. See also Steven Boër and William Lycan, "Who, Me?" *Philosophical Review* 88 (1980): 427–466.

■ FOR FURTHER READING

Martin, M., ed. *The Cambridge Companion to Atheism*. Cambridge: Cambridge University Press, 2007.

Martin, M., and R. Monnier, eds. *The Impossibility of God*. Amherst, NY: Prometheus Books, 2003.

14 The Coherence of Omniscience

■ JEROME GELLMAN

The first order of business is providing a working definition for "omniscience":

(DO) S is *omniscient* iff for every proposition, p, if p is true then S knows that p; and S has no false beliefs.[1]

Two different claims go under the heading that "omniscience" is incoherent:

(O1) There exists an omniscient being entails impossibility.

And,

(O2) There is a proposition, P, (not entailed by *There exists an omniscient being*) which everyone should concede true, or to which theists are committed, such that P is inconsistent with *There exists an omniscient being*.

On (O2), when P is a proposition we should all affirm, *There exists an omniscient being* must be rejected. And when P is a proposition to which theists are committed, theists have incoherent beliefs if they believe in an omniscient being.[2]

Now it is easier to try proving (O1) or (O2) true rather than false. For the former it suffices to try finding one incoherence. But I cannot *prove* there is no incoherence, perhaps very deep, in *omniscience*, nor can I prove that there exists no proper P whatsoever for (O2).

Perhaps I could try to refute, in turn, existing arguments for (O1) and (O2), and declare *there exists an omniscient being* innocent until proven guilty. But I can do better. I can provide a way of approaching both extant arguments for incoherence and potential *future* ones. This gives no guarantee for the future. But, based on a proven track record with existing arguments against omniscience, it will show not only that omniscience is coherent *as far as we know*, but provide hope for future rebuttals as well. That is my task here.[3]

1. BERTRAND RUSSELL'S EXISTENTIAL CRISIS

In 1901, Bertrand Russell was shocked when he discovered the incoherence of "naïve set theory" (NST).

(NST) Any collection can constitute a well-defined set

is at the basis of set theory, including for Cantor and Frege. Russell discovered incoherence in set theory.[4] For example, "the set of all sets that are not members of themselves" defeated (NST). Set theory was incoherent, crushed as a branch of mathematics.[5]

At that point, Russell did not abandon set theory.[6] Instead, he sought a modified concept of sets that would enable the work for which "set theory" was needed. The key to his modification was Russell's ramified theory of types. This involved restrictions on what sorts of elements could be members of given sets, and required new axioms. From now on not *all* collections could be a set. Some criticized Russell for introducing unnecessary restrictions and balked at some of his new axioms. For example, Russell assumed the decidedly nonmathematical axiom that there exist an infinite number of objects, that is, nonsets (axiom of infinity). In due time, others, such as Quine, generated new axioms, avoiding the shortcomings of the ramified theory of types.[7] The concept "set" survived through diligent attention to the purposes of set theory by the ingenuity of successive modifications.

▪ 2. BACK TO OMNISCIENCE

There are lessons for omniscience from Russell's story:

1. The notion of omniscience is employed for specific purposes. To reach an adequate concept of omniscience we should attend to those purposes.
2. What should control the discussion of omniscience is whether a specific characterization serves the intended purposes.
3. We should not confuse a particular formulation of omniscience with the root idea we are trying to articulate. We are not to abandon "omniscience" because a particular articulation fails.
4. It might take time to advance to what we need for successfully pinning down "omniscience."

Applying these lessons we determine the purposes for endorsing omniscience. These purposes diverge between the theological/philosophical idea of God's knowledge and that of the religious life. Accordingly, I present two approaches for dealing with incoherence charges: one theological and the other religious. The first is my version of a theistically inclined "perfect being theology" and the other pertains to how God is conceived in the religious life. Each considers omniscience in its context and yields (with a few slipped-in assumptions) a "ramified theory of omniscience."

▪ 3. PERFECT BEING THEOLOGY

St. Anselm (1033–1109), in *Proslogion*, articulated "perfect being theology" (PBT). In PBT, Anselm's phrase "that than which no greater can be thought," is equivalent to "a perfect being," a being possessed of maximal possible greatness. In chapter 5 Anselm writes:

> What then are You, Lord God, You than whom nothing greater can be thought? ... What goodness, then, could be wanting to the supreme good, through which every good exists? Thus you are just, truthful, happy, and *whatever it is better to be than not to be*— for it is better to be just rather than unjust, and happy rather than unhappy.[8]

Following Anselm, PBT determines that knowledge is better to have than not, and the more knowledge the better. So PBT asserts:

(PK) A perfect being has perfect knowledge.

Similarly, PBT endorses:

(PP) A perfect being has perfect power.
(PG) A perfect being has perfect goodness.
(PD) A perfect being has perfect duration.
(PJ) A perfect being is perfectly just.

And, commonly:

(PE) A perfect being has its power, goodness, duration, and justice essentially.

A problem arises of inconsistencies between these. For example, (PP) seemingly entails that a perfect being has *power* to forget. Yet, the conjunction of (PE) with (PK) entails that a perfect being cannot forget, because a perfect being is perfect in knowledge essentially. The conjunction of (PE) with (PG) seemingly entails that a perfect being cannot sin while (PP) entails the opposite.

To avoid such inconsistencies, PBT should articulate the notion of a perfect being as

(PS) X is a perfect being iff there exists a *perfection-set* that X instantiates.

A *perfection-set* is a consistent set of attributes that as a whole confer maximal possible greatness. This means translating each of (PP) through (PE) as saying its attribute belongs in a perfection-set. Exactly what degree of each attribute is in a perfection-set is determined by weights to be given to each to add up together consistently to a maximally great being.

Applying (PS) to our above inconsistencies, determine the relative values of having the power to forget and lacking that power because of being essentially omniscient, as well as the relative values of not being able to sin because of being essentially good and being able to sin. The more valuable of the two wins out. In each case, by weighing incompatible attributes against one another we resolve the inconsistencies. Above all we should realize that a perfect being isn't sup-posed to be a freak circus performer who dazzles us by his "everything-tricks." It's not "Step right up folks! See the two-headed lady and the perfect being that does everything-tricks! Two for the price of one!" Rather, a perfect being instantiates a perfection-set, whatever it might be.

A warning: Anselm also says that God (our perfect being) is *greater* than can be thought. So, God has perfections we can't think of, and moreover, we cannot be sure that the perfections we ascribe are the right ones. If so, we cannot equate our conception of perfection with its actual instantiation. Nonetheless, we are to strive for epistemic goodness as much as possible within our human limitations and accept the reasonable assurance of our judgments.

3.1 Two objections

Problem 1. William Wainwright objects to a view similar to my PBT, asking "What if the incompatible attributes are equal in value?" and says that either one must maintain that this cannot happen or admit that PBT isn't fully determinate. But Wainwright protests that it is difficult to see how the first could be established and that the second "undercuts" the value of PBT.[9]

In reply, I concede that for all we know we will one day discover an inconsistency between attributes of equal value. Moreover, for all we know there exists more than one perfection-set, one that confers maximal possible greatness. So, PBT might turn out not to be an algorithm for defending omniscience. We should not be too bothered by this, though. The bare possibility of stalemated attributes and multiple perfection-sets does not undercut PBT now. Only discovering one of those will do that.

If there were multiple perfection-sets, how would one come to be instantiated rather than another? I imagine it would be a brute metaphysical fact that one perfection-set of many, if many there are, is instantiated. Or it would be a broadly logically necessary truth which perfection-set is instantiated.

But why worry about stalemated attributes and multiple perfection-sets now? We have no reason now to believe that there are such things. (Though there are debates about which is the perfection-set. See below.) In any case, even if there are, PBT can still be a decision tool in a great number of cases. So if PBT shows a positive track record, which I show below, we have reason to adopt it for facing incoherencies in omniscience.

Problem 2. Wainwright addresses the charge of opposing intuitions. Maybe there exist no multiple perfection-sets. Yet, there exist opposing intuitions about what goes into a perfection-set. People have different intuitions, moral and theological, about what makes for a "perfect being." This is so even though I restrict myself here to theistically inclined conceptions Epistemically, at least, we are faced with multiple perfection-sets. So PBT is ineffective in determining what a perfect being is.

My indirect reply: to get at the meaning of "omniscience," we must look at its context. In theology a good candidate for that context is PBT. So, PBT at least could provide a schema for what "omniscience" amounts to in theology, even if there is no unanimity. Also, at some level of abstraction there is wide agreement as to what makes for perfection, such as a kind of existence not had by any other being and degrees and types of power, knowledge, and goodness that together are unsurpassable in value.

My direct reply is given by Wainwright:

> If, after careful reflection, it still seems to me that [my intuition is correct about what attributes are perfections] it would appear reasonable for me to proceed on the assumption that they really *are* perfections. The ultimate test for each of us can only be our own best judgment. Our judgments, though, are irredeemably personal for, in the last analysis, we can only view the various pieces of evidence in the medium of [our *own*] primary mental experiences.

What Wainwright writes is especially true when you discern an epistemic advantage over your counterintuitionists. But this holds also in cases where you do not perceive an advantage. As Peter van Inwagen points out, everyone has many beliefs that somebody rejects, over whom they have no epistemic advantage. Yet, we consider it kosher to retain those beliefs.[10] I agree with Thomas Kelly when he concludes that

> the mere fact that others whom I acknowledge to be my equal with respect to intelligence, thoughtfulness, and acquaintance with the relevant data disagree with me about some issue does not undermine the rationality of my maintaining my own view.[11]

Given a good track record (shown below), PBT can be expected to yield some consensus on omniscience, and where it doesn't, because of conflicting intuitions, PBT still recommends itself as a schema for approaching theological omniscience in accordance with one's own intuitions.

Now it was quite natural for "naïve omniscience theory" to have translated (PK) as

> (PB-DO) S has the knowledge of a perfect being $=_{df}$ for every proposition p, if p is true then S knows p; and S believes no falsehoods,

or, as "omniscience," unaware of lurking problems. This was as natural as NST unwittingly assuming (NST). But just as a proper definition of a set was controlled by the purposes of set theory, "omniscience," theologically, is to be controlled by PBT.

4. RELIGIOUS CRITERIA FOR GOD'S KNOWLEDGE

An alternative control upon omniscience is from the religious life. The omniscient being of religion is God, and so we attend to the point of God's knowledge within religion. I will not make extravagant generalizations about "religion." Instead, I will concentrate on some central themes in the "Judeo–Christian–Islamic" tradition.

In that tradition, God's knowledge is needed for God to be an appropriate creator and designer of the universe, who controls and directs the natural world, knows the affairs of humans so deeply as to know our minds, rewards good deeds and admonishes the bad, and can be relied upon for the future. God's knowledge guarantees, along with other attributes, future salvation and is a reason for love and obedience.

Such divine knowledge occurs in Psalm 139: "You know my sitting down and my rising up, you understand my thought afar off. You measure my going about and my lying down, and are acquainted with all my ways." Hebrews 4:13 says: "And there is no creature hidden from His sight, but all things are naked and open to the eyes of Him to whom we must give account." And the Qur'an: "Thou knowest that which we hide and that which we proclaim. Nothing in the earth or in the heaven is hidden from Allah" (14:38).

The concept arising from these considerations could be expressed in naïve formulation as

(All-K) God knows *everything*!

while meaning that God knows *everything* required of God. In naïve omniscience theory it would have been natural to transform (All-K)'s "everything" into (DO), unaware of problems lying in ambush. But (All-K) should never have forgotten its roots in the religious life, and should refer back to that life for its unpacking. A proper unpacking of (All-K) for the religious life would be like this:

(R-DO) God is omniscient if and only if for every true proposition, p, that God needs to know to be true to be the…, God knows p; and God believes no falsehoods,

where the dots are to be filled with creator, designer, sustainer of the universe, source of salvation, rewarder of good, punisher of evil, and the like.

■ 5. FOUR ARGUMENTS AGAINST OMNISCIENCE

I turn to illustrate the two approaches.

5.1 Grim makes a mess

Patrick Grim has an argument against omniscience in the sense of (O2). Here are excerpts:

I follow a trail of spilled sugar around and around a tall aisle in the supermarket, in search of the shopper who is making a mess. Suddenly I realize that the trail of sugar that I have been following is spilling from a torn sack in my cart, and that I am the culprit—I am making a mess. What it is that I come to know at that point [is] traditionally regarded as the proposition that

(1) I am making a mess.

[(1)], moreover, is traditionally regarded as the same proposition as:

(3) Patrick Grim is making a mess.

What is known or expressed in terms of (1) and (3) is not the same. For the "I" of (1) is an essential indexical essential to what it is I know or express in knowing or expressing (1). When I stop myself short in the supermarket, gather up my broken sack, and start to tidy up, this may be quite fully explained by saying that I realize...what I express by (1). But it cannot be fully explained, or at least as fully explained, by saying that I realize that Patrick Grim is making a mess—what is expressed by (3). In order to give a realization on my part that Patrick Grim is making a mess the full explanatory force of my realization that I am making a mess, in fact, we would have to add that I know that I am Patrick Grim. And that, of course, is to reintroduce the indexical.

What is known or expressed in terms of (1), then...is not merely what is known or expressed without the indexical in terms of (3).

The indexical "I" is essential to what I know in knowing (1). But only I can use that "I" to index me—no being distinct from me can do so. I am not omniscient. But there is something that I know that no being distinct from me can know. Neither I nor any being distinct from me, then, is omniscient: there is no omniscient being.[12]

Much has been written about this argument.[13] Here, I step back to approach it from the perspectives of PBT and religion.

On PBT, before God (our perfect being) created humans, Grim's problem did not exist. The problem arose after creating persons. On PBT the question is which is better? Not creating persons and thereby not creating true inaccessible propositions or creating persons and thereby losing access to their self-reflexive propositions? Clearly it is better to create persons and lose access to their self-reflexive propositions than not to create them. Persons can enter into a supremely valuable relationship with a perfect being, and into good relationship with one another and the world, thereby creating great moral value. This greatly outweighs the loss. So, a perfection-set should include creation of self-reflexive beings, at the cost of not knowing every proposition.[14]

Hence, on PBT, even if Grim were correct, it would not follow that a perfect being would not have the knowledge required by a perfection-set. "Omniscience," in the "ramified" theory, means precisely that.

Now the religious reply. Even if Grim is right, for every X, and for every proposition with a self-reflexive essential indexical, like "I am making a mess," said by X, God *does* know that "X is making a mess," and "you are making a mess" said of X.

In one sense, God does *not* know "everything" that X knows since God does not know a proposition X knows. On the other hand, God will know everything X knows about X, only from a different perspective. God has infinite empathy with persons, so knows what it is like for X to know what X knows about herself down to her deepest thoughts and deepest embarrassments. Knowing the truth of the proposition X knows is irrelevant.

Similarly, Linda Zagzebski introduces the concept "omnisubjectivity":

> An omniscient being must have perfect total empathy with you and with all conscious beings. This is the property I call omnisubjectivity... An omnisubjective being would know everything you know or understand from living your life.[15]
>
> Suppose... the proposition expressed by (1) differs from the proposition expressed by (3), and only I can know (1). This is a problem... if omniscience entails knowing the truth-value of all propositions. But if the only difference between knowing (3) and knowing (1) is the point of view, it is reasonable to think that a being who knows (3) and who also perfectly empathizes with me when I know (1) knows everything I know when I know (1). This solution will not satisfy anyone who insists that an omniscient being must know the very same proposition I know... but I think that this account succeeds in preserving omniscience even if it does not succeed in preserving one traditional account of omniscience.[16]

Zagzebski's reply expresses a religious understanding of "omniscience," reflecting (R-DO). (PBT can argue similarly against Grim.)

5.2 What time is it?

An argument from essential temporal indexicals against omniscience (in the sense of (O2)) is due to Norman Kretzmann, who offered this crisp argument:[17]

(1) A perfect being is not subject to change.
(2) A perfect being knows everything.
(3) A being that knows everything always knows what time it is [at every time and time zone].
(4) A being that always knows what time it is is subject to change.
(5) A perfect being is subject to change.
(6) A perfect being is not a perfect being.

Therefore,

(7) There is no perfect being.

This type of argument goes back at least to the medieval Jewish philosopher Gersonides (1288–1344), who argued from God's immutability to God's lacking knowledge of changing objects.[18]

Kretzmann supports premise (1) with an argument of St. Thomas Aquinas (*Summa Theologica*, I, Q. 9, art. 1.):

> [God is immutable] because everything which is moved acquires something by its movement, and attains to what it had not attained previously. But since God is infinite, comprehending in Himself all the plenitude of perfection of all being, He cannot acquire anything new, nor extend Himself to anything whereto He was not extended previously. Hence movement in no way belongs to Him.

Aquinas argues that when something changes it acquires what it previously did not have. But a perfect being comprehends the "plenitude of perfection of all being," so there could never be anything missing that it did not have. Hence it cannot change.

From the perspective of PB, the argument should be judged faulty. At any moment a perfect being possesses the plenitude of perfection for *that* moment only if aware of the changing world in real time, including knowing the time. There is no moment when it "lacks" anything (pejoratively) from the plenitude of perfection, because the "plenitude" changes from moment to moment. That a perfect being does not know *now* what would be expressed at another time as what the time is "now" (i.e., then) does not entail any deficiency, and certainly does not entail "finiteness." The perfect being exists in its infinite fullness at each moment of time relative to what fullness is at that time.

Neither does knowing what time it is entail that a perfect being is not "full act" but mere potential (another Aquinas argument). It is "full act" each moment of time relative to what constitutes being full act at that time, including knowing what time it is. The only *potential* it has is to be perfect at every moment. Hardly a shortcoming. I conclude that a perfect being will be mutable and know what time it is.

I turn to the religious response, regarding God. Immutabilists like quoting Malachi 3.6, "I the Lord do not change," and James 1.17, "There is no variation or shadow of turning [in God]. They then conclude that the Bible teaches God's immutability. However, it should be clear that neither verse implies immutability.

Malachi 3 opens with God foretelling purging of the temple priests, as well as others, for their evil ways. The prophet then consoles the people with news that God will not consume the Israelites, but continue to be their God, because God does not change *with regard to his love for His people.*

The context in James is in the verses just preceding:

> Let no one say when he is tempted, "I am tempted by God"; for God cannot be tempted by evil, nor does He Himself tempt anyone.

Then:

> Do not be deceived, my beloved brethren. Every good gift and every perfect gift is from above, and comes down from the Father of lights, with whom there is no variation or shadow of turning.

God is said to not change with regard to *goodness*. God does not disappoint or zigzag. God, in Richard Swinburne's phrase, has a "constancy of character."[19] You can be sure that God will not tempt you, but will shower gifts upon you. Nothing more should be read into this verse.[20] Indeed, if the Bible is our guide, it is replete with stories that, literally, depict God as changing.

I conclude that the Bible does not teach God's immutability. On the contrary, the religious life requires a God who knows what time it is and everything about you and the changing world in real time. God empathizes with your pain while you feel it, and rejoices in your good deeds as you do them. This is a corollary of omnisubjectivity. For that reason Gersonides's saying that God has no knowledge of changing particulars was a religious dead end. And divine immutability never took hold in Judaism, despite Maimonides's and Gersonides's endorsement and its appearance in kabbalah. Kretzmann's argument fails.

5.3 Self-referential propositions

Patrick Grim argues for incoherence of omniscience (in sense (O1)) as follows:
Suppose that some being, God, let us say, is omniscient. And consider:

> 1. God believes that (1) is false.
>
> …Suppose first, then, that (1) is true. On that supposition, as (1) maintains, God believes that (1) is false. But we are supposing that (1) is true. So if (1) is true, God holds a false belief, and thus is not omniscient…Suppose instead, then, that (1) is false. On this supposition, since (1) maintains that God believes that (1) is false, it is false that God believes that (1) is false…But we have assumed that (1) is false, and thus there is a truth, that (1) is false, which God does not believe and hence does not know. So if (1) is false God is not omniscient either.[21]

Grim argues that (1) having no truth value will not help. Whether (1) be true or false, or neither, God, our perfect being, is not omniscient.

Philosophers have offered various rebuttals to Grim's argument.[22] On PBT, a perfect being can safely ignore having any opinion on (1). A perfect being has a degree of knowledge included in a perfection-set. Ignoring (1) does not make one any less perfect. Hence, since the proposition, on one horn of the argument, that "God does not believe and hence does not know" is (1), Grim's argument does not succeed in showing omniscience incoherent.

Similarly, the religious response, too, would reply that God's functioning in the life of a devotee does not hinge upon God addressing (1). Failing to do so does not diminish God's religious worthiness, according to (R-DO). God may safely ignore (1). Grim's argument fails.

5.4 God's vision

The fourth argument is a type (O1) argument. Here it is presented by Michal Martin, following an argument by Ronald Puccetti:[23]

> If P is omniscient, then P would have knowledge of all facts about the world: "Y". So if P is omniscient, then P knows Y. One of the facts included in Y is that P is omniscient. But in order to know that P is omniscient P would have to know:
>
> (Z) There are no facts unknown to P.
>
> Puccetti argues that Z cannot be known since Z is an unrestricted negative existential... Z is a negative existential that is completely uncircumscribed... God could not exhaustively search space and time because they are both infinite. No matter how long God searched there would be more space and time to search... Thus, for God to know that He knows all the facts located in space and time is impossible, and since omniscience entails such knowledge, omniscience is impossible.

It will not help to say that God knows (Z) because God created everything contingent. God could not know God was the creator of everything contingent without knowing (Z).

Similar reasoning applies to many negative existentials, such as that there are no sentient beings other than on earth. Also, God could not know the *number* of sentient beings in the universe. For PBT, God, our perfect being, should know such facts. In the religious life it is not clear that God must *know* that God is omniscient (in the sense of (R-DO)). But God must know negative existentials and be able to number things. So Puccetti's argument threatens both PBT and the religious life.

For PBT, I focus on the assumption that God, our perfect being, knows by "searching" or "seeing." Yes, Rabbi Akivah said: "All is seen."[24] Augustine said: "He sees all things simultaneously, and nothing is there which He does not see."[25] And one of Allah's 99 names is *al Basir*, "seer of all." Taking this "literally" might lead to supposing God knows only what God can "observe." Hence God could not know many negative existentials because God could not "see" what makes them true.[26]

But God's "seeing" is a metaphor. On PBT, God, a perfect being, does not know by drawing conclusions from observations. God's knowledge is not evidence based. In Puccetti's scenario God is beholden to what strikes his "eyes." That is not perfect knowledge. Rather, God has innate knowledge, based on a built-in infallible (hence maximally reliable) "mechanism" that permanently and directly grants God knowledge. God does not infer truths. They are "in" God all together. Thus God knows (Z) and all true negative existentials. For sure, such a metaphysical mechanism is mysterious and wondrous; this is, after all, *God*.

But there is nothing incoherent about an innate infallibly reliable mechanism. I conclude that Puccetti's argument fails for PBT.

In the religious life it is not initially apparent that God's knowledge should be as in PBT. Perhaps it does not matter how God knows as long as He knows. But Puccetti impugns the religious definition of omniscience by barring many negative existentials from God's knowledge. So the religious life should do whatever it takes to protect (R-O) and go along with PBT on this. So Puccetti's argument fails.

■ 6. CONCLUSION

I have presented four arguments against omniscience and have illustrated two methods for defusing them, from PBT and the purposes of religious life. The hope is that you can invoke them successfully against future arguments. But perhaps you disapprove of my methods. Then you might find yourself stuck with omniscience incoherencies. I would urge you then to reconsider my approaches so as to advance the coherence of omniscience. Or maybe you don't accept my judgments in PBT as to what would be better for a perfect being to be or not be. Again, you might find yourself stuck with incoherencies. At that point, I would invite you not to give up but seek an improved, more sophisticated approach to omniscience. All in the spirit of Bertrand Russell.[27]

■ NOTES

1. The second clause of the right side is unnecessary if it is impossible to hold contradictory beliefs. But I have held contradictory beliefs. So it is possible and the second clause necessary.

2. Perhaps the most famous P is: "Human beings have free will." This is supposed to be inconsistent with omniscience. Since there is a dispute about an omniscient being knowing the future ("open theism" says, "No"), and since the argument has intricacies beyond the scope of this chapter, I leave that P aside. For open theism, see Clark Pinnock et al., *The Openness of God* (Downers Grove, IL: InterVarsity Press, 1994).

3. What follows is in part a development of Jerome Gellman, "The Paradox of Omnipotence, and Perfection," *Sophia* 14 (1975): 31–39; Gellman, "Omnipotence and Impeccability," *The New Scholasticism* 51 (1977): 151–161; Gellman, "Limits of Maximal Power," *Philosophical Studies* 55 (1989): 329–36; and Gellman, *Experience of God and the Rationality of Theistic Belief* (Ithaca, NY: Cornell University Press, 1997), chap. 6. See also George Schlesinger, "Divine Perfection," *Religious Studies* 21 (1985): 147–158; and Schlesinger, *New Perspectives on Old-Time Religion* (Oxford: Oxford University Press, 1988).

4. Bertrand Russell, "My Mental Development," in *The Philosophy of Bertrand Russell*, 3rd ed., ed. Paul Arthur Schilpp, 3–20, especially 13 (New York: Tudor, 1951); and Russell, *My Philosophical Development* (London: Routledge, 1995), 58ff.

5. Truth be told, around the same time, Cantor discovered other inconsistencies in prevailing set theory.

6. Reportedly Frege became deeply despondent over the problem.

7. See W. V. Quine, "New Foundations for Mathematical Logic," in *From a Logical Point of View*, 2nd rev. ed. (Cambridge, MA: Harvard University Press, 1980), 80–101.

8. My emphasis. Anselm, *St. Anselm's Proslogion*, trans. M. J. Charlesworth (Notre Dame, IN: University of Notre Dame, 1979), 121.

9. William Wainwright, "Two (or Maybe One and a Half) Cheers for Perfect Being Theology," *Philo* 12, no. 2 (2009): 228–251.

10. Peter van Inwagen, "It is Wrong, Always, Everywhere, and for Anyone, to Believe Anything, Upon Insufficient Evidence," in *Faith, Freedom, and Rationality*, ed. Jeff Jordan and Daniel Howard-Snyder, 137–154 (Lanham, MD: Rowman and Littlefield, 1996).

11. Thomas Kelly, "The Epistemic Significance of Disagreement," *Oxford Studies in Epistemology* 1 (2005): 167–195.

12. Patrick Grim, "Some Neglected Problems of Omniscience," *American Philosophical Quarterly* 20, no. 3 (1983): 272.

13. See John E. Abbruzzese, "Against Omniscience. The Case from Essential Indexicals," *International Journal for Philosophy of Religion* 41 (1997): 25–34.

14. One might protest that the creation of persons was *not* good because it resulted in vast unjustified evil. We need not grant that unjustified evil exists. But even if we do, this protest errs. I have said that it is better *to* create persons with self-reflexive knowledge and to lose one's access to their self-reflexive propositions than not to create them. That is consistent with saying that a perfect being *should not* have created the persons of *our world* because the good was outweighed by the evil; not because creating persons per se was not good.

15. Linda Zagzebski, "Omnisubjectivity," 14"Omnisubjectivity," *Oxford Studies in Philosophy of Religion*, 1, Jonathan Kvanvig, editor (Oxford: Oxford University Press, 2006), 231–248. See also S. Torre, "De Se Knowledge and the Possibility of an Omniscient Being," *Faith and Philosophy* 23 (2006): 191–200.

16. Zagzebski, "Omnisubjectivity," 17.

17. Norman Kretzmann, "Omniscience and Immutability," *Journal of Philosophy*, 63 (1966): 409–421.

18. See T. M. Rudavsky, "Divine Omniscience and Future Contingents in Gersonides," *Journal of the History of Philosophy* 21 (1983): 513–536.

19. Richard Swinburne, *The Coherence of Theism* (Oxford: Oxford University Press, 1997).

20. For a defense of this reading, see I. A. Dorner, *Divine Immutability: A Critical Reconsideration* (Minneapolis: Fortress Press, 1994).

21. Grim, "Some Neglected Problems of Omniscience," 267. Grim presents a cluster of arguments similar to this one, involving sentential self-reference. On PBT, they are to be handled in a similar way to what transpires below.

22. For a good review of the literature, see Abbruzzese, "Against Omniscience."

23. Michael Martin, *Atheism, A Philosophical Justification* (Philadelphia: Temple University, 1990), 294–295; Ronald Puccetti, "Is Omniscience Possible?" *Australasian Journal of Philosophy* 41 (1963): 92–93.

24. Avot, Chapter 3, Mishnah 15. My translation from the Hebrew.

25. Augustine, *Trinity, The Fathers of the Church*, Volume 45, Translated Stephen McKenna, C.SS.R (Washington: Catholic University of America, 1963), p. 487.

26. God having infinite sight won't help since God must know that about God. But God, so it goes, could not know that since it is not knowable by "seeing" that it *is* infinite.

27. I am grateful to William Wainwright for his advice on PBT.

■ FOR FURTHER READING

Morris, T. V. *Anselmian Explorations*. Notre Dame: University of Notre Dame Press, 1987.

Plantinga, A., and P. Grim. "Truth, Omniscience, and Cantorian Arguments: An Exchange." *Philosophical Studies* 71 (1993): 267–306.

Simmons, K. "On an Argument Against Omniscience." *Noûs* 27 (1993): 22–33.

Wainwright, W. "Omnipotence, Omniscience, and Omnipresence." In *The Cambridge Companion to Philosophical Theology*, ed. C. Taliaferro and C. Meister, 46–65. Cambridge: Cambridge University Press, 2010.

Wainwright, W. "Two (or Maybe One and a Half) Cheers for Perfect Being Theology." *Philo*, 12, (2009): p. 238.

Wierenga, E. "Omniscience." In *The Oxford Handbook of Philosophical Theology*, ed. T. Flint and M. Rea, 129–144. Oxford: Oxford University Press, 2009.

The Problem of Evil

15 Evil as Evidence Against God

■ RICHARD M. GALE

It will be argued that traditional theists—those who believe that there exists an omnipotent, omniscient, omnibenevolent, and providential God—have yet to succeed in showing that the known evils of the world do not constitute good evidence against the existence of this God. Theists have employed two quite different strategies to neutralize the challenge of evil. The first is to construct theodicies that show that it is likely, or at least not implausible, that God has a morally exonerating excuse for allowing evil. The second is that of theistic skepticism, that holds there to be too big a cognitive gap between our minds and God's for us to be able to fathom his morally exonerating reasons for permitting evil. Both will be discussed in turn.

1. THEODICIES

What, in general, is an evil and what are the different types of evil? An evil is something that, taken by itself in isolation, is an ought-not-to-be, an "Oh, no!" Examples are physical and mental suffering by a sentient being, including lower animals, immoral action, bad character, and a privation in which something fails to measure up to what it ought to be, such as a human being born blind. The qualification "taken by itself" is important, since some evils are justified because they are a so-called blessing in disguise, being necessary for the realization of an outweighing good or prevention of an even greater evil. As members of such a larger whole, they are not an ought-not-to-be. A distinction that will play a crucial role in our discussion of evil is between justified and unjustified evils. A justified evil is one for which God, were he to exist, would have a morally exonerating excuse for causing or permitting it. An evil can be both justified and gratuitous, as, for example, a merited punishment that is not necessary for the realization of an outweighing good or prevention of an even greater evil. Another important distinction is between natural and moral evil, the latter, unlike the former, being attributable to the misuse of free will by finite creatures. Some theists refuse to call anything but moral evil or wickedness an evil, thereby eliminating natural evils as challenges to theism. This linguistic maneuver, however, accomplishes nothing, for the problem still remains as to how God could be justified in permitting suffering that is not attributable to the misuse of free will by finite creatures. To accommodate this redefinition of "evil," natural evils could be called "schmevils," the problem now being how God could be justified in allowing there to be schmevils.

We must not fall prey to the divide and conquer demand that one theodicy applies to every type of evil. All that is required is that for every type of evil there is a theodicy that applies to it. Given the great variety of evils, we should not be surprised that there are a variety of different theodicies. But must there be a theodicy for every known *instance* of every *type* of evil? No theodicist has claimed to be able to do this, but if a theodicy can be found for many instances of a given type of evil, it at least gives the theist some basis for having hope that it can be done for every instance of that type of evil as well. There is an important distinction between what I will call "internal" and "external" theodicies. The former makes use of some tenet that is unique to some theistic creed, whereas the latter does not. Unless an internal theodicy can give some arguments for the theistic tenets it employs, the theodicy is nothing more than a defense, which is a description of a possible world in which God has a morally exonerating excuse for permitting the evil in question sans any argument for this possible exonerating condition obtaining in the actual world.

1.1 External theodicies

If there is an infinite regress of worlds with respect to goodness, and it is plausible to think that there is, God cannot be blamed for creating a world that is inferior to another world he could have created. For this charge can be leveled no matter what world God creates, and an objection that applies in every possible case is not much of an objection. But it has been ingeniously argued by Robert M. Adams that even if there were a uniquely best of all possible worlds, God would not be morally obligated to actualize it, since by actualizing less good creatures than he could have he is bestowing grace upon them, that is, bestowing a benefit without consideration of merit, and grace is recognized by all to be a virtue. This seems plausible when confined to nonmoral goodness such as beauty, athletic ability, and the like, but is highly dubious if it is moral goodness that is in question. But one thing is for sure: *There cannot be any unjustified evil in a world that God actualizes.*

The most horrendous evils are moral evils that result from man's inhumanity to man. The free will theodicy (FWT) has attempted to show that it is not implausible that there is available to God, were he to exist, a morally exonerating excuse for permitting these moral evils. The first premise is that there exist persons who perform free actions in the libertarian sense of not being determined by anything external to them to so act. The second premise is that these persons for the most part freely do what is morally right, thus resulting in a favorable balance of moral good over moral evil. The third premise claims that there is such great value to free will that it is better to have free agents who for the most part freely go right than not to have any free agents at all. The fourth premise is that it is not implausible to believe that God is unlucky because any free agent he would create would freely go wrong at least once. From these four premises it is inferred that God, were he to exist, would have a morally exonerating excuse for permitting moral evil, given that it is the price that he must pay to have any free persons at all in existence.

There are currently three different versions of the God-could-be-unlucky premise. According to Alvin Plantinga, God knows in advance of his creating a free person what actions this person will freely perform; however, he does not determine that they will so act, for, were he to do so, he would, according to the libertarian theory of freedom, render these actions unfree. The problem for this version of the FWT is that by having God act with foreknowledge of what will result from his action, he determines the result. Thus Plantinga's God determines every creaturely free action. And this is freedom canceling.

The other two versions have God creating free persons without foreknowing what they will freely do, thereby making him blameless for moral evil due to excusable ignorance. According to Robert M. Adams's version, there was no prior fact of the matter as to what various types of persons would do with their free will, and thus there was nothing for God to know. Richard Swinburne's version of how God could be unlucky holds that there is a prior fact of the matter as to what various types of persons would do with their free will; however, God, in spite of his being omniscient, is unable to know these facts in advance of his creative decision. For, if he were to know it and create free persons, he would be usurping their freedom for the reason just given. And it is essential to God that he is able to create free persons.

It has been objected to both excusable-ignorance versions of the FWT that God is blameworthy for acting recklessly in creating free persons without knowing what will result. This objection abuses our concept of recklessness. One acts recklessly when she fails to properly investigate what the consequences of her action will be. But in the case of God's creation of free persons, no investigation could have determined the consequences. Still, it might be objected that he should not have run the risk of creating free persons without prior assurance of what would result. This is a very wimpy objection. Given the great value of there being free creatures, God was justified in rolling the dice.

The problem for the FWT, in all three of its versions, is that it cannot be successfully applied to the more horrendous instances of moral evil, such as slavery, the Holocaust, and the case of the six-year-old girl, Sue, who is raped, tortured, and killed. Isn't God blameworthy for these evils, since he created people with the freedom to do these horrible things and even determined that they would have strong dispositions and inclinations to do so? Shouldn't he have desisted from creating persons who are strongly disposed to do these horrible things, or at least stepped in at a certain point and rescinded his gift of free will to the monsters that perpetuated these evils? At a minimum, shouldn't he have prevented their evil choices and actions from causing suffering to innocents?

Swinburne answers "no" to these questions by appeal to a very dramatic sort of free will in which the chooser is strongly tempted to make the immoral choice. In his *Providence and the Problem of Evil* he writes that "fairly clearly to do good out of very serious free will despite strong contrary temptation is the best exercise of choice" and "to have a free choice between a greater and lesser good, they need a desire for the lesser good stronger than that for the greater good."[1] As for our having the freedom to harm innocents, as in the case of Sue, it is good that God gave us "the very deep responsibility for how long others live...It is a mark of supreme trust to allow someone to have a gun. If God made this world, he made a world with many guns."[2] Many will think that something has gone wrong with a theodicy when it reads like a National Rifle Association bumper sticker. Swinburne has earned himself the distinction of being the Charlton Heston of philosophy. Swinburne's claim that it is good that Sue's murderer had a strong temptation or desire to do what he did to her flies in the face of the moral intuitions that guide our social policies and practices, for we do our best to reform persons who face such temptations and prevent others from having them, thereby preventing them from being free with respect to such actions that can bring great harm to innocent persons. Obviously Swinburne does not take seriously the plea in the Lord's Prayer to "lead us not in to temptation."

Another way that Swinburne tries to justify horrendous moral evils is by their opening up dramatic possibilities for others to exercise their free will in combating them. "The sufferings and deaths in the concentration camps...made possible serious heroic choices...and they make possible reactions of courage (e.g. by the victims), of compassion, sympathy, penitence, reforms, avoidance of repetition, etc., by others."[3] Slavery "made possible innumerable opportunities for very large numbers of people to contribute or not to contribute to the development of this culture."[4]

Yet another way in which Swinburne justifies God's allowing the innocent to suffer is by appeal to the service-to-others theodicy. "It would have been our misfortunate if there had been no starving...All the ways in which the suffering of *A* is beneficial for *B* are also beneficial for *A*—because *A* is privileged to be of use."[5] This theodicy would not apply to a person whose life is a living hell, no matter how much it is of service to others. Herein appeal must be made to Christian revelation that there is an afterlife in which due compensation is given to these unfortunates and, moreover, a compensation that requires their prior suffering. But without adequate evidential support, this theodicy is nothing more than a defense. Swinburne applies his service-to-others theodicy even to natural evils, such as a deer dying painfully in a forest fire. He holds that it is quite possible that this served as a lesson to other animals as to how to avoid such a fate in the future, and likewise Sue's murder may help to spur the passage of stronger laws against sexual predators.

Swinburne's theodicies read like a parody of the greater good theodicy, being on a par with "if he hadn't burned down his house in a drunken stupor killing his wife and five children, he never would have given up drinking" or "if it weren't for the perverse foreign policy of the United States in Southeast Asia during the sixties and seventies, we wouldn't be able today to buy delicious sate chicken for $3.50 from a roadside Vietnamese vendor in most American cities." Unfortunately Swinburne did not intend his theodicies as a joke.

Yet another instance of Swinburne's Charlton Heston–type theodicy is given for God's allowing great amounts of animal suffering as a result of the law of the survival of the fittest that drives evolutionary development. He glibly says that "the redness of nature 'in tooth and claw' is the red badge of courage."[6]

Axiological problems arise also with aesthetic versions of the greater good theodicy in which evils are justified because they contribute to the greater beauty or aesthetic merit of the whole universe. It is good that there is consumption, for if there weren't, Verdi never would have written *La Traviata* and Puccini *La Boehme*. Only someone possessed of an Oscar Wilde–type mentality that makes aesthetic values the summum bonum would find this plausible. If he hadn't burned down his house in a drunken stupor killing his wife and five children, he never would have given up drinking. This looks like more sate chicken for $3.50. Sometimes in the greater-good theodicy, as in the case of Leibniz, evil is justified because it is necessary for realizing the summum bonum of having a world that realizes the maximum number of possibilities with the simplest scientific laws. This conception of goodness is quite remote from traditional theism's conception of God's benevolence. Leibniz's God certainly is neither the personal God depicted in the scriptures nor a God that is eminently worthy of adoration, love, respect, and obedience.

Another misbegotten theodicy is the significant contrast one, according to which we humans would not be able to notice and appreciate the good unless we had contrastive experiences of evil. For the sake of argument, let us assume that this is a fact about our psychology. But God did not have to create so many evils, since one experienced instance would do the trick, and the needed contrastive experience, moreover, need not be of a real-life one, but of one depicted in a movie. He could have satisfied the need for significant contrast by showing us a video of unreal evils. Furthermore, this fact about our psychology seems to be a contingent one, thus allowing for God to have created us with a psychology that would enable us to notice and appreciate good without having any contrastive experience.

1.2 Internal theodicies

An internal theodicy employs some premise that is unique to some religious creed, and without some argument for the truth of this premise the theodicy is only a defense. It would be unfair, however, to charge every internal theodicy with being a trivial exercise of begging the question against the nontheistic opponent of the theodicy. An example of a trivial internal theodicy is

> God exists.
> If God exists, there are no unjustified evils. Therefore,
> All evils are justified.

But many internal theodicies are far from trivial, since they show how various tenets of a theistic creed in an unobvious way supply us with the resources of combating the challenge of evil. The following are some examples of nontrivial internal theodicies.

Plantinga, in a public discussion of evil, advanced this greatest story ever told internal theodicy.[7]

> Any world with incarnation and atonement is a better world than any without it.
> All worlds with incarnation and atonement must contain evil. Therefore,
> Evil is justified.

Obviously the atheist, as well as the non-Christian theist, would not grant the first premise. There are several current internal theodicies that make a similar appeal to Biblical revelation.

Peter van Inwagen's fundamentalist theodicy holds that evil is a result of the first generation of humans freely rebelling against God, with their ruin being inherited by all of their descendants.[8] There is no attempt to show that the descendants are in any way blameworthy or morally responsible for these sins, and yet they are the victims of this hereditary ruin. But this seems unfair in the same way as it is to keep in the whole class for the misdeeds of a single person. The whole idea of a deity who is so vain that if his children do not choose to love and obey him will bring down all sorts of horrible evils on them and their innocent descendants elicits horror from many who would ask what we would think about a human father who treated his children in this way. Like Iago's "Credo" in Verdi's *Otello*, van Inwagen seems to believe in a cruel and vengeful god.

Van Inwagen adds yet another seeming moral horror to his fundamentalist theodicy. One of the ways in which God makes it clear that man cannot live apart from him is to create a system of chance evils, the victims of which can be and often are innocent persons, such as Sue. Among the natural consequences of the fall is the following evil state of affairs: Horrors happen to people without any relation to desert. They happen simply as a matter of chance. It is a part of God's plan of atonement that we realize that a natural consequence of our living to ourselves is our living in a world that has that feature. Van Inwagen papers over the problem of fairness by the following referential equivocation.[9] We complain that some of us—quite often the good and wise and innocent—fall into the pits. God's response to this complaint is this: *You* are the ones who made yourselves blind, in which the pits represent chance evils and our being blind represents our being defenseless before these evils as a result of hereditary ruin. The use of "we" refers to the innocent descendants of the original culprits who are doing the complaining, but the use of "You" by God refers to the original perpetrators. Herein God is depicted as confounding the perpetrators with their innocent descendants, which is surprising given his omniscience. (I suspect that the equivocation is the fault of van Inwagen rather than God.)

Eleonore Stump has espoused a theodicy that is a close cousin to van Inwagen's in that it too is based on original sin.[10] God brings about natural evils so as to help us achieve salvation, which we do by entering into the proper relationship with him. Our wills have been damaged by original sin and have turned away from God. Natural evils help to realign our wills so that they will again be directed toward serving God by reminding us that we are unable to make it on our own. They humble us by reminding us of how vulnerable and fragile we are, which will aid our coming back to our Lord. They are, however, mere aids; for if they alone were enough to determine that our wills would become directed toward God, this turning of our wills would not be done freely, which is not what God wants. He wants us to freely elect to return to him. Again, the problem is whether a god who has these moral attributes is eminently worthy of love and worship although not unfit to be eminently worthy of being feared and obeyed—a supernatural Al Capone.

Not all theodicies suffer from dubious axiological assignments either to God or worldly states. Some of them appeal to distinctively Christian values, but that alone should not render them nonstarters. An example is the redemptive suffering theodicy of Marilyn McCord Adams.[11] It is based upon the value of martyrdom, which then is extrapolatable to some but not all other types of suffering. Through being successfully tested in her faith, the martyr builds a closer relation of trust with her God. Furthermore, through suffering one gets a vision into the inner life of God incarnate on the cross. This theodicy has a limited application, doing nothing to address the cases of Sue and Bambi.

2. THEISTIC SKEPTICISM

Theistic skepticism attempts to rebut William Rowe's inductive argument that infers from the fact that we humans, after long and exhaustive investigation, have not discovered any reasons that would justify God' permitting the known horrendous evils of the world, that it is probable that God does not exist or, at least, that the probability of his existence is lessened by this failure.[12] Because our imaginative and cognitive powers are so radically limited, we are not warranted in inferring that there are not or probably are not God-justifying reasons for evils. Theistic skepticism involves our inability, first, to access the divine mind so as to determine the different sorts of reasons that God could have for permitting evil, and second, because of our woefully limited knowledge of history, especially the future, whether these evils are necessary for the realization of an outweighing good.

Rowe's argument mistakenly assumes that we are up to divining every possible God-justifying reason for permitting evil. As Stephen Wykstra put it, God's reasons are no-see-ums for us.[13] If you carefully inspect a room and fail to detect a zebra, it is reasonable for you to inductively infer that there is no zebra in the room. But if you were trying to detect an ammonia molecule in the room, your failure to find it by unaided observation would not justify your inference that no ammonia molecule is in the room. The Divine mind is the ultimate no-see-um for us, regardless of what instruments of detection we employ. Our minds are to God's as a one-month-old baby's is to an adult's mind. It is contended that a universe created by God would likely have great moral depth in that many of the goods below its puzzling observable surface, many of the moral causes of God's current allowing and intervenings, would be "deep" moral goods. William Alston develops an analogy between the physical world and morality in respect to their having a hidden nature that is gradually brought to light by painstaking investigation.[14]

This analogy appears strained. To discover the hidden nature of gold—its molecular structure—required a long-term, sustained inquiry. But no analogous inquiry was required to unearth the hidden nature of morality, for a hidden morality is no morality. That morality be on the surface, common knowledge of all, is an empirical presupposition for our engaging in our social moral practices, the purpose of which is to enable us to modify and control each other's conduct by the use of generally accepted rules and principles of moral evaluation, thereby effecting more satisfactory social interactions. It also is required for our entering into relationships of love and friendship with each other. Such relationships require significant commonality of purposes, values, sympathies, ways of thinking and acting, and the like.

Many objections have been lodged against theistic skepticism. First, it is reasonably believed only in worlds in which the inhabitants have good evidence that their world overall is a good one. If all they ever experienced were horrendous evil sans any good, it would not be reasonable for them to attempt the evidential challenge of evil through theistic skepticism. Thus the theistic skeptic has the burden of showing that our world overall is a good one.

Second, theistic skepticism precludes the theist from employing teleological arguments, although not ontological and cosmological arguments; for if the bad things about the world should not be evidence against the existence of God, the good things should not count in favor of his existence. Teleological arguments turn into two-edge swords. Maybe the good aspects of the world that these arguments appeal to are produced by a malevolent deity so as to highlight evil or because they are necessary for the realization of an outweighing evil, and so on for all the other demonodicies.

The most serious problem for theistic skepticism is that it seems to require that we become complete moral skeptics. Should we be horrified at what happened to Sue? Should we have tried to prevent it or take steps to prevent similar incidents in the future? Who knows?! For all we can tell it might be a blessing in disguise or serve some God-justifying reason that is too "deep" for us to access: for example, it might be a merited Divine punishment for some misdeed that Sue will commit in the after-life. The result of this moral skepticism is paralysis of the will, since we can have no reason for acting, given that we are completely in the dark whether the consequences of our action are good or bad.

Another objection concerns whether theistic skepticism allows for there to be a meaningful personal love relation with God. The problem concerns whether we humans can have such a relation with a being whose mind so completely transcends ours, who is so inscrutable with respect to his values, reasons, and intentions. Not all kinds of moral inscrutability preclude a love relationship. It is important to distinguish between the moral rules and principles employed by a person and the manner in which she applies them to specific cases based on her knowledge of the relevant circumstances, this being a casuistic issue. A distinction can be made between moral principle inscrutability and casuistic inscrutability. That another person is casuistically inscrutable to us need not prevent our entering into a communal love relationship with it, provided it is far more knowledgeable than us about relevant worldly conditions, as is God, an omniscient being. But moral principle inscrutability of a certain sort does rule out such a relationship. Although we need not understand all of the beloved's moral reasons for her behavior, it must be the case that, for the most part, we do in respect to behavior, which vitally affects ourselves. One thing, and maybe the only thing, that can be said in favor of the theodicy favored by fundamentalists according to which evil results from the Fall and are messages from God to show us how lost we are without him, is that it does not run afoul of this requirement. We can hardly love someone who intentionally hurts us and keeps his reasons a secret unless for the most part we know his reasons for affecting us as he does and moreover know that they are benevolent. The answer to Plantinga's rhetorical question that if God did have a reason for permitting evil, why should we be the first to know is that we should be for those that vitally concern us. The sort of personal relationship we are supposed to have with God according to theism requires that God does not leave us in the dark with respect to these kinds of evils; for in a personal relationship one person should not bring harm to the other without informing him or her of the reason for doing so. In the case of the evils that have resulted from original sin, God has not kept it a secret as to why he is causing great evils to the progeny of Adam and Eve.

Making God so inscrutable also raises a threat that theism thereby will turn out to be falsified or, if not falsified, rendered meaningless. Several atheists, including Michael Scriven and Theodore Drange, have used the hiddenness of

God as the basis for an argument against his existence.[15] There is, they say, a presumption of atheism so that no news is bad news. Numerous quotations from the Bible are assembled in which it is said that God's intention in creating men was so that they would come to know of his existence and worship, obey, and enter into a communal loving relation with him. Thus if we do not have good evidence that God exists because he has chosen to remain hidden, this constitutes good evidence against his existence.

Swinburne has an answer to this atheistic argument that is based on God wanting created persons to come to know of his existence and enter into a communal relation with him of their own free will.[16] If he were to make his existence too obvious, this would necessitate their doing so and thus be freedom canceling. If God's existence, justice, and intentions became items of evident common knowledge, then man's freedom would in effect be vastly curtailed. Again, we see Swinburne radically overestimating the value of free will. A consequence of his position is that we should not raise our children in a religion, since then their subsequent religious belief will not have been acquired freely. Swinburne has mislocated the point at which free will enters into the religious life. It is not in regard to one's believing that God exists, but how one lives up to this belief in life.

By not allowing known evils to count against God's existence, not even allowing it to lower the probability that he exists, the skeptical theist might be draining the theistic hypothesis of all meaning. If the known evils are not the least bit probability lowering, then it would appear that for theistic skeptics no amount of evil would be. Even if the world were a living hell in which each sentient being's life was one of unrelenting suffering of the worst sort, it would not count as evidence against God's existence, and would not lower the probability of his existence one bit. This seems highly implausible and calls into question the very meaningfulness of their claim that God exists. And this is so whether or not we accept the notorious verifiability theory of meaningfulness, which Plantinga likes to have die the death of self-reference by pointedly asking whether it is applicable to itself.[17] We can recognize that something has gone wrong even if we cannot come up with a good theoretical explanation of why it is wrong.

■ NOTES

1. Richard Swinburne, *Providence and the Problem of Evil* (Oxford: Clarendon Press, 1998), 213–214.

2. Swinburne, *Providence and the Problem of Evil*, 217.

3. Swinburne, *Providence and the Problem of Evil*, 217.

4. Swinburne, *Providence and the Problem of Evil*, 217.

5. Swinburne, *Providence and the Problem of Evil*, 217.

6. Swinburne, *Providence and the Problem of Evil*, 217.

7. Alvin Plantinga, *God, Freedom and Evil* (New York: Harper Torchbooks, 1974).

8. Peter van Inwagen.

9. van Inwagen.

10. Eleonore Stump, *Faith and the Problem of Evil* (Grand Rapids, MI: Stob Lectures Endowment, 1999).

11. Marilyn McCord Adams, *Horrendous Evil and the Goodness of God* (Ithaca, NY: Cornell University Press, 1999).

12. William Rowe.

13. Stephen Wykstra.

14. William P. Alston, "The Inductive Argument from Evil and the Human Cognitive Condition," *Philosophical Perspectives* 5 (1991): 29–67.

15. Michael Scriven and Theodore Drange.

16. Swinburne, *Providence and the Problem of Evil.*

17. Plantinga, *God, Freedom and Evil.*

▨ FOR FURTHER READING

Adams, R. M. "Middle Knowledge and the Problem of Evil." *American Philosophical Quarterly* 14 (1977): 109–17.

———. "Must God Create the Best?" *Philosophical Review* 81 (1972): 317–332.

Gale, R. M. "Freedom and the Free Will Defense." *Social Theory and Practice* 16 (1990): 397–423.

Lewis. C. S. *The Problem of Pain.* New York: Macmillan, 1943.

16 God and Evil

■ CHAD MEISTER

Two prominent views of the world in Western cultures are naturalism and theism. Each of these worldviews, we might call them, brings with it a set of difficulties that its adherents must grapple with if their view is to be a coherent and reasonable one. One rather serious problem for theism has to do with the reality of evil and suffering in the world. There are in fact a variety of problems related to evil for the theist, but a central one can be put in the form of a dilemma, as does Sam Harris:

> Of course, people of all faiths regularly assure one another that God is not responsible for human suffering. But how else can we understand the claim that God is both omniscient and omnipotent? This is the age-old problem of theodicy, of course, and we should consider it solved. If God exists, either He can do nothing to stop the most egregious calamities, or He does not care to. God, therefore, is either impotent or evil.[1]

Harris maintains that the most reasonable solution is to avoid the horns of the dilemma by concluding that God does not exist. The theist, of course, cannot avoid the dilemma in this way while maintaining a theistic conception of the world. In order for the theist's view of the world to be a reasonable one, given evil, it seems that she should take on the burden of attempting to demonstrate that even though evil is real and God exists, nevertheless it makes sense to affirm that God is neither impotent nor evil. As we will see below, a theist could plead ignorance at this point, for the world is very complex. Fair enough. There are many aspects of the world that we are simply incapable of grasping. But I think the theist can say more than this—much more. It is also worth noting that it is not at all clear that the nontheist, in particular the naturalist, is devoid of a burden given the reality of evil. In fact, it could turn out that the naturalist has a more onerous burden to address. But let's set that aside for now. The major focus of this chapter will be to take on the theistic burden raised by evil.

Before moving forward it will be helpful to clarify some terms. By *naturalism* in this context I mean to signify the view that natural entities (i.e., entities that can be examined by the natural sciences) have only natural causes and that there are no supernatural entities (e.g., there is no God[2]). By *theism* in this context I mean to signify the view that there exist more than natural entities and that at least one such entity can exercise causal powers on natural entities; specifically, there exists one such supernatural entity: God. To clarify matters further, by *God* I mean a being who is personal (in the sense that God is a subject who possesses both mind and will; though, of course, in a manner that far surpasses human mind and will—God is not less than personal, at any rate), ultimate reality (the source and ground of all things, including moral truths), separate from the world yet actively involved in the world (neither a pantheistic deity nor a deistic one), and worthy of worship (being wholly good, having inherent moral perfection, and excelling in knowledge and power).

For the theist, then, a major challenge to the reasonableness of theism is the reality of evil given this understanding of God. Where, precisely, the difficulty lies is not universally agreed upon, and atheologians have approached the subject in varying ways. Before examining some of the problems raised by evil, let's hone in on what I mean when using the term *evil* in this context. I won't attempt to provide a definition of evil, but rather a general description. As commonly delineated, some evils are of a moral sort. These kinds of evils are dubbed *moral evils* because they are in some sense the result of a moral agent. Some moral evils are great, such as the horrors of torture, genocide, child abuse, and rape. There are also less severe types of moral evils, including lying, stealing, or betraying someone's trust. Another category of evil has to do not with moral agents, but with naturally occurring events or disasters. Examples of *natural evils* include disease, floods, hurricanes, tornadoes, famine, and other tragic events that do harm to humans and other creatures.

The moral and natural evils that exist seem, at first glance, to be inconsistent with the existence of an omnipotent, omniscient, and omnibenevolent God. To quote Harris again: "If God exists, either He can do nothing to stop the most egregious calamities, or He does not care to." So it seems that if God exists, God is either impotent or evil. This is the crux of the intellectual problem of evil.[3] But is this dichotomy a legitimate one? Does it follow that, given the reality of evil, if God exists, God is either impotent or evil?

1. EVIDENTIAL PROBLEMS OF EVIL

Since the mid-1980s, the challenges regarding evil have for the most part shifted from the strong claim that theism is *necessarily* false to the more reserved claim that theism (at least as traditionally understood) is *probably* false. This type of argument, often referred to as the *evidential* or *inductive* or *probabilistic* argument from evil, does not attempt to demonstrate that God's existence is logically impossible (that type of argument is referred to as the logical problem of evil). Rather, it concludes that given the evils in the world, the existence of God is improbable.

Many versions of the evidential problem of evil have been propounded in recent decades, and an especially powerful one has been crafted by Michael Tooley. Professor Tooley argues that the existence of evil (even just one occurrence of evil) lowers the probability that God exists. Given the large amount of evils that exist in our world, the probability that God exists becomes very low—much less than half. He grants that there could be a greater good that justifies the evil, but there could also be a greater evil that makes the situation even worse. So the appeal to unknowns does not help the theist. He grants that if there were good arguments for the existence of God, then there could be reasons for resisting arguments from evil, or even blocking the arguments. But he maintains, and argues vehemently, that there are no good arguments for God's existence. A truncated version of Tooley's evidential argument from evil runs as follows:

(1)   If there is an all-powerful and all-knowing being, then there are cases where that person intentionally allows natural disasters such as tsunamis and earthquakes that kill hundreds of thousands of innocent people, including children.

(2)   The property of intentionally allowing such natural disasters is a wrong-making characteristic of an action, and a very serious one.

(3)   In many such cases, we do not know of any right-making characteristics that we have good reason to believe are both present in the cases in question and also sufficiently significant to counterbalance the relevant wrong-making characteristics.

(4)   Therefore, if there is an all-powerful and all-knowing being, then there are specific cases of such a being's intentionally allowing natural disasters where there is a wrong-making property that is not, as far as we know, counterbalanced by right-making properties.[4]

(5)   Therefore it is likely that if there is an all-powerful and all-knowing being, then there are specific cases of such a being's intentionally allowing disasters where the total wrong-making properties of the actions—both the known ones and the unknown ones—are not counterbalanced by the total right-making properties, both known and unknown.

(6)   An action is morally wrong, all things considered, if it has wrong-making characteristics that are not counterbalanced by its right-making characteristics.

(7)   Therefore, if there is an all-powerful and all-knowing being, then that being knowingly allows things to happen in situations where it is morally wrong to do so, all things considered.

(8)   If one knowingly allows things to happen in situations where it is morally wrong to do so, then one is not morally perfect.

(9)   Therefore, there is no omnipotent, omniscient, and morally perfect being.

(10)   But if God exists, then he is by definition omnipotent, omniscient, and morally perfect.

(11)   Therefore, God does not exist.

This argument, especially as Tooley develops it in print, is quite impressive.[5] Alvin Plantinga refers to the argument as "clear, rigorous, and detailed," and declares that "if we can show this formulation of the argument [the one developed in *Knowledge of God*] doesn't succeed, it seems unlikely, at least for the moment, at any rate, that any formulation will."[6]

There are various approaches a theist might take in responding to this argument.[7] One could argue, for example, that there are good reasons to believe that premises (2) and (5) (key premises in the argument) are false. Or one could argue that we are not in an appropriate epistemic position to know that premises (2) and (5) are true. The first approach might involve *theodicy*—the attempt to justify God and the ways of God given the evil and suffering in the world. We will explore theodicy below. Let's begin with the second approach.

For Tooley, since we "do not know of any right-making characteristics that we have good reason to believe are both present in the cases in question, and also sufficiently significant to counterbalance the relevant wrong-making characteristics" (premise (3)), we are justified in inferring that there probably are not any (premise (5)). But is this a good inference to make? Stephen Wykstra has called arguments such as this "noseeum arguments;" if you do not see X, that is a good reason for thinking not X. In this case it is alleged that after carefully searching for right-making characteristics that might come about from natural disasters in which innocent people are killed, none can be found, so it is a good inference to conclude that there are none.[8]

Noseeum arguments can be strong or weak, good or bad. Suppose someone reported to the Central Intelligence Agency (CIA) that he had reason to believe members of al Qaeda (the Sunni Islamist militant group) were planning an attack on subways in Boston within the week. After investigating this report, CIA operatives discover that this conclusion was based entirely on a dream the informant had. In this case, it doesn't seem to the investigators that the claim about an imminent al Qaeda attack is reasonable to believe, for they don't see what the informant presented to them as valid evidence; they have reason to believe that dreams of this sort do not warrant serious consideration. In this case, the investigators' noseeum inference that the informant's claim is unwarranted is a good one. But consider another example. In the late 1800s, after the discovery of X-rays, radiography (the use of X-rays to view materials, such as the human body) was utilized for various purposes, including fitting shoes and assisting in surgery. It was unknown for some time that the electromagnetic radiation produced by radiography is harmful to living tissue. So it was used extensively and in some cases was the cause of cancer in human beings who were overexposed to the radiation. Since no dangers could be detected (radiation is invisible to the human eye, as are the immediate effects of overexposure), it was inferred that there were none. But as we know now, the noseeum inference in that case was a bad one.

So what about the naturalist's inference from evil—specifically Tooley's claim that since we do not know of any right-making characteristics concerning natural disasters, there likely are none? Is it more like the first example or the second? Many theists, including those who hold to what's called *skeptical theism*,[9] maintain that the naturalist's inference—specifically in this case that since no right-making characteristics that might come about from natural disasters in which innocent people are injured or killed can be found, it is a good inference to conclude that there likely are none—is like the second. Since many of God's ways are inscrutable, they argue, we are not in an epistemic position to judge as improbable the claim that there are right-making characteristics, or even great goods, secured by God through the various evil events that occur. There may well be goods brought about by evil events (or their allowance) that we cannot comprehend, given our cognitive (and perhaps other) limitations.

One might respond to skeptical theism by arguing that on this view there could never be *any* reason for doubting God's existence given evil, no matter how horrific and extensive the evil may be.[10] The skeptical theist, it could be argued, has made the divide between God's knowledge and human understanding too wide—wider than what is reasonable on theism. The skeptical theist, or any theist for that matter, need not agree, however. For human limitations and the inscrutability of God are, in fact, broadly held in theistic traditions and have been all along. One example is found in the Old Testament Book of Job where, after suffering great personal harm and loss, Job demands a response from God. The text reads: "Then the Lord answered Job ... 'Who is this that darkens counsel by words without knowledge? ... Where were you when I laid the foundation of the earth? Tell me if you have understanding. Who determined its measurements ... ?'" (38:1–4). As the questioning ensues, Job is ultimately brought to silence before God. In the midst of this profound experience of God, Job begins to see the depths of his own cognitive limitations and responds: "I know that you can do all things ... Therefore, I have uttered what I did not understand, things too wonderful for me, which I did not know" (42:2–3). Perhaps many or even most of the events that occur in the world are so interconnected and complex that we are, like Job, incapable of comprehending the value(s) of God's permitting specific evils (or evils in general) to occur. Such a possibility seems plausible, and perhaps even likely, given theism and the known vast complexities of the world.

Skeptical theism is one sort of response to the theist's burden, and an important one at that. But many theists, including me, don't find it completely satisfying. In fact, lacking an encounter with God of the kind Job allegedly experienced, if skeptical theism of the sort noted above were the only response available to evidential problems of evil, and if there were no strongly positive reasons for affirming belief in God, theism it seems to me would be untenable. Fortunately there is more.

■ 2. THEODICY AND DIVINE CONSTRAINT

Most theists agree that there are certain limitations to divine action. In asserting such limitations one need not be committed to the denial of omnipotence for, contrary to the view of René Descartes, omnipotence need not entail the ability to bring about what is logically contradictory or to accomplish what is metaphysically incoherent. God cannot create square circles, for example, or make seven plus three equal eleven (in base ten arithmetic). We might refer to such limitations as divine constraints, and there are many dimensions to such constraints that are relevant to this discussion.

One dimension of divine constraint has to do with free will. In creating creatures with the ability to choose, God is limited in the kinds of worlds God can bring about. Using the tools of modal logic and the notation of possible worlds, Alvin Plantinga penned what has become perhaps one of the most quoted statements addressing this type of constraint:

> A world containing creatures who are significantly free (and freely perform more good than evil actions) is more valuable, all else being equal, than a world containing no free creatures at all. Now God can create free creatures, but He can't *cause* or *determine* them to do only what is right. For if He does so, then they aren't significantly free after all; they do not do what is right *freely*. To create creatures capable of *moral good*, therefore, He must create creatures capable of moral evil; and He can't give these creatures the freedom to perform evil and at the same time prevent them from doing so. As it turned out, sadly enough, some of the free creatures God created went wrong in the exercise of their freedom; this is the source of moral evil. The fact that free creatures sometimes go wrong, however, counts neither against God's omnipotence nor against His goodness; for He could have forestalled the occurrence of moral evil only by removing the possibility of moral good.[11]

While for Plantinga the above scenario is offered as a logical possibility for purposes of rebutting the logical argument from evil, many theists hold that it is reasonable to believe that it reflects the actual world. This entails an incompatibilist view of free will in which morally significant freedom is incompatible with any form of determinism—a view with which not all theists agree. But I take it that indeterminism is the most plausible position to hold, and many theists and nontheists do indeed hold it. So it seems reasonable to believe that while it is possible that there exists a world in which there is no moral evil and only moral good, whether that world actually exists is up to the free creatures who populate that world. God cannot cause that world (or any relevant world) to have only moral good while at the same time respecting the libertarian freedom of the creatures in that world.

Furthermore, it is widely agreed in evolutionary psychology that for moral development to occur, agents need the ability to make moral choices, and these choices must have real consequences. So moral maturity requires that agents be involved in their own moral formation through the (often arduous) process of moral decision-making. But in order to have choices that have real moral merit, a proper environment is necessary—an environment both external to and internal to the agent. John Hick has argued that a proper external environment is a challenging one: "The world is seen as a place of 'soul making' or person making in which free beings, grappling with the tasks and challenges of their existence in a common environment, may become 'children of God' and 'heirs of eternal life'. Our world, with all its rough edges, is the sphere in which this second and harder stage of the creative process is taking place."[12] It is not unreasonable to maintain that real moral progress entails making hard moral decisions, and our world is certainly one in which hard decisions are natural and commonplace.

A proper internal environment could well be one that includes opposing desires and dispositions within the individual, such as lust and aggression on the one hand and altruism and benevolence on the other—desires and dispositions that we do in fact find within human beings. Internal conflict and struggle may even be a necessary part of the very nature of moral advancement, at least in the early phases of moral formation (reflect on your own moral development and consider whether this is true). If so, a life involving moral decision-making, freely choosing between opposing dispositions and desires, would be an essential part of character formation. If it is the case that competing desires and dispositions are requisite for moral decision-making (at least in its developmental phase), then something akin to aggression, disappointment, frustration, danger, and pain—all of which are essential aspects of biological development—may be *necessary* features of an internal environment in which real moral progress can occur in an individual. In other words, a world like ours may be indispensible for creatures like us.[13]

Because of these (and perhaps other) constraints, God did create a world in which some evil is an integral element of it. But God is justified in creating this world because God could not create a world like ours where there are sentient moral beings like us in it without creating that world with some evil as a part of it, including the processes that brought us to where we are at this stage in history. In that case, a high price would be exacted by God if he were to create a world that is "better" than our world; namely, we would be absent from it!

An objection can be raised that at least some of the *natural evils* that exist are inconsistent with, or at least seriously problematic for, the existence of God. In other words, while theists and naturalists often agree that some or perhaps even much of the evil that exists in our world is consistent with divine creation, certain aspects of creation make it unlikely that God exists. Tooley suggests that the various natural disasters in which many innocent people are killed makes God's existence highly unlikely. Moving from the abstract to the particular, he cites the Lisbon earthquake—in which about 60,000 ordinary people were killed—as a prime example. "No rightmaking properties that we know of," says Tooley, "are such that we are justified in believing both that an action of choosing not to prevent the Lisbon earthquake would have had those rightmaking properties, and that those properties are sufficiently serious to counterbalance the relevant wrongmaking property."[14] But again, how do we know that our epistemic limitations don't hamper our knowledge about what is *actually* involved in such an event? "Furthermore," as Plantinga argues, "Christians and other theists believe that God performed the action of permitting the Lisbon earthquake. They therefore believe that the action of permitting the Lisbon earthquake has the property of having been performed by God, who is a perfectly good person. This is a rightmaking property that clearly outweighs and counterbalances any wrongmaking property that action has.... Still further, Christians believe (or would believe if they thought about it) that they are *justified* in believing these things."[15] Whether theists are justified in believing that God is perfectly good is another matter, but clearly many theists think so.[16]

There is yet another aspect of theodicy that is important to consider in offering a justification of God given natural evil—especially natural evils of the sort that Tooley mentions in which people, most notably children, are killed and so seem to be prematurely removed from the domain of soul making. God would not bring about a world in which sentient creatures experience evil, suffering, and death for purposes of mere expediency. God could not create a universe where evil ultimately triumphs. Two points about this. First, it seems clear that for most forms of theism the individual is more fundamental than the species. So the child who dies prematurely, for example, is not being sacrificed for purposes of granting free will and soul making for *Homo sapiens*. It would be immoral to affirm that the end of this earthly life is the end of such an individual. Most theists agree, and have always maintained that an afterlife in which there is a compensation for evil is essential. Second, it would be highly anthropocentric to maintain that the natural world, with its suffering, death, and predation, exists only for the development of human moral perfection—as mere preparation for the development of moral and spiritual virtue among human persons. All creatures are valuable, and all creatures, at least all sentient ones, should have the opportunity to experience what might be called *eschatological fulfillment*. This means that every creature should have the opportunity to experience its own flourishing and fulfillment, either in this life or in the next. Keith Ward offers the following insight on the issue:

> Theism would be falsified if physical death was the end, for then there could be no justification for the existence of this world. However, if one supposes that every sentient being has an endless existence, which offers the prospect of supreme happiness, it is surely true that the sorrows and troubles of this life will seem very small in comparison. Immortality, for animals as well as humans, is a necessary condition of any

acceptable theodicy; that necessity, together with all the other arguments for God, is one of the main reasons for believing in immortality.[17]

Along these lines the Hebrew prophet Isaiah describes a future scenario in which the wolf will live with the lion, the lion will eat straw like an ox, and the young child will not be harmed by the viper—a time when humans and animals will experience life redeemed (Isaiah 11:6–9). If God exists as the omnibenevolent, all-powerful, creator God depicted in the Abrahamic traditions, it makes sense for God to set the world to rights—to provide the opportunity for the ultimate redemption of all sentient beings. This may be accomplished by bringing them into a flourishing state in a life beyond death where they will receive what was unavailable to them in this life—ultimate fulfillment of their natures. Envisioning such a heavenly existence may be beyond the ability of human conception. Nevertheless, many people have suggested that the new heaven and new earth will include all sorts of creatures besides human beings—animals, angels, and other realities as well. Given the existence of God, it is not unreasonable to expect an eschaton that far surpasses human imagination in goodness, grandeur, and beauty.[18]

■ 3. EVIL AS EVIDENCE AGAINST NATURALISM

In taking on the theist's burden of evil, I have argued that a justification of God can be provided, and while a world riddled with the kinds of evils that exist does at first glance reduce the likelihood of the existence of a perfectly good, all-powerful, omniscient God, nevertheless such evils may well be an essential feature of a good world with us in it. But in wrapping up this chapter, two further issues are worth addressing. First, an analysis of the justification of God given evil must take into account other factors related to one's beliefs about God and the nature of God; for whether it is reasonable to believe that God is justified given evil will be partly dependent upon one's worldview—one's entire set of beliefs, experiences, and understanding of God and the world. If a certain claim p is improbable on a certain claim q, it does not follow that one who accepts both p and q is irrational or guilty of epistemic impropriety (even granting that she believes that p is improbable given q), for p may be probable with respect to other things she knows or believes.[19] The background information provided by one's worldview is central in this discussion. From a theistic perspective, for example, there are arguments from natural theology to consider that may (and I believe do) provide some evidence for the existence of God. There may also be nonpropositional evidence or grounds for believing that God exists, including a natural knowledge of God (as suggested by Thomas Aquinas) or a *sensus divinitatus* (as described by John Calvin)—a cognitive process in which God reveals God's reality and presence to an individual.[20] All of this needs to be considered when examining God and problems of evil.

Second, let's return to a point made at the beginning of this chapter. While it is usually the theist who takes on the burden of making sense of the reality of evil in our world (and as noted above, the theist should take on the burden, for the problem is a serious one indeed), it is also important to note that the naturalist is not off the hook in providing an account of the reality of evil. Consider the following case of horrific evil:

> A young Muslim mother in Bosnia was repeatedly raped in front of her husband and father, with her baby screaming on the floor beside her. When her tormentor seemed finally tired of her, she begged permission to nurse the child. In response, one of the rapists swiftly decapitated the baby and threw the head in the mother's lap.[21]

Such grim horrors are almost beyond human comprehension and imagination. As Dostoyevsky notes, there are evils practiced by human beings that even the beasts would not commit. The above is a case in point. When we ascribe the term "evil" to these events, we are not referring to mere personal preferences. We are not simply saying that we don't like them. We are indicating that something is truly wrong with them. They are objectively evil; their being evil is not a matter of subjective opinion. If the rapists, in this case, could not be convinced that what they were doing was evil and wrong, that would be irrelevant to the facts of the matter, for what they are doing *is* evil and wrong whether the rapists recognize it as such or not. And because these acts are evil and morally wrong, we are justified in affirming that they are wrong and in attempting to stop them from occurring—even against the rapists' desires and intentions.

It strikes me that the naturalist has at least two problems with respect to evil. First is what we might call a *grounding* problem. If rape, racism, torture, murder, government-sanctioned genocide, and so forth are objectively evil—evil for all persons in all times and places whether they recognize them as such or not—then what makes them so on the naturalist's account? What grounds their evilness? What explains why they are evil? What makes them truly evil rather than simply activities someone dislikes? On the naturalistic account, it is not clear how there can be such real evil. Sure, there can be things the naturalist doesn't like, or is even disgusted by; there can be pain and suffering and other antipathies. But on what basis can the naturalist ascribe something objectively evil about them? If there are objective moral values, then there must be some basis—some metaphysical foundation or grounding—for their being so. It seems to me that naturalism lacks such a foundation or grounding or explanation, for on naturalism the cosmos is not morally good per se, nor is there a morally good being sufficient to ground evil or to bring real objective goodness out of evil.[22]

A second difficulty for the naturalist is what we might call a *meaning* problem. On theism (specifically the theism of the Abrahamic faiths), much of the evil, including all moral evil, is an *aberration*—something abhorrent to the nature and purposes of the world. Moral evil is neither willed nor hoped for by God. On the

framework of naturalism, the events that occur in the world, including the horrific scenario described above, are simply a natural part of the fabric of reality.
Tigers eat gazelles, rapists attack and murder (and sometimes eat) innocent victims. Period. This is not to suggest that the naturalist has no basis whatsoever
for ameliorating evil; the naturalist need not acclimate to evil in the sense of
welcoming it as merely one among other necessary aspects of the world. There
are many things one might disagree with even though there is no objective moral
foundation for the position (e.g., it could be argued on pragmatic or hygienic or
aesthetic grounds, for example, that eating with silverware should be preferred
to eating with fingers; so too with ameliorating evil). But there remains for the
naturalist a philosophical accommodation of evil that does not occur for theism,
for the theist recognizes not just our need and calling to overturn evil, but sees
that evil as contrary to the way things ought to be.

To sum up, there has been quite a development in philosophical discourse
about problems of evil since the mid-twentieth century, when it was commonly
argued that the existence of God was *contradicted by* the reality of evil. For now
not only does it seem reasonable to many to believe that God exists given the
moral and natural evils in the world, but the reality of objective evil seems to provide evidence against naturalism. The tables have turned. It's now time for naturalists to take on the burden they face in a world that, to quote Richard Dawkins,
"has precisely the properties we should expect if there is, at bottom, no design,
no purpose, no evil, no good, nothing but pitiless indifference."[23] This burden, I
submit, is a greater one than theists have ever faced.

■ NOTES

1. Sam Harris, *Letter to a Christian Nation* (New York: Alfred A. Knopf, 2006), 55.

2. Some naturalists define naturalism as the view that natural entities have only natural
causes and do not go further in affirming that there are no supernatural entities.

3. The problem of evil has taken many forms throughout the centuries, so it may be
better to speak of *problems of evil*, as there are a host of them for the theist. In this chapter,
however, I will limit the discussion to intellectual problems. Besides intellectual problems
of evil, there are other categories as well, including what is sometimes called the existential
problem of evil (other titles include the "religious problem," "moral problem," "pastoral prob-
lem," "psychological problem," or "emotional problem"). Simply put, this sort of problem
concerns the existential disgust or dislike one has of a God who would allow evil to exist.

4. This premise is slightly modified from the actual statement professor Tooley made in
the debate from which this argument is taken (see footnote 5). The actual statement was this:
"Therefore, if there is an all-powerful and all-knowing being, then there are specific cases of
such a being's intentionally allowing natural disasters where there is a wrong-making property does not, as far as we know, counterbalance by right-making properties."

5. Tooley's argument is articulated and defended by him in Alvin Plantinga and Michael
Tooley, *Knowledge of God* (Oxford: Blackwell, 2008), 98–146. The truncated argument form
that I provide in this chapter was presented by him in a formal debate with William Lane

Craig entitled *Is God Real? The Debate*, held at the University of North Carolina, Chapel Hill, NC, March 24, 2010.

6. Plantinga and Tooley, *Knowledge of God*, 151, 153.

7. For Plantinga's response to it, see Plantinga and Tooley, *Knowledge of God*, 164–174.

8. See, e.g., Stephen J. Wykstra, "The Humean Obstacle to Evidential Arguments from Suffering: On Avoiding the Evils of 'Appearance'," *International Journal for Philosophy of Religion* 16 (1984): 73–93. Wykstra is responding to an evidential argument offered by William Rowe, but the same strategy is relevant here.

9. The term "skeptical theism" was coined by Paul Draper. It does not refer to theists who are skeptical about theism, but rather to the view that while we can know (or be warranted in believing that) God exists, we should be skeptical of our ability to discern God's reasons for acting or refraining from acting in any particular case.

10. William Rowe makes this claim. For more on this see Daniel Howard-Snyder, Michael Bergmann, and William Rowe, "An Exchange on the Problem of Evil," in *God and the Problem of Evil*, ed. William Rowe (Oxford: Blackwell, 2001), 124–128, 156–157.

11. Alvin Plantinga, *God, Freedom, and Evil* (Grand Rapids, MI: Eerdmans, 1977), 30.

12. John Hick, *Philosophy of Religion*, 4th ed. (Englewood Cliffs, NJ: Prentice Hall, 1990), 45–46.

13. The following works offer insightful and sometimes contradictory points of view on this issue: Philip Clayton and Jeffrey Schloss, eds., *Evolution and Ethics: Human Morality in Biological and Religious Perspective* (Grand Rapids, MI: Eerdmans, 2004); Carolyn Zahn-Waxler, E. Mark Cummings, and Ronald Ianotti, eds., *Altruism and Aggression: Social and Biological Origins* (Cambridge: Cambridge University Press, 1986); Konrad Lorenz, *On Aggression* (London: Methuen, 1966); Harriet Harris, ed., *God, Goodness and Philosophy* (London: Ashgate, 2011).

14. Plantinga and Tooley, *Knowledge of God*, 119.

15. Plantinga and Tooley, *Knowledge of God*, 170–171.

16. Such justification could come from propositional or nonpropositional evidence.

17. Keith Ward, *Rational Theology and the Creativity of God* (New York: Pilgrim, 1982), 201–202. John Wesley shared a similar sentiment in responding to the claim that there might be an objection made against God for the suffering of so many animals: "But the objection vanishes away if we consider that something better remains after death for these creatures also; that these likewise shall one day be delivered from this bondage of corruption, and shall then receive an ample amends for all their present sufferings." John Wesley in a sermon entitled, "The General Deliverance," in *Sermons on Several Occasions*, Vol. 2 (London: J. Kershew, 1825), 131, as quoted in Christopher Southgate, *The Groaning of Creation: God, Evolution, and the Problem of Pain* (London: Westminster John Knox Press, 2008), 78.

18. See also Keith Ward, *Divine Action: Examining God's Role in an Open and Emergent Universe* (Philadelphia: Templeton Foundation Press, 2007), especially chap. 14, "The Redemption of Time."

19. For more on this point see Alvin Plantinga, "Epistemic Probability and Evil," in *The Evidential Argument from Evil*, ed. Daniel Howard-Snyder, 69–96.

20. We rely on nonpropositional evidence for a variety of things, including the reality of other minds, an external world, and so on.

21. Eleonore Stump, "The Mirror of Evil," in *God and the Philosophers*, ed. Thomas Morris (New York: Oxford University Press), 239.

22. This moves the discussion into the domain of the moral argument. For more on this, see chapters 7 and 8 in this book.

23. Richard Dawkins, "God's Utility Function," *Scientific American* 273, no. 5 (1995): 85. I spell out some problems confronting naturalists given evil in my *Evil: A Guide for the Perplexed* (London: Continuum, 2012), chap. 5.

■ FOR FURTHER READING

Adams, M. M. *Horrendous Evils and the Goodness of God*. Ithaca, NY: Cornell University Press, 1999.

Draper, P. "Pain and Pleasure: An Evidential Problem for Theists," *Noûs* 23 (1989): 331–350. Reprinted in *The Evidential Argument from Evil*, edited by D. Howard-Snyder, 12–29. Indianapolis: Indiana University Press, 1996.

Hick, J. *Evil and the God of Love*. London: Palgrave Macmillan, 2007.

Planting, A. *God, Freedom, and Evil*. New York: Harper & Row, 1974.

Stump, E. *Wandering in Darkness: Narrative and the Problem of Suffering*. Oxford: Clarendon Press, 2010.

Southgate, C. *The Groaning of Creation: God, Evolution, and the Problem of Evil*. Louisville, KY: Westminster John Knox Press, 2008.

Evolution and Belief in God

17 Bayes and the Evolution of Religious Belief

■ JOSEPH BULBULIA

Roughly, a scientific theory may be said to undermine a domain of belief if the theory is both credible and significantly weakens the epistemic grounds for believing the propositions of that domain. I use Bayes's rule to illustrate

- how evolutionary psychology plausibly undermines the domain of religious beliefs, and
- why the degree of undermining for any specific religious belief depends on variables that form no part of evolutionary psychology per se.

I suggest a "golden rule for belief fixation," according to which religious and antireligious arguments should be judged by their capacity to change the minds of Bayesian thinkers who are not already convinced.

1. THE BELIEVER'S DILEMMA

Suppose that Ed is both a committed theist and a committed Darwinian. Ed's education persuades him that evolutionary theories account for biological designs. Ed's experience persuades him that Gods of some kind exist.

Ed has a special interest in evolutionary theories of religion. So far as Ed can see, evolutionary theories suggest that Gods do not cause religious beliefs, as believers think, but rather genes interacting with environments cause religious beliefs, without supernatural remainder. Suppose that Ed is a rational, truth-seeking individual. Suppose that he finds evolutionary theories credible. To what extent, if any, is Ed rationally bound to revise his religious commitments?[1]

Here I propose a method to help Ed, and other truth-seekers, to answer this and related questions about the relationship of evolutionary explanations of religious commitments, on the one hand, and religious commitments, on the other. The method does not tell anyone what to believe. It rather suggests how to revise religious beliefs in light of credible psychological research. The method offers no specific result, but it is not trivial. For it is important to know how to make up our minds in light of what we learn from credible sources.[2] The importance of having a good method should not be confused with the importance of using it. I will assume that Ed has the time and the inclination to devote himself to improving the quality of his beliefs. In practice, however, truth-seekers like Ed might well have better things to do, like clearing their minds of philosophical

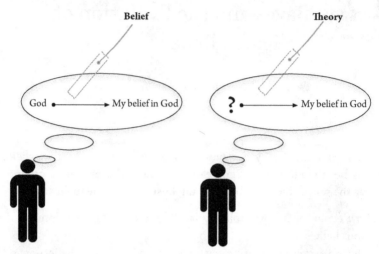

Figure 17.1 The believer's dilemma.

thoughts and getting some sun. I set this complication to the side. I also set to the side the question of whether we can know enough about divinity to form beliefs about which we can assign degrees of probability. Elsewhere I argue that we have good reason to believe that certain fundamental religious questions will forever exceed human comprehension.[3] I restrict my interest to those religious propositions, supposing there are any, that can be assigned some degree of confidence. By "confidence" I include "no confidence," "perfect certainty," and all points between these two extremes. I begin by considering two common, but I think faulty, methods for fixing religious beliefs.

1.1 The inference to atheism from methodological naturalism

Evolutionary psychology shows how religious beliefs are possible without any Gods to cause them. Does Ed's confidence in evolutionary psychology require atheism? Evolutionary psychology adopts *methodological naturalism,* a doctrine that accords a negligible probability to any proposition that invokes Gods to explain natural systems—including explanations for those regions of nature occupied by religious beliefs. Though rarely explicit, methodological naturalism is assumed as a matter of course in all scientific research.

For Ed to abandon his religious beliefs from methodological naturalism, however, would be rash. Methodological naturalism is not a scientific discovery, but rather a guideline for scientific discovery, one that is justified from its past successes. Methodological naturalism must allow that the Gods might exist, even as it restrains theories from postulating Gods as explanatory variables. Justification for methodological naturalism comes from the evidence that cumulative scientific understanding follows only those communities of inquiry who leave the

Gods out of their scientific explanations, while never following communities that posit Gods. Perhaps the Gods wish it to be so. Scientists have good reasons, in any case, not to appeal to the Gods when explaining those who believe in Gods.

Perhaps scientists of the future will abandon methodological naturalism, revising their theories to permit supernatural variables. Methodological naturalism is a pragmatic rule of thumb, not a finding, so this prospect cannot be excluded. Though nothing about contemporary science suggests that such a departure is likely or desirable, the point is that any revision to religious belief should follow the evidence, not the rules that guide explanations for the evidence: rules for the conduct of science can be, and often are, revised during the course of scientific inquiries.

1.2 The inference to religious belief from inward conviction

Suppose that Ed is as strongly convinced of the existence of Gods as he is of any other fact. Suppose that Ed understands there is no contradiction in believing two compatible beliefs (let's call them "doctrines"). The doctrine of the existence of Gods is logically compatible with any scientific doctrine, so Ed concludes that his religion is safe from scientific revision. In any case, Ed is more confident of his religion than he is of any science. He would, for this reason, reject any scientific finding before rejecting his religion. Ed's contentment to leave his religious commitments untouched by scientific discovery is, however, rash.

To see this, notice that epistemic error is compatible with powerful conviction. Subjective confidence is an important starting point for truth, but it is poorly suited as an end point for discovery. Ed might learn that his confidence is misplaced. Second, and related, scientific theories sometimes reveal that our convictions are misplaced (we consider examples in sections 3.1 and 3.2). Wherever a credible scientific theory shows systematic errors, the authority of our convictions should be opened for reevaluation. If we are interested in the truth, and have nothing better to do, we should reevaluate controversial convictions, inspecting them for faults, as an airplane mechanic inspects a fuselage for cracks.

The philosopher Kim Sterelny uses the concept of "counterfactual sensitivity" to describe how scientific theories sometimes undermine beliefs:

> Rationally formed beliefs are counterfactually sensitive: Had the world been different, the agent's views would be different. For that reason, [psychological] theories...are undermining. If true, they show that there is no mechanism through which an agent's beliefs about the world track states of the world.[4]

Sterelny's idea is that beliefs generated from mechanisms that are not counterfactually sensitive should warrant low confidence because such beliefs will only track the truth accidentally.[5]

Because the evolutionary psychology of religion describes plausible mecha-nisms for the generation of strong, but counterfactually insensitive convictions, Ed and other truth-seekers would do well to reconsider whether evolution-ary psychology implies revisions, assuming they have the time on their hands, and an inclination to improve the accuracy of their beliefs. However, for this, truth-seekers require a reliable method. Enter Bayes.

■ 2. BAYES' RULE AND BELIEF REVISION

The question of how Ed should revise his religious beliefs in light of evolution-ary psychology presents a special instance of the more general question of how truth-seekers should update any belief in light of relevant evidence. Bayes's rule enables us to think precisely about how to update confidence offering a simple, uncontroversial, and exact method for revaluation.

Let us first state Bayes's rule in its mathematical form, and then use a simple example to illustrate its power. (Do not worry if you have a hard time following the mathematical presentation: the example will clarify the rule's meaning and power.)

Bayes's rule states that the conditional probability for the truth of any prop-osition (hypothesis) given new evidence (this value is called "the posterior") is equal to the conditional probability of the evidence given the hypothesis (this value is called "the likelihood") multiplied by the prior probability of the hypothesis (irrespective of the new evidence) divided by the probability of evi-dence (irrespective of the hypothesis):

$$\Pr(h|e) = \frac{\Pr(e|h) * \Pr(h)}{\Pr(e)} \tag{1}$$

Perhaps Ed and other truth-seekers would rather drill holes in their teeth than contemplate this equation. How can mathematical squiggles help us to think about Gods? A simple example illustrates the rule's power.

2.1 Example of Bayes in action

Recall that Ed is interested in the probability that Gods exist, given his con-fidence in evolutionary psychology. We assume subjective probability takes a number between 0 (no confidence) and 1 (perfect confidence). Call the hypothesis that Gods exist **FOLK**, and assign this hypothesis the variable h. For now we ignore the complication that beliefs in Gods differ, namely that there are different folk hypotheses—h^1, h^2, h^3, ..., h^n—pertaining to the exis-tence of different Gods. [We will return to this complication below (section 3, equation 6)]. Call the hypothesis that Gods do not exist **NULL**, and assign this alternative hypothesis the variable ¬h, which we interpret to mean "Gods do not exist." **NULL** accounts for the evidence that people believe in Gods without appealing to the existence of Gods. The confidence for **NULL** is initially given from evidence that people are not invariably correct in what they believe.

We need to assign values to the prior probability that Gods exists and to the likelihoods of these two hypotheses conditional on evidence that may discriminate between their predictions. Such evidence is the result of an experiment, in the broadest sense of "result" and "evidence." Suppose we take the prior probability of Gods existing to be a coin toss $p(h) = .5$. The numbers we assign for these prior probabilities does not ultimately matter for belief fixation, at least if we have sufficiently many observations by which to update our beliefs, and if the hypotheses are formulated to be revisable by the results of experiments. The relatively low importance of our prior probabilities to repeated assays arises because the results of any initial Bayesian experiment yields posterior beliefs that may form the prior probabilities for subsequent experiments. In principle, we can repeat the Bayesian method indefinitely many times, improving on the quality of our beliefs, as posterior confidence becomes the prior probability for the next round of observations.

Though in practice it may be too costly or otherwise impractical to persist with the experimental strategy, and disagreements over how the results should be interpreted, and other disagreements, may hamper progress, Bayes's rule offers a perfect method by which to improve beliefs about those regions of the world for which we are capable of forming and improving beliefs by evidence-based reasoning. The history of doctrinal conflicts suggests the prospect for convergence isn't trivial. However, we need not be perfectionists. Improving the quality of our beliefs is worthwhile, even without any convergence at the limit of inquiry. Moreover, disagreements are not logically fated to remain antinomies—a cause for optimism.

Continuing with our example, the likelihood that Gods explains beliefs in Gods is given by $p(e|h)$. This is the probability that we would find religious beliefs if the Gods were to exist. The prior probability of finding beliefs in Gods is given by $p(e)$. This is the probability of finding religious beliefs under all the relevant explanations for such beliefs. Again we simplify by imagining that explanations are exhausted by **FOLK** and **NULL**, ignoring that people believe in different Gods.

We suppose a high likelihood for the hypothesis that Gods would cause religious beliefs wherever there are Gods (i.e., Gods are not deceivers). From this supposition we accord, say, a 95 percent probability of the likelihood of $p(e|h)$. We suppose that people mainly get things right, though not always, and so allow some nonnegligible error rate, say $p(e|\neg h) = 10$ percent. Again the prior probabilities do not matter much because updating our posteriors enables us to improve our estimates, as the experimental process is repeated.

We are interested in the conditional probability that Gods exist given the evidence that many believe in them. We have two hypotheses (h = **FOLK**, $\neg h$ = **NULL**). Bayes's rule states:

$$\Pr(h|e) = \frac{\Pr(e|h) * \Pr(h)}{\Pr(e|h) * \Pr(h) + \Pr(e|\neg h) * \Pr(\neg h)} \tag{2}$$

We insert the relevant variables and discover that:

$$\Pr(\text{FOLK} \mid \text{widespread beliefs}) = \frac{.95 * .5}{.95 * .5 + .1 * .5} \approx .9 \tag{3}$$

Under our stated assumptions, the evidence that people believe in Gods brings a large shift in confidence favoring the proposition that Gods exist.[6] We move from a coin toss to 90 percent certainty.

Consider how matters would differ, were we to hold an alternative theory, one that explains the abundance of religious beliefs on the supposition that religious beliefs are not counterfactually sensitive. Replace **NULL** with this alternative theory for religious belief, which we will call **UNDERMINING**. The hypothesis space is still Gods exist or Gods do not exist. However, an undermining psychological theory changes assumptions about the probability that people would perceive Gods even were Gods not to exist. Suppose that we accord a 99 percent confidence to the hypothesis that people would believe in Gods even if Gods were not to exist. Holding everything else the same and running Bayes's theorem, we have:

$$\Pr(\text{FOLK} \mid \text{widespread beliefs}) = \frac{.95 * .5}{.95 * .5 + .5 * .99} \approx .49 \tag{4}$$

Under these new assumptions, **UNDERMINING** brings a large reduction in confidence, taking us from a near certain wager for the existence of Gods to a gamble marginally stacked against the existence of Gods (h < 50 percent). Notice, however, that confidence is not utterly destroyed. We are back to a confidence that roughly approximates a coin toss.

2.2 Three lessons

First, Bayes offers a perfect calculus for belief revision, one that is as certain as any law in mathematics. The pragmatic relevance of the rule to practical decision making may be doubted, but not the rule itself. If you entertain a hypothesis with specific likelihoods, and you are a truth-seeker interested in the quality of your beliefs, then you ought to revise your beliefs in light of the evidence exactly as Bayes's rule demands.

Second, given specific assumptions about the relevant prior probabilities and likelihoods, Bayes's rule tells us by precisely how much our confidence should change given other observations, the results of experiments in the broadest sense. Notably, intuitions may differ from Bayesian results. When comparing the assumptions of the case described in equation 4 with the case described in equation 3, I doubt many would have guessed that confidence for God should decline by 41 percent.

Third, the drawbacks of Bayes's rule for practical reasoning are both obvious and instructive. What data could discriminate between hypotheses for the existence of Gods? For the data presuppose frameworks for interpretation, and these frameworks are themselves subject to controversies. Yet, while controversies need not be settled immediately, Bayes's rule helps us to understand how disagreements over what to believe may be rationally resolved eventually, for beliefs about the world, about what evidence counts, and about frameworks for evaluation alike. Even with very different assignments of prior confidence for prior beliefs, confidence may converge eventually, as assignments of prior probabilities are updated to become posterior probabilities, in light of experimental results (in the broadest sense). Where prior probabilities for any knowable fact are not fixed at a limit of 0 or 1, any credible psychological theory showing counterfactual insensitivity may always affect confidence to some degree.

3. BAYES AND UNDERMINING PSYCHOLOGICAL THEORIES

3.1 The moon illusion

The moon appears larger to us when it is low on the horizon compared to when it is high. Many are surprised to learn that this appearance is an artifact of our visual system, which is wired in a way that happens to produce false judgments for the relative size of celestial objects. Those who are incredulous can photograph the moon at both high and low positions, and measure the radiuses of the respective images. The image size will be identical, high or low.

The moon illusion clarifies how confidence in a perceptual judgment should decline in response to a psychological theory that explains the mechanisms that influence our beliefs. While perception judgments are normally reliable, the moon illusion reveals a domain for perception's fallibility. Lacking an independent reason for thinking that the moon changes in size or relative distance to the earth (in the way our visual systems estimate), the psychological theory suggests that confidence for a waxing and waning moon should decline.

The illusion also shows how we may come to doubt our perceptual judgments quite apart from any theory showing counterfactual insensitivity, for here our perceptual judgements conflict with known physical facts. Plain reasoning from basic optics might be sufficient to warrant strong skepticism for the moon illusion. This possibility generalizes. Indeed, ordinary reasoning from observations leads to most revisions to our beliefs: "Looks like rain, but wait a minute, I appear to be on a movie set," etc.

Bayes's rule offers a perfect method for belief revision. However, the psychological effect of Bayesian reasoning on belief revision remains a separate question for psychology. Whether our beliefs in certain domains are recalcitrant presents a distinct question. This psychological question must not be confused with the normative question of whether confidence *ought* to change, given our prior assumptions and beliefs, in light of relevant evidence. If we accept values for our priors, then we should hold ourselves accountable to Bayesian inference.

3.2 Self-deception

Knowledge of the moon illusion undermines a perceptual judgment without bother. We learn it, and go about life exactly as before. However, psychological theories occasionally imply revisions to fundamental beliefs. Consider an example.

Robert Trivers offers an evolutionary theory of self-deception according to which we systematically distort our self-appraisals, causing us to believe that we are more "beneffective" (benevolent and effective) than we actually are. He offers a plausible evolutionary logic for such distortions: those who convince themselves that they are beneffective will be more likely to win the confidence, trust, and admiration of others. By believing their own lies, the self-deceived avoid sending secondary signals that give their lies away. Wherever enhancements to social esteem converts to fitness effects, psychological mechanisms by which "we deceive ourselves to better deceive others" may be selected and amplified.[7]

Trivers's theory finds support from a wealth of data. Notably, these data affect the prior probability of confidence for self-assessments of virtue. Unlike the moon illusion, however, the prior probability for any arbitrary person's beneffectiveness cannot be zero. Some people, we may suppose, genuinely are beneffective. While Trivers's theory cannot settle the question of who exactly is virtuous, the theory reveals a weakness for any inference based on personal introspection. Convictions formed that way are not counterfactually sensitive.

We can use Bayes's rule to explore the implications of Trivers's theory for revising judgments about person virtues. Suppose Trivers's theory implies a probability of 95 percent for introspecting a virtuous self. Suppose that independent evidence suggests that only 10 percent of the population is actually beneffective. Suppose that nearly all beneffective people appreciate their virtues $[p(y|x^* = .99]$. Running Bayes's theorem under these assumptions we find:

$$\Pr\left(\text{beneffective} \mid \text{feel benefective}\right) = \frac{.99*.1}{.99*.1 + .95*.9} \approx .11 \qquad (5)$$

Under such assumptions none of us should be very confident about our self-appraisals of our personal beneffectiveness.

4. EVOLUTIONARY PSYCHOLOGY AND THE FIXATION OF RELIGIOUS BELIEF

Should evolutionary psychology diminish confidence for religious beliefs? To evaluate this prospect we need some initial reason for assuming that the probability that Gods cause religious beliefs is not either 0 or 1. Again, I am interested in only those religious beliefs about which it is appropriate to hold confidence of varying degrees, allowing that much about Divinity may exceed any hope for human understanding, so judgments of any kind go out the window.

4.1 Darwin and religion

Darwin offers several reasons for doubting his former Christian orthodoxy in his *Autobiography*. These provide good reason for thinking that the probability that Gods exist is not 0 or 1. Darwin writes:

> At the present day the most usual argument for the existence of an intelligent God is drawn from the deep inward conviction and feelings which are experienced by most persons. But it cannot be doubted that Hindoos, Mahomadans and others might argue in the same manner and with equal force in favour of the existence of one God, or of many gods, or as with the Buddhists of no God. There are also many barbarian tribes who cannot be said with any truth to believe in what we call God: they believe indeed in spirits or ghosts, and it can be explained, as Tyler and Herbert Spencer have shown, how such a belief would be likely to arise. This argument would be a valid one if all men of all races had the same inward conviction

of the existence of one God; but we know that this is very far from being the case. Therefore I cannot see that such inward convictions and feelings are of any weight as evidence of what really exists.[8]

Let us interpret Darwin in light of Bayes. Pluralism implies that there are alternative hypotheses to one's preferred religious hypothesis. Weights must be assigned to these hypotheses in the denominator of our evaluation of any specific religious hypothesis $(h, h', h'', h''', \ldots h^n)$:

$$\Pr(h|e) = \frac{\Pr(e|h) * \Pr(h)}{\Pr(e|h) * \Pr(h) + \Pr(e|h') * \Pr(h') \cdots \Pr(e|h'') * \Pr(h'')} \quad (6)$$

If we assume that religious persons of different stripes harbor subjective confidence for their preferred religions, then subjective confidence does not provide any evidence by which to discriminate between specific religious hypotheses. I assume truth-seeking believers will agree about the weakness of subjective feelings for belief fixation, but nevertheless disagree about the amount of weight to give to rival hypotheses. Bayes's rule suggests that truth-seekers need not worry about their different initial assignments of prior probabilities. Differing judgments about the prior probabilities of specific beliefs will tend to converge as these beliefs update in light of new evidence.

It is worth noting, for the record, that Darwin did not draw an atheist's conclusion from the facts of pluralism. Rather he writes that "the mystery of the beginning of all things is insoluble by us."[9] Though Darwin describes himself as an "agnostic," his position does not imply commitment to middle probability for the proposition that Gods exist; he rather judges that ultimate question about the origins of all things cannot be posed.[10]

4.2 An evolutionary account of religious commitment

Evolutionary theories of religious psychology offer plausible hypotheses for the mechanisms supporting deep inward convictions about the Gods. Evolutionary models are credible because they predict specific features of religious commitment such as its relationship to moral commitment, its tenacity, and its capacity to coordinate large social groups. In terms of Bayes's theorem, were the observed properties of religious commitment different, we would have cause to abandon evolutionary models of religion. The models offer inferences to the best explanations for these and other properties of religious commitment. Though the details of specific evolutionary models are hotly debated, I will review areas of general scientific agreement, explaining how these areas of agreement suggest revisions for confidence in the targets of religious belief.

4.2.1 Local Gods and counterfactuals

4.2.1.1 Step 1

The cognitive anthropologist Stewart Guthrie offers the following explanation for the evolution of anthropological beliefs:

i.   Wherever false negatives are costly, tendencies to err may be favored.

ii.   We plausibly lose much when we fail to discern actual persons but lose little from false positives.

iii. For this reason we evolve to believe in anthropological beings, though they do not exist.

iv.   Ethnographic and psychological studies show that anthropomorphism is common.[11]

v.   Ethnographic and historical evidence shows that anthropomorphism is a prominent feature of all religions.

On this theory, anthropomorphism evolved from the relative benefits of false positives when compared to true negatives.[12] Guthrie notices that there is abundant evidence of widespread anthropomorphic belief. He generalizes from these data, claiming that religion originates in anthropomorphic tendencies.[13] Guthrie's model, if accurate, implies counterfactual insensitivity for beliefs in anthropological Gods.

4.2.1.2 Step 2

Evolutionary researchers notice that something more than Guthrie's model is required to explain the evolution of religion. Though Guthrie's model explains the automatic production of anthropomorphic judgments, it does not explain the failure of these judgments to update in light of new evidence. Put another way, anthropomorphic perception typically differs from anthropomorphic belief. For ordinary beliefs we allow evidence to revise our initial perceptions. For example, Trundle mistakes a log for her lover, and responds affectionately. On closer inspection, she recoils, composes herself, and assumes an appropriate posture. Guthrie's model requires an explanation for the *recalcitrance* of religious beliefs. It also requires an explanation for why religious anthropomorphism projects Gods, whose powers render Gods somewhat different from ordinary persons.

4.2.2 The fixation of religious commitments to cooperative norms

While there are many controversies about specific evolutionary hypotheses,[14] a rough consensus has emerged in favor of religious commitments as culturally and genetically evolved adaptations for cooperative exchange. The main elements of this evolutionary model are hardly new. In the 4th century BCE, the Greek author Critias conjectured:

> Some shrewd man first, a man in judgment wise, found for mortals the fear of gods…So that everything which mortals say is heard and everything done is visible. Even if you plan in silence some evil deed it will not be hidden from the gods: for discernment lies in them.[15]

Critias presents an evolutionary logic to explain religion: beliefs in Gods endure because such beliefs help to secure social order. The benefits that this social order ensures favor the conservation of tendencies to acquire and transmit moralizing religious beliefs. Such benefits favor the persistence of religious beliefs over time irrespective of whether the Gods believed in exist. Contemporary evolutionary researchers add to the Critiasian hypothesis by providing explicit models for the evolution of religious cognition as coalition mechanisms that cultural and genetic coevolutionary dynamics favor. These contemporary evolutionary models answer the following lingering puzzles in Guthrie's anthropomorphism model:

1. Why do religious persons believe in Gods and not merely distal humans? Answer: If prosocial conduct is to be motivated, the Gods must be believed to be real. They must also be credited with powers sufficient to motivate prosocial responses. Thus religious beliefs optimize prosocial motivations when religious persons believe in Gods who are endowed with the powers to observe and reward or punish the relevant social behaviors.

2. Why is religious belief recalcitrance? Answer: Effective cooperation demands reliable social prediction across variable circumstances—threats, distractions, and incentives may differ for individual cooperators situated in different places and times. For social prediction to be reliable amid the tides of change, the beliefs that motivate prosocial responses must not vary. The stability of social prediction requires the durability of incentives, and so benefit from the fixation of beliefs in rewarding Gods.[16]

We next consider this evolutionary psychological model for moralizing, counterfactually insensitive religion in more detail.

4.2.3 Moral properties and recalcitrance

4.2.3.1 Commitments as beliefs and feelings

If religions evolved to promote cooperation, then we would expect the objects of religious commitments to possess properties that motivate cooperative commitments. Several recent evolutionary theories hypothesize that Gods evolve as sanctioning authorities[17] and/or as monitoring agents to whom cooperative reputations matter,[18] or as agents that combine both properties.[19] The proposition that religious commitments evolve to facilitate coalition behaviors casts doubt on the inward authority of any religious convictions as reason for thinking that the conviction is true.[20]

Moreover, the prospect for cooperation's success increases wherever Gods are believed to offer additional motivation from positive reward factors, such as those that love, hope, and joy bring wherever these are integrated with cooperative norms.[21] For example, wherever cooperative action is believed to please the Gods that one intrinsically desires to please, religious commitments may inspire prosocial responses from motivations that will not vary with the salience of extrinsic rewards and punishments. Furthermore, we might expect cooperative norms to receive additional support from the interactions of explicit belief-like structures and a wide spectrum of affective responses. This is because motivations are not merely produced from thoughts, but also from various feeling states. Preliminary evidence suggests that the religious music, festivals, prayers, chanting, dance, and other social practices and rites align the affective states of participants, even at large social scales.[22] Thus the generation of inward convictions and feelings may be more complex than the production of beliefs. A song does not affect us because we believe in it, at least not entirely. In these ways, evolutionary psychology therefore explains why religious commitments are not like ordinary beliefs.[23]

4.2.3.2 Suspicion

Evolutionary theories of religion predict tendencies for suspicion and even aggression against those perceived to be opponents of one's religion.[24] This fact is hard to explain from the perspective of any particular religion in a manner that does not beg questions against other religious perspectives. However, if religious cognition evolved to facilitate cooperation, then perceptions that religious difference is immoral find a simple explanation. Evolutionary models predict mistrust of other religions wherever cooperation across religious lines is uncertain.[25] Religious coalitions offer especially powerful cooperative motivations from the effects of beliefs in supernatural causation, as Critias long ago observed.[26] Related biases for the moral superiority of one's tradition may be predicted from cooperative demands. For such biases, when shared, facilitate effective social coordination.[27]

4.2.4 Emotional properties

For religious persons to cooperate, they must be able to reliably identify each other. There are two separate identification problems related to two different types of threat to cooperation. Sometimes cooperation is threatened by "free riding"—taking from cooperative goods without contributing. Free-riding has room to evolve wherever the benefits of cheating predictably exceed the benefits of cooperation.[28] Where free riding threatens cooperation, evolutionary dynamics may target recognition systems that enable effective partner discrimination.[29] Religious emotions are simply explained as features of discriminating signalling systems because emotions are hard to fake without the appropriate commitments.[30] By contrast, emotional displays would be useless or even distracting for belief mechanisms that evolve to track variability in the world. Ordinarily it would be awkward and costly to feel worshipful upon noticing the rainfall, etc. The emotional qualities of religious convictions are poorly explained as the effects of ordinary empirical search and discover mechanisms.

Sometimes cooperation is threatened by a combination of risk and uncertainty, without any clear threat from free riding. Cooperative insecurity arises wherever partners may benefit from cooperation only if others cooperate too, but not if not. Collective benefits can exceed any benefit from cheating yet still bring risks. Suppose we are workers at a factory. Suppose all workers would benefit by asking for a raise, if and only if everyone were to demand a raise simultaneously. Suppose further that there could be no plausible threat for retribution were all to ask for a raise at the same time. Imagine that wherever coordination is less than perfect, retribution is certain. Would you risk sending your request without knowing that others will also send theirs? If the costs of failure are too high, or the relative benefits are too low, it might be unwise to take such risks. Indeed, even if you are personally courageous you might predict that cowards will spoil the operation. Your courage does not predict theirs (ignoring dependencies). This toy example illustrates how cooperation can fail even if there is no incentive to cheat successful cooperation, and even among those who are by nature cooperative and courageous. Failure arises from an inability to predict what others will do. Thus any mechanism that ensures collective action against such risks will be desirable to all partners, and so highly evolvable. For the problem we have just imagined, unions sometimes provide effective assurance mechanisms: unions convert a problem of uncertain cooperation under risk to an easier coordination problem of enlisting members. And for the benefits of such assurance workers have an incentive to pay their union dues. Generalizing to evolutionary timescales, coordinating structures may be ratified by cultural and natural selection from the benefits of cooperative assurance. Some argue that many features of religious cognition and culture evolved to solve this second cooperation problem.[31]

Our task is not to review the evolutionary literatures in detail but rather to consider how evolutionary models explain religious beliefs as counterfactually insensitive. If such evolutionary explanations are on the right track, subjective confidence would appear to provide insufficient warrant in favor of religious belief: the foregoing evolutionary models predict that we would possess strong confidence irrespective of the truth.

▪ 5. A GOLDEN RULE FOR BELIEF FIXATION

What have we learned about the capacity of evolutionary psychology to undermine religious beliefs? Psychological hypothesis might rationally undermine confidence for a domain of belief wherever

- the hypothesis predicts the occurrence of beliefs in this domain, and
- the hypothesis shows such beliefs to lack counterfactual sensitivity.

The most plausible evolutionary theories of religion variously explain supernatural commitments as a variety of coalition cognition. Supernatural convictions will evolve to be counterfactually insensitive. The idea is that we have evolved an attraction for religious beliefs irrespective of any alleged religious fact. Evolutionary theories of religion are credible because they predict properties of religious cognition that remain poorly explained in folk theories.

If one were to believe these evolutionary models should one give up on religion? No. Bayes's rule helps us to understand that the adjustment of belief is a matter of degree. How much one's beliefs are modified depends on one's prior confidence in religion as it meets an undermining evolutionary model for religion. Returning to the question we posed at the outset, if Ed's prior probability for his religious propositions were to remain high for reasons unrelated to the coalition mechanisms that evolutionary psychology describes, then the impact of evolutionary psychology on Ed's confidence in religion might be rather low.[32]

I suspect that many believers would claim authority for religious propositions from factors that are independent of their inward convictions (so too might atheists for their beliefs)—so too might Ed. However, committed truth-seekers of every theological stripe should be cautious before allowing any inference from data acquired from inward search strategies. For we have noticed that coalition mechanisms may corrupt judgments about the independent grounds for our beliefs. Because the mechanisms that bias judgments generally operate outside awareness, such distortions are compatible with epistemic sincerity.

We have focused on the narrow question of how Ed and similar truth-seekers should update their religious beliefs in light of evolutionary psychology, but we have ignored what it might mean for people who hold different theologies to engage in truth-seeking activities together. This is a separate and more difficult topic about which to offer advice. The question is not how best for me to adjust my beliefs but how best to for me to adjust yours, and to be rationally affected by yours.

I think about the topic of theological exchange in the following way. The golden rule of morality states that we should treat others as we would like ourselves to be treated. A similar rule—Bayes's rule (along with a larger edifice of bayesian statistical inference)—has enabled progress in the natural and social sciences, where theories and evidence are only accepted when presented in a manner that can in principle persuade critics who do not already agree with the

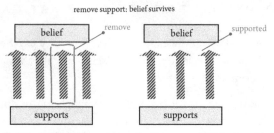

Figure 17.2 The limits of psychology for undermining multiply supported beliefs

hypothesis or model under consideration. Revisions are rarely wholesale, but rather proceed incrementally. I think internalizing Bayes's rule can help theological truth-seekers put into practice something like a "golden rule of belief fixation". Even those who honestly disagree about the prior probabilities attaching to various religious and areligious hypotheses can mend their disagreements by clarifying the predictions that enable discriminations in favor of one belief over its rivals. In theory, as inquiry progresses, we would expect posteriors beliefs on different sides to slowly converge. The interest of the Bayesian method is that it shows something to be possible that one might not have thought to be possible, namely improving our opinions regarding the Gods, gradually converging in our thinking. Theological relativism is not logically fated.

Whether theologians who disagree with each other are psychologically prepared to accept the results of Bayesian inquiries remains an open and separate question. I have described an uncontroversial calculus for belief revision without any psychological evidence that it can be put to practical use. It is far from obvious to me that convergence in religious judgments is possible by rational means—that is, without drugs, coercion, the destruction of institutions, and similar draconian measures. However my anecdotal observations after more than twenty years of studying religions is that religious viewpoints do change, though slowly—often inperceptibly—in response to the examples of others. Such change is seldom a matter of debates, but occurs through one's affiliations and experiences.

I have set aside the question of whether it is worth anyone's time to pursue the rational implications of one's scientific beliefs for religious beliefs, rather than doing something else more urgent or edifying—like feeding the hungry, taking in strangers, visiting the sick, or as we earlier considered for Ed, getting some sunshine. Personally I would rather do many things besides debating religion. My distaste arises, in part, because I do not wish to change anyone's mind, one way or the other. However I also doubt that religious questions admit of answers that can be stated in propositions. Science has led to some impressive results, but humans are organisms and as such, we are limitated in our understanding. We have good evolutionary reasons to suspect that our questions about ultimate reality are not well formulated.[33]

Insofar as it makes sense to debate theism, the topic of this volume, all such debates should take place within a Bayesian framework.[34]

ACKNOWLEDGMENTS

Thanks to Marcus Frean, Chad Meister, and J. P. Moreland for their helpful comments. A Victoria University Research Fund Grant (no. 8-3046-108855) supported part of this research.

NOTES

1. A similar question might be raised for an atheist. How does the evolutionary psychology of religion impact on atheistic convictions? The method I describe here applies generically to any belief.

2. See Peirce, C. S. "The Fixation of Belief," in *Charles S. Peirce: Selected Writings, ed.* P. P. Weiner, 91–112 (New York: Dover, 1966).

3. Bulbulia, J. (2012). *Ennuitheism*. In Science and the World's Religions: Vol 3. Religions and Controversies, Chapter 7, pages 43–64. Praeger, Santa Barbara, CA.

4. Sterelny, K. "Escaping Illusion," *American Scientist* 94 (2006): 461–463.

5. Apparently Anaximander believed that humans evolved from fish. He was correct, though for spurious reasons: Anaximander apparently thought that humans were once born inside fish, which we later outgrew and ate. In many details Anaximander's theory was bizarrely false. His truth was accidental.

6. For an Bayesian argument in favor of Christianity see Swinburne, R., *The Resurrection of God Incarnate* (New York: Oxford University Press, 2002). I suggest, without argument, that Swinburne's method for selection of confirming evidence violates a golden rule of belief fixation—explained below—insofar as this selection would not persuade those not already convinced of the correctness of the Christian hypothesis.

7. Trivers, R., "Self-Deception in Service of Deceit: Selected Papers of Robert Trivers," in *Natural Selection and Social Theory*, ed. R. Trivers, 255–293 (New York: Oxford University Press, 2002).

8. Darwin, C., *The Autobiography of Charles Darwin and Selected Letters* (New York: Dover, 1958), 91.

9. Darwin, C. *The Autobiography of Charles Darwin*, 73.

10. Bulbulia, J. "Why I am an Ennuitheist," in *Science and the World's Religions*, ed. Patrick McNamara and Wesley J. Wildman (Westwood, CT: Greenwood, 2012), 43–64.

11. Guthrie, S., *Faces in the Clouds: A New Theory of Religion* (New York: Oxford University Press, 1993.

12. Recently Foster and Kokko presented an exact model for the conservation of anthropomorphic traits, showing conditions for the evolution of hair-trigger perceptual judgments that may fire in the absence of any anthropomorphic cue. See Foster, K. R., and Kokko, H., "The Evolution of Superstitious and Superstition-like Behaviour," *Proceedings of the Royal Society of London* B 276 (2009): 31–37. Their result can be simplified to a variant of Hamilton's ubiquitous rule, which in its most general form states that any trait will be favored wherever the benefit-to-cost ratio exceeds 1:

$$\frac{\text{benefits}}{\text{costs}} > 1 \tag{7}$$

Hamilton, W., "The Evolution of Altruistic Behavior," *American Naturalist* 97 (1964): 354–356.

13. Notice that we could reduce Bayes's theorem for hypothesis selection to a variant of this ratio by thinking of benefits and costs to confidence. Wherever

$$\frac{\Pr(e|h')}{\Pr(e|h'')} > 1 \tag{8}$$

then confidence for h' should rise (assuming only two hypotheses). However, Guthrie shows us that whether confidence for the more likely hypothesis actually does rise is secondary to the practical benefits of believing.

14. Schloss, J. and Murray, M. J., "Evolutionary Accounts of Belief in Supernatural Punishment: A Critical Review," *Religion, Brain, & Behavior* 1 (2011): 46–99.

15. Critias, "The Critias Fragment," in *Sextus Empiricus, Adversus Mathematicos* (4th century BCE), 2010.

16. For a discussion, see Joseph Bulbulia, "Religious Costs as Adaptations that Signal Altruistic Intention," *Evolution and Cognition* 10 (2004): 19–38.

17. Johnson, D. and Kruger, O., "The Good of Wrath: Supernatural Punishment and the Evolution of Cooperation," *Political Theology* 5 (2004): 159–176.

18. Bering, J., "The Folk Psychology of Souls," *Behavioral and Brain Sciences* 29 (2006): 453–498.

19. Johnson, D. and Bering, J., "Hand of God, Mind of Man: Punishment and Cognition in the Evolution of Cooperation," in *The "Nature" of Belief: Scientific and Philosophical Perspectives on the Evolution of Religion*, ed. J. Schloss and A. Plantinga, 26–43 (Oxford: Oxford University Press, 2009).

20. Johnson, D. and Fowler, J. "The Evolution of Overconfidence," *Nature* 477 (2009): 317–320.

21. Schloss, J., "He Who Laughs Best: Involuntary Religious Affect as a Solution to Recursive Cooperative Defection," in *The Evolution of Religion: Studies, Theories, and Critiques*, ed. Joseph Bulbulia et al., 197–207 (Santa Margarita, CA: Collins Foundation Press, 2008).

22. Konvalinka, I. et al., "Synchronized Arousal Between Performers and Related Spectators in a Fire-Walking Ritual," *Proceedings of the National Academy of Sciences* 108 18 (2011): 8514–8519; T. Luhrmann, *When God Talks Back* (New York: Oxford University Press, 2011; U. Schjoedt et al. "The Power of Charisma: Perceived Charisma Inhibits the Attentional and Executive Systems of Believers in Intercessory Prayer," *Social Cognitive and Affective Neuroscience* 4 (2010): 199–207.

23. Bulbulia, J., "Religious Costs as Adaptations that Signal Altruistic Intention," *Evolution and Cognition* 10 (2004): 19–38.

24. For evidence see Turchin, P., *War and Peace and War: The Rise and Fall of Empires* New York: Penguin, 2006.

25. Lanman, J., *A Secular Mind: Towards a Cognitive Anthropology of Atheism*. PhD thesis, Oxford University.

26. Bulbulia, J. (2004). "Religious Costs as Adaptations that Signal Altruistic Intention," *Evolution and Cognition*, 10(1): 19–38.

Henrich, J. (2009). "The Evolution of Costly Displays, Cooperation, and Religion: Credibility Enhancing Displays and Their Implications for Cultural Evolution," *Evolution and Human Behavior*, 30: 244–260.

Norenzayan, A. and Shariff, A. F. (2008). "The Origin and Evolution of Religious Prosociality," *Science*, 322(5898): 58–62.

27. Graham, J. and Haidt, J. "Beyond Beliefs: Religions Bind Individuals Into Moral Communities," *Personality and Social Psychology Review* 14 (2010): 140–150.

28.

$$1 < \frac{\text{benefits of detection}}{\text{benefits of cooperation}} \tag{9}$$

29. Bulbulia, J. "The Cognitive and Evolutionary Psychology of Religion," *Biology and Philosophy* 18 (2004): 655–686; W. Irons, "Why Are Humans Religious? An Inquiry into the Evolutionary Origins of Religion," *Currents in Theology and Mission* 28 (2001): 357–368; Schloss, "He Who Laughs Best," R. Sosis, "Book Review: 'Darwin's Cathedral: Evolution, Religion, and the Nature of Society,'" *Evolution and Human Behavior* 24 (2003): 137–143.

30. Irons, "Why Are Humans Religious?, Schloss, "He Who Laughs Best," R. Frank, *Passions Within Reason: The Strategic Role of the Emotions* (New York: W.W. Norton, 1988).

31. Bulbulia, J. and Frean, M. (2010). *The Evolution of Charismatic Cultures. Method and Theory in the Study of Religion*, 22: 254–271.

32. Here is a true story from my own life. I learned about the earth's spherical shape from a teacher who, as it turned out, happened to be very senile. She should not have been trusted with such an important fact, perhaps especially with one so dramatically in conflict with appearances. Yet my round earth belief survived the disclosure that its causes were unjustified. My confidence remains warranted because my belief is anchored in many reliable sources. In terms of Bayes's theorem, my posterior confidence in the round earth hypothesis is close to 1.

33. Discussed in Bulbulia, J. (2012). Ennuitheism. In Science and the World's Religions: Vol 3. Religions and Controversies, chapter 7, pages 43–64. Praeger, Santa Barbara, CA.

34. I am told that Alvin Plantinga and others (including Vic Reppert) have advanced Bayesian-style arguments to the effect that the conjunction of evolutionary theory and naturalism implies a global and self-refuting defeater for all our beliefs. In this chapter I have not attempted to wrestle with any such justifications for global skepticism. It is enough for me to notice that scientists who employ Bayes's rule find it terrifically helpful in discriminating between rival hypotheses. As a piece of algebra, Bayes's rule cannot be doubted. As for the commitments of methodological naturalism, these certainly can be doubted, and improved. Naturalists should not seek a priori justifications for their methods, and should not think of their assumptions as anything more than provisional because no successful scientific project has ever imposed such demands on discovery. In any case, whatever bullet one must bite to employ Bayes's rule for discriminating between rival hypotheses seems to me worth biting, if the alternative is to live without it, or to embrace some intelligence-defeating skepticism.

▪ FOR FURTHER READING

Chomsky, N. *New Horizons in the Study of Language and Mind*. Cambridge: Cambridge University Press, 2000.

Lauwereyns, J. *The Anatomy of Bias: How Neural Circuits Weight the Options*. Cambridge, MA: MIT Press, 2010.

McKay, R., and D. Dennett. "The Evolution of Misbelief." *Behavioral and Brain Sciences* 32 (2011): 493–510.

18 Evolutionary Accounts of Religion and the Justification of Religious Belief

■ MICHAEL J. MURRAY AND
JEFFREY P. SCHLOSS

■ 1. INTRODUCTION

Suppose that Fred is a committed theist and a committed Darwinian. Fred's education persuades him that evolutionary theory accounts for many aspects of the natural world that have the appearance of being designed. Fred's experience and upbringing persuade him that God exists.

Fred has a special interest in evolutionary theories of religion and concludes from them that there is good reason to think that religious beliefs are at least largely caused by the interaction of genes and environment on the human mind. So far as Fred can see, nothing about evolutionary theory requires or rules out the claim that God initiates the evolutionary process, and so, he concludes, evolutionary theory is silent whether or not God initiated the process that led to the religious beliefs in question. To what extent, if any, is Fred rationally bound to revise his religious commitments?

As the reader might notice, Fred's situation is closely related to the situation of Ed referenced at the beginning of Joseph Bulbulia's corresponding chapter. In this chapter we will look at a few reasons why someone might think that the information Fred has requires him to revise his religious commitments, and why those reasons are not convincing. We will then mount a positive case according to which such religious beliefs are, at least for all we know, fully justified even if the evolutionary accounts of the origin of religious belief are true.

Before we get to a discussion of how evolutionary accounts of religion impact religious belief, we need to step back and think about how "causal accounts of the origin of belief" function more generally, and why they might or might not be threatening to any sort of belief, religious or otherwise. As a result, over the next few pages we will consider these questions more generally, and only return to religious belief at about the halfway point of the chapter. We ask the reader's patience while we stake out these important preliminary considerations.

■ 2. IDEAS AND THEIR ORIGINS

Theorizing and research about the nature of minds, the origins of ideas, and the justification of beliefs have been going on since philosophizing began. Ancient

Greek philosophy was a font of different theoretical perspectives on these topics, with some arguing that (at least some) ideas are innate, and others defending the view that all ideas have their origin in the five senses. Refinements of the relevant debates on these topics continued on through the medieval, Renaissance, and modern periods with philosophers offering often brilliant arguments for their respective positions.

When psychology was beginning to emerge as a genuine scientific discipline in the late-nineteenth and early twentieth centuries, the debate about innate ideas was largely regarded as settled. In part because of the work and influence of Swiss developmental psychologist Jean Piaget, scientists concluded that the evidence was squarely against the claim that we are born with any innate cognitive structures or content.

Empirical psychological work undertaken since the middle of the twentieth century has, however, told a very different story. Indeed, recent findings in cognitive and developmental psychology have essentially undone the two previously dominant views of the human mind—the view of John Locke, according to which the mind is a blank slate, and the view of the behaviorist B. F. Skinner, according to which human thoughts and feelings are causally inert. The Lockean view holds that the mind comes to beliefs without native disposition and solely by the impress of experiences of the world around us. But recent findings have shown us that the human mind is nothing like a blank slate. Instead, mounting evidence has made it clear that we come into the world with—if not "innate ideas"—at least dispositions to preferentially attend to certain aspects of the environment, storing information in recurrent data structures, and forming particular classes of beliefs (and/or desires) when our minds are activated by classes of stimuli. We will see some examples in a moment. Locke might have hoped that dispositions of this sort are nothing special since, as described, these "cognitive dispositions" might amount to nothing more than "dispositions to record on the mental slate what the chalk of experience supplies." Why, he might ask, should we regard our cognitive dispositions as anything more exotic than that? The primary reason is that the beliefs that are thus spawned are both cross-culturally recurrent and/or present even when the stimuli that generate them are evidentially insufficient (psychologists describe such beliefs as arising despite "the poverty of the stimulus"). Thus the mind seems to contain more than the data of experience could have provided. This is impossible to square with standard Lockean empiricism.

A good example of this can be found in so-called folk theories.[1] Folk theories are specific bodies of information that people use to reason and to which they appear naturally disposed. While there is some variability among folk theories, in many cases such theories have a universal core. For example, there is good evidence that humans pan-culturally classify plants and animals into hierarchically organized taxonomies of kinds that include three levels: a generic species, a higher-order biological domain, and a lower-order category of species.[2] At each level, being a member of a kind is exclusive (if something is a plant, it cannot also be an animal), and allows us to draw inferences about other kind-specific properties of the organism (if something is an animal, it always gives birth to things that are of the same kind). As another example, data seem to indicate that humans pan-culturally associate kind membership (being a tiger) with possession of an invisible causal "essence" that resides within each substance without being a formal part of it.[3] In other words, we seem naturally disposed to believe something like Platonism or Aristotelianism about organisms, according to which to be a tiger is to have (or be related to) something like "the form of tiger."

Cognitive and developmental psychologists are identifying an increasing variety and number of such folk theories.[4] Those working in this field now claim substantial evidence that our minds are disposed to such beliefs concerning the nature of the mind (folk psychology),[5] the biological world (folk biology),[6] dynamics and physical ontology (folk physics),[7] basic mathematical facts (folk mathematics), etc.

Noting that we have such cognitive dispositions does not, however, explain their origin. *Why* are human minds configured so as to form certain universal concepts in the wide range of environments to which we are exposed over the course of cognitive development? The answer to this has to do with rejecting the behaviorist notion that human thoughts and feelings are causally inert. Because beliefs influence behaviors, beliefs have implications for our evolutionary fitness. As a result, cognition itself may be subject to natural selection when evolutionary pressures select for (or against) certain behaviors and the beliefs that generate them. This does not mean that individual thoughts are biologically determined, but it does mean that general tendencies in cognition may reflect cognitive dispositions that have been shaped by selection. And in certain cases, it may also be that the range of variability in certain domains of thought has been constrained. For example, an increasing number of theorists argue that folk theories are one (among many) human traits that are universal because they have been shaped or "canalized" during the evolution of human cognition.[8] Canalization (or even fixation) of a trait occurs when (1) design features constrain the development of organisms and thus limit the variability of features that can emerge downstream, and/or (2) there is a single variant of the trait that is most adaptive across the range of environments to which the organism is exposed.[9]

It is not our purpose here to argue that claims like this about "cognitive evolution" are true or false, but rather to assess their consequences *if they are true*. And if this account of evolutionary cognitive canalization is true, two surprising conclusions seem to follow. First, it appears that the origin of some types of beliefs is explained primarily in terms of *causes* rather than in terms of *reasons*. That is, on this picture, it looks like unintelligent ("blind")[10] causal forces operating on organisms select for minds that naturally form these beliefs rather than some other beliefs. This is surprising because (1) beliefs that arise by causes rather than reasons also seem to lack the kind of history we usually think is necessary for justification of beliefs (which usually requires appeal to reasons), and yet (2) we take many of the beliefs that result from canalized cognition to be central, if not downright foundational, to our thinking about and understanding of the world (beliefs in the existence other minds, mathematics, etc.). As a result, many of our most fundamental beliefs appear to be (epistemically) in trouble.

Second, if this is all there is to the story, beliefs of this sort will be unjustified unless the causal pathway that generates them is of a sort that tracks the truth of that belief. So, for example, we might learn that human minds have a nearly irresistible tendency to attribute certain kinds of mental states to any living organism (indeed, even to a wide variety of types of "representations of organisms"—cartoons, robots, etc.) having facial features that roughly approximate the features of primate faces. If the reason for this is that there is some adaptive advantage for us to form such beliefs when stimulated in this way, we have reason to treat these attributions of "mindedness" as unjustified since, it seems, these belief-forming mechanisms would *not track the truth* of the belief. That is, on this view, the belief is not dependent on whether or not such animals actually *have* intentional mental states, but only on their having certain facial features. Thus, to use the language of Kim Sterelny cited by Joseph Bulbulia in his contribution to this volume, the innate psychological disposition to form such beliefs is not "counterfactually sensitive."[11] It appears as though we would have beliefs in other minds even if the world contained human-like and other entities with mammalian facial features but lacked mindedness altogether.

So is that how it really is? If many of our beliefs are formed by cognitive dispositions acquired through "blind" evolutionary forces, should we take a skeptical stance toward those beliefs, or at least regard them as unjustified?

Probably not. Above we hypothesized that if cognition is canalized by "blind evolutionary forces," then the resultant belief-forming mechanisms would not "track the truth of the belief." But that hypothesis is probably incorrect. Indeed, it seems fairly easy to imagine how selection might function to keep our belief-forming mechanisms on track.[12]

Let's consider what appears to be a straightforward story about how natural selection might select for on-track belief-forming mechanisms. If my local environment is filled with various things that are relevant to my acquiring nutrition, securing mating opportunities, avoiding disease, injury, and predation, etc., there will be strong selective pressure in favor of belief-forming mechanisms that get the facts about these objects largely right. As a result, we have reason to think that, in such cases, our native belief-forming mechanisms do get these things right.[13]

If this account is correct, the targets of my beliefs are causes of my beliefs in two ways: *remotely* and *proximately*. They are causes remotely because those targets were among the features of the selective environment that explain why

I have belief-forming mechanisms that (when stimulated in ways that are typical when those objects are present to my senses) trigger true beliefs about those objects. And they are causes proximately because those objects do in fact trigger the beliefs in individual cases where we come into sensory contact with them. As a result, objects in the environment can be causes of the belief in two distinct but complementary senses—in a remote or "ultimate" sense by selecting for certain dispositions in belief-forming mechanisms, and in a proximate sense by triggering the appropriate disposition in individual instances. Unless significant features of the environment to which our cognitive dispositions are adapted change significantly and more rapidly than canalized dispositions can accommodate, beliefs formed in the way we have described will be truth-tracking. Let's call this the "proximate-remote" causal account of the origin of evolved belief.

In ordinary discourse about beliefs and their justification we think about that justification in terms of reasons, evidence, and arguments (and sometimes "grounds"). When we challenge someone on the justification for their beliefs, we expect that any justification offered will be supplied in terms of these categories (and not in terms of facts about the causal ancestry of the beliefs). Indeed, when we respond to such challenges about our beliefs by citing the *causal* ancestry of the belief, it is usually with apologetic overtones. In exotic cases one might cite causal explanations along the following lines. "Why do you believe there is a giant shimmering boulder hovering over your bed?" "I guess it must be from that LSD you slipped in my drink." But even in more mundane cases, appealing to causes rather than reasons in explaining beliefs often gives the impression that such explanations undermine justification.[14] Such explanations often feature the dismissive word "only" as in, for example, "You *only* believe in Allah because you were born in Egypt."

The "proximate-remote" account, if and when it is correct, shows that explanations in terms of causes and reasons need not always be as unsatisfying as such dismissive comments make them appear. If the targets of my belief are both the *remote cause* of the on-track belief-forming mechanism as well as the *proximate trigger* of a token instance of belief about the target, then those targets count both as *causes of* and *reasons for* my belief.

The phrase "reasons for" is ambiguous when used in contexts like this. In some cases we think of reasons in terms of propositions that make other propositions more likely to be true. The belief that Smith's fingerprints are on the murder weapon is a "reason for" the belief that Smith is the murderer, because the first belief provides some confirming evidence for the second. In the boulder case, however, the "reasons for" relationship is not to be conceived of as a relationship between propositions, but rather as one in which "a way the world is" confers justification on a belief directly (as long as the believer is in an appropriate causal relationship with the target of the belief). In a world in which the presence of boulders explains (albeit partially) the on-track belief-forming mechanism that translates my seeing the boulder into a "boulder belief," as well as the particular belief that I know that there is a boulder in front of me when I see one, the presence of boulders is a reason for my belief as well a cause. In such a situation, a proximate cause can also be the justifying ground of the belief, as long as that cause (like a boulder, but unlike LSD) is connected to the truth of the belief it triggers.[15]

So how is all of this relevant to assessing the implications of evolutionary accounts of the origins of religious (or any other) beliefs? Arguments that claim that there is something about evolutionary accounts of beliefs that undermine those beliefs operate by claiming that the causal accounts and the reasons-conferring accounts come apart.[16] Such accounts can come apart when (1) the target of the belief is not involved in the shaping or causing (via selection) of the relevant belief-forming mechanism, or (2) the target is involved in the selection of the mechanism without providing selective pressure in favor of a reliable belief-forming mechanism, or (3) the target is involved in selection for the belief-forming mechanism, but not in the generation of a token instance of belief about the target, or (4) the target is involved as a proximate cause of the belief, but not by activating the belief-forming mechanism that was selected for, or (5) the target was not involved as a proximate cause of the belief at all.

Note that reason-conferring is not *always* undermined in these cases, even when causing and reason-conferring come apart. For example, it could be that boulders are involved in the selection of the on-track belief-forming mechanism that generates belief in boulders. But that mechanism might be sufficiently coarse grained that it will reliably generate beliefs about numerous other physical structures in our environment, even when those structures played no direct role in the selective process.[17] While working through the conditions that undercut the conferring of reasons would be a useful exercise, it is not the one we intend to pursue here. Instead, we want to focus on a particular class of cases that seem to be especially problematic.

To begin, let's note that, generally, reason-explanations of this sort run into trouble the more causally remote the target becomes. The extreme case discussed in the recent philosophical literature concerns evolved dispositions to form moral beliefs and, in particular, moral beliefs that involve belief in objective moral facts.[18] The problem in this case is as follows. There has emerged a variety of empirically supported, theoretically coherent evolutionary accounts of the origin of moral belief and behavior in human beings. According to some of these accounts, what is selected for is not simply morally relevant beliefs and behaviors, but belief in the reality of *objective moral facts*. Although there is debate over these accounts,[19] let's examine the implications of their being largely right. According to what we have seen so far, accounts of the origins of a belief do not constitute justificatory challenges to the beliefs they purport to explain, when the targets of the beliefs are involved in the selection of the belief-forming mechanism and triggering of the beliefs in token cases. But it is hard to see how "objective moral facts" can play either role in this case. The natural forces that provide the selective pressure in our ancestral past, as well as the proximate environment that triggers particular beliefs, do not include objective moral facts.[20] The argument for this is long, but can be bypassed here by simply noting that, on any account, objective moral facts are not natural facts. The question, then, is whether or not one can argue that objective moral facts are related to the natural facts that *are* relevant to the selection of belief-forming mechanisms and/or the triggering of beliefs in ways that preserve the reasons-conferring connection. It appears that the answer is no. That is, it appears that they are "counterfactually insensitive," and we would have such beliefs even if they were false, because they are caused in ways that are independent of their truth.

Before moving on it is worth noting that even if (1) these evolved intuitive mechanisms really do explain dispositions to believe in objective moral facts, and (2) those mechanisms are not truth-tracking, this does not entail that the beliefs are unjustified. If we had good reasons for believing in objective moral facts apart from the moral intuitions that, on this account, are triggered by our evolutionary heritage, then those beliefs could be justified nonetheless. So although we cannot infer from arguments like this straight to conclusions about moral skepticism or nihilism, believers in moral realism bear the burden of showing that there are reasons independent of evolved dispositions to such beliefs.[21]

■ 3. COGNITIVE AND EVOLUTIONARY BASIS OF RELIGIOUS BELIEFS

We are now ready to engage the specific issue of religious beliefs. Over the last dozen years or so, cognitive, developmental, and evolutionary psychologists have made an increasingly compelling case that many aspects of religious belief and practice admit of causal explanations in much the same way that beliefs in objective moral facts do. Cognitive and developmental psychologists have argued that human minds are disposed naturally to generate, retain, articulate, and spread beliefs in the reality of supernatural agents—agents who are responsible for teleological features of nature and who police morally relevant behaviors between human agents. They have further argued that there are strong, native dispositions to believe that such beings have magnified agent qualities: they are immortal, superpowerful, all-knowing, and all-perceiving.[22] Others have argued that we have native dispositions to form beliefs that human agents are composed of physical bodies and immaterial minds, and that those minds continue to function after bodily death.[23] Evolutionary theorists offer suggestive evidence that such dispositions are not only present realities, but that they emerged because of various adaptive pressures that confronted humans as their social groups increased in size. In such cases, belief in supernatural, moralizing gods became adaptive as a way of enhancing group cooperation.[24] The case that we are "natural born believers" is by no means closed. But the evidence is strongly suggestive.

In light of what we have seen so far, the question should now be clear: Do such accounts raise a problem for the justification of religious beliefs?[25] That is, should we conceive of the relationship between causes and reasons in the case of religious belief the way we do when we think about evolved belief-forming dispositions concerning boulders, or the way we do when we think about belief in objective moral facts? Put another way we might ask: Is it the case, given these accounts, that we would have these religious beliefs, whether or not they are true?

Initially the answers to these questions seem obvious. The mechanisms that explain the dispositions toward religious belief and the beliefs that are generated by the activation of these mechanisms appear to have arisen and to be triggered entirely by natural entities. As a result (it seems), whether or not supernatural agents exist, we would have minds that naturally form beliefs in such agents. If this is right, it is problematic since it would mean that these belief-forming processes are insensitive to counterfactual conditions and are not truth-tracking.

In what follows we consider three worries that arise with respect to this argument. The first two involve philosophical issues concerning justification and truth-tracking and the last focuses on the central concern generated by this argument.

In general, a cognitive mechanism is truth-tracking if it would not produce the beliefs it does when those beliefs are false. Our boulder-belief-producing mechanism is, let's presume, reliable, and one of the characteristics that is true of it and relevant to its justificatory status is this: if there were no boulders in front of me, that mechanism would not produce that belief. In virtue of this, the mechanism is truth-tracking.

More precisely, we can say that a belief-forming mechanism is truth-tracking if and only if, in the nearest world at which the target belief is false, the mechanism does not produce the belief. That is, for any cognizer, C, a belief-forming mechanism, M, aimed at forming beliefs, B, where B affirms the obtaining of a state of affairs, S, is truth-tracking when the following conditional is true:

(TT) M is truth-tracking if and only if *were S not to obtain, C would not believe B.*

Problems arise, however, when we apply (TT) to monotheistic belief formation. The first problem is that, on traditional monotheism, God exists necessarily. As a result, the italicized counterfactual is trivially true because the antecedent is a counterpossible. Given that, the mechanisms at work here satisfy truth-tracking, but not in a way that is very gratifying. After all, even if God has not one thing to do with the actual emergence and activation of these belief-forming mechanisms, beliefs emerging from them satisfy (TT), and that runs afoul of the spirit of truth-tracking in the first place.

Let's set that problem aside and turn to a second problem. When considering the italicized counterfactual, we are asked to consider whether or not, *in the nearest world at which there is no God*, belief in God would still obtain. If God belief would occur in the nearest no-God world, then the mechanisms in question are not truth-tracking. Setting aside the worry about the necessity of divine existence, what would such a world be like? Consider three possibilities.

1. In the nearest no-God world, the physical cosmos remains largely as it is. It begins with a colossal big bang, followed by the formation of galaxies, stars, and planets. On at least one such planet, Earth, the necessary conditions for life are met, and life emerges by some (as yet undescribed) natural process. At that point, Darwinian mechanisms give rise to animals with nervous systems and complex social structures, ultimately spawning intelligent life which, for reasons already laid out above, come to have cognitive mechanisms that are naturally disposed to form supernatural beliefs, beliefs in monotheistic gods among them.

2. In the nearest no-God world, there are no intelligent beings, living beings, planets, stars, galaxies, matter, space, time, or big bang. Because a contingent cosmos requires a creator, the nearest no-God world contains no contingent beings at all. Thus in the nearest no-God world, there is no supernatural belief.

3. In the nearest no-God world, the big bang occurs and spawns a physical cosmos. However, the very specific laws and initial conditions necessary to support the emergence of differentiated matter, stars, planetary systems, life, and intelligence require the existence and activity of a fine-tuning cosmic intelligence. Thus the resulting cosmos does not contain beings who have beliefs.

If (1) is the right way of describing the nearest no-God world, then our dispositions to form supernatural beliefs fail to satisfy (TT). If (2) and/or (3) is the right way, they do. So which is it?

One can imagine cogent arguments for all three. However, one might also claim that adopting (2) or (3) is just a desperate theistic trick to salvage truth-tracking. But if it is correct that the very existence of the cosmos, or the special properties that support life and intelligence really do hang on the existence of a divine creator, then it is correct that (2) or (3) does represent the nearest no-God world. In that case, the theist's affirmation of (2) or (3) is no mere trick. Of course, if the naturalist is right in thinking that there is no God, and in thinking that the existence of the cosmos, life, and intelligence don't require a God, then (1) represents the nearest no-God world.[26]

Perhaps we can adjudicate this stalemate by resolving questions about the argument from design or the cosmological argument. If such arguments prove sound, perhaps they will show us that and why the existence of the universe, fine-tuning, etc., depend on the existence of God. Although debates over these issues have endured for centuries, in light of continuing discoveries about the origins of the cosmos and the initial conditions, fundamental constants, and downstream conditions necessary for intelligent life, we may be able to assign physical probabilities for the emergence of believing creatures, or epistemic probabilities to (1), (2), and (3). If not, then it seems that we can say at least (and probably at most), that (TT) is satisfied if theism is true and not satisfied if theism is false. That is not an especially exciting conclusion, but it is not a trivial conclusion.

Let's set aside this issue however. Assume for the moment that the theistic view of the cosmos is correct. On that view, God creates the universe (say via the big bang) and diverse, complex, and intelligent life (say via Darwinian processes). If belief-forming mechanisms are susceptible to positive selective pressure by Darwinian means, it would be perfectly reasonable to expect God to configure the cosmos in such a way (1) that supernatural belief-forming mechanisms would evolve by natural selection (whether as adaptations or spandrels), and (2) that triggers in the natural environment would generate token instances of belief in God. If this is the case, then God would be part of the causal trajectory that led to our having supernatural belief-forming mechanisms in a way that is similar to the way in which boulders are part of the causal trajectory of boulder belief.[27] That is, on this view, *God is the remote cause of such beliefs* and, insofar as God creates the world with triggers sufficient to generate token beliefs in supernatural agents, *God is the proximate cause as well.*

This view makes causal accounts of the origin of supernatural belief quite different from causal accounts of the origin of belief in objective moral facts. In the former case, unlike the latter, the target has a clear, if indirect, role in causal pathways that lead to the belief-forming mechanism and also to the triggers of token instances of belief.[28]

So if one starts off with a presumption of theistic or supernatural belief, causal accounts of this sort don't undermine the justification of such belief. Of course, once again, the naturalist will not buy any of this account and will think instead that there is nothing more to the story about the origin of supernatural belief than what we learn from evolutionary accounts (and whatever the relevant story is about the various cultural elaborations of these accounts). On that view, supernatural beliefs are formed by a domain of cognitive mechanisms that are not truth-tracking, and are thus unjustified.

The upshot of all of this is as follows: we are led to the conclusion that theistic beliefs are unjustified if false, but justified if true (and something like the account set out above is also true).

There is one final issue that needs to be addressed here that we might put as follows. As we have seen above, if someone approaches the epistemic implications of these causal accounts on the presumption that a theistic story is true, then such accounts do not seem to provide reason for thinking that the cognitive mechanisms involved fail to track truth. But one might argue that this is the wrong way to approach these issues. Perhaps it is unfair to ask what we should conclude if we approach these accounts "presuming that theism is true." Proceeding in this way runs the risk of smuggling in the outputs of the very belief-forming mechanisms, the epistemic integrity of which are in question. If we allow ourselves to accept the outcomes of these mechanisms and only then ask whether or not we can regard them as on track, then our inquiry will be open to question.

Of course, if we have reasons for accepting the truth of theism that are independent of the "mechanistic workings" of evolved intuitions toward supernatural belief, then it is appropriate for the theist to assess the implications of evolutionary-causal accounts in light of the totality of her evidence.[29] Thus if there are independent reasons that justify belief that God exists, any worries about "evolutionary accounts" of the origin of God beliefs seem to go away.

But it is important to note that many religious believers are not in possession of such independent evidence. For many, if not most, religious believers, supernatural belief is just something they find welling up within them. Perhaps they view this as a form of religious or mystical experience, or perhaps it is something like the *sensus divinitatus* hypothesized by advocates of a view known as reformed epistemology.[30] In such cases, the religious believer is at risk of illicitly smuggling in a presumption of theistic belief that arises from the evolved belief-forming mechanism the reliability of which is now at issue.

In light of this one might argue that the epistemic situation of religious believers who are without independent evidence for their beliefs should be one of agnosticism. After all, given the evolutionary accounts of the origin of religion, the religious believer has no reason to favor a theistic gloss on the origin of their belief—one according to which their religious belief-forming mechanisms are on track—as opposed to a naturalistic one—according to which those mechanisms, while perhaps adaptive, are not on track. Indeed, insofar as theistic glosses on these accounts seem vastly less parsimonious, perhaps things are worse than that. The parsimony of the naturalistic explanation might commend naturalistic accounts *over* theistic accounts, all other things being equal.

Three comments are in order with respect to this argument. First, the extent to which the argument works is dependent on the extent to which theistic belief is the result of the operation of the mechanisms identified by these accounts. According to the argument set out above, (1) many religious believers form their religious belief by means of religious experience or reliance on religious intuition (or *sensus divinitatus*) and (2) such experience or intuition is just another name for the operation of our evolved supernatural belief-forming mechanisms. However, either or both of these claims might well be false.

Second, the above argument presumes that the naturalistic account starts out with a degree of plausibility that is either equal to that of the theistic account or slightly better than the theistic account (due to considerations of parsimony). However, for reasons we have seen, this is not obviously correct. It might be the case that what is most plausible from a naturalistic account is the obtaining of a possible world with no intelligence, life, stars, planets, galaxies, space, time, etc. But if that is what naturalism entails, it is false that the naturalistic account should represent our default presumption in this matter.[31]

Third, let's grant that religious beliefs do arise from religious intuitions or experience that are nothing more than the activation of our evolved supernatural belief-forming capacities. Let's further assume that there is no good reason to presume the truth of the theistic account on our epistemic approach to these issues. Even then there is no reason to think that the theist cannot persist in fully justified belief. Why? Because even in that case—at least as it has been set out here—the situation for the theist is exactly analogous to the situation we confront when faced with the prospect of the possibility of a Cartesian evil deceiver. When the skeptic presents us with an alternative account of the origin of our perceptual beliefs such as we find in cases where one supposes that everything we sense is the result of the activity of an evil deceiver—an account that is in conflict with our default, intuitive understanding of those beliefs (as accurately representing the state of the outside world)—we are justified in rejecting that explanation despite the fact that (1) we have no non-question-begging reason for thinking that our default understanding is preferable to the skeptic's alternative scenario, and (2) the default understanding is one that, if the skeptic's take were correct, would account for (and seemingly undermine) the very noetic condition that we make appeal to in explaining why we prefer the realist position to the skeptical one.

4. CONCLUSION

In closing, let's return to the question raised at the beginning of this chapter: Fred has a special interest in evolutionary theories of religion and concludes from them that there is good reason to think that religious beliefs are at least largely caused by the influence of interaction between genes and environment on the human mind. So far as Fred can see, nothing about evolutionary theory itself requires or rules out the claim that God initiates the evolutionary process and structures the conditions that constrain it, and so, he concludes, evolutionary theory is silent on whether or not God orchestrated the process that led to the religious beliefs in question. To what extent, if any, is Fred rationally bound to revise his religious commitments?

If what we have said above is correct, the answer is "no extent at all." This is not in any way to suggest that religious (or other) beliefs to which we are intuitively disposed deserve to be held with smug certitude, or that some scientific theories cannot require some religious beliefs to be modified or abandoned. If

Fred had lived at various times in the seventeenth to twentieth centuries and had religiously funded commitments to geocentrism, a 6,000-year-old Earth, the supernatural creation of species, or vitalism, Fred would have been rationally bound to revise his beliefs in light of science—as many believers in fact did.[32] But unlike these examples, nobody is claiming that the evolutionary or cognitive sciences entail the falsity of religious beliefs. Indeed, there is wide agreement that they harbor no relevance at all for the question of truth. The concern here is for warrant. And even if Fred accepts these scientific accounts as fully adequate, for all he knows, the mechanisms that produce his religious beliefs are truth-tracking. There is nothing in the theories themselves that would require Fred to deny that the mechanisms in question were caused remotely by God for the purposes of generating religious beliefs and triggered by features of his environment (remotely) caused by God to generate such beliefs. And if that is the way things are, Fred's beliefs are on track and connected to their targets in ways that make them justified. Thus these arguments do not raise serious worries for Fred the believer. He can go take a walk in the morning sun with his good friend and fellow traveler Ed, and thank God for the day's new mercies.

■ NOTES

1. Daniel M. T. Fessler and Edouard Machery, "Culture and Cognition," in *The Oxford Handbook of Philosophy of Cognitive Science*, ed. Eric Margolis, Richard Samuels, and Stephen P. Stich (Oxford: Oxford University Press, 2011), chap. 21.

2. Scott Atran, "Core Domains versus Scientific Theories: Evidence from Systematics and Itza-Maya Folkbiology," in *Mapping the Mind: Domain Specificity in Cognition and Culture*, ed. Lawrence A. Hirschfeld and Susan A. Gelman (Cambridge: Cambridge University Press, 1994), 316–340.

3. Susan A. Gelman and Lawrence A. Hirschfeld, "How Biological is Essentialism?" in *Folkbiology*, ed. Scott Atran and Douglas Medin (Cambridge, MA: MIT Press, 1999), 403–446.

4. Lawrence Hirschfeld, and Susan A. Gelman, eds. *Mapping the Mind* (Cambridge: Cambridge University Press, 1994); Steven Pinker, *How the Mind Works* (New York: W.W. Norton, 1997); Dan Sperber, David Premack, and Ann James Premack, eds. *Causal Cognition* (Oxford: Oxford University Press, 1995); Elizabeth Spelke, "Initial Knowledge: Six Suggestions," *Cognition* 50 (1994): 431–445.

5. Alvin I. Goldman, "The Psychology of Folk Psychology," *Behavioral and Brain Sciences* 16 (1993): 15–28; Simon Baron-Cohen, *Mindblindness: An Essay on Autism and Theory of Mind* (Cambridge, MA: MIT Press, 1995); György Gergely et al., "Taking the Intentional Stance at 12 Months of Age," *Cognition* 56 (1995): 165–193.

6. S. Carey, "The Growth of Understandings of Natural Kinds," in *Causal Cognition: A Multi-Disciplinary Debate*, ed. Dan Sperber, David Premack, and Ann J. Premack (Oxford: Clarendon Press, 1995), 268–302; John D. Coley, "Emerging Differentiation of Folkbiology and Folkpsychology: Attributions of Biological and Psychological Properties to Living Things," *Child Development* 66 (1995): 1856–1874.

7. Daniel J. Povinelli, *Folk Physics for Apes: The Chimpanzee's Theory of How the World Works* (Oxford: Oxford University Press, 2000); Renée Baillargeon, "The Object Concept Revisited: New Directions in the Investigation of Infants' Physical Knowledge," in *Visual Perception and Cognition in Infancy*, ed. Carl E. Granrud (Hillsdale, NJ: Erlbaum, 1993), 265–315; Elizabeth S. Spelke, "Physical Knowledge in Infancy: Reflections on Piaget's Theory," in *The Epigenesis of Mind: Essays on Biology and Cognition*, ed. Susan Carey and Rochel Gelman (Hillsdale, NJ: Erlbaum, 1991), 133–169.

8. Denise Dellarosa Cummins and Robert Cummins, "Biological Preparedness and Evolutionary Explanation," *Cognition* 73 (1999): B37–B53.

9. "Most" adaptive does not necessarily entail optimality, but only "better than" others, or "satisficing." And better adapted across environments does not mean best adapted in each. In different situations, it may involve phenotypic generalists, specialists, or—as is often the case with cognitive characteristics—a union of the two strategies involving phenotypic plasticity built on a general but developmentally labile core.

10. Richard Dawkins, *The Blind Watchmaker: Why the Evidence of Evolution Reveals a Universe Without Design* (New York: W. W. Norton, 1986).

11. Kim Sterelny, "Escaping Illusion," *American Scientist* 94 (2006): 461–463.

12. It is actually more difficult than it might seem to provide an account of how natural selection could succeed in preferentially retaining on-track belief-forming mechanisms and winnowing out those that are not on track. Part of the reason for this is that the reliability or unreliability of those mechanisms is only visible to selection when they reliably result in behaviors that are adaptive or maladaptive. However, adaptive or maladaptive behavior involves much more than simply getting ones belief right or not. As Plantinga has pointedly argued, systematically false beliefs can deliver adaptive behaviors if they are paired with affective states that jointly yield adaptive behavior. In order for selection to establish beliefs or belief-producing mechanisms that track truth, behaviors or internal states generated by beliefs must be more likely to result in reproductive advantage if the beliefs are true. For what follows, we will set aside this issue and assume there are cases in which this condition is met.

13. Ryan T. McKay and Daniel C. Dennett, "The Evolution of Misbelief," *Behavioral and Brain Sciences* 32 (2009): 493–510. For an alternative view, see Stephen Stich, *The Fragmentation of Reason* (Cambridge, MA: MIT Press, 1993); Alvin Plantinga, *Warrant and Proper Function* (Oxford: Oxford University Press, 1993); and James K. Beilby, ed. *Naturalism Defeated?: Essays on Plantinga's Evolutionary Argument Against Naturalism* (Ithaca, NY: Cornell University Press, 2002.

14. Roger White, "You Just Believe That Because …," *Philosophical Perspectives* 24 (2010): 573–615.

15. On a somewhat more technical note, it is worth stating that foundationalists will typically deny that we can or must provide a reason for basic beliefs of, say, this perceptual sort (where reasons are conceived of as propositions that confer incremental confirmation). But those foundationalists will also typically admit that those beliefs must be triggered by *something* (perceptual "grounds" in this case). Such grounds don't provide propositional evidential support, but they do provide reasons in the sense intended when I reply to the question "Why do you believe that there is a boulder in the field?" by replying "Because there *is* a boulder in the field." Such a reply could be taken as missing the epistemic import of the question, and mistakenly offering an irrelevant causal reply. Instead, we should look at the answer as shorthand for a longer, truth-tracking answer, the longer version of which would

go as follows: "The reason for believing a boulder is there is that boulders were among the causes that selected for belief-forming mechanisms that generate 'boulder beliefs' when my senses are stimulated thus-and-so, and that boulder in the field has stimulated my senses thus-and-so."

16. Griffiths and Wilkins 2011; Gary Kahane, "Evolutionary Debunking Arguments," *Noûs* 45 (2010): 103–125. "When Do Evolutionary Explanations of Belief Debunk Belief?" accessed at http://philsci-archive.pitt.edu/5314/ (last accessed February 25, 2013).

17. There is a framing problem that requires more space than we can give it here. The account we are defending here allows that targets can be sufficiently similar that selective pressure for reliable belief forming about one will transfer to others. But if the grain is coarse enough, reliability worries reemerge. Something can be course grained in the sense of forming reliable beliefs about a class of objects that includes methods of distinguishing them (recognizing life and having a general mechanism for differentiating kinds). Or it can be general/ course grained and miss distinctions that are real but unimportant to selection (which we might come to see by other faculties). Or it might be course grained in the sense of generating reliable but very general beliefs (e.g., there's a supernatural reality) but is also susceptible to noise from various other inputs that generate the fine-grained attributes of belief when appropriate targets are not present.

18. Richard Joyce, *The Myth of Morality* (Cambridge: Cambridge University Press, 2007); Sharon Street, "A Darwinian Dilemma for Realist Theories of Value," *Philosophical Studies* 127 (2006): 109–166; Gilbert Harman, "Moral Relativism," in *Moral Relativism and Moral Objectivity*, ed. Gilbert Harman and J. J. Thompson (Cambridge: Blackwell, 1996), 3–64; Gilbert Harman, "Is There a Single True Morality," in *Ethics: Selections from Classic and Contemporary Writers*, ed. Oliver Johnson and Andrews Reath (Boston: Wadsworth, 2011), 453–469.

19. Some argue that while the human moral sense has emerged from evolutionary processes, it is a spandrel and not an adaptation at all (Francisco Ayala, "The Difference of Being Human: Ethical Behavior as an Evolutionary Byproduct," in *Biology, Ethics, and the Origins of Life*, ed. Holmes Rolston III (Boston: Jones & Bartlett, 1995), 113–136). Thus specific moral beliefs are not entirely constrained by the legacy of having been selected for adaptive value. They may be shaped by traditional "reasons," not just causes (Philip Kitcher, "Ethics and Evolution: How to Get There from Here," in *Primates and Philosophers: How Morality Evolved*, ed. Frans de Waal (Princeton, NJ: Princeton University Press, 2006), 120–139). Others claim that although natural selection provides an adequate causal account for central tendencies in certain moral norms, it does not actually offer an explanation for belief in moral normativity (John Hare, "Is There an Evolutionary Foundation for Human Morality?" in *Evolution and Ethics: Human Morality in Biological and Religious Perspective*, ed. Philip Clayton and Jeffrey Schloss (Grand Rapids, MI: Erdmans, 2004), 187–203; Schloss 2011).

20. Or, rather, if the environment does include moral facts, the moral facts are not posited to (and it is hard to imagine they could) play a causal role in the selection for or triggering of belief-forming mechanisms.

21. It should be noted in this case, however, that critics of belief in objective moral facts have raised serious concerns about the viability of any argument of this sort. These critics argue that any attempt to mount independent arguments for the reality of objective moral facts will always take place against a background evaluative framework that involves the evolved (dispositions toward) moral belief that we are worried about. As a result, any argument for objective moral facts will, overtly or not, deploy this background evaluative framework, fatally undermining any claim to have independent justification for such beliefs.

22. Justin Barrett, *Why Would Anyone Believe in God?* (Walnut Creek, CA: AltaMira Press, 2004.

23. Paul Bloom, *Descartes' Baby* (New York: Basic Books, 2004).

24. Jeffrey P. Schloss and J. Michael Murray, "Evolutionary Accounts of Belief in Supernatural Punishment: A Critical Review," *Religion, Brain, and Behavior* 1 (2011): 46–66.

25. The category of "religious beliefs" is both more varied and more ambiguous than what we normally identify as moral beliefs. We consider the epistemic problems for those components of religious belief that are (rightly or wrongly) posited to be both recurrent and explainable by cognitive and evolutionary causal accounts.

26. This paragraph assumes that all theists accept the notion that the existence of the universe, fine-tuning, etc., require God's existence and activity in some way. Of course, a theist could reject that, in which case that theist might have good reason to accept (1) over (2) or (3).

27. There is one obvious difference between the two cases. Unlike a boulder, in the divine case the trigger of the belief is not the target of the belief (God), but rather a state of affairs that is structured by God so as to generate religious beliefs. But recall that our stipulation was not that the causal trigger of a belief must *be* the object of belief, but that it be reliably connected to the object of belief. This religious belief scenario would meet that criterion. However, this would not be the case in the following situation: God creates the universe with a structure sufficient to generate minds inclined to believe in God when presented with certain features typical of the universe. But God dies. While the remote cause of the belief is connected to the object of belief, the proximal cause—the trigger—is not.

28. One could perhaps claim that objective moral facts were causally involved in both the origin of minds capable of believing in moral facts and in proximally triggering such beliefs. But unlike construals of God, we are not aware of proposals that moral facts have this kind of causal power or that the existence of moral cognition requires it.

29. One might worry here that a rejected parallel line of thought raised in the discussion of objective moral facts undermines this move. There we claimed that there were epistemic worries about invoking "independent reasons" in support of the existence of objective moral facts because the normative taint of evolved dispositions to moral belief would so skew our normative sensibilities that we would have good reason to doubt the independence of the reasons. But no such worries arise here (though see the remainder of the paragraph for a caveat). The reasons that might be deployed to support religious belief need not be "religious reasons," but can instead be perfectly ordinary natural facts: that the universe displays fine-tuning, for example.

30. For a discussion of the relation between reformed epistemology and CSR, see Kelly J. Clark and Justin L. Barrett, "Reformed Epistemology and the Cognitive Science of Religion," *Faith and Philosophy* 27 (2010): 174–189; and "Reidian Religious Epistemology and the Cognitive Science of Religion," *Journal of the American Academy of Religion* 79 (2011): 639–675.

31. In addition, even if one could make the case that a world with intelligent life would not be impossible or extraordinarily unlikely on naturalism, one would still need to be able to provide not just a plausible but a convincing naturalistic account for the existence of intelligent beings with metacognition and religious beliefs. While we have been assessing the epistemic implications if such an account existed and was widely accepted, we should point out that it does not. Currently on offer is a range of speculative, promising, but debated proposals.

32. In the conclusion of his chapter in this volume, Joseph Bulbulia maintains—on the basis of his own anecdotal observations over two decades—that religious viewpoints change

slowly and in response to examples, affiliations, and nondiscursive means. Of course this may often be true (as it is of change in scientific viewpoints as well; see Denis Alexander and Ronald Numbers, eds., *Biology and Ideology from Descartes to Dawkins* Chicago: University of Chicago Press, 2010). But in the accumulated anecdotes known as history, this does not appear to characterize adequately the interactions between science and religion over the last 300 years. Indeed, the reformulation of religious ideas in response to scientific understanding has been characterized as a continual retreat in the face of advancing science (John William Draper, *History of the Conflict Between Religion and Science* (New York: D. Appleton, 1874; Andrew Dickson White, *A History of the Warfare of Science with Theology in Christendom*, 2 vols. (New York: D. Appleton, 1896). Although this too is an oversimplification (David Lindberg and Ronald Numbers, *God and Nature: Historical Essays on the Encounter Between Christianity and Science* (Berkley: University of California Press, 1986; Ronald Numbers, *Galileo Goes to Jail, and Other Myths About Science and Religion* (Cambridge, MA: Harvard University Press, 2010), it is surely the case that the propositional content of religion can and does change in rational consideration of the conclusions of science.

▪ FOR FURTHER READING

Barrett, J. *Cognitive Science, Religion, and Theology: From Human Minds to Divine Minds.* West Conshohocken, PA: Templeton Press, 2011.

———. *Why Would Anyone Believe in God?* Lanham, MD: Alta Mira Press, 2004.

Bering, J. *The Belief Instinct: The Psychology of Souls, Destiny, and the Meaning of Life.* New York: W.W. Norton, 2011.

Bulbulia, J. et al., eds. *The Evolution of Religion: Studies, Theories, and Critiques.* Santa Margarita, CA: Collins Foundation Press, 2008.

Dennett, D. *Breaking the Spell: Religion as a Natural Phenomenon.* New York: Penguin, 2007.

Leech, D., and A. Visala. "Naturalistic Explanation for Religious Belief." *Philosophy Compass* 6 (2011): 552–563.

McNamara, P., ed. *Where God and Science Meet: How Brain and Evolutionary Studies Alter Our Understanding of Religion.* Westport, CT: Praeger, 2006.

Schloss, J., and M. Murray, eds. *The Believing Primate: Scientific, Philosophical, and Theological Reflections on the Origin of Religion.* New York: Oxford University Press, 2010.

Wilson, D. S. *Darwin's Cathedral: Evolution, Religion, and the Nature of Society.* Chicago: University of Chicago Press, 2003.

The Nature of Human Beings

19 Human Persons are Material and Immaterial (Body and Soul)

■ STEWART GOETZ

▦ 1. INTRODUCTION

Metaphysical views quite often come in clusters. This is certainly true with beliefs about the self, the purpose of life, the freedom of the will, and the afterlife. Thus, if one believes that the self is (or has) a soul, one is more likely to believe that it exists for the purpose that it experience perfect happiness, that it has the freedom to choose nondeterministically how and when it will pursue that happiness, and that it persists through or across time as the numerically same self with the possibility of surviving the death of its body and persisting into the afterlife either disembodied or with a different body. If one were to cease to believe that the self is a soul, then one would likely cease to have the other beliefs. Thus, not only does Owen Flanagan deny the existence of the soul, but he also denies that the experience of perfect happiness is the purpose of life and that we are free to make nondetermined choices.[1] So, while in what follows I primarily address the existence of the soul, it should be remembered that, strictly speaking, belief in its existence is part of a package deal, and the plausibility of that belief is closely tied to the plausibility of belief in the package as a whole.

▦ 2. WHAT IS A SOUL?

It is helpful to state briefly with some degree of precision what the soul is. In the simplest terms, the soul is a substance. What, however, is a substance? A substance is a particular entity or thing, whether material (e.g., a table, a tree) or immaterial (e.g., a soul), which has or exemplifies essential properties or characteristics that it cannot lose without ceasing to exist. These essential properties include powers to act and capacities (propensities) to be acted upon. When a soul exercises one of its powers, it is an agent, and when it has one of its capacities actualized, it is a patient. A soul has various essential psychological powers, including the power to think about, consider, or focus on different issues (e.g., I can think about the soul–body distinction) and the power to choose to act (e.g., I can choose to get or not get married and choose to pursue or not pursue a career in philosophy). Essential capacities of the soul include the capacity to experience pleasure (e.g., I experience pleasure while reading a C. S. Lewis book and while playing racquetball), the capacity to experience pain (e.g., I experience pain when struck by a ball), and the capacities to desire (e.g., I desire a drink of water after a hard workout) and to believe (e.g., I believe that writing this chapter is hard work). Given this characterization of a soul in terms of its essential psychological powers and capacities, it is important to make two additional points.

First, one should recognize that while the power to think is an essential property of the soul, the soul need not continuously exercise this power in order to exist. Moreover, a particular thought such as that Barack Obama is the first African American president of the United States might not have been had by a soul and yet it would still have been the same soul. Similarly, though a soul might have chosen as a way of life to forego performing certain kinds of actions (e.g., eating certain kinds of food) as a way of fulfilling its desire for pleasure, it might have chosen a different way of life. Still, it would have been the same soul. The idea, here, is that the particular exercising of the powers of thought and choice are nonessential or accidental in nature, and it is because they are that we believe that we could have thought and chosen different things and still have been the same soul. This point about the accidental nature of particular thoughts and choices accounts for the ordinary belief that I have that while I chose to be a college professor, I might have chosen instead to go to work for a major corporation and still have been the same soul. Similarly, because particular thoughts, choices, and personality traits are accidental in nature, we believe that a person who enters prison as a bitter, cold-blooded killer can exit as a thankful, kind-hearted individual who works on behalf of the well-being of others.

Second, one must be equally mindful of the fact that while the soul has multiple essential psychological powers and capacities, these powers and capacities are not themselves substances (they are not substantive). Because they are properties and not substances, powers and capacities cannot be separated from and exist independently of the soul such that they are able (have the capacity) to become parts of other substances. They are not substantive, separable parts of the soul in the way that a portion of the table on which I am writing (e.g., the top, a leg) is a substantive, separable part of the table that can exist independently of the table and become a part of another substance (e.g., a leg of a table can become a leg of a chair). Thus a table, unlike a soul, is a complex entity or thing in virtue of the fact that it is made up of parts that are themselves substances (substantive parts). Physical scientists inform us that a table is actually a lattice structure of molecules bound together by attractive powers affecting appropriate capacities, and when this lattice structure is broken by a sufficient force, the table breaks. Unlike a table and material objects in general, a soul is not a complex entity because it has no substantive parts. Instead, it is substantively simple in nature. It is a simple thing. While a soul is complex in so far as it has a multiplicity of properties, it is simple in so far as it has no substantive parts. Thus complexity at the level of propertyhood is compatible with simplicity at the level of thinghood.[2,3]

3. THE NATURE OF BELIEF IN THE SOUL

How widespread is belief in the soul's existence and what, if anything, explains belief that the soul exists? Evidence suggests that belief that the soul exists is commonsensical in nature. As the philosopher William Lyons has recently stated, the view "that humans are bodies inhabited and governed in some intimate if mysterious way by minds (souls), seemed and still seems to be nothing more than good common sense."[4] Thus we find this common sense was manifested in the ordinary beliefs of people in first-century Palestine. For example, when Jesus asked his disciples who people thought he was, some thought he was John the Baptist, others that he was Elijah, and others that he was Jeremiah or one of the prophets.[5] Even Herod, who had John the Baptist executed, wondered if Jesus was John.[6] Given that it is reasonable to assume that John the Baptist's body could easily be located, it makes sense to conclude that people might have thought that Jesus was John's soul reembodied. In our own day, the author J. K. Rowling makes effective use of the soul–body distinction (what philosophers typically refer to as "dualism") in her hugely popular Harry Potter novels, in which the worst death one can die is to have one's soul sucked out of one's body by the kiss of a being called a dementor. And the contemporary nondualist philosopher John Searle reports that "when I lectured on the mind–body problem in India [I] was assured by several members of my audience that my views must be mistaken, because they personally had existed in their earlier lives as frogs or elephants, etc."[7]

What explains this commonsensical belief in the soul's existence? Some thoughts of the philosopher René Descartes about his awareness of himself as a soul can serve as our guide at this point:

> When I consider the mind [soul], that is to say, myself inasmuch as I am only a thinking thing, I cannot distinguish in myself any parts, but apprehend myself to be clearly one and entire; and although the whole mind seems to be united to the whole body, yet if a foot, or an arm, or some other part, is separated from my body, I am aware that nothing has been taken away from my mind. And the faculties [powers and capacities] of willing, feeling, conceiving, etc. cannot be properly speaking said to be parts, for it is one and the same mind which employs itself in willing and in feeling and understanding.[8]

Descartes notes that when he introspectively considers himself, he apprehends himself to be one and entire, by which he seems to mean that he is aware that he has no substantive parts. He is careful to make clear that the lack of such parts does not imply a lack of a multiplicity of properties (of which he is also aware) because simplicity at the level of thinghood is compatible with complexity at the level of propertyhood. Moreover, because Descartes is aware that he is a substantively simple soul, when, for example, he thinks about what he is, he is aware that *all* of him thinks. He thinks as a *whole* or in his *entirety* because as an entity that lacks substantive parts, it is not possible for one part of him to think while another does not. And when he *simultaneously* thinks about his being a soul, hopes that he will survive death, and feels pain in his foot, he is aware that it is one and the same soul in its entirety that is the subject of each event.

Given the argument to this point about the commonsensical and introspective nature of belief in the soul's existence, it seems accurate to say that this belief is basic in nature in the sense that it is not inferred or derived from any other belief that one has.[9] In addition, one's belief that one is a soul is found near the bottom of one's system of beliefs. One of the many things of which the philosopher Alvin Plantinga has reminded us is that our belief structures are analogous to the structures of buildings.[10] Thus some of our beliefs are more foundational than, and provide the basis for, other beliefs that we have. Given this hierarchical structure, Plantinga also points out that a belief has a feature that he terms its *depth of ingression*, which is measured by how much reverberation or impact its loss would have on the rest of a person's belief structure.[11] The more peripheral the belief, the less its depth of ingression. For example, while I believe that I am supposed to play basketball today at noon, my finding out that the game is tomorrow at noon would not have extensive reverberations throughout my belief structure. The depth of ingression of my belief about the day and time of the basketball game is low. Because my belief that I am a soul is not only basic but also at the center of my belief structure, an undermining of it would have extensive reverberations throughout my belief system. For example, its loss would undermine both my belief that I can survive death and experience perfect happiness in the presence of God (as I stated at the outset of this chapter, belief about the soul is attended by a cluster of other beliefs, including beliefs that bodily or psychological criteria for my [or anyone else's] personal identity are neither necessary nor sufficient, that I cannot be present as a percentage of a whole like a material object can [if I lose my arm I am not 90 percent of a person like a table is 90 percent of a table if it loses a leg], and that I have libertarian freedom). The depth of ingression of my belief that I am a soul is therefore high.

While belief that the soul exists is basic in nature, there is reason to hold that the belief that one is distinct from one's body is nonbasic or inferred in nature. Though the belief in dualism is inferential in nature, the nature of the inference is nevertheless quite simple. Here is what I have elsewhere referred to as the simple argument for dualism:

1. I (my soul) am (is) essentially a simple entity (I have no substantive parts).
2. My body is essentially a complex entity (my body has substantive parts).
3. If "two" entities are identical, then whatever is a property of the one is a property of the other.
4. Therefore, because I have an essential property that my body lacks, I am not identical with my body.[12]

Why think that one even has a body? The most plausible answer is as follows: On the one hand, when certain things are done to a particular physical entity, one directly feels pains and pleasures. On the other hand, when one chooses and intends to do certain things, that same physical entity directly moves in response. In light of these facts, one naturally comes to refer to the physical entity in question as "my body." In short, regard for a particular physical entity as one's body is ultimately rooted in certain causal facts about how that entity is related to one's soul.

4. OBJECTIONS TO DUALISM

The philosopher Roderick Chisholm has written that we should take seriously "certain things we have a right to believe about ourselves" and "be guided in philosophy by those propositions we all do presuppose in our ordinary activity."[13] While it is unclear to me that I have a *right* to believe certain things about myself (the idea strikes me as odd), it is clear to me that I just find myself having certain beliefs, and it is not possible for me to stop having them unless I am provided with a good reason to think that they are questionable or false. As I have argued in the previous section, one of the things that we, as ordinary persons, believe about ourselves is that we are souls that are distinct from our physical bodies. What reasons might there be for believing that dualism is false?

According to the nondualist philosopher David Armstrong, Descartes is guilty of having made an invalid inference when he claims, as I quoted in the previous section, that he is aware of himself as a substantively simple soul:

> Descartes seems to be moving illegitimately from the fact that the mind is a *single* thing to the conclusion that it is a *simple* thing. And introspection would seem to go against Descartes here. We can be aware of multiple processes coexisting in our minds [souls]. Indeed, Plato argues in the *Republic* (434d–441c) for parts of the soul on the ground that we can entertain inconsistent desires. He gives the example of a man torn between his desire to gaze at corpses lying beside the road and his feeling that this is a shameful desire to indulge.[14]

Is Descartes making the illegitimate inference that Armstrong suggests? It is doubtful that he is. Descartes would likely respond that although he sometimes has inconsistent desires (desires that are such that the fulfillment of one excludes the fulfillment of the other), the loss of one or both of them (which is a common experience) does not result in a diminishment of him in the sense that he loses substantive parts. All of him remains after their loss. Hence Armstrong has not provided a good reason to think that Descartes starts with the general belief that he is a single thing and infers the specific belief that he is a simple thing.

There are many who believe that the most powerful objection to dualism comes not from questions about what we are aware of about ourselves introspectively, but from developments in contemporary brain science. What might be discovered in science that poses problems for belief in the existence of the soul? According to Nancey Murphy, the main culprit is localization studies in which regional structures or distributed systems in the brain are found to be correlated with psychological capacities like language, sight, and emotion. What the evidence from these studies supposedly suggests is that the brain itself, as opposed to the soul, is the subject of these capacities:

> A major part of current neuroscience research involves mapping regions of the brain (neuroanatomy) and studying the functions of the various regions (neurophysiology). Studies of this sort intersect, in fascinating ways, the philosophical issues [concerning the relationship of the mind to the brain]. First they provide dramatic evidence for physicalism. As neuroscientists associate more and more of the faculties once attributed to mind or soul with the functioning of specific regions or systems of the brain it becomes more and more appealing to say that it is in fact the brain that performs these functions... With the development of CAT scans (computerized axial tomography) it has become possible to study correlations between structural abnormalities and behavior of people while they are alive. MRI scans (magnetic resonance imaging) now provide more detailed pictures, more easily revealing locations of brain damage. PET scans (positron emission tomography) allow research correlating localized brain activity with the performance of specialized cognitive tasks.[15]

There are various examples of what Murphy has in mind. For example, David Parkes points out that because the left of the two brain hemispheres is usually dominant for speech, "left-sided brain lesions can cause a searching for words, a limitation of vocabulary, a shortening of sentences, or a jumble of meaningless words."[16] According to Glenn Weaver, early degeneration of neurons in the hippocampus of the brain (located in the right and left temporal lobes of the cerebral cortex) results in disturbances in working memory, where persons may have increasing difficulty either remembering where they placed items, recalling the names of persons to whom they were recently introduced, "or following the narratives of stories they are reading or watching on television."[17] Parkes draws our attention to the fact that multiple sclerosis can produce frontotemporal-limbic damage in the brain that results in an overflow of sadness, mirth, or despair.[18] As I learned in the case of my own father with Alzheimer's disease, neurons die, small holes appear throughout the brain tissue, and the cerebral cortex looks shriveled in CT scans of the brain. According to Malcolm Jeeves, a general conclusion we should draw is that "the nature of the [causal] interdependence increasingly uncovered by scientific research makes a substance dualism harder to maintain without tortuous and convoluted reasoning."[19]

Surely, however, Jeeves overstates the case against soul–body dualism. As even Murphy points out, "it is important to note that this evidence [from neuroanatomy and neurophysiology] will never amount to proof: it will always be possible for the dualist to claim that these [mental] functions belong to the mind and that mental events are merely *correlated* with events in particular regions of the brain."[20] After all, a correlation between two things or events is not sufficient to establish their identity. Two distinct things can be correlated and genuinely remain two distinct things. In the case of a soul and a brain, there could be soul functions and events correlated with brain functions and events. C. Stephen Evans not only agrees that correlation is not identity, but also wonders why people like Murphy and Jeeves are taken in by the findings of localization studies in the first place:

> What, exactly, is it about these findings that are supposed to create problems for dualism? Presumably, the mere fact that the mind is causally impacted by the brain is not a problem, since most dualists have been interactionists eager to maintain that the body (and indeed the wider physical world) can in some way affect the mind. Is it a problem for dualism that this causal action takes place through the brain, rather than, say, the heart as Aristotle thought? It is hard to see why this should be a problem. Is it a problem that the causal effects should be the product of specific regions of the brain? Why should the fact that the source of the effects are localized regions of the brain, rather than the brain as a whole, be a problem for the dualist? It is hard for me to see why dualism should be thought to entail that the causal dependence of the mind on the brain should only stem from holistic states of the brain rather than more localized happenings... We did not need neurophysiology to come to know that a person whose head is bashed in with a club quickly loses his or her ability to think or have any conscious processes. Why should we not think of neurophysiological findings as giving us detailed, precise knowledge of something that human beings have always known, or at least could have known, which is that the mind (at least in this mortal life) requires and depends on a functioning brain? We now know a lot more than we used to know about precisely *how* the mind depends on the body. However, *that* the mind depends on the body, at least prior to death, is surely not something discovered in the twentieth century.[21]

If Evans is correct, and it seems that he is, then what persuades people like Murphy and Jeeves that physicalism is to be preferred to dualism? At one point, Murphy says that "science has provided a massive amount of evidence suggesting that we need not postulate the existence of an entity such as a soul or mind in order to explain life and consciousness."[22] And Jeeves claims that "some [dualists] take a 'soul-of-the-gaps' position, much like the older 'god-of-the-gaps position,' using the concept of the 'soul' to explain those human experiences that we cannot (yet, at least) explain neurologically or biologically."[23] However, in light of the points made in the previous section that the belief in the soul's existence is both commonsensical and basic in nature, it is hard to make a plausible case for the view that people who believe in the existence of the soul view it initially as a hypothetical entity whose existence is postulated in a god-of-the-gaps fashion to account for human experiences that cannot yet be explained in physical terms.

And if one subsequently develops arguments for the soul's existence that supplement the basic belief in its reality, they involve postulating the soul to explain distinctively metaphysical, and not scientific, facts (e.g., that explain the making of nondeterministic choices or the possibility of life after death). Thus cases in which the soul is postulated are philosophical in nature and complementary to and not in conflict with cases involving the relationship between our experiences and happenings in the physical world.

There are many other objections to dualism that should but cannot be considered here, because of limitations of space. However, the books and articles in both the notes and recommended readings below will provide the reader with an excellent entry point into the debate about the existence of the soul and its relationship to the body. The issues are both important and interesting and deserve a reader's careful attention.

■ NOTES

1. See Owen Flanagan, *Self Expressions: Mind, Morals, and the Meaning of Life* (Oxford: Oxford University Press, 1996), chap. 1; Owen Flanagan, *The Problem of the Soul* (New York: Basic Books, 2002).

2. A soul is immaterial (not material or physical). To be immaterial, however, is not to be composed of immaterial stuff. It is not to be composed of any stuff at all. See Roderick M. Chisholm, "On the Simplicity of the Soul," *Philosophical Perspectives* 5 (1991): 168.

3. In order to deflect a standard criticism, I should make clear that value judgments such as that the soul is good and the material world is evil are not part of dualism per se. One can be a dualist and not believe any such idea.

4. William Lyons, *Matters of the Mind* (New York: Routledge, 2001), 9.

5. Matthew 16:13–14. All scriptural references are from the Revised Standard Version.

6. Matthew 14:2.

7. John Searle, *The Rediscovery of the Mind* (Cambridge, MA: MIT Press, 1992), 91.

8. René Descartes, "Meditation VI," in *The Philosophical Works of Descartes*, vol. 1, trans. Elizabeth S. Haldane and G. R. T. Ross (Cambridge: Cambridge University Press, 1911), 196.

9. Strictly speaking, it is the belief that one is a soul that is basic, but the belief that the soul exists, which is not about any particular soul, is entailed by "I am a soul," and I will therefore continue to discuss the belief that the soul exists.

10. Although Plantinga has written extensively on the issue of belief, I will refer to his "Reason and Belief in God," in *Faith and Rationality*, ed. Alvin Plantinga and Nicholas Wolterstorff (Notre Dame, IN: University of Notre Dame Press, 1983), 16–93. As an indication of the foundational nature of one's belief that one is a soul, Thomas Nagel points out that no matter what empirical (scientific) discoveries we make, it might very well be impossible for us to give up what he calls the simple view of ourselves. See Thomas Nagel, "Brain Bisection and the Unity of Consciousness," in *Mortal Questions* (Cambridge: Cambridge University Press, 1979), 164.

11. Plantinga, "Reason and Belief in God," 50.

12. Stewart Goetz, "Modal Dualism: A Critique," in *Soul, Body, and Survival*, ed. Kevin Corcoran (Ithaca, NY: Cornell University Press, 2001), 89–104.

13. Roderick M. Chisholm, *Person and Object* (LaSalle, IL: Open Court, 1976), 15.

14. David Armstrong, *The Mind-Body Problem: An Opinionated Introduction* (Boulder, CO: Westview Press, 1999), 23. The emphases are Armstrong's.

15. Nancey Murphy, "Human Nature: Historical, Scientific, and Religious Issues," in *Whatever Happened to the Soul? Scientific and Theological Portraits of Human Nature*, ed. Warren S. Brown, Nancey Murphy, and H. Newton Malony (Minneapolis: Fortress Press, 1998), 13.

16. David Parkes, "The Vulnerability of Persons: Religion and Neurology," in *From Cells to Souls—and Beyond: Changing Portraits of Human Nature*, ed. Malcolm Jeeves (Grand Rapids, MI: Eerdmans, 2004), 46–47.

17. Glen Weaver, "Embodied Spirituality: Experiences of Identity and Spiritual Suffering among Persons with Alzheimer's Dementia," in *From Cells to Souls—and Beyond: Changing Portraits of Human Nature*, ed. Malcolm Jeeves (Grand Rapids, MI: Eerdmans, 2004), 87.

18. Parkes, "The Vulnerability of Persons: Religion and Neurology," 45.

19. Malcolm Jeeves, "Toward a Composite Portrait of Human Nature," in *From Cells to Souls—and Beyond: Changing Portraits of Human Nature*, ed. Malcolm Jeeves (Grand Rapids, MI: Eerdmans, 2004), 240.

20. Murphy, "Human Nature: Historical, Scientific, and Religious Issues," 13.

21. C. Stephen Evans, "Separable Souls: Dualism, Selfhood, and the Possibility of Life After Death," *Christian Scholars Review* 34 (2005): 333–334. The emphases are Evans's.

22. Murphy, "Human Nature: Historical, Scientific, and Religious Issues," 18.

23. Jeeves, "Toward a Composite Portrait of Human Nature," 245.

▧ FOR FURTHER READING

Goetz, S., and M. Baker, eds. *The Soul Hypothesis*. London: Continuum, 2011.

Goetz, S., and C. Taliaferro. *A Brief History of the Soul*. Oxford: Wiley-Blackwell, 2011.

Moreland, J. P. *Consciousness and the Existence of God: A Theistic Argument*. New York: Routledge, 2008.

Swinburne, R. *The Evolution of the Soul*, rev. ed. Oxford: Clarendon Press, 1997.

Taliaferro, C. *Consciousness and the Mind of God*. Cambridge: Cambridge University Press, 1994.

20 Human Persons are Material Only

■ KEVIN CORCORAN

I'm a *physicalist* about human persons, that is, I believe that we are wholly physical objects. I don't believe there are nonphysical souls in the *natural* world. So I do not believe that we are or have such nonphysical souls as parts. I believe we are through-and-through physical. The physical stuff that I believe wholly composes us is chock full of surprising potentialities, such as the potential to produce the wine of consciousness from the spectacularly complex network of one hundred billion nerve cells and their several hundred trillion synaptic connections housed in the wetware of the human brain. In a world overflowing with natural wonders—consider the marsupial wolf and the carnivorous plant, for example—it is a wonder that the natural world should contain conscious, self-conscious, personal, moral beings like ourselves. But it does! And while the "why" that it does seems to me more easily to fit within a theistic understanding of the universe, the "how" that it does seems increasingly to yield to naturalistic explanation.

Before I tell you why I believe that we are wholly physical objects let me share with you why, perhaps surprisingly, I have never been convinced by traditional arguments *against* dualism. For starters, I have never found the following sort of objection to dualism the least bit persuasive: "how could a *nonphysical* mind ever get a causal grip on *physical* muscle and ligaments? The two substances are just too radically *different* to causally interact." Well, if you're a traditional theist, at any rate, you shouldn't find this line of argument at all persuasive, as God—a *nonphysical* substance—is believed to have causally brought about the existence of the *physical* world and to be causally sustaining it in existence. So the idea that mind and body causally interact should be no more problematic for a traditional theist than the notion that God and creation are in causal commerce. How mind and physical stuff (or mind and body) interact, of course, would remain a nice and legitimate question. But that they interact should not be found surprising.

I myself do not reject dualism on account of any argument. I'm what Stewart Goetz might call an *antecedent materialist*.[1] I come to the discussion assuming I am a physical object, since that is what I have always seemed to myself to be for as long as I can remember. I frankly see no use for a nonphysical soul. It doesn't explain anything about consciousness that cannot be explained without it, and it is furthermore a wholly unnecessary hypothesis for many religious doctrines, despite intuitions to the contrary by many religious believers. For example, belief in an afterlife, belief in the peculiarly Christian idea of the Incarnation of Christ, as well as the belief that we human beings bear the image of God—*none* requires belief in a nonphysical soul in order to be made sense of. So until I am confronted with some knock-down, drag-out argument to the contrary (and let's be honest, in philosophy there are precious few, if any, knock-down, drag-out arguments for anything), or until I am presented with some phenomena that cannot be accounted for in naturalistic terms but requires a nonphysical soul or, yet again, until I have something resembling a conversion experience that forces me to renounce my physicalism, I'm sticking with it.

In the pages that follow, I want to respond to a couple arguments *against* a physicalist conception of human nature, explain to you why I believe a nonphysical soul is explanatorily irrelevant and theologically unnecessary, and so explain why I see no reason to abandon my belief that I am a wholly physical object.

1. MYSTERY OF CONSCIOUSNESS ARGUMENTS, NEUROSCIENCE AND WHY THE SOUL IS EXPLANATORILY REDUNDANT

I am a person, a human person. You are too. Stating conditions that are individually necessary and jointly sufficient for something's being a person is difficult.[2] But it seems uncontroversial to say that anything that is a person has a capacity for *consciousness*. In other words, consciousness is a necessary condition of personhood. Anything lacking a capacity for consciousness, whatever else it may be, is surely not a person. Some dualists believe that the sheer fact of consciousness provides a reason to favor dualism over physicalism. While there are various arguments that trade on this idea, I will present two examples. Both are versions of what I like to call mystery of consciousness arguments. Here's the first, let's call it MoCA1:[3]

1. I am a conscious being who also enjoys *self*-consciousness.
2. No theory exists for how consciousness (let alone *self*-consciousness) can arise from the *purely physical* contents of the brain.
3. Therefore I am *not* wholly physical.

Here's the second, MoCA2:

1. There is no naturalistic explanation for the felt qualities of experience, like pleasure and pain, flavors and smells.
2. The primary qualities of physical objects (like brains themselves) are quite obviously physical, third-person observable, and measurable.
3. Felt qualities of experience, like pleasure and pain, flavors, smells, and color experience are precisely not obviously physical or third-person observable and are in fact very difficult to fit into a naturalistic or physicalist framework.
4. Therefore the felt qualities of experience are not wholly physical (nor perhaps even partly physical).[4]

Let's begin with MoCA1. I will frankly admit that there is now no adequate physical theory that explains just how consciousness arises from the complicated network of wetware housed between our ears. How we get from soggy grey matter to consciousness is, I admit, a veritable mystery. But I fail to see how dualism takes the mystery out of consciousness. If anything, it seems to multiply mystery by adding to the mystery of consciousness the mystery of a nonphysical substance that enjoys consciousness. Is it is really any easier to see how a nonphysical soul could be conscious than it is to see how a physical organism could? I don't think so.

Moreover, many features of consciousness, from the ability to discriminate and react to environmental stimuli and the ability to access our own internal conscious states, to the focus of attention and the difference between wakefulness and sleep, to the very existence of emotions, all of these conscious phenomena are in fact explainable in terms of brain structures and neural activity.[5] In other words, science explains these features of consciousness without invoking a nonphysical soul. So at least with respect to these aspects of conscious experience, a nonphysical soul is explanatorily redundant, that is, there is nothing for a nonphysical soul to explain. The steady march of progress and explanatory successes already achieved in the neurosciences and its cognate disciplines, coupled with the continued progress and successes we can expect in the future, seems to portend a dark explanatory future for a nonphysical soul.

We may not yet be able to explain just how consciousness emerges from the neural circuitry contained in our skulls, but we are able to explain many features of consciousness in physical terms, that is, in terms of neural structures and activity.

Even the so-called *hard problem* of consciousness that MoCA2 tries to exploit in its argument—*experience* itself, the *what it's like* features of consciousness (i.e., the feels and smells, pleasures and pains, etc.)—does not require or favor a nonphysical mind or soul in order to be explained. Physicalists who take consciousness seriously (and granted, there are many who don't!) could simply accept experience as ontologically *fundamental*, a feature of the world that cannot be explained in terms of anything simpler. With respect to such basic or fundamental features of the world one seeks a theory of how they relate to everything else in the natural world, such as Maxwell did with electromagnetic processes that could not be explained in terms of the prevailing mechanical processes that were part of scientific theories of the nineteenth century. Maxwell introduced electromagnetic charge and electromagnetic forces as fundamental, ontologically sui generis components of a physical theory. Likewise, materialists who take consciousness seriously might accept consciousness as a fundamental feature of the natural world, right alongside mass, energy, and charge, and seek to articulate fundamental laws and basic principles—*psychophysical* principles—that supplement without interfering with the physical laws that govern the nonconscious entities and their properties from which consciousness emerges.[6]

To get a handle on how such laws might supplement without interfering with the physical laws that govern the nonconscious entities and their properties out of which consciousness emerges, consider the following example from Elizabeth Anscombe. She has us consider "a large glass box full of extremely minute physical particles," which is constantly shaken.[7] By studying the motion of the particles, it is found that "small unit patches of uniform colour" are randomly generated, and statistical laws can be developed to explain this motion. However, it is also observed that the "word 'Coca-Cola' forms like a mosaic" along one of the sides, though it varies in size and location. This phenomenon can occur and have a causal explanation not derived from the laws "concerning the random motion of the particles and their formation of small unit patches of colour" without the violation of these laws.[8]

Now, suppose you are a traditional theist. Is there any reason you should be sanguine about explaining consciousness in natural, physical terms? Well, actually, I think there is. One need not embrace *atheistic* naturalism in order to believe that it is in virtue of some natural property of brains that organisms are conscious. I am a theist. I believe in the God of the Hebrew scriptures, and so I believe neither that the natural world is all there is, nor that the natural world is "causally closed." I believe that while God constantly sustains the natural world in existence and can intervene in the natural world, and has in fact done so and can do so again, I nevertheless believe that, for the most part, God does not directly intervene in the natural world. Since the natural world has yielded in so many ways to scientific explanation over the past several hundred years, it seems only plausible to believe that God created the world—the *natural* world—with its own integrity and such that it operates according to regularities that can be grasped and understood.

Since it is plausible to believe that God created the natural world, and all that it contains, with its own integrity, it is also reasonable to believe that consciousness itself—a feature encountered in the natural world—has a *natural* explanation. One need not be a metaphysical naturalist to believe that.

It may be helpful here to distinguish metaphysical naturalism from both methodological naturalism and what, in the past, I have called chastened naturalism.[9] *Metaphysical* naturalism amounts to the claim that the natural world is all there is and is exhaustive of reality. *Methodological* naturalism, on the other hand, amounts to a presupposition of the practice of science. It says that scientific explanations must exclude reference to supernatural entities. If science is in the business of discovering natural causes, this ought not to surprise or offend. Methodological naturalism, as I understand it, is compatible with a robust theism insofar as it does not rule out explanations that appeal to God. It simply would not count such explanations as scientific explanations. What I have called *chastened* naturalism recognizes the enormous contribution science has made to our understanding of the natural world and takes the natural world to possess its own integrity and to exemplify regularities that can be understood without reference to supernatural entities. What makes it chastened natural-ism is its refusal to make the "metaphysical" turn and to claim that the natural world is all there is and, therefore, the sciences are the only source of genuine knowledge. Chastened naturalism is compatible with there being religious expe-rience and divine revelation. Such experience and revelation provides for reli-gious knowledge, which is genuine knowledge even if not visible to the practice of science, and by definition not scientific knowledge. Therefore, to grant that consciousness has a natural explanation does not require the sacrifice of theistic commitments. Even to be hopeful that future science will produce a theory that accommodates consciousness and shows just how it relates it to everything else in the natural world can be grounded in those same theistic commitments.

We can massage the foregoing into something of an argument from expecta-tion to the explanatory irrelevance of a nonphysical soul. If dualism were true, the argument might run, we would not expect to discover the thoroughgoing and deep causal dependencies of consciousness and experience on brain activities and states that we do in fact find. The more we study, the more we discover the underlying neural (i.e., physical) dependence and (physical) causal explanations of consciousness. Therefore the more we learn about the neural correlates of con-sciousness, the more explanatorily irrelevant a nonphysical soul becomes.

■ 2. BRAIN SCIENCE: TWO CASES

Allow me to present two illustrative cases from neuroscience, cases that illustrate just how certain remarkable features of consciousness are explainable in terms of neuroscience. My reasoning here is not that these cases or any future discoveries in neuroscience, and the cognitive sciences in general, will produce data that are inconsistent with dualism. I do not believe that will ever be the case. Even the phe-nomenon of *divided consciousness* that results from commissurotomy can be made to fit the dualist hypothesis. But we physicalists believe that while dualism can be made to fit the data, the phenomenon of divided consciousness certainly fits more seamlessly with a physicalist picture of the natural world and consciousness than it does a dualist picture. Moreover, the phenomenon itself is certainly not what one might expect were dualism in fact true. My reasoning, based on cases like the fol-lowing two, is just that given the progress and successes at explaining various facets and features of consciousness already achieved, and the progress and successes we can expect in these fields in the future, dualism becomes a less and less plausible thesis when it comes to an account or explanation of consciousness.

2.1 The real life memento man and the blind patient

Clive Wearing is a seventy-three-year-old former composer and musician who has completely lost the ability to lay down new, conscious memories. For the past thirty years he has lived in a tragic and perpetual state of "just waking up." Whether his wife has been gone for ten minutes or ten years, it doesn't matter: when she enters his room he embraces her ecstatically, believing that he is seeing her for the first time after a long separation. Several minutes into a game of solitaire, a game he loves, he will have no recollection that it was he who dealt and played the cards lying before him. Even when he records copious notes for himself on the progression of the game, he will still insist that, although the notes are indeed in his handwriting, he did not write them. He has no idea how the notes got there or who may have dealt the cards.

Imagine that—your whole conscious life lived out on a mental treadmill; no matter how far you run it is always the same well-worn path you travel. That's the character of Clive Wearing's conscious life—his sense of being a continuous self stretches no farther back than just a few minutes. What is the cause of Clive Wearing's severe and unusual form of amnesia? Clive's amnesia is the result of a viral infection that insinuated itself into his brain, completely destroying his hippocampus, that part of the human brain responsible for storing *conscious* memories. That consciousness can be altered or even eliminated by altering or destroying certain regions of the brain demonstrates the degree to which our conscious lives are radically physically based.

Now, is dualism logically incompatible with such empirical discoveries in the neurosciences as the discovery that severe atrophying of the hippocampus results in the near total loss of continuity of conscious memory? Of course not. But if dualism were true, I just don't think we would expect to find such a radical, causal dependence of conscious lives on the physical, which is exactly what we do find. And explaining the curious features of Clive Wearing's conscious life is achieved without any need to invoke nonphysical souls.

The second case I want to consider is that of *blindsight*. This is a fascinating condition that renders patients who suffer from it able to "see" without *consciously* seeing. A patient suffering from blindsight can be shown, say, a spot of light in their "blind" field of "vision" and asked "what is it you see?" The patient will answer "nothing." Which is exactly what we would expect. But if the patient is asked to point to the spot of light, the patient can do it. If the object is moving up or down, left or right, in the blind field, the patient can tell you with near perfect accuracy in which direction the "unseen" object is moving. But how can that be? How can someone "see" without seeing?

Well, what we know about the neuroanatomy of vision is this. There are, in fact, two pathways that subserve different aspects of vision. One pathway travels from the eyeball to those regions of the brain required for visual perception. The other travels from the eyeball to the brainstem. The first pathway is evolutionarily newer and it goes from the eyeball, through the thalamus, to the visual cortex. You need this pathway in order to *consciously* see something. The second pathway is evolutionarily older and is found in birds and reptiles (nonhuman animals, which some believe do not enjoy consciousness) and it goes from the brainstem to the higher centers of the brain. It is the higher centers of bird, reptile, and human brains that substantially differ, and that accounts for why the one (humans) and (likely) not the other (reptiles and birds) do not enjoy consciousness. This older pathway is involved in reflexive behavior and orienting to something important in your visual field (perhaps something that threatens your continued existence). In blindsight, it is part of the newer pathway that is damaged—the visual cortex. Therefore blindsight patients do not *consciously* see anything. But the older pathway, the one that subserves the "fight or flight" reflex, is intact. It is in virtue of this evolutionarily older pathway that blindsight patients are able to nonconsciously "see" the direction of objects they do not "see" consciously.

Let me ask again. Does any of this prove that dualism is false? Obviously not. But it is the fact that more and more aspects of consciousness are being explained in terms of neurophysiology that is galvanizing physicalists and providing them with ever more optimism that experience itself will one day yield to explanation—explanation wholly in terms of principles and laws that are consistent with everything else we know about the natural world and the workings of the brain. It is on the basis of such considerations as these that I see no reason to posit the existence of a nonphysical soul.

■ 3. THE SIMPLE ARGUMENT

I have often heard it said that people do not believe in a nonphysical soul because of its alleged *explanatory* power. Rather, people believe in a nonphysical soul perhaps because they are *antecedent* dualists, because it just seems to them that they are not a physical object, or at least not a wholly physical object. Indeed, some philosophers claim that they are introspectively aware of their substantive simplicity, and since physical organisms and their organs are composite objects, they cannot be identical with such things as those. Still others, religious believers for example, might claim that such peculiarly Christian doctrines as the Incarnation of Christ, life after death, and our being created in the image of God *require* a dualist conception of ourselves.

While I have nothing to say in response to those to whom it just seems, pretheoretically, that they are a nonphysical soul, other than that it does *not* seem so to me. I do have something to say in response to those who claim to be introspectively aware of their substantive simplicity and also to those who might believe certain theological doctrines demand belief in a nonphysical soul. Stewart Goetz, for example, has presented what he refers to as the "simplicity argument." It goes like this:

1. I am essentially simple.
2. My body is essentially complex.

3. If I am identical with my body, then whatever is a property of the one is a property of the other.
4. Therefore, because I have an essential property that my body lacks, I am not identical with my body.[10]

Again, the first premise of the argument is supposed to be a deliverance of introspection. Goetz, following Descartes, claims to be introspectively aware of his simplicity, that is, of the substantive simplicity of the soul that is Stewart Goetz.

But might Goetz be confusing his failure to be introspectively aware of his substantive complexity for his being introspectively aware of his substantive simplicity? From his failure to be introspectively aware of his substantive complexity, it appears that in the relevant passage of *Meditations* Descartes illegitimately infers that he is substantively simple. And the inference to simplicity is illegitimate because even if Descartes is himself substantively complex, there is no reason to believe that he could be introspectively aware of this.

So I find the simplicity argument to be unsound, as its first premise it seems to me is false. I have another argument to the very same conclusion that I believe is sound. It goes like this:

1. I am essentially a psychological being.
2. My body is not essentially a psychological being.
3. A single thing cannot both be and not be an essentially psychological being.
4. Therefore I am not identical with my body.

But note: this is not an argument *for* dualism. It is an argument whose conclusion is compatible with both dualism and certain versions of physicalism. It is, for example, compatible with the constitution view of human persons I defend in *Rethinking Human Nature* and elsewhere.[11] According to this view, we are wholly physical objects constituted by without being identical with our physical bodies. To affirm the conclusion to the simplicity argument is not, therefore, to affirm dualism.[12]

■ 4. THEOLOGICAL DOCTRINES PUTATIVELY REQUIRING A NONPHYSICAL SOUL

4.1 The Incarnation

Let us begin with the doctrine of the Incarnation of Christ, a central tenet of Christianity. It may seem that the doctrine is inconsistent with a physicalist conception of human personhood. I believe a physicalist view of human persons like my own actually makes better sense of the Incarnation than does dualism. Let me explain.

The putative problem for the physicalist is this: if God (or the second person of the Trinity) is essentially a nonphysical being, then how could such a being become purely physical without losing an essential property? And if the second person of the Trinity loses an essential property, then more than ceasing to be fully God, would he not simply cease to exist?

Well, according to the Chalcedonian formulation, the incarnate Christ is one person with two natures, a fully divine nature (that of the second person of the Trinity) and a fully human nature (that of Jesus of Nazareth). The constitution view divides things just where one would expect—between the human nature and the divine nature of the single person. And keep in mind, by the way, that the person of Christ is *not* human; he is divine, being the second person of the Trinity. But this one person, in the Incarnation, had two natures—human and divine. On this understanding of the dual natures, Christ is wholly nonphysical in his divine nature and wholly physical in his human nature. Now consider the less than elegant cleavage substance dualists must offer. According to substance dualism, Christ is wholly nonphysical in his divine nature and partly physical and partly nonphysical in his human nature. Not especially elegant. So, to my mind, my physicalist view of human persons, far from being unable to accommodate the doctrine of the Incarnation, is actually better able to explain the doctrine than is dualism.

Notice, too, that the way the objection is often put contains an important mistake, if what I said above is true. For we see that the second person of the Trinity did not become purely physical (or even partly physical!). The second person of the Trinity did not give up nonphysicality in the Incarnation. Remember: one person (divine and nonphysical) with not one, but, in the Incarnation, two natures—one nonphysical, the other physical. How can that be? I don't have the slightest idea, but the mystery of the Incarnation is not explained away by any account, be it dualist or physicalist.

4.2 The *imago Dei*

Now, what of the *imago Dei*, the image of God? If it's true that we human persons are wholly physical beings, as any version of physicalism must claim, then what does it mean any longer to say that we have been created *in God's image*? Doesn't having been created in the image of God just mean having a nonphysical soul and the features of intellect, will, and emotion that characterize soul? I do not believe that our having been created in the image of God means that we are nonphysical as God is nonphysical. What then does it mean?

Well, there are many ways of understanding the claim that we human beings image God. One might mean that we image God when we care for Creation and contribute to the terrestrial flourishing of the Created order. This, after all, is what the Bible means when it speaks of our having been given "dominion." We are God's vice regents, as it were. To have dominion is to care for others, including nonhuman "others" like oceans and streams, octopuses and salamanders; in other words, to have dominion is to tend to the well-being of all the earth. Second, one might mean that we image God when we live in loving relation to other human beings and invest ourselves in their flourishing and well-being. For we are essentially *persons-in-relation*. Since God is a trinity, it is not surprising that we should image God in virtue of our essentially social nature. The tenor of the relation between the three persons of the Trinity is one of a harmonious and free exchange of love and joy. So engaging in acts of mercy, hospitality, love, kindness, etc., is to act like God. In fact, we image God when we image Jesus, who welcomed the outcast, fed the hungry, clothed the naked, hated evil, and delighted in doing the work of the Father. Finally, one might claim that we image God in our suffering. God is love. To love is to open oneself up to suffering. And suffering love is God love.

Now, none of these ways that I have mentioned that we image God rules out, of course, that we are wholly or partly nonphysical beings, but it doesn't imply it either. The fact that we have been created in the image of God is perfectly compatible with the claim that we are wholly physical beings. Indeed, there is nothing in the doctrine of the *imago Dei*, rightly understood, that entails a dualist view of human nature.

4.3 Life after death

Finally, let us consider if all too briefly the Christian doctrine of life after death. Since, it seems, that bodies peter out and eventually cease to exist and that in any plausible physicalist account of human persons, one's body is necessary for one's own existence, how is it that a body that peters out and ceases to exist can somehow turn up in the hereafter? Or if the physicalist happens to believe in either an immediate survival or an intermediate state between death and a resurrection, then how exactly can a body that has apparently died nevertheless continue to live? Often, after death, a corpse is right before our eyes. How then can that dead body be enjoying any kind of meaningful afterlife? Doesn't the doctrine of an afterlife require a nonphysical soul that survives death?

Let's make things really difficult. Suppose you believe that a single thing cannot have two beginnings, that a thing cannot begin to exist, cease to exist, and then begin again to exist. Is it possible for there to be a body in heaven numerically the same as a body I watch die if there's no such thing as *gappy* existence?

In different places Dean Zimmerman and I have argued that one answer to this question lies in the fissioning of causal paths. It seems possible that the causal paths traced by the simples caught up in the life of my body just before death can be made by God to fission such that the simples composing my body then are causally related to two different, spatially segregated sets of simples.[13]

One of the two sets of simples would immediately cease to constitute a life and come instead to compose a corpse, while the other would continue to constitute a body in heaven or wherever an intermediate state of existence is enjoyed.[14] In other words, the set of simples along one of the branching paths at the instant after fission fails to perpetuate a life while the other set of simples along the other branch does continue to perpetuate a life. If this is at least possible, as it seems, then we have a view of survival compatible with the claim that human bodies cannot enjoy gappy existence.

This view of immediate survival into an afterlife is also compatible with an intermediate state of conscious existence between death and resurrection. Like most other views in the neighborhood, however, it does not come without a price. At least part of the cost involves giving up the assumption that material continuity is necessary for the persistence of physical objects. Moreover, whereas we may be willing to allow physical organisms in particular to gradually replace some or all of the matter that constitutes them, we may not be willing to allow for an all-at-once replacement like that entailed by the fissioning of causal paths view of survival. We may think that's too high a price to pay. However, insofar as what ultimately matters for the persistence of organisms is the holding of immanent causal relations between any two stages of an organism's career, giving up the assumption about material continuity is not a cost incurred by the view, but rather an entailment of it.

There is a more serious metaphysical problem with the fissioning of causal paths view of survival, however; namely, it seems to violate what has come to be called "the only x and y" principle. According to this principle, whether or not some objects x and y compose some concrete individual F should have nothing to do with events involving numerically distinct objects spatiotemporally segregated from F. But in the account of immediate survival just suggested, it looks as though whether or not a body persists into the afterlife has everything to do with what happens to the other fission product, namely, that it immediately perish. I have answered this charge elsewhere in some detail and so won't take it up here, except to say that I think there are good reasons for believing that it can never be the case that there be a competitor for identity with my body.[15]

Note that this view just needs to be possibly true in order to show that belief in an afterlife does not require the existence of a nonphysical soul. And let me also point out here that if you are a dualist and a Christian theist, you believe in the resurrection of the body and not just the survival of a nonphysical soul into an afterlife. So making sense of the resurrection of the body is an equal opportunity employer. The dualist, no less than the physicalist, has to make sense of it.

■ 5. CONCLUSION

Belief in a nonphysical soul does nothing to demystify consciousness. How a nonphysical soul could be conscious is no easier to see than it is to see how a physical organism could. Moreover, many features of consciousness are wholly explainable in physical terms, making a nonphysical soul explanatorily redundant. A nonphysical soul is, in addition, wholly unnecessary with respect to many important theological doctrines that may seem to require it. I see no reason, therefore, to believe that I am anything other what I have always seemed to myself to be: one physical object among many in a most astonishing and wonderful physical world.

▪ NOTES

1. In contrast to what Goetz calls himself—i.e., an "antecedent soulist." See Stewart Goetz, "Substance Dualism," in *In Search of the Soul: Four Views of the Mind-Body Problem*, ed. Joel Green and Stuart Palmer (Downers Grove, IL: InterVarsity Press, 2005), 43. The title is originally adapted from John Perry's own "antecedent physicalist," which he calls any person "committed to physicalism in the sense that he or she sees some compelling reasons for it and will not give it up without seeing some clear reason to do so." Goetz, "Substance Dualism," fn. 22.

2. But I attempt to do so in *Rethinking Human Nature: A Christian Materialist Alternative to the Soul* (Grand Rapids, MI: Baker Academic, 2006), 73–75; Kevin Corcoran, "Persons and Bodies," *Faith and Philosophy* 15, no. 3 (1998): 330.

3. Something like this argument can be gathered from J. P. Moreland's *Consciousness and the Existence of God* (New York: Routledge, 2008), chap. 2; or Richard Swinburne, *The Evolution of the Soul*, rev. ed. (New York: Oxford University Press, 1997), 196–197.

4. See Robert Adams, "Flavors, Colors, and God," in *The Virtue of Faith and Other Essays in Philosophical Theology* (New York: Oxford University Press, 1987), 243–262.

5. For a couple of detailed examples, see section 2, "Brain science: two cases."

6. See David Chalmers, *The Conscious Mind: In Search of a Fundamental Theory* (New York: Oxford University Press, 1996), 125–127.

7. Elizabeth Anscombe, *Causality and Determinism: An Inaugural Lecture* (New York: Cambridge University Press, 1971), 27.

8. Jason Runyan brought this illustrative example from Anscombe to my attention in conversation.

9. See Corcoran, *Rethinking Human Nature*, 60.

10. For a detailed discussion of this argument, see Dean Zimmerman, "Two Cartesian Arguments for the Simplicity of the Soul," *American Philosophical Quarterly* 28, no. 3 (1991): 217–226. For a defense, see Goetz, "Substance Dualism," 33–60. For a brief critique, see Corcoran, *Rethinking Human Nature*, 33–34.

11. See Kevin Corcoran, "The Constitution View of Persons," *In Search of the Soul: Four Views of the Mind-Body Problem*, ed. Joel Green and Stuart Palmer (Downers Grove, IL: InterVarsity Press, 2005), 153–188.

12. Stephen Yablo makes this point effectively. After pointing out that probably most dualistic arguments are aimed at a conclusion like (4), Yablo notes that "philosophers have been slow to appreciate how unimpressive non-identity theses can be." He writes: "Assuming an unrestricted version of Leibniz's Law (the indiscernibility of identicals), non-identity is established by any difference in properties, however slight or insignificant. If, as seems likely, my body will remain when I am dead, then that already shows that my body and I are not the

same thing… You may say that this is dualism enough. But bear in mind that analogous considerations show equally that a statue is not identical to the hunk of clay which makes it up; and this is not normally taken as grounds for a dualism of statue and clay. On pain of insignificance, self/body dualism must mean more than just the non-identity of self and body." See Stephen Yablo, "The Real Distinction Between Mind and Body," in *Thoughts: Philosophical Papers*, Vol. I (New York: Oxford University Press, 2008), 2.

13. Dean Zimmerman was the first to suggest this view in a paper presented at the Pacific Division American Psychological Association (APA) meeting in 1994. I take up the view in my "Persons and Bodies" and Zimmerman develops it further in his "The Compatibility of Materialism and Survival: The 'Falling Elevator' Model," *Faith and Philosophy* 16, no. 2 (1999): 194–212.

14. We will assume not only that persons are essentially persons, but that being alive or conscious is a necessary condition for human personhood. Therefore there is after the fissioning only one possible candidate for a person-constituting object since the surviving corpse is not a living organism and so not capable of subserving consciousness.

15. See Kevin Corcoran, "Physical Persons and Post Mortem Survival Without Temporal Gaps," in *Soul, Body and Survival*, ed. Kevin Corcoran (Ithaca, NY: Cornell University Press, 2001), 201–217.

■ FOR FURTHER READING

Corcoran, K., ed. *Soul, Body, and Survival: Essays on the Metaphysics of Human Persons* (Ithaca, NY: Cornell University Press, 2001).
Gasser, G. *Personal Identity and the Resurrection* (Burlington, VT: Ashgate, 2010).
Hasker, W. *The Emergent Self* (Ithaca, NY: Cornell University Press, 1999).
van Inwagen, P. *Material Beings* (Ithaca, NY: Cornell University Press, 1995).

PART II

Debates About Specific Christian Beliefs

Miracles and Christian Theism

21 Christianity and Miracles

■ PAUL K. MOSER

> When the crowds were increasing, he [Jesus] began to say, "This generation is an evil generation; it seeks a sign, but no sign shall be given to it except the sign of Jonah. For as Jonah became a sign to the men of Nineveh, so will the Son of man be to this generation ... The men of Nineveh will arise at the judgment with this generation and condemn it; for they repented at the preaching of Jonah, and behold, something greater than Jonah is here"
>
> (Luke 11:29–32 Revised Standard Version [RSV]; cf. Matthew 12:38–40).

Mark's Gospel reports a similar situation where Jesus responds simply that no sign will be given to this generation (Mark 8:11–12). The "sign" sought by the audience of Jesus was a *miraculous* sign (as indicated in some English translations, such as the New International Version (NIV) translations of Luke 11:29, Matthew 12:38, and Mark 8:12). Accordingly, Jesus suggests that the seeking of miraculous signs, at least with regard to his own status, is "evil." What does this lesson hold for the relation of miracles to Christianity? In particular, what role, if any, do miracles have in a case for (the truth of) Christianity? This chapter answers such questions. It proceeds with the general notion of a miracle as an *extraordinary* divine intervention, thus allowing for the constancy of divine intervention without our corresponding knowledge of such constancy.

1. JONAH'S SIGN

The previous quotation from Luke's Gospel does not refuse miraculous signs altogether. On the contrary, it acknowledges a miraculous "sign" provided *by Jesus himself* in a manner analogous to Jonah's relation to the people of Nineveh. The general idea is that Jesus is a sign to his generation in a manner analogous to Jonah's being a sign to the people of Nineveh. More specifically, the key point emerges from the claim that the people of Nineveh "repented at the preaching of Jonah, and behold, something greater than Jonah is here" in the person of Jesus. The sign of Jonah, in other words, involves the repentance of Nineveh at his preaching, and this sign has an analogue in the sign of Jesus to his generation. ☞

The straightforward inference is that just as Jonah was a miraculous sign to Nineveh in virtue of Nineveh's repentance at his preaching, so also is Jesus a miraculous sign (from God) to his generation. The view that Jesus is such a sign is endorsed in John's Gospel after some people ask him, "What sign do you do, that we may see, and believe you?" (John 6:30 RSV). Of course, many people do not acknowledge Jesus as such a sign, and this leads John's Gospel to offer an explanation: "Everyone who has heard and learned from the Father comes to me [Jesus]" (John 6:45 RSV). The suggestion is that being receptive to (learning from) God is central to recognizing Jesus as a miraculous sign from God. Accordingly, John's Gospel states: "If anyone wills to do his [God's] will, he will know whether the teaching [of Jesus] is from God" (John 7:17).

Two questions emerge. First, what exactly does Jesus's being a miraculous sign from God consist of? Second, exactly how does one's willingness to do God's will enable one to discern Jesus's being a sign from God? The latter question involves the issue of what exactly people are to learn from God. We shall consider these questions.

■ 2. JESUS'S SIGN

Jonah's being a miraculous sign consists of his role in the repentance of the people of Nineveh. Specifically, via Jonah's message of judgment on Nineveh, the king of Nineveh brought the following message to his people: "let man and beast be covered with sackcloth, and let them cry mightily to God; yea, let every one turn from his evil way and from the violence which is in his hands. Who knows, God may yet repent and turn from his fierce anger, so that we perish not?" (Jonah 3:8–9 RSV). Through his message of judgment from God, Jonah became, with the unintended aid of the king, an agent of repentance toward God for the people of Nineveh. When God saw the repentance of the people of Nineveh, he had mercy on them in his "steadfast love" and called off the judgment proclaimed by Jonah (Jonah 3:10, 4:2). Accordingly, Jonah was a living and breathing sign of God's merciful love that calls for human repentance.

Like Jonah, Jesus was a living sign of divine love that seeks human repentance for the sake of a right relationship with God. Even so, there was a big difference: Jesus *willingly* portrayed the divine message for humans, whereas the message came through Jonah despite his unwilling attitude and behavior. If Jonah is the paradigmatic disobedient prophet used by God, Jesus is the model obedient prophet who carries out God's mission to humans. Both prophets, however, took their divine message beyond the Jewish people to Gentile outsiders. Even if Jesus focused his mission on the people of Israel (see Matthew 15:24), he extended his mission to Gentiles too (see, for instance, Matthew 15:28; Luke 7:1–10). This extended mission became a matter of controversy among some Jews early in the ministry of Jesus (see Luke 4:23–28), and the subsequent controversy over Paul's Gentile mission became a hallmark of his ministry (see his letters to the Galatians and the Philippians).

A theme common to all of the Gospels is that Jesus performed remarkable signs of various sorts.[1] According to Matthew's Gospel, some critics of Jesus attributed some of his powerful signs, particularly his exorcisms, to the power of Satan (Matthew 9:34, 12:24–27; cf. Luke 11:15; John 7:20–21, 8:48–54, 11:47–48). Jesus offered a contrary source: "if it is by the finger of God that I cast out demons, then the kingdom of God has come upon you" (Luke 11:20; cf. Matthew 12:28). According to all strata of the Gospel traditions, including the "Q" tradition of materials common to Luke and Matthew but not Mark, Jesus performed remarkable signs, and these signs attracted the attention of critics and supporters. We can dispute the source of these signs—God, Satan, or some purely natural source—but the extensive reports of them do call for some explanation.

If Jesus refused a sign to people seeking a sign, as in Luke 11:29–32, why does he reportedly include a wide range of signs in his ministry? Is there an inconsistency here? An important consideration is that Jesus came as the divinely anointed one who was promised in parts of the Hebrew scriptures, including the book of Isaiah (29:18–19, 35:5–6, 61:1–2), as God's redeeming representative. As E. P. Sanders notes, however: "Jesus's actual claim may have been in fact higher [than a claim merely to being God's promised 'Messiah']: not only spokesman for, but viceroy of, God; and not just in a political kingdom but in the kingdom of God."[2] Matthew's Gospel portrays Jesus as summing up the pertinent redemptive signs as follows: "Jesus answered them, 'Go and tell John [the baptizer] what you hear and see: the blind receive their sight and the lame walk, lepers are cleansed and the deaf hear, and the dead are raised up, and the poor have the good news [prophesied by Isaiah] preached to them. And blessed is he who takes no offense at me'" (Matthew 11:4–6 RSV; cf. Luke 4:18–19).

Jesus suggested that his miracles are signs not only of God's power, but also of his own distinctive role in the coming of God's kingship, or reign, on earth. This fits with his preaching that inaugurated his ministry: "The time is fulfilled, and the kingdom of God is at hand; repent, and believe in the gospel" (Mark 1:15 RSV; cf. Matthew 4:17). Accordingly, Jesus indicated that the kingship of God is drawing near in his own ministry (see Luke 11:20). His signs, however, are not impartial transparent "proofs" of his distinctive status or of God's reality. Instead, they are elusive and subtle indicators of the power of God in his life. This raises the question of what God aims to accomplish with such elusive signs. Particularly, what does God seek to have us learn from Jesus, and perhaps from Jonah too, if Jesus and Jonah are themselves elusive signs from God? Let's approach this issue indirectly, by considering human failure to perceive God's signs.

■ 3. WILLING AND DISCERNING

Many people deny that Jesus is a sign from God, and they demand a sign of some distinctive sort to buttress any claim that Jesus is a genuine sign from God. In doing so, they suggest that Jesus himself was and is an inadequate sign, if he was a sign at all. By way of response, Alan Richardson comments:

> It is possible for us to fail to see Christ as the manifestation of the power and the purpose of God; then we shall be content with an explanation of the miracle-stories in terms of modern psychology or folk-mythology. The miracle-stories, as an essential part of the preaching of apostolic Christianity, confront us with the question whether the power of God was or was not revealed in the person and work of Jesus Christ. They compel us to say Yes or No.[3]

The issue becomes whether Jesus himself is a sign of the power and purpose of God. Some people answer negatively, but this is premature in advance of clarification of the talk of "the power and purpose of God." It is akin to denying God's existence without a clear understanding of what the exalted title "God" actually involves, and this is an occupational hazard among philosophers.

According to Richardson, "to understand the meaning of the miracle-stories of the gospel tradition it is first necessary to have penetrated the incognito of Jesus, and to have seen behind the Jesus of Galilee the Christ of New Testament faith."[4] This may be so, but we still need clarification of the relevant talk of the power, purpose, and meaning of God in the signs under consideration. We also need clarification of what is involved in "the Christ of New Testament faith." Richardson explains:

> [Jesus] was not concerned to impress his contemporaries with his marvelous power; but rather that he asked them by the same token to believe that he had authority upon earth to forgive sins. He not merely opened the eyes of blind men, but claimed by that sign the power to make men see the truth of God ... And, finally, he not merely raised a child or a man from the dead, but claimed in doing so to be the resurrection and the life ... In the last resort it was the sign of the resurrection which authenticated all Jesus's other signs and the claims which they involved (cf. John 2:18–22).[5]

Richardson points us in the right direction, the direction suggested by Jesus himself (see Mark 2:9–11; cf. Luke 5:22–24). Note, however, the initial oddness of invoking the resurrection of Jesus as what "authenticated" the signs and claims of Jesus. The problem is that his resurrection is not a transparent "proof" for all parties to the dispute. Indeed, one's invoking the resurrection of Jesus will seem question-begging to some critics.

Evidence regarding the resurrection of Jesus seems sensitive to an inquirer's will (regarding God's will) in a manner that challenges its being used as a transparent authentication for all concerned. Jesus himself apparently acknowledged as much, in ascribing the following remark to Abraham in a parabolic story: "If they do not listen to Moses and the prophets, neither will they be convinced even if someone rises from the dead" (Luke 16:31 New Revised Standard Version [NRSV]). This remark is an important indicator of the epistemology of

Jesus, and it speaks against any kind of simple historical empiricism as a means for adjudicating the resurrection of Jesus or related divine signs. One's listening to Moses and the prophets somehow figures in one's being suitably convinced of the resurrection. The clarification of "somehow" is, of course, important now.

We can take some steps by attending to the idea of "listening to Moses and the prophets." The natural question is, listening to *what* in Moses and the prophets? Jesus does not have in mind *all* of the details of the Mosaic law and the prophets' teachings. In fact, he corrects some of the teachings of the Hebrew scriptures, including those about God as hating his enemies. For instance, Psalm 11:5 RSV states, "The Lord tests the righteous and the wicked, and his soul hates him that loves violence" (cf. Psalm 5:5). In sharp contrast with such teachings of the Hebrew scriptures, Jesus taught that God loves evil people, including his enemies, and that the children of God should follow suit. He taught as follows in the Sermon on the Mount: "You have heard that it was said, 'You shall love your neighbor and hate your enemy.' But I say to you, Love your enemies and pray for those who persecute you, so that you may be sons of your Father who is in heaven ... You must be perfect, as your heavenly Father is perfect" (Matthew 5:43–45, 48 RSV; cf. Luke 6:27–36; Romans 12:20–21). Clearly Jesus did not share the hateful attitude of the psalmist or assign that attitude to God.

Jesus thought of the primary lesson of the Hebrew scriptures (including "Moses and the prophets") as pointing to God's redemptive love humanly personified in himself. This love, according to Jesus, includes definite commandments that are to be obeyed by humans. According to Matthew's Gospel, he portrayed "the [Mosaic] law and the prophets" as depending on two commandments: first, the commandment to love the Lord your God with all your heart, soul, and mind; and, second, the commandment to love your neighbor as yourself (22:37–40; cf. Mark 12:29–31). Mark's Gospel portrays Jesus as adding that there is no commandment greater than these two (12:31), and Luke's Gospel represents Jesus as offering these two commandments in response to the question of what one can do to inherit eternal life (10:25–28).

Jesus was well aware that humans do not fully obey the love commandments at the heart of his teaching and therefore are in need of forgiveness and repentance. He says of humans: "If you, who are evil, know how to give good gifts to your children, how much more will your Father who is in heaven give good gifts to those who ask him?" (Matthew 7:11). In addition, he remarks, in connection with a question about inheriting eternal life, that "no one is good but God alone" (Mark 10:18; Luke 18:19; cf. Matthew 19:17; John 2:24). As a result, Jesus claims that it is impossible for humans to save themselves, but that human salvation is nonetheless possible for God (see Mark 10:26–27; Luke 18:26–27; Matthew 19:25–26). He offers the parable of the laborers in the vineyard to teach that God's kingdom operates by God's gracious generosity rather than by human scales of merit or earning (see Matthew 20:1–16). Moreover, he offers the parable of the Pharisee and the tax collector to illustrate that justification before God stems from God's mercy rather than human self-righteousness (see Luke 18:9–14). The latter parable fits nicely with Paul's famous message of "the free gift of righteousness" for humans before God (see Romans 5:17; cf. Romans 3:21–26).

We now may acknowledge that divine love, by the lights of Jesus, involves a life-giving merciful gift (of right relationship with God) as well as a command (to love God and others). Perhaps the most salient summary of this position is offered in John 3:16 RSV: "For God so loved the world that he gave his only Son, [in order] that whoever believes in him should not perish but have eternal life." Even if this famous proclamation did not come directly from Jesus himself, it captures the central message of Jesus, and it relates divine love to human faith (to which we shall return in the next section).

The Gospel of John has a special interest in human perceiving and failing to perceive Jesus as the culminating sign of God for human redemption. In John 7:4 RSV, the brothers of Jesus say to him: "if you do these things [that is, these signs], show yourself to the world." John interjects an editorial remark: "For even his brothers did not believe in him" (John 7:5). He thus suggests that Jesus's brothers were not in a position to understand the nature of his signs, particularly their pointing to a distinctive kind of divine love. Their charge to "show yourself to the world" manifests a serious misunderstanding of God and Jesus on their part.

Jesus draws a sharp contrast between his brothers and himself, as follows: "The world cannot hate you, but it hates me because I testify of it that its works are evil" (John 7:7). On the heels of this indication of needed repentance before God (with echoes of Jonah), Jesus issues his key cognitive principle: "If anyone wills to do his [God's] will, he will know whether the teaching [of mine] is from God or whether I am speaking on my own authority" (John 7:17). One's "willing to do God's will" thus emerges as significant in discerning whether Jesus is genuinely a sign from God. As himself a proposed sign from God in the tradition of Jonah, Jesus seeks a response of human repentance and trust in the light of God's merciful and demanding love. We need to examine the cognitive basis for such a challenging and life-defining response.

■ 4. FROM DIVINE LOVE TO HUMAN FAITH

A decisive matter concerns what exactly God wants out of his signs, including the personified signs of Jonah and Jesus. The case of Jonah illustrates that at a minimum God aims to reveal that God is "gracious ... and merciful, slow to anger, and abounding in steadfast love" (Jonah 4:2). In accordance with this aim, God employs Jonah to call the people of Nineveh to repentance and trust toward God, and when they repent, God promptly calls off the judgment threatened by Jonah (3:4–5, 4:2, 11). The sign of Jonah, then, manifests God's "merciful, steadfast love" for the sake of calling wayward people into reconciliation with God. This is the culminating lesson of the book of Jonah (4:11), and Jesus found it to anticipate his own ministry on behalf of God toward wayward people. Like Jonah, Jesus regarded himself as one sent by God to manifest, in his life and his death, God's merciful, steadfast love toward wayward people. Accordingly, Luke portrays Jesus as proclaiming, "Fear not, little flock, for it is your Father's good pleasure to give you the [divine] kingdom" (Luke 12:32). God's merciful, unearned giving of his kingdom, through Jesus, to wayward people is his "grace," in Paul's influential language (see Romans 3:21–26). Such language of "grace" (*charis*) is a simple variation on the language of divine *agape*, or self-giving, merciful redemptive *love* even toward God's enemies.[6] The heart of the matter is that God "first loved us" (1 John 4:19; cf. 1 John 4:10).

The redemptive love manifested by God in the signs of Jonah and Jesus is not only offered by God but also, as suggested previously, commanded by God of recipients of divine love. Even so, we should not think of the divine love commands as requiring that humans produce unselfish love on their own. Leon Morris notes: "The love that is commanded [by God] is not a love that believers generate themselves; it is a love that proceeds from divine love. Confronted with God's love, we may respond by accepting it or rejecting it."[7] Accordingly, we must face the question of how humans are to appropriate the divine love on offer. If such love is integral to the signs offered in Jonah and Jesus, we should also ask, in the same vein, how humans are to appropriate the divine signs on offer.

A familiar story is that the things of God, including divine signs, are to be received *by faith*, or by *people of faith*. This story may be defensible ultimately, but it demands clarification of its slippery talk of *faith*. Faith certainly looms large in the ministry of Jesus and, subsequently, in the mission of Paul to the Gentiles. In modern times, however, the notion of faith has become polluted by fideism, the troubled view that religious belief is exempt from demands of evidence or cognitive support of any kind. A misreading of Kierkegaard has contributed to such pollution among contemporary philosophers and theologians,[8] but an antidote is available in some of the New Testament writings. The needed antidote, however, is one of the best kept secrets in philosophical theology and in New Testament studies.

Paul comments as follows on the relation between faith and love: "In Christ Jesus neither circumcision nor uncircumcision is of any avail, but faith working through love" (Galatians 5:6 RSV). The RSV margin of this translation fittingly notes that the alternative translation of the relevant participle "*energoumene*" in the passive instead of middle voice leaves us with "faith *made effective* through love."[9] Duncan recommends that we should read Galatians 5:6: "in the clear light of Galatians 2:20, where … Paul declares that what brought him to rest exclusively on *faith* was the revelation of a Saviour who *loved* him."[10] In Paul's Good

News proclamation: "I have been crucified with Christ; it is no longer I who live, but Christ who lives in me; and the life I now live in the flesh I live by faith in the Son of God, who loved me and gave himself for me" (Galatians 2:20 RSV). Evidently Paul thought of his faith as based in divine self-giving love manifested in God's son.

We need not digress to a debate about the middle or passive voice of the participle "*energoumene*" in Galatians 5:6. Even if one favors the middle voice, and opts for "faith expressing itself through love" (as many contemporary translators and commentators do), one still needs to identify the ultimate source of the love in question. Paul is altogether clear on this source,[11] as we see in Romans 5:1, 3–5 RSV:

> Since we are justified by faith, we have peace with God through our Lord Jesus Christ … More than that, we rejoice in our sufferings, knowing that suffering produces endurance, and endurance produces character, and character produces hope, and hope does not disappoint us, because God's love [*agape*] has been poured into our hearts through the Holy Spirit which has been given to us (cf. 2 Corinthians 5:5,14).

The key phrase is "God's love has been poured into our hearts." Paul understands hope in God as faith in God directed toward the future when God will fulfill a promise, and he therefore uses "faith" and "hope" interchangeably at times.[12] As a result, Paul would also say that faith in God "does not disappoint us, because God's love has been poured into our hearts." This consideration fits well with Paul's mention of "faith" [in God] at the opening of the previous quotation, in Romans 5:1.

We now may endorse Emil Brunner's observation that "faith [in God] is nothing other than the vessel into which God pours his love … Faith is … the openness of our heart for God's love."[13] Brunner speaks fittingly of "the faith [in God] which consists in the reception of the divine love."[14] This divinely intended connection between divine love and human faith in God bears directly on the purpose and the cognitive status of divine signs, including those found in Jonah and Jesus.

God does not seek human faith, belief, or knowledge regarding God apart from (divinely intended) transformative human reception of divine love. In other words, God does not offer signs to prompt human faith based just on intellectual reflections or any other factors apart from the transformative human reception of divine love. Accordingly, contrary to the attitudes of many philosophers, divine signs are not offered as the stuff of a spectator sport. They come instead with the divine aim to redirect human wills away from futility and toward life in full cooperation with God. Such signs, then, will not serve their divine purpose of human transformation, or even be perceived by humans for what they truly are, if they are not willingly received, in repentance and trust toward God, as a source of divine transformative love.

N. R. Hanson comments: "There is no single natural happening, nor any constellation of such happenings, which establishes God's existence ... If the heavens cracked open and [a] Zeus-like figure ... made his presence and nature known to the world, *that* would establish such a happening."[15] This reveals a misunderstanding of divine signs, and the misunderstanding is widely shared. It is not clear what Hanson means by "natural happening," and it is doubtful that we should expect God to be available in "natural" happenings. In any case, it is unclear that Hanson's imagined Zeus intervention would have anything to do with God's existence. "God" is a maximally exalted title requiring worthiness of worship, but Hanson's Zeus appears to be nothing more than an object of entertainment for casual spectators. In particular, there is nothing redemptive about this Zeus-like figure in the face of human hate and self-destruction. Hanson's imagined case therefore does not bring us anywhere near God.

We now can break with fideism regarding the divine signs of Jonah and Jesus and human faith in God. God's love being poured into our hearts is no mere belief; it is a salient *experience* that serves as the cognitive, evidential foundation for well-founded belief in God.[16] As Brunner notes: "[Divine] love is the criterion by which we recognize whether our faith is genuine faith ... (Gal. 5:6). For faith [in God] is not mere knowledge; it is [the human reception of] the self-communication of the divine life, the love which manifests itself as the principle of the new life."[17] The human reception of such divine love is a struggle to receive such love and thereby to trust God, and thus is very different from any spectator experience of a Zeus-like figure who cracks open the heavens and leaves us morally unchanged.

The signs of a God worthy of worship come with a divine redemptive purpose, and that purpose can be at odds with our own purposes. In that case, we easily can misunderstand the signs if we notice them at all. The signs are intended by God to have humans join in cooperation with God's redemptive goals, as the cases of Jonah and Jesus illustrate. Humans need to discern the divine love involved in the signs and to receive and appropriate it for the authoritative life-giving divine power it is. In Paul's Good News message, humans appropriate the life-giving power of the signs when they willingly yield to (cooperate with) God's self-giving love on offer (manifested perfectly in Jesus) and become, by God's power, a "new creation." This new creation is no mere human belief or construct. It powerfully involves the moral and spiritual resurrection and reorientation of a willing person by God, as Paul witnessed firsthand.[18]

The new creation has a key cognitive component. Accordingly, Paul remarks that "neither circumcision counts for anything, nor uncircumcision, but a new creation" (Galatians 6:15 RSV). In the same vein: "From now on, therefore, we regard no one from a human point of view; even though we once regarded Christ from a human point of view, we regard him thus no longer. Therefore, if any one is in Christ, he is a new creation" (2 Corinthians 5:16–17 RSV; cf. John 3:1–14).

Paul (a.k.a. Saul) was a zealous persecutor of the followers of Jesus (see Galatians 1:13–24), but in the presence of God's call through Jesus, he came to acknowledge that Jesus is a living redemptive sign from God. He came to see someone formerly subject to his persecution as a sacred, life-giving sign from God.

■ 5. CONCLUSION

Humans will have to face, sooner or later, God's primary sign in Jesus and the corresponding question from Jesus himself: "Who do you say that I am?" (Mark 8:29). Their answer will affect not only their perception but also their future regarding being in or out of fellowship with God. Not all alleged miracles are genuinely of God, but the sign of Jesus satisfies the criterion of divine self-giving love and calls us all to enter and enjoy life without end in fellowship with God.

■ NOTES

1. For classifications of these signs, see Alan Richardson, *The Miracle-Stories of the Gospels* (London: SCM Press, 1941); Alan Richardson, *An Introduction to the Theology of the New Testament* (New York: Harper & Brothers, 1958), 95–102.

2. E. P. Sanders, *The Historical Figure of Jesus* (London: Penguin, 1993), 242; cf. E. P. Sanders, *Jesus and Judaism* (Philadelphia: Fortress Press, 1985), 321–322.

3. Richardson, *The Miracle-Stories of the Gospels*, 126.

4. Richardson, *The Miracle-Stories of the Gospels*, 137.

5. Richardson, *The Miracle-Stories of the Gospels*, 131–132.

6. Cf. J. Armitage Robinson, *St. Paul's Epistle to the Ephesians*, 2nd ed. (London: Macmillan, 1904), 224–226.

7. Leon Morris, *Testaments of Love* (Grand Rapids, MI: Eerdmans, 1981), 189; cf. Anders Nygren, *Agape and Eros*, trans. P. S. Watson (New York: Harper & Row, 1953), 125–126.

8. On which, see Paul K. Moser and Mark McCreary, "Kierkegaard's Conception of God," *Philosophy Compass* 5 (2010): 1–10; cf. Paul K. Moser, *The Evidence for God* (Cambridge: Cambridge University Press, 2010), chap. 2.

9. In favor of the passive rendering, particularly "*made operative* through love," see Robinson, *St. Paul's Epistle to the Ephesians*, 241–247; George Duncan, *The Epistle of Paul to the Galatians* (New York: Harper, 1934), 157–158; Kenneth W. Clark, "The Meaning of energeo and katargeo in the New Testament," *Journal of Biblical Literature* 54 (1935): 93–101.

10. Duncan, *The Epistle of Paul to the Galatians*, 157.

11. Cf. Ceslaus Spicq, *Agape in the New Testament*, Vol. 2 (London: Herder, 1965), 222.

12. On which, see Emil Brunner, *The Christian Doctrine of the Church, Faith, and the Consummation*, trans. David Cairns (Philadelphia: Westminster Press, 1962), 339–346; Herman Ridderbos, *Paul*, trans. J. R. De Witt (Grand Rapids, MI: Eerdmans, 1975), 248–252.

13. Emil Brunner, *Faith, Hope, and Love* (Philadelphia: Westminster Press, 1957), 75; cf. p. 33.

14. Brunner, *The Christian Doctrine of the Church*, 236; cf. p. 316.

15. N. R. Hanson, *What I Do Not Believe and other Essays* (Dordrecht: Reidel, 1971), 322.

16. On which, see Paul K. Moser, *The Elusive God* (Cambridge: Cambridge University Press, 2008); Moser, *The Evidence for God*.

17. Brunner, The *Christian Doctrine of the Church*, 339.

18. See Romans 6:4–11; cf. Moser, *The Elusive God*, 187–189.

▨ FOR FURTHER READING

Earman, J. *Hume's Abject Failure: The Argument Against Miracles.* Oxford: Oxford University Press, 2000.

Fogelin, R. *A Defense of Hume on Miracles.* Princeton, NJ: Princeton University Press, 2005.

Keener, C. *Miracles: The Credibility of the New Testament Accounts.* Grand Rapids, MI: Baker, 2011.

Twelftree, G. ed. *The Cambridge Companion to Miracles.* Cambridge: Cambridge University Press, 2011.

22 It is Not Reasonable to Believe in Miracles

■ EVAN FALES

I will offer three rather different arguments for the contention that belief in miracles is not reasonable. The first project will be to assess the claim that miracles are even possible. I'll argue that, although the occurrence of miracles is logically possible, it may well not be metaphysically possible. (I say "may well" as the argument invokes a robust, philosophically contentious, conception of causation.) The second project is a (rather brief) defense of Hume's assessment of the rationality of belief in miracles on the basis of testimonial evidence. (Like Hume, I'll mainly set aside the question of what would make rational a belief that a witnessed candidate event was a miracle. In either case, of course, the argument presupposes that miracles are not impossible.)

Finally, I'll argue—again briefly—that dogged concern over whether miracles *actually* happen has the pervasive—and perverse—consequence that miracle stories are systematically misunderstood. I claim that the Biblical stories were not intended to be, and should not be, read literally. For tradition-minded Christians, naturally, matters come to a head in I Corinthians 15, where Paul *seems* to be insisting precisely that the Faith depends entirely upon the literal "bodily" resurrection of Jesus. Well, things are often not what they seem. I'll be arguing that there's a better way to read the miracle narratives: better both because more historically plausible, and because more charitable, in the sense of ascribing to the authors and their immediate audiences beliefs that are actually *true*, or at least entirely reasonable to believe. So on that way of understanding miracle stories, I say that they are indeed reasonably believed. But this won't appease those who, taking the stories literally, also offer that affirmative response. These three arguments, though distinct, support one another in ways that will become clear as I proceed.

Before I begin, a clarification is in order. What is reasonable for one person to believe, on the evidence, may not be reasonable for another. They may have different evidence—or, having the same body of evidence, one may have intellectual tools for assessing that evidence lacked by the other. (Ironically, stupidity and ignorance can make beliefs reasonable that would be irrational for those who don't suffer these handicaps.) But I'll be addressing the question on behalf of you, dear reader, who *do not* (as I hope I myself do not) suffer from these intellectual defects. Furthermore, I shall set aside the question of whether it might ever be reasonable to believe something for which one doesn't have adequate evidence, where reasonableness is judged on pragmatic grounds. Our question is whether, and in what circumstances, it would ever be reasonable to believe that a miracle had occurred *on the evidence*.

1. ARE MIRACLES POSSIBLE?

There is a short way to deal with miracles, if defined to be violations of laws of nature. If we further take *"It is a law that all As are Bs"* to entail *"Every A is a B,"* and if what counts as a violation is an *A* that's not a *B*, then it follows that a miracle is a logical (or, more broadly, conceptual) impossibility. Even though Hume sometimes defines a miracle as a violation of a law of nature, he cannot have intended this implication, for granting it would have made the path to his conclusion in "Of Miracles" much easier—even trivial.[1] And Hume clearly intended a much more substantive result, as should we.

This means we shall have to deny either that *"It is a law that As are Bs"* entails *"All As are Bs,"* or be much more circumspect about what it is for a miracle to "violate" a law of nature. I opt for the latter. A key observation is that causal laws are typically defeasible: such a law states that if an event of type *C* happens, an event of type *E* will follow, other things being equal. Other things are not always equal: an arrow's flight describes a parabola—unless blown by the wind, struck by a passing bird, etc. And when God strikes, things are most definitely not equal. So the idea is this: a miracle is a divine intervention, an influence upon the course of (some region of) nature that, had only natural forces acted, would have transpired in some other way. The laws that describe (or govern) that "other" way are not violated; it's just that divine influence, when added to the naturally occurring forces, results in something not otherwise "in the cards." The resulting event need not be (as Hume recognized) spectacular or even recognizable by us—though we could electively add the requirement that the event must be religiously significant. Formally: *"Event a of type C was followed by event b of type E* (instead of E)"* is not inconsistent with *"It is a law that events of type C are followed by events of type E, other things being equal."* What a miraculous "violation" amounts to is nothing more (and nothing less) than a reflection of the fact that nature is not causally closed, and, on occasion, the deity decides to push things around a bit.

Now a popular way of characterizing miracles, this apparently avoids a conceptual shipwreck.[2] But is it actually as viable as it looks? That depends on what the laws of nature in fact are—which is not a conceptual matter. In particular, it depends upon the standing of certain conservation laws: consider, for example, local conservation of energy and momentum.[3] These two laws are understood to hold without exception; they are not defeasible. They are often stated this way: in a causally closed system, total energy and momentum remain unchanged over time.[4] Having conceived the miraculous to involve divine (causal) intervention, the natural suggestion is that when God acts upon the physical world, the affected region of space is *not* causally closed.

That's what the theist should say—but the price is steep. Take a gas in a closed, isolated container. The total energy and momentum of the gas molecules will remain unchanged over time. But if we heat the container over a flame, the energy content of the gas will increase; the system is no longer closed. However, we can restore the energy balance by extending the boundaries of our system to include the flame (the source of heat): the total energy for the gas plus the heat source will, once again, be conserved. Matters are different when God supplies energy (or momentum) to an otherwise closed physical system. If we now extend the "boundaries" of the system to include God, energy/momentum will *not* be conserved. For God has no mass/energy, and it makes no sense to speak of His having lost or gained energy in a transaction with nature. According to the theist, God creates energy ex nihilo.

Could God interact with a physical system without affecting its budget of energy or momentum? To answer this, let's think about what's happening a bit differently. According to Hume, a causal law was just a matter of there being a regularity in nature. But many philosophers now agree that this is too thin a conception of causation. I should say that our *fundamental* conception of causation derives from our experience of felt pushes and pulls.[5] If that's correct, then a cause is just something that exerts a *force*. Newton's third law of motion says that for every force, there's an equal and opposite force. This, indeed, entails the conservation laws, for energy is just force multiplied by distance, and momentum is just force times time.[6] But then, causation implies exchanges of energy and momentum. And, to put it graphically, our problem becomes how does God, who has no mass/energy, exert forces on matter? Given that every force is balanced by an opposite force, what does the matter push back against? God's body? Moreover, Newton's third law is not defeasible: it allows for no exceptions.[7]

Theists might demur: the law, they may say, does have one sort of exception. Its scope covers interactions between material objects, but not between material and nonmaterial objects. But this is no minor concession. For one thing, it implies that the laws of physics are not time-reversal invariant or space-translation invariant, symmetries that are fundamental to the physical world as we understand it.[8] These aren't minor adjustments. The notion that local energy and momentum are not conserved is a radical notion: there is no evidence for it in physical science, and massive evidence to the contrary. (And it won't do to reply, of course there is no evidence from physical science, physical science can't detect or investigate the supernatural. For that's just false: if there is nonconservation of energy or momentum somewhere in the universe, there is no reason why it can't be measured.)

As a final maneuver, theists might claim that God's influence on the world is not mediated by exertion of force, but by some other sort of causal relation. But this looks like a *deus ex machina*. We have no idea what such a causal relation could be—nothing that ties it to experience in the way that our conception of forces is tied to the experience of felt pushes and pulls. One can only respond that theists owe us an explanation for what looks like an ad hoc postulate. If causation is necessarily mediated by forces, and if Newton's third law obtains necessarily, then miracles are impossible. I take the necessities in question to be metaphysical necessities,[9] in which case the impossibility of miracles is a metaphysical impossibility. Not even God can do things impossible in that sense. ⌐

▓ 2. MIRACLE STORIES ARE UNBELIEVABLE

There is some irony in the frequent observation that miracles "don't happen any more" as they did in Biblical times. I have some news: they *do* happen, with lively frequency, in many parts of the world, thanks to the agency of all manner of spirits, gods, and other denizens of the supernatural. It is the post-Enlightenment industrialized West that seems to be experiencing something of a miracle drought. This fact itself wants explanation.

Here I'll be defending Hume's judgment on those abundant miracles that fed the faith of our fathers—miracles we know of only by way of hearsay. ‑ Unfortunately, the question of the reasonableness of taking miracle stories at face value engages issues in confirmation and probability theory too technical for proper treatment here. I'll do my best, therefore, to cut to the chase without running roughshod over essential matters. As I read Hume, the essence of his argument is that, in order to identify an event as a miracle, it must be known to "violate" the applicable laws of nature. But the very evidence required to establish those laws as known is the very best sort of evidence we could have that an exception has never occurred. Against this we must weigh the evidence that favors the veracity of a miracle report. These reports have human authors, and any measure of reliability must reflect knowledge of the track record of human veracity—a track record known to be sensitive to such factors as competence, credulity, motives for dissembling, conditions under which liars risk detection, etc. If we can speak here of "laws" of human behavior at all, they are ones that entail only statistical regularities—and don't encourage a high degree of confidence in human testimony.[10] ◄

Now if, as Hume says and I concur, we are to apportion our strength of belief to the balance of the evidence for and against a claim (however that is to be evaluated), then doubt about a miracle must always outstrip (or at best equal) confidence in testimony that it occurred. To this abstract argument, Hume adds various observations that reflect especially unfavorably on miracles retailed in support of a religion. Particularly pungent are Hume's comments on a group of near-contemporaneous miracle stories he knew to be rejected by almost all of his readers, even though they occurred at the center of European civilization (Paris) and whose impostures had resisted detection even after several concerted efforts at exposure.

Hume's argument provoked numerous responses, then and now.[11] There are, in particular, two objections to Hume's argument that I think require direct rebuttal. One points out that it's not in general true that the intrinsic improbability of an event infirms the credibility of a report that it occurred. So if Hume means merely to be discounting miracle reports on the grounds of the improbability of the reported events, then he won't have demonstrated the irrationality of believing such reports. The other objection observes that when Hume appeals to "what happens in all times and places" to support the law whose "violation" constitutes a miracle, he is relying, for the most part, precisely upon testimony (how many of us have first-hand experience, constituting an inductively large and representative sample, that humans don't rise from the dead?)—and tendentiously excluding precisely the testimony that points to exceptions. That seems to beg the question against the miracle-monger.

We can address both of these concerns if we pose the question this way: what is the best (most plausible, most likely) explanation of the data we have? Those data include, for example, some early Christian reports that other Christians said that they had seen and fraternized with Jesus three days after his burial and various scattered reports of others who died and revived from Ancient Near East (ANE) pagan, Jewish, and Christian sources;[12] on the other hand, there is massive evidence (most of it testimonial) that people don't recover from death. That's not all: we have manifold instances of alleged miracles subsequently exposed as impostures. We also understand *why* dead people do not revive. (The ancients didn't have our knowledge of biochemistry, but certainly recognized that decomposition is a progressive process and that rotting flesh can't duplicate the functions of living bodies.) Some, to be sure, may reason that God could reconstitute decomposing flesh (and had good reason to do so in this case).[13] How plausible that explanation is depends upon (1) what independent evidence one has that God exists, and (2) what independent evidence there is that God would have *wanted* to raise Jesus (but not, presumably, Bacchus, Apollonius, or any of the other figures in resurrection narratives rejected by Christians). The Humean alternative is to discredit all the resurrection reports on the strength of the reasoning that our total data much more strongly support the following explanation: dead people never rise, and occasional claims to the contrary (wherever they are found) are to be explained by reference to opportunities for dishonesty, credulity, ignorance, etc., that are admitted on all hands to be pervasive in human societies. (There is a third alternative explanation, of which more below.)

This way of thinking about the matter clearly doesn't beg the question raised by occasional reports of resurrections. Rather, it confronts those reports head-on: discounting them is the right reaction because we have a natural explanation for their falsity, one we believe *anyway* about human connivance, and readily apply to miracle stories we have no stake in. Explanatory considerations also rebut the first objection. It's true that we don't regularly discredit a witness because of the improbability of what's reported. If you tell me that you were dealt such-and-such a hand in last night's poker game, I don't disbelieve you just because that poker hand is wildly improbable. After all, you were dealt *some* hand, and if from a properly shuffled deck, then that hand is as likely as any other. But here we have a perfectly good explanation for why the improbable should occur—an explanation that, on independent grounds, is likely to be true. Matters assume a different complexion if you aver that, with everything at stake, you were dealt a royal flush. If I believe your report at all, I will seek an alternative explanation to chance: might there have been cheating? I reason thus because the winning hand seems "too good to be true"—hence chance is an unlikely explanation. Similarly, I suspect your appeal to divine intervention to explain Jesus's alleged resurrection: here, both the report and the explanation seem too good to be true, if Jesus is your homeboy.

The question of whether to believe miracle stories is traditionally understood to pit two rival explanations: a theistic explanation, on which favored miracle stories are true reports of divine intervention, and the Humean fraud-and-folly (as I call it) explanation. Given just those choices, I think the Humean alternative wins hands down. But are these the only alternatives? Each has difficulties. The Humean has to explain how stories wild on their face managed to pass muster and, at least in the case of Christian origins, motivated otherwise intelligent people to join a movement at considerable risk and sacrifice. Is there a better way to explain this?

3. MIRACLE STORIES ARE BELIEVABLE AFTER ALL—BUT NOT THE MIRACLES

Here is a familiar story:

> Then Moses stretched out his hand over the sea; and the Lord drove the sea back by a strong east wind all night, and made the sea dry land, and the waters were divided. And the people of Israel went into the midst of the sea on dry ground, the waters being a wall to them on their right hand and on their left. The Egyptians pursued, ... The waters returned and covered the chariots and the horsemen and all of the host of Pharaoh ... And Israel saw the great work which the Lord did against the Egyptians, and they believed in the Lord (Exodus 14:21–31 RSV).

What shall we make of this? Some nineteenth-century Bible critics tried to offer naturalistic explanations for the Biblical miracles. A strong east wind, it might be thought, really would be able to drive back the waters of a shallow part of the Red Sea. But what made such a wind to blow? Was this wind the breath of God? If so, then we have, not a naturalistic explanation, but divine intervention after all—not to mention the fact that the million-plus Israelites had to march, with their animals, straight into that wind. A wind strong enough to erect walls of water would be strong enough to pick up the entire multitude of Israelites, together with their goats, and drive them back into the waiting arms of Pharaoh's army. As naturalistic explanations go, this one is not worth the ink.[14]

Such explanations are not only physically ignorant, but theologically misguided: they try to preserve historical veracity at the cost of discrediting the very providential care of God for His people that the text means to convey. Let us abandon the concern with "history": after all, in this case, there happens to be abundant evidence in the archaeological record that there was no Exodus, and therefore no crossing of the Red Sea.[15] That frees us to consider other dimensions of this story, rich in symbolism and meaning. (I might remark in passing that, if we take the story at face value, nearly a million and a half Israelites, of all ages and conditions of life apparently "got it" and worshipped the Lord as a result of this spectacular bit of showmanship—though, bafflingly and to God's eternal frustration—they had to be reminded over and over again by similar spectacles. The diagnosis: they were a "stiff-necked" people. A more clear-headed assessment is that they must have been spectacularly and recklessly bereft of common sense—again, if the story is taken at face value.)

So how should we proceed? The first thing to notice about this text is that the action is highly choreographed—choreographed to tell a story with significant meaning. For example, Moses makes repeated pleas to Pharaoh to release the Israelites; the repeated refusals, which are engineered by God, lead to increasingly intense and destructive woes for Egypt. The second thing to notice is that real history doesn't "work" this way. History isn't merely "one damned thing after another," but it approaches much more closely to that than to scriptural narratives. History doesn't tell itself as a significant story; historians must work to extract meaning from it. The third thing to notice about the passage is that its structure is fashioned from transposable elements or themes. This feature is familiar to sacred narratives the world over. Within a sacred tradition (and sometimes across traditions that borrow from each other), such elements appear repeatedly, like words in a common vocabulary. Like words, they can be "strung together" in myriad combinations to assemble narrative structures; and like words combined into sentences, the meanings of the narratives are a function of the meanings of the constituent themes and the way they are ordered or organized to form the narrative structure (the "syntax" of the story). Let's begin with this third feature of the Red Sea crossing.

The first task is to place our story in context, and that means doing at least two things: considering its place within a larger narrative, and identifying themes within the story that are powerful for the tradition—a power attested to by their repeated appearance in its stories about itself. Let's reconnoiter: what are some of these themes?

Of course the larger story is a story about the escape of Israel, the sons and daughters of Jacob, from Egyptian bondage, and the destruction, in the process, of Egyptian society at the hand of Yahweh, the Lord. Here are some rather obvious themes that this story employs or affirms

1. the chosenness of Israel,
2. the defeat of Israel's enemies by her God,
3. the presence of a mediator between God and Israel—a prophet/leader who reigns 40 years, and
4. the delivery of Israel from captivity and slavery.

First I establish the enduring power of these themes by noting some places where they recur. Then I'll turn to a fifth theme—indeed, the most obvious one.

1. That Israel enjoys a special relationship with Yahweh as His chosen "sons" hardly requires comment. This relationship is established by the covenant between Yahweh and Abraham respecting his son Isaac (Genesis 17:8–21; cp. 22:15–18, 26:1–5), is consistently affirmed throughout the Hebrew Bible, and is reiterated (though in a new key) by St. Paul in the New Testament (Romans 9:8–13; 11:1–32).
2. The story of Israel's subsequent conquest of Canaan, and of later wars with its enemies, is filled with descriptions of conflicts in which Israel's faithful worship of Yahweh is rewarded with victory over enemies. Episodes are found throughout Numbers, Deuteronomy, Joshua, Judges, 1 and 2 Samuel, Kings, and Chronicles; the theme is generalized and linked to the fifth theme, discussed below, in Psalms and elsewhere. We may hint at this link by noting that, as part of His defeat of Egypt, God has just slain all the first-born male children of Egypt (i.e., the legal heirs of family lines) on the Passover night, a theme echoed earlier in Pharaoh's slaughter of Jewish male infants (Exodus 1:15 ff.) and later in Herod's slaughter of Jewish male children upon hearing of Jesus' birth (Matthew 2), a direct parallel between Jesus and Moses.[16]
3. Moses' formal leadership of Israel begins with the escape from Egypt and ends 40 years later with his death atop Mt. Pisgah, overlooking Canaan. Eli, priest, judge of Israel, and mentor of Samuel, judged Israel for 40 years (1 Samuel 4:18); King David reigned over Israel for 40 years (2 Samuel 5:4; 1 Kings 2:11; 1 Chronicles 29:27), as did his son Solomon (1 Kings 11:42; 2 Chronicles 9:30) and the just king Joash (2 Chronicles 24:1).[17]
4. This is not the only such delivery. Best known, no doubt, is the Persian (actually Medean) King Cyrus's release, attributed to Yahweh's providence, of the captive Israelites who had been enslaved by the Babylonian king Nebuchadnezzar (2 Chronicles 36:22–23; Ezra 1:1–4; Isaiah 44:28, 45:1). There are other examples, both earlier and later.[18]

But here's the fifth theme—one noteworthy for its power: the parting of the waters for Israel's passage through the sea and rescue by God. What are these waters, and what does it mean that Israel should by God's help be able to pass through them? The association of the waters of the sea with death, destruction, and chaos is ancient and appears literally dozens—probably hundreds—of times in the narratives and poetry of the Hebrew Bible. Few themes recur more persistently throughout the Bible. Obviously I can't present or discuss even a significant portion of these. However, a few deserve mention; they incorporate notions that circulated across many cultures in the ANE. These notions include (1) an association between the "waters" (or the "deep," the "sea," the "flood") and danger, death, and chaos—things out of control; (2) prayer on behalf of God's chosen for deliverance, and God's positive response; (3) God's ability to control the chaos, and a similar ability given to His anointed; (4) the "dry land" as, in contrast, a symbol for life-giving stability (social order requires being able to fix stable social boundaries); and (5) use of entry into, and escape from, the waters as a representation of a rite of passage, in which a person or group of persons make the transition from one state or kind of social being to another, usually better, state.

Such rites of passage occur worldwide, and are often symbolized by entry into a realm of "death" and reemergence into a new condition of life.[19] Not every use of the theme exemplifies all of (1)–(5), though often what's not said is implied. Now some examples: God's parting the waters and bringing forth the dry land (Genesis 1:9–10); God's again parting the waters with wind to provide safe haven for Noah's Ark (Genesis 8:1–12); the parting of the River Jordan (Joshua 3:4–14; also 2 Kings 2:6–15); various passages in Job, especially 38 and 41 (Leviathan is a monster of the deep); Jonah's captivity in the whale; numerous Psalms (e.g., 2:1–9, 18:6–19, 42:5–11, 69, 74, 77:16–20, 88, 89, etc.; also 2 Samuel 22. This last psalm (see verses 17–20) makes quite clear the symbolic imagery that equates the chaos waters with the power to disrupt social life (here, the power of the king's enemies).

These observations make evident the following features of the story at Exodus 14:

1. The Red Sea crossing can be understood as a rite of passage, constituting Israel for the first time as an independent nation (albeit as yet without a homeland and about to be given its laws). That rite is recapitulated when Israel does—finally—enter the Promised Land via a similarly miraculous crossing of the Jordan River.
2. The Red Sea (the *yam sûp*) was taken to be an arm of the chaos waters, and hence represented the realm of death. Israel survives passage through these waters (over "dry ground") by divine grace, and by divine grace, Egypt, Israel's enemy, perishes.[20]

3. An individual chosen by God as His prophet is authoritatively established as Israel's sanctioned leader. Here, as elsewhere repeatedly, Moses cries out to God for rescue (Exodus 14:10–17), and God gives succor. *assistance in a tof trouble*

We have, then, a story that represents the creation of a new social order—the nation of Israel—from a people brought out of a condition of social chaos by their god and set upon the path to a destiny also fashioned by that god. But none of this language requires us to suppose that the author(s) of Exodus imagined a *literal* crossing of the Red Sea—or even the literal captivity in Egypt (a perennial enemy of Israel's) of a large population of "children of Israel." What's required is that the imagery employed by the story can convey to Israel a conception of who and what they are as a nation, a conception that, among other things, gives authority to the laws and customs under which they existed.

Once we see this much, the question whether God might have somehow parted the waters of the Red Sea, by stirring up a wind or by some other means, begins to lose interest. Of more interest is the question of how Israel, through the telling of this story and the other stories of the Pentateuch, constructed and conceived of its self-identity as an independent nation among other nations in the ANE.[21]

Now some theist will be sure to insist that, even if I am right about the *symbolic* dimensions of Exodus 14, that is entirely consistent with the *literal* occurrence of the events narrated in Exodus. What we have is a story that operates on two levels: as accurate history, and as God's providential operation *through* history to effect His will for humanity. But why should we saddle the authors of Exodus with the belief that they were reporting historical events—especially since we know, from the archaeological evidence, that those events never occurred in any case?

Looking at things this way, reading Exodus 14 through the lens of 2 Samuel 22:17–20 and other chaos-waters texts, raises the question: why did Israel come to express its identity with this story (or this sort of story)? Alas, trying to answer that important question would require me to spill far more ink than I have (nor do I have a complete answer). But examining this question, I believe, is far more interesting and fruitful than interminable debates over whether an "east wind" could split the Red Sea.

So is it reasonable, never having witnessed one, to believe in miracles? Well consider: maybe you don't know whether miracles are metaphysically impossible. But, given my argument, you should admit that they might be. Second, you must weigh the prospects (supposing that they *are* possible) that any given story both relates what would be a genuine miracle and is (literally) true. Surely the probability of that isn't very high. Third, you will have to discount the possibility that the story is intended nonliterally. Putting together all of those probabilities, what are the chances?

■ NOTES

1. David Hume, "Of Miracles," *An Inquiry Concerning Human Understanding*, Sec. X, ed. Charles W. Hendel. (Indianapolis, IN: Bobbs-Merrill, 1955), 117–141.

2. For example, Robert Larmer, *Water Into Wine* (Montreal: McGill-Queen's University Press, 1988); William Alston, "How to Think About Divine Action," in *Divine Action*, ed. B. Hebblethwaite and E. Henderson (Edinburgh: T & T Clark, 1990), 51–70; William Lane Craig, "The Problem of Miracles: A Historical and Philosophical Perspective," 1986, http://www.leaderu.com/offices/billcraig/docs/miracles.html, accessed June 18, 2010.

3. This question has been engaged in considerable detail in a different but related debate over the possibility of dualistic (mind/body) interactionism. For obvious reasons, the question whether immaterial minds can causally influence bodily motion parallels the question whether an immaterial God can rearrange bits of matter. Unfortunately much of the debate has been flawed by a woeful ignorance of basic physics. I say "local" conservation because the values of the conserved quantities can't be uniquely defined at a time within a relativistic framework for the entire universe or any region with large space-time curvature. But such concerns are irrelevant to earthbound miracles. My thanks to William Klink for helpful discussions of these matters. For a lay exposition, see Tamara M. Davis, "Is the Universe Leaking Energy?" *Scientific American* 303 (2010): 38–47.

4. The Heisenberg uncertainty principle allows that their values are uncertain for sufficiently small intervals of time and space, respectively. But this consideration doesn't loosen the constraints on macroscopic miracles; see Peter G. Clarke, "Determinism, Brain Function and Free Will," *Science and Christian Belief* 22 (2010): 133–149.

5. For an extended discussion, see Evan Fales, *Causation and Universals* (New York: Routledge, 1990), chap. 1. That our fundamental conception of causation is associated with felt forces does not prejudice the question whether there can be action at a distance. (After all, we feel the pull of gravity, but not as a contact force.)

6. A bit more technically

$$E = \int \vec{F} \cdot d\vec{s} \quad \text{and} \quad \vec{p} = \int \vec{F} dt \text{,}$$

where E = energy, p = momentum, s = distance, t = time, and F = force.

7. What about God's communicating with humans directly by directly influencing, in some way, their mental states? If minds are not material things, does not this possibility avoid the difficulties that beset divine interference in the physical world? Perhaps. But if, as I believe is likely, human conscious states are at least dependent upon the existence of suitable bodily (i.e., brain) states, then this possibility is no more free of the difficulties mentioned than are "ordinary" miracles; see in this connection David L. Wilson, "Mind-Brain Interactionism and the Violation of Physical Laws," *Journal of Consciousness Studies* 6 (1999): 185–200.

8. Conservation of energy implies time-reversal invariance (the laws of physics remain unchanged if the "movie" of the universe is "run backwards" and conservation of momentum implies space-translation invariance; the laws remain unchanged under spatial translation).

9. See Fales, *Causation and Universals*, chaps. 2 and 3.

10. Agreement between multiple independent witnesses to an event (at least in the absence of notable disagreements) can dramatically strengthen the weight of testimony. But, at least as concerns the New Testament testimony to Jesus' miracles, the condition of absence of disagreement is so repeatedly violated that the real question is how that is to be explained, given that the clear evidence of the early Christian community's oral transmission and sharing

of its earliest traditions, prior to any extant writings, makes impossible the conclusion that we have any independent witnesses in the corpus of surviving testimonies.

11. These are too numerous to list. Perhaps the most prominent full-length contemporary treatment is John Earman, *Hume's Abject Failure: Hume's Argument Against Miracles* (Oxford: Oxford University Press, 2000).

12. For example, Bacchus, Apollonius of Tyana, and other pagan figures. Both Elijah and Elisha revived dead boys (I Kings 17, II Kings 4); Jesus raised Lazarus (John 11; cp. also Luke 7:11–17). The bodies of "many saints," their tombs opened, rose from the dead when Jesus died on the cross (Matthew 27:52–53).

13. For example, Richard Swinburne, *The Resurrection of God Incarnate* (Oxford: Oxford University Press, 2003), part I.

14. A variant explanation displaces the crossing to the "Sea of Reeds"—the marshy area of the Nile Delta along the Mediterranean. The "wall of water" is explained as a tsunami, caused by the volcanic explosion of the island of Thera, which is supposed to have coincided with Israel's escape from Egypt. I won't bother to debunk that theory; see Bernard F. Batto, "Red Sea or Reed Sea? How the Mistake Was Made and What Yam Sûp Really Means," *Biblical Archaeology Review* 10, no. 4 (1984): 57–63.

15. A concerted search for archaeological remains of the 40-year sojourn in Sinai turned up nothing. The account of the Israelite invasion of Canaan in Joshua is not sustained by the archaeology of that period in Palestine; the conflicting account in Judges may be more accurate. Some scholars—for example, Frank Moore Cross—allow that the Exodus story might reflect a history of escape of a small band of Canaanitic Egyptian slaves who may have settled for a time in Midian and then joined a people populating the highlands of Palestine.

16. There is a close link as well with Genesis 22, the story of the binding of Isaac—but that would take me too far afield.

17. The symbolic connections to 40-day periods are too numerous and complex to discuss here.

18. For example, Judges 3–6 recounts at least four cases; the apocryphal Maccabean books relate another (the rebellion against the Seleucid tyrant Antiochus IV); see also the books Esther and Daniel.

19. This symbolism is quite natural if we think, as I do, of personhood not simply in terms of the natural or biological capacities of a human being, but also in terms of their social position or status; an individual "dies" as one kind of social being—for example, being a child or being an ordinary citizen—and reemerges into the world an adult, an elected official, a nobleman, knight, or queen. Note that baptism—one ancient rite of passage—involves an immersion in water that was understood in the first century CE to symbolically represent a death and rebirth into a new state of social being. For a discussion and examples, see Arnold van Gennep, *The Rites of Passage*, trans. Monika B. Vizedom and Gabrielle L. Caffee (Chicago: University of Chicago Press, 1960); Victor Turner, *The Forest of Symbols: Aspects of Ndembu Ritual* (Ithaca, NY: Cornell University Press, 1967); and classically, James Frazer, *The Golden Bough: A Study in Magic and Religion*, abridged (New York: Macmillan, 1973).

20. See Batto, "Red Sea or Reed Sea?," 59–60. The Red Sea was considered in ancient Jewish mythology to be an arm of the Southern Ocean, which was itself understood to be a surface feature of the chaos waters (most of which were subterranean). The destruction of Egypt's social order is symbolically reflected in (a) the Passover destruction of family legal continuity and (b) the destruction of Egypt's military.

21. There is a prior question that is even more fundamental: how did the author(s) of Exodus, in the absence of any (literal) miracles and in light of their use of miraculous imagery to express their deepest reflections upon questions of social order and national identity, understand, and intend to be understood, their talk of the divine, or revelation and prophecy, and of providence? I have offered a theoretical framework for thinking about those questions in Evan Fales "Truth, Tradition, and Rationality," *Philosophy of the Social Sciences* 6, no. 2 (1976): 97–113; "The Ontology of Social Roles," *Philosophy of the Social Sciences* 7, no. 2 (1977): 139–161; and, in specific application to the New Testament, in "Taming the Tehom: The Sign of Jonah in Matthew," in *The Empty Tomb: Jesus Beyond the Grave*, ed. Jeffrey J. Lowder and Robert Price (Amherst, NY: Prometheus Books, 2005), 307–348.

■ FOR FURTHER READING

Broad, C. D. "The Argument from Energy." In *The Mind and its Place in Nature*. London: Routledge & Keegan Paul, 1925.

Dietl, P. "On Miracles." *American Philosophical Quarterly* 5 (1968): 130–134.

Dostoyevsky, F. *The Brothers Karamazov*, translated by Constance Garnett, Book IV, chap. 1, and Books VI and VII. New York: Random House, 1950.

Fawcett, T. *Hebrew Myth and Christian Gospel*. London: SCM Press, 1973.

Geivett, D., and G. R. Habermas, eds. *In Defense of Miracles: A Comprehensive Case for God's Action in History*. Downers Grove, IL: InterVarsity Press, 1997.

Price, R. M., and J. J. Lowder, eds. *The Empty Tomb: Jesus Beyond the Grave*. Amherst, NY: Prometheus Books, 2005.

Russell, R. J., N. Murphy, and C. J. Isham, eds. *Quantum Cosmology and the Laws of Nature: Scientific Perspectives on Divine Action*. Notre Dame, IN: University of Notre Dame Press, 1996.

Smith, M. *Jesus the Magician*. New York: Harper & Row, 1978.

Science and Christian Faith

23 Science is at Odds with Christianity

■ JULIAN BAGGINI

The science versus religion debate is one of the most tired of our time. However, it is not clear what exactly has been exhausted. Are the players spent because they have tried everything, or is it rather that they have used up all their energy running around in circles, going nowhere? Like being lost in the desert, it's difficult to tell whether the monotony is down to the barrenness of the landscape or the fact that you keep coming back to the same place.

It certainly seems to be the case that familiarity has bred contempt more than it has deepened understanding. Participants on both sides often feel that the other side just doesn't get it. If there is to be any progress in this discussion, people are going to have to try to listen to some familiar arguments as though for the first time. Although there may indeed be nothing new of substance to say, a refreshing of the debate may be achieved by some subtle reframing of old points: how well things are illuminated depends on how they are lit. That will be my strategy in what is to follow.

■ 1. THE COMPATIBILITY DISTRACTION

One of the biggest problems with the science and Christianity debate is that it is so often framed in terms of *compatibility*. This is peculiar. After all, that one belief is compatible with another is the most minimal test of its reasonableness imaginable. Consider the claim that the Apollo moon landings never happened. Is there any scientific reason to think this *must* be false? Of course not. Laws of physics are not broken by conspiracy theories (at least not most of them). Concrete evidence, such as pictures of the Earth from space and lunar rock, could all, in principle, have been obtained without a man ever having set foot on the moon. Nevertheless, I don't think anyone should be impressed by the claim that the view that the Apollo moon landings never happened is compatible with science. So what? The evidence more than suggests, it screams that they *did* happen.

What really counts, what should really make the difference between assent and rejection of an empirical claim, is not whether it is compatible with science, but whether an evidence-led, rational examination of a view supports it better than competing alternatives. That is what makes Apollo mission denial at odds with science. This should be obvious. Why it is then that the science versus Christianity debate is still so often framed in terms of compatibility is a holy mystery.

Perhaps the reason is that many are persuaded that the root of the compatibility is a difference that means Christianity does not need to answer to any demands of evidence-led, rational examination. Following this line, it is argued that to treat Christianity (or most other religions) as though it were an empirical hypothesis is to make a category mistake of the worst kind. If this were true, then compatibility with science would be all Christianity needed to close the science versus religion debate, along with some other kind of nonscientific justification, the validity of which science is no authority on. Christianity could say what it liked and the scientists would just have to wash their hands and say, "Nothing to do with me, guv'."

The biologist Stephen Jay Gould makes just this kind of move when he argues that science and religion having nonoverlapping magisteria (NOMA). Science deals with "the empirical realm: what the Universe is made of (fact) and why does it work in this way (theory). The magisterium of religion extends over questions of ultimate meaning and moral value. These two magisteria do not overlap, nor do they encompass all inquiry."[1] In short, science is empirical, religion is ethical.

A version of this strategy has also been adopted by the physicist John Polkinghorne and the mathematician Nicholas Beale. As they put it: "Science is concerned with the question, How?—By what process do things happen? Theology is concerned with the question, Why?—Is there a meaning and purpose behind what is happening?"[2] It sounds like a clear enough distinction, but in practice many "why" questions are really "how" questions in disguise. For instance, if you ask why does water boil at 100°C?, what you are really asking is what are the processes that explain that it has this boiling point?, which is a question of how. The blurring between how and why is perhaps even clearer when the why question is about causes. If you ask why did the light come on?, for instance, a full answer would again include many purely scientific explanations of *how* it is that the pressing of a button can lead to illumination. In the same way, if you ask why did human beings evolve from a common ancestor with chimpanzees?, much of the answer will involve you with the hows of natural selection.

What exactly is the character of the kinds of "why" questions that generally concern theology? I suggest it is something we can call "agency-why." To understand an action or event as being the result of agency—deliberate action—we need to assume *causation with intention*. To understand the switching on of a light as the result of agency, for instance, you have to assume that the relevant answer as to why it came on involves reference both to the intentions of the switch flicker and a causal explanation of why this action would have the desired effect. There is no agency-why when there is intention without causation. You do not explain a football team's victory on the basis that a football supporter willed it, because this willing could not have caused the result. Nor is causation without intention a proper case of agency. If my telephoning a friend causes them to lose concentration while skiing and fly off the edge of a cliff, my action is clearly a cause of the disaster, but it was not the result of my agency.

In the humans case, when we ask why things have happened, and we are looking for meaning and purpose, we are not always asking a question about agency-why. We are capable of finding meaning without purpose in things that just are or just happen, even when they are not the result of any choices we make. Consider the example of suffering. An atheist can conclude that suffering serves no teleological purpose. Pain and suffering are natural phenomena that evolved because they added survival value to the conscious creatures who felt them, alerting them to damage to the body. Nevertheless, the atheist can resolve to find meaning in suffering, or to give it meaning. What this means is that she can attempt to use what would otherwise be a purely negative experience in a more positive way, by, for instance, using it to put what matters in context, to reassure herself that she is capable of withstanding more than she thought, or by thinking of others who suffer even more and developing compassion for them. In answer to Polkinghorne and Beale's question, "Is there a meaning and purpose behind what is happening?" the reply could be, "Not *behind* it, but *in* it, if we put it there."

It is also possible, of course, for a human being to choose a painful route through life for a deliberate purpose, or even to inflict pain on others for what they believe to be a greater good. In such cases, there is a meaning and purpose behind what is happening, and so there is an agency-why explanation of why it happened. Such an explanation does not in principle need to assume anything outside of science. As a matter of fact, we rarely bring science into it, because our scientific understanding of consciousness and decision-making is primitive. Hence the explanation "she wanted to push herself to the limits" is far more useful than any explanation that attempts to look at deep neurological processes, for instance. In principle, however, we have every reason to think that there is a level of description that would account for any human choice or behavior in purely scientific terms. As physical beings in a physical universe, we have to assume that a complete physical science would be able to fully account for everything we do. It may not be practically possible to ever get to this complete description, and I suspect it will never be the most useful way of thinking about ourselves and others if we could, but in principle, such a level of description must exist. If it does not, then by definition, the natural does not explain everything and there must be some supernatural forces at work in the universe too.

It should be openly acknowledged that the commitment to naturalism this view entails requires acknowledging that naivve conceptions of free will do not hold. If the hypothetical reduction is possible, then there is no "voluntarist" or "libertarian" faculty of free will that human beings have that enables us to overrule the natural chain of cause and effect. This is not a problem for most secular-minded philosophers, however. As a recent study showed, only about 16.6 percent of philosophy faculty and PhDs "accept or lean toward" libertarianism (interestingly, very close to the proportion who "accept or lean toward" theism—16.3 percent).[3]

The important point here is to notice how agency-why in the human case relates to scientific truth. For practical purposes, we often can treat the scientific question of *how* separately from the meaning and value question of *why*. But that is not because the question of why is in fact separate from the question of how. It is simply that we best approach questions of *why* from the point of view of conscious motive and the question of *how* from the point of view of more mechanistic science. Even now, that is not always the case. We do sometimes explain why people behave as they do by explaining the how, the underlying neural mechanisms that drive their behavior. We do this when we answer a "why" question with "because he was drunk," "because he was on medication that affected him badly," or "because he suffered damage to his prefrontal cortex." These answers make sense because they are examples of unusually clear relations between brain states and behavior. But what proponents of voluntarism fear in such explanations is true: if this is the case in such behaviors, then it is also the case that normal behavior too is at some level explained simply by what is going on in the brain, body, and its environment. That means agency-why questions for humans are not fundamentally in a different category to how questions. We distinguish between how and why in humans because the different questions are alerting us to different salient features of the situation.

Now consider the agency-why of a deity. To think of God's intentions and their relation to the causal order in the same way as we do humans does not make sense on any mainstream conception of the Christian God. A Spinozistic "God-or-nature" could act with a purpose that was, at root, simply the playing out of natural forces. But this is not the theistic God. The theistic God is "behind" what happens, not simply part of it. That means that when you ask why things happen in the theological context you are not asking a question that has no bearing on the how, the supposed domain of science. Either God is affecting the how, in which case theology has entered the domain of what was supposed to be science; or he is not, in which case he is a Spinozistic "God-or-nature," not any mainstream Christian God, and can in effect be dropped out of our account of the universe.

Consider, for example, anthropic fine-tuning, which another religious physicist, Paul Davies, calls more snappily "the Goldilocks enigma": the conditions in the universe are just right for life to have evolved, and had a few things been just slightly different at the big bang, none of us would be here.[4] At the moment, there is no generally accepted scientific explanation for why or how this is so. Polkinghorne answers the "why" question by saying that the life-enabling laws of physics are "graciously provided by the creator."[5] But this is also a claim about *how* the universe came to be this way, namely, by divine fiat. Since it cannot explain the mechanism by which God intervened, nor test the hypothesis that he did so, it is no substitute for a proper scientific answer.

"How" inevitably gets mixed up with theological questions of "why" because "why" in the religious sense is usually agency-why, which involves intention and causation, and is not just about interpreting what things mean. This must be so. The Christian God is both creator and ruler of the universe. So if things happen in that universe that have meaning and purpose, then clearly it is because this God has set things up in some way, or intervened in some way, to make sure that purpose is achieved or meaning realized. The neat division between how and why questions therefore turns out to be unsustainable.

■ 2. DO ATHEISTS RULE OUT RELIGION A PRIORI?

It might be objected that this argument only works because the kinds of intentions and causation belief in a deity bring to our understanding of the world have been ruled out a priori by a secular science dogmatically committed to naturalism, not because science has to be this way. Richard Swinburne, for instance, argues that his arguments for a dualistic soul are rejected because the materialist dogma of the time excludes them, even though reason and evidence—good scientific virtues—point to their existence.[6]

Even if there were a naturalist assumption in science, it would not rule out a priori the existence of certain things that are usually thought of as supernatural. If ghosts existed and it were possible to verify their existence scientifically, then ghosts would be natural, not supernatural. Indeed, "ghost hunters" and the like make their claims seem more credible precisely because they claim to be able to detect their presence in ways that should satisfy scientists.

But more importantly, "natural" and "science" are not defined here in ways that rule out the possibility of the religious a priori. There are possible worlds where supernatural agency explanations are real and empirical at the most basic level. For instance, if our world was like that of the ancient Greek or Roman gods, then we would live in a world in which fundamental explanations for events could not be given purely in terms of impersonal scientific forces. Unless these gods were in fact just superpowerful mortals, acting within the laws of nature, complete knowledge of the physical universe and the laws that govern it would not be sufficient to tell you what would happen (or, to be more accurate in this post-Newtonian time, the probabilities of things happening). Science could only concern itself with what happens in the absence of divine intervention. But to explain how it was that certain things happened, you would need to appeal to divine action and intention.

Could we live in this kind of world? Science offers no a priori reason why not. If we allow a theistic God as a logical possibility, then we have to allow that it is not an a priori truth that every event in the universe must have an impersonal, scientific explanation. Hence it might be argued that when religious thinking does get involved in hows, this could be in harmony with science. To go back to anthropic fine-tuning, it could be argued that there is indeed a gap in our scientific understanding. We cannot explain why it is that the laws of physics are so precisely tuned to allow human life to have evolved. It is a baffling mystery in desperate need of an explanation. Given that, the hypothesis that there must be some divine intention behind it could be a scientific one: given the data, there is a possible world in which it would be the best hypothesis, one we would be entitled, for scientific reasons, to hold. If science is a posteriori, as I think it is, it does not rule out a priori the existence of causes other than mechanistic, impersonal ones.

The reply to this is that religious explanations have no role in science for purely a posteriori reasons. There are at least two such general reasons, and one more particular to anthropic fine-tuning. The first is Hume's argument in section XI of *An Enquiry Concerning Human Understanding*, based on the simple principle that "when we infer any particular cause from an effect, we must proportion the one to the other, and can never be allowed to ascribe to the cause any qualities, but what are exactly sufficient to produce the effect."[7] Whenever (as a matter of fact) we invoke deities to explain events in the natural world, we breech this principle. Even if we were entitled to see something as evidence of some agency or intention, you would only have arrived at some mysterious force and nothing as specific as a theistic God. "The supposition of farther attributes is mere hypothesis," said Hume. The reason for this is clear enough. Inductive inferences, upon which science is based, depend on a similarity between observed cases and unobserved ones. But we simply have no observed data on supernatural entities on which to base any inductive hypothesis. The subject lies entirely beyond the reach of human experience. So when a Christian looks at a problem such as anthropic fine-tuning and hypothesizes a theistic God to explain it, she is doing bad science. That this is not strictly unscientific is beside the point: bad science is at odds with science as pseudoscience.

The second reason is that we have good inductive grounds for treating "the God of the gaps" as a desperate hypothesis.[8] Putting God where a current scientific mystery lies is as crude and irrational a move when the problem is anthropic fine-tuning as it is when the question is how the sun moves across the sky. Christian scientists recognize this, of course, and will protest that they are definitely not invoking a God of the gaps. However, it is hard to see how these protestations are justified in the case of anthropic fine-tuning, where the structure of the argument is there is a hole in our scientific explanation; there is no other scientific reason to postulate a theistic God; nevertheless it looks like it plugs the hole to me, so let's postulate it.

There is a third reason that is particular to anthropic fine-tuning. This is simply that the whole issue of the significance of the improbability in such cases is confused. Lots of things are extremely improbable, yet they happen without the need for any explanation other than chance. A common example is the UK National Lottery. Your chances of winning are tiny: 1 in 14 million. Yet more than 2,000 people have won to date. In each case, there is no need to invoke anything other than chance to explain this. Clearly, if enough tickets are sold, someone will win. Although it is highly improbable for any given person that they will win, it is almost certain that someone will, if enough different possibilities are being generated.

Take a different example. An artist decides to create a work of conceptual art as a complete one-off, calling it *aft*. *Aft* is an arrangement of a million grains of sand blown by the winds over a canvas and then set by a process of encasement. Given the number of grains and their possible positions, the chances of that particular work of art existing, rather than another, are infinitesimally small. Yet clearly, its remarkable improbability does not require an explanation other than it was the result of a random process.

In the case of anthropic fine-tuning, we just don't know enough about the nature of the uncertainty to know whether it requires a special explanation. Perhaps we are like lottery winners, marveling in our improbable victory, unaware that it was inevitable that life was going to emerge in one universe or another, and thinking that we need something other than chance to explain why we are in the one with life. Or maybe we are like *aft*, inconceivably improbable, but then again, any universe would have been just as improbable. The fact that things needed to be just so for our kind of life to evolve might turn out to be unremarkable, because the same would have been true for any other kind of life that would have evolved in any number of other possible universes. We just don't know. So the idea that our improbability points to a divine intention is, again, just bad science.

■ 3. LANGUAGE GAMES

Before concluding, I wish to say just a few words about words. It has been increasingly common in recent years to hear people defend religious truths on the basis that religious language is significantly different from scientific language. What exactly this difference is varies between accounts, but broadly speaking, the division is between *mythos* and *logos*. *Logos* is the language of literal, empirical truth; *mythos* is the language of meaning and value.[9] So we can see straight away that really this argument is simply a variant on the distinction we have already seen between the two magisteria of science and religion.

This distinction explains, it is claimed, why it is those who see a conflict between science and religion are misguided. When a scientist says "water is H_2O," they are making a very different claim from that of the priest who says "this is the blood of Christ" when offering the Eucharist. The scientist is telling you something that would be verified by examining the water under a microscope. Whatever the priest means, it is not that his chalice contains hemoglobin.

If it were indeed the case that Christianity were purely a matter of *mythos*, then it would not, of course, be at odds with science. But any impartial observer would note that this simply is not true of most actually existing Christianity. A priest may not believe that the communion wine is literally the blood of Christ, but the Roman Catholic Church to which he belongs does believe that literal miracles occur because of the intercession of saints, that Mary really was a virgin when she conceived Christ, that Jesus really did rise bodily from the dead, and so on. Christianity is full of factual claims. It seems to me that proponents of the *mythos/logos* distinction are actually advocating an alternative to the Christianity of our time, not describing its nature. They show a way by which it need not be at odds with science, not that it is not at odds with science in its current form.

The other important thing to note is that the apparently reassuring statement that people just get religion wrong when they think of it as being empirical actually requires the biting of some pretty hard bullets. The problem comes when you really try to specify what sort of language *mythos* is, if not literal and empirical. If religious language is figurative, then religion is poetry, and devotion aesthetic. There is nothing wrong with that, but I'm not sure many deeply religious people would be happy to see what they do in those stark terms. If, rather, it is that religious language is imprecise or analogical, gesturing toward religious truths that are ultimately inscrutable, then no one should claim to know God, his nature, or his wishes. Religion would have to be a much more modest enterprise than it has historically been. I'm all in favor of this, but again, I doubt many true believers would be happy to accept these limitations. Eternal salvation, for instance, is not so attractive if you admit it is not clear what "eternal" or "salvation" really means in practice.

■ 4. CONCLUSION

The general reason why Christianity is at odds with science should now be clear. It is not at odds with science because it inevitably has to be. It is at odds, as a matter of fact, because despite the protestations of sophisticated intellectual defenders of faith, it makes numerous empirical claims about the world. Much of what is said in Christianity is best understood as *mythos*, not *logos*, but it simply misrepresents the beliefs of most Christians to deny that Christianity contains creeds that belong to the domain of *logos*. It would be fine if Christianity only considered issues of meaning and value and left questions of *how* to science, but it repeatedly strays into questions of how, postulating God as a first cause or setter of the cosmic constants. Some Christians may be indifferent to the factual status of claims about the empty tomb, or the real existence of a personal God, or of life after death, but Christians who are indifferent to all of them are a very rare breed. A Christianity that did avoid questions of how would be very different from the one that actually exists. Its God would be a part of nature, a subject to its laws, not a maker of them. The traditional theistic God, who intervenes and acts in the world, is at odds with science because there is no good evidence of such interventions actually occurring. To truly follow the strictures of NOMA, one would have to treat the Gospels as no more than the articulation of the moral philosophy of a first-century Palestinian. Anything more and you are in the realm of facts at odds with science.

The apparently neat division between "why" and "how" does not work in keeping science and Christianity neatly apart. If religion truly sticks only to why, then it cannot be a theistic religion with an activist, free God. If it gets itself involved with hows, which it clearly does when it brings God in to explain fine-tuning or the origin of the big bang, then it is offering competing explanations to those of science, which, in Laplace's famous saying, science has no place for the God hypothesis.

The conclusion that Christianity is indeed at odds with science therefore needs to be understood as an a posteriori one. That is why it is a trivial truth that Christianity and science can be compatible. It is also why one can imagine, and indeed practice, forms of Christianity that are not at odds with science, and clearly there are people who do that. But as a matter of fact, Christianity is not usually like that. If the religion is to cohabit with science, then it needs to accept itself as a nonfactual, nonempirical discipline much more deeply and more honestly than it has generally managed to date.

▪ NOTES

1. Stephen Jay Gould, *Rocks of Ages: Science and Religion in the Fullness of Life* (New York: Ballantine Books, 2002), 6.

2. John Polkinghorne and Nicholas Beale, *Questions of Truth: Fifty-One Responses to Questions about God, Science, and Belief* (Louisville, KY: Westminster John Knox Press, 2009), 7.

3. The PhilPapers Surveys, conducted by David Bourget and David Chalmers, conducted in November 2009, http://philpapers.org/surveys/results.pl. Results are based on 1,803 respondents.

4. P. C. Davies, *The Goldilocks Enigma: Why Is the Universe Just Right for Life?* (London: Allen Lane, 2006).

5. Polkinghorne and Beale, *Questions of Truth*, 41.

6. Swinburne was most explicit about this in an interview with the author, parts of which were published in Julian Baggini, *The Ego Trick* (London: Granta, 2011), 64: "The only reason people deny what stares them in the face is because they're captured by the physicalist dogma current in our time."

7. David Hume, *Hume on Religion*, ed. J. Baggini (London: Philosophy Press, 2010), 128.

8. The phrase and concept of the God of the gaps is attributed to Henry Drummond, *The Ascent of Man* (New York: James Pott & Co., 1894), 333.

9. The mythos/logos distinction as been widely popularized over the last decade by Karen Armstrong, starting with her 2000 book *The Battle for God: Fundamentalism in Judaism, Christianity and Islam* (New York: Knopf/HarperCollins, 2000).

■ FOR FURTHER READING

Baggini, J. *The Ego Trick*. London: Granta, 2011.

Drummond, H. *The Ascent of Man*. New York: James Pott & Co. Publishers, 1894.

Gould, S. J. *Rocks of Ages: Science and Religion in the Fullness of Life*. New York: Ballantine Books, 2002.

Hume, D. Hume on Religion. Edited by J. Baggini. London: the Philosophy Press, 2010.

24 Science is not at Odds with Christianity

■ KEITH WARD

When the Bible was compiled, science in its modern sense had not begun to exist, and human views of the nature of the physical world were very different than they now are. The earth was conceived to be a flat disc floating on a great ocean, and the stars were lamps hung on a hemisphere over the earth. The earth was the center of God's purpose, and Jerusalem was the center of the earth. The world had not existed for very long, and it would probably cease to exist in a fairly short time without any great changes happening to it. Some Jews believed that when the Messiah came, the whole dome of the sky and the earth would be renewed, and a new age when lions and lambs would play together would dawn.

Modern science has changed this view of the world almost beyond recognition. Is Christianity so bound up with the ancient world view that it has become obsolete? I suggest that some versions of Christianity, closely bound up with that ancient view, are at odds with modern science. But just as science can change, so can religion, and there are revised versions of Christianity that are wholly compatible with the modern scientific world view. Not only that, they can illuminate and complement the scientific view in a way that is very important to a full understanding of the world.

▨ 1. SIX POINTS OF TENSION

It is easy to locate points of possible tension. Here are six main such points: First, if God created the universe, we would not expect the universe to be random, pointless, or cruel. But some scientists, particularly evolutionary biologists, stress that the evolution of life seems to be random, and that the processes of evolution are wasteful and cruel, so throwing doubt on any belief in creation by a good God.

Second, astronomers now know that there are more than a hundred billion stars in our galaxy, and more than a hundred billion galaxies in the visible universe, that the cosmos is almost fourteen billion years old, and will exist for billions of years yet, long after the earth has ceased to exist. This is hard to square with a belief that humans are the center of God's purposes for the universe, or even that they are of any great cosmic importance at all.

Third, belief that the world might end soon conflicts with modern knowledge that the universe will continue for billions of years. Life on this planet may indeed destroy itself soon, but that will not introduce any new golden age, or affect the rest of the universe in any significant way. A return of Jesus on the clouds would break all the known laws of physics, and it seems unintelligible in the context of modern cosmology, which presumes that physical laws will continue to operate long after the annihilation of planet Earth.

Fourth, stories of a virgin birth, a resurrection from the dead, and of walking on water and creating food out of nothing—stories of miracles like these are in tension with scientific skepticism about the possibility of miracles, and with the belief that all physical events occur in accordance with natural laws of physics.

Fifth, stories of Jesus exorcising demons conflict with modern medical belief that there are no demonic forces, and that physical causes like viruses and brain malfunctions are better explanations of mental illnesses.

Sixth, advances in neuroscience and artificial intelligence suggest that without the physical brain humans would have no conscious existence, so they throw doubt on any possibility of resurrection or of life after death.

■ 2. REDRAWING ANCIENT CHRISTIAN BELIEFS

Theologians of most major forms of Christianity have accepted that new scientific knowledge requires some redrawing of ancient beliefs, but not their abandonment. The main theological responses take the following forms, adopting the order set out above:

First, it is true that a God-created universe cannot be random, wasteful, pointless, or cruel. But does a generally Darwinian account of evolution entail that this is what the universe is like? Passions tend to run high in the world of biology, but I doubt whether the established facts of genetic mutation and natural selection show randomness (in the sense of complete lack of direction or lack of any tendency to evolve consciousness and intelligence, for example), wastefulness, or pointlessness. These are value judgments, not scientific judgments. It is interesting that many physicists, pointing out that "random" mutations are of course physically caused, not simply uncaused, find intelligent life to be more or less inevitable, given the fundamental laws and constants of nature. One person's wastefulness may be another's creative fecundity, and whether there is any point in a given process is not a question that could be resolved by any purely scientific observation.

The facts of evolutionary biology do rule out some views of divine providence—for instance, that God in every instance acts for the best, or that there are no chance events in nature. But they leave open a number of other possibilities—for instance, an intelligent creator may set up a self-organizing, partly indeterminate, but increasingly integrated and complex system operating under general laws that will enable intelligent creatures to emerge. Such creatures may play a creative role in shaping the future of the physical universe, and in actualizing conscious states of great value (like appreciating beauty, under-standing the laws of nature, and relating to one another in love).

The fact of suffering is, of course, a major problem for theists, but evolution-ary theory may in fact help to explain its existence by showing how it seems to be an essential possibility in the existence of societies of self-developing organ-isms within which sentience emerges, and whose genesis will eventually give rise to free and responsible cognitive agents. Theists may hardly expect to be able to demonstrate that this is the case. But at least they can rebut the simplis-tic claim that a good God would never have any reason for creating a world in which suffering exists. They can rebut it by showing that there may be such a reason, present in the necessities of the laws that govern the natural world, even if we cannot fully show what those necessities are (something that most natu-ral scientists, like most theologians, would dearly love to do, but which most confess is probably beyond our powers). To put it very briefly, if there are to be carbon-based intelligent beings like humans, perhaps the laws of nature, of evolutionary biology, and of psychological development need to be just what they are. If so, we could not eliminate all suffering without eliminating *Homo sapiens*. And whether or not that would be a good thing is beyond the remit of science to say.

Modern scientific knowledge can play a very valuable part in causing theists to think very carefully about the role of chance and providence, of necessity and freedom, and of the relation of divine and human causality in the created world. Some ancient views may have to be given up. But a deeper view of God's purpose in creation may be formulated in the light of our cosmological and biological knowledge. Those who take that deeper view are unlikely to think of humans as the center of creation. But they may think of intelligence and moral freedom, in whatever material forms they may exist, as such a center. It is unlikely that they should think that God created things just as they are, to remain unchanged forever. But they may think that God created a developing, emergent universe of which intelligent persons are an integral part, with the responsibility of shaping the cosmos toward greater knowledge of truth, creation of beauty, and a con-scious communion of personal beings.

Such beliefs would not be entailed by cosmology or biology, and there will probably continue to be biologists who strongly object to seeing any direction or purpose in the evolutionary process. Yet there is a coherent theistic view that is consistent with the best biological knowledge—and it is no accident that great biologists and physicists like Dobzhansky and Faraday found their theistic beliefs confirmed, and not negated, by their scientific investigations.

The second point of tension has already been touched upon. The universe was not created for the sake of human beings, even though Thomas Aquinas at one point mistakenly suggested that it was. But the universe may well be created for the sake of conscious, intelligent, and morally free beings, who can share in the creativity and appreciation of all forms of goodness that, Christians believe, marks the life of God.

Christians believe that "God became human" and took form as a man. The Christian doctrine of the Incarnation asserts that Jesus was fully human, and that his humanity was, on this planet, a full, unique, and authentic expression of the nature of God, insofar as it can be expressed in human form. We can say "the Word became flesh," meaning that the eternal *logos*, the wisdom of God, was expressed in and through the human person of Jesus. That does give human life a sanctity that is important and distinctive. It also adds force to the Old Testament assertion that humans were created "in the image and likeness" of God. That cannot mean that humans are physically like God, since God has no physical form. It means that humans are able in principle to express or mediate the presence and power of God, and that they possess the God-like power and responsibility to care for the creation of which they are part.

These things, Christians believe, are true. But they carry the unspoken implication that there may be millions of other very different beings that are also able to express and mediate God's presence, and which may be responsible for their environment. For that they would need consciousness, intelligence, and moral sense. But there is no reason at all why humans should be the only beings in the universe with those properties. Jesus, then, is God-made-human on this planet, but there is no reason why there should not be other forms of incarnation elsewhere in the cosmos.

Perhaps Christian iconography needs revising to take account of this. Heaven—the presence of God—will not contain a human-looking Jesus by the side of God, in charge of the whole universe. Heaven contains the eternal Word of God, whose form is beyond imagining. His form for us may be human, but that may be only one of a myriad of forms, for all we know (and of course we do not know). I rather hope, however, that the glorified Christ will be more like the Christ that St. Paul saw in his vision on the road to Damascus, a blinding fire, not a young Palestinian man. Jesus is what the Word truly is on and for this small planet. But the one who is the cosmic Christ, the Lord of the universe, is not confined to any human form. And that is the key: the Word of God is not *confined* to the human person of Jesus, but the Word is truly *expressed and manifest* in Jesus, as fully as it can be in human form. Jesus is truly God for us; but we should never confuse the human nature of Jesus with the Word that is beyond all human imagination. That point was well and clearly made by the Council of Chalcedon in 451 AD.

This leads naturally on to the third point, the return of Christ in glory at the end of the age (or the end of the world, as it is popularly known). There are many millenarian cults in human history, cults that predict a catastrophic end to history, and the return of some historical figure to usher in a new age of peace and plenty. Insofar as they are testable, they have all been tested and found wanting—the figure has never returned. What all these cults seem to show is that humans have a deep desire for some better life, for a final destruction of evil, disease, and death, and for a deliverer who will liberate them from evil.

For some, Christianity is a millenarian cult. But I suggest that it was always much more than this, that millenarianism is a literalist misreading of the heart of Jesus' teaching, and that what has enabled Christianity to survive for 2,000 years is not millenarianism, but a much deeper spiritual teaching about the ultimate union of divine and human nature in Christ.

Millenarianism in fact suffers from spiritual myopia and megalomania, the short-sightedness of thinking that this planet is the center of God's attention and the absurdity of thinking that this little piece of human history has truly cosmic significance. One service modern science can perform for Christian theology is to overcome such short-sighted self-centeredness once and for all. It can provide a more truly cosmic vision of the whole universe as directed toward the generation of intelligent and creatively free life forms. They will be able finally to achieve complete understanding and appreciation of this amazing and awe-inspiring cosmos, a truly creative ability to shape the cosmos toward the realization of all the forms of goodness that are potential in its structure, and a fully cooperative sharing of experience and action among all forms of sentient life.

Such a vision is adumbrated in the work of some secular scientists. Martin Rees and Frank Tipler, for instance, have suggested the possibility that if evolution continues on the same trajectory, intelligent life will become dominant in the universe even if it takes billions of years.[1] Tipler even suggests that superintelligences in the far future, inhabiting intergalactic space, may be able to replicate past life forms and thus bring about a secular equivalent of the resurrection of the dead.

While this may be possible, Martin Rees also points out that humans may destroy themselves within a few decades, and that in any case the present conjecture is that the universe will eventually run down as it continues to expand, making the everlasting existence of complex life forms impossible. In addition, Christian hope for eternal life is not for a simple replication of what we now are, but for a complete transformation of personal being, as the key New Testament text, 1 Corinthians 15, suggests.

So it seems that true resurrection will not lie within the bounds of this space-time. It will lie in a different realm of existence, where the laws of thermodynamics do not apply, and where the forms of embodied existence will be beyond the reach of decay and death. Science cannot speak of such a realm, though modern science does often raise the possibility that there may be other forms of existence beyond this space-time (many worlds, or even the quantum realm from which space-times may emerge).

At this point Christian belief does speak of things beyond the reach of physical science. It speaks of the purely spiritual, nonphysical being of God, and it proposes that the whole of physical reality emerges from and depends upon that spiritual reality. If this is so—and purely physical science cannot deny it—then God will know and hold in consciousness every cosmic event that has ever happened, and will be able, Christians believe, to reembody any or all sentient and self-conscious beings in different forms, and in ways that correct or fulfill capacities that such beings had in their material lives.

The millenarian desire for an ending of evil, for a new and fuller form of life, for judgment on evil-doers coupled with a possible liberation from evil for all who are penitent is not to be fulfilled in an imminent earthly future. That became clear as soon as the first generation of Christian disciples had died, and realization came that there was to be an indefinite future in which the church would continue to explore its mission to new generations. It may not be fulfilled within this space-time at all, for it must be a future in which all generations can share, not some favored final generation far in our future.

The return (literally, the *parousia* or being present) of Christ in glory is beyond this space-time, though for each individual it is near, because each moment of our lives is taken into the presence of Christ in glory, both in judgment and in the possibility of forgiveness. So while humans may not be God's main or only purpose, and human lives may not have intergalactic significance in terms of their effects on the rest of the cosmos, nevertheless God has a unique purpose for every human life and each life is of eternal significance to God. Creation is not literally the beginning of the physical universe, but the dependence of every time upon the transtemporal being of God. In the same way, eschatology, the end of all things, is not literally the end of the physical universe, but the assumption of every time into the transtemporal being of God. As all times are united and transfigured in Christ, then Christ will be truly present in glory to all sentient beings.

Ultimately the eternal Christ will appear in primordial splendor to every human who has ever lived. The whole of history and every created person, and perhaps innumerable other histories of other species and galaxies, will be taken into the life of God and transformed by the self-giving love of Christ into forms strange and new. Then what St. Gregory of Nyssa called our infinite journey into God will enable all the events of our lives, all that we have done and suffered, to be seen in the wider and deeper context of God's love. Then we shall work out the consequences of our hatred, greed, and ignorance (pictured in the New Testament as the outer darkness or the purging fires of *Gehenna*), and perhaps realize many of the potentialities we were unable to realize in this earthly life. We shall, if we accept God's offer of love and healing, grow endlessly in the knowledge and love of the infinite life of God. That, I think, is the spiritual reality behind the overliteralistic assertions of millenarianism. It is the promise of the kingdom of God that Jesus proclaimed, the promise that we shall see him in the eternal glory of God and be with him in the joy of Paradise.

Physical science does not and cannot deal with these things. For they do not concern the predictable future of things in this space-time. They deal with the consummation of all the things of this space-time in another form of being beyond this space-time, in a realm of Spirit, in the life of God. This transcosmic dimension was already depicted in the New Testament, in the first chapter of the letters to the Ephesians and the Colossians, which speak of all things in heaven and earth existing in Christ, and being united in Christ. In modern cosmology, our knowledge of the vastness in time and space of this universe can help to make this spiritual dimension of Christianity clearer, and bring out the real spiritual meaning of Jesus' teaching about the drawing near of the kingdom of God in his own person.

Christian belief in the nature and purpose of God is not based on science, but on divine revelation in the person of Jesus. This raises the fourth point of possible tension with science, however, for some scientists hold that the rule of physical law is so absolute and unbreakable that miracles like the resurrection, which reveal God's purpose for humanity, simply cannot happen. This viewpoint is not so widely held since the advent of quantum physics, which usually sees laws as probabilistic, not deterministic, and holds that even very improbable events can happen on rare occasions. Laws of nature are perhaps better seen as constraints on the sorts of things that can happen rather than as rigid determinants of what happens. Physical laws may be, as physicist John Polkinghorne says, descriptions of how things behave in artificially isolated conditions, when no unforeseen influences affect the system under investigation.[2]

Miracles are, in my opinion, best defined as events that are extraordinary in transcending the usual behavior of physical objects, and which carry a strong spiritual significance, expressing the presence and purpose of God. They are caused by God for a special purpose, and are closely connected with the prayers of especially holy men and women, whose closeness to God enables them to mediate divine power in extraordinary ways.

Christians believe that Jesus was chosen by God to express and mediate in a unique way the divine purpose of healing human estrangement, liberating humans from evil, and assuring humans of eternal life with God. If this is so, it seems entirely natural that Jesus should display special gifts of healing, deep insight into God's nature, and intimate awareness of God's presence. He is not unusual in living after death, and not even unique in appearing after death to his disciples. But the transformation of his physical body into a spiritual body (the empty tomb), the appearance of that body in substantial form over a period of time, and his ascension into heaven are unique.

If God wills that Jesus' role as Messiah should be vindicated, that resurrection life should be seen as a promise for all, and that Jesus' reign as Lord of the kingdom should be inaugurated, then the resurrection and ascension of Jesus are very suitable means of such a revelation. As Blaise Pascal put it, the revelation is not given in such an overwhelming form that it deprives humans of all excuse for unbelief, but it is given in a sufficiently impressive way for those whose hearts are already moved by Christ, even if unconsciously (like St. Paul), to be confirmed in their belief.

I think there are no good scientific arguments against the possibility of miracles, since science must simply record what happens, miracles do not occur in experimentally testable or repeatable conditions, and they do not, by definition, fall under any general laws of nature. So all will depend upon whether people believe that God exists or is known in personal experience, and on whether the Biblical and ecclesiastical testimony to Jesus' living presence carries conviction. I believe that it does, but the fifth point of tension raises the difficulty that many of Jesus' miraculous acts were exorcisms of evil spirits. Modern science has replaced talk of spirits with talk of psychiatric illnesses and brain malfunctions. This implies that many Biblical reports of Jesus' acts cannot be taken literally.

This is a point of tension only if you insist that all Biblical narratives are literally true. Most historians would accept that the terminology of evil spirits was a prescientific way of referring to mental illnesses of various sorts, and that effective healers could have employed such terminology. Also, reports of miraculous acts do generally tend to be exaggerated over time, so that while the Bible may accurately report Jesus' healing powers, the descriptions that were passed on in oral tradition grew in wonderment and were elaborated in a terminology of spirit powers that modern medicine would reinterpret in psychiatric terms.

Those Christians who accept the main principles of Biblical criticism that have existed for more than a hundred years would have no problem with accepting that reports of miracles in the life of Jesus are prone to hyperbole and saturated with prescientific interpretations. While particular assessments of what occurred will vary between scholars, it would seem reasonable to affirm that Jesus possessed extraordinary powers of healing, extraordinary wisdom, and extraordinary awareness of and devotion to the will of God. The main spiritual lesson of Jesus' exorcisms is that healing is a work of God, that today Jesus' disciples should use every means to care effectively for the sick, and that Jesus' work was one of healing, not one of violence and destruction.

It therefore seems quite reasonable to believe that God acted in and through Jesus to heal, to forgive, to teach, and to reconcile, and thus to show what the divine nature is. God showed what the divine purpose was by vindicating Jesus' mission in raising him from death, as an anticipation of the divinely intended destiny that awaits all human beings. But the sixth point of tension puts all this in question by querying the intelligibility of a mind without a body. Some neuroscientists claim that the mind depends upon the brain in such a way that there cannot be thoughts, feelings, or intentions without a complex physical brain. So there cannot be a God who thinks and has purposes, and human persons cannot survive the death of their brains.

Is this, however, established by science? Rather, is it not a highly disputable philosophical theory that mental events are nothing over and above brain events? I think what is needed at this point is a clearer recognition of the limits of natural science. Science describes physical structures and behavior and formulates general physical theories to explain why such behavior occurs. If science could describe and explain all behavior in physical terms, without remainder, then science would indeed explain everything. But the underlying philosophical question remains, is everything describable in purely physical terms? Philosophers disagree about this, but it seems a proper question, which allows the answer "no."

Many philosophers, and almost all classical philosophers, cite such things as consciousness, perceptions, thoughts, feelings, mathematical and moral facts, minds, and God, as examples of nonphysical entities. I believe that Christians are committed to the existence of some such nonphysical entities, for Christians think that God is not physical, but is the reality from which all physical entities arise. God, on a Christian understanding, knows all possible states, evaluates them as good or bad, chooses some states for the sake of the goodness they make possible, and enjoys that goodness for its own sake. God does all this without a brain, so brains are not logically necessary for knowledge, evaluation, choice, and enjoyment to exist. It seems to me that this is clearly a logical possibility, so that the affirmation of nonphysical entities, and of minds that can survive the death of the physical brains with which they are causally connected in this life, cannot be unintelligible.

Neuroscientists can register what happens in brains when thoughts occur, and that is fascinating and medically vital. But the philosophical assertion that all mental states and acts are caused purely by brain events is nowhere near being established. If a materialist scientist takes a bet that one day this will be established, a scientist who is a Christian can safely and reasonably bet the other way. I suggest that all personal experience supports the Christian view, and that the scientific evidence is so provisional and disputable that it is in no position to claim superiority.

I have considered six main points of tension between science and Christianity. Those points exist, and for some Christians they will place their faith at odds with the findings of science. However, most theologians in mainstream forms of Christianity revise ancient Christian beliefs to bring them fully into line with modern scientific knowledge. In that process, I have sketched how science brings out a greater depth of spiritual meaning in Christian beliefs. Finally, I have argued that the disagreements that may remain are not between science and Christianity, but between materialist philosophy and forms of philosophy that take mind and consciousness more seriously. In this respect, perhaps Christianity has something to teach about the moral importance and the moral dignity of the personal that materialist science is in danger of denying.

■ **NOTES**

1. Martin Rees, *Our Cosmic Habitat* (Princeton, NJ: Princeton University Press, 2001); John Barrow and Frank Tipler, *The Anthropic Cosmological Principle* (Oxford: Oxford University Press, 1986).

2. John Polkinghorne, *Exploring Reality* (London: SPCK, 2005).

■ **FOR FURTHER READING**

Barbour, I. *Religion and Science: Historical and Contemporary Issues.* London: SCM Press, 1997.

Conway Morris, S. *Life's Solution: Inevitable Humans in a Lonely Universe.* Cambridge: Cambridge University Press, 2003.

Jeeves, M., ed. *Human Nature.* Edinburgh: Royal Society of Edinburgh, 2006.

Swinburne, R., ed. *Miracles.* New York, Macmillan, 1989.

The Doctrine of the Trinity

25 The Doctrine of the Trinity is Coherent

■ THOMAS D. SENOR

■ 1. INTRODUCTION

On each Sunday in cathedrals and churches all across the world, people profess their faith in the triune God of Christianity. Many publically recite creeds that assert or imply that the Father, Son, and Holy Spirit are each divine *and* that God is one. Yet how is this possible? How can there be three divine persons and a single God? This chapter will focus on precisely this question. We'll begin with a brief discussion of what the doctrine of the Trinity is. Having outlined the content of the doctrine, we'll next look at reasons for thinking it is conceptually flawed. This will lead us into further reflection about the nature of the doctrine and to what the Christian is committed to when she accepts it. The conclusion I'll reach is that it is more difficult to generate a persuasive argument for the incoherence of the Trinity than many skeptics have supposed. That's the defensive part of the strategy. Offensively, I will then sketch an account that, while retaining a needed element of mystery, does not suffer from any apparent logical difficulties.

■ 2. WHAT IS THE DOCTRINE OF THE TRINITY?

Pared to its bare bones, the doctrine of the Trinity is a conjunction of the following two claims:

> Monotheism (ONE): There is one God.
> Three Persons (THREE): The Father, Son, and
> Holy Spirit are distinct divine persons.

The Father, Son, and Holy Spirit are "distinct" in the relevant sense if they are not identical. This kind of distinctness is consistent with a great deal of interdependence (the model I'll discuss, for example, has the three persons very much intertwined). ONE and THREE are both the most fundamental claims the doctrine of the Trinity makes and the basis of the skeptic's argument for incoherence. So no model or account of the doctrine can be useful in defending the Trinitarian against the skeptic unless it endorses both ONE and THREE. There are, however, a couple other claims that are accepted by nearly all traditional Christians that go beyond these two theses. And while I don't believe it is necessary that any model explicitly represent these two other claims, no model will be a defense of what the ecumenical church has thought about the Trinity if it is not at least consistent with them.

The first such claim has to do with the relationship between the members of the Trinity. According to traditional dogma, the Father *begets* the Son, and the Holy Spirit *proceeds* from either only the Father (as the Eastern church teaches) or from the Father and the Son (as the Western church teaches). So the Father is ontologically somehow more basic than are the Son and Holy Spirit.

The second important traditional Trinitarian claim not yet mentioned concerns a different aspect of the relationship of the members of the Trinity. Although there may be ontological dependence of the Son and Holy Spirit on the Father, the three persons are all equal in their divinity—none is more divine or in any way greater than another. While the New Testament frequently speaks of the Son doing the *will of* the Father and the Holy Spirit being *sent by* the Son, the only way in which the Son and Holy Spirit are thought to be subordinate to the Father is functional rather than ontological. Metaphysically, the three members of the Trinity are equal and to deny this is to adopt the heresy of *subordinationism*.

Let's express these two additional Trinitarian claims as follows:

Father/Son/Holy Spirit Relationship (FATHERSOURCE): The Father is the source of the Son and the Holy Spirit (perhaps with the Son, perhaps not).

Equality of the persons (EQUALITY): The three persons in the Trinity are ontologically equal; none is greater than any of the others.

In what follows, then, we'll make the following assumptions. A model of the Trinity shows the doctrine to be coherent only if it is itself logically consistent and it entails both monotheism (ONE) and the distinction of the three persons (THREE) on some reasonable understanding of these theses. Additionally, such a model will be fully theologically adequate only if it is consistent with both FATHERSOURCE and EQUALITY.

■ 3. THE INCOHERENCE CHARGE: A FIRST PASS

A seriously benighted Trinitarian critic might make the following objection:

Christians claim to be monotheists; and to be a monotheist is to believe in precisely one God. Yet Christians also say that God is triune–and you can't have a Trinity without having a triad of divine beings. But, necessarily, something can't be one and three. I can't own precisely one and precisely three cars or have precisely one and precisely three spouses, etc. Holding to the doctrine of the Trinity is as incoherent as either of these other claims.

I say that such a critic is "seriously benighted" because the aforementioned objection rests on a superficial understanding of the doctrine. True, one can't have precisely three cars (spouses) and precisely one car (spouse), and in the same way there can't be precisely three and precisely one divine being(s). But it is crucial to the traditional understanding of the doctrine of the Trinity that the claim is *not* that there are precisely three Gods and precisely one God; rather, the doctrine says that God consists of three *persons* and one *substance* (or essence). So the straightforward inconsistency is avoided by the claim that God is three of one sortal and one of a distinct sortal. As we will see, the key to any proffered model of the Trinity is explaining just what these sortals are and how they are to be understood. And, as we shall further see, to make this first "sortal" defensive maneuver is hardly enough to avoid all inconsistency charges.

■ 4. THE INCOHERENCE CHARGE: A MORE SOPHISTICATED VERSION

At this point in the dialectic, the anti-Trinitarian's first volley has been successfully returned. But this victory is hollow since the objection is that of the seriously benighted objector. What might a more sophisticated Trinitarian skeptic say? Here is a much improved version of the argument from incoherence:

> Christians claim to be monotheists—to believe in precisely one God. If there is one God, then there is precisely one divine being. Why? Because if there were multiple divine beings, there would be multiple beings who were divine. But a being who is divine is (a) God. So monotheism is true only if there is precisely one divine being. However, Christians also hold that the Father, Son, and Holy Spirit are each divine and yet distinct ("distinct" here just means "not identical"). That is, it is not the case that the Father = the Son, or the Father = the Holy Spirit, or the Son = the Holy Spirit. So, the logical implication of Christians' assertions about the three persons of the Trinity (that they are divine and yet distinct) is that there are three divine *beings*. Now one can't consistently claim to be a monotheist and claim that there are three divine beings. But that's just what the traditional doctrine of the Trinity commits one to, so that doctrine is incoherent.

Unlike the argument of the benighted skeptic, this line of reasoning represents a serious challenge to the doctrine of the Trinity. The remainder of this chapter will largely be dedicated to understanding the various options the Christian has for responding to it. Before doing that, however, we'll need to be clearer about what precisely needs defending: what does the doctrine of the Trinity, as traditionally and ecumenically understood, really amount to? The next section offers a tentative answer to that question.

■ 5. TWO TYPES OF RESPONSE TO THE ARGUMENT FOR INCOHERENCE

Let's get back to our anti-Trinitarian who has made the second, more sophisticated objection. She has argued that the doctrine of the Trinity entails that there is a single God, and yet that there are three divine beings, and hence three gods. Now there are two ways one might attempt to meet this objection. The direct way would be to provide a model or account of the Trinity according to which both ONE and THREE are both true (and on a suitably strong understandings of each). Alternatively, one might respond indirectly. That is, even if one can't construct the kind of model envisaged in the direct response, one might attempt to show that whether or not there is a particular model, there is no good reason to think that ONE and THREE are logically inconsistent. This indirect response is, in a way, weaker than its direct cousin since it doesn't demonstrate the error of the objection. Yet, in another way, it is potentially stronger since if it works against this particular incoherence charge, it will likely work against all such objections.

In the next section of this chapter we'll have a brief look at the indirect response to the anti-Trinitarian's challenge. Although I won't have the space to fully develop the idea, the basic point can be laid out in short order. After we see how the indirect response goes, I will offer a model of the doctrine of the Trinity that is at least apparently coherent, and that entails that ONE and THREE are true.

■ 6. THE INDIRECT RESPONSE: THE DIFFICULTY OF ARGUING FOR INCOHERENCE

To make this case for incoherence stick, the skeptic will have to plausibly argue that there is no way to fill out the content of creedal statements expressed by THREE and ONE according to which the statements mean (at least something like) what has traditionally been intended by them[1] and, on those understandings ONE and THREE are consistent. To be clear, I'm not stating there is no possible way of making such an argument. Perhaps there is. However, constructing it would require than careful logic-chopping: it could be accomplished only by first arguing that a historically sound interpretation of the creeds and writings of the Patristics requires that there is no good way of understanding them that is consistent with both THREE and ONE being true. And that is a project that (at least to my knowledge) has yet to be taken on by the Trinitarian skeptic. Unless or until it is, it will always be open to the Trinitarian to either attempt to refute the argument in question or find some other historically significant rendering of ONE and THREE that can sidestep the argument in question.

To put the matter somewhat differently, it is not obvious which propositions are expressed by the sentences associated with ONE and THREE. That is, while we've been working with an understanding of what these sentences mean, we have certainly not fixed them to one, particular meaning in each case. When the church agreed upon the phrase (translated into English) of "three persons and one substance," it wasn't so much locking down any particular propositional content as it was codifying language that could be understood in a variety of ways.[2] Now there are ways of understanding ONE and THREE that will clearly be out of step with the various understandings of the key terms and phrases. But there will be many more than will be accepted by some significant portion of the church while rejected by others, and other ways of understanding them that those who rejected the former interpretation will accept. So to show that the doctrine of the Trinity is incoherent would require showing that there is no way of understanding the sentences in ONE and THREE that is both logically consistent and in keeping with some historically significant interpretation of the doctrine.

7. THE DIRECT RESPONSE: A COHERENT MODEL OF THE TRINITY

The primary challenge for the philosophical theologian is explaining how it is possible for God to be three persons and yet a single substance. Somewhat more abstractly, the goal is to offer a model that has God being three Xs and yet a single Y, for some X and Y that does justice to the traditional formulation of "three persons and one substance." And, if the account is to be truly compatible with the other claims that the church has (nearly universally) wanted to claim about the Godhead, then it will have to also be consistent with both the FATHERSOURCE and EQUALITY.

There are two ways one might go about constructing a Trinitarian model. First, one might stress the importance of Christianity's insistence that it is strictly a monotheistic religion and begin by taking a very robust reading of ONE according to which it represents in some sense the most fundamental truth about the nature of God. One who begins this way will then see the task of giving an account of THREE that is metaphysically strong enough so that her model is not modalistic. On the other hand, one might think that at the core of the narrative of scripture and tradition are the joint claims that Jesus Christ was God, and that Jesus and the Father are distinct; on such a perspective, whatever the divine unity consists in, then, it must be consistent with the genuine distinctness of the persons of the Father, Son, and Holy Spirit.

According to the traditional way of viewing the matter, those who take the first tact are called "Latin" or "Western" Trinitarians (because this is the view that dominates the early Western church) and those who opt for the second option are known as "Greek" or "Eastern" Trinitarians (because this is the view that dominated the early Eastern church). The model that I will be presenting and defending seeks to integrate these perspectives by taking the best aspects of both.

Let's begin the construction of our model by making a distinction that was fundamental to the Greek position. Philosophers commonly distinguish *types* from *tokens* or, to use different language for the same distinction, *universals* from *particulars.* A type or universal is something that can be instantiated by multiple individuals. The Bose speaker to my immediate left is a distinct token or particular speaker from the Bose speaker to my immediate right; they are not numerically identical. But they do share in the type or universal of *speaker.* Similarly, Elisa, Katie, and Graham are three distinct people who all fall under the type or universal of *human being.* This distinction was put to use by the Greek Trinitarians who understood substances not as tokens or particulars, but as types or universals.[3] If substances are universals, then the claim that X and Y are "of the same substance," or consubstantial, does not entail that X and Y are composed of the same stuff, but rather that X and Y are *the same kind of thing.* So if substances are universals, we can easily understand how genuinely distinct individuals can nevertheless be unified in substance. The Trinitarian claim that the Father, Son, and Holy Spirit are three persons and one substance becomes the claim that each is a person numerically distinct from the others who instantiates the same nature that the others instantiate—namely, the nature of divinity: in short, there is one divine substance (universal) and three persons (particulars) who share it.

So far, so good. The problem, though, is that we haven't gotten so far. For there is a clear objection to the move to understanding substances are universals: no one would mistake my left and right speakers for being a single speaker; Elisa, Katie, and Graham, while being members of a single kind, are in fact three distinct human beings. So if the unity of the Father, Son, and Holy Spirit can be modeled by the unity of Elisa, Katie, and Graham, then just as in the latter case, we must say that there are three human beings, so in the former case we must say there are three divine individuals—that is, three gods. But if that is right, then of course we've run afoul of ONE.

If Greek Trinitarianism entails that the unity of the Trinity is no greater than the unity of three individual humans, it is a nonstarter. For if this is all the Christian can say to get out of the incoherence claim, the truth of this charge has been established. Sure, a Christian could fall back to a redefined position according to which universal substantial unity is all that is asserted. But that would no more vindicate her against the incoherence charge than the theist who gives up divine omnipotence has vindicated theism from the argument from evil. If the Greek Trinitarian is to have any chance of offering an account that doesn't conflict with ONE, there will have to be more to the story than we've seen.

Fortunately, there is. To start to see this, let's think for a moment about all the ways in which Elisa, Katie, and Graham are ontologically distinct. First, the existence of each is fundamentally independent of the existence of the others. Any one could have existed without the other two; any two could have existed without the third. Indeed, the continued existence of each is similarly independent of the other two. So while they are all dependent on their shared nature (i.e., were there no such thing as human nature, then none of them would exist), their individual existence is entirely independent of the others. Another point to note is that Elisa, Katie, and Graham are but three of billions who have or have had a human nature. If the three of them are "one" in any significant sense, so are the billions of others.

Not only might they have existed independently and they are but three of billions of their kind, but their desires, wills, and plans are distinct, and sometimes in conflict. It is not only possible but highly likely that if they work on cooperative projects together they will have disagreements. What Elisa thinks is a good means to a good end will occasionally be disputed by Graham, while Katie will deny that the particular end is good in the first place. There will be arguments, frustrations, and, in all probability, grievances because of conflicts in desires, wills, and plans.

Were the Trinity to consist of three individuals who were entirely ontologically distinct, and who possess their own agendas that conflict with those of the other members of the group, there is no question that the charge of polytheism would be accurate. For the situation so described is exactly the kind of polytheism the church was concerned about repudiating, calling to mind, as it does, the feuding gods of ancient Babylon and Greece.

Fortunately for the Greek Trinitarian view, there is much more to say about the unity of the Godhead than can be said about the unity of individual human beings. In the first place, the relationship between the three persons of the Trinity is a necessary relation: it is not possible that any exist unless they all do. Furthermore, the three are necessarily exhaustive of the divine kind: there are no possible worlds in which there are any other divine persons. These aspects of the relationships between the members of the Trinity do a great deal to distinguish this universal/particular relationship from that borne by humans to humanity.

Still, if the three persons, even necessarily related in the ways delineated above, were to be at odds with each other so that their wills, desires, and plans were frequently in conflict, the unity of the Trinity would be seriously undermined. However, the Greek Trinitarian need not accept that such conflict is possible. Another aspect of the unity enjoyed by the Father, Son, and Holy Spirit is the necessary harmonization of their wills. Such harmony need not imply identity. That is, for example, the Son might come to will something only because the Father wills it—and vice versa. What can't happen, the Greek Trinitarian will insist, is that one person wills X when another person wills not X. With the necessary harmonization of the wills, the infighting and quarreling exemplified by the Greek gods (for instance) will not be a possibility.[4]

It's time to take stock. The model we've constructed thus far is pretty clearly in keeping with the Greek Trinitarian model that is clearly consistent with the truth of THREE. In asserting that there are three individual persons, each of whom shares in the divine nature or substance (construed as a universal), the model is committed to as strong a statement of THREE as could be hoped for (many in the Latin tradition would say it is too much to want!). The big issue, of course, concerns ONE. Is the sense in which the Father, Son, and Holy Spirit compose a single God enough to make ONE true on a reasonable reading? Many doubt that it is.[5] For even if we grant that the closeness enjoyed by the three persons of the Trinity is much greater and deeper than that of Elisa, Katie, and Graham, it is nevertheless the closeness of three individuals. Put differently, it is part of the logic of *identity* that it is not a matter of degree whether entities A, B, and C are numerically the same: they are either the same or they aren't. Saying that (1) there is a harmonization of wills, (2) the persons exist in any circumstance where any of the others do, and (3) it is not possible that there are more members of that kind does nothing whatever to indicate *numerical* unity. And it is numerical unity that ONE requires.

While there is clearly something to this objection to the Greek Trinitarian view, we must be careful not to assume that ONE simply rules out the possibility of any genuine distinction among the persons of the Trinity. For to assume that is nothing other than to make the benighted objection to the doctrine discussed earlier in this chapter. And whatever else one might think about the Patristic fathers, they weren't stupid. They wouldn't have asserted that there are three and that there is one *of the same sortal*. So insisting that any genuine distinction among the persons automatically brings with it the falsity of ONE suitably understood is to accuse the Patristics of being blind to an explicit contradiction. And interpretive decency forbids that.

Yet we can't let the Greek Trinitarian off the hook so easily. For even if ONE will allow for some elements of diversity, it isn't clear that it is consistent with the current view. For the Greek Trinitarian's position is that there are three persons who each have his own particular, token divine nature. Now, so far we've not said much about what this entails, but it is natural to think that with each person comes a particular set of attributes that are necessary for personhood. So it would seem that the Father, Son, and Holy Spirit must have distinct sets of knowledge/beliefs, desires/wills, and causal powers to act. But if these are generally distinct—if there is no underlying individual, token substance upon which all depend—then it can sensibly be argued that the Trinity is a trio of deeply related but fundamentally distinct entities. The Godhead is in fact a necessarily cooperative committee of three, held together by sharing a universal nature of which they are, necessarily, the only three particulars. Thus when we refer to "God," we don't succeed in referring to a person, but rather to a committee. But this means that God is not (strictly speaking) a person. Each of these consequences counts against a maximally robust rendering of ONE. But the Greek Trinitarian may not be moved by this consideration. After all, we've already seen that a maximally robust understanding of ONE is clearly inconsistent with THREE. What the objector must be claiming, then, is not that Greek Trinitarianism is inconsistent with the strongest version of ONE, but rather with *any* understanding of ONE that is sufficiently robust. This strikes me as a rather hard case to make.

Yes, on this model some claims commonly made about God will turn out to not be literally true (that God is a person, for example); still, the Godhead includes three persons, and so the Greek view certainly doesn't imply that the deity is impersonal in any sense that a Christian should find troublesome.

As things now stand, there is no good reason to be overly pessimistic about the coherence of the Trinity if the doctrine is understood along Greek Trinitarian lines that we've been discussing. However, the secondary desideratum should also be kept in mind: we want an account that also explains the ontological priority of the Father and the grounding of the Son and Holy Spirit on the first person of the Trinity. And the Greek view doesn't obviously have the resources to provide a model that will do all we want. What I shall do now is reconsider one key aspect of Greek Trinitarianism and claim that making an adjustment that moves it importantly in the direction of the Latin view will give us a stronger model of the Trinity that is both coherent and able to satisfy our secondary desideratum.

The Greek Trinitarian view, at least as traditionally conceived, involves understanding the divine substance as a universal rather than as a particular.[6] However, the Latin perspective—with its emphasis on the substantial unity of God—insists that the divine substance is a particular. What makes God one, in this view, is nothing else than that there is only a single token instance of the divine substance. The problem for Latin Trinitarianism is in its understanding of THREE. If there is a single token of the divine substance, in what sense are the Father, Son, and Holy Spirit distinct persons?

In what follows, I'm going to roughly sketch a model makes the Latin assumption of a single token substance and that also attempts to give an answer to the distinction question. This view is, I believe, consistent with that of the Cappadocian Fathers (whose work is definitive of the Greek tradition). Furthermore, it will also make clear how FATHERSOURCE and EQUALITY can be true.

We can start to address the distinction question if we think of the single particular nature as being multileveled (obviously this is all metaphor). The fundamental level is the Father, the second level is the Son, and the third is the Holy Spirit; that is, the Father is the ontological ground of both the Son and the Holy Spirit. This does not imply that the Father *creates* either the Son and Holy Spirit, however, because the means by which the Son and Holy Spirit are produced is will-independent. In any possible situation in which the Father exists, the Son and Holy Spirit exist, and they are eternally brought about as a necessary extension of the Father's very existence. Yet there is an important asymmetry at work here: the Son and Holy Spirit are ontologically dependent on the Father, while the Father is ontologically independent of them. What does that mean? Let's say that B is ontologically dependent on A if were it not for A's productive powers, B would not exist. So even though each member of the Trinity exists necessarily and eternally, the Son and Holy Spirit are ontologically dependent on the Father although the Father is not ontologically dependent on either of them.

Admittedly this is all very sketchy. In an attempt to give more substance to the model, let's consider an analogy. One of the many positions that one might hold regarding the human person is that of emergentism. According to this view, human beings are biological entities composed only of parts that are in the province of the natural sciences. Yet in another sense people can't be reduced to their biological properties because their material parts give rise to an emergent mind that has causal powers that are more than the sum of its material parts. So, suppose that the truth about human mentality is this: (1) the brain is the only ontological/causal source of human thought and action; (2) the mind is the product of the causal activity of the brain; (3) the mind is emergent, and this implies that the causal powers of the mind are not identical with the causal powers of the brain—the mind has powers that depend on the brain but that are distinct from it. Given the emergence of the nonepiphenomenal mind, there will be events that are the causal product of the mind. Suppose such a mind freely decides to go see the Cubs play the Cardinals. The causal history of this decision includes the causal activity of the brain that produces the emergent mind and also the causal activity of the emergent mind that produces the decision to go to the Cubs–Cards game as opposed to going to see a local production of Macbeth happening the same night. All three of these entities (the brain, the mind, the decision) are aspects of a single, unified person.

Even metaphorically, talk of levels here is misleading because the next part of the model will insist that the three persons are necessarily and deeply inter-dependent.[7] Nevertheless, it is the Father who produces both the Son and the Holy Spirit, although the means by which the other two persons are produced is somehow distinct (since one is, in some sense, a son and the other is not). Yet since all are instances of the single, particular divine nature, each is truly divine.

How are the persons "intimately interconnected"? The real answer, of course, is "God only knows!" But since there is no shortage of speculations in models of the Trinity, I will offer one possibility. What seems crucial for the distinction of the persons is that each is capable of initiating his own action—even if, as the tradition claims, when one acts the others act too. In the abstract, the inter-penetration of the divine persons involves sharing and mutual interdependence. Somewhat less abstractly, a model might hold that the while each person pos-sesses his own distinctive will, the persons have a common storehouse of knowl-edge and set of causal powers (i.e., causal powers that are above and beyond those required for a basic act of will). So, on this view, the knowledge and the power to achieve ends directed by the will are entirely shared; and while the wills are distinct (i.e., there are three willing faculties), they are grounded in the single divine nature in such a way as to assure their being in complete harmony.

So on this very rough sketch of a model, the persons are distinct because each possesses a unique will (and as the Greek Trinitarians insisted, though distinct, these wills are necessarily harmonious). Yet unlike standard Greek

Trinitarian models, each person does not have his own particular instance of the divine nature—there is but a single, particular nature. The members of the Trinity are thus unified because of the interpenetration of persons and attributes. Furthermore, each is God because each is instantiated in the one, particular divine nature. Although nothing has been said about what, precisely, the relations of Sonship and procession come to, in having the Father as the most fundamental person in the Trinity (in that the others are necessarily ontologically dependent on him) the model incorporates FATHERSOURCE in a way that neither of the other models we've examined does. Also, since each is fully instantiated in the one particular nature, and each has the full epistemic and causal powers of divinity, together with a divine will with which to initiate action, there is a fundamental equality among them in that each is equally divine (even if the others are functionally subordinate to the Father). So EQUALITY is also secured (or at least as much as it can be given FATHERSOURCE). Finally, to the worry that Greek Trinitarianism entails that God is not a person, this combined model allows, if not for the worry to cease, for it to be lessened. For since the Father is the ontological ground of the Trinity, we can think of "God" (as in the phrase "God the Father Almighty") as applying to the Father only in some contexts. It can also, in other contexts, refer to the full divine nature (or the Trinity of persons), but there is now a natural way of understanding it as applying to a single person.

There is nothing particularly novel about this model. Not only does it take elements from the Latin and Greek models as I've somewhat simplistically laid them out, but it incorporates these features in a way that might well have been very much what the Cappadocian Fathers had in mind.[8]

▪ 8. CONCLUSION

The aim of this chapter has been to consider, and ultimately rebut, the charge that the doctrine of the Trinity is incoherent. In doing this, I've looked at what is required to show incoherence and argued that the prospects for such an argument do not look good (because to do so would be to show persuasively that there are no ways of understanding ONE and THREE according to which they are each suitably strong and possibly jointly true). But even if I succeeded in that, successfully arguing that the prospects for a satisfactory incoherence argument are grim is far short of arguing that the doctrine of the Trinity is coherent. So the second part of this chapter looked at three possible ways that a Christian might attempt to construct a model that is, prima facie at least, coherent. To my mind, each of them is enough to rebut the charge that there is no way to satisfactorily understand ONE and THREE that allows for truth of both. I do think, though, that defending the fully traditional account of the Trinity also requires giving an account that is at least consistent with FATHERSOURCE and EQUALITY.

I've argued that the best prospect for vindicating all aspects of the traditional account of the Trinity can be found in the model that this chapter explicates. While a good dose of mystery clearly abounds, logical incoherence does not.

■ NOTES

1. There is little doubt that there has not been a single, exact traditional understanding of the doctrine of the Trinity. What was codified is a liturgical formulation "three hypostases, one ousia" or "three persons, one substance" rather than a particular account of what, precisely, these formulations meant.

2. Thus the terms translated as "person" and "substance" were always understood in a variety of ways in Trinitarian proclamations.

3. The Cappadocian Fathers were Basil the Great (330–379), bishop of Caesarea; his brother Gregory of Nyssa (c. 330–395), bishop of Nyssa; and Gregory of Nazianzus (329–389), Patriarch of Constantinople. For a brief but helpful discussion of their understanding of the Trinity, see J. N. D. Kelly, *Early Christian Doctrines*, 5th ed. (London: Continuum, 2005), chap. 5.

4. Much of what I have said here can be found in Richard Swinburne's *The Christian God* (Oxford: Oxford University Press, 1994), 170–192.

5. For example, see Brian Leftow, "Anti Social Trinitarianism," in *The Trinity: An Interdisciplinary Symposium on the Trinity*, ed. Stephen T. Davis, Daniel Kendall, and Gerald O'Collins (Oxford: Oxford University Press, 1999); and Daniel Howard-Snyder, "Trinity Monotheism," *Philosophia Christi* 5 (2003): 375–403.

6. This account of the history of the doctrine has come under attack recently. For example, see Richard Cross, "Two Models of the Trinity?," *Heythrop Journal* 43 (2002): 275–294.

7. What I'm appealing to here has been called the "indwelling" (or "perichoresis") of the Father, Son, and Holy Spirit that was introduced by the Cappadocians.

8. See Kelly, *Early Christian Doctrines*, 265–267.

■ FOR FURTHER READING

Davis, S. T., D. Kendall, and G. O'Collins, eds. *The Trinity: An Interdisciplinary Symposium on the Trinity*. Oxford: Oxford University Press, 1999.Leftow, B. "A Latin Trinity." *Faith and Philosophy* 21 (2004): 303–333.

McCall, T. H. *Which Trinity? Whose Monotheism? Philosophical and Systematic Theologians on the Metaphysics of Trinitarian Theology. Grand Rapids, MI: Eerdmans, 2010. Rea, M., and J. Brower. "Material Constitution and the Trinity." *Faith and Philosophy* 22 (2005): 387–405.

26 The Trinity is Incoherent

■ TIMOTHY WINTER

In 2002 a large-scale survey of attitudes among Church of England clergy revealed that the Trinity, at once the most recondite but most fundamental of orthodox Christian doctrines, was rejected or questioned by a startling number of priests. Only 78 percent of male clergy, and 70 percent of females, felt able to express "confidence" in the doctrine.[1] Churchwide, it is clear that a growing number of Christians agree that the doctrine is "an article of faith very difficult for contemporary believers."[2] As one priest rhetorically asks: "Is it, as I suspect, an embarrassment, an absurd legacy, which we could well do without having to promote or defend?"[3]

Even among churchgoers who profess to believe the doctrine, errors of inter-pretation clearly abound. One seasoned observer of the Anglican scene frankly concludes that "most church people believe in three Gods."[4] This apparently widespread polytheism is hardly less striking than what is, in creedal terms, the reciprocal error, a functional Unitarianism: "some of us are at heart only con-fident about God the Father, the Creator, the one who is truly God. When we think about Jesus, we imagine him as a human being—just like us, only better." Overall, in the words of the same churchman, "our expressions of our beliefs are almost certainly going to be heretical, if judged by the language of the creeds."[5]

This apparent crisis of confidence is evident also in the liturgy. Some recent liturgies frankly incorporate either Unitarian or tritheistic professions of faith,[6] while several leading texts on worship and prayer appear to skirt tactfully around this doctrine. An example would be the influential Catholic monograph *The Church at Prayer* (1968), which refers to the doctrine of the Trinity on only a single page.[7] A leading history of twentieth-century liturgical movements omits all mention of the Trinity,[8] as does Gordon Wakefield's *Outline of Christian Worship* (1998).[9]

Although liturgies crafted by professional theologians may still incorporate abundant references to the Triune God, and are likely to include doxologies in which the Trinity is the centerpiece, there are signs that more grassroots forms of worship pass over the doctrine in near silence. A recent survey subtitled "The Trinity in the Most Used Contemporary Christian Worship Songs" documents an almost complete absence of Trinitarian themes and references. "The naming of God in a Trinitarian fashion is very minimal," it laments. None of the popular songs included in the survey explicitly direct worship to the Trinity, although a very small number name the persons of the Trinity together.[10]

If doctrine and worship are struggling over the Trinity, preaching fares little better. Major modern collections of sermons seem seldom to refer to it, with the exception of a few treatments of the economic Trinity and very occasional revivals of the medieval practice of finding Trinitarian signs in nature. Sermons on Trinity Sunday show an increasing tendency to avoid preaching on scriptural texts. And as in popular belief, sermons on the Trinity are frequently heretical, commending outright tritheism, or modalism, or a radically monarchian perspective that is in practice Arian.[11]

Overall, a mark of the Christian community in its current stage of doctrinal development is unmistakably the widespread incomprehension of a doctrine that has become "unintelligible and religiously irrelevant on a wide scale."[12] While most professional theologians seek to hold the line, and some (Vanhoozer, Tracy, Milbank, and others) even find the Trinity particularly relevant to a late modern or postmodern intellectual and social climate,[13] it seems that the doctrine is treated with reserve by most parishioners, preachers, and liturgists.

■ 1. BIBLICAL WITNESS

Despite the desire of many to interpret the disparate Biblical data in compliance with the classical creeds, it is evident that the classical Trinitarian proof-texts were identified only after centuries of disputation. It is significant that the best known, 1 John 5:7–8, which is the only clearly Trinitarian passage, is also the best-known instance of forgery in the Bible, being absent from the oldest Greek manuscripts.[14] Although he doubted its authenticity, Erasmus was obliged to include it for fear of undermining the doctrine of the Trinity. With the exception of this interpolation, the text of the Old Testament and New Testament never attributes threefoldness to God; God's only number is one.[15] As Emil Brunner sees matters:

> The mystery of the Trinity, proclaimed by the church, and enshrined in her liturgy, from the fifth and sixth century onwards, is a pseudo-mystery, which sprang out of an aberration of theological thought from the lines laid down in the Bible, not from the Biblical doctrine itself.[16]

Whether Jesus himself was proposing a theology radically unfamiliar to the Jews is a question that continues to detain scholars. It is evident, however, that he never preached this most characteristic of church doctrines, since he, the New Testament authors, and their first readers, were solidly monotheistic in the Jewish sense. In the Book of Acts, more than half of the debates concern the Jews and their beliefs, but at no point do we suspect that belief in one God in three persons formed part of the fearless proclamation of the disciples. Had they preached such a thing, the Jews would certainly have responded robustly; but of this the author has left no record.

The dominant message of the New Testament is Jewish monotheism. There are texts, however, where an apparent triad is named. For example: "Go and make disciples of all nations, baptizing them in the name of the Father, the Son and the Holy Spirit" (Matthew 28:19). Another instance is: "Chosen according to the foreknowledge of God the Father, through the sanctifying work of the Spirit, for obedience to Jesus Christ and sprinkling by his blood" (1 Peter 1:2). Although minds shaped by creedal formulas instinctively read these as Trinitarian statements, the original context of first-century Palestine makes this unlikely. The idea of a perichoretic union of self-aware hypostases, each of which was entirely God, came later. To see this more clearly, let us consider the Bible's understanding of Jesus, and the Holy Spirit, in turn.

■ 2. NEW TESTAMENT CHRISTOLOGY

In the Bible, Jesus sometimes appears explicitly to deny that he is divine. Texts include, "Why do you call me good? No one is good but God alone" (Mark 10:18), and "The son can do nothing of his own accord, but only what he sees the Father doing" (John 5:19). Similarly, Jesus is frequently depicted as having nondivine qualities, including temptation, fear, indecision, and lack of knowledge, as at Gethsemane, where he is intensely afraid, so that God sends an angel to strengthen and reassure him (Luke 22:39–46). Jesus does not know the date of the second coming (Mark 13:32). Again and again he is portrayed as obedient to the Father, and sent by Him, "learning obedience" (Hebrews 5:8). Since such qualities conflict with what is logically known of God, the Gospel writers are here clearly presenting him as a nondivine being. Later generations, seeking to harmonize this with the evolved doctrine of his fully divine nature, developed, on the basis of Philippians 2:5–11, the idea of *kenosis*, whereby God, as the second person, "emptied" Himself of aspects of His Godhead during the three decades of His existence on earth. The consequence of this was a double paradox: not only can a single entity be fully divine and fully human (i.e., infinite and finite simultaneously), but that same entity can disengage aspects of deity at will without becoming less fully divine and thereby impairing the perfection of the Incarnation or the atonement.

"God the Son" never appears in the Bible. Still, "son of God" is a title that it frequently accords to Jesus. For pagans in his time, to be a "son of God" meant that one inherited all or part of deity from a divine father; in fact, this was perhaps the notion that most characteristically united the pagan cults of the Roman Empire. However, it is a commonplace of modern scholarship that in an Aramaic and Hebrew milieu such a phrase carried no pagan implications, but denoted angelic, rabbinic, messianic, or kingly authority. Hence "sons of God" (*b'nai ha-elohim*) are angels, or inspired men (Genesis 6:2; Job 1:6; Psalms 29:1). Scholars unswayed by the demands of Nicene orthodoxy largely concur that for Jews in first-century Palestine, to be a son of God in no way implied divine status.[17] To understand it in such terms would be to violate an essential premise of Jewish monotheism, and indicates Hellenistic and Roman religious influence.

While the Synoptics overwhelmingly bear witness to Jesus as an authentically Jewish figure calling to a very Jewish repentance, John's Gospel nonetheless contains much that implies that in the first century, despite the evident absence of Trinitarian belief, many Christians did attribute quasi-divine status to Jesus. It is clear that phrases attributed to him such as "I and the Father are one" (John 10:30) were taken in Hellenized circles as evidence that Jesus had a consciousness of himself as in some sense united with God. Whatever the original beliefs and purposes of the author of John might have been, it is clear that a straightforward identification of Jesus with the mainstream Galilean piety of his day needs to take account of such terms, and of their early elaboration by Paul and his branch of the Jesus movement.

Assuming, for the sake of argument, that such Johannine and Pauline claims correctly preserve Jesus' own self-understanding, let us consider whether, in a solidly monotheistic environment, such claims would have been heard most naturally as claims to divine status, or as signs of a particular type of friendship.[18] We may helpfully do this by considering a distinctive genre of texts taken from the early period of the religion that emerged after Christian doctrine assumed its classical form: Islam. The literature known as Holy Hadiths (*ḥadīth qudsī*) presents the prophet speaking in the first person as though he were God, although his listeners assumed axiomatically that he was merely repeating God's words.[19] Here is perhaps the best-known example:

> Whoever harms a friend of Mine, I declare war upon him. My servant draws near to Me with nothing more beloved to Me than that which I have made obligatory upon him. And My slave continues to draw nearer to Me with optional acts of devotion until I love him. And when I love him, I am his ear with which he hears, his eye with which he sees, his hand with which he strikes, and his foot on which he walks. If He asks Me, I surely grant his request; and if he asks My protection, I surely grant it to him.[20]

The Islamic tradition had no difficulty in hearing in such texts the word of God, and failed to identify the first person "Mine" with His prophetic messenger. Such a hadith is an instance of what Louis Massignon dubbed a "theopathic locution" (*shaṭḥ}* in Arabic), in which the illuminated human soul receives and conveys God's own speech.[21] Pondering this particular hadith, Muslims noted the paradoxical and apparently blasphemous possibility that God could become the eye, the ear, the hand, and the foot of the saint; yet this was uniformly understood as a reference to closeness to God, to "friendship" (*wilāya*) with Him. The saint is not "God in the flesh."

Here the prophet speaks again:

> O son of Adam! So long as you call upon Me and ask of Me, I shall forgive you for what you have done, and I shall not mind. O son of Adam, were your sins to reach the clouds of the sky and were you then to ask forgiveness of Me, I would forgive you.[22]

A reader of Hellenistic pagan formation, finding such a claim embedded in a biography of the prophet, might assume that he was here claiming divinity, together with the divine prerogative of forgiving sins.[23] However, in its natural Arabian milieu, where the understanding of monotheism had been shaped for generations by a Jewish presence, such an interpretation would have been rejected out of hand. A prophet remains, always, God's servant, which is why the first words uttered by Jesus in the Koran, when still an infant in his mother's arms, are "I am the servant of God" (19:30).

This scriptural genre of "theopathic locution," in which a perfected human soul provides a sounding board for the speech of God, is associated with the prophet, but in Islamic history came to be regarded as a possible attribute of saints as well. The phenomenon whereby God apparently ventriloquizes through a saint became fairly widespread in early medieval Islam, and is also attested in rabbinic Judaism.[24] In a firmly monotheistic environment, however, there was a constant discomfort about this potentially ecstatic and disruptive practice, and many feared that untutored admirers might fatally confuse the passive human intermediary with the divine speaker. For the founder of Ash'arism, Islam's major theological tradition:

> Among the ascetical Sufis there are some who believe and profess that the Creator takes up an abode in individual entities, and that He can inhere in human beings, animals, and other entities. [Such people] often cast aside the Law, claiming that when a person attains to God, then no religious duty is any longer incumbent upon him.[25]

This misunderstanding of the mystic's experience is the error of incarnation, frequently leading to indifference to the revealed law; it is seen as the ultimate negation of the religion of the monotheistic prophets of Israel. Al-Ghazālī (d. 1111), a theologian who was well aware of the extravagances of certain mystics, wrote that Muslims should beware of repeating the error of those who, dazzled by the light of God mirrored in the perfect heart of Jesus, mistakenly worshipped him as a god.[26] A friend of God bodies forth qualities of perfection whose source and ground is God Himself; he is, to use the prophet's language, "made in the image of God,"[27] a "child of God,"[28] a "perfect man," but no worship is due to him, for his egoless perfection points away from himself, to the One who is greater than all creation. As the Johannine Jesus carefully puts it: "He who believes in me, believes not in me but in him who sent me" (John 12:44).

■ 3. THE HOLY SPIRIT

As we have seen, some early Christians venerated Jesus as a sign of aspects of divinity. However, even among practitioners of what Mary Daly calls "christolatry," there appears to have been no worship of the Holy Spirit in the first century.[29] In the second century, Justin Martyr held that the Logos was "another God," while Tertullian, also charged with believing in "two Gods" by some Christians, believed that Jesus partook of divinity, yet neither taught a triune God; their conception was essentially binitarian, entailing an adoration of the Father and the Son only.[30] As Alan Segal records:

> It seems likely that the Church continued to use the stronger term "two gods" whenever it needed a strong polemical statement against its heretics but admitted to binitarianism until such time as the doctrine of the Trinity was firmly entrenched in the third and fourth centuries.[31]

The Bible does speak of a Holy Spirit: it is a power or aspect of God, "poured out" to inspire and strengthen His servants. The biblical authors offer little support, however, for postapostolic suppositions that this attribute is a discrete deity. In the Old Testament, the Holy Spirit is the *ruach-YHWH*, God's spirit, and the New Testament takes the same view while introducing elements of a new terminology. In one passage (John 14:16), the church is promised a *parakletos*, a "counselor" or "advocate," who will guide Christians to truths that Jesus was not yet prepared to disclose. Trinitarians have historically identified this figure with the Holy Spirit, understood as an equal member of the Trinity; but the original text does not bear this sense. A more defensible claim would be that Christ is here predicting the arrival of a subsequent human guide (later figures such as Montanus and Mani claimed to be the *parakletos* in this sense). This interpretation gains in credibility when we recall an established dimension of Jewish expectation, which held that "Israel should focus its eschatological hope not only on the figure of the Messiah, but also on a Spirit-filled Prophet to come."[32] It appears that some in first-century Palestinian Jewry were expecting not one, but two messianic deliverers: one who would act as a priest, and the other who would be a king.[33]

While the identity of this "second messiah" continues to elude many interpreters, it is safe to assume that early Christianity did not hold that the spirit of God was "God the Spirit"; the term simply signified the guiding or prophetic action of the incorporeal deity.[34] Even the Nicene Creed of 325 failed to indicate that the "Holy Spirit" was a third deity within the Godhead; this had to wait for the troubled Council of Constantinople (381 CE). Many demurred, however, even after a series of imperial edicts imposed torture or the death penalty on those who refused to accept the Holy Spirit as a fully consubstantial member of the Trinity.[35]

4. FINAL REFLECTIONS: WHAT WOULD JESUS DO?

In this chapter we have not argued that the doctrine of the Trinity, as set forth in the official creeds, is a metaphysical impossibility. Nor has it been claimed that official Trinitarian teaching is intrinsically polytheistic. Instead, it has been suggested that the doctrine fails on two internal Christian criteria and hence is, as a purportedly Christian belief, incoherent.

The first is that the doctrine appears to be incompatible with the faith of Jesus and the apostolic generations. Forced apologetics aside, it is intrinsically unlikely that the historical Jesus of Nazareth, had he attended the Council of Constantinople, would have voted for the party that posterity came to regard as orthodox. As a fervent Jewish worshipper of his divine Father, caught up in a *unio mystica* that allowed many to see aspects of divinity indicated in his life and qualities, but still a servant of the One God, he would have been sentenced to death for his radical denial of Christian orthodoxy, by the same Roman Empire that, in its time of paganism, had brought his earthly ministry to a sudden end.

The foundation of authentic Christianity must be the way its founder himself believed and worshipped. The incorporation of the ancient Hellenic principle of a divine triad into the formerly Jewish movement of Christianity allowed the new religion to attract many gentiles, and a vibrant syncretism was born (Gregory of Nyssa, contemplating paganism as a *preparatio* for the church, presented Christianity as a *via media* between Jewish monotheism and Greek polytheism).[36] Although the Reformers, in their zeal to return to the sources, sought in their more courageous moments to rescue the beliefs of the first Christians from the Hellenizing categories and assumptions of the imperial councils, to this day the doctrine is required by the great majority of Reformed churches. It is in this spirit that a recent survey of Trinitarian interpretations of the Lord's Prayer warns us against presumptuous attempts to subscribe to the beliefs of Jesus and his Apostles:

> However much we may, rightly and understandably, load the Lord's Prayer with christological and Trinitarian teaching, its New Testament origins inevitably tell us of a different context: not one to which we should anachronistically aspire in some way to "return."[37]

The survival of the belief in the infallibility of the creeds concurrently with a reduced confidence in the inerrancy of scripture is a subject that, while fascinating, can find no place here. Perhaps the contemporary "retreat to religion" tempts some fearful souls to believe that without a literal defense of historic doxologies, their identity will be swept away by the turbid seas of modernity. Still, the postbiblical doctrine must defend itself, not only against the historically settled charges of Jewish and Muslim monotheists, but against the growing number of Christians who consider it unscriptural and unhelpful.

The second of our Christian grounds for declaring the doctrine incoherent is the fact of its simultaneous centrality and obscurity. We have seen how baffled ordinary churchgoers are by this core Christian claim about the object of their worship, and how they often react by storing Trinitarian talk in a seldom-opened cupboard of their minds. If the greatest commandment of Jesus is to believe that "the Lord thy God is One" (Mark 12:29), then a doctrine, misunderstood, that has led many Christians into a polytheism from which the Jews have been spared, might seem an unlikely gift of the Holy Spirit. Neither is the implementation of the Great Commission to spread the faith notably helped by the centrality of this doctrine, which remains a scandal to the world's many unbelievers.[38]

Not only does this immensely subtle and contested dogma lead many into gross heresy, it surely obstructs our relationship with the religion's founder. Although theologians differ sharply over the nature of Jesus' self-awareness, his usefulness as a role model is drastically curtailed by the "dual-nature" Christology that necessarily makes of him a being categorically unlike ourselves. A Christ marked by static perfection, inerrant even as a small child, who could not "increase in wisdom and stature, and in favor with God," is an entity utterly alien to our experience and imagination, and cannot in any way "represent" us; as McCord Adams asks, "Could not self-diffusing Goodness, superabundant generosity, find a 'smidgeon' more scope for its extravagance by identifying itself with the messy developmental process we struggle through?"[39]

The doctrine seems no less effective in endangering a clear and loving worship of the God served and praised so perfectly by the human Jesus of Nazareth. Great religions heal souls by inspiring a simplicity of life, rooted in simple and direct worship. Instead of worshipping the Father adored by Jesus, believers in the Trinity are asked to make a metaphysical riddle the object of their worship; indeed, the Athanasian Creed threatens those who fail to grasp it with "eternal fire." It may be granted that there is always something mysterious about the inner life of God. But to introduce threeness into the divine essence is to make of God, whom we wish ardently to approach as a person, into an alien abstraction. The decline of Trinitarian language in popular worship is rooted in an entirely correct bewilderment and alienation.

Consequently we also need to ask whether the public confession and adoration of a conundrum, a one-pointed triangle, as a condition for access to truth and salvation, has not contributed substantially to the wider crisis of faith experienced in the Western world. Modern secularity began in Christendom, not in China, India, or Islam. Is the unpersuasiveness of Trinitarian metaphysics one salient explanation for this not insignificant fact? As a ready target for secular incredulity, it may have played a significant role in the rise of atheism and the even more widespread deism that have replaced orthodoxy in the historic lands of Christendom.

■ NOTES

1. *Daily Telegraph*, July 31, 2002; Peter Brierley, *The Mind of Anglicans* (London: Cost of Conscience, 2002).

2. Reverend David A. Keddie, "Sermon for Trinity Sunday," *Expository Times* 118, no. 8 (May 2007), 387.

3. Keddie, "Sermon for Trinity Sunday," 387.

4. C. S. Rodd, "Three Gods," *Expository Times* 112, no. 8 (May 2001), 274. See the identical observation of Geoffrey Lampe, *Explorations in Theology*, vol. 8 (London: SCM, 1981), 36.

5. Rodd, "Three Gods," 273. Cf. the following comment: "Is it really a living doctrine for the average church member? To be honest, I have a suspicion that many church people deviate from it, to one side or the other. Some are virtually 'tri-theists': the Father, the Son and the Holy Spirit are regarded practically as three separate Gods. Others are virtually Unitarians: in the practice of their faith the Father alone is God, while Jesus Christ is seen as a special man who reveals the Father, and the Holy Spirit is for them a power rather than a divine Person." Klaas Runia, "The Trinity," in *The Lion Handbook of Christian Belief* (Tring, UK: Lion, 1982), 164.

6. For instance, the Church of Scotland's *Common Order* (1994), in which "Father" in Trinitarian statements is frequently replaced with "God"; see Kathryn Greene-McCreight, "What's the Story? The Doctrine of God in the *Common Order* and the *Book of Common Worship*," in *To Glorify God: Essays on Modern Reformed Liturgy*, ed. Bryan Spinks and Iain Torrance (Edinburgh: T&T Clark, 1999), 99–114, see 103–109.

7. A. G. Martimont et al., *The Church at Prayer: Introduction to the Liturgy* (Shannon, Ireland: Irish University Press, 1968), 123.

8. John R. K. Fenwick and Bryan D. Spinks, *Worship in Transition: The Twentieth Century Liturgical Movement* (Edinburgh: T&T Clark, 1995).

9. Gordon S. Wakefield, *An Outline of Christian Worship* (Edinburgh: T&T Clark, 1998). See also David Jasper and R. C. D. Jasper, eds., *Language and the Worship of the Church* (Basingstoke, UK: Macmillan, 1990), in which the Trinity is mentioned only in the contribution by Martin Warner.

10. Lester Ruth, "*Lex Amandi, Lex Orandi:* The Trinity in the Most Used Contemporary Christian Worship Songs," in *The Place of Christ in Liturgical Prayer: Trinity, Christology, and Liturgical Theology*, ed. Bryan D. Spinks, 342–359 (Collegeville, MN: Pueblo, 2008). A similar observation is made by Robert Letham, *The Holy Trinity: In Scripture, History, Theology and Worship* (Phillipsburg, NJ: P&R Publishing, 2004), 410.

11. Marguerite Shuster, "Preaching the Trinity: A Preliminary Investigation," in *The Trinity: An Interdisciplinary Symposium on the Trinity*, ed. Stephen T. Davis, Daniel Kendall, and Gerald O'Collins, 357–380 (Oxford: Oxford University Press, 1999).

12. Elizabeth A. Johnson, "To Let the Symbol Sing Again," *Theology Today* 54 (1997): 301.

13. For an excellent survey, see Stanley J. Grenz, *Rediscovering the Triune God* (Minneapolis: Fortress, 2004).

14. Bruce M. Metzger, *A Textual Commentary on the Greek New Testament* (New York: United Bible Societies, 1971), 715–717.

15. "The New Testament contains no doctrine of the Trinity." Donald H. Juel, "The Trinity and the New Testament," *Theology Today* 54 (1997): 313.

16. Emil Brunner, *The Christian Doctrine of God*, vol. 1, trans. Olive Wyon (London: Lutterworth, 1949), 226.

17. Geza Vermes, *Jesus the Jew, 2nd* ed. (London: SCM Press, 1973), 192–213; cf. James D. G. Dunn, *Christology in the Making: An Enquiry into the Origins of the Doctrine of the Incarnation*, 2nd ed. (London: SCM, 1989), 12–64.

18. "When John's Jesus says: 'I and the Father are One,' He is not in the first instance making a metaphysical claim, but alluding to ancient ideals of friendship." Marilyn McCord Adams, "Blessed Trinity, Society of Friends!" *Expository Times* 117, no. 8 (May 2006): 331.

19. William A. Graham, *Divine Word and Prophetic Word in Early Islam* (The Hague: Mouton, 1977).

20. Narrated by Bukhārī. See text and commentary in Abdal Hakim Murad, trans., *Selections from the Fatḥ al-Bārī by Ibn Ḥajar al-ʿAsqalānī* (Cambridge: Muslim Academic Trust, 1421/2000), 17–23.

21. Carl W. Ernst, *Words of Ecstasy in Sufism* (Albany: State University of New York Press, 1985).

22. Cited in Ezzedin Ibrahim and Denys Johnson-Davies, trans., *Forty Hadith Qudsi* (Cambridge: Islamic Texts Society, 1997), 126.

23. Although this right, biblically, may be delegated to priests, as Jesus delegated the right to forgive sins to his disciples (John 20:22–23).

24. Examples would include the thirteenth-century cabbalist Abraham Abulafia, who cried, "He is I and I am He" (Moshe Idel, *The Mystical Experience in Abraham Abulafia* [Albany: State University of New York Press, 1988], 127); and Joseph Karo (d. 1575), who was possessed by the divine Shekhina and spoke with its voice; see Lawrence Fine, "Benevolent Spirit Possession in Sixteenth-Century Safed," in *Spirit Possession in Judaism: Cases and Contexts from the Middle Ages to the Present*, ed. Matt Goldish (Detroit, MI: Wayne State University Press, 2003), 108.

25. Abu'l-Ḥasan al-Ashʿarī, *Maqālāt al-Islāmiyyīn wa'khtilāf al-muṣallīn* (Istanbul: Devlet Matbaası, 1929–1930), 13–14.

26. Abū Ḥāmid al-Ghazālī, ed. Fadlou A. Shehadi, *al-Maqṣad al-Asnā fī sharḥ maʿānī asmāʾ Allāh al-ḥusnā* (Beirut: Dar el-Machreq, 1971), 166.

27. For the hadith "God made Adam in His image" and its controversies, see Daniel Gimaret, *Dieu à l'image de l'homme: les anthropomorphismes de la sunna et leur interprétation par les théologiens* (Paris: Cerf, 1997).

28. This is not a common Islamic usage, but it occurs in the hadith: "People are God's children, and the people God loves most are those who show His children the greatest charity", narrated by Abū Nuʿaym al-Iṣfahānī, *Ḥilyat al-awliyāʾ wa-ṭabaqāt al-aṣfiyāʾ* (Cairo: Maktabat al-Khānjī, 1351–1357/1932–1938), vol. 2, 102, and vol. 4, 237; Muḥammad al-Quḍāʾī, *al-Musnad* (Beirut: Muʾassasat al-Risāla, 1405/1985), 208; and is echoed in the *Dīwān* of Abu'l-ʿĀtāhiya (Beirut: Dār Ṣādir, 1964/1384), 371.

29. The earliest text suggesting worship of the Holy Spirit appears to be the second-century *Ascension of Isaiah*; see L. T. Stuckenbruck, "Worship and Monotheism in the Ascension of Isaiah," in *The Jewish Roots of Christological Monotheism: Papers from the St. Andrews Conference on the Historical Origins of the Worship of Jesus*, ed. Carey C. Newman, James R. Davila, and Gladys S. Lewis (Boston: Brill, 1999), 70–89.

30. Alan F. Segal, "'Two Powers in Heaven' and Early Christian Trinitarian Thinking," in Davis et al., *The Trinity*, 85–91.

31. Segal, "'Two Powers in Heaven,'" 92.

32. John Breck, *Spirit of Truth: The Origins of Johannine Pneumatology* (Crestwood, NY: St. Vladimir's Seminary Press, 1991), 18.

33. James VanderKam, "Messianism in the Scrolls," in *The Community of the Renewed Covenant*, ed. Eugene Ulrich and James VanderKam (Notre Dame, IN: University of Notre Dame Press, 1993), 211ff; John J. Collins, "Messiahs in Context: Method in the Study of Messianism in the Dead Sea Scrolls," in *Methods of Investigation of the Dead Sea Scrolls and the Khirbet Qumran Site*, ed. M. O. Wise (New York: New York Academy of Sciences, 1994), 223–227. However, not all scholars accept the "two messiahs" reading of the Scrolls; see L. D. Hurst, "Did Qumran Expect Two Messiahs?" *Bulletin for Biblical Research* 9 (1999): 157–180.

34. Geoffrey Lampe, *God as Spirit* (Oxford: Oxford University Press, 1977).

35. Charles Freeman, *A.D. 381: Heretics, Pagans, and the Dawn of the Monotheistic State* (New York: Overlook, 2009).

36. Gregory of Nyssa, *The Catechetical Oration*, ed. James Herbert Srawley (Cambridge: Cambridge University Press, 1903), xvii.

37. Kenneth Stevenson, "Christology and Trinity: Interpreting the Lord's Prayer," in Spinks, *The Place of Christ in Liturgical Prayer*, 223.

38. "The Trinity is revealed only in the church, i.e., the community through which we become sons of the Father of Jesus Christ. Outside this it remains a stumbling block and a scandal." John D. Zizioulas, "The Doctrine of the Holy Trinity: The Significance of the Cappadocian Contribution," in *Trinitarian Theology Today*, ed. Christoph Schwöbel (Edinburgh: T&T Clark, 1995), 60.

39. Marilyn McCord Adams, *What Sort of Human Nature? Medieval Philosophy and the Systematics of Christology* (Milwaukee: Marquette University Press, 1999), 98.

▪ FOR FURTHER READING

Casey, M. *From Jewish Prophet to Gentile God: The Origins and Development of New Testament Christology.* Cambridge: Clarke, 1991.

Channing, W. E. *Selected Writings.* Mahwah, NJ: Paulist Press, 1985.

Dunn, J. D. G. *Did the First Christians Worship Jesus? The New Testament Evidence.* London: SPCK, 2010.

Richardson, C. C. *The Doctrine of the Trinity.* New York: Abingdon Press, 1958.

Snedeker, D. R. *Our Heavenly Father Has No Equals: Unitarianism, Trinitarianism, and the Necessity of Biblical Proof.* San Francisco: International Scholars Publications, 1998.

The Atonement

27 Responsibility, Atonement, and Forgiveness

■ RICHARD SWINBURNE

The New Testament is full of claims that Christ died for our sins, claims which imply very clearly that Christ's act made it possible for the guilt of our sins to be removed and for us to be forgiven by some objective process and not merely by being an example to us of how to behave. I shall call a theory of how this process worked a theory of the Atonement. But while the early Ecumenical Councils spelled out the doctrines of the Incarnation and the Trinity in precise ways, no Ecumenical Council (or Pope) has pronounced on *how* Christ's death secured that Atonement.[1]

▒ I. GENERAL MORAL PRINCIPLES

In this chapter I shall seek to analyse how one person can provide atonement for the sins of another. I shall then show that—given certain other Christian doctrinal and historical claims—Christ did provide atonement for human sins in this way; and I shall conclude by pointing out the inadequacies of rival theories of how this happened. The theory which I shall claim to be the correct theory coincides with the account given in the Letter to the Hebrews of Christ's death as Christ's voluntary sacrifice, and also with Anselm's satisfaction theory as modified by Aquinas and Scotus.

I begin with an analysis of the nature of wrongdoing and how it is to be dealt with in ordinary inter-human relations. Obligations are obligations to someone. I have an obligation to you to tell you nothing except what is true; I have an obligation to my children to feed and educate my children. When we fail in our obligations, we wrong those to whom we had or believed we had the obligation. Wronging is of two kinds—objective wronging, which is failing to fulfil your obligation whether or not you believed that you had that obligation; and subjective wronging, which is doing what you believed to be objectively wrong. In the first case you wrong the person to whom you had the obligation, and in the second case you wrong the person to whom you believed that you had an obligation. I wrong you objectively if I have borrowed money from you and do not repay it. I wrong you subjectively if I believe that I have borrowed money from you and do not repay it. And of course much wrongdoing is both objective and subjective, as when I do not repay money which I both have borrowed and believe that I have borrowed. By objective wrongdoing, I acquire what I shall call objective guilt; and by subjective wrongdoing I acquire what I shall call subjective guilt.

Obviously subjective guilt is the worse kind of guilt since it results from consciously chosen action. It is a stain on the soul, and needs to be dealt with. We are culpable, blameworthy for our subjective wrongdoing. Clearly to my mind, we can only acquire subjective guilt and so blameworthiness, if we have freely chosen to do the subjectively wrong action. And the "free will" which we need is libertarian free will, free will to act one way or a different way despite all the causal influences to which we are subject. Otherwise we would not be the ultimate source of our actions. So many of the Christian Fathers before Augustine asserted that we have free will and that we need it in order to be responsible for our actions, and they seem to have in mind this natural libertarian sense of free will.[2] I believe that we have such free will, although for reasons of space I cannot argue that here.

Although it matters less than subjective guilt, objective guilt also matters. If I have not repaid the money I owe you, there is still something amiss with me which needs to be dealt with even if I believe that I have repaid you. In interacting with other people we are responsible for our obligations to them, and an unintended failure to perform these obligations involves (non-culpable) guilt. I shall call dealing with our guilt "making atonement" for our wrongdoing.

Atonement has four components—repentance, apology, reparation and penance, not all of which are required to remove objective guilt or the subjective guilt arising from less serious wrongdoing. If I wrong you I must make reparation for the effects of my wrongdoing. If I have stolen your watch, I must return it and compensate you for the inconvenience and trauma resulting from my thieving. If the watch has been destroyed, I must give you back something of equivalent value. When I have deprived you of a service I owe you, I must perform the service and compensate you for the delay. But what needs to be dealt with is not merely the effects of wrongdoing; there is also the fact of wrongdoing—that I have sought to hurt you. I must distance myself from that as far as can be done. I do this by sincere apology; that is, public apology expressing inner repentance. But for serious wrongdoing, mere words of apology are often not enough. I need to show you my repentance by doing something extra for you, doing for you more than is needed to compensate for the effects of my wrongdoing. I may give you a small gift, or provide an extra service as a token of my sorrow; and I shall call doing this making a penance. Where the guilt is only objective, repentance is not required (I cannot repent of something for which I am not to blame); and where the wrongdoing is not serious, there is less need of penance. The process is completed when the wronged person, whom I will sometimes call the victim, undertakes to treat the wrongdoer, in so far as he can, as one who has not wronged him; and to do that is to forgive him. It is often done by saying the words "I forgive you." Treating the wrongdoer in this way involves both public and private acts, the private acts being of trying one's best to control any feelings of resentment against the wrongdoer.[3]

It is not necessary, in order for the victim to forgive the wrongdoer, that the latter should make a full atonement. Some apology and (if the wrong is subjective) repentance is always required, but the victim can determine how much (if any) reparation is required. (Henceforth when I write "reparation," "and penance" should also be understood.) I may let the wrongdoer off the need to compensate me for stealing my watch, if he has destroyed it and has no money with which to repay me—so long as he apologizes, and the apology sounds sincere (that is, sounds as if it is backed by repentance). It is however bad, I suggest, to treat someone who has wronged you seriously and yet makes no serious attempt at apology and repentance, as one who has not wronged you. It is not to take his hostile stance towards you seriously; it is to treat him as a child not responsible for his actions. If someone has killed your much loved wife and yet for some reason is beyond the reach of the law, it would be bad simply to ignore this and to enjoy his company at a party; it would be insulting to your wife to do so. Since forgiving is a good thing, I suggest that we only call treating the wrongdoer as one who has not wronged you "forgiving" him where it is good so to treat him, that is when treating him in this way is a response at least to some apparent repentance and apology on his part. Without this, treating the wrongdoer as someone who has not wronged you is condoning his wrong actions. Those theologians who think that God forgives everyone whether or not they want to be forgiven seem to me to have an inadequate view of what his perfect goodness consists in. And I do not think that the New Testament in any way supports that interpretation. In giving them the Lord's Prayer, Jesus taught his disciples to ask for forgiveness from God—which would be a pointless exercise if God had already forgiven them. Further, Jesus is quoted as saying "If your brother does wrong, rebuke him. If he repents, forgive him."[4] And Jesus added a condition for receiving forgiveness from God, a condition plausibly to be regarded as a mark of true repentance: "If you do not forgive others, neither will your Father forgive your wrongdoings."[5]

■ II. HUMANS NEED ATONEMENT

Now it does look as if almost all humans have wronged God, directly and indirectly. Wronging God is sinning. We wrong him directly when we fail to pay him proper worship. Deep reverence and gratitude is owed to the holy source of our existence. We wrong him indirectly when we wrong any of his creatures. For thereby we abuse the free will and responsibility we have been given by God—and to misuse a gift is to wrong the giver. And in wronging God's creatures, we wrong God also in virtue of the fact that he created these creatures. If I hit your child, I wrong you, for I damage a person on whom you have exercised your loving care. Such wronging is actual sin—sometimes only objective but often subjective as well, at least in the respect that the wrongdoer believes that he is doing wrong to someone, even if he does not realize that he is doing wrong to God. But it is, of course, far worse if he realizes that he is wronging the good God who created him and keeps him in existence from moment to moment.

But there is more to our bad condition than mere actual sin. There is an element inherited from our ancestors and ultimately from our first human ancestor, whom—defined as the first of our ancestors who had free will and moral beliefs—we may call Adam. There is first a proneness to wrongdoing which (in view of the fact that so much wrongdoing involves wronging God, at least indirectly) I shall call original sinfulness. Our original sinfulness consists of the bad desires which we have inherited from our ancestors, especially a proneness to seek our immediate well-being in lesser respects at the expense of others and at the expense of our ultimate well-being. This inheritance is partly "social." If our parents behave badly, that influences us to behave badly. But the inheritance is also genetic. We inherit our ancestors' genes, which cause our strong desires to seek far more than our fair share of food, sleep, shelter, sex etc.; and evidence has emerged within the last two years that what a person does and suffers (at the hands of others) at an early age affects the genes he or she hands on to their children.[6]

But, as well as inheriting original sinfulness, we also inherit a debt. All our ancestors have done wrong, and in consequence they owe God atonement; but they have not (at any rate in general) made that atonement—it still needs to be made. We are indebted to our ancestors for our life and so many of the good things which come to us. For God in creating us has acted through them who have (in general) not merely brought us into the world, but often lavished much care on our nurture (or on the nurture of others of our ancestors who nurtured others who in turn nurtured us). Those who have received great benefit from others owe them a smaller benefit in return. And since what we have inherited from our ancestors includes not merely many good things, but also the debt they owe to God, our duty to our ancestors is to help them to make their atonement. Even the English law requires that before you can claim what you inherit from your dead parents you must pay their debts. To inherit a debt is not however to inherit guilt.[7] For we were not the agents of our ancestors' wrongdoing, but we have inherited a responsibility to make atonement for this debt of "original sin," as far as we can—perhaps by making some reparation.

It is beginning to look as if we humans are in no very good position to make proper atonement for sins, good though it would be that we should make that atonement. We owe much anyway by way of service to God our creator, who has given us so much. We owe a lot more in virtue of our own actual sins; and yet more in virtue of the sins of our ancestors. And yet, because of the size of the debt and because of our own original sinfulness, it would be very difficult for us to make any proper atonement. We need help.

How can someone else help us to make atonement? "No one can atone for the sins of another."[8] Taken literally, that remains profoundly true. You cannot make my apologies, or even pay my debts. If I steal £10 from John and you give him an equivalent sum, he has not lost money; but it remains the case that I still owe £10 to John. But one human can help another to make the necessary atonement—can persuade him to repent, help him to formulate the words of apology, and give him the means by which to make reparation.

So what would be a proper reparation (with penance) for us to offer to God, if someone else provided the means of reparation? What has gone wrong is that we humans have lived bad human lives. A proper offering would be a perfect human life, which we can offer to God as our reparation. Maybe one human life, however perfect, would not equate in quantity of goodness the badness of so many human lives. But it is up to the wronged person to deem when a sufficient reparation has been made; and one truly perfect life would surely be a proper amount of reparation for God to deem that sufficient reparation had been made.

But why would God require any reparation, when he could simply forgive us in response to some minimum amount of repentance and apology? Well, he could have done so—various theologians recognised that.[9] But they also say that there is much good in him taking our wrongdoing so seriously as to insist on some reparation. When serious wrong has been done, parents and courts rightly insist on the wrongdoer providing some minimum amount of reparation. It involves the wrongdoer taking what he has done seriously. And if he has no means to make reparation, a well-wisher may often provide him with the means; the wrongdoer can then choose whether or not to use that means for that purpose. Suppose that I owe you some service, for example suppose that I have promised to clean your house and that you have already paid me to do this. Suppose also that I have spent the money but omitted to clean the house at the promised time, and that I have now had an accident which makes me unable to clean the house. Clearly I owe you repentance and apology; but I must also try to get someone else to clean the house. Even if you don't badly need the house to be cleaned, you may think it important that I should be involved in getting it cleaned; it matters that I should take responsibility for what I have omitted to do. So you may encourage a third person to offer to me to do for you the service on my behalf. If I accept the third person's offer I am involved in providing the reparation. When with repentance and apology, I ask you to accept the third person's action as my reparation, you, the victim, may then judge that I have taken my wrongdoing seriously enough to forgive me for it.

▪ III. HOW GOD PROVIDED ATONEMENT

As we have seen, ordinary humans are in no good position to make atonement for our own sins, let alone provide reparation for the sins of all other humans; and in my view God would have no right to require or even allow anyone else to perform such a demanding task. The Christian claim is that in Jesus Christ God provided the atonement, and I now suggest that this may be best understood in this way that he provided an act of reparation of which we can avail ourselves. God the Father (or perhaps God the Holy Trinity) was the wronged person (the victim of our wrongdoing); and God the Son was the one who, as Jesus Christ sent by God the Father, thinking it so important that we should take our wrongdoing seriously, made available the reparation for us to offer back to God the Father.

What would show that Christ provided an atonement for our sins in this way? Jesus Christ would have to have been God incarnate, to have led a perfect life, and to have claimed that this life was available for us as our reparation. Also God would need to show by some act which God alone could do that he had accepted the sacrifice (and which would be recognizable in the contemporary culture as showing this)—for example by raising Christ from the dead, and thereby showing his approval of what Christ had done. To the extent to which we have evidence that these things are so, to that extent we have evidence that Christ has provided an atonement for our sins. A perfect life need not end in a death by execution, but in so many human societies that may well happen; those who protest too strongly against injustice, above all if they claim divine authority for their actions, were very likely to get executed in many ancient societies. If God is to live a perfect life among us, just once for the sins of the world, it is plausible to suppose that he might choose to live in a society where it is highly probable that living a perfect life would involve bearing serious suffering, and where protest pays the highest price. Most theologians have thought of the reparation made by Christ as his Passion or Crucifixion, or perhaps the series of events from his betrayal to his death. But they have also stressed that what mattered about these events is that Christ freely allowed them to happen; and so the series must include the free actions of Christ which led to his crucifixion, and that will include at least all the public part of his perfect life. The reparation is not so much his death, as his actions which led to his death.

This account of how Christ made an atonement coincides with the account in terms of sacrifice given in the Letter to the Hebrews. The letter regards Christ's death as an effective sacrifice which achieved what the sacrifices in the Jewish temple could not. But "the blood of Christ" contributed a sacrifice "without blemish,"[10] to "bear the sins of many."[11] It was offered only once, and that was all that was needed—"He entered once for all into the Holy Place, not with the blood of goats and calves, but with his own blood, thus obtaining eternal redemption."[12] In the most primitive way of thinking about sacrifice lying behind (the far more sophisticated) Old Testament thought, a sacrifice is the giving of something valuable to God who consumes it by inhaling the smoke, and often gives back some of it to be consumed by the worshippers (who eat some of the flesh of the sacrificed animal).[13] The sacrifice of Christ is then Christ (God the Son) giving to God (the Father) the most valuable thing he has—his life, a perfect life of service to God and humans in difficult circumstances, leading to its being taken from him by his crucifixion. In order for the sacrifice to be successful (that is, for God to accept the sacrifice) Christ "entered into heaven itself, now to appear in the presence of God on our behalf"[14]; and the letter also alludes to what the writer must regard as our evidence of Christ's exaltation, that God "brought [him] back from the dead... by the blood of the eternal covenant."[15]

I have written that Christ "provided" an atonement and pointed out that the benefits of sacrifice are available only to those who associate themselves with it. And clearly Christians have always claimed that Christ's act makes no difference to us if we do not in some way appropriate it for ourselves. (Christ is "the source of salvation to all who obey him"[16].) We can say to God "Please accept instead of the life which I ought to have led (and the lives which my ancestors ought to have led) this perfect life of Christ as my reparation." Thereby we join our repentance and apology with the reparation (and penance) which Christ provides. The ceremony of entry to the Christian church is baptism. The Nicene creed echoes various New Testament texts in affirming belief in "one baptism" (that is, a non-repeatable ceremony) "for the forgiveness of sins." It is in this way that God gives those of us who seek it, his forgiveness. At their baptism, wrote St Paul, Christians are baptised into the death of Christ[17]; as adults, they appropriate it for themselves, or—when infants are baptised—parents do so with the prayer that when the infants become older, they will themselves accept the association that their parents made on their behalf. And the association established by baptism is renewed at each eucharist when, St Paul claims, "as often as you eat this bread and drink this cup, you proclaim the Lord's death until he comes."[18] According to Matthew and Mark, Christ claimed that he could or would "destroy the Temple and build in three days another Temple not made with hands"[19]; and since they clearly thought that he himself was what came to life after three days, they thought of him as the substitute for the Temple, and so his life and death as a substitute for the Temple sacrifice. Since the bread and wine of the Eucharist are given the status of the "body" and "blood" of Christ (however that is to be understood), our participation in the sacrifice of Christ has an exact analogy to participation in older sacrifices when worshippers ate some of the sacrifice. "Body" and "blood" are the elements of sacrifice; and since the phrases "this is my body" and "this is my blood" are fairly clearly the original words of Christ, the sacrifice theory is not—I suggest—only that of the Letter to the Hebrews alone, but of Christ himself.[20]

While many of the Fathers continued to teach that Christ's death was a sac-rifice, some of them put forward one or both of two other theories (to my mind very unsatisfactory theories) which some of them combined with the sacrifice theory.[21] Some of them thought of the atonement (in the sense defined at the beginning of this paper) as brought about by Christ taking and so perfecting human nature. But that involves a Platonic view of our human nature as a sepa-rately existing universal in which all humans participate; and Plato's theory of forms seems to most of us highly implausible. Further, this theory seems to imply that the atonement was achieved by the incarnation; and that makes it unclear how the Crucifixion has any role in this, as all the Fathers acknowledged that it did. Other patristic writers wrote of the Crucifixion as a redemption or the pay-ment of a ransom. The question then arises to whom the ransom was paid? The only possible answer seems to be—the Devil. But then why did the ransom need to be paid? Could not God just have annihilated the Devil? The reply sometimes given is that in some way God had promised the Devil that he would be allowed to control the fate of those who sinned against God. But why should God have made so foolish a promise? True, there is much talk in the New Testament of Christ "redeeming" us and even paying a "ransom." There is much talk, too, of his rescuing us from evil, and sometimes this is put personally in terms of his rescu-ing us from the Devil. But any idea of a prior bargain with the Devil, so that God was obliged to pay a ransom to him, is—I suggest—alien to the New Testament. All that the New Testament texts are claiming is that Christ rescued us from the guilt of sin, and (to some extent) from the power to sin—that is, he gave us the power not to sin. And any theory of the Atonement (including the sacrifice theory) will incorporate the former element; the latter is a further aspect of the work of Christ—the beginning of our sanctification.

Anselm's theory in *Cur Deus Homo?* is however similar to the sacrifice theory, although he uses the word "satisfaction" for the reparation which is offered to God, the voluntary payment of a debt by one who is God. His theory does how-ever make rendering satisfaction of an amount equal to the harm done, neces-sary before forgiveness can be given. And it leaves it unclear how the benefits of Christ's death come to us. Aquinas takes over Anselm's basic idea, but rem-edies these deficiencies. Christ's death was desirable but not necessary, claimed Aquinas.[22] While God can provide the satisfaction, Aquinas accepted the objec-tion that "the man who sins must do the repenting and confess," but "satisfaction has to do with the exterior act, and here one can make use of instruments, a cat-egory under which friends are included."[23] He also claimed that the benefits of Christ's death flow to us through our incorporation into it in baptism and other sacraments—"Christ's passion, the universal cause of the forgiveness of sins, has to be applied to individuals if they are to be cleansed from their sins. This is done by baptism and penance and the other sacraments, which derive their power from the passion of Christ."[24] And Aquinas regarded his theory both as a sacrifice theory—"Christ's passion was a true sacrifice,"[25] and also a "satisfaction" theory.[26] Like Anselm however, Aquinas and then the Reformers claimed that human sin, because it consisted in wronging God, was enormously bad; and by contrast Christ's passion was infinitely good. Scotus rightly avoided such comparative talk—how can one weigh the goodness and badness of acts on an exact scale? He claimed instead that the value of Christ's passion was the value God put upon it; and so God could deem it a sufficient reparation for human sin.[27]

The Reformers had a penal substitution theory of the Atonement. Christ's death was a punishment which he voluntarily underwent instead of the punishment which we would have had to undergo.[28] Anselm's theory is often regarded as such a theory; but he himself distinguished "satisfaction" as something "freely given" from "the exaction of punishment."[29] Punishment is something undergone, imposed (whether on the guilty person or someone else) by the wronged person (or someone acting on his behalf) in order to deal with his guilt. And while someone may indeed voluntarily undergo a punishment, the voluntariness consists in someone allowing others to do something to him; the volunteer may allow others to take him into custody, but what happens after that depends on the others. But Anselm presumably held that at every stage of the process, Christ was active—for example, in allowing himself to be betrayed, in his struggle in Gethsemane and in not invoking his Father's help to rescue him. "Making satisfaction" is a voluntary act, as is offering a sacrifice. The Father did not need to impose anything on Christ or anyone else.

To give a theory of the Atonement, as I have understood that notion, is to give a theory of how Christ's act made it possible for the guilt of our sins to be removed; and in this paper I have sought to give such a theory. But in doing so I have no wish to deny that God's incarnation in Jesus Christ served many other good purposes, some of which have been misleadingly captured in other theories of "atonement." These include solidarity with us in the sufferings which God causes us to endure for good reasons, giving us an example of how to live, revealing to us important truths, and—as I have already mentioned—providing help to us in avoiding future sins and in forming characters fit for Heaven.

■ NOTES

1. This paper is a fuller version of a paper entitled "Christ's Atoning Sacrifice" published in *Archivio di Filosofia*, 2008.

2. Thus Irenaeus: "If some had been made by nature bad, and others good, these latter would not be deserving of praise for being good, for such were they created; nor would the former be reprehensible, for thus they were [originally]. But since all men are of the same nature, able both to hold fast and to do what is good; and, on the other hand, having also the power to cast it from them and not to do it,—some do justly receive praise even among men who are under the control of good laws (and much more from God), and obtain deserved testimony of their choice of good in general, and of persevering therein; but the others

are blamed, and receive a just condemnation, because of their rejection of what is fair and good." (*Against Heresies*, Book 4, ch 37, in: *The Writings of Irenaeus*, tr. A. Roberts and W.H. Rambault, vol 2, T. and T. Clark, 1869.)

3. Many writers seem to suppose that one has only truly forgiven someone if one has ceased to have such feelings of resentment. Thus Jeffrie Murphy attributes to Joseph Butler, and himself endorses, the view that "forgiveness involves a change in inner feeling"; one "who has forgiven has overcome...vindictive attitudes." (See his *Getting Even: Forgiveness and its Limits*, Oxford University Press, 2003, p. 13) I do not find this view stated very explicitly in Butler's Sermon "Upon Forgiveness of Injuries" to which Murphy refers, but it is perhaps implicit there. However, one's feelings are not fully under one's control. Forgiving is a performative act, something one does. Doing it involves a commitment to try to control one's feelings, but it cannot involve more. But Murphy goes on usefully to distinguish forgiving from regarding the supposed wrongdoer as justified in having done what he did, from regarding the act as excusable, and from showing mercy to the wrongdoer. He also distinguishes forgiving someone from being willing to interact with them in the same way as before the wrong act (which he calls being "reconciled to them.") That also seems right. One might forgive someone who has abused one's children, but ensure that he did not see them again. The forgiving involves treating the abuser as someone who has not wronged you in the past, but it is compatible with treating him as someone who might wrong you in future.

4. Luke 17:3.

5. Matthew 6:15.

6. See for example the news report in *The New Scientist*, 7 January 2006, p. 10, and the earlier article "Hidden Inheritance" by Gail Vines in *The New Scientist*, 28 November 1998, pp. 27–30.

7. Augustine was responsible for the wide acceptance in the Western church of the view that the descendents of Adam are guilty for his sins (and so suffer from "Original guilt"), although—as far as I can see—none of the Fathers before Augustine had advocated it. On this see my *Responsibility and Atonement*, p. 144. The biblical passage which is always cited as expounding the doctrine of Original Guilt is Romans 5:12–21. I argue in *Responsibility and Atonement*, Additional Note 8 (p. 206) that this passage cannot bear that interpretation.

8. This point was made both by Jeremiah (31:29–30) and Ezekiel (18 passim) who affirm that no one will be held guilty and so condemned to die for the sins of their parents or children.

9. Thus Gregory Nazianzen wrote that "although as God [our Saviour] could have saved [us] by his will alone...He provided us a thing greater and more fitted to shame us, even fellowship in suffering and equality of rank" (*Oration* 19). Aquinas wrote that "If God had wanted to free man from sin without any satisfaction at all, he would not have been acting against justice." (*Summa Theologiae* 3a.46.2 ad 3.) And in effect too Scotus seems to say the same—see L.W. Grensted, *A Short History of the Doctrine of the Atonement*, Longmans, Green and Co., 1920, pp. 161–2. So too (with hesitation) does Bonaventure—Grensted, p. 148.

10. Hebrews 9:14.

11. Hebrews 9:28.

12. Hebrews 9:12.

13. See J. Pedersen, *Israel. Its life and culture*, Oxford University Press, rev. ed. 1959, pp. 299–375 (esp. p. 359).

14. Hebrews 9:24.

15. Hebrews 13:20.

16. Hebrews 5:9.

17. Romans 6:3.

18. I Corinthians 11:26

19. Matthew 26:61. Mark 14:58.

20. Although differing in other respects, all four accounts of the Last Supper given in the New Testament (in the Gospels of Matthew, Mark, and Luke, and in I Corinthians) describe Jesus as uttering these words over the bread and the wine. Although John's Gospel has no account of the Last Supper, it insists on the need to eat the "flesh" and drink the "blood" of Christ in order to belong to the Christian community and share in Christ's Resurrection—see John 6:41–59.

21. See (e.g.) J.N.D. Kelly *Early Christian Doctrines*, 5th ed., 1977, ch. 14.

22. See note 9.

23. *Summa Theologiae* 3a.48.2 ad 1.

24. op. cit. 3a.49.1. ad 4.

25. op. cit. 3a.48.3.

26. "Christ by his suffering made perfect satisfaction for our sins"—op. cit. 3a.48.2.

27. For Anselm see *Cur Deus Homo?* 1.21 "How great a burden sin is" and yet 2.14, "no enormity or multitude of sins . . . can for a moment be compared with [a] bodily injury inflicted upon [Christ]." For Aquinas see op.cit 3a.48.2 ad2. For Scotus and (among the Reformers) Turretin, see F.W. Grensted *A Short History of the Doctrine of the Atonement*, Longmans, Green, and Co, 1920, pp. 158–62 and pp. 243–4.

28. While Calvin allowed that (in theory) God could have used another "mediator" between God and man, than one who was both God and man—though he did not see how (see J. Calvin *Institutes of the Christian Religion* 2.12.1), he seems to assume that it was necessary that there be a "mediator."

29. *Cur Deus Homo?* 2.15.

▓ FOR FURTHER READING

Anselm, *Cur Deus Homo*. in St Anselm, (tr.) S.N. Deane, Chicago: Open Court, 1903.

Aulen, G. *Christus Victor*. Norwich: SCM Press, 1984.

Hare, J. *The Moral Gap*. Oxford: Oxford University Press, 1996 (especially part 3).

Swinburne, R. *Responsibility and Atonement*. Oxford: Oxford University Press, 1989.

Quinn, P. "Swinburne on Guilt, Atonement, and Christian Redemption" in *Reason and the Christian Religion, edited by Alan Padgett*. Oxford: Oxford University Press, 1994.

28   Problems with the Doctrine of Atonement

■ JOHN HICK

The term "atonement" is so deeply embedded in Christian discourse that every systematic theologian feels obliged to have a doctrine under this heading. And yet the word is so variously used that some of these doctrines have little in common except the name. In its broad etymological meaning, at-one-ment signifies becoming one with God—not ontologically, but in the sense of entering into a right relationship with our Creator, this being the process or state of salvation. But in its narrower sense atonement refers to a specific method of receiving salvation, one presupposing that the barrier to this is guilt. It is in this context that we find the ideas of penalty, atonement, redemption, sacrifice, oblation, propitiation, expiation, satisfaction, substitution, forgiveness, acquittal, ransom, justification, remission of sins, forming a complex of ideas that has long been central to the Western or Latin development of Christianity.[1]

In this narrower sense, Jesus' crucifixion was an act of atoning, or making up for, human sin. On the other hand, in the broader sense in which atonement simply means salvation, or entering into a right relationship with God, Jesus' death may or may not be separated off from his self-giving life as a whole, as having a special significance on its own. As a rough approximation we can say that the broader sense has been more at home in the Eastern or Greek development of Christianity and the narrower in its Western or Latin development.

In my view it would be best, in the interests of clarity, to restrict the term "atonement" to its narrower and more specific meaning. The basic notion is that salvation requires God's forgiveness and that this in turn requires an adequate atonement to satisfy the divine righteousness and/or justice. This atoning act is a transaction, analogous to making a payment to cancel a debt or to remit an impending punishment. In the background there is the idea of the moral order of the universe, which requires that sin, as a disruption of that order, be balanced or cancelled either by just punishment of the offender or a substitute, or by some adequate satisfaction in lieu of punishment.

I am going to argue that in this narrower sense the idea of atonement has played itself out; although of course the broader sense, in which atonement simply means salvation, is alive and indeed vitally important.

In so arguing I am, I think, reflecting a widespread contemporary perception. Indeed, were it not for its recent revival by some Christian philosophers who, unlike most contemporary theologians, see church doctrine as a set of immutable truths, one could easily think that the notion of atonement, in its narrower sense, had died out among thoughtful Christians. For modern treatments of salvation seldom center upon St. Anselm's doctrine of a satisfaction to cancel the insult to God's majesty caused by creaturely disobedience, or the penal-substitutionary idea of an imputed justification won by Christ's having taken upon himself the punishment due for human sin. It is symptomatic of the vanishing role of these ideas today that in the most recent (1989) revision of the *Encyclopedia Britannica,* while there is a brief entry on atonement in the ready reference micropedia, the more than 100 pages of in-depth study of Christianity in the macropedia include only one reference to the idea that "the Christian is the one to whom the righteousness of God is ascribed in faith for the sake of the merit of Jesus Christ, which he earned for himself through his expiatory sacrifice on the cross" (vol. 16, p. 285); and the writer immediately adds that "in the 20th century, however, the schema of justification seems less understandable" because its presuppositions "are scarcely found any more in religious consciousness" (pp. 284–285).

As with other traditional doctrines, it is important to try to go back in historical imagination to the original experience out of which it grew. It is evident that the profound and all-absorbing experience of the early post-Easter Christian community was of a living spirit, which they identified as the spirit of the risen Jesus, welling up within them, individually and corporately, and drawing them into a new, joyous, and exhilarating stream of life, full of positive meaning and free from the besetting fears of the ancient world—of demons, of fate, of sin, and of death. This new liberated life, brimming with meaning and hope, was the religious reality that was to be expressed, first in what seems to us today a cluster of bizarre images, and later, within medieval Latin Christianity, in various sophisticated theories of a transactional atonement. However, we in the Western churches today, both Catholic and Reformed, may well feel that none of these inherited theories retains any real plausibility and that we should look again at the alternative development within Eastern Christianity of the idea of a gradual transformation of the human by the divine Spirit, called by the Orthodox theologians deification (*theosis*).

These two conceptions do not, of course, entirely exclude each other. Latin theology has also held that the justification won by Jesus' death leads to sanctification, which is the gradual transformation of the sinner into a saint. And Orthodox theology also holds that Jesus' death was somehow crucial in bringing about human "deification." And since both traditions use the same stock of biblical images, one can find much the same language somewhere within each. But nevertheless, their basic tendencies move in markedly different directions, one guided by a transaction-atonement conception and the other by a transformation conception of salvation.

We shall come back later to the Eastern tradition and its transformational conception, but in the meantime let us look more closely at the transactional model.

Before the division between Eastern and Western Christianity, the earliest attempt to conceptualize the Christian experience of liberation and new life fastened upon the Markan saying attributed to Jesus, that "the Son of man came not to be ministered unto, but to minister, and to give his life a ransom (*lutron*) for many" (Mark 10:45). The idea of ransom had a poignant meaning in the ancient world, in which a considerable proportion of the population lived in a permanent state of slavery, and free citizens were liable to become enslaved if their tribe, city, or nation was defeated in war. Being ransomed, and thus made free, was accordingly a vivid and powerful metaphor, whose force most of us can probably only partially recapture today.

But, making the perennial theological mistake of taking metaphorical language literally, the early Christian writers asked themselves to whom Jesus was, by his death, paying a ransom, and the inevitable answer, in a world plagued by fear of demons, was the Devil. In the words of Origen, "To whom gave he his life 'a ransom for many'? It cannot have been to God. Was it not then to the evil one? For he held us until the ransom for us, even the soul of Jesus, was paid to him."[2] And so for many centuries—indeed virtually until Anselm introduced his satisfaction theory in the eleventh century—it was generally accepted by Christian writers and preachers that the human race had fallen through sin under the jurisdiction and power of the Devil and that the cross of Christ was part of a bargain with the Devil to ransom us. Within this literature there is also, as a subplot, the idea that in this bargain God outwitted the Devil, transforming a situation in which he had a just claim over humanity to one in which he put himself in the wrong by taking a greater ransom, namely God the Son, than was due. Thus Gregory of Nyssa proposed that "in order to secure that the ransom in our behalf might be easily accepted by him who required it, the Deity was hidden under the veil of our nature, that so, as with ravenous fish, the hook of the Deity might be gulped down along with the bait of the flesh."[3] St. Augustine even more picturesquely suggested in one of his sermons that "as our price he [Christ] held out his cross to him like a mouse trap, and as bait set upon it his own blood."[4] Such imagery is only embarrassing today. But while the ransom theory was never elevated to creedal authority, it was very widely used, occurring in the writing of Irenaeus, Origen, Gregory of Nyssa, Ambrose, Rufinus, Gregory the Great, Augustine, and Chrysostom. Nevertheless, it is impossible today to make any good sense or use of it. As Anselm later asked, "why should we accept that the Devil has any valid legal rights over against the infinite Creator?"[5] The wonder is that such a notion satisfied some of the best Christian minds for so long. As Grensted says, "That such a theory could stand for nine hundred years as the ordinary exposition of the fact of the atonement is in itself a sufficient proof that the need for serious discussion of the doctrine had not as yet been felt."[6]

When the need for serious discussion did begin to be felt, the theories that were produced began from belief in original sin as an inherited guilt affecting the entire human race and requiring an adequate atonement to expunge it. To attack this idea today is, for most of us, to do battle against a long-extinct monster. Nevertheless, the ecclesiastical reluctance to abandon traditional language is so strong that even today there is a point in recalling why we should cease to think and speak in terms of original sin—except as a mythological term for the universal fact of human moral imperfection. For this ancient notion presupposes the willful fall from grace of the first humans and the genetic inheritance by the whole species, as their descendants, of a sinful and guilty nature. This is something that only doctrinal fundamentalists can believe today. But prior to the Enlightenment of the seventeenth and eighteenth centuries it was a seriously entertained idea. Thus the Council of Trent (1646) pronounced:

> If anyone does not confess that the first man Adam, when he had transgressed the command of God in Paradise, straightway lost that holiness and righteousness in which he has been established, and through the offence of this disobedience incurred the wrath and indignation of God, and therefore incurred death ... [and] if anyone asserts that the disobedience of Adam injured only himself and not his offspring ... or that ... only death and the pains of the body were transferred to the whole human race, and not the sin also, which is the death of the soul: let him be anathema.[7]

While the Westminster Confession (1647) declared:

> Our first parents being seduced by the subtlety and temptation of Satan, sinned in eating the forbidden fruit ... By this sin they fell from their original righteousness, and communion with God, and so became dead in sin, and wholly defiled in all the faculties and parts of soul and body. They being the root of all mankind, the guilt of this sin was imputed, and the same death in sin and corrupted nature conveyed to all their posterity, descending from them by ordinary generation (chap. 6).

However, today, the idea of an actual human fall resulting in a universal inherited depravity and guilt is totally unbelievable by educated Christians. Instead of the human race being descended from a single specially created pair, we see the species as having evolved out of lower forms of life over a long period of time. Instead of the earliest humans living in a perfect communion with God, we see them as probably having a primitive animistic outlook. Instead of them living in harmony with nature and one another, we see them as engaged in a struggle to survive in competition with other animals, and with one another, within an often harsh environment. If out of piety toward the traditional language we wish to retain the term "fall," we can say that the earliest humans were, metaphorically speaking, already "fallen" in the sense of being morally and religiously imperfect. That is to say, there was a wide gap between their actual condition and the imagined "original righteousness" of paradisal perfection, so that they can be said to have been as though they had fallen from such an ideal state. But since that state never existed, would it not be better to abandon the concept of the fall altogether? If we believe that there never was a human fall from an original paradisal state, why risk confusing ourselves and others by speaking as if there were?

I take it that our endemic individual and corporate self-centeredness, from which the many forms of moral evil flow, is an aspect of our nature as animals engaged in the universal struggle for survival; and that this self-centered propensity exists in tension with a distinctively human capacity for ego-transcendence in response to the felt claim upon us of moral values. In this tension we have a genuine, though limited, freedom and responsibility; and in so far as we are free, we are guilty in respect of our wrong choices. There is thus a genuine problem of guilt. I shall return to this presently, but at the moment we are concerned with the ancient notion of original sin.

For it is this that feeds into the traditional conceptions of atonement. In the light of a typical contemporary ethical awareness, the idea of an inherited guilt for being born as the kind of beings that we are is a moral absurdity. We cannot be guilty in the sight of God for having been born, within God's providence, as animals programmed for self-protection and survival in a tough environment. And even if we discount our modern awareness of the continuity between *Homo sapiens* and the rest of animal life, the moral principle behind the traditional doctrine is still totally unacceptable. Although evidently believable in the age in which it was propounded, the notion of a universal inherited guilt was losing moral plausibility in the eighteenth century; and at the end of the nineteenth century the forthright humanist critic, W. K. Clifford, was expressing an already widespread perception when, having in mind the kind of ecclesiastical pronouncement that I quoted earlier, he said that "to condemn all mankind for the sin of Adam and Eve; to let the innocent suffer for the guilty; to keep anyone alive in torture for ever and ever; these actions are simply magnified copies of what bad men are. No juggling with the 'divine justice and mercy' can make them anything else."[8]

We have already seen in the ransom idea the way in which Christian theology has drawn its soteriological analogies from the structures of contemporary society—in this case the pervasive fact of slavery and the liberating possibility of being ransomed from it. The next model to dominate the Christian imagination was proposed by Anselm in his *Cur Deus Homo?* (completed in its present form in 1098), one of the most influential books of Christian theology ever written. Anselm took over the concept of satisfaction that had long operated in both church and society. This was the idea that disobedience, whether to God or to one's earthly lord, was a slight upon his honor and dignity, and required for its cancellation some adequate satisfaction in the form of an acceptable penance or gift. In the medieval penitential system a sinner's prescribed act of penance was believed to be accepted by God as a satisfaction restoring the moral balance;

and likewise, when one did something to undermine the dignity and authority of one's feudal overlord, one had either to be punished or to give some other sufficient satisfaction to appease the lord's slighted dignity. This notion, reflecting a strongly hierarchical and tightly knit society, evidently made sense in the cultural climate of medieval Europe.

Against this background Anselm defined sin as "nothing else than not to render to God his due."[9] What is due to God is absolute obedience: "He who does not render this honor which is due to God, robs God of his own and dishonors him; and this is sin … So then, everyone who sins ought to pay back the honor of which he has robbed God; and this is the satisfaction which every sinner owes to God" (pt. I, chap. 11). Further, "even God cannot raise to happiness any being bound at all by the debt of sin, because he ought not to" (pt. I, chap. 21). However, it is impossible for humanity to make the required satisfaction; for even if we were perfectly obedient in the future, we would only be giving to God what is already due to him, and a satisfaction requires something extra that was not already due. Further, because God is the lord of the whole universe, the adequate satisfaction for a slight upon the divine honor "cannot be effected, except the price paid to God for the sin of man be something greater than all the universe besides God" (pt. II, chap. 6). And, to add to the difficulty, since it is humanity that has offended God, it must be humanity that makes the restitution. Thus, since the needed satisfaction is one which "none but God can make and none but man ought to make, it is necessary for the God-man to make it" (pt. II, chap. 6). The God-man can give something that was not owing to God, namely his own life: "For God will not demand this of him as a debt; for, as no sin will be found, he ought not to die" (pt. II, chap. 11). Accordingly, Christ's voluntary death on the cross constituted a full satisfaction for the sins of the world. However, in our own more democratic age it is virtually impossible to share Anselm's medieval sense of wrongdoing as a slight upon God's honor that requires, before even the truly penitent can receive forgiveness, a satisfaction to assuage the divine honor and dignity. The entire conception, presupposing as it does a long-since vanished world, now makes no sense to us, and it would, in my view, be best to cease altogether to use it in our theologies and liturgies.

Another emphasis was introduced by the Reformers of the sixteenth century. They made the originally Pauline idea of justification central, understanding it in a legal sense, defined by Melanchthon as follows: "To justify, in accordance with forensic usage, here signifies to acquit the accused and to pronounce him righteous, but on account of the righteousness of another, namely of Christ, which righteousness of another is communicated to us by faith."[10] This legal concept of justification, and hence salvation, as being counted innocent in the eyes of God, emerged from the background of an understanding of law that has changed since Anselm's time. In the medieval world, law was an expression of the will of the ruler, and transgression was an act of personal disobedience and dishonor for which either punishment or satisfaction was required. But the concept of an objective justice, set over ruled and ruler alike, had been developing in Europe since the Renaissance. Law was thought to have its own eternal validity, requiring a punishment for wrongdoing that could not be set aside even by the ruler. It was this principle that the Reformers applied and extended in their doctrine that Christ took our place in bearing the inexorable divine penalty for human sin.

All of us who have been through a fundamentalist phase in our Christian life are familiar with the explanation, derived from the Reformers, that God, being just as well as loving, could not simply forgive even the truly penitent sinner, but in his mercy sent his Son to suffer the inevitable punishment in our stead.

> He died that we might be forgiven,
> He died to make us good,
> That we might go at last to heaven,
> Saved by his precious blood.
> There was no other good enough
> To pay the price of sin;
> He only could unlock the gate
> Of heaven and let us in.

Calvin points out that in order to prompt our imaginations to gratitude the scriptures tell the justified sinner that

> he was estranged from God through sin, is an heir of wrath, subject to the curse of eternal death, excluded from all hope of salvation, beyond every blessing of God, the slave of Satan, captive under the yoke of sin; destined finally for a dreadful destruction; and that at this point Christ interceded as his advocate, took upon himself and suffered the punishment that, from God's righteous judgment, threatened all sinners; that he purges with his blood those evils which had rendered sinners hateful to God; that by this expiation he make satisfaction and sacrifice duly to God the Father; that as intercessor he appeased God's wrath; that on this foundation rests the peace of God with men; that by this bond his benevolence is maintained toward them.[11]

It is hardly necessary today to criticize this penal-substitutionary conception, so totally implausible has it become to most of us. The idea that guilt can be removed from a wrongdoer by someone else being punished instead is morally grotesque. And if we put it in what might at first sight seem a more favorable light by suggesting that God punished himself, in the person of God the Son, in order to be able justly to forgive human sinners, we are still dealing with the religious absurdity of a moral law that God can and must satisfy by punishing the innocent in place of the guilty. As Anselm pointed out long ago, through the mouth of his interlocutor in *Cur Deus Homo?*, "it is a strange thing if God so delights in, or requires, the blood of the innocent, that he neither chooses, nor is able, to spare the guilty without the sacrifice of the innocent" (pt. I, chap. 10).

However, Richard Swinburne has recently made an impressive attempt, in his *Responsibility and Atonement*,[12] to retrieve a transactional conception. His understanding of salvation can be summarized as follows:

1. Guilt in relation to God is the great barrier to salvation, that is, to receiving God's gift of eternal life. (This is assumed throughout Swinburne's discussion.)
2. In the case of wrong done by one human being to another, reconciliation requires four things: repentance, apology, whatever reparation (i.e., undoing of the harm done) is possible, and penance, that is, some additional act—such as the giving of a costly gift—that is not part of the reparation but is an expression of the reality of one's regret and sorrow at having done the wrong.[13]
3. God is a personal being—though absolutely unique in nature—with whom we exist in the same kind of moral relationship as to our fellow human beings, and the same general conditions for reconciliation apply. (This is assumed throughout part II, though not explicitly stated.)
4. All wrong-doing to fellow humans is also wrong-doing done to God. For "Man's dependence on God is so total that he owes it to him to live a good life. Hence when a man fails in any objective or subjective duty of his fellows, he also fails in his duty towards God, his creator."[14]
5. We can repent and apologize to God for our sins, but we cannot on our own offer adequate atonement (i.e., reparation and penance). For "since what needs atonement to God is human sin, men living second-rate lives when they have been given such great opportunities by their creator, appropriate reparation and penance would be made by a perfect human life."[15]
6. That "perfect human life" is provided by Christ, who lived without sin and voluntarily endured a death that he openly intended as a sacrifice that we, accepting it from him, can offer to God as atonement for our sins, both individual and corporate. Christ's death is thus "an offering made available to us men to offer as our reparation and penance." "There is no need," Swinburne adds, "to suppose that life and death [of Christ's] to be the equivalent of what men owe to God (or that plus appropriate penance), however that could be measured. It is simply a costly penance and reparation sufficient for a merciful God to let men off the rest."[16]
7. To be sanctified and thus finally saved is only possible to those who (as well as repenting and apologizing) participate in the Christian worship of God and plead the atoning death of Christ, thereby throwing off their guilt. To be saved we must thus be joined—either in this life or hereafter—to the Christian church, which is the body of Christ.[17]

I think it must be granted that all this is possible, and indeed those of us who were once fundamentalist Christians, "washed in the blood of the Lamb," are likely to feel a certain emotional tug toward this set of ideas. The question is not, however, whether such a schema is logically possible, but whether it is religiously plausible; and to many of us today it is likely to seem highly implausible, even though also with elements of truth within it. I shall comment from this point of view on the seven points listed above.

Point 1. That the idea of salvation revolved around the issues of guilt and atonement is a central theme of the Latin theological tradition, launched by, above all, St. Augustine. The Greek tradition, on the other hand, stemming from the early Hellenistic fathers of the church and preserved within Eastern Orthodoxy, thinks of salvation as deification or (more precisely) transformation. Forgiveness is, of course, an element within this, but does not have the central place that the Latin tradition, followed by Swinburne at this point, gives to it. Swinburne prefers the Greek to the Latin development on a number of issues; but he does not seem to have considered the radical alternative that the Eastern theological trajectory offers. If one sees salvation/liberation as the transformation of human existence from self-centeredness to a new orientation centered in the ultimate divine reality, the transaction theories of salvation then appear as implausible answers to a mistaken question.

Point 2. Swinburne's analysis of guilt and reconciliation between human beings is excellent; this is one of the "elements of truth," as it will seem to more liberal Christians, within his total theory.

Point 3. That God is another person, with unique attributes but subject to the same moral requirements as ourselves, and thus with obligations and duties and possibilities of supererogatory deeds; that God's probable procedures can be predicted by means of a human analogy; and that the proper human analogy leads to the belief that God's saving work is confined in its fullness to the Christian strand of history, strikes me as anthropomorphic, parochial, and unimaginative to a degree that renders it massively implausible. But I shall say more under point 5 about Swinburne's transfer of the conditions for reconciliation with a fellow human being to reconciliation with God.

Point 4. That our relationship to fellow human beings involves our relationship to God, so that in all that we do we are also ultimately having to do with God is, from a more liberal point of view, another "element of truth" within Swinburne's theory.

Point 5. When we do wrong, the kind of reparation required is that we do what we can to nullify or reverse the consequences of our action. Thus when we contribute—as we do almost all the time—to the common evils of the world, we can do something to counter this by contributing to the common good of the world. When we wrong an individual we can usually do something to recompense the person wronged. And, as Swinburne points out, in such a case it is also appropriate to do something extra, which he calls penance, by offering some additional service or gift to express the reality of our regret and sorrow at having wronged the other person. But the question that has to be asked is whether this fourfold schema—repentance, apology, reparation, and penance—can be carried over unchanged into our relationship with God. Swinburne's fundamental error, in my view, is in assuming that it can. Repentance, and apology as an expression of repentance, still apply; the sinner should truly and deeply repent and ask God's forgiveness. But is there also scope, specifically in relation to God, for reparation and the extra that Swinburne calls penance? I suggest that when we have offered reparation-plus-penance to the human beings whom we have injured, there is no further reparation-plus-penance to be made solely for God's benefit. In doing all we can to repair matters with our wronged neighbor we are doing what genuine repentance requires. For God cannot be benefited, and thus recompensed and atoned to, by any human acts in addition to those that benefit God's creation. In relation to God the truly penitent person, genuinely resolving to do better in the future, can only accept forgiveness as a free gift of grace, undeserved and unearned. It may well be Jesus' life and teachings that prompt someone to do this. But it is not, in my view, appropriate to express that fact by depicting his death as an atoning sacrifice that benefits God and so enables God to forgive humanity.

Swinburne emphasizes that "one man can help another to make the necessary atonement—can persuade him to repent, help him to formulate the words of apology, and give him the means by which to make reparation and penance."[18] True; and likewise the divine Spirit may prompt us to a true repentance that wants to make reparation to the human individual or community that we have wronged and to offer any additional service or gift that may be appropriate. But what the Spirit will thus prompt us to do is some act in relation to those human neighbors. It is this that satisfies the principle, which Swinburne rightly stresses, that to take a wrongdoer and his or her wrongdoing seriously entails the need for whatever restitution and whatever additional gift or service is appropriate. But the idea that something further, corresponding to this reparation-plus-penance toward our human neighbor, is required by God for himself seems to me groundless. It rests upon a category mistake in which God is treated as another individual within the same moral community as ourselves. For a moral relationship with another person presupposes the possibility of actions that can benefit or injure that other person, but we cannot benefit or injure our Creator over and above our actions in benefiting and injuring our fellow creatures.

Further, even if, despite this, a benefit solely to God were possible and required, Swinburne's unargued assumption that a perfect human life would constitute it is, surely, illogical. A perfect life, fulfilling every "objective and subjective duty," is already, according to Swinburne, owed by all of us to God, and therefore could not constitute a reparation-plus-penance for not having lived a perfect life in the past. And yet again, even if *per impossibile* it could, how would one single perfect human life, namely that of Jesus, count as all human beings having led perfect lives? Swinburne's answer at this point it that God was free to accept whatever

God wished as an atonement for human sin. "God could," he says, "have chosen to accept one supererogatory act of an ordinary man as adequate for the sins of the world. Or he could have chosen to accept some angel's act for this purpose."[19] This is a deeply damaging admission, rendering it truly extraordinary that God should require the agonizing death of his Son. For on Swinburne's view there was no necessity for the cross, such as was provided in their own way by the satisfaction and penal-substitutionary theories. Swinburne is abandoning the idea of a moral law that could only be satisfied by Jesus' death. For it was, according to him, entirely within God's free choice to establish the conditions for human salvation. But in that case, God's insistence on the blood, sweat, pain, and anguish involved in the crucifixion of his innocent Son now seems to cast doubt—to say the least—on the moral character of the deity.

Point 6. Swinburne says several times that Jesus openly intended his death as "an offering to God to make expiation in some way for the sins of men."[20] There is, in fact, no consensus among New Testament scholars as to how Jesus understood his own death. To what extent did he think of it as having religious significance? There is a range of possibilities. A (theologically) minimalist view is expressed by E. P. Sanders. He lists it as "conceivable"[21] or even "possible"[22] (in distinction from "probable," "highly probable" or "virtually certain") that Jesus "may have given his own death a martyrological significance."[23] Acknowledging, indeed emphasizing, the historical uncertainties, he notes that "the idea that a martyr's death is beneficial for others and that his cause will be vindicated is attested in Judaism ... It is not necessary to assume that Jesus indicated to his followers that they should think in this way. Once he died, it probably seemed entirely natural to attribute benefit to his death and look for vindication."[24]

At the other end of the scale is the older view of Joachim Jeremias, developed in his influential treatment of the Last Supper. He recalls that a lamb was killed at the original Passover and its blood smeared, at Yahweh's command, on the Israelites' doors:

> As a reward for the Israelites' obedience to the commandment to spread blood on their doors, God manifested himself and spared them, "passing over" their houses. For the sake of the passover blood God revoked the death sentence against Israel; he said: "I will see the blood of the passover and make atonement for you." In the same way the people of God of the End time will be redeemed by the merits of the passover blood. Jesus describes his death as this eschatological passover sacrifice: his vicarious death brings into operation the final deliverance, the new covenant of God.[25]

And Jeremias concludes, "This is therefore what Jesus said at the Last Supper about the meaning of his death: his death is the vicarious death of the suffering servant, which atones for the sins of the 'many', the peoples of the world, which ushers in the beginning of the final salvation and which effects the new covenant with God."[26]

On Jeremias's interpretation we have to suppose that Jesus, in the words of E. P. Sanders, "conceived in advance the doctrine of atonement,"[27] a supposition that Sanders regards as historically highly improbable. "Aspects of Jeremias' view, for example that Jesus identified himself with the Suffering Servant of Isaiah, have," he says, "been disproved, but there are general objections to the whole line of thought that has Jesus intending to die for others, rather than just accepting his death and trusting that God would redeem the situation and vindicate him."[28] However, let us nevertheless, for the sake of argument, suppose that Jesus did understand his coming death as a sacrifice to God, analogous to the original Passover sacrifice, and that he thought of this as required to inaugurate God's coming kingdom. Such a self-understanding could only occur within the context of Jesus' apocalyptic expectation, which was itself a variation on contemporary Jewish restoration eschatology. But Jesus' expectation, confidently taken up by the early church, was not fulfilled, and had faded out of the Christian consciousness before the end of the first century. The identification of Jesus as the eschatological prophet inaugurating God's Kingdom went with it, being progressively superseded by his exaltation to a divine status. This in turn made possible the various atonement theories that presuppose his divinity, eventually seeing the cross as (in the words of the Anglican liturgy) "a full, perfect, and sufficient sacrifice, oblation, and satisfaction, for the sins of the whole world." However, even conservative New Testament scholarship today does not suggest that Jesus thought of himself as God, or God the Son, second person of a divine Trinity incarnate, and so we cannot reasonably suppose that he thought of his death in any way that presupposes that. It is therefore much more believable, as a maximal possibility, that Jesus saw himself as the final prophet precipitating the coming of God's rule on earth than that he saw himself in anything like the terms later developed by the church's subsequent atonement theories.

Incidentally, it is noteworthy that Swinburne departs from the traditional view that the value of Jesus' death was equal to, or exceeded, the evil of human sin, so as to be able to balance it. Swinburne says that "it is simply a costly penance and reparation sufficient for a merciful God to let men off the rest."[29] But if a merciful God can properly "let men off the rest" without a full punishment having been inflicted or a full satisfaction exacted, why may not God freely forgive sinners who come in genuine penitence and a radically changed mind? The traditional atonement theories explained *why* God could not freely forgive penitent sinners. But what was intelligible—whether or not acceptable—on those theories becomes unintelligible, and doubly morally questionable, on Swinburne's view.

Point 7. Swinburne also modifies the traditional exclusivist doctrine that salvation is confined to Christians, so that *extra ecclesiam nulla salus*, by adding that non-Christians may have an opportunity to be converted beyond this life. This epicycle of theory, although departing from established teachings about the finality of death, is the only refuge left for one who is in general a doctrinal fundamentalist but who does not wish to have to defend a manifestly morally repugnant position.

I thus do not find in the least attractive or convincing this latest attempt to rehabilitate the conception of salvation as being brought about by Jesus' death as an atonement to God for human sin.

The basic fault, as I see it, of the traditional understandings of salvation within the Western development of Christianity is that they have no room for divine forgiveness! For a forgiveness that has to be bought by the bearing of a just punishment, or the giving of an adequate satisfaction, or the offering of a sufficient sacrifice, is not forgiveness at all but merely an acknowledgment that the debt has been paid in full. But in the recorded teachings of Jesus there is, in contrast, genuine divine forgiveness for those who are truly penitent and deeply aware of their own utter unworthiness. In the Lord's Prayer we are taught to address God directly as our heavenly Father and to ask for forgiveness for our sins, expecting to receive this, the only condition being that we in turn forgive one another. There is no suggestion of the need for a mediator through whom to approach God or of an atoning death to enable God to forgive. Again, in the Lukan parable of the prodigal son, the father, when he sees his penitent son returning home, does not say, "because I am a just as well as a loving father, I cannot forgive him until someone has been duly punished for his sins," but rather he

> had compassion, and ran, and fell on his neck, and kissed him. And the son said unto to him, Father, I have sinned against heaven, and in thy sight, and am no more worthy to be called thy son. But the father said to his servants, Bring forth the best robe, and put it on him; and put a ring on his hand, and shoes on his feet: and bring hither the fatted calf, and kill it; and let us eat and be merry: For this my son was dead and is alive again; he was lost, and is found (Luke 15: 20–24).

And again, in the Lukan parable of the Pharisee and the publican, the latter "standing afar off, would not lift up so much as his eyes unto heaven, but smote upon his breast, saying, God be merciful to me a sinner. I tell you, this man went down to his house justified" (Luke 18:13–14). And yet again, there is the insistence that Jesus came to bring sinners to a penitent acceptance of God's mercy: "go ye and learn what that meaneth, I will have mercy, and not sacrifice: for I am not come to call the righteous, but sinners to repentance" (Matthew 9:13).

This was fully in accord with contemporary Judaic understanding. E. P. Sanders, in his authoritative work on Jesus' Jewish background, says that "the forgiveness of repentant sinners is a major motif in virtually all the Jewish material which is still available from the period;"[30] and it continues today in this prayer from the service on the Day of Atonement:

> O do thou, in thy abounding compassion, have mercy upon us, for thou delightest not in the destruction of the world ... And it is said, Let the wicked forsake his ways, and

the man of iniquity his thoughts; and let him return unto the Lord, and he will have mercy upon him; and to our God for he will abundantly pardon. But thou art a God ready to forgive, gracious and merciful, slow to anger, plenteous in loving kindness, and abounding in goodness; thou delightest in the repentance of the wicked and hast no pleasure in their death ... turn ye, turn ye from your evil ways; for why will ye die, O house of Israel? And it is said, Have I at all any pleasure in the death of the wicked, sayeth the Lord God, and not rather that he should return from his way, and live?

For Judaism sees human nature as basically good and yet also with an evil inclination that has continually to be resisted. However, God is aware of our finitude and weakness, and is always ready to forgive the truly penitent. In Islam there is an essentially similar view. God is always spoken of in the Qur'an as *Allah rahman rahim,* God the gracious and merciful. God knows our weaknesses and forgives those who, in the self-surrender of faith, bow before the compassionate Lord of the universe. Again, in the most widely influential of the Hindu scriptures, the *Bhagavad Gila,* we read,

> There I bow down, prostrate and ask for pardon:
> Now forgive me, God, as friend forgives his comrade,
> Father forgives son, and man his dearest lover.[31]

This sense of divine mercy is indeed found throughout the world's monotheistic faiths, with the Latin Christian belief in the need for an atoning death standing out as exceptional. Indeed, within modem Protestant thought, outside the continuing fundamentalist stream, there has been a general acceptance of the idea of a free divine forgiveness for those who truly repent. In an attempt to reconcile this with the traditional language about Jesus' death as the instrument of our salvation, various "moral influence" theories have been proposed in the modem period. Their essence is admirably expressed in the old preachers' story about the tribal chief who urges his people to abandon cannibalism. When his urgings are ineffective he tells them that if they must kill someone, they should go to a certain clearing the next day at dawn and kill the man they find there wrapped in a red blanket. They do so, and on opening the blanket find that they have killed their own beloved chieftain, and they are so struck with remorse that they are at last motivated to give up their cannibalism. Likewise, it is suggested, remorse at having crucified the Son of God can lead to repentance and hence God's forgiveness. Thus the liberal theologian Auguste Sabatier wrote that Jesus' passion and death "was the most powerful call to repentance that humanity has ever heard, and also the most operative and fruitful in marvellous results. The cross is the expiation of sins only because it is the cause of the repentance to which remission is promised."[32]

This is no longer a transactional conception of atonement, and indeed is no longer a conception of atonement, in the sense of expiation, at all. It is rather a suggestion about how Jesus' death may have helped to make salvation possible. The limitation of this suggestion is that remorse at having (collectively) killed God the Son can only be felt by that minority of human beings who believe that Jesus of Nazareth was indeed the second person of a divine Trinity. The notion, which the older satisfaction and penal-substitutionary theories made possible, of an atonement offered on behalf of all humanity, is here lost. The moral influence conception of atonement is in fact one of those theological epicycles by which it is sought to abandon an untenable traditional idea—in this case the transaction conception of salvation—while at the same time retaining the traditional language.

We can now move from a critique of the Western/Latin understanding of salvation as hinging upon sin and guilt, and as requiring the atoning sacrifice of Christ, to build upon the work of the Hellenistic fathers, treating this, however, not as a fully developed theological option, but as a movement of thought that can be continued today.

For Christianity is richer and more varied than most Christians, immersed within their own particular strand of it, have commonly been aware. Thus those of us formed by Western Christianity or its missionary extensions are often ignorant of the rather different Eastern development of Christian thought. The Orthodox Churches themselves, which are guardians of this tradition, have remained more or less moribund, both theologically and ecclesiastically, for many centuries; and I am not advocating acceptance of their total theological package. But buried in their history there is the groundwork of a profound and attractive alternative to the medieval theology of the Roman Church as well as that of the sixteenth-century Reformers and their successors. The difference is between salvation as hinging upon an atoning transaction that enables God to forgive and to accept the fallen human race, and salvation as the gradual transformation of human beings, who are already in the "image" of God, into what the Hellenistic fathers, on the basis of Genesis 1:26, called the "likeness" of God. Thus in the eighth century, John of Damascus wrote: "The expression 'according to the image' indicates rationality and freedom, whilst the expression 'according to the likeness' indicates assimilation to God through virtue."[33] This "assimilation to God" was also frequently called *theosis* (deification). In the words of the seventh-century Byzantine theologian Maximus the Confessor, "A man who becomes obedient to God in all things hears God saying 'I said: you are gods' (John 10:34); he then is God and is called 'God' not by nature or by relation but by [divine] decree and grace."[34] Accordingly, to quote a contemporary Orthodox writer, "The Christian faith ... is understood to lead to the transfiguration and 'deification' of the entire man; and ... this 'deification' is indeed accessible, as a living experience, even now, and not merely in a future kingdom."[35] It is this actual human transformation, or "deification," that constitutes salvation. Thus while in the Latin view, to be saved is to be justified, that is, relieved of guilt, by Christ's sacrificial death, in the Orthodox view, to be in process of salvation is to be responding to the presence of the divine Spirit and thus undergoing a gradual transformation from natural self-centeredness to a radically new centering within the divine life. It should be noted that this Eastern understanding largely coincides with the modem "liberal" Western approach initiated in the nineteenth century by Friedrich Schleiermacher, who viewed the saving influence of Christ in the context of God's total creative work, so that Christ's "every activity may be regarded as a continuation of that person-forming divine influence upon the human nature."[36]

In Orthodox thought the deification theme is embedded in a comprehensive theology in which the ideas of incarnation and Trinity are central elements and in which the resurrected Christ plays a vital role in the process of transformation. That role was, however, only described in broad metaphorical terms. Thus Athanasius said that humans "could not become sons, being by nature creatures, otherwise than by receiving the Spirit of the natural and true Son. Wherefore, that this might be, 'The Word became flesh' that He might make man capable of Godhead,"[37] and again, "He was made man that we might be made God."[38] But the way in which God becoming human enables humans to become divine was not spelled out. Indeed, it perhaps cannot be intelligibly spelled out other than in terms of the experience, known within all religious traditions, of being influenced and changed by the life and words of a great exemplar. There is perhaps a continuity here with what Adolf Deissmann called St. Paul's "mysticism,"[39] with humans undergoing a transformation (*metamorphosis*) in Christ, for we "are being changed into [Christ's] likeness from one degree of glory to another" (II Corinthians 3:18). We are to be transformed from the state of slavery into the state of sonship (Romans 8:15–17), or again, conformed (*symmorphosis*) to the image of Christ (Romans 8:29). "Do not be conformed to the world," Paul urges the Christians in Rome, "but be transformed by the renewal of your mind" (Paul 2:12). And, indeed, we may say that to be a Christian is to be one in whose life Christ is the major, the largest single, influence (often among a variety of influences) for salvific transformation.

Jesus' death has indeed played no small part in this influence. Although the meaning of that death was pictured during most of the first Christian millennium in the crude ransom imagery, and during most of the second millennium in terms of the morally questionable satisfaction and penal-substitution theories, the cross has continued throughout as the central Christian symbol because it stirs deeper and more complex emotions than are captured by any of these official doctrines. For many people it is a self-evident intuition that an authentic religious leader is willing, if necessary, to be martyred by those who fail to recognize or accept the challenging truths that he or she embodies. It is indeed because true prophets and gurus embody, or live out, or incarnate, their teachings that to reject the message is to reject the messenger, and the most emphatic form of rejection is by inflicting death. To illustrate this from recent history, in the moral and political conflicts of India and the United States in the twentieth century there was a certain tragic appropriateness in the fact that Gandhi and Martin Luther King, teaching the universal requirements of love and justice, were assassinated by fanatics motivated by religious and racial prejudice. On the same principle there was a tragic appropriateness in the death of Jesus. He taught the way of life of God's Kingdom, and the imminent coming of that Kingdom on earth. This was to the ruling Roman power a potential incitement to rise up against it in the name of God, as was to happen in 66–70 CE and again in 135 CE. He also prophesied the destruction of the Jerusalem temple, thus deeply antagonizing its priestly guardians, who collaborated in his arrest and trial. But these historical factors were soon submerged in the Christian consciousness by a religious understanding of the crucifixion. Jesus' acceptance of his death as having some positive meaning inevitably evoked, in the thought world of his time, the universal language of sacrifice. In the Judaism of Jesus' period, a sacrifice made as a sin offering to God involved the shedding of blood as a giving of the life essence. However, as a cumulative result of the teachings of Jesus, as well as of Hosea and Amos before him and many others after him, can we not now see that the sacrifice of animal or human blood pointed, in a crude and inadequate way, to the much deeper sacrifice of the ego point of view in becoming a channel of divine grace on earth? The real meaning of Jesus' death was not that his blood was shed—indeed crucifixion did not involve much bloodshed—but that he gave himself utterly to God in faith and trust. His cross was thus a powerful manifestation and continuing symbol of the Divine Kingdom in this present world, as a way of life in which one turns the other cheek, forgives one's enemies "unto seventy times seven," trusts God even in the darkness of pain, horror, and tragedy, and is continually raised again to the new life of faith.

Yet even this does not exhaust the felt impact of Jesus' death. For the voluntary death of a holy person has a moral power that reverberates beyond any words that we frame to express it. Even on a lower level, when someone knowingly gives his or her life for the sake of another—say, in a rescue from a fire or avalanche or bomb or an oncoming train or car, or in some other way—something has happened that is awe-inspiring and, in an indefinable way, enriching and enhancing to the human community. And so it was, in a much greater way, with the death of Jesus. This is no doubt why the mythological pictures of a ransom paid to the Devil, or of a sacrifice to appease the divine honor or justice, were able to last so long. For since we cannot fully articulate the impression made upon us by the crucifixion of one who was so close to God, no ecclesiastical language about it has been ruled out as too strange or extravagant.

Nevertheless, we have to insist that these ecclesiastical theories are all misleading. It is misleading to think that there is a Devil with legitimate rights over against God. It is misleading to think of the heavenly Father on the model of a feudal lord or a stern cosmic moralist. And it is misleading to see an acceptance of the Christian mythology of the cross as the only way to salvation for all human beings. Let the voluntary sacrifice of a holy life continue to challenge and inspire us in a way that transcends words. But let us not reduce its meaning to any culture-bound theological theory.

To summarize and conclude: Jesus' death was of a piece with his life, expressing a total integrity in his self-giving to God, and his cross continues to inspire and challenge us on a level that in no way depends upon atonement theories developed by the church. Those theories have no doubt helped people in the past to rationalize the immense impact upon them of the cross of Christ, and they did so in ways that cohered with the plausibility structures of their time. But our own intellectual world is so different, both within the church and without, that those traditional atonement theories no longer perform any useful function.

▓ NOTES

1. This essay was originally published in Stephen T. Davis, *Philosophy and Theological Discourse* (London: Macmillan, 1996), reproduced with the permission of Palgrave Macmillan.

2. Origen, *In Matt.*, xvi. 8, quoted by L. W. Grensted, *A Short History of the Doctrine of the Atonement* (Manchester: Manchester University Press, 1962), 38.

3. Gregory of Nyssa, "The Great Catechism, Chapter 24," in the *Nicene and Ante-Nicene Fathers*, Series II, vol. V, p. 494. Cf. Rufinus, *Comm. in Symb. Ap. 16.*

4. St. Augustine, Sermon 130, quoted by Grensted, *A Short History*, 44.

5. Anselm, *Cur Deus Homo?*, pt. I, chap. 7.

6. Grensted, *A Short History*, 33. What Gustav Aulen called the "classic" theory of atonement, according to which Christ was victor over the Devil, seems to me to be a variation on the ransom model rather than an alternative theory. "Its central theme," says Aulen, "is the idea of the Atonement as a Divine conflict and victory; Christ—Christus Victor—fights against and triumphs over the evil powers of the world, the 'tyrants' under which mankind is in bondage and suffering" (*Christus Victor*, trans. A. G. Herbert [London: SPCK, 1953], 20).

7. *Denzinger*, 788f.

8. W. K. Clifford, *Lectures and Essays*, Vol. I, (1901), 221.

9. Anselm, *Cur Deus Homo?*, chapter 11, in S. N. Deane's *St. Anselm: Basic Writings*, trans. J. G. Vose (Lasalle, IL: Open Course Publishing, 1962), 202.

10. Melanchthon, *Apol. Con/. Aug.*, p. 125, quoted by Grensted, *A Short History*, 193.

11. Calvin, *Institutes of the Christian Religion*, Book II, chap. 16, para. 2, trans. Ford Lewis Battles, *The Library of Christian Classics*, vol. XX (London: SCM Press, 1961), 505.

12. Richard Swinburne, *Responsibility and Atonement* (Oxford: Clarendon Press, 1989).

13. Swinburne, *Responsibility and Atonement*, chap. 5.

14. Swinburne, *Responsibility and Atonement*, 124.

15. Swinburne, *Responsibility and Atonement*, 157.

16. Swinburne, *Responsibility and Atonement*, 154.

17. Swinburne, *Responsibility and Atonement*, 173.

18. Swinburne, *Responsibility and Atonement*, 149.

19. Swinburne, *Responsibility and Atonement*, 160.

20. Swinburne, *Responsibility and Atonement*, 122.

21. E. P. Sanders, *Jesus and Judaism* (London: SCM Press, 1985), 326.

22. Sanders, *Jesus and Judaism*, 332.

23. Sanders, *Jesus and Judaism*, 326.

24. Sanders, *Jesus and Judaism*, 324–325.

25. Joachim Jeremias, *The Eucharistic Words of Jesus*, trans. Norman Perrin (London: SCM Press, 1966), 226.

26. Jeremias, *The Eucharistic Words of Jesus*, 231.

27. Sanders, *Jesus and Judaism*, 332.

28. Sanders, *Jesus and Judaism*, 332.

29. Swinburne, *Responsibility and Atonement*, 154.

30. Sanders, *Jesus and Judaism*, 18.

31. *Bhagavad Gila*, trans. Swami Prabhavananda and Christopher Isherwood.

32. Auguste Sabatier, *The Doctrine of the Atonement*, trans. Victor Leuliette (London: Williams & Norgate, 1904), 127.

33. John of Damascus, *On the Orthodox Faith*, II.12.

34. Maximus the Confessor, *Ambigua*, cited by John Meyendorff, *Byzantine Theology* (New York: Fordham University Press, 1987), 164.

35. Meyendorff, *Byzantine Theology*, 125.

36. Freidrich Schleiennacher, *The Christian Faith*, trans. H. R. Mackintosh and J. S. Stewart (Edinburgh: T & T Clark, 1956), 427.

37. Athanasius, *Discourses Against the Arians*, discourse II, chap. 21, para. 59, trans. in *The Nicene and Post-Nicene Fathers*, vol. IV, p. 380.

38. Anthanasius, *On the Incarnation of the Word of God*, para. 54, trans. in *The Nicene and Post-Nicene Fathers*, vol. IV, p. 65.

39. Adolf Deissmann, *The Religion of Jesus and the Faith of Paul*, 2nd ed., trans. William E. Wilson (London: Hodder & Stoughton, 1926), 193f.

■ FOR FURTHER READING

Finlan, S. *Problems with Atonement: The Origins of, and Controversy about, the Atonement Doctrine*. Collegeville, MN: Liturgical Press, 2005.

Green, J. B. *Recovering the Scandal of the Cross: Atonement in New Testament and Contemporary Contexts*. Downers Grove, IL: InterVarsity Press, 2000.

Heim, M. S. *Saved From Sacrifice: A Theology of the Cross*. Grand Rapids, MI: Eerdmans, 2006.

Hick, J. *The Metaphor of God Incarnate: Christology in a Pluralistic Age*, 2nd ed. London: SCM Press, 2005.

Sanders, E. P. *Jesus and Judaism*. London: SCM Press, 1985.

The Incarnation

29 An Anselmian Defense of the Incarnation

■ KATHERIN A. ROGERS

The claim that God became man is bizarre—if true it points to an event that is unimaginably strange and absolutely sui generis. Since the claim was first made, many have argued that it is unreasonable to believe it. Here, drawing on the work of St. Anselm of Canterbury, I respond to that charge, making the modest case that belief in the relevant testimony is not obviously foolish given certain background assumptions and that the particular criticisms I address can be adequately answered. (An overall defense beginning with the demanding task of defining "reasonable" and explaining when, in general, it is reasonable to believe any claim, lies outside the scope of this chapter.) After a brief glance at why one might believe that God became man, I turn to three sorts of arguments raised by Michael Martin that purport to show that the very idea is incoherent.[1] First, it is said to be impossible that a single person could be both God and man since a single person could not have conflicting divine and human attributes. Second, were there a God-man, He could not possibly be Jesus as the Bible portrays Him. Third, the point of the Incarnation is said to be "for our salvation," but theories of how this is accomplished are fundamentally incoherent—or at best inexplicable and arbitrary. My defense will be "Anselmian" in that it presupposes Anselm's classical theism and it will draw on specifically Anselmian elements regarding the nature and purpose of the Incarnation, with special attention to Anselm's understanding of the value of human freedom. My discussion should support the case that individual questions concerning the Incarnation are most profitably considered, not as isolated issues, but rather within a systematic and well-developed theory of the nature of God and the relationship of God to creation in general and humanity in particular.

Why believe that God became man? St. Peter and the earliest Christians seem to have come to believe it based on what Jesus said and did. In 451 AD the Council of Chalcedon adopted the statement that would be accepted as orthodox—Christ is one person with two natures. The statement followed the letter Pope Leo the Great wrote to Flavian, patriarch of Constantinople, and Pope Leo appealed to the testimony of the earliest Christians and the interpretation put upon it by subsequent generations under the guidance of the Holy Spirit. Presumably, like Pope Leo and those who attended the Council of Chalcedon, most who believe in the Incarnation do so as a matter of faith, that is on the basis of someone's testimony. By a traditional definition of "faith" such as that offered by St. Augustine, we all believe most of what we believe on faith, and we could not function as human beings if we did not.[2] We "take on faith" whatever we believe about history that we have not witnessed for ourselves, about lands and peoples we have not visited, and about scientific claims we have not proven for ourselves—science, in practice, is a faith-based enterprise, and could not make progress if it weren't. But, of course, there is testimony and testimony, and some it would be foolish to accept. Is faith in the Incarnation silly? Is it like believing in bracelets that cure all ills and in pills that make you lose a lot of weight quickly, easily, safely, and permanently? How can we adjudicate between the trustworthy testimony and the testimony that should be rejected?

One approach is to assess the probability of the claim in question against the background of our other beliefs. How might this work in the case of the Incarnation?[3] The question of the reasonableness of believing in the Incarnation can properly arise if you take it that there exists a God who acts as an agent in the world. On the assumption that there is no such God, the epistemic probability of the Incarnation is nil. But suppose that you are convinced—perhaps by some combination of the moral argument and the argument from design—that there is a good God who has a care for the world. The world is a beautiful place and God takes an interest in it down to the smallest detail.[4] On this assumption the occurrence of the occasional miracle is not obviously improbable. You may doubt some particular report, but you have no reason to suppose that the good God who takes an interest in the world would not produce an unusual effect now and again.

But given this basic view of the world and its Maker, you may conclude that there is something very odd in the human condition. Human beings have wonderful talents and brilliant capacities, and yet something seems to have gone badly wrong with us from the beginning. Look at human history and what you see is a surprising amount of wickedness, different in quantity and quality from what you might expect from the evolution of a primate as a natural outgrowth of the struggle to survive. Auschwitz is not an instance of a typical predator or a competitive breeder going about his business. And looking within you may note that there is a tendency within yourself to do bad things that is in excess of any natural function—in fact, it makes you unlovely and miserable. Call this appreciation of the apparently ubiquitous failing in humanity, especially in yourself, the sense of sin.[5] If there is a good God who made human beings and takes an interest in them, and if things have gone badly wrong with humanity, then God *ought to do something about it!* Given these background beliefs, the Incarnation does not seem obviously improbable. When you consider the testimony that God has become a man in order to save us from our sins you might reasonably say to yourself, "Well, I thought He would do *something*. I guess this is it!"[6]

The critic, such as Martin, may respond that you have not really considered what the Incarnation entails. The Chalcedonian claim is that Christ is a single person with two natures, a divine and a human nature, "which undergo no confusion, no change, no division, no separation."[7] But some of the attributes of a divine nature seem to be logically incompatible with attributes of a human nature. For example, a single person cannot be both omnipotent and limited in power, can he?[8] Yet if Jesus is indeed the Son of God, then He is identical with the Word, "but given the principle of the indiscernibility of identicals—if two things are identical then they have all of their properties in common—an obvious logical absurdity can be generated: Jesus, the Son of God, both has and does not have certain attributes."[9]

The traditional answer to this problem, the one given by St. Anselm among many others, is that Christ can be said to have certain attributes qua divine and others qua human.[10] But *how*, if Christ is a single person? Elsewhere I propose an analogy that, though distant, is nonetheless helpful in addressing the qua move. Moreover, looking at where the analogy fails can help in discussing other difficulties with the Incarnation. The analogy is Nick Playing, a boy playing a video game; Nick, the actual boy sitting in front of the screen, is analogous to the second person of the Trinity. He is playing a character on the screen, Virtual Nick, which is analogous to the human body and soul of Christ.[11] To improve the analogy the game should perhaps be a first-person player game. The player sees the action in the first person, for example, seeing only his own virtual arms and hands and (occasionally) feet and legs. If there are other players they see the character from a third-person perspective as a whole figure. Nick Playing is analogous to Christ, God having assumed the human body and soul.

This analogy suggests ("captures" is too strong a word) at least four important points that contemporary literature on the metaphysics of the Incarnation often fails to appreciate. First, and most importantly, classical theism holds that there is a radical difference in the ontological status of God and the human being. Anselm, in the neoplatonic tradition, used the language of "levels of being." God is the absolute existent on which all else depends, such that creatures have a "thin" and reflected sort of being. (Those who eschew that language can still appreciate the radical difference between God, the source of all who keeps everything that is not Himself in being from moment to moment, and the creature that exists in absolute dependence on the Creator.) The "thinness" and the utter dependence of Virtual Nick suggest the much more radical ontological separation of God and man.

Second, based on this dependence relationship, all the causal efficacy in the "composite" that is the Incarnation is on the side of the Son. I put "composite" in scare quotes because, though it seems an appropriate word, it might bring to the mind of the metaphysically literate philosopher the various popular theories and examples dealing with material composites. Some philosophers of religion, adopting composite accounts of the Incarnation to defend the qua move, appeal to these theories and examples and thus open their analyses of the Incarnation to difficulties that could have been avoided.[12] Nick could not be playing without Virtual Nick, but all the action is up to Nick. (Nick, of course, needs all the electronics, hardware, software, etc., so he is a much more limited cause than God.) Third, the analogy makes the useful suggestion that God incarnate is God doing something. Nick Playing is Nick doing something where Virtual Nick and Nick are both active, but the source of the action is Nick. If Christ is a composite, He is not a composite where the two parts can equally "sit there" like a cat with its tail. Christ is a composite because of the activity of the Son. Fourth, Christ's human nature—the human body and soul—exists only as Christ's human nature. In the contemporary literature it is sometimes supposed that there is some separate and discreet human individual that the Son grabs and adds to Himself. But no. That would mean either that there are now two people in the Incarnation or that this separate individual was destroyed by being assumed—neither of which is acceptable. Even discussion of what status the human body and soul would have if they (or better, "it," since they form an organic unity) were not assumed is incoherent. Virtual Nick, the first-person character, is Nick's character and does not exist unless being played by Nick.

How does this help with the qua move? Take the example of power.[13] Nick, as Nick Playing, can accomplish various first-person activities in the game through Virtual Nick—mainly running around and shooting. The other characters in the game (say that they are "mere" characters and not characters being played by other actual people) do that, too. But Nick can also do all kinds of things that no mere video game character can do. He can—playing or not—eat a three-dimensional cookie, for example. His extravirtual power can manifest itself in the game as well. Let us say that the game controls in the actual (three-dimensional world) allow the player to move the elements in the game around almost at will—though still within certain game constraints. Nick cannot make an element in the game become three-dimensional, for example. But his status as actual in the three-dimensional world means that with the mere touch of a (three-dimensional) button he can levitate a virtual tree, blink a building out of being, blink a tank into being, and even turn the whole game off (again assuming he's playing by himself). Nick, let us say, has "transcendent power" in that his capabilities far exceed what the characters in the video game can do. Virtual Nick, considered as a character, does not have transcendent power. He can only do what video game characters do. But suppose it would help Virtual Nick, in his running and shooting, if a bridge appeared. Nick Playing can see to it because Nick has transcendent power. Qua Nick, Nick Playing has transcendent power, although qua Virtual Nick, Nick Playing does not have transcendent power. Nick's transcendent power is not circumscribed by Virtual Nick's limitations—the bridge appears! And that makes sense because the causal efficacy in the composite came from Nick to begin with. And this is analogous to the Anselmian understanding of the Incarnation. Christ is omnipotent, not through

His human nature, but through His divine nature. This does entail that the single person who is the Son and Jesus of Nazareth is omnipotent. Jesus could blink the universe out of being if He chose to—not in virtue of His human body and soul, but in virtue of being God incarnate. Weird. But that was to be expected.

But now a different sort of question arises. Martin argues that the biblical Jesus does not seem to be omnipotent. True, He works miracles, but they are limited and local. If He were omnipotent (and knew it), might He not have done more amazing things: "changed the course of the stars and not merely stilled the storm? Would he have cured all the sick people of Judea and not just some of those he came in contact with? Would he have made wine from nothing and not just changed water into wine? Would he have floated through the air and not just walked on the water?"[14] But first it should be remembered that belief that Jesus was God incarnate is reasonable only for someone who holds the belief in a good, designing, agent God. If there is such a God, then, with or without the Incarnation, there is an omnipotent (or at least transcendently powerful) person in the universe capable of changing the stars in their courses and curing everyone on the planet of their diseases. He does not do so presumably because He does not want to.[15] That He incarnates as Jesus would not entail that He would change His mind about how best to govern the universe.[16]

Second, there is a very interesting consistency to Jesus' miracles that ties in with Anselm's assessment of the relationship of the human creature to His Creator. Anselm is perhaps the first philosopher to expound a systematic and well-developed theory of libertarian freedom. Human beings must choose between open options because that is the only way for a creature, which exists in absolute dependence on its Creator, to will the good from itself (*a se*). And in having this aseity the human agent can be a true image of God. Thus Anselm grants to the human being a very exalted metaphysical stature. Although ontologically we are radically distant from God, we are true images, even to the point of exercising some causal power over how things go in the universe.[17] Here is one place where the video game analogy fails. Video game characters do not have free will! In almost every instance where Jesus works a miracle (there are a few exceptions, but *very* few) he is responding to someone's request, either on their own behalf or on behalf of a friend or loved one. This pattern fits well with the Anselmian view in which God has set up the system so that human agents initiate action and contribute to the course of events. Thus there is no reason to expect more startling miracles from an omnipotent Jesus, and there is some reason to expect exactly the sort of miracles that we find recorded.

Even if the critic allows this explanation for the biblical portrayal of Jesus' power, he may point to more difficult biblical attributes. What of Christ's temptation? The God of classical theism is necessarily good. His very nature is the source of all value. It is not possible that God should sin. In fact, on Anselm's analysis, to sin is to will what God wills that you should not will. So it is logically impossible that God should sin, or even cause someone else to sin.[18] But Jesus seems to be tempted. For example, after fasting for forty days he is hungry, and Satan suggests that he should turn the stones into bread. But working a miracle at Satan's behest can't possibly be the right thing to do. If Jesus was not actually subject to some desire to do the bad thing then He was not really tempted. But then He does not really choose to do the good freely, and He cannot serve as a model for the rest of us. So it must be possible for Jesus to sin.

Here, again, Anselm's analysis of freedom offers a plausible way to approach the issue. First, note that it is not the *sinfulness* of an act that an agent desires. Sinfulness is not any sort of thing at all. It is a lack of goodness where goodness ought to be.[19] A person sins, according to Anselm, not because he has some interest in simply doing the bad thing, but because he wants something desirable, the pursuit of which, for that person at that time in that way, is not the right thing to do. The desirable object and the internal motivation that move one to pursue it are from God (as is everything in the classical theist's universe). "Evil" motivations—like lust or gluttony or the obsessive desire for power—are good motivations pursued in an extreme and improper way. Temptation, then, for anyone, is the desire to have or do something that, at its core, is good. Jesus might be tempted in His human nature in that, for example, He is hungry and wants to eat some bread. He could not sinfully pursue that desire in a way that would serve Satan's interests. He could be tempted in the garden before His arrest in that He could want to avoid the pain He knows is coming, but He could not run away. Christ cannot possibly sin.

How then, can He be free? Anselm notes that some have defined freedom as the ability to sin or not to sin. But, he insists, that is not the right definition. Freedom is the ability of the agent to be good *from himself.* Human beings, with Christ as the one exception, do not exist *a se.* Everything about us, including our motivations, are from God. Thus we need genuinely open options to choose the good or to reject it in order to perform any action that is truly our own.[20] But God exists *a se* and does not need options to choose from Himself and hence to be free.[21] In fact, on Anselm's analysis, the open options are required for the created agent only at some point in his history. The good angels and the blessed in heaven do not confront open options because they have all they can possibly want. Still, they are free because they are responsible for their present condition due to their past choices.[22] So, although Jesus cannot sin, He can be tempted and He is free.[23]

This may not satisfy those who think Christ should suffer temptation just the way we fallen human beings do. But He can't, at least not on the orthodox understanding of the Incarnation. The Council of Chalcedon states that Christ is "like us in all respects except for sin." He is not subject to original sin. And, though He can "see" all of our subjective phenomenological states, He cannot know, in the first person, what it is like Himself to sin. Does this undermine the view that one purpose of the Incarnation is for Jesus to serve as a model for us? Take the person who is hungry and is thinking of stealing some bread. Christ may say to that person, "Resist, as I did! I, too, know what it is like to be hungry!" But if the thief should retort, "Yes, but You don't know—in the first person—what it is like to be the ignorant, sinful, steeped in vice, guy that I am!" Christ may have to agree that the thief has a point. In resisting temptation Christ has the unfair advantage of being fully God as well as fully man. It does not follow that we should not try to imitate Him.

A third sort of criticism against belief in the Incarnation argues that a coherent picture of how it is supposed to effect atonement is not forthcoming. A full discussion of Anselm's theory of atonement lies outside the scope of this chapter, but a quick look at how he might (or does) respond to some standard questions should provide evidence for my claim that discussing the Incarnation within a systematic world view renders it less puzzling. In brief, Anselm's theory in his *Cur Deus Homo* is this: By sinning, mankind incurred an enormous debt against God. It is so large that only God can pay it. But it is mankind that owes it. Hence the need for a God-man. (Those who find the "debt" language too crude can translate the thesis into "estrangement" talk. I like the debt language. It expresses the intersection of the transcendent with the mundane that is at the core of the Incarnation story, and it is certainly biblical.)

But a plethora of questions arise. Anselm, in the voice of his interlocutor, asks why God—who tells human beings to forgive—could not simply forgive the debt? Anselm responds that that would be injustice, treating the sinful just the same as the sinless. God, being the source and standard of all value is uniquely "unable" to ignore justice.[24] Moreover, it is ultimately more respectful of our human freedom and dignity that humanity be allowed to pay the debt. Martin poses a further series of questions aimed at undermining the strength of Anselm's theory.[25] If justice is so important, why should not God simply let the sinful suffer eternal damnation? That would be just! Anselm's answer is that God made us because He loves us, and He would not let His work suffer such permanent damage.[26] Still, the debt is ours and Christ doesn't *deserve* to die. True, says Anselm, He chooses to pay this debt freely.[27] "But," says Martin, "in Anselm's account humans do not provide any part of the satisfaction that is due God and God shows conspicuously unsaintly behavior by accepting vicarious satisfaction from his innocent son."[28] This is a curious thing to say. Christ is and must be a human being. In fact, Christ must be a literal, biological descendent of Adam in order to have the sort of family unity that makes Him "one of us" so that His payment can suffice for our debt.[29] Modern, Western philosophers have not usually taken family unity so seriously, but that may be an oversight in modern philosophy. And since Christ *is* God, God could hardly refuse to allow Christ to pay what He freely chooses to pay for love of his human family.

Martin suggests that, on Anselm's theory of atonement, we should expect more than one Incarnation. An Anselmian response might go like this: We can make some sense of a single person with a divine and a human nature, including a human body and a human soul, because of the radical ontological distinction between the two natures. But a single person with a divine nature, and with two (or more) human bodies and two (or more) human souls is a metaphysical impossibility, and this is what would be entailed if the Word became incarnate more than once.[30] In any case, once is enough. The payment is sufficient for all sin. Why wouldn't it be? Everyone who (with the help of grace) commits himself to Christ can be saved. (How and why this happens may differ wildly from human life to human life. The Catholic Church insists that without Christ none can be saved, yet grants that "in ways known to himself God can lead those who, through no fault of their own, are ignorant of the Gospel, to that faith without which it is impossible to please him"[31]). It does not matter when the commitment is made. Those before the Incarnation may nonetheless believe, perhaps on the basis of prophecy or perhaps they may have to wait until Jesus preaches to the souls in Hell (I Peter 3:18–20). Is Martin's idea that—regarding those living after the Incarnation—it is hard for people to believe in things that happened a long time before they were born? And so to swell the ranks of believers Christ "ought" to keep coming back? But plenty of people had trouble believing that Christ was God incarnate when He was right in front of them (hence the crucifixion), and plenty of historically educated people have no trouble at all believing all sorts of things that happened long before they were born. Multiple Incarnations is not only metaphysically impossible, but also simply unnecessary. But why did He come when He did? God only knows! Which is another way of saying, "Obviously that was the right time to come."

And why is Christ's death the appropriate payment?[32] On the Christian account, humans need not have died had it not been for sin. Death is a punishment for sin, so if Christ freely accepts an undeserved death, then it is a fitting payment.[33] But if God wants humanity to be saved, why does He not save everybody rather than only believers? Because—yet again—human freedom is important. The Incarnation is necessary, but not sufficient, for the salvation of any given individual. That person must choose to accept Christ's payment for their sin.[34] Anselm insists that grace is necessary (and cannot be merited), but given the offer of grace, the human individual can accept or reject it. Human freedom is valuable, so God cannot save us without our consent.

This is only the quickest hint at how Anselm answers (or might answer) some of the questions that the critic can pose against the Incarnation. Anselm himself poses a host of other questions and the critic might pose many more. But I believe the discussion above provides evidence that it may be harder than the critic first thought to make the charge of incoherence, or even the lesser charge of arbitrariness, stick against the Incarnation. And so, if you believe in a good, powerful, agent God and you find it likely that He would work to undo the deep and ubiquitous damage done by sin, then perhaps the Incarnation, strange though it seems, is exactly what you ought to expect.

▦ NOTES

1. See Michael Martin, *The Case Against Christianity* (Philadelphia: Temple University Press, 1991), 125–161, 254–256. Martin aims his criticisms especially against Thomas Morris's *The Logic of God Incarnate* (Ithaca, NY: Cornell University Press, 1986). Rather than defend Morris I offer an Anselmian response to the criticisms when they are couched in a general way.

2. *Confessions* 6.5. Here I define "faith" as St. Augustine and many traditional Christians have done. There are modern and contemporary definitions that would hold that an epistemically justifiable acceptance of testimony should not be labeled "faith."

3. A core Christian doctrine is that saving faith requires grace, but how these two elements may interact in the history of a conversion lies outside the scope of the present chapter.

4. The strongest version of the design argument follows Aquinas's Fifth Way: It is the very laws of nature themselves that are recognized as contingent and hence in need of a causal explanation. Aquinas also captures the idea that the laws produce "the best," a point supported by particle physicist Stephen Barr's insistence that the very equations that describe the motions of subatomic particles are *beautiful* (*Modern Physics and Ancient Faith* [Notre Dame, IN: University of Notre Dame Press, 2003], 93–104). David Hume finds design arguments to be nonstarters in part because he sees the physical universe as unpleasant and ugly. Barr would hold that Hume fails to see what is there to be seen.

5. Is this failing actually ubiquitous? Hard to say, but do not point to the saints throughout history as counterexamples. The saints who pondered and wrote about such things seem to have an even greater sense of their failings than the rest of us. The prayers of St. Anselm are a prime example.

6. This line of thought is inspired by the assumptions Anselm makes in his *Cur Deus Homo* (CDH) where he is addressing Jews and Muslims regarding the "need" for the Incarnation.

7. The Statement of the Council of Chalcedon is available online at http://www.piar.hu/councils/ecumo4.htm.

8. I choose omnipotence as the attribute which, according to Martin (*The Case Against Christianity*, 139), Morris's "two minds" approach cannot succeed in reconciling with human limitation.

9. Martin, *The Case Against Christianity*, 125.

10. CDH, Book I, chap. 8.

11. Katherin Rogers, "Incarnation," in *The Cambridge Companion to Christian Philosophical Theology*, ed. Charles Taliaferro and Chad Meister, 95–107 (Cambridge: Cambridge University Press, 2010).

12. Thomas Senor points to some of these problems in "The Compositional Account of the Incarnation," *Faith and Philosophy* 24 (2007): 52–71.

13. For "omniscience," see Rogers, "Incarnation," 102–107.

14. These questions are taken from Martin, *The Case Against Christianity*, 139, where he is concerned to show that Morris's "two-minds" theory does not explain why Jesus appears so limited in power, but it seems to me that the questions are generally relevant.

15. Part of the classical theist answer to the question of why God does not interfere more in the physical universe is that He very much *likes* the world He has made and strongly prefers to have things follow their usual order except in those rare instances when He has a specific point to make.

16. God changes only *quoad nos*. How, then, could He "become" incarnate? If time is isotemporal (all times are equally real) and God is eternal (He does not live a life composed of temporal moments, but all the equally real times are immediately present to Him), then in His one act of being He is and does all He is and does. He *could* produce any number of miraculous effects in the universe during the moments at which He is incarnate on planet Earth, but there is no presupposition in favor of the claim that He *would* do so.

17. See Katherin Rogers, *Anselm on Freedom* (Oxford: Oxford University Press, 2008). This is a radical position that puts Anselm at odds with major classical theists like Augustine and Aquinas who hold that all that is done in the world is done as and because God wills.

18. Rogers, *Anselm on Freedom*, 89.

19. Anselm's preferred term is "justice," but he has a rather idiosyncratic definition of the term, and so its use might cloud the issue unnecessarily.

20. Rogers, *Anselm on Freedom*, 54–66.

21. Rogers, *Anselm on Freedom*, 185–205.

22. Rogers, *Anselm on Freedom*, 83–86.

23. Morris's solution to the temptation problem is to say that Christ cannot sin, and that in His divine mind He knows it, but in His human mind He is ignorant of the fact. So it is epistemically possible for Him to sin (Morris, *The Logic of God Incarnate*, 137–162). This seems to divide up the person that is Christ too much, in that a key element of personhood is free agency. My understanding of the Incarnation entails that the omniscience of the divine nature trumps the limitations of the human nature. Jesus is omniscient through His access to the Word, although some things He says in the Bible may make Him sound ignorant.

24. CDH, I.12–13, 23, 24.

25. Martin, *The Case Against Christianity*, 254–256.

26. CDH II.4.

27. CDH I.9, II.5, 10, 11.

28. Martin, *The Case Against Christianity*, 255.

29. CDH II.8. Does talk of "Adam" discredit the theory? I do not see why. Anthropologists tell us that human beings are all descended from a first human being.

30. Perhaps the suggestion is that Christ—the particular individual that is Jesus—should be expected to pop in and out of history frequently. I don't know why someone would expect this. He said he'd be back when the time is right.

31. *Catechism of the Catholic Church* (New Hope, KY: Urbi et Orbi Communications, 1994), section 847.

32. Martin imagines a larger payment, the eternal suffering of the God-man. Is that a coherent thought? The eternal suffering of Hell is mainly—at least this is the view of the major philosophers of the classical tradition—being cut off from God. It is hard to see how God can be cut off from God. Perhaps Martin imagines Christ suffering everlasting physical pain in His human nature. Well, the Anselmian can respond that, happily, that's not necessary, and Christ's resurrection and ascension is an important part of the story.

33. CDH II.18, 19.

34. Rogers, *Anselm on Freedom*, 136–141.

■ FOR FURTHER READING

Anselm of Canterbury. *Anselm of Canterbury: The Major Works*, edited by Brian Davies and G. R. Evans. Oxford: Oxford University Press, 1998.

Davis, S. T., D. Kendall, and G. O'Collins, eds. *The Incarnation*. Oxford: Oxford University Press, 2002.

Weinandy, T. G. *Does God Change? The Word's Becoming in the Incarnation*. Still River, MA: St. Bede's Publications, 1984.

30 The Incarnation Doctrine is Incoherent and Unlikely

■ MICHAEL MARTIN

■ 1. BACKGROUND

One of the major doctrines of Christianity is the Incarnation. This doctrine presents both conceptual and factual problems. One can raise questions about the consistency of holding both the view that Jesus is the Son of God and the portrayal of Jesus in the scriptures. If Jesus is the Son of God, then presumably he has the traditional attributes of God. However, if Jesus is a human being, then he seems to have attributes that are in conflict with divine ones, and an obvious logical absurdity can be generated: Jesus, the Son of God, both has and does not have certain attributes. Even if this problem can be solved, other questions arise. If Jesus was omniscient, why does he act as if he is not in the scriptures? How can Jesus be the Son of God, and hence morally perfect, and, as he is portrayed in the scriptures, be tempted to sin? If these conceptual questions are answered, one can also raise factual questions pertaining to the truth of the Incarnation. For example, what reasons do we have for supposing that Jesus is the Son of God? Can the truth of the Incarnation be supported by deductive or inductive arguments?

Can these problems be solved? The history of attempted solutions does not inspire confidence. The apparent incoherence of Jesus being at the same time the Son of God and a human being has always been a problem of the Christian faith. Since the time of the early church fathers, various Christological heresies, schools of thought, and bitter debates have been generated in attempting to save Christianity from seeming logical inconsistency.[1] But even if these conceptual problems had been solved, the rationale for belief in the Incarnation remains to be well articulated and defended. Christian theologians have suggested everything from faith to deductive logic as the foundation of the belief in the Incarnation, yet none of the proposed foundations seem satisfactory.

■ 2. MORRIS'S TWO MINDS VIEW

In his book *The Logic of God Incarnate*, Thomas V. Morris suggests solutions to conceptual and factual problems connected with the Incarnation.[2] Although Morris is not the first Christian apologist to defend the rationality of belief in the Incarnation, his attempt is one of most sophisticated and novel. One can reasonably claim that if there are problems with it, it is likely that there will be problems with others.

Let us consider two conceptual problems generated by supposing that Jesus is both the Son of God and a human being that play a large role in Morris's analysis. Even if one could show that it was coherent to suppose that Jesus was omniscient, there is a scriptural problem. The Jesus of the Gospels was portrayed as an omniscient being. He certainly did not act as if he was omniscient and this fact cries out for some explanation.

Problem 1. In order to account for Jesus' apparently limited human characteristics, Morris introduces the two minds theory of Christ. Although this theory was not originated by Morris,[3] his defense of it is perhaps the most extensive yet produced. In this view, Jesus had two distinct ranges of consciousness. The divine mind of God the Son "contained, but was not contained by, his earthly mind, or range of consciousness."[4] Thus there is an asymmetrical assessing relation between the two minds.

Has Morris's theory solved the problem of the prima facie incoherence of the Incarnation? Even if he has, does his theory have other conceptual problems? Morris's two minds theory is explicitly intended to explain why Jesus does not seem like an omniscient being. However, this theory also seems to serve a purpose that is not explicitly acknowledged: it attempts to prevent an inconsistency. One might argue that Jesus is both omniscient and not omniscient: Jesus, the Son of God, is obviously omniscient, but Jesus, the human being, is clearly not. According to scripture he lacks certain knowledge; for example, Jesus says that he does not know the date of the last judgment. Morris's two minds theory can be understood as a way of attempting to avoid this inconsistency, for it allows one to say that Jesus' divine mind is omniscient but that his earthly mind is not. Thus, although one seems to be simultaneously attributing contradictory properties to a single entity, one really is not. In fact, one is simultaneously attributing contradictory properties to different entities, that is, to different minds. In this way the inconsistency seems to be avoided.

However, the traditional account that Morris defends assumes that God the Son is *one* person.[5] But if God the Son is one person in any ordinary sense of the term "person," then, even if he has two minds, any predications of knowledge will have the *person* of God the Son as their subject. If one said that God the Son's divine mind knows that p, this is a misleading way of saying that God the Son knows that p and p is known by God the Son via his divine mind. But if this is so, then Morris's solution entails that the *person* Jesus, the Son of God, is omniscient and is not. Jesus is omniscient because all true propositions are known via his divine mind. He is nonomniscient because some propositions are not known via his human mind. Indeed, Jesus is omniscient and is not on Morris's theory precisely because he has two minds. Morris's use of the two minds theory obscures this obvious point.

Although I have criticized Morris's attempt to answer one charge of incoherence by using the two minds theory, I have not yet questioned whether one person could have two minds.[6] If one supposes that mind 1 of body B has different thoughts, different moods, and comes to different decisions than mind 2 also of body B—all of which seems possible in the two minds theory—it is plausible to suppose that mind 1 and mind 2 are being treated as different agents. But then we should say that there are two persons, P1 and P2 that are sharing B. However, this two persons theory conflicts with Christian orthodoxy.

Morris attempts to deal with this problem by saying that "ordinarily, minds and persons are individuated in a one-one correlation" and that "the existence of a human mind in a merely human person may preclude the exemplification by that person of any other mind, or range of consciousness of the appropriate sort at the same time. So among mere humans the individuation of two minds at any one time will suffice for the identification of two persons." However, he argues that it is possible that "outside that context, there is no such one-one correlation." In particular, he maintains that when a mind and body are part of a larger whole "which on the two-minds view they are in the case of Jesus—they alone do not suffice to individuate a person not possibly having as well some other distinct sort of mind at the same time."

Morris is left then with the following problems. It is at least dubious whether one person could have two minds. But if Jesus is one person with two minds, then the doctrine of the Incarnation is incoherent. However, if Jesus is two persons, then Morris's theory conflicts with Christian orthodoxy. The two persons theory and the fragmented mind theory are unacceptable since they conflict with Christian doctrine.

Problem 2. Morris also attempts to explain how Jesus could be morally perfect and tempted to sin. He argues that it was epistemologically possible for Jesus to have been tempted to sin since in terms of his human consciousness he did not know that it was logically impossible for him to do so. But Jesus would have been able to acquire such knowledge, and given certain plausible assumptions, he would have done so.[7] Consequently it is likely that he would have come to know that he could not sin and this would have made it impossible for him to be tempted to sin.

There is a further problem with Morris's analysis. He argues that Jesus' decision not to sin was not the causal result of his divine nature. Consequently, although Jesus' sinless actions were inevitable, they were not made inevitable by his being necessarily morally perfect. Morris illustrates his thesis by the following story. Suppose that Jones is in a room in which, unknown to him, the door is locked. He decides to stay there and consequently does not leave. Of course, had he tried to leave he would have been unsuccessful. Morris argues that although Jones's not leaving the room was predestined, his decision not to leave the room was not influenced by what prevented him from leaving the room, namely the locked door. Similarly, although Jesus' sinless actions could not have been otherwise, his actions were not influenced by what prevented him from sinning, namely his moral perfection.

The problem with Morris's theory is that it makes it a mystery why Jesus decided not to sin. After all, the Gospels teach that he was tempted to sin. This would mean in part that he was attracted to or led on by his desire to do something immoral. According to Morris, although his actions were not influenced by his morally perfect nature, he *always* decided not to sin. From what we know of human beings, this seems extremely unlikely at the very least. It is important to see that Morris cannot argue here that although Jesus is fully human he is not merely human. Jesus' earthly consciousness was merely human and, according to Morris, his moral actions were not influenced by his divine nature. Why then did Jesus *always* decide not to sin?

To return to Morris's example, it would be a bit curious if Jones, not knowing the door was locked and led on by his strong desire to get out of the room, decided to stay in the room. However, his behavior would become very puzzling if this happened consistently. Suppose that he was in 1,000 rooms in which the doors were locked, he did not know this in each case, he had a strong desire to get out of all the rooms, and yet he never decided to leave any of them. His consistent decisions not to leave the rooms would certainly call for some special contextual explanation. In the same way, if Jesus was tempted to sin, his decision not to sin calls for some special contextual explanation. Morris provides no such explanation and therefore leaves us with a puzzle.

There is a final problem with Morris's theory. He seems to assume that a person's being morally perfect is logically compatible with this person's being tempted to commit sins insofar as such a person lacks knowledge of his or her moral perfection. So far we have uncritically accepted this assumption. But should we? To see that we should not we need only draw out the implications of being tempted to sin. As we have seen, although Morris does not define what he means by being tempted to sin, it is plausible to suppose that this entails being attracted to or led on by one's desire to do something immoral. However, it is absurd to suppose that a morally perfect being could be attracted to or led on by his desire to, for example, torture or murder. Insofar as Jesus had an attraction or desire of this sort, he could not be morally perfect. Since the Gospels teach that he was tempted, he could not be morally perfect and consequently he could not be God the Son. This argument does not, of course, show that Jesus could not be morally perfect and be fully human. However, it does show that Jesus could not be morally perfect *and* be tempted to sin. Morris attempts to show that both theses are true and he is not completely successful.

Earlier we considered and rejected the idea that a person or thing could tempt another person to sin without the person who was tempted being attracted to do something sinful. However, the problems with Morris's theory suggest that we should briefly reconsider this idea. If one adopted the rejected analysis, some problems of his theory would be solved. Although Jesus was tempted to sin by the Devil and others, he was *never* attracted to do anything immoral. Consequently it would be easy to explain why Jesus never decided to sin. He never decided to sin because he had no attraction to do immoral acts. Further, on the rejected theory there would be no problem in saying that a morally perfect being such as Jesus could have immoral attractions. In the rejected analysis Jesus, a morally perfect being, could be tempted to sin and yet have no immoral desires.

However, in the rejected analysis we have an explanatory problem of at least as great magnitude as in Morris's theory. Although presumably Jesus was made many immoral offers by the Devil and others and was presented with situations that would have attracted all other humans to do immoral acts, he was *never* attracted to do any immoral act. This would be easy to explain if his actions were influenced by his morally perfect nature. But, according to Morris, they were not. Why then was Jesus never attracted to do any immoral actions? It is difficult to see how this could be explained on the assumption that Jesus is fully human. Although being fully human may not entail being attracted to do some immoral act at some time or other, it verges on the miraculous that anyone who is fully human would not be attracted to do some immoral act at some time or other. Was Jesus' divine mind causing him never to be attracted to sin? But then, contrary to Morris's supposition, would not this mean that Jesus' lack of attraction was caused by his morally perfect nature? Perhaps his lack of attraction to sin was caused by his strict religious training as a human being. But strict religious training does not seem to stamp out *all* such attraction in humans.

Furthermore, the rejected analysis has another problem. If Jesus was never even attracted to perform sinful acts, it is difficult to see how he could be a human model for resisting sin. A person who never has sinful attractions and desires is so removed from the human situation that he would be difficult, if not impossible, to relate to when one is attracted to sin, trying to resist it, and looking for an ideal to follow. Indeed, it is difficult to see why Jesus would be praiseworthy for not sinning if he was never even attracted to sin. One praises someone for resisting the attraction of sinning. Jesus, in the rejected analysis, would have had no attractions to resist. Could he perhaps be praised for not having sinful attractions? This all depends on the explanation of the remarkable absence of such attractions in Jesus, which has yet to be supplied.

It is surely the case that sometimes the absence of an attraction to a sinful action is not something to be praised. A man who does not have pedophilia is hardly to be praised for not having a sexual attraction for young children. On the other hand, the absence of attraction for strong drink in a former alcoholic is ordinarily something to be praised since one assumes that the alcoholic, through rigorous training and discipline, has somehow eliminated the attraction. What makes Jesus' lack of attraction to sin something that one suspects is not appropriate for praise is that in the rejected analysis he *never* had the attraction. It was not something that he had to eliminate by training and effort. How then could he be praiseworthy?

Thus, although the rejected analysis of temptation may solve some of the problems of Morris's analysis, it has others that are equally as serious.

■ 3. THE TRUTH OF THE INCARNATION

Let us suppose for the sake of the argument that the Incarnation is a coherent doctrine and the claim that Jesus is the Son of God does not have conceptual problems. Is there any good reason to suppose that he was in fact the Son of God? Is there any reason to suppose that he was not? Is belief in the Incarnation reasonable?

3.1 Morris's defense

In addition to attempting to defend the Incarnation against the charge of incoherence, Morris also tries to provide a defense of the possibility of rational belief in it. Maintaining that in deductive arguments there will be at least one premise whose positive epistemic status is not greater than the doctrine of the Incarnation itself, he rejects any attempt to base belief of the Incarnation on them. What about nondeductive arguments? He maintains that "it seems not to be the case that there is any single, isolable form of nondeductive argument typically relied upon"[8] by Christians to infer from certain facts, for example, the portrayal of Jesus in the New Testament that Jesus is God incarnate. Could the reasonableness of belief in the Incarnation be based, then, on direct experience and not on inference? Morris is sympathetic with this suggestion but he realizes that the objection might be raised that observational reports about physical objects and behavior underdetermine statements about persons and mental states and that the same thing would be true about observational reports about Jesus. No matter what we observe that Jesus did, this is compatible with his not being omniscient, omnipotent, and so on. So Morris concludes that "if seeing that an individual is God requires seeing that he is omnipotent, necessarily good, omnipresent, omniscient, ontologically independent, and the like, then the prospects for just directly seeing that Jesus is God look pretty dim, to say the least."[9]

However, Morris rejects the idea that seeing Jesus as divine requires this "seeing that" relation. In certain situations we can reasonably believe that we are observing the mental qualities of other persons and not just observing people behaving in certain ways, he says. Furthermore, he holds that it is possible that there is "an innate human capacity which, when properly functioning, allows us to see God, or, to put it another way, to recognize God when we see him."[10] For example, many people see Jesus as divine upon seeing the portrait of him in the

Gospels. They do not base their belief on any argument or inference. Someone who believes that Jesus is divine on the basis of this direct seeing can, as he or she matures, reasonably take what he or she learns of the Christian story to be corroboration of that belief.[11]

Morris admits that if there is an innate human capacity that when properly functioning allows us to recognize God when we see him, then if Jesus is God incarnate, "it is clear that there are widespread and deeply rooted impediments to this capacity's functioning."[12] Morris suggests that this human capacity will only function properly with the removal of some of these impediments. But how are they to be removed? Quoting passages from the New Testament, Morris implies that these can be removed only by the Holy Spirit. Thus he admits in the end that a full account of the epistemic status of Christian belief "would require, at its core, what we might call a Spirit Epistemology."[13]

This account of the possibility of the reasonableness of the belief that Jesus is God incarnate has serious problems. First, it relies on the idea that if human capacity is functioning properly, one will be able to see Jesus as God incarnate. But what reason is there to suppose this is true? It seems strange that so many people who have studied the New Testament, for example, Jews, Moslems, and atheists, and who have not seen Jesus as God incarnate have impediments to their innate human capacity. In any case, why has the Holy Spirit not removed these people's impediments?

Furthermore, if Morris can rely on Spirit Epistemology to show that Jesus is the Son of God, other religions can use similar epistemologies to justify their doctrines. Muslims might argue that when impediments have been removed by Allah one can see Mohammed as the prophet of Allah and see Jesus as not God incarnate. Allah has removed such impediments in the case of devout Muslims and has not done so in the case of devout Christians. Mormons might claim that one can only see Joseph Smith as seer, translator, prophet, and apostle of Jesus Christ when impediments have been removed by God. Such impediments have been removed in the case of devout Mormons by the Holy Ghost, but not in the case of non-Mormons. Indeed, if one allows Spirit Epistemology, why not allow followers of some pagan wonder workers, for example, Apollonius, to argue that he was God incarnate since he was seen as God. The contrary opinion of their opponents can be answered by arguing that their opponent's innate capacity to see this wonder worker as God is impeded and God has chosen not to remove the impediment.

The second problem with Morris's defense is that he does not consider any of the inductive arguments used to support belief in the Incarnation. Just because there is no single isolable form of nondeductive argument typically relied upon to support belief does not mean that inductive arguments are not relevant and one can rely on direct observation. It may well be true, as Morris says, that many people do not base their belief in the Incarnation on inference.

But this hardly shows that their belief is justified. If, as he claims, Christians typically base their belief in the Incarnation on the portrait of Jesus in the Gospels, in order to be rational they must suppose that the Gospels are so reliable and trustworthy that there is good reason to suppose that Jesus did many of the things that are claimed of him there. Surely they have no reason to believe these things without examining the historical evidence, considering the reliability of the witnesses, and so on. Until this is done, Morris's statement that one can find corroboration in the Gospels for belief in the Incarnation is unwarranted. Corroboration is possible only when what the Gospels teach is supported by the evidence.

3.2 The evidence needed

Let's consider what this evidence could be. The evaluation of the truth of the Incarnation is closely connected with the evaluation of other assumptions of Christianity. Thus, if the historicity of Jesus is dubious, then it is irrational to hold that Jesus was God the Son. The existence of Jesus is surely a necessary condition for his being the Son of God. What about the other basic doctrines of Christianity? Unlike the historicity of Jesus, the doctrines of the Virgin Birth, the Resurrection, and the Second Coming are not necessary conditions of the Incarnation. One can in all consistency reject them and yet accept the Incarnation. Thus it is logically possible that Jesus was not born of a virgin, was not resurrected, and will not return in glory and yet was the Son of God.

However, although it is logically possible to hold the doctrine of the Incarnation and reject the other doctrines, their rejection does pose a serious problem for believers in the Incarnation. The Incarnation has a central importance in Christianity since it purports to explain them.[14] Jesus' Virgin Birth is explained by supposing that he was the Son of God: Mary was made pregnant by the Holy Spirit and gave birth to the Son of God. Jesus' Resurrection is explained by supposing that Jesus was God the Son who came to the earth, was rejected and crucified, and was brought back to life in order to fulfill his divine mission of saving the world. Jesus' Second Coming is explained by supposing that as the Son of God he will return in glory in order to complete his task.

The Incarnation as an explanatory theory is no exception. Thus, if the doctrines of the Virgin Birth, Resurrection, and Second Coming are rejected, a large part of the evidence for supposing that Jesus is the Son of God must be set aside. However, the truth of these doctrines should be rejected.[15] With this evidence gone, there must be other evidence for the Incarnation to explain and hence to support it. What could this be?

There seem to be two basic types of evidence that the Incarnation might still explain which in turn would support its truth. The first consists of the miracles of Jesus, the various wondrous deeds that he is alleged to have performed.

Thus Jesus' ability to perform miracles could be explained by supposing he is all-powerful. Since he is all-powerful, he could cure the sick, give sight to the blind, turn water into wine, and walk on water. However, he is all-powerful because he is the Son of God.

The second type of evidence consists of Jesus' moral teachings and moral example. These are to be followed because he is morally perfect. He is morally perfect because he is the Son of God and the Son of God, by definition, must be morally perfect. However, as I have argued elsewhere, even if there was good reason to suppose that Jesus' worked miracles, this would not confirm the hypotheses that Jesus was the Son of God more than rival hypotheses. Moreover, there are grave obstacles to accepting the belief that he worked miracles.[16] So recourse to miracles provides no support for the Incarnation.

If Jesus' ethical teachings and moral example were perfect, this does not mean that he was the Son of God. The perfection of Jesus' morality and example is compatible with alternative explanations: for example, with Jesus being the son of some morally perfect but finite god or Jesus being endowed with moral perfection by God as an example to humankind and yet having none of the other properties of a deity, including any supernatural powers such as the ability to work miracles. Nor would Jesus' moral perfection make the hypothesis that he is the Son of God more probable than not. The expectation of his moral perfection on the alternative theories is just as high as on the theory that he is the Son of God and these alternatives seem a priori no less probable than the theory that Jesus is the Son of God.

What if it turns out that Jesus was not an ideal model of ethical behavior and that some of his ethical teachings were dubious? This would not prove conclusively that he was not the Son of God. However, combined with the other evidence it would surely make his divinity unlikely. One would expect that the Son of God would not act in morally questionable ways and expound ethical doctrines that are problematic. Thus these finding provide indirect support for falsehood of the Incarnation.

■ 4. CONCLUSION CONCERNING THE TRUTH OF THE INCARNATION

Belief in the Incarnation is clearly unjustified. Not only is the evidence for the Incarnation lacking, but it is incoherent and conceptually problematic. The falsehood of other doctrines of Christianity such as the Resurrection undercuts much of the traditional support for the Incarnation. In addition, the miracles allegedly connected with Jesus' life provide no evidence for the Incarnation and, even if Jesus was morally perfect, this would not constitute very strong evidence that he was the Son of God. However, there is no evidence that he performed miracles and good reason to deny it.

NOTES

1. For the historical background to this debate within Christianity, see Aloys Grillmeier, *Christ in Christian Tradition* (New York: Sheed and Ward, 1965); J. N. D. Kelly, *Early Christian Doctrine*, rev. ed. (New York: Harper & Row, 1978).

2. Thomas V. Morris, *The Logic of God Incarnate* (Ithaca, NY: Cornell University Press, 1986).

3. Morris, *The Logic of God Incarnate*, 102, n. 20.

4. Morris, *The Logic of God Incarnate*, 103.

5. See Eleonore Stump, "Review of Thomas Morris's The Logic of God Incarnate," *Faith and Philosophy* 6 (1989): 220.

6. See Bruce Langtry, "Review of Thomas Morris's The Logic of God Incarnate," *Australasian Journal of Philosophy* 65 (1987): 501–503.

7. Michael Martin, *The Case Against Christianity* (Philadelphia: Temple University Press, 1991), 140–142.

8. Langtry, "Review of Thomas Morris's The Logic of God Incarnate," 199.

9. Langtry, "Review of Thomas Morris's The Logic of God Incarnate," 200.

10. Langtry, "Review of Thomas Morris's The Logic of God Incarnate," 201.

11. Langtry, "Review of Thomas Morris's The Logic of God Incarnate," 202.

12. Langtry, "Review of Thomas Morris's The Logic of God Incarnate," 203.

13. Langtry, "Review of Thomas Morris's The Logic of God Incarnate," 204.

14. As I have argued in *The Case Against Christianity* (chaps. 3 and 4), the Incarnation neither entails the Virgin Birth and Resurrection nor makes them likely.

15. See Morris, *The Logic of God Incarnate*, chap. 13; and Martin, *The Case Against Christianity*, chaps. 3 and 4.

16. Morris, *The Logic of God Incarnate*, 149–156.

FOR FURTHER READING

Grant, M. *Jesus: An Historian's Review of the Gospels.* New York: Scribners, 1977.

"The Incarnation." In *The Catholic Encyclopedia.* http://www.newadvent.org/cathen/07706b.htm.

"Incarnation (Christianity)." In *Wikipedia.* http://en.wikipedia.org/wiki/Incarnation_ (Christianity).

Schwertley, B. "The Incarnation of Christ." http://www.entrewave.com/view/reformedon-line/Incarnation.htm.

Smith, M. *Jesus the Magician.* San Francisco: Harper & Row, 1978.

Wells, G. A. *The Historical Evidence for Jesus.* Buffalo, NY: Prometheus, 1982.

Yarmey, A. D. *The Psychology of Eyewitness Testimony.* New York: Free Press, 1979.

*The Historical Reliability of
the New Testament*

31 The Gospels are Reliable as Historically Factual Accounts

■ STEPHEN T. DAVIS

■ 1.

In this chapter I will argue that the Gospels in the New Testament (NT) are reliable. That is, the claims they make—preeminently their historical claims—can be trusted. I also believe that the NT's theological and ethical teachings are reliable, but I will not be able to say much about them.

I do not hold that the Bible is inerrant. The Bible contains discrepancies and inconsistencies that I am not able to harmonize sensibly.[1] But I do hold to a "high" view of biblical reliability; I approach the Bible with what we might call a hermeneutic of trust. My inclination is to accept what it says unless I find convincing evidence not to do so.

I will be opposing people whom I will call "NT critics," by which I mean scholars who are in my opinion unnecessarily skeptical and negative in their judgments and who consequently deny that the NT is historically reliable. There are two main types of NT critics. The first sort holds that since the NT is not historically reliable, that constitutes compelling reason to reject Christianity. The others think that despite the historical unreliability of the NT, it is still possible and even important to follow Christ. The version of Christianity that these folks accept is usually highly revisionist.

I do not suggest that the central purpose of the evangelists was to write accurate history. I think their deepest aim is eloquently stated in John 20:31: "These [words] are written so that you [the reader] will come to believe that Jesus is the Messiah, the Son of God, and that through believing you may have life in his name."

In this chapter I must be both selective in the topics that I will discuss and brief. Let me offer a brief roadmap of where we will be going. In section 2 I will respond to four arguments often given by NT critics. In section 3 I will offer three arguments of my own in favor of the reliability of the Gospels. And in section 4 I will discuss some implications of what I have said.

One last preliminary point: I believe in God—that is, in an all-powerful, all-knowing, and loving creator of the heavens and the earth. Moreover, I am no Deist; I believe that God can and occasionally does intervene in human history to do things like rescue people from slavery, promulgate laws, inspire prophets with messages, and send his son to earth. I mention this point because some NT critics either do not believe in God at all or believe in God but deny that God ever intervenes. But unfortunately I do not have space to argue in favor of the existence of an intervening God or refute the claim that the NT must be unreliable because it records miracles.[2]

▦ 2.

So let me now consider four arguments of NT critics.

Argument 1. The NT documents are faith statements, not historical writings. It is quite true that the books of the NT were written by people who wanted their readers to believe in Jesus. Their books are not neutral or unbiased. But of course that fact by itself does not entail that what they say about Jesus is false. Suppose I want to tell you about some person in hopes that you will admire her. In such a case, does it follow that the best way for me to achieve this end is to exaggerate or misrepresent the facts about her? Not necessarily. I would have thought that the best way to convince people to believe in Jesus is to tell the truth about him.

Among NT critics, it is often assumed that if a given Gospel text seems to have a theological purpose, that is, it fits with the author's theological or apologetic stance, it does not record accurate history. But are authors who are deeply devoted to some person or idea unable to be objective about it? That hardly follows. Consider holocaust survivors: most of them are passionately committed to the moral wrongness of genocide and the survival of the Jewish people but are extremely careful to record their experiences accurately.[3]

Moreover, in the case of Jesus, the presence during the oral period (roughly 30–70 AD) of witnesses who had been with Jesus and who could correct false accounts constituted a deterrent against people simply inventing flattering items about Jesus. There is no denying that stories about Jesus were translated, edited, paraphrased, and recontextualized. But many NT critics ignore the effect of the continuing presence of eyewitnesses. It is almost as if they assume that the witnesses simply disappeared during the oral period, so that the stories were told and passed on only by anonymous communities. But as Richard Bauckham argues, the disciples and other witnesses remained crucial during the period of oral transmission.[4]

Argument 2. The text of the NT is unreliable. It is sometimes argued that the surviving manuscripts of NT documents contain so many variants that they are unreliable; we cannot be sure what the originals said.[5] But this claim is exaggerated. There certainly are variant readings in the manuscripts. Most are due to unintentional errors of copyists; they concern spelling, word order, minor grammatical differences, repeating a word, or skipping a line. Such errors can easily be corrected. Some changes were intentionally made by copyists, but even in those cases we can usually see what the scribe had in mind (e.g., to bring the text into conformity with other biblical texts or with accepted doctrine) and we can fix the error.

There are admittedly a few cases where it is difficult to decide what the original text said. Do any of them concern issues that are important for Christians? Sure. I suppose it is important to know whether Christians will be protected if they handle rattlesnakes or drink poison. But this issue can be settled easily: text critics agreed long ago that Mark 16:9–20 is a later addition. Is the Trinity important to Christians? Certainly. So should it bother Christians that the Trinitarian benediction in I John 5:7–8 was probably added later? Not at all: Christians believe in the Trinity on other grounds. The story of the woman taken in adultery (John 7:53–8:11) is an important pericope, beloved of Christians. But it does not appear in the earliest texts of the Fourth Gospel. Indeed, it reads more like a text from the synoptic Gospels (which is possibly the reason some manuscripts place it in Luke). Does it nevertheless record an actual event? Yes, that is quite possible.

So, yes, some of the textual variants do concern important matters. But the point is that the problems they raise can be solved, and have been accounted for long ago by those who believe that the NT is reliable. In the vast majority of cases, text critics agree on, and Christians can know, what the original texts said. Very few difficult variants raise any serious questions about the text's meaning. We possess a text of the Greek NT that is accurate enough to be more than adequate for religious and theological purposes.

Argument 3. The NT documents are late. It is true that the Gospels were written some years after the events they record. Jesus was probably crucified in the year 29 or 30 AD. The earliest NT books—some of the Pauline epistles—were probably written slightly more than twenty years later. Mark was probably written some time between 65 and 70 AD. Matthew and Luke were probably written some ten to fifteen years after Mark; and John, the last canonical Gospel, was probably written in the early 90s.

In general, the closer in time witnesses or historians are to the events they speak or write about the better. But some NT critics accordingly hold that what we encounter in the Gospels is not Jesus himself (i.e., the actual events as they occurred in, say, 29 AD), but the church's understanding of Jesus in the 80s or 90s, when those books were receiving final form. Thus—so it is concluded—many of the events recorded in those books did not occur as described.

Is this true? Well, in the Gospels we certainly do come in contact with the consciousness of the evangelists at the time that they were written. But that fact does not rule out the possibility that we also come in contact with Jesus himself, with events that occurred in 29 or 30 AD. Indeed, in reading the work of any historian writing about any person or period in history, we do naturally come in contact with the consciousness of the historian at the time the work was written. But if the historian has done a worthwhile job of writing history, we also come in contact with the person or events written about. I believe that in the Gospels—despite the fact that they are written years afterward from the perspective of faith—we can learn much of what Jesus said and did.

When it comes to constructing "a life of Jesus," NT critics disagree with each other. Writing revisionist books about Jesus seems to be a cottage industry these days.[6] Was Jesus essentially an apocalyptic prophet, a teacher of wisdom, a healer, a cynic philosopher, or perhaps a magician? All such notions have been defended. Nevertheless, a rough consensus emerges in such circles on what we can know about the life of Jesus. Here are the main points: he was a Palestinian Jew from Nazareth who was baptized by John the Baptist and became a public figure in first-century Palestine; he selected a group of disciples and engaged in a ministry of preaching, teaching, and healing; under the influence of Jewish apocalyptic thinking he preached the kingdom of God and came into conflict with Jewish groups such as the Pharisees and Sadducees; although he ministered mainly in Galilee, he eventually came to Jerusalem, where he was arrested, tried, and crucified.[7]

I certainly accept that these are facts; my difficulty is seeing how anybody could suppose that this is *all* or almost all that we can know about Jesus. Are these minimum facts sufficient to explain the existence of the Christian church and the traditions about Jesus in the NT? For example, why would anybody suggest that this relatively innocuous figure was God incarnate? Aren't scholars rationally obliged to posit a "life of Jesus" that would help explain why the church so quickly arrived at notions like sinlessness, preexistence, divine Sonship, and unity with the Father? Surely a great deal more than this needs to be said about Jesus.[8]

Since many NT critics deny that Jesus was divine, there is intense speculation about the sources of and influences on NT Christology. Some suggest that notions like preexistence and divinity were arrived at after a long and complicated quasi-evolutionary process involving embellishments in the Jesus tradition due to religious experiences, or social conditions in the Christian community, or the influence of other cultures and religions. A mere Jewish prophetic teacher eventually became a preexistent being, ontologically one with God.

Two points need to be made here. First, those who argue for some such scenario have not made a compelling case. Despite efforts to find pre-Christian parallels to and influences on NT Christology, no assured parallels and influences have been found. Moreover, the very idea of extensive Pagan influences on pre-Pauline Christology, which some NT critics have suggested, seems to me implausible. There simply was not enough time, in the pre-Pauline church, for such influences to have had the envisioned effects. Second, nowhere in the NT, or in any of the sources or layers of tradition that supposedly antedate and influence it, has anybody located a purely human Jesus. Scholars such as C. F. D. Moule,[9] Martin Hengel,[10] N. T. Wright,[11] and Larry Hurtado[12] have argued that even the most elevated Christological notions are very old indeed. Some of the highest Christological notions are found, either explicitly or by implication, in the letters of Paul, the earliest datable documents in the NT.

Of course, even if divinity claims are early, that does not show that they are true. I have only been arguing against the idea that the NT's high claims for Jesus are late and unreliable embellishments.

Argument 4. The NT documents are contradictory. I do not deny that there are different emphases and discrepancies in the NT. Many of the apparent inconsistencies can be easily harmonized, and most of the intractable ones are unimportant. Still, they are there. Yet I believe there is an amazing unity to the NT's picture of Jesus.

But some NT critics reject this last claim. Dismissing an almost a priori assumption of NT unity in the biblical theology movement in the mid-twentieth century, many NT critics go overboard in the other direction. Contradictions in the NT are sought out with inquisitorial zeal; any attempt to harmonize two apparently discrepant passages is rejected as laughably unscholarly; and it seems to be assumed that there is no such thing as "the NT view" of this or that. The NT is not a coherent book, but a kind of awkward and uneven anthology. Accordingly, NT critics often insist that there are many Christologies in the NT. That is, the NT contains many competing and mutually inconsistent interpretations of Jesus, harmonization of them is impossible, and accordingly no one biblical Christology is normative for all Christians.

Again, some of this is correct. There *are* different Christological emphases in various NT texts, and facile harmonization must be avoided because it can cause us to miss the great richness and variety of NT Christology. Nevertheless, I want to insist that harmonization of apparently discrepant texts is a natural and rational impulse, whether in biblical criticism or ordinary life. All historians at times try to reconcile apparently discrepant testimony.

And the different interpretations of Jesus are best seen as related insights that developed among different persons and communities over time. I believe that these interpretations are mutually consistent and are best expressed in terms of the church's classical doctrine of the incarnation. It is a telling fact that theologians from the second century onward (e.g., Ignatius) were sufficiently impressed by the unity of the NT pictures of Jesus to claim that they can be synthesized in the notion of incarnation. So it seems to me that there does exist what we can call an "NT picture of Jesus." Despite differences of emphasis, all the NT writers agree on crucial points.[13]

3.

So now let me offer three arguments in favor of the reliability of the picture of Jesus in the Gospels.[14]

Argument 1. Paul on Jesus. Scholars sometimes say that the apostle Paul knew or cared little about the life of Jesus. But that is not true. What is true is that Paul never wrote a Gospel; his extant epistles were all occasional pieces that responded to various needs that he saw in the individuals and churches to whom he wrote.

But the life and teachings of the Lord were important to Paul. This fact is easy to establish. He emphasized the need for believers to obey and even imitate Jesus (1 Corinthian 11:1; 4:10–12; 10:5; 1 Thessalonians 1:6). And it is not clear how that could be done or even attempted without at least some knowledge of Jesus' life. Moreover, Paul made a careful distinction between Jesus' teachings and his own teachings (1 Corinthians 7:7–16; cf. 2 Corinthians 11:17; 1 Thessalonians 4:2, 15). Again, how could Paul do that without knowing what Jesus' teachings were?

Moreover, in broad outline we can piece together a credible "life of Jesus" by noting scattered references in the seven letters that most NT scholars accept as authentically Pauline (Romans, 1 and 2 Corinthians, Galatians, Philippians, 1 Thessalonians, and Philemon). And when we compile Paul's "life of Jesus," we find that to a great extent it confirms what we find in Mark, the earliest of the Gospels, and denies virtually nothing that is found there.

Here is what we can find. His name was Jesus (1 Corinthians 1:1); he was a man (Romans 5:15), born of a woman (Galatians 4:4); he was Jewish, a descendant of Abraham (Galatians 3:16, 4:4) and David (Romans 1:3); he had brothers (1 Corinthians 9:5). He was sent by God to take on human form (Romans 8:3; Philippians 2:6–11); he was poor (2 Corinthians 8:9) and humble (Philippians 2:6–11); he suffered (Romans 8:17); he was loving and compassionate (Philippians 1:8); and he lived an exemplary life (Romans 15:3, 8; 2 Corinthians 8:9; Philippians 2:6–8).

Jesus gathered disciples, including Cephas and John (Galatians 1:19; 2:9), and taught people on various religious topics (1 Thessalonians 4:2), including marriage and divorce (1 Corinthians 7:10), how those who preach the gospel should make their living (1 Corinthians 9:14), blessing those who persecute you (Romans 12:14), repaying no one evil for evil (Romans 12:17), accepting all foods as clean (Romans 14:14), and his own ultimate triumphal return (1 Thessalonians 4:15–17). On the night Jesus was betrayed he took bread, broke it, gave thanks, and said, "This is my body that is for you. Do this in remembrance of me." Then he took a cup and said, "This cup is the new covenant in my blood. Do this, as often as you drink it, in remembrance of me" (1 Corinthians 11:23–26).

Jesus was betrayed (1 Corinthians 11:23), was crucified by "the Jews" (1 Corinthians 1:23; 2:2; 1 Thessalonians 2:14), and was buried (1 Corinthians 15:4). On the third day (1 Corinthians 15:4) God raised him from the dead (Romans 1:4; 4:25; 6:4; 8:34; 1 Corinthians 15:4; 2 Corinthians 4:14; Galatians 1:1; 1 Thessalonians 4:14). He appeared to Peter, then to "the twelve," then to more than 500 people, then to James, and then to all the apostles (1 Corinthians 15:5–7). Finally, as the Gospel writers do, Paul insisted that Jesus would return (1 Thessalonians 4:16–17) to be revealed (1 Corinthians 1:7) and to judge all people (Romans 2:16). Indeed, this last point constitutes a major theological innovation shared by Mark and Paul: the idea of a suffering messiah who dies on a cross and will one day return in victory over his enemies.[15]

The importance of this point about agreement with Paul is clear: the authentically Pauline letters were all written well before Mark, and indeed within twenty to thirty years of the death of Jesus. Accordingly, what Paul said about the life of Jesus is much more likely to be reliable on purely historical-critical grounds than something written much later. And this reliability confirms the accuracy of later texts like Mark that largely agree with Paul on the life of Jesus. Mark does not appear to be myth or fable or fiction. What we have here, then, is an impressive reason for regarding Mark as reliable.

Argument 2. Jesus' view of himself.[16] A second way of approaching the question of the reliability of the picture of Jesus in the Gospels is to ask, what did Jesus think of himself? The traditional way of answering this question was simply to quote Christological statements from the Fourth Gospel, for example, "I and the Father are one" (John 10:30) or "Whoever has seen me has seen the Father" (John 14:9). But many biblical scholars deny that these words constitute the *ipsissima verba* of Jesus. Such statements—so they say—tell us more about the faith of the early church at the time John was written than they do about the actual teachings of Jesus.

Is that true? Well, as noted, the Gospels are not neutral "facts-only" biographies of Jesus. And John's Gospel was the last canonical Gospel written and so was the furthest removed from the events it describes. As the early church recognized, it is a more overtly theological interpretation of Jesus than were the synoptics. Moreover, since Jesus spoke and taught in Aramaic, and since the New Testament was written in Greek, then almost none of the sayings attributed to Jesus in the Gospels constitute his *ipsissima verba*.

Still, I believe that much of the material in the Gospels that implies a high Christology can in some form be traced back to Jesus. That is, despite what NT critics say, Jesus implicitly claimed the high status that the church attributed to him; he viewed himself as more than a prophet, as more even than the Messiah, and as more than a "Son of God" (where that term describes kings and other special men). He was, I believe, in some robust sense, conscious of himself as having a special and unique relation to God.

Jesus' lofty view of his own aims and vocation best explains why he was crucified. And on some theories of Jesus it is not easy to see why anybody would want to kill him. This seems to be a problem for the countercultural Jesus of the Jesus Seminar who produces arresting and pithy religious aphorisms. People might well have taken such a Jesus as an eccentric, but hardly as the kind of person who must be killed.

Moreover, the view of Jesus found in the New Testament does a better job than revisionist views in explaining the rise of the church. It is obvious that there was a phenomenon called first-century Judaism. There was also a phenomenon called first-century Christianity. The question is how we get from one to the other. What explains the existence of the Christian movement? On some contemporary views of Jesus, this constitutes a difficulty. But if Jesus really performed miracles, claimed (implicitly) to be the Messiah and to have a unique and special relationship with God, and was raised from the dead, an explanation is nearby. In other words, the Gospels do a better job of explaining known facts than revisionist theories.

Consider what Jesus did. He took it upon himself to overrule standard interpretations of the Torah, to offer forgiveness of sins,[17] to claim that his words would endure forever, to claim that the eternal destiny of persons depended on their response to him and his ministry, and to promise to be with his followers forever. He allowed them to worship him and encouraged them to pray in his name. (This same sort of "high" Christological strand is present even in earlier texts such as Philippians 2:5–11 and 1 Corinthians 8:6, as well as, a bit later, Colossians 1:15–20.)

So the argument is that the best explanation of early Christian worship of Jesus and lofty claims about Jesus is that Jesus himself was at least implicitly conscious of having a unique and intimate relationship with God and communicated his awareness of his own vocation and status to his followers.[18] His sense of ministry and identity was doubtless shaped by various events in his life, including the baptism, temptation, transfiguration, and passion.[19]

I am not saying that any validation of Jesus' high status must rest solely, or even mainly, on what Jesus himself (explicitly or implicitly) claimed to be. Also playing crucial roles in the church's confession of Jesus as divine Lord and Son of God were the post-Easter responses to Jesus' death and resurrection and the coming of the Holy Spirit.

Argument 3. The resurrection of Jesus. One crucial NT claim about Jesus is that God raised him from the dead. NT critics usually deny that claim; in many cases this is because they do not believe in an intervening God. But theologically orthodox scholars have made a powerful case in recent years in favor of the reality of Jesus' resurrection—indeed, in favor of his bodily resurrection.[20]

Let us define briefly two worldviews: (1) *Naturalism* is the view that the physical world exhausts reality; there are no nonphysical things like God or gods and no violations of natural laws. Accordingly, every event that occurs can in principle be explained by methods similar to those used in the natural sciences. (2) *Supernaturalism* is the view that the physical world exists because it was brought into being, along with its natural laws, by God, and God has the ability to violate natural laws. Accordingly, not every event can be explained scientifically. My point is that once it is established that belief in supernaturalism is a defensible position (and I believe Christian philosophers have done that very thing[21]), a strong case can be made for the resurrection of Jesus.

The earliest Christians unanimously and passionately believed that Jesus was alive. Their belief in his resurrection is what accounts for their transformation from frightened cowards, huddling away in hiding right after the crucifixion, to courageous preachers of their Lord shortly thereafter. What this point establishes is that the earliest Christians truly *believed* that God had raised Jesus. It does not establish the truth of their belief. But it does go a long way toward refuting reductive theories of their belief—for example, what the disciples really meant is that the work of Jesus goes on or that Jesus was in some spiritual sense still present with them.

The disciples' belief in the resurrection sustained the Jesus movement and allowed it to survive and thrive. It enabled them to overcome both the discouragement they felt immediately after their leader's death and their later persecution. Moreover, criticisms of the empty tomb and appearance traditions can, in my opinion, be answered.[22] Notice that there are certain facts about the resurrection that almost no one disputes: (1) Jesus was crucified and died; (2) first-century Jews did not believe in a suffering and dying messiah; (3) first-century Jews did not believe in any kind of pre-end-time resurrection of individuals; (4) the earliest Christians believed that the tomb was empty, that the risen Jesus had appeared to several of them, and that these events occurred because God had raised Jesus from the dead.

The point is that resurrection deniers face one big embarrassment: no one has ever produced a plausible naturalistic explanation of what happened after the crucifixion that accounts for these accepted facts. None of the explanations that have been suggested—wrong tomb, swoon, hallucination, mistaken identity, myth—have any compelling evidence in their favor. Many are so weak that they collapse of their own weight once they are spelled out.[23]

When we look at the NT accounts of the empty tomb, it is notorious that we find many discrepancies. But we also find an amazing degree of agreement on what we might call the basic facts. All accounts (the four Gospels plus 1 Corinthians 15) unite in proclaiming that early on the first day of the week certain women, among them Mary Magdalene, went to the tomb; they found it empty; they met an angel or angels; and they were either told or else discovered that Jesus was alive. There is also striking agreement between John and at least one of the Synoptics on each of these points: the women informed Peter and/or other disciples of their discovery; Peter went to the tomb and found it empty; and the risen Jesus appeared to the women and he gave them instructions for the disciples. Moreover, in one sense, it may be that the discrepancies themselves lend credence to the basic facts. They show that a variety of Christian interpretations of the empty tomb, at many points quite independent of each other, all agree on these basic facts.

Accordingly, the claim that Jesus really was raised from the dead is the best explanation of the evidence, at least for supernaturalists. I do not say that if I am correct on this point all of Jesus' words and deeds described in the Gospels have been authenticated. But if I am indeed correct, that does impressively buttress the claim that the Gospels are reliable.

■ 4.

I have been arguing that the Gospels are historically reliable. But why is this important? Aren't the theological and ethical teachings of Christianity more important than its historical assertions? Well, perhaps they are. And it is true that many of the teachings of Jesus do not need any historical basic for them to be wise, incisive, and helpful. But some absolutely bedrock Christian claims do need a historical basis. Now some NT critics argue that the *meaning* of the resurrection (which they always explain in ways that do not involve the dead Jesus actually living again) is more important than the *historical claim* that Jesus was raised. But I would respond that if Jesus was not actually raised by God, then "the resurrection of Jesus" ultimately means virtually nothing, apart perhaps from some lessons about facing death bravely.

How can a book like the NT—with historical discrepancies, textual variants, and differences of emphasis on theological themes—be considered religiously authoritative? Those are questions NT critics often pose.

My answer would be this: I believe that God superintended the writing of the texts that Christians call the Bible. But that was not enough. It seems that in order for the Bible to accomplish God's purposes, God would have to (1) ensure the protection and preservation of God's basic message to humankind (e.g., by putting it into a text); (2) superintend the process of compiling that book (including deciding on the canon of that text); (3) ensure that this text could be properly interpreted (e.g., by creating a tradition of interpretation like "the rule of faith"[24]); and (4) ensure its authoritative interpretation and application by creating an institution (the church) designed to do that very thing. And I believe God did all four.

There are places in the Bible where many Christians find it difficult to hear God's voice. The Bible is a human as well as a divine product—there are peaks and valleys, highs and lows. What is needed, especially in the light of the murkier nooks and crannies of the Bible (among which I would include the command to slaughter all the Canaanites [e.g., Deuteronomy 2:31–35], as well as the conclusion of Psalm 137), is what I will call *theological exegesis*. This is exegesis in the light of the rule of faith. Any given text must be interpreted in the light of the Christian community's vision of the witness of the entirety of scripture. We must always view such a vision as fallible and amendable by further exegesis. Otherwise, the freedom of the Holy Spirit to speak to us in scripture can be curtailed. But the church's overall vision of the macromeaning of the Bible can be seen as a canon against which to test various interpretations of texts.

Three hermeneutical principles—principles that have been implicitly recognized since the church fathers—help clarify (although they do not exhaust) what I mean by theological exegesis: (1) the Old Testament is to be interpreted in terms of the NT; (2) obscure passages are to be interpreted in terms of clear passages; and (3) everything is to be interpreted Christologically. The four Gospels, certain of the Pauline letters (notably Romans and Galatians), and many of the Psalms are to be taken as hermeneutically foundational.[25] Are they "more inspired" or "more truly God's word" than the others? No. The claim is merely that they are more hermeneutically foundational to Christian beliefs and practices.

Let me illustrate. There exists in my home town a progressive theological seminary called the Claremont School of Theology. One day several years ago I was speaking with one of the students whom I knew reasonably well, a young man who identified strongly with the gay community. He said that the main reason he could not accept anything like my own high view of biblical authority is, as he put it, "the Bible teaches the subjugation of women." I replied that the Bible teaches that idea only if we take all the texts in the Bible, line them up, and treat them as being on a hermeneutical and theological par. But if we were to follow that procedure, we would also have to say that the Bible teaches that we should kill our disobedient sons by stoning (Deuteronomy 21:18–21) and that we should never plant our fields with two different kinds of grain (Leviticus 19:19). I said that just as Christians regard those last two commands as superseded by later and more hermeneutically foundational texts, so we should regard those texts that seem to teach the subjugation of woman. Properly interpreted—so I told him—the Bible does not teach the subjugation of women.

The opinion that the NT is reliable depends on a certain view of its character. It is not just that Christians take the NT to be authoritative scripture (although we do; as if we could also take *The Iliad* or *The Republic* or maybe even *The Critique of Pure Reason* to be scripture if we chose to do so): the opinion depends on the view that the NT is a book unlike other books, a book in which in some robust sense God speaks to us. Those who hold that the NT is reliable cannot regard it as merely or simply a human product like the works of Homer or Plato or Kant. They hold it to be, when properly interpreted, the word of God.

As noted, I do not espouse biblical inerrancy. But I do affirm that the Bible is "infallible," where I understand this to mean something like "does not mislead us in matters that are crucially related to Christian faith and practice."[26] So those who hold that the NT is reliable distance themselves from any notion that the NT is just another book like all the others. They approach the NT with a hermeneutic of trust. They take it to be the source of religious truth above all other sources, the norm or guide to religious truth above all norms or guides. All others are subordinate to scripture and are to be tested by scripture.

My arguments in this chapter do not amount to a proof that the Gospels are historically reliable. There are many NT reliability issues that I have not addressed. Moreover, all history deals with probabilities. But in many cases historical probabilities can be high. I believe my arguments do show that there is a strong probability that the Gospels are reliable.[27]

■ NOTES

1. Besides the discrepancies, the central reason that I do not affirm inerrancy is that commitment to it drives interpreters toward forced and awkward interpretations of the Bible in order to make problematic assertions be true.

2. But I discuss this point in Stephen T. Davis, *Making Sense of the Resurrection* (Grand Rapids, MI: Eerdmans, 1993), chap. 1. See also Stephen T. Davis, *God, Reason, and Theistic Proofs* (Edinburgh: Edinburgh University Press, 1997).

3. I am indebted for this example to Craig Blomberg.

4. Richard Bauckham, *Jesus and the Eyewitnesses* (Grand Rapids, MI: Eerdmans, 2006), 6, 8, 93, 503.

5. See Bart Ehrman, *Jesus, Interrupted* (New York: HarperCollins, 2009), 181–224.

6. Indeed, one sometimes gets the impression that in such circles any and all hypotheses about Jesus, however remote and bizarre they might be, are acceptable topics of serious scholarly discussion—except, of course, orthodox ones.

7. A typical list is found in Norman Perrin, *The New Testament: An Introduction* (New York: Harcourt Brace Jovanovich, 1974), 287–288.

8. Marcus Borg will insist that these last items all arose vis-à-vis the post-Easter Jesus. And he is certainly right that it was in the post-Easter period that these notions were spelled out. But my question is, what was it about the disciples' experience of the pre-Easter Jesus that made it possible for them later to arrive at such lofty notions?

9. Charles Moule, "Three Points of Conflict in the Christological Debate," in *Incarnation and Myth: The Debate Continued*, ed. Michael Goulder (Grand Rapids, MI: Eerdmans, 1979), 137. See also Charles Moule, *The Origin of Christology* (Cambridge: Cambridge University Press, 1977), 2–7.

10. Martin Hengel, *The Son of God* (Philadelphia: Fortress, 1976), 2, 10. See also Martin Hengel, *Between Jesus and Paul* (Philadelphia: Fortress, 1983), 31.

11. Wright's views on this point are summarized in Marcus Borg and N. T. Wright, *The Meaning of Jesus* (New York: HarperCollins, 2007), 157–168.

12. See, e.g., L. W. Hurtado, "Pre-70 C.E. Jewish Opposition to Christ-Devotion," *Journal of Theological Studies* 50, no. 1 (April 1999): 5–6, 10.

13. Arthur Wainwright argues convincingly that on several crucial Christological points the NT writers agree. See Arthur Wainwright, *Beyond Biblical Criticism: Encountering Jesus in Scripture* (Atlanta, GA: John Knox, 1982), 22–33.

14. These points are explored more fully in Stephen T. Davis, *Christian Philosophical Theology* (Oxford: Oxford University Press, 2006), chap. 5.

15. Obviously I do not claim that the canonical Gospels or even Mark are simply reproduced in Paul or vice versa. Indeed, some of the items just mentioned are not in Mark at all (e.g., resurrection appearances only occur in Mark's inauthentic "long ending"), and many items from the Gospels (notably miracle stories and parables) are not mentioned in the Pauline letters. But the basic outline is there.

16. I explore this issue in more detail in Davis, *Christian Philosophical Theology*, chap. 9.

17. See Stephen T. Davis, "'Who Can Forgive Sins But God Alone?': Jesus, Forgiveness, and Divinity," in *The Multivalence of Biblical Texts and Theological Meanings*, ed. Christine Helmer (Atlanta, GA: Society of Biblical Literature, 2006), 113–123.

18. I do not claim that Jesus went around saying "I am God" or thought of himself in the creedal terms arrived at centuries later—terms like "hypostatic union," "second person of the Trinity," etc.

19. I have argued elsewhere (following Royce Gruenler) that a plausible case can be made for Jesus' messianic consciousness even from sayings in the Gospels that NT critics accept as authentic. See Stephen T. Davis, "Was Jesus Mad, Bad, or God?," in *The Incarnation, ed.* Stephen T. Davis, Daniel Kendall, and Gerald O'Collins (Oxford: Oxford University Press, 2002), 234–239.

20. Among many others, see Richard Swinburne, *The Resurrection of God Incarnate* (Oxford: Oxford University Press, 2003) and N. T. Wright, *The Resurrection of the Son of God* (Minneapolis: Fortress Press, 2003).

21. I think especially here of the work of Richard Swinburne. See, e.g., *The Existence of God* (Oxford: Oxford University Press, 1979).

22. See Stephen T. Davis, *Risen Indeed* (Grand Rapids, MI: Eerdmans, 1993).

23. William Lane Craig makes this point convincingly. See William Lane Craig, *Reasonable Faith: Christian Truth and Apologetics,* 3rd ed. (Wheaton, IL: Crossway Books, 2008), chap. 8.

24. The rule of faith was the church fathers' term for the church's view of the overall message of scripture.

25. Several of these points were suggested years ago by E. J. Carnell in his *The Case for Orthodox Theology* (Philadelphia: Westminster Press, 1959), 51–65.

26. See Stephen T. Davis, *The Debate About the Bible: Inerrancy Verses Infallibility* (Louisville, KY: Westminster Press, 1977).

27. I would like to thank Professors Craig Evans and Alex Rajczi for their helpful comments.

▨ FOR FURTHER READING

Bauckham, R. *Jesus and the Eyewitnesses*. Grand Rapids, MI: Eerdmans, 2006.

Borg, M., and Wright, N.T. *The Meaning of Jesus*. NY: HarperCollins, 2007.

Craig, W. L. *Reasonable Faith: Christian Truth and Apologetics*. 3rd. ed. Wheaton, IL: Crossway Books, 2008.

Swinburne, R. *The Resurrection of God Incarnate*. Oxford: Oxford University Press, 2003.

Wright, N. T. *The Resurrection of the Son of God*. Minneapolis: Fortress Press, 2003

32 The Gospels Are Reliable as Memory and Testimony

■ MARCUS BORG

To affirm "the reliability of the Gospels" has more than one meaning. Its most common one—which you can see by putting the phrase in your Google search window—is that the Gospels are reliable as historically factual accounts of Jesus' life. They tell us what he said and did. If they say that he did something, he did it. If they say he said something, he said it.

This understanding of "reliable" as meaning historical factuality is commonly extended to the Bible as a whole. If the Bible says something happened, it happened. If the Bible says something is right or wrong, that settles it.

This view has "harder" and "softer" forms. The hard form insists that the Gospels (and the Bible as a whole) are to be understood this way because they are the inerrant and infallible revelation of God. For the hard form, the phrase "the Bible is inspired by God" means that the Bible is a divine product with a divine guarantee to be true in whatever it says. It is historically factual and morally absolute.

Many Christians affirm this view. About half of American Protestants believe that the earth and the universe are less than 10,000 years old. Why? Because they belong to churches that teach that the Genesis stories of creation (and the Bible as a whole) are historically factual accounts of what happened. This way of seeing is the basis of the creation versus evolution controversy that divides American Christians and sometimes erupts in the public square.

It is also central in the controversy about same-sex sexual relationships: if the Bible says they're wrong, then they're wrong. Its factual and moral teachings are absolute.

The softer form of this view does not insist that the Genesis stories of creation are literal factual accounts of events that happened less than 10,000 years ago. It can accommodate the days of creation to immense amounts of time.

It can recognize that some of the Bible's teachings are not absolute and thus no longer apply. Few Christians insist that the rules about food, menstruation, sexual emissions, skin diseases, circumcision, the Sabbath, and laws that permit slavery and mandate debt forgiveness every seventh year are the absolute laws of God for all time.

Nor does the softer form insist on the exact historical factuality of the Gospels. When the same story appears in more than one Gospel, as frequently happens, it is not bothered by slight differences in detail. Such differences are what we would expect when two or three different writers tell the same story.

Thus whether Jesus rode into Jerusalem on one donkey (Mark 11) or two donkeys (Matthew 21) doesn't really matter; the story is basically the same. So also it doesn't matter whether there was one angel at the empty tomb (Mark 16) or two (Luke 24). The core, the gist, of the story remains the same, even as some details differ.

But like the harder form, the softer form affirms that the core, the gist, of the stories in the Gospels is historical and factual. These include the stories of the extraordinary events that frame Jesus' life: his divine conception and star-attended birth in the beginning; at the end, his empty tomb and appearances in bodily form to his followers as Lord and God. The softer form affirms a core of historical factuality in these stories, even while recognizing differences in detail.

So also it consistently sees a historical core in stories about miraculous deeds done by Jesus. The most spectacular include changing water into wine, walking on the sea, feeding a multitude with a few loaves and fishes, restoring sight to the blind, and raising the dead. He really did these things, even as details within the stories differ.

This softer form is widespread. Probably most Christians see the Bible and the Gospels this way, or think they're supposed to. Most of us absorbed a form of it in childhood. We have been conditioned by our upbringing, whether in a church or simply in modern Western culture, to see the Bible and the Gospels in a historically factual way—and then to believe them or not. Unless our lives have called it into question, this way of seeing is the common default position in modern culture.

Many Christian scholars, authors, theologians, and preachers also affirm this softer form, especially, to use an inadequate label, those within "conservative" Christianity. Not all "conservative" Christians affirm biblical inerrancy. Some recognize the difficulties of doing so and also know that the explicit affirmation of biblical inerrancy is not part of ancient and premodern Christianity. Rather, it is modern, the product of the last three centuries or so.

But they consistently defend the historicity—that is, the general historical factuality—of the Bible and the Gospels. I am not aware of any "conservative" Christian who has written that the historicity—the historical factuality—of the birth stories doesn't matter, or that it doesn't matter whether Jesus really walked on the sea and stilled a storm, or miraculously fed a multitude, or that his tomb was really empty. For them, affirming the reliability of the Gospels means affirming the historical factuality of the core, the gist, of the stories. What they say happened really happened. Truth and historical factuality are thus identified. You can't have one without the other.

As I conclude this section on harder and softer forms of "the reliability of the Gospels" as meaning their basic historical factuality, I emphasize that I do not know if they apply to Stephen Davis and his chapter. We have not read each other's chapters. This chapter is not directly a response to him.

Rather, I emphasize that these are general categories intended to describe widespread ways of seeing in contemporary Christianity, including the intellectual stream of much of conservative Christianity. Christian apologetics—defending the truth of Christianity—often includes emphasizing the historical factuality of the Bible and the Gospels.

Thus I have not begun my chapter with this understanding of "the reliability of the Gospels" with his view in mind. Instead, I have done so because the common understanding's emphasis on historical factuality differentiates it from another meaning of the phrase. This is the alternative that I affirm.

■ 1. AN ALTERNATIVE UNDERSTANDING OF THE RELIABILITY OF THE GOSPELS

My view, in a sentence, is the gospels are historically reliable documents that combine early Christian memory of the pre-Easter Jesus with post-Easter testimony to his significance.

Much is meant by this sentence. Let's begin to expand its meanings:

- The Gospels are historically reliable accounts of what their authors wrote. Centuries of textual criticism—the careful comparison and analysis of ancient manuscripts of the Gospels—have resulted in a text accepted by a consensus of scholarship, both conservative and mainstream. With only a few minor exceptions, we can be confident that the Gospels and the New Testament as a whole reliably report what was originally written.
- The Gospels are products of developing traditions. Written in the last third of the first century, they tell us how the traditions about Jesus developed in early Christian communities several decades after his historical life.
- As products of developing traditions, they contain memory. They are about "Jesus remembered." Some of what they narrate is memory of things he said and did and what he was like.
- As products of developing traditions, they contain testimony. They testify, witness, to what Jesus had become in the experience, thoughts, and lives of his followers in the decades after his historical life. They are not just memories of Jesus as he was in "his then," but also express and proclaim the significance and meaning that Jesus had come to have in "their now."

Thus the Gospels combine post-Easter memories of the pre-Easter Jesus with post-Easter convictions about his significance and meaning. The rest of this chapter describes and amplifies the basis, the foundations, of this way of seeing the Gospels and the meanings that result.

2. THE GOSPELS AS PRODUCTS OF DEVELOPING TRADITIONS

According to a massive consensus of scholarship, the earliest Gospel is Mark. Sometime around the year 70, for the first time, an early Christian put the story of Jesus into writing. We call the author and his Gospel "Mark."

Though Mark is the earliest Gospel, it is not the earliest document in the New Testament. That distinction belongs to the genuine letters of Paul. At least seven of the thirteen letters attributed to him were written by him in the 50s. But Paul's letters do not tell the story of Jesus. He was writing to communities that already knew about Jesus and so he didn't need to tell his story.

Mark is not only the first to tell the story of Jesus, but tells it as "gospel," as he announces in his first sentence. The Greek word for "gospel" means "news"— news about what has happened and is happening. Old news is not news. The word has an additional connotation in the Gospels: it means "good news"—and that is what has happened in Jesus. His story is gospel, good news.

In the decades after Mark, the rest of the Gospels were written. Their chronological sequence is unclear. Usually Matthew and Luke are seen as next, from the 80s or 90s, with John from the 90s and perhaps the last. But some scholars today date Luke and its companion volume Acts early in the second century, and thus later than John.

Some conservative scholars would move the dates for the Gospels earlier, for more than one reason. The Gospels do not mention the destruction of Jerusalem and the temple in the year 70 as an explicitly past event. Perhaps that means that all were written before 70?

Another reason: the book of Acts does not mention the death of Paul. Paul was executed in Rome in the middle of the 60s. More than half of Acts is about Paul; he is its central character. So the fact that Acts doesn't mention his death suggests to some that it must have been written before the middle 60s. This affects the dating of Luke: because it was written before Acts, it must not be later than the early 60s. And for those conservative scholars who think that the author of Luke used Mark, this makes Mark earlier yet, maybe only two or three decades after the historical life of Jesus.

But despite uncertainty about the chronological sequence of the Gospels, and even if dating of all of them as pre-70 were to be correct, the basic point remains. Namely, the Gospels are the product of developing traditions in early Christian communities.

For as many as four decades, if dating Mark around 70 is correct, or two or three decades if the earlier dating is correct, the story of Jesus—of what he was like, what he said and did—was remembered and told orally and not in written form.

The point is not that memory and oral tradition are intrinsically unreliable. People in preprint cultures had memories quite different from we who can simply "look things up" in books or electronically. For them, the past lived only in oral memory.

This included memory of the recent past and also of the remote past. With literacy rates in the ancient Mediterranean and Jewish world at 5 percent or less, and given how time-consuming and expensive hand-copied manuscripts were to produce, most of Jesus' followers would have known the stories of the Old Testament only aurally and orally. They knew the past through memory—and they remembered much better than we do.

So the point is not that memory is unreliable. Rather, the point is that early Christians didn't simply remember the pre-Easter Jesus until authors put their memory into writing. Instead, in the decades before the Gospels were written, Jesus' followers' convictions about him developed. Their understanding of his significance and the meanings of things he said and did grew and deepened.

The reason: they continued to experience him as a figure of the present. The movement he had begun continued, and they experienced the same presence they had known in him continuing to animate it.

They proclaimed him as both "Lord" and "Christ" (i.e., the Messiah, God's anointed one). In language from John's Gospel, they spoke of him as "the light of the world," "the bread of life," "the way," "the door," "the vine," "one with God," and "the Word made flesh"—as the decisive revelation of what can be seen of God in a human life.

Thus the Gospels tell us how the story of Jesus developed in different Christian communities. Mark tells us how the story developed and was understood within his community, Matthew within his, and so also Luke and John. What they share in common: each is the product of traditions about Jesus as they developed in the time and place in which each Gospel was written.

■ 3. THE EVIDENCE

The evidence for seeing the Gospels as products of developing traditions is found in the documents themselves. Often two or more Gospels tell the same story. This happens especially in Mark, Matthew, and Luke, known collectively as the "synoptic" gospels because of their considerable similarity. Some stories in the synoptics also appear in John, and thus in all four Gospels. These include stilling a storm on the sea, feeding a multitude with a few loaves and fishes, giving sight to the blind, freeing people from paralysis, raising the dead, and the execution and resurrection of Jesus.

But—and this is the point—the stories are told differently. Sometimes the differences are minor and can be understood as the equivalent of "copy editing"—changing some words, using fewer words to tell the same story, and so forth. But sometimes the differences are major and more significant.

The easiest way to see this is to look at an edition of a "Gospel parallels." The synoptic Gospels (and sometimes John) are printed in vertical parallel columns. Spending even an hour with a Gospel parallels leads to the question: how does one account for differences in the same story of something Jesus did or in the same text reporting what Jesus said?

The most plausible explanation is that the differences are the products of the way traditions about Jesus developed in different Christian communities. The writers of the Gospels wrote from within these communities and for them.

4. THE LORD'S PRAYER

To illustrate with a specific example, I turn to the Lord's Prayer. I do so in part because of its familiarity. It is probably the best-known prayer in the world.

What is less well known is that there are three different forms of it in documents from Christianity's first hundred years: in Matthew, Luke, and *The Didache* (pronounced "did-ah-kay"). The latter is not in the New Testament, but is an early Christian document perhaps as early as 100 CE. Two Gospels—Mark and John—do not have the Lord's Prayer.

These three early Christian forms of the Lord's Prayer differ in various ways. Two are almost but not exactly the same. The versions in Matthew and *The Didache* are most familiar to Christians. Except for the concluding doxology, they are essentially the same. Matthew's version ends with "And deliver us from evil." *The Didache* adds a doxology: "For the power and the glory are yours forever." Catholics commonly pray Matthew's version, Protestants commonly pray a version of the latter.

Luke's version of the Lord's Prayer is quite different. Shorter and simpler, it does not begin with "Our Father who art in heaven," but simply "Father." Rather than "Hallowed be thy name," Luke has "Your name be holy." Rather than "Your kingdom come on earth as it is in heaven," Luke has simply "Your kingdom come." After the petitions for daily bread, forgiveness, and deliverance from temptation, it lacks Matthew's "And deliver us from evil."

How can these differences in early Christian versions of the Lord's Prayer best be explained? The most plausible explanation is that the differences reflect how it developed in different Christian communities in the decades after the end of Jesus' historical life.

The different forms mean that we do not have an exact memory, a transcript, of the Lord's Prayer as it came from Jesus. We have it in somewhat different forms because it is the product of early Christian traditions as they developed in different Christian communities.

■ 5. MEMORY, METAPHOR, AND TESTIMONY

The Gospels as a developing tradition that combine memory and testimony frequently use the language of metaphor. "Metaphor" refers to the more-than-literal, more-than-factual, more-than-historical meaning of words. Metaphor is about "the surplus of meaning" that language can carry, a phrase that I learned from the contemporary Catholic theologian David Tracy. Thus metaphorical meaning is more than historical and factual meaning, not inferior to it.

Some stories in the gospels combine memory with metaphor. Some in my judgment are purely metaphorical, by which I mean that the whole of the story is metaphorical. I begin to explain what I mean with two examples of the former.

■ 6. JESUS AS EXORCIST: THE STORY OF "LEGION"

That Jesus was an exorcist who cast out demons from people whom he and his contemporaries perceived as possessed is accepted by most scholars. More stories are told about Jesus as exorcist (and, to broaden the category, as healer) than about any other figure in the history of Judaism. But are the stories of Jesus as an exorcist and healer to be understood primarily as factual reporting about past events? Or do they also have a metaphorical meaning?

The story of Jesus and Legion is the longest exorcism story in the Gospels. As Mark 5:1–20 tells the story, it is filled with images of impurity. Jesus for the first time enters Gentile territory—impure land.

There he encounters a man possessed by unclean spirits. The possessed man lives in a graveyard; death and cemeteries imparted the gravest impurity. He is naked and out of his mind. His name is Legion, the word for a division of elite Roman soldiers. Unclean animals—pigs—abound in the neighborhood. When Jesus casts the evil spirits into the pigs, thousands of them rush into the sea and are drowned.

So what is this story about? To regard it primarily as a factual account of what happened risks missing its point. As a metaphorical narrative, it means more than it means as a simply factual account.

Its surplus of meaning builds on the following:

- The theme of purity and impurity is ubiquitous in this story and counters conventional understandings of that time. Impurity was contagious and overcame purity. The story reverses that understanding: Jesus enters into a setting of radical impurity and overcomes it. What is in him is more powerful than impurity; what is in him is contagious.
- The possession theme. The man is possessed by Legion. In its first-century context, the word had an unmistakable connection to the Roman Empire. How to understand that connection is less clear. Is this a story about

"imperial possession"? Is that what drove the man crazy and led him to live in a graveyard, the land of the dead?

- What it says about Jesus. The above, of course: Jesus overcomes impurity, delivers people from possession, restores people to their right minds. Jesus can enter the land of the dead, the place of utter desolation, and transform lives.

All of this flows out of seeing this story as a metaphorical narrative. Doing so does not require saying that it's not historical. But the historical factuality of the story ceases to be the crucial question.

I don't think that Mark 5:1–20 is intended primarily as a historically factual account of a specific event. Rather, I think of it and other exorcism stories in the Gospels as metaphorical narratives with a historical grounding in Jesus as an exorcist. They combine memory and metaphor.

▨ 7. JESUS AND SIGHT TO THE BLIND

The Gospels have more than one story of Jesus giving sight to blind people. Two are in Mark 8:22–26 and 10:46–52 and they also appear in Matthew and Luke. One is in John 9.

It is possible that Jesus restored sight to one or more blind people. These stories may be based on memory. But the way they are told gives them a more-than-historical and thus metaphorical meaning. The two stories in Mark frame Jesus' journey from Galilee to Jerusalem, one at the beginning and the other at the end. They suggest that seeing is about seeing the significance of Jesus and following him on the way that leads to Jerusalem, death, and resurrection. Indeed, the second one ends with a blind beggar "seeing again" with the result that he follows Jesus on "the way" that leads to Jerusalem.

So also the story in John 9 is rich with metaphorical meaning. It is the occasion for the Jesus of John's Gospel to say, "I am the light of the world," thereby building on John's theme of Jesus as the light in the darkness who brings enlightenment.

The story also contains words enshrined in the hymn "Amazing Grace" as "I once was blind but now I see." The power of the line resides in its metaphorical resonance: this story is not simply or even primarily about an event in the past in which Jesus gave sight to a blind man, but about something that generations of Christians have experienced. Jesus is the one who enables us to see, to see again, to see anew. He is the light that enlightens everybody, the true light, to echo language from the magnificent prologue in John's first chapter.

Did Jesus heal this particular blind man? Understanding the story as a metaphorical narrative means that this question hardly matters, and perhaps doesn't matter at all. The affirmation is clear: Jesus is the light of the world, the light in our darkness, the one who gives sight to the blind. For Christians, the affirmation is true, independent of the historical basis of this story.

■ 8. HOW MUCH IS MEMORY?

Because I am about to turn from stories that I think contain memory to stories that I see as purely metaphorical, I provide a list of what I see as historical memory in the Gospels. This list is not complete and exhaustive, but it is illustrative.

- Jesus was born shortly before the death of Herod the Great in 4 BCE. Herod had ruled the Jewish homeland on behalf of the Roman Empire since 37 BCE. He was succeeded by his sons.
- Jesus grew up in the peasant village of Nazareth, about five miles from Galilee's capital city of Sepphoris. Around 20 CE, Herod's son Herod Antipas moved his capital to Tiberias on the Sea of Galilee.
- In the mid to late 20s, Jesus left Nazareth to be with John the Baptizer, a Jewish wilderness prophet. He was baptized by John.
- After John was imprisoned by Herod Antipas, Jesus began his own public activity. With John locked away, Jesus as a follower of John decided to continue what John had begun.
- Central to Jesus' message was the coming of the kingdom of God.
- The kingdom of God was for the earth—about a transformed world. That it was about the transformation of this world and not primarily about an afterlife is expressed in the Lord's Prayer: your kingdom come on earth—as it already is in heaven.
- He recruited people for the kingdom of God, calling them to follow him in his passion for God and God's kingdom.
- His primary audience was the rural peasant class. According to the Gospels he didn't go to cities, except Jerusalem. Rather, he taught in towns, villages, hamlets, and the countryside where the peasant class lived. This included not only agricultural workers, but other manual and menial laborers. They were the ones most marginalized and often made destitute by the way things were.
- He often taught with stories (parables) and short sayings (aphorisms), memorable forms of speech that he used to subvert conventional ways of seeing.
- He was a healer and exorcist. As mentioned earlier, more healing and exorcism stories are told about Jesus than any figure in the Jewish tradition.
- He was executed in Jerusalem by the authorities near the end of the week of Passover when the city was filled with Jewish pilgrims celebrating ancient Israel's liberation from Egypt.
- His execution followed a series of challenges to the authorities and the way things were. He entered the city in a preplanned anti-imperial procession whose symbolism proclaimed that the kingdom of God was about peace and the end of war. He performed a provocative public act in the temple that indicted its authorities—collaborators with Roman imperial

rule—as having made the temple into a den of robbers. Representatives of the authorities sought to discredit him in verbal conflicts in the temple courts.

- Near the end of the week, he was arrested, tortured, and crucified. The mode of execution points unambiguously to Roman imperial responsibility: in his time and place, a cross was always a Roman cross. It is likely that high-level temple authorities were also involved; their positions depended upon collaboration with the imperial domination system. Nevertheless, "Christ crucified," to use a phrase from Paul, meant executed by the empire, the rulers of this age.

- After his death, some of his followers continued to experience him as a living figure of the present. They experienced him not just as a "ghost" of somebody who had died, but as "risen"—that is, vindicated by God, raised to God's right hand, now both Lord and Christ.

9. METAPHORICAL MEANING AS PARABOLIC MEANING

Now I move from memory to the truth of metaphorical narratives, the claim that they can be true even if not reporting factual memory. Their meaning and truth are parabolic. The model for this claim is the parables of Jesus.

Everybody recognizes that his parables are made-up stories. When he told the parable of the good Samaritan, he wasn't reporting something that happened the other day on the road from Jerusalem to Jericho. When he told the parable of the prodigal son, he wasn't reporting an incident that had happened in a family that he knew about. We don't imagine that there was a particular prodigal son whose father welcomed him so lavishly, just as we don't imagine that the story of the man who was beaten and robbed by thieves and left half-dead was a crime report.

And yet we recognize that these are important stories filled with meaning and truth. So also with his other parables. All Christians see them as truth-filled and in that sense truthful. But their truth is about meaning; they are not about reporting factual events.

This is the foundation for seeing many Gospel stories as parabolic. Seeing them this way means that the question of historical factuality recedes in importance. To illustrate this claim, I conclude with the stories that frame Jesus' historical life: birth stories and Easter stories.

10. THE TRUTH OF THE BIRTH STORIES AS PARABOLIC TESTIMONY

The stories of Jesus' birth are probably the best-known stories in the world. They are filled with miraculous happenings: divine conception in a virgin, a special star, angels appearing to Joseph and Mary and singing to shepherds, and the fulfillment of prophecy.

They are found in two Gospels, Matthew and Luke (Mark and John do not have birth stories). The stories are very different from each other. Matthew's is much shorter than Luke's and revolves around King Herod's plot to kill Jesus. The wise men following the star are part of that larger plot, as is the story of the holy family fleeing into Egypt.

Luke has much that is not in Matthew (and very little that is in Matthew): the story of the birth of John the Baptizer to aged and infertile parents, the annunciation by the angel Gabriel to Mary that she will conceive a son without a human father, the journey from Nazareth to Bethlehem because of a census ordered by the emperor Augustus, birth in a stable, and shepherds rather than wise men coming to the baby Jesus.

The differences are substantial enough to raise the question, what kind of stories are these? Are they meant to report memory of events that happened? Or were they, from the beginning, intended as metaphorical narratives, as parables about Jesus? And—importantly—is their parabolic truth, their truth as metaphor, independent of their historical factuality?

In their first-century historical context, their metaphorical meanings—their parabolic meanings—are clear. Their historical context, their interactive matrix, was the Jesus movement within Jewish covenantal theology within the Roman Empire and its imperial theology.

Jewish covenantal theology was the context that shaped Jesus and his early followers. It emphasized unconditional loyalty to the God of Israel, the God of the law and the prophets. And it was the basis of Israel's hope: it was filled with God's promises, God's dream for a different kind of kingdom on earth—a world of justice and peace in which humanly inflicted misery would be no more.

Yet their world was ruled by Rome, the latest in a series of domination systems. Roman imperial theology legitimated its rule as divinely willed. The titles of the emperor included "Son of God" and "Lord." Caesar Augustus, the greatest of the emperors, was called the "savior of the world" who had brought "peace on earth." Moreover, Augustus was the product of divine conception; his father was Apollo, the god of light and order. Imperial theology was proclaimed throughout the empire in the media of the day: coins, inscriptions, statuary, and temples.

In this context, the birth stories directly counter Roman imperial theology even as they also use primordial archetypal language that connects to larger themes. They affirm and testify:

- Jesus—not Caesar—is the true Lord, Son of God, and savior whose way brings peace on earth.
- The story of Jesus is about conflict between the rulers of this world and the kingdom/lordship of God—God's dream for the world.

- The story of Jesus is about the true light in the darkness. Caesar, son of Apollo, the god of light, is not.
- The story of Jesus is about the fulfillment of ancient Israel's and humanity's deepest yearnings and longings for a different kind of world.

All of these are among the parabolic meanings of the birth stories. Their truth as parables about Jesus and as testimony to Jesus does not need to deny their historical factuality. But neither does it need to affirm their historical factuality. Believe whatever you want about whether his birth happened this way and then ask, in their first-century context, what did these stories mean?

▓ 11. THE TRUTH OF THE EASTER STORIES AS PARABOLIC TESTIMONY

Within this way of seeing the Gospels as a combination of memory and testimony, it does not matter whether Easter involved something spectacular happening to the physical body of Jesus. It does not need to defend the historical factuality of an empty tomb and a physical resurrection. It sees the Easter stories as parabolic, as parables, as meaningful and truthful stories without needing to see them as historically factual accounts of what happened.

Yet I do think the Easter stories have a historical ground. Their historical factuality is twofold: (1) some of his followers had experiences of Jesus after his death; and (2) they experienced him not simply as a ghostly survivor of death, but as a sacred reality, as Lord, raised to God's right hand, as one with God.

To expand the first:

- Jesus appeared to his followers. Paul uses this language in I Corinthians 15 in a list of people to whom the risen Jesus appeared, including Paul. The language suggests visions such as Paul had.
- I think his followers also had nonvisionary experiences of him as a figure of the present. They continued to experience the same Spirit they had known in him during his historical life—the same presence and power that had filled him.

To expand the second:

- These experiences led to the exclamation "Jesus is Lord." This differentiates these from other postdeath experiences. Studies suggest that roughly 50 percent of surviving spouses will have at least one vivid experience of their deceased spouse. Yet these experiences do not lead to the conclusion that the deceased is now Lord and God.
- There was something about the experience of the post-Easter Jesus that did lead to this affirmation. Paul's experience in or near Damascus led him to ask, according to Acts 9, "Who are you, *Lord*?" So also in John 20, when the risen Jesus appears to Thomas, he exclaims, "My Lord and my God!"

- They experienced Jesus no longer as a figure of flesh and blood constrained by time and space. Now he was one with God and so was with them every-where. He was "Emmanuel," which means "God with us."
- The experiences of Jesus as Lord and one with God led intrinsically to the claim that God had vindicated Jesus. Easter is about God's "Yes" to Jesus and God's "No" to the powers that killed him. In words from Acts 2 addressed to the authorities, "This Jesus whom you crucified, God has made both Lord and Christ."

Within this way of seeing the Easter stories, their truth does not depend upon whether something spectacular happened to the corpse of Jesus. Only a histori-cally factual reading of the story of the empty tomb requires that.

The other stories in the Gospels are all about appearances of the risen Jesus. They and Paul suggest that whatever the risen Jesus is, he is not a physical being in the sense that we commonly understand the word "physical." He can appear in locked rooms, appear and not be recognized, and disappear when he is recognized. He can appear in Galilee, Jerusalem, in or near Damascus, and on the island of Patmos.

I conclude this section on seeing the Easter stories as testimony and parable with a reflection. Within this framework, what does the story of the empty tomb mean? Set aside whatever convictions you may have about whether the tomb of Jesus was really empty. Or believe whatever you want about that. Now, what does the story mean as parable? More than one thing.

- You won't find Jesus in the land of the dead. An angel asks the women who have gone to his tomb: "Why do you seek the living among the dead? He is not here. He is risen."
- The tomb couldn't hold him. He is a figure of the present, not just of the past.
- The powers that ruled his world killed him—but that hasn't stopped him. He's loose in the world, still here, still recruiting for the kingdom of God.

It seems to me that, for Christians, the above statements are true independently of whether the tomb was really empty. I do not need to argue against the factual-ity of the empty tomb; rather, I'm suggesting that the parabolic meanings of the story of the empty tomb are the really important ones.

■ 12. A FINAL REFLECTION

For Christians, is anything lost by seeing the birth stories and Easter stories and the Gospels as a whole as a combination of memory and testimony? If some-thing is lost, what is it?

Or does this way of seeing the Gospels as historically reliable documents that express the memory and testimony of Jesus' followers preserve what really matters, what is most important? What, if anything, is added by seeing them as historically factual accounts? Is "Jesus was the Son of God" one of the facts of history? Is the empty tomb a fact of history, that anybody who had gone to the tomb that morning would have found it empty? Or are these affirmations the testimony of his early followers to the significance that Jesus had for them?

Is Christian faith about believing in the historical factuality of the Gospels? Or is Christian faith about commitment, allegiance, and loyalty to Jesus as the decisive revelation of God's passion for the world? If you are inclined to say "both," why? What's at stake in also affirming that the Gospels are reliable as historically factual accounts?

For me, it is enough that we have the memory and testimony of his followers. To echo words from Paul: we have this treasure in earthen vessels.

▨ FOR FURTHER READING

Borg, M. *Jesus: Uncovering the Life, Teaching, and Relevance of a Religious Revolutionary.* New York: HarperCollins, 2006.

———. *Reading the Bible Again for the First Time: Taking the Bible Seriously but not Literally.* New York: HarperCollins, 2001.

———. *Speaking Christian: Why Christian Words Have Lost Their Meaning and Power—and How They can be Restored.* New York: HarperOne, 2011.

Dunn, J. D. G. *Jesus Remembered.* Grand Rapids, MI: Eerdmans, 2003.

Wright, N. T. *Simply Jesus: A New Vision of Who He Was, What He Did, and Why He Matters.* New York: HarperOne, 2011.

The Historical Jesus

33 Is the Christ of Faith also the Jesus of History?

■ STEPHEN J. PATTERSON

1. ARE WE AN EXCEPTION?

For centuries Christian believers have opened the Gospels and read of the incredible life of their savior, Jesus Christ. The world of the Gospels is an exceptional world, full of wonder and miracle. The hero, Jesus, is born to a virgin who conceives by the Holy Spirit; this hero is God's own child. As a boy he astonishes his elders by debating with the scholars in the temple. When he grows up, he astonishes the crowds by healing the sick and raising the dead. He astonishes his disciples by walking to them across the waves as their boat is tossed on the stormy sea. He wins every argument by astonishing the scribes and Pharisees with the cleverest turn of phrase. And when his enemies prevail, and he is arrested and crucified, the tomb cannot hold him. On the third day, the stone is rolled away and Jesus is raised from the dead to appear once more to his astonished followers. An astonishing story. But the most astonishing thing about it is the ease with which the Christian believer slips into this world to experience it as though it were real. In his or her normal, ordinary life, heroes hit home runs, run for president, and walk on the moon. But they do not walk on water. In the real world even the most ardent believer goes to the doctor when he or she gets sick. After all, when people get sick in the real world, they sometimes die, and when they die, they stay dead. But somehow the life of Jesus—and the world of Jesus—is different. In the Christian believers' world view, the world that comes to life in the Bible is an exceptional place, where things happen that do not happen in normal life. But this *seems* normal. After all, Jesus is the divine Son of God. He is an exception, one of a kind. Who could not see this: he walks on water.

The question before us, "Is the Christ of faith also the Jesus of history?" is the question of whether this impression we get from the Gospels is true or actually an illusion. Did Jesus really do astonishing things, and is this why people should believe in him? Or is this an illusion that masks another, more important reality: that faith begins in another, less astonishing, more ambiguous, and ultimately more challenging way? In what follows I will argue that the Christ of faith is not in fact also the Jesus of history. This is a Christian conceit that allows us to think that we believe what we believe because history itself proves we are right. It is a conceit we can no longer afford in an increasingly plural and divided world— one in which religious claims often do more to fan the flames of hostility than to douse them. It is one thing to have faith. It is another to think that one's own faith is self-evident and for anyone to believe otherwise is just unreasonable infidelity. For this reason it is important that the distinction between the Christ of faith and the Jesus of history be crystal clear.

But once the distinction is made, what then? Shall Christian theology dispense with the Christ of faith and speak only of the Jesus of history? Or, alternatively, should the believer speak only of the Christ of faith? In the final analysis, I will argue that even though it is important to distinguish between the Jesus of history and the Christ of faith, it is also important to hold them together, for there is another very important sense in which the Jesus of history is the Christ of faith.

■ 2. NO, THE CHRIST OF FAITH IS *NOT* ALSO THE JESUS OF HISTORY

The Christ of faith, that is, Jesus (Christ) as he is described in early Christian confessional writings like the Gospels or Paul's letters, is most definitely not to be understood also as Jesus, just as he appeared in history. There are several reasons for answering our question quite emphatically with a "no."

2.1 The common sense reason

The first is what we might call the common sense reason: insofar as Jesus is described in the Gospels as having been born of a virgin, working miracles, even raising the dead, and having himself died, being raised from the dead to walk again among mortals as a living, breathing human being—insofar as Christian confessional writings describe him thus as a person with superhuman qualities—common sense tells us that this is not Jesus as the historian might reasonably describe him. Real people do not have superpowers. Historians never describe real people from the past as though they did. Historians do not suppose that Plato was born miraculously,[1] or that Pythagoras could really calm stormy waters,[2] or that Julius Caesar actually did ascend into heaven and become a god.[3] The mere fact that ancient sources quite soberly assert these things does not sway us. It is not historically credible to assert that human beings from any age (regardless of what their contemporaries might have believed) possessed superhuman qualities. This is simply good, common sense. Without this simple common sense about how the world works and what people are really like, history is left without a method.

Today it is surprising to find that this is still a bone of contention. Those who pursue scholarship within the secular academy readily take such historical common sense for granted, but evangelical scholars do not generally accept it. Robert Webb has recently described two poles in historical Jesus scholarship: the "naturalistic" approach, in which normal cause and effect within a closed space-time continuum is assumed, and the "theistic" approach, which will accept at least some historical explanations that involve divine intervention—that is, supernatural as well as natural causes.[4] He is right to call attention to the divide, but his labeling is less than apt. There are many theistic theologians and historians who would object in principle to the notion of divine intervention with "efficient causality" of the sort presupposed in the biblical narratives. Webb goes on to observe that one's orientation to one or another of the poles depends on one's worldview.[5] This is perhaps true, but watch where this way of framing the issue leads. For the naturalistic historian to accept a supernatural explanation, he says, would require "him/her to step outside of who they are and entertain an alternate worldview."[6] In today's postmodern intellectual milieu, the inability or unwillingness to do this is an obvious shortcoming, for we must all be willing to open ourselves to other worldviews and step outside of who we are. To fail at this is to succumb to one's own narrow prejudices and unexamined biases. The "critical theistic historian," on the other hand, "is *open* to the possibility of theistic causation."[7] And that, of course, is a good thing: openness is above all else the quintessential postmodern intellectual virtue. It is this kind of reasoning that leads evangelicals to claim that to deny the historicity of supernatural biblical accounts is simply to yield to modern, scientific prejudice against an alternative worldview.

But is this really an accurate way of putting the matter? I believe it is safe to say that the "critical theistic historians" Webb has in mind never (yes, never) opt for a supernatural explanation of events unless it involves deciding for the special claims of the Christian tradition (usually the Bible, but not exclusively so). I have never read an evangelical scholar with the same openness to the supernatural claims made about pagan or Jewish figures of the past, or about the founder figures of other religions, for whom similar claims are made. When considered in this very practical light, what Webb calls critical theistic history is simply *Christian* theistic history, not really critical at all and far from open. It is not, as Webb might imply, a favoring of history over science,[8] but a favoring of faith over history. Legitimate history must, at the very least, treat all of its subject matter with more or less the same set of rules. The universe cannot be "open" for various Christian claims requiring a supernatural cause, but closed for everything else. If common sense tells us that Pythagoras did not have superpowers, then it tells us just as clearly that Jesus did not have superpowers either. The Christ of faith is not the Jesus of history.

2.2 The form critical reason

A second reason is what might be called the form critical reason. It derives from several insights of form criticism. If one considers that thirty to forty years passed between the life and ministry of Jesus and the writing of the first Gospels, one must reckon with the stark reality that the traditions about Jesus, the building blocks of the Gospel narratives, were passed around orally through generations of new believers before they ever lit upon the ears of the Gospel writers or their sources. These oral traditions had been through many iterations in various settings and situations in the early Jesus communities and adjusted accordingly. Each time a story was retold, it was with the intention of convincing some new audience that Jesus was the Christ, the Messiah and Son of God. In other words, long before the tradition was rendered in writing, the oral tradition had already become a tradition about the Christ of faith, no longer by any means a simple collection of stories about the historical Jesus. So powerful have these insights been in shaping the critical perspective on the Gospels that many critical scholars despair of ever being able to recover anything historical from them. The building blocks were formed in the fires of faith; therefore, the Gospels themselves are through and through confessional narratives about the Christ of faith. The historical Jesus is forever lost.

For almost a century, anyone wishing to do historical Jesus research has had to overcome this considerable hurdle. In the aftermath of Bultmann's *History of the Synoptic Tradition*,[9] historical Jesus research in European circles all but ceased; after a brief resurrection as the New Quest in the 1950s and early 1960s, it has lain dormant until the present. In English-speaking circles the quest has gone on, sometimes with post-Bultmannian presuppositions,[10] sometimes without.[11] In a recent work, Richard Bauckham attempted to write the epitaph for form criticism in Gospel research by refurbishing the traditional view that the Gospels are based on eyewitness testimony.[12] But his dismissal of form criticism is, in my view, altogether premature and misguided. True, many of the *tradition historical* aspects of form critical theory have been problematized: there are few reliable rules by which one might track the development of the oral tradition—it neither "grows" nor "shrinks," nor does it become increasingly complex or progressively more simple.[13] Also, the forms Bultmann identified would have been better delineated according to ancient rhetorical conventions.[14] But the insights of form criticism most important for our purposes have not been effectively challenged; to the contrary, they have only grown more secure. We may now point to Harris's work to underscore the extent to which the ancient world was an oral culture,[15] and to Walter Ong and Jack Goody to deepen our sense of how different orality and literacy are as media of cultural development.[16] It is now clearer than ever that oral tradition tries for gist, not reproduction, is malleable, not static, and develops in close relationship to changing community circumstances. The form critical point is not that people forget things, it is that people reproduce things in community contexts to address ongoing circumstances. Those early believers who repeated the traditions from and about Jesus were not historians, but preachers and storytellers. In their hands, the traditions about Jesus survived, but also changed and developed to reflect new circumstances and new convictions about who he was. The Gospels gather up this material in all its variety and embed it in a narrative. The result is a mix of history and interpretation, memory and creative imagination.

One should remember also that what is true of the smaller units of oral tradition is also true of the larger narratives created by the Gospel writers themselves. Recall what Papias said about the writing of Mark, our first narrative Gospel:

> Mark became Peter's interpreter and wrote accurately whatever he remembered, not, however, in the order in which things were said and done by the Lord. For he had not heard the Lord, nor had he followed him. Rather, as I said, later on he followed Peter, who used to give instruction as the need arose, but did not make something like an arrangement of the Lord's sayings, so that Mark did nothing wrong in writing down single points as he remembered them (Eusebius, *Ecclesiastical History* 3.39.15).[17]

This passage is remarkable on a number of counts. It reflects very clearly what theorists have said about orality: that what survives in an oral culture survives because it is useful and memorable. So Peter (if Papias has this right) remembered things and spoke them as the need arose. That is what Mark had—or what any Gospel writer would have had—remembrance of things heard from others. What he did not have was a narrative, the story of Jesus' life. This he had to create. We can now say that the narrative vehicle he created was something more than a simple string of pearls.[18] The Passion narrative, especially, was shaped on the basis of a common martyrological form, what George Nickelsburg has called "The Story of the Persecution and Exaltation of the Righteous Man," a pattern drawn from many contemporary literary examples.[19] The point is that this was a choice, a choice made in response to certain circumstances obtaining in the life of the Markan community and the author's own convictions about what Jesus could mean to his community in its hour of need. It is a story about Jesus, not the remembered history of his life.

2.3 The problem of internal consistency

A third reason is what might be called the problem of internal consistency. The claims that are made about Jesus the Christ are actually quite varied and diverse. Consider the following examples: Did Jesus think he was one with God, or did he eschew even the slightest compliment as praise too high? The person who said "Why do you call me good? No one is good but God alone" (Mark 10:18) probably did not also say "I and the Father are one" (John 10:30). As history, the difference is a problem. But as interpretation, not so much really: for Mark, humility is the supreme sign of Jesus' extraordinary status, but for John, it is his matter-of-fact boldness that reveals his true identity. These are not competing versions of Jesus' actual personality, but variations in the attempt to express adequately the convictions his followers developed about him. Or consider: Was Jesus the Son of God by virtue of his resurrection (Romans 1:4), his baptism (Mark 1:11), his divine birth (Matthew 1:18–25; Luke 1:35), or his preexistence as the divine logos of God (John 1:1–18)? Whether or not the skilled systematician could arrange all these claims into a cogent whole, it is clear that they do not derive from some common historical experience in which Jesus' status was decisively revealed. Rather, these claims were generated in all their variety as followers of Jesus borrowed from the lexicon of religious ideas—apotheosis, divine anointing, the divine birth of a *theios aner*, the Platonic *logos* of Jewish sapiential theology—to find words that would adequately express their convictions about him. Or finally: Was Jesus raised from the dead as a "life-giving spirit" (1 Corinthians 15:45), having what Paul might call a "spiritual body" (1 Corinthians 15:44), or was it as Luke describes in the following scene:

> As they were saying this, Jesus himself stood in the midst of them and said to them, "Peace to you." But they were startled and became afraid, for they thought they were seeing a ghost (*pneuma*). And he said to them, "Why are you troubled, why do questions arise in your hearts? See my hands and feet, that it is I myself. Touch me and see, for a ghost (*pneuma*) does not have flesh and bones as you see that I have" (Luke 24:36–39).

Paul's audience, who could not conceive of a flesh and blood resurrection,[20] would have scoffed at Luke's account. But Luke had his own scoffers to worry about, and they would have dismissed Paul's "Spirit of Christ" as a mere ghost.[21] So which of these Christs of faith is the historical Jesus? Neither. The Christ of faith is Jesus as seen only with the eyes of faith. If faith meets unfaith with a spiritual body, then a spiritual body it is. If faith meets unfaith with a physical body, then a physical body it is. The Christ of faith is a response of faith, always offered in a particular rhetorical situation. He does not exist to be described outside of faith—truly spiritual or truly physical. Having faith in Jesus is not a matter of getting right the actual terms of his postmortem existence. It is always about declaring one's loyalty to Jesus, whether that means removing the stumbling block of physical resurrection or countering the claim that he is merely a ghost.

2.4 The historical reason

Finally, one of the most compelling reasons to answer our question with a "no" is very simply the historical reason. The Christ of faith, as he appears in the Gospels—born of a virgin, worker of miracles, healer—is a demigod striding across the earth. And yet, history tells us that in the end the historical Jesus died alone, the victim of crucifixion, with few followers and little respect from his contemporaries. Even for those who might be willing to consider that Jesus really did have supernatural qualities, this should represent a historical incongruity.

Had Jesus in fact been as he is described, his status as the Son of God, Redeemer, Savior, would have been manifestly self-evident. Who could have doubted him?

This is perhaps worth considering because two of our Gospel writers struggle precisely with this problem in their narrative portrayals of Jesus. Mark's author introduced the "Messianic secret," whereby Jesus reveals his divine identity to various persons, but strictly forbids them from saying anything about it. There are, of course, several explanations for this well-known Markan theme, but Wrede's solution is still widely embraced: Mark could well see that Jesus had in fact won few converts in his lifetime. Mark wanted to show that this was by design. Jesus chose to keep his messianic identity a secret until it should be revealed in the fullness of time.[22] The author of John also recognizes this problem and states it clearly in the Prologue: "He was in the world, and the world was made through him, but the world did not recognize him" (John 1:10). The problem is then played out in a series of Johannine scenes in which Jesus plays the role of *Deus incognito*, appearing to people—Nicodemus, the Samaritan woman—as an ordinary person, and yet speaking words the audience knows to be the words of the Son of God. The audience knows that he is the Logos, the one sent from God, but to those to whom he speaks in the narrative itself he remains an enigma, whose enigmatic words are met only with confusion and disbelief.[23]

All of this reflects what historical common sense has already told us, that Jesus—the historical Jesus—was a real human being, not a demigod with supernatural powers. His followers saw in him a vision of God incarnate. But as with every human experience of the divine that is disclosed in the midst of historical existence, it was ambiguous. Some who encountered him decided for him. For them, he became the Christ of faith. Others decided against him. For them, he remained only Jesus, the carpenter's son from Nazareth (Mark 6:3). The claims of Christian faith were not, and are not, self-evident. They involve(d) a decision about a very real, historical experience that came in the form of a real person. As much as the Gospels try to make explicit and clear what was in reality ambiguous and debatable, the historian cannot lose sight of the fact that the life of Jesus was a real *human* life. The Christ of faith is an expression of a decision to see in him what could not be seen apart from faith.

▓ 3. YES, THE CHRIST OF FAITH IS THE HISTORICAL JESUS

This is Christianity: the decision to see in Jesus an epiphany of God. If this is so, then there is another way in which our question must be addressed, and answered very differently. There is a sense in which the Christ of faith is most definitely the historical Jesus. For, insofar as faith in Jesus was indeed faith in *Jesus*, all of the confessional language that creates the Christ of faith finds its meaning finally in reference to the Jesus of history.[24] It is not just anyone whom Christians proclaimed as raised from the dead, but Jesus, whose life stood for something important and revelatory to those who followed him, whose particular words proved revelatory to those who heard them and believed, whose particular ways proved revelatory to those who experienced him and believed. Of course, not everyone did believe. But for those who did, it was Jesus in whom they believed, and so it was Jesus who is elevated by the Christ of faith language through which his significance was proclaimed. For this reason, the identity between the Christ of faith and the Jesus of history must always be maintained.

This seems clear enough from the form and genre of the Gospels themselves. In the canonical Gospel tradition the preferred form is the martyr's story.[25] The stories that lead up to Jesus' arrest and execution are not mere preface: they portray the martyr's life, the life that leads to his fate and makes it worth considering. For surely the martyr's fate—his/her death and redemption—cannot be considered apart from the martyr's life. Indeed, the tragic end to an ordinary life is simply a tragedy. But the tragic end of a principled life is far more: it becomes a witness (*martyria*), a witness to the exemplary life and the values championed by the martyr. It urges faithfulness, even in the face of opposition, even the threat of death. It is not that the cross finds its significance in the resurrection,[26] but that the cross and resurrection find their significance in the life of the martyr. In the Gospel of Mark the cross is spoken of in explicitly martyrological terms:

> If anyone would come after me, let him deny himself/herself and take up the cross and follow me. For whoever would save her life will lose it; and whoever loses his life for my sake and the gospel's will save it. For what does it profit a person to gain the whole world and give up his life? And what can a person give for her life? For whoever is ashamed of me and my words in this adulterous and sinful generation, of him will the Son of Man also be ashamed, when he comes in the glory of his Father with the holy angels (Mark 8:35–38).

Now, when one searches the Gospel of Mark for Jesus' words, the witness is admittedly thin. Perhaps the heat and pressure of war and violence has boiled the whole thing down to the singular question of faithfulness (see, especially, Mark 13). So when the authors of Matthew and Luke, independently of one another, decided to revise Mark, each chose to supplement Mark. In Matthew and Luke it is not just anyone who dies at the hands of his enemies, it is Jesus who said the poor are blessed and spoke of a new reign of God in which the lost and forsaken of the world would find a place. These are not incidental details. They witness to that which the martyr values most deeply, the cause for which he or she is willing to die. And when, in the end, the martyr's sacrifice is vindicated, it is these values, this cause, that is elevated to the will of God. If the Gospels present Jesus' life as *kairos*,[27] a moment of decision, it is the substance of his life—what Willi Marxsen would later call "*die Sache Jesu*"—that one must decide about.[28]

The fact that our Gospels are not modern biographies such as one might write about King or Kennedy, in which the life of the martyr, though filtered for its most edifying content, is still a realistic human life, should not prevent us from seeing this basic structure to early Christian faith. The one who preaches the Sermon on the Mount is also the one who walks on water. The one who befriends the unclean and degraded leper is also the one who miraculously heals him with a mere touch. Our Gospels are a mix of history and interpretation, myth and reality. These two poles—history and interpretation—work together and must be held together. The historical reminiscence, however it survives, is the memory of an experience in history—the words and deeds of a real human being. The interpretation, whatever its form, is the expression of faith that says in these words and deeds one can encounter something more than the human being. One can encounter God in a real human life. History and interpretation, they always work together, interpretation always claiming the presence of revelation, history always recalling the moment and character of that revelation. In this sense the Christ of faith *is* the historical Jesus; the historical Jesus *is* the Christ of faith.

NOTES

1. Diogenes Laertius, *Lives* 3.1–2.

2. Iamblichos, *Life of Pythagoras*, 28.

3. Ovid, *Metamorphoses*, 15.

4. Robert L. Webb, "The Historical Enterprise and Historical Jesus Research," in *Key Events in the Life of the Historical Jesus: A Collaborative Exploration of Context and Coherence,* ed. Darrell L. Bock and Robert L. Webb (Tübingen: Mohr-Siebeck, 2009), 40, *et passim.*

5. Webb, "The Historical Enterprise and Historical Jesus Research," 46–47.

6. Webb, "The Historical Enterprise and Historical Jesus Research," 46–47.

7. Webb, "The Historical Enterprise and Historical Jesus Research," 47.

8. Webb, "The Historical Enterprise and Historical Jesus Research," 40, n. 82: "In the naturalistic approach, science is dominant...In the theistic approach historical event is dominant."

9. Rudolf Bultmann, *History of the Synoptic Tradition*, rev. ed., trans. John Marsh (Peabody, MA: Hendrickson, 1994); German original, *Die Geschichte der synoptischen Tradition* (Göttingen: Vandenhoeck & Ruprecht, 1921).

10. For example, John Dominic Crossan, *The Historical Jesus: The Life of a Mediterranean Jewish Peasant* (San Francisco: Harper, 1991).

11. For example, N. T. Wright, *Jesus and the Victory of God* (Minneapolis: Fortress, 1996).

12. Richard Bauckham, *Jesus and the Eyewitnesses: The Gospels as Eyewitness Testimony* (Grand Rapids, MI: Eerdmans, 2006).

13. E. P. Sanders, *The Tendencies of the Synoptic Tradition* (Cambridge: Cambridge University Press, 1969).

14. Klaus Berger, *Formgeschichte des Neuen Testaments* (Heidelberg: Quelle and Meyer, 1984).

15. William V. Harris, *Ancient Literacy* (Cambridge, MA: Harvard University Press, 1989).

16. Walter Ong, *Orality and Literacy* (London: Methuen, 1982); Jack Goody, *The Domestication of the Savage Mind* (Cambridge: Cambridge University Press, 1977); Jack Goody, *The Interface Between the Written and the Oral* (Cambridge: Cambridge University Press, 1987).

17. From the Greek in K. Lake, *Eusebius, The Ecclesiastical History*, 2 vols. (Cambridge, MA: Harvard, 1949).

18. The felicitous coinage of Karl Ludwig Schmidt, *Der Rahmen der Geschichte Jesu. Literarkritische Untersuchungen zur ältesten Jesusüberlieferung* (Berlin: Trowitzsch, 1919).

19. G. W. E. Nickelsburg, *Resurrection, Immortality, and Eternal Life in Intertestamental Judaism* (Cambridge, MA: Harvard University Press, 1972), 48–62; G. W. E. Nickelsburg, "The Genre and Function of the Markan Passion Narrative," *Harvard Theological Review* 73 (1980): 153–184.

20. For this interpretation of the Corinthian situation, see Paul Hoffmann, *Die Toten in Christus. Eine religionsgeschichtliche und exegetische Untersuchung zur paulinischen Eschatologie* (Münster: Aschendorff, 1966), 241–243; Pheme Perkins, *Resurrection: New Testament Witness and Contemporary Reflection* (Garden City, NY: Doubleday, 1984), 221–227; Dale Martin, *The Corinthian Body* (New Haven, CT: Yale University Press, 1995), 104–136, among others.

21. Hans-Dieter Betz, "Zum Problem der Auferstehung Jesu im Lichte der griechischen magischen Papyri," in Hans-Dieter Betz, *Hellenismus und Urchristentum: Gesammelte Aufsätze I* (Tübingen: Mohr-Siebeck, 1990), 248–249; Gregory Riley, *Resurrection Reconsidered: Thomas and John in Controversy* (Minneapolis: Fortress, 1995), 53; Stephen J. Patterson, *Beyond the Passion: Rethinking the Death and Life of Jesus* (Minneapolis: Fortress, 2004), 114–115.

22. William Wrede, *The Messianic Secret*, trans. J. C. G. Grieg (Cambridge: James Clarke, 1971); German original, *Das Messiasgeheimnis in den Evangelien. Zugleich ein Beitrag zum Verständnis des Markusevangeliums* (Göttingen: Vandenhoeck & Ruprecht, 1901).

23. See Wayne Meeks, "The Man From Heaven in Johannine Sectarianism," *Journal of Biblical Literature* 91 (1972): 44–72.

24. The point of view developed here is presented most fully in Willi Marxsen, *Jesus and the Church*, trans. Philip Devenish (Philadelphia: Trinity, 1992); earlier, see also Ernst Käsemann, "The Problem of the Historical Jesus," in Ernst Käsemann, *Essays on New Testament Themes* (Naperville, IL: Allenson, 1964), 15–48 (especially 30–34); and among theologians, Schubert Ogden, *The Point of Christology* (San Francisco: Harper & Row, 1982). For the author's view, see Stephen J. Patterson, *The God of Jesus: The Historical Jesus and the Search for Meaning* (Harrisburg, PA: Trinity, 1998).

25. Bernard Lohse, *Märtyrer und Gottesknecht* (Göttingen: Vandenhoeck & Ruprecht, 1955); Patterson, *Beyond the Passion*, especially chap. 2, "Martyr."

26. Rudolf Bultmann, "The New Testament and Mythology," in Rudolf Bultmann, *New Testament and Mythology and Other Basic Writings*, ed. and trans. Schubert M. Ogden (Philadelphia: Fortress, 1984), 36.

27. Käsemann, "Problem of the Historical Jesus," 31.

28. Marxsen, *Jesus and the Church*, 16–35.

■ FOR FURTHER READING

Bultmann, R. "The New Testament and Mythology." In *New Testament and Mythology and Other Basic Writings*, selected, edited, and translated by Schubert M. Ogden, 1–44. Philadelphia: Fortress, 1984.

Marxsen, W. *Jesus and the Church*, translated by Philip Devenish. Philadelphia: Trinity, 1992.
———. *The Resurrection of Jesus of Nazareth*. Philadelphia: Fortress, 1970.
Ogden, S. M. *The Point of Christology*. San Francisco: Harper & Row, 1982.
Patterson, S. J. *The God of Jesus: The Historical Jesus and the Search for Meaning*. Harrisburg, PA: Trinity, 1998.

34 The Christ of Faith is the Jesus of History

■ CRAIG A. EVANS

What is asserted in the title of this chapter requires qualification, which I think can be done through paraphrase. Paraphrased and expanded, the title could be "What informed Christians believe about Jesus accurately reflects the Jesus of history." But even this paraphrase requires qualification, for the words "Jesus of history" constitute a construct, not an observable, verifiable reality. No one actually has access to the Jesus of history. To access the Jesus of history would require traveling back in time, which of course is impossible. No idea or concept, such as "Christ of faith," can be equated with someone or something long ago. Accordingly, what we mean by "the Jesus of history" (or "the Julius Caesar of history") is the construction of a coherent picture or narrative from the literary and archaeological remains from the past. So the title of this chapter might be further expanded to read "What informed Christians believe about Jesus represents a fair and reasonable construction of the ancient sources and related data." Alas, not a catchy title.

This chapter does not attempt to address the philosophical issue of how and in what sense a person who lived can be represented or portrayed as history or biography. This is a complicated and much debated topic.[1] The premise of this chapter is that in many cases we have access to a sufficient amount of material that has survived from the past so that we can construct a coherent and plausible portrait, even narrative, of a person who lived long ago. There may well be a great number of gaps in our constructed narrative and a great many unanswered questions, but we will be in a position to say a number of significant things about the person.

What makes the topic at hand difficult is that what Christians believe about Jesus is a mixture of historical elements and theological confessions. This can be illustrated by reviewing the Apostles' Creed, a western creed that probably first came to expression in the third century and in its final form in the fourth century or later. The familiar creed reads:

> I believe in God, the Father almighty,
>> Maker of heaven and earth.
>> (1) *And in Jesus Christ, his only Son, our Lord;*
>> (2) *Who was conceived by the Holy Spirit,*
>> (3) *Born of the Virgin Mary;*
>> (4) *Suffered under Pontius Pilate,*

(5) *Was crucified, died, and was buried;*
(6) *He descended into Hades;*
(7) *The third day he rose from the dead;*
(8) *He ascended into heaven;*
(9) *And sits at the right hand of God the Father Almighty;*
(10) *From thence he shall come to judge the living and the dead.*

I believe in the Holy Spirit;
the holy Catholic Church;
the communion of saints;
the forgiveness of sins;
the resurrection of the body;
and the life everlasting. Amen.[2]

The part of the creed that makes specific reference to Jesus is placed in italics and numbered. Some of this material is clearly of a historical nature; much of it is not. Let's review it line by line. The first line reads, "[I believe] in Jesus Christ, his only Son, our Lord." "Jesus" refers to the historical person Jesus of Nazareth. Apart from a few eccentrics, no historian doubts that such a person actually lived in the first century and that in one sense or another was the founder of a movement that in time became known as Christianity. The creed identifies this Jesus as "Jesus Christ." "Christ" or "Messiah" (from Hebrew, meaning the "anointed one") is also historical in the sense that this is how Jesus' first followers regarded him. Some scholars think Jesus was confessed as Israel's Messiah after the resurrection; some think that he was before. I take the latter position, because in my view it offers a better explanation for the ubiquitousness of this title and for the execution of Jesus as "king of the Jews," of which more will be said shortly. Although Jesus was called "Christ" by his followers, this does not necessarily mean that he was. Indeed, historical research cannot prove (or disprove) the claim that Jesus was Israel's Messiah. Similarly, historical research cannot prove that Jesus was God's Son or that there is even a God. These elements are confessional, not historical.

The second and third lines read, "[I believe that Jesus] was conceived by the Holy Spirit, born of the Virgin Mary." This statement alludes to the infancy narratives recounted in the Gospels of Matthew and Luke. The former says that Mary "was found to be with child of the Holy Spirit" (Matthew 1:18) and that an angel told Joseph, the man to whom Mary was engaged, "that which is conceived in her is of the Holy Spirit" (Matthew 1:20). The latter Gospel says an angel told Mary, in response to her question about giving birth to a son in her as yet unmarried state, "The Holy Spirit will come upon you" (Luke 1:31, 35). Historical research cannot confirm a virginal conception, whether by the Holy Spirit or by some other agency. At most, historians think they can detect traces of controversy surrounding Jesus' conception and birth.³ The evangelists Matthew and Luke affirm the belief that the strangeness and controversy surrounding these intimate details were due to divine intervention, not a sexual lapse on the part of Mary. People can accept or reject the explanation offered by the evangelists; historians can do little to decide the question.

The fourth and fifth lines read, "Suffered under Pontius Pilate, was crucified, died, and was buried." These are the kinds of statements that historians—as historians—can deal with. Although the suffering, crucifixion, death, and burial of Jesus can all be viewed as having theological meaning (as we see in early Christian writings), they are also descriptions of events that can be investigated by historians. Did Jesus suffer crucifixion and death under Pontius Pilate, the prefect of Judea? Was he buried, or was he left unburied, perhaps hanging on the cross? If buried, did any of his family and followers know where? Historians are in a position to grapple with these questions by making critical use of the New Testament Gospels, other writings, and data gleaned from the remains of material culture.

The remaining lines concerned with Jesus, that is, lines six through ten, are mostly theological. Line six states that at death Jesus "descended into Hades." Here historians cannot get to first base. What happened to Jesus after his death cannot be discovered through historical investigation. Nor can the existence or nonexistence of a place called Hades. But the affirmation in line seven that on the "third day he rose from the dead" is to some extent open to historical investigation. The sources state that on the third day following his death the tomb of Jesus was found empty and that Jesus himself was seen and recognized by a number of his followers. How credible these accounts are (e.g., their number, their antiquity, how well they accord with Jewish and Roman practices relating to execution and burial) is a question that historians can address. Some historians have concluded that the accounts are not to be believed; others have concluded that they should be believed.

The rest of the lines that pertain to Jesus are theological and not subject to historical investigation. Even line eight, which affirms that Jesus "ascended into heaven," is only theological surmise. The risen Jesus may have been seen by Jesus' followers, some of them may have even seen him "taken up" in some sense, but no one saw him enter "heaven" any more than anyone saw him descend into Hades. So also the affirmation in line nine that the risen Jesus now "sits at the right hand of God the Father Almighty"; it is a theological conclusion, perhaps informed by revelation or mystical experience, but it is not something that historians can investigate any more than the prediction in line ten that at some time in the future Jesus shall return "to judge the living and the dead."

By their nature creeds are brief and focus on essential theological elements. As the word "creed" implies (from the Latin *credo*, "I believe"), they are statements of faith and not summaries of history. Accordingly, one should not be too surprised that the Apostles' Creed says nothing about what Jesus taught and almost nothing about the things he did. But when people today speak about the "Jesus of history" and the "Christ of faith," they often have in mind more than the limited theological affirmations of a creed. They have in mind what Jesus taught and what he did, including elements affirmed by the creed. They wonder if the Jesus uncovered through critical historical investigation closely approximates the portraits of Jesus we find in the New Testament Gospels, the Jesus in whom Christians have faith.

Although the recent "Third Quest" for the historical Jesus was more historical and contextual in its approach (in contrast to the highly theological "New Quest" of the 1950s and 1960s), often lying behind it was the question that asked whether the Jesus of tradition (i.e., the Jesus of the New Testament Gospels) was supported by critical historical research. The group of scholars that made up the North American Jesus Seminar by and large answered this question in the negative. The Jesus of history, as discerned from the oldest and best sources critically evaluated,[4] was quite different from the Jesus of the creeds and traditional Christian belief and piety.[5]

A number of other scholars, however, have come to different and less minimalistic conclusions.[6] Of course, not all of these scholars have concluded that the historical Jesus exactly equates with the Jesus of the New Testament Gospels, but many think he is pretty close. If I may, allow me to present the Historians' Creed (or *concludo*, "I conclude"):

I conclude that Jesus

(1) Was baptized by John
(2) Proclaimed the kingdom of God
(3) Healed and cast out evil spirits
(4) Summoned disciples and appointed twelve as apostles
(5) Was confessed as Israel's Messiah and God's Son
(6) Challenged the Jerusalem temple establishment
(7) Was betrayed by one of his apostles
(8) Was examined and condemned by the Jewish council
(9) Was handed over to Pontius Pilate, the Roman prefect of Judea
(10) Was condemned to death and was crucified
(11) Was buried
(12) And on the third day appeared to a number of followers and family

Let's review these conclusions, some of which overlap with affirmations in the Apostles' Creed, and then ask if they justify the claim found in the title of this chapter, namely, that "the Christ of Faith is the Jesus of History."

The first conclusion states that Jesus "was baptized by John." There are several factors that count in favor of this conclusion. First, three of the four first-century Gospels, that is, the New Testament Gospels of Matthew, Mark, and Luke, state that Jesus was baptized (Matt 3:13–15; Mark 1:9; Luke 3:21). The first two (Matthew and Mark) state explicitly that it was John who baptized Jesus, while it is implied in Luke. John does not state or imply this, but the connection between John and Jesus is affirmed (John 1:29–34). Later traditions also affirm that John baptized Jesus or seem to presuppose it (Acts 1:22; *Gospel of the Ebionites* §4; *Gospel of the Nazarenes* §2; *Gospel of the Hebrews* §2). Second, because John's preaching and baptizing focused on a call to Israel to repent, it is difficult to understand why early Christians would invent a story about Jesus (who is supposed to be sinless; cf. John 8:46; 2 Corinthians 5:21; Hebrews 4:15; 7:26; 1 Peter 2:22) going to John for baptism. It is therefore not surprising that most scholars engaged in Jesus research agree that the story of Jesus and John has a strong claim to authenticity. The value of this story is that it places Jesus and his preaching and activities into the context of a renewal movement, which in turn clarifies in important ways the next line of the *concludo*.

The second line concludes that Jesus "proclaimed the kingdom of God." There is wide agreement among scholars that the central datum of Jesus' public activities was his proclamation of the kingdom (or rule) of God (Matthew 3:2; Mark 1:15; Luke 4:43; John 3:3, 5). The proclamation of God's kingdom in a Jewish setting of late antiquity recalled a theme that is pervasive in the Old Testament scriptures, namely, that God was Israel's king and ultimately the king of the world. Jesus' proclamation would also have resonated with his contemporaries who longed for God's rule, as promised to the patriarchs, foretold by the prophets, petitioned by the faithful almost daily in their prayers, and who, acting as prophets and would-be messiahs, hoped to bring about the kingdom of God. That Jesus was able to draw crowds to himself was due in no small way to his mighty deeds that accompanied his proclamation of God's kingdom—which leads us to the next line of the *concludo*.

The third line affirms that Jesus "healed and cast out evil spirits." At one time the supernatural element of the Jesus story caused embarrassment for post-Enlightenment thinkers. This element was either eliminated altogether or was rationalized in one manner or another. Today most scholars acknowledge that it is probable that Jesus did things that his contemporaries regarded as miracles or mighty works of power. (Most historians now recognize that historical investigation into such stories does not require philosophical or scientific explanations.) His supporters saw these works as evidence that God's power was at work in him (e.g., Mark 1:27–28; 2:12); his critics argued that it was the power of Satan at work in him (e.g., Matt 12:24; Mark 3:22). These works, especially the exorcisms, provide important context for understanding the proclamation of the kingdom of God. In short, in the words and works of Jesus the kingdom of Satan was in the process of being overwhelmed by the kingdom of God (cf. Mark 3:26, where Satan's kingdom "has an end"), which was longed for by the faithful (cf. *Testament of Moses* 10:1 God's "kingdom will arise and the Devil will have an end").[7]

The fourth line affirms that Jesus "summoned disciples and appointed twelve as apostles." All agree that Jesus, frequently called rabbi or teacher, called disciples to himself. Most scholars agree that it was Jesus who appointed the twelve apostles, whose membership may have varied somewhat during his public mission and activities. Among these were brothers Peter and Andrew, and the two sons of Zebedee, James and John, who in the early church became known as "pillars." These men were commissioned and empowered by Jesus to proclaim his message and to perform works of power (though evidently with less success than what was enjoyed by their master).

The fifth line of the *concludo* affirms that Jesus "was confessed as Israel's Messiah and God's Son." It was fashionable in some circles in earlier generations to think that the confession of Jesus as Messiah was a post-Easter development, that it was the resurrection that led to this understanding. What lent support to this view was the belief that there was no genuine pre-Easter tradition in which Jesus claimed a messianic identity.[8] The publication of 4Q521, the Messianic Apocalypse, in the early 1990s led to reconsideration of this thinking. In this scroll fragment a number of things are anticipated when God's Messiah appears. Among these things will be healing, raising the dead, and proclamation of good news to the afflicted. These elements, mostly from Isaiah, are present in Jesus' reply to John, who had inquired if Jesus was the awaited coming one (Matthew 11:2–6; Luke 7:18–23). It is now recognized that Jesus' reply to John was messianic after all, and very few question the authenticity of this Gospel tradition. It is also conceded that calling the Messiah the "Son of God" is rooted in Old Testament scripture (e.g. Psalms 2:2, 7; 2 Samuel 7:14). That the messianic epithets "Son of God" and "Son of the Most High" (cf. Luke 1:32–38) were current in the eschatological thinking of Jesus' time is now attested by 4Q246, also known as the Son of God text.

The sixth line affirms that Jesus "challenged the Jerusalem temple establishment." This conclusion is hardly contested. The debate tends to center on the meaning of Jesus' action in the temple precincts and what motivated them. One interpretation is that Jesus warned of coming judgment, an interpretation consistent with the earlier preaching of John the Baptist. It is probably not a coincidence that Jesus defended himself in the precincts by comparing himself to John. The temple controversy makes sense of much that follows.

The seventh line of the *concludo* affirms that Jesus "was betrayed by one of his apostles." This is hardly something the early church would invent. But it is entirely consistent with what we know of the pre-70 AD aristocratic priests who, according to Josephus, a first-century Jewish historian who was himself of aristocratic priestly stock, were violent and not above bribery. The betrayal of Jesus leads us to the next line.

The eighth line affirms that Jesus "was examined and condemned by the Jewish council," a Jewish council that in all probability was dominated by the high priest and his colleagues. Jesus had insulted and threatened them in the temple precincts. He has now been brought before them for examination. The result of this examination enabled the council to deliver Jesus to the Roman authorities with the recommendation (demand?) that Jesus be put to death.

The ninth line affirms that Jesus was "handed over to Pontius Pilate, the Roman prefect of Judea." The eighth, ninth, and tenth lines of the *concludo* are closely related. The glue that holds them together is Jesus' acknowledgment of his messianic status, complete with the claim to be in some sense the "Son of God." The charge of blasphemy, the presentation to Pontius Pilate, which implies an additional charge of treason, and the resulting crucifixion of Jesus for claiming to be the "king of the Jews" confirm his earlier claim to be Israel's Messiah.

The tenth line, "was condemned to death and was crucified," is disputed by almost no one. Widely accepted, though disputed by some, is the claim in all four New Testament Gospels that Jesus was crucified for claiming to be the "king of the Jews." Most scholars accept this tradition as authentic because it does not reflect what Christians said of Jesus. Christians confessed Jesus as the Son of God, Savior, Lord, and Messiah—not "king of the Jews," a Roman designation (principally for Herod the Great). It is not a Jewish designation either. Most Jews spoke of the Messiah as the "King of Israel." The authenticity of the tradition that Jesus was crucified as king of the Jews strongly supports his pre-Easter self-understanding as Israel's Messiah and, if Messiah, then in some sense God's Son.

The eleventh line of the *concludo* asserts that Jesus "was buried." At one time this was hardly doubted, but in recent years a few scholars have argued that the corpse of Jesus was probably left unburied.[9] This point is important, because if the corpse of Jesus was left unburied, or at best was pitched into an unmarked ditch, where it was mauled by animals, then the authenticity of the empty tomb story is greatly weakened. But this novel hypothesis has been vigorously challenged by scholars, including archaeologists. Jews buried all dead, including the executed, and the Romans complied with Jewish customs—at least during peacetime.[10]

The twelfth and final line of the *concludo* affirms that Jesus "on the third day appeared to a number of followers and family." This claim is hotly disputed, of course, but most concede that this was the belief of the first followers of Jesus. Our earliest written source for this belief is found in Paul's letter to the Christians in Corinth:

> [3]For I handed on to you as of first importance what I in turn had received, that Christ died for our sins in accordance with the scriptures, [4]and that he was buried, and that he was raised on the third day in accordance with the scriptures, [5]and that he appeared to Cephas, then to the twelve (1 Corinthians 15:3–5).

Paul's "Christ died for our sins" parallels the tenth line of our *concludo*. Paul knows that the death of Jesus was by crucifixion, as we see elsewhere in his letters (e.g., 1 Corinthians 1:23; 2:2, 8; Galatians 3:1). His statement, "for our sins," is theological to be sure, but it probably is rooted in Jesus' Words of Institution (Matt 26:26–29, "for the forgiveness of sins"; Mark 14:22–25, "poured out for many [sinners]"), words with which the apostle was familiar (1 Corinthians 11:23–25). Jesus did not simply die the death of a martyr or righteous man, his death was sacrificial. Paul's "he was buried" parallels the eleventh line. And, of course, Paul's "he was raised on the third day" and "he appeared to Cephas, then to the twelve" parallel the twelfth line.

Paul's reference to tradition that he has "received" offers important, early support for the essential elements of Christian proclamation. Most think Paul was converted two or at most three years after the movement began. It strikes me as improbable that Paul, formerly an enemy of the Christian movement, and converted not long after the key events took place, would not have been in a position to ascertain the basic facts surrounding the death and burial of Jesus, as well as the identity and number of persons who claimed to have seen the risen Jesus. Elsewhere in his writings Paul talks about meeting some of these witnesses of the resurrection of Jesus (cf. Galatians 1:18–19; 2:9, 11). Most importantly, Paul is himself an eyewitness of the risen Jesus (1 Corinthians 9:1; 15:8). Paul provides us with first-hand testimony, not second- or third-hand hearsay. One is free to believe Paul or not believe him. One is free to reinterpret him. Similarly, one is free to set aside all of the early Christian testimony, but that is just what it is—setting aside the evidence that we have. In my view the evidence that we have justifies the twelfth line of the historians' *concludo*, that is, that Jesus "on the third day appeared to a number of followers and family," or so many—including eyewitnesses—believed. Philosophy, science, even psychology may come into play, either supporting or undermining the claims of these witnesses, but from a historical perspective the evidence is weighty.[11]

The significance of the resurrection of Jesus lies in its corroborative power. That is, if Jesus was resurrected, then what he said prior to his crucifixion and what he said to his followers (including, eventually, Paul) probably should be accepted as true. I concede that this inference does not follow as a mathematical proof. After all, Jesus could have been quite mistaken in many things he said, perhaps even delusional as to his identity and purpose, and yet still have been raised from the dead. But I suspect such an option would strike most as bizarre and at odds with common sense. It is more probable that if Jesus was actually raised from the dead, as a number of his closest followers (and an enemy and an indifferent soul or two) actually witnessed, then we should take seriously what he taught about God and about himself.

So where does this leave us? Strictly speaking we cannot without qualification equate the Christ of faith with the Jesus of history. The two are related; they overlap. But they are not the same. Much that Christians believe about Jesus, what is usually called Christology, reflects theology that simply is not open to historical examination. In what way can historical investigation prove or disprove the belief that Jesus is the second person of the Triune Godhead? How can a historian prove that Jesus' death on the cross paid the price for human sin? Or that his resurrection made justification of humans possible in the sight of a holy God?

Nevertheless, a qualified equation is possible. The "Christ of faith" includes a number of historical components, some of which are very important. These include Jesus' death, burial, and resurrection. If the evidence for these components is compelling, especially for the last one, then we have come a long way in showing that the Jesus of history really is what lies behind the Christ of faith. A Jesus of history who performed works of power, whose teachings regarding God and people continue to inform and enrich humanity, whose authority and claims seem to overlap with the authority of God himself, and who on the third day following his brutal death was raised from the dead and was seen alive by many of his followers, family, and even skeptics, is wholly consistent with the Christ of Christian faith. The Christ of faith entails more, to be sure, but the Christ of faith (or Christology) of necessity presupposes the Jesus of history.

The Jesus of history overlaps with key theological elements in Christology, such as teaching with the authority of God himself, and in the resurrection. But the Jesus of history also lays a sufficient foundation on which the more expansive Christology and Christian creeds may be built. If Jesus was God's Son, as he seems to have implied, if his death benefitted humanity, as his Words of Institution seem to say, and if his resurrection from the dead authorizes him to send his apostles throughout the world, then the link between the Jesus of history and Christ of faith is a strong one indeed.

It is the firm conviction of this author that behind the creed, behind the faith claims of the Christian movement, is history. The death, burial, and resurrection of Jesus are not merely theological ideas, but actual events. It was the actual events that awakened faith and later prompted theological inquiry. This inquiry in time articulated the Christology we see summed up in the Apostles' Creed and creeds like it. Therefore, when properly qualified, we can affirm that "the Christ of Faith is the Jesus of History."

■ NOTES

1. The problem is addressed in a very helpful essay by R. L. Webb, "The Historical Enterprise and Historical Jesus Research," in *Key Events in the Life of the Historical Jesus*, ed. D. L. Bock and R. L. Webb (Tübingen: Mohr Siebeck, 2009), 9–93, especially 9–38. What I call "literary and archaeological remains from the past," Webb aptly calls "historical traces."

2. See B. Altaner, *Patrology* (New York: Herder and Herder, 1960), 47–50. The creed, also known as the *Symbolum Apostolicum*, appears in many books of prayer and liturgical handbooks. The creed draws upon words and phrases found in New Testament writings and in the writings of the early fathers.

3. As perhaps seen in the reference to Jesus as the "son of Mary" (Mark 6:3), as if to hint at uncertainty with respect to Jesus' paternity, or the implied insult directed against Jesus by his critics: "We were not born from fornication!" (John 8:41).

4. By "oldest and best sources critically evaluated" I refer to the seminar's severe criticism of the four New Testament Gospels (Matthew, Mark, Luke, and John) and to its surprisingly friendly assessment of extracanonical Gospels, such as Thomas and Peter, portions of which are thought to be as old as the canonical Gospels.

5. For the results of the Jesus Seminar's work, see R. W. Funk and R. W. Hoover, eds., *The Five Gospels: The Search for the Authentic Words of Jesus* (Sonoma, CA: Polebridge Press, 1993). For a personal and theological perspective that sheds much light on the thinking exhibited in the seminar's work, see R. W. Funk, *Honest to Jesus: Jesus for a New Millennium* (San Francisco: HarperCollins, 1996). For an insider's view of the seminar and its achievements, see R. J. Miller, *The Jesus Seminar and its Critics* (Sonoma, CA: Polebridge Press, 1999).

6. I recommend P. R. Eddy and G. A. Boyd, *The Jesus Legend: A Case for the Historical Reliability of the Synoptic Jesus Tradition* (Grand Rapids, MI: Baker Academic, 2007).

7. The well-known War Scroll from Qumran (1QM) envisions the same thing. It foresees a great battle between the sons of light and the sons of darkness. Not only will humans fight, angels and spirits will join the battle. The wicked of humanity, along with Satan and his evil spirit allies, will be crushed. The War Scroll dates to the first century BC; the *Testament of Moses* dates to the early first century AD (probably c. 30 AD).

8. Both Peter's confession, "You are the Messiah" (Matthew 16:16; Mark 8:29), and Jesus' positive reply to the question of the high priest, "Are you the Messiah?" (Matthew 26:63–64; Mark 14:61–62), were understood as post-Easter Christian confessions.

9. As seen, e.g., in J. D. Crossan, *Who Killed Jesus? Exposing the Roots of Anti-Semitism in the Gospel Story of the Death of Jesus* (San Francisco: HarperCollins, 1995).

10. On the high probability of Jesus' proper burial in an identifiable tomb, see Craig A. Evans, "Jewish Burial Traditions and the Resurrection of Jesus," *Journal for the Study of the Historical Jesus* 3 (2005): 233–248.

11. For a recent and lengthy study that finds in favor of the resurrection, see M. R. Licona, *The Resurrection of Jesus: A New Historiographical Approach* (Downers Grove, IL: InterVarsity Press, 2010).

■ FOR FURTHER READING

Blomberg, C. L. *The Historical Reliability of the Gospels.* Downers Grove, IL: InterVarsity Press, 2007.

Keener, C. S. *The Historical Jesus of the Gospels.* Grand Rapids, MI: Eerdmans, 2009.

Wright, N. T. *Jesus and the Victory of God: Christian Origins and the Question of God*, vol. 2. London: SPCK, 1996.

The Resurrection of Jesus

35 Jesus Did Rise from the Dead

■ GARY R. HABERMAS

It is often claimed that the resurrection of Jesus is the center of Christianity. If this is even close to the mark, then this is a crucial topic. But did this event actually occur? It is not surprising that many views and nuances mark the theological and historical landscape. One scholar who rejects the literal resurrection event is Professor James Crossley of the University of Sheffield, a cochair of the British Jesus Seminar. I will begin with some comments regarding my methodology, and then provide a critique of Crossley's research.

■ 1. A MINIMAL FACTS APPROACH

Crossley maintains that most historical Jesus studies (including his) are all about "fact-finding" reports. Though he expresses some ambiguity, he acknowledges that this is not wrong.[1] It is indeed common fare for many historical Jesus scholars to research and discuss those facts that they think are well evidenced. Several set forth lists of data that are commonly acknowledged by other researchers.[2] For many years I have also practiced the method of listing occurrences from the end of Jesus' life that have two characteristics: (1) each is well established from what we know, which accounts for (2) its wide acceptance among the vast majority of critical scholars, whatever their own position on the issue. My basis for delineating what most researchers hold on these subjects is an ongoing study of scholarly publications from 1975 to the present.[3]

Among the best established of these "minimal historical facts" are the following two:

1. Jesus died due to Roman crucifixion.
2. Very soon afterwards, a number of Jesus' disciples had experiences that they believed were appearances of the risen Jesus.[4]

Since these early experiences are the chief focus of this dialogue, I will simply list eight of the best-established reasons for its widespread acceptance among critical scholars, in keeping with the initial methodological step above.[5] The first four reasons come from two of Paul's "authentic" epistles, while the last four are drawn from a variety of sources.

Paul reports:

1. That he received an exceptionally early Gospel creedal tradition that reported a list of appearances of the risen Jesus (1 Corinthians 15:3–7).

2. That he experienced what he also believed was an appearance of the risen Jesus (1 Corinthians 15:8; 9:1).
3. That he checked this Gospel report with other key apostles (Galatians 1:18–2:1–10) and that they agreed with him (Galatians 2:6).
4. That he declared that the other apostles taught the same message he did regarding Jesus' appearances (1 Corinthians 15:11).

From other sources (including Paul) we learn:

5. That other early traditions and sermon summaries (such as those in Acts) provide similar reports.
6. That as a result, these early disciples were transformed, even being willing to suffer and die for this Gospel message.[6]
7. That James, the brother of Jesus, experienced what he also believed was an appearance of the risen Jesus (1 Corinthians 15:7).
8. Although not quite as widely held by recent scholars, a majority still think that the tomb in which Jesus was buried was later found empty (all four Gospels).

Perhaps surprisingly, Crossley appears to accept each of these reasons, at least in its broad outline, with the exception of the last one regarding the empty tomb. No doubt he would offer caveats here and there, but he seems to grant the heart of the first seven, usually without any dispute.[7]

Even more striking are some of Crossley's individual comments. Jesus probably expected and predicted his own death.[8] He states often that the early tradition in 1 Corinthians 15:3–7 is crucial since it is actually a report of the "eyewitnesses" who thought they saw appearances of the risen Jesus, and thus "must be taken very seriously."[9] These are "reliable reports" and comprise "good evidence that the first Christians did not invent the resurrection from scratch."[10] This includes Paul's experience, whose record "makes it the best available evidence we have which deserves to be taken with some seriousness."[11]

In Galatians 2:2, Paul states that he went to Jerusalem to share with the chief apostles—Peter, James the brother of Jesus, and John—the Gospel message that he preached. Crucially, the others added nothing to his Gospel proclamation (Galatians 2:6), and they also wanted him to continue assisting the poor (Galatians 2:10). Paul is also crystal clear that the Gospel message indispensably included the resurrection of Jesus as an integral part (1 Corinthians 15:1–20; Romans 1:3–4; 10:8–9).

For Crossley, the parallel descriptions in Galatians 2:1–10 and Acts 15 show that agreement was reached in this meeting on the nature and application of the salvation message. Further, "it appears...that Paul's mission...was accepted."[12] Here Crossley speaks generally in terms of the accord regarding Gentile inclusion, as well as acknowledging the part played by the preaching of the Gospel data, as proclaimed, for example, in Acts 13:38–39.[13]

Thus the Gospel message, including the death and resurrection appearances of Jesus, would have been part of the early apostolic affirmation. Moreover, Crossley acknowledges that each of these key apostles, such as Peter and James, had similar experiences,[14] which is close to the point Paul is making in 1 Corinthians 15:11 that all the apostles were teaching the same message regarding the resurrection appearances.[15]

Crossley affirms at least the major aspects of the first seven statements in the list above,[16] even though he dismisses the historicity of the empty tomb. Still, he agrees that Paul, in 1 Corinthians 15:4, "refers to bodily resurrection in the strongest sense ... of the sort that would have left behind an empty tomb."[17] Further, the empty tomb traditions are very early, including those found in the Gospel of Mark, which Crossley dates in the late 30s to early 40s CE, only a decade after Jesus.[18]

Crossley's acknowledgment of these specific areas, including his very positive comments, was done quite freely, rather than being "forced" by his dialogue partners. One indication of this is how often he repeats these points. How does he concede this material without restraint and yet reject the historicity of the resurrection appearances and the empty tomb? This is our next topic.

▓ 2. EXPLAINING THE HISTORICAL DATA

It is my contention that Crossley, along with certain other recent critical scholars, is confronted with the proverbial "horns of a dilemma" at this point. On the one hand, they generally accept data such as those outlined above, due to the strong historical support that is available. In the treatment here I mentioned eight lines of argument that support the central contention that some of Jesus' early followers had experiences that they believed were appearances of the risen Jesus. The majority of recent commentators hold that this evidence favors the conclusion that the disciple's experiences were visual in nature, since this seems to be where the reports converge.

2.1 Visions/hallucinations

In other words, several very early New Testament accounts indicate the disciples' claim that they actually saw Jesus after his death, that this became their central proclamation, and that this message totally transformed their lives to the point of being willing to die for it. Even a former persecutor (Saul/Paul) and skeptic (James the brother of Jesus) reported these experiences. The actual language is the language of sight. For the majority of scholars who accept the historicity of the empty tomb, this event would appear to be evidence that whatever happened involved Jesus' body as well.

The key, then, is how these appearance data should be explained. Crossley thinks that, "in sum, *something* happened after the death of Jesus, and the closest we get to eyewitness accounts suggests that various people had visionary experiences."[19] He adds, "Yes, historically, *something* happened shortly after Jesus' death."[20] However, "all this proves is that certain people believed they saw Jesus."[21] But he thinks that the appearances were more likely "visions" or "visionary experiences *interpreted* as a bodily raised figure."[22] But what sort of visions were they? Crossley is far from precise or nuanced here. They must be subjective visions in order to support his contention that Jesus did not actually rise from the dead, as his title indicates.[23] More rarely, Crossley mentions hallucinations.[24]

A thesis or interpretation should make the most sense of the evidence that we have at our disposal. Is Crossley's response the best way to account for what we know, especially in our common factual areas? It would appear not to be the case, and for many reasons, although we will have to limit ourselves to just a few.

From these data, some species of subjective visions are very difficult to maintain. (1) The pre-Pauline creed in 1 Corinthians 15:3–7 includes three group appearances of the resurrected Jesus.[25] This is an exceptionally serious issue for any subjective vision/hallucination hypothesis, and is virtually a "deal-breaker" by itself. (2) Even viewed as individuals, the variety of persons, times, and places of Jesus' appearances is additionally crucial. Persons respond differently to psychological phenomena as well as to time and place distinctions, thereby lessening significantly the likelihood of the same or similar sightings.

Moreover, given their different circumstances and species of unbelief, (3) Saul the persecutor and (4) James the brother of Jesus would have represented different dynamics that would also have militated against their own subjective visions/hallucinations. Although Crossley denies the historicity of the empty tomb (see below), (5) establishing this event would argue that whatever happened to Jesus involved his body, which is another huge roadblock to the vision/hallucination hypothesis.

These are just some of the many problems with the vision/hallucination hypothesis.[26] But it should be noted carefully that, if Crossley fails at this point, to say that his entire resurrection thesis might be near collapsing would not be an exaggeration. Crossley agrees with the vast majority of recent critical scholars that some sort of visual explanation is needed to satisfy the known historical data,[27] hence his hypothesis involving visions/hallucinations. But if the latter fails as an explanation, then we are confronted even more forcefully with the very early eyewitness data that Jesus' disciples were utterly convinced that they saw Jesus again after his death.

What about Crossley's suggestion that visions are quite common in "the cross-cultural study of religion and society" where they occur in "countless cultures and in countless contexts"?[28] At this point, Crossley's discussion of appearance/vision/hallucination is almost entirely without crucial nuances, such as the differences between hallucinations, illusions, and delusions, so it is extremely difficult to know exactly what he is describing or concluding. As noted earlier, his "visions" must be construed as subjective events. Did some of these cross-cultural, world religious experiences involve illusions or even delusions, which are very commonly confused with hallucinations? Were drugs involved, as is common in some religious contexts? How do we know that the reports, whatever they purportedly concern, are actually true? Could some of the cases actually involve veridical phenomena, in which case at least those aspects do not belong in this category at all? We simply need specific cases and details here in order to ascertain if they are analogous.[29]

2.2 Gospel storytelling

With regard to the Gospel accounts, Crossley makes another suggestion: expansions of material would be a typical way to tell stories in antiquity, either in Jewish (Crossley's preference) or Gentile legendary traditions. His chief examples include "Midrashic and haggadic literature" that especially highlights the stories of rabbis or heroes of the past, like "Moses, Abraham, Joseph, Elijah."[30]

The major problem with such comparisons is that they are not truly analogous to the Gospel accounts. Crossley himself admits that these Jewish accounts "could hardly be said to give genuine historical insight as to what really happened millennia ago." And though his examples "cannot be historically accurate," they may still be analogous to the Gospels.[31] But it is very difficult to know how he thinks the latter could be the case, when the sources he cites speak of persons who lived hundreds or even thousands of years earlier, while he dates the Gospel of Mark to just a decade after Jesus' death. Historiographically, such an extreme difference provides a striking dissimilarity.

Besides the less than analogous examples above, what about Crossley's claim that some of these ancient sources include cases where "historically inaccurate storytelling was done for fairly recent figures"? His prime examples are, "stories of rabbis," along with "the rapid emergence of miraculous and legendary traditions surrounding pagan figures, such as Alexander or Augustus, even within their own life times."[32]

What Jewish rabbis could Crossley have in mind here? Again, he does not say, omitting crucial details. Probably the best candidates are Honi the Circle-Drawer (first century BCE) and Hanina ben Dosa (first century CE). But the time difference between these persons and their historical sources is also very significant. For example, Josephus wrote about Honi[33] about 125 years afterwards, while the difference between Honi and the Talmud[34] is almost 350 to 550 years later. The Babylonian Talmud[35] dates about 450 years after Hanina ben Dosa.

Granted, some researchers make the point that the traditions contained in the Talmud sometimes date significantly earlier than these writings,[36] but even allowing for such, a gap of 125 to 550 years later does not qualify as writings concerning "fairly recent" persons, as per Crossley's claim. Some scholars make very similar claims on behalf of the Gospels' reliance on earlier oral sources, but skeptical scholars are often unmoved.[37] Still, it is clear that the Gospels are much closer to the events they describe, and while this does not by itself guarantee historical correspondence, it puts the Gospels in a much better position to present accurate claims.

Regarding Crossley's examples of Alexander and Augustus, once again he seems to be sailing in very rough waters. While writings that are no longer extant were composed much earlier, our existing historical accounts are much later than Alexander the Great's exploits. Historians Diordorus, Strabo, Curtius, Plutarch, and Arrian wrote from almost 300 to more than 450 years after Alexander. The last two are arguably the most influential, and they both date well over 400 years after Alexander.

I want to be very clear concerning what I am saying here. It is not doubted that legend probably grew up around Alexander quite quickly, but the problem is that his exploits are almost entirely known through the lens of these much later writers. Lucian intriguingly asserts that when Aristobulus presented a false account of Alexander's exploits to his leader, Alexander tossed the writing overboard into the water, due to its falsehoods.[38] And Plutarch states that, when writing about Alexander, he was not trying to portray a history, but a life, which allowed him to paint his picture of Alexander a bit more freely.[39]

So at this extended period of time, it is nearly impossible to ascertain which reports (or portions of them) go back in just that particular form to the earliest sources, or which ones may not have been reported accurately. Even when they cite this or that earlier author, what is the epistemic gauge that measures whether something has been expanded in any of several ways over the hundreds of intervening years since the events themselves? As with the rabbis, to utilize such late accounts in order to argue that the Gospel writers participated in widespread storytelling is unwarranted.

Regarding Augustus, Suetonius makes many comments about supernatural signs being reported throughout the emperor's life, including some reports attributed to Asclepius of Mendes,[40] of whom virtually nothing is known. Tacitus adds a little more detail.[41] But these two Roman historians wrote about exactly a century after Augustus's death. Once again, I am not denying that legend arose quickly,[42] only that it is difficult to make assertions regarding specifics when using sources dated a century (or far more) afterwards. Given these sources, neither does Augustus warrant being termed a "fairly recent figure" in terms of the reports that we possess. If the Gospels were written a century or more after Jesus, there is no question that skeptics would be further energized.

Crossley thinks that if there were "a similar story" in the ancient non-Christian world "no one would take it seriously."[43] But that's just the point here—the non-Christian accounts are not at all analogous to what Crossley even recognizes are Paul's eyewitness accounts. Yet, Crossley theorizes that the accounts in Matthew 27:52–53 and 28:11–15 present just such examples of ancient storytelling.[44] He also mentions Luke's eliminating the Galilean appearances from his narrative along with John's account of the appearance to Thomas as other possibilities.[45]

However, several problems abound here. Crossley chooses the later Gospels for his contrasts. Further, even the latest Gospel (John) was still written only about 60 years or so after Jesus, as opposed to these Jewish or pagan sources that so often date hundreds or even thousands of years after their stories are purported to have occurred, as Crossley specifically notes concerning the Jewish examples. Moreover, Luke (or John) recording accounts such as Jesus' appearances in Jerusalem could simply be a matter of a later writer adding new and truthful traditions that were known to his own community, purposely filling in the gaps. That hardly sounds like a problem, let alone a denial of earlier accounts.

But there are at least two larger problems with Crossley's criticism of Gospel storytelling. There seem to be very few examples in the Gospels like the two just mentioned from Matthew, where substantial numbers of critical scholars raise questions. As such, this comparative rarity is itself a crucial contrast with the Jewish and pagan examples above. Further, conservative scholars like those Crossley engages very rarely, if ever, argue from the inspiration of the text to the historical events in question. Rather, they usually prefer to support the reliability of particular passages and then make their case from those texts. Or with William Lane Craig, Michael Licona, or myself, another move (as was done in this chapter) is to base our arguments on data that skeptics, moderates, and conservatives all share because they are so well evidenced. These are the data that need to be explained.[46]

Where does this leave Crossley's insistence that invented stories have made their way into the Gospel accounts? The apologist has more than one option. She could argue that Crossley's Jewish and pagan cases are not analogous, usually due to the exceptional lateness of his texts. Or it could be contended that his argument does not obtain because the specific Gospel text is reliable. Or the apologist could respond that they will table this discussion and argue only from data on which both agree. If the case can be established on the minimal data alone, then aberrations in other places can be shown not to disturb that conclusion. Since Crossley has not come close to showing that his alleged legendary examples actually disprove the case for the resurrection appearances, the apologist could simply move to the much more crucial assertions regarding the resurrection, based on the commonly held historical facts. From these perspectives, Crossley attempts to pick around the edges but fails to come anywhere close to destroying the central argument for the resurrection of Jesus.

2.3 The empty tomb

According to Crossley, Mark probably created the account of the empty tomb. He asks, "why not make the argument that it was invented to explain why no one knew where the empty tomb was?"[47] Though the women witnesses are often cited by critical scholars as good evidence for this event, Crossley disputes this claim, holding that it is "not, however, as strong as is sometimes thought."[48]

There is far too much that could be said on this subject, but what can be done here is present several summary arguments. That Mark invented this story makes very little sense, and it is opposed by several important considerations. (1) Crossley presents absolutely no evidence for his position. Asking a leading question is no substitute for an argument, especially when we have no reason to think that the location of the tomb was ever a question in the first place. (2) More damaging is that, as mentioned earlier, Crossley thinks that the pre-Pauline creed in 1 Corinthians 15:4 "refers to bodily resurrection in the strongest sense . . . of the sort that would have left behind an empty tomb."[49] But since this tradition predates both Paul and the Gospel of Mark,[50] this alone means that Mark did not invent at least the initial teaching.

(3) Although the other three Gospels also mention the empty tomb, they did not borrow it from Mark. Scholars find that, including Mark, there are either three or four independent accounts here.[51] (4) Many scholars recognize that Mark utilized an earlier passion tradition that included the empty tomb account.[52] The last two reasons especially show that Mark did not invent this story. (5) Yet another source for the early teaching of the empty tomb comes from the Acts sermons, which are also very early.[53]

Besides indications such as these that the empty tomb account was not invented by Mark, as per Crossley's suggestion, there are many other indications that this was a historical occurrence. In my ongoing survey of contemporary critical scholars, mentioned above, almost two dozen arguments have been forwarded in favor of this event.[54] The likelihood of the pre-Pauline creed in 1 Corinthians 1:4, multiple attestation, the pre-Markan passion narrative, and the Acts sermon found especially in 13:29–31 not only indicate that Mark was not the originator of this teaching, but are also four strong reasons to affirm the empty tomb teaching.

Two additional arguments include, first, the location of the empty tomb proclamation: Jerusalem. This was absolutely the last place for this message unless the tomb was indeed unoccupied, for an occupied sepulcher would completely refute the message. This is multiply strong in that Crossley states repeatedly that the empty tomb accounts are very early.[55]

Second, the women are reported in the multiply-attested Gospel accounts as the eyewitnesses to the empty tomb. This testimony is vastly underestimated by Crossley, who protests that "women were given a relatively prominent role in

Jesus' ministry, and this could have made their testimony more acceptable for some." Such "socio-economic upheaval" could have affected gender relations.[56] That may be true, but Crossley completely misses the chief point here that the message was being taught to a larger Mediterranean world that did not share this enlightened perspective. That is probably why the women are not mentioned in the official lists in 1 Corinthians 15 and the Acts sermons.[57] Then why are the women cited unanimously in the Gospel accounts? As Osiek states, "they remained because the memory of their role was so persistent that it could not be removed."[58] In other words, it was recorded because that's the way it happened! That is certainly the most straightforward and less-convoluted conclusion.

My point in this brief critique is that Crossley's attempts to account for the data that even he accepts as historical is sufficient to point out several serious problems in each of his major alternative scenarios. Further, these same facts support strongly the New Testament message. Why does he not recognize this?

▪ 3. CONCLUSION: THE POWER OF WORLD VIEWS

I think perhaps the most crucial element in Crossley's rejection of Jesus' actual resurrection appearances and the empty tomb are not the historical data, but his naturalistic world view. In his dialogues, his opponents accuse him frequently of failing to evidence his overall natural perspective.[59] Yet, he seems to be almost unaware of the philosophical issues, even when they are pointed out.[60]

One place where it seems that his view comes across most clearly is when discussing the empty tomb. He concedes more crucial ground than many skeptical scholars, holds that Mark dates only a mere decade after Jesus, and admits the exceptionally early date for the empty tomb accounts. Yet he asserts that Mark's story is invented. He does so by juxtaposing the most fragile and unconvincing questions against a number of good facts to the contrary. Why? The empty tomb is not even a supernatural report. Yet, it just seems that he is unable to allow it, for this would be another huge argument that the resurrection appearances/visions were not subjective hallucinations and confirm further that the New Testament reports are about a risen body. So the empty tomb gets cut off at the pass, without out a clear argument against all the data to the contrary.

Another example is Jesus' predictions of his death, which we have noted that Crossley accepts for several historical reasons. But he seems to excise Jesus' predictions of his death from those of his resurrection, which are side-by-side in the exact same statements. Again, why so?

Although it is indeed supernatural, I think the same thing happens to the resurrection appearances, while Crossley prefers a much weaker hypothesis, once again against many refutations. Where else can a naturalist go? Realizing that there are a number of accredited historical facts, Crossley is forced to account for them by picking weaker hypotheses that account poorly for the data that we know.

Crossley may feel justified in taking views that are less likely on the evidence since the final option of resurrection involves a supernatural event. But it must be remembered that he never pauses to demonstrate his naturalism; his overall default position is simply assumed without reasons. But we need adequate argumentation if his assumed position allows him to simply cut off consideration of opposing views.

Further, although this can only be hinted at here, I have pointed out at length that other arguments powerfully indicate the likelihood of an afterlife. If so, then this should open the door significantly to the resurrection, since this event involves a specific instance of afterlife.[61] At any rate, it further challenges Crossley's underlying but unevidenced naturalistic default position and should cause great pause for continuing to rule out the resurrection appearances when they are supported by our best historical data.

▪ NOTES

1. James G. Crossley, "Writing About the Historical Jesus: Historical Explanation and 'the Big Why Questions', or Antiquarian Empiricism and Victorian Tomes?" *Journal for the Study of the Historical Jesus* 7 (2009): 68; cf. 68, 75, 89–90.

2. For example, E. P. Sanders, *The Historical Figure of Jesus* (London: Penguin, 1993), 10–11.

3. Some of these results have been published in articles such as Gary R. Habermas, "Resurrection Research from 1975 to the Present: What Are Critical Scholars Saying? *Journal for the Study of Historical Jesus* 3 (2005): 135–153.

4. On the nearly unanimous scholarly recognition here, see Gary R. Habermas, "Experiences of the Risen Jesus: The Foundational Historical Issue in the Early Proclamation of the Resurrection," *Dialog: A Journal of Theology* 45 (2006): 288–297.

5. Though I cannot argue here for either the historicity or the scholarly acceptance of these eight, I have addressed these data on many other occasions. For example, see Gary R. Habermas, *The Risen Jesus and Future Hope* (Lanham, MD: Rowman and Littlefield, 2003), especially chap. 1; Habermas, "Experiences of the Risen Jesus," 289–293; cf. Habermas, "Resurrection Research from 1975 to the Present," 140–145.

6. Details come from the epistles, Acts, Clement of Rome, and Josephus.

7. The finer points here, including various minutiae, are contained in Crossley's writings such as "Against the Historical Plausibility of the Empty Tomb Story and the Bodily Resurrection of Jesus: A Response to N. T. Wright," *Journal for the Study of the Historical Jesus* 3 (2005): 171–186; Michael F. Bird and James G. Crossley, *How Did Christianity Begin? A Believer and Nonbeliever Examine the Evidence* (London: SPCK, 2008), especially 11, 51–63, 70–74; Crossley, *The Date of Mark's Gospel: Insight from the Law in Earliest Christianity* (London: T & T Clark, 2004), especially chap. 5.

8. Bird and Crossley, *How Did Christianity Begin?*, 11, 53; Crossley, "Against the Historical Plausibility," 173.

9. Crossley, "Against the Historical Plausibility," 171, 174, 176, 178, 186.

10. Crossley, *The Date of Mark's Gospel*, 140; Crossley, "Against the Historical Plausibility," 173; cf. Bird and Crossley, *How Did Christianity Begin?*, 54.

11. Crossley, "Against the Historical Plausibility," 176, note 23; also, Crossley, *The Date of Mark's Gospel*, 140.

12. Crossley, *The Date of Mark's Gospel*," 154; Bird and Crossley, *How Did Christianity Begin?*, 74.

13. Crossley, *The Date of Mark's Gospel*,"155–156; Bird and Crossley, *How Did Christianity Begin?*, 71, especially since the example he uses, Acts 13:38–39, comes in the exact same message by Paul, immediately after the proclamation of the death, burial, and resurrection of Jesus in verses 29–37.

14. Crossley, "Against the Historical Plausibility," 176, 178.

15. Compare also the subject of the plural pronouns in the verses following (15:12–15).

16. The references in note 7 also treat the remaining portions of these seven areas.

17. Bird and Crossley, *How Did Christianity Begin?*, 52; also Crossley, "Against the Historical Plausibility," 178.

18. Crossley, *The Date of Mark's Gospel*, chap. 3 and "Conclusions;" Crossley, "Against the Historical Plausibility," 177–178.

19. Bird and Crossley, *How Did Christianity Begin?*, 58 (italics are original).

20. Crossley, "Against the Historical Plausibility," 186 (italics are original).

21. Bird and Crossley, *How Did Christianity Begin?*, 52.

22. Crossley, *"Against the Historical Plausibility,"* 171 (italics are original); similarly, 177 and Bird and Crossley, *How Did Christianity Begin?*, 54.

23. It should be noted very carefully that had Crossley argued that Jesus was *actually* raised and appeared evidentially but in less than bodily (that is, objective) visions, this would still be a species of resurrection, for Jesus still would have been alive after his death and still would have appeared to his disciples.

24. Crossley, "Against the Historical Plausibility," 174, including note 10.

25. These include appearances "to the twelve," to more than 500 persons at once, and "to all the apostles." Any accredited records from the Gospels and/or the Acts sermon summaries would add to these examples.

26. For nineteen problems with various versions of such hypotheses as applied to the resurrection, see Gary R. Habermas, "Explaining Away Jesus' Resurrection: The Recent Revival of Hallucination Theories," *Christian Research Journal* 23 (2001): 26–31, 47–49. For further medical information, see Harold Kaplan, Benjamin Sadock, and Jack Greeb, *Synopsis of Psychiatry*, 7th ed. (Baltimore: Williams and Wilkins, 1994), 306–307, 489.

27. On this scholarly agreement plus the reasons on which it is based, see Habermas, "Experiences of the Risen Jesus," especially 288–289, 292.

28. Bird and Crossley, *How Did Christianity Begin?*, 53; cf. Crossley, "Against the Historical Plausibility," 174.

29. For many possible responses, see Gary R. Habermas, "Resurrection Claims in Non-Christian Religions," *Religious Studies* 25 (1989): 167–177.

30. Crossley, "Against the Historical Plausibility," 171, 178–181; also Bird and Crossley, *How Did Christianity Begin?*, 56–58.

31. Crossley, "Against the Historical Plausibility," 179–180.

32. Crossley, "Against the Historical Plausibility," 181.

33. Josephus, *Antiquities* 14:2.

34. Taanith 3:8.

35. Berakhoth 34b.

36. Geza Vermes, *Jesus and His Jewish Context* (Minneapolis: Fortress, 2003), viii.

37. Like Crossley himself when addressing N. T. Wright's claim in the very same context (Crossley, "Against the Historical Plausibility," 178).

38. Lucian, "How to Write History," in *Lucian*, 8 vols. (Cambridge, MA: Harvard University Press, 1959), vol. 6:15.

39. Plutarch, Alexander 1.

40. Suetonius, *The Twelve Caesars*, Augustus 94; cf. 5–6, 96–97.

41. Such as Tacitus, *Annals* 1:11.

42. Not all ancient historians engaged in this sort of supernatural reporting. Thucydides is a notable exception. The late Oxford University historian P. A. Brunt comments that Thucydides "excludes divine intervention from human affairs" (xxviii). Further, "most of his evidence came from eyewitnesses whom he could cross-examine." Incredibly, Brunt adds that such striving for accurate reports "reappeared with Jewish and Christian writers, whose veneration for the Scriptures inspired them with a wider respect for documentary truth." Brunt includes the New Testament writers as following the tradition of those ancient historians who sought accurate, eyewitness reports. See Thucydides, "The Peloponnesian Wars," trans. Benjamin Jowett, revised and introduced by P. A. Brunt, *The Great Histories*, ed. Hugh R. Trevor-Roper (New York: Washington Square Press, 1963), "Introduction," xxii–xxiii.

43. Bird and Crossley, *How Did Christianity Begin?*, 63.

44. Crossley, "Against the Historical Plausibility," 179; Bird and Crossley, *How Did Christianity Begin?*, 56–57.

45. Crossley, "Against the Historical Plausibility," 182; Bird and Crossley, *How Did Christianity Begin?*, 58.

46. Craig explains that he no longer includes an argument for the reliability of the New Testament in his Christian evidences text in order not to give the impression that this is necessary in defending the central doctrines of Christianity. See William Lane Craig, *Reasonable Faith: Christian Truth and Apologetics*, 3rd ed. (Wheaton, IL: Crossway, 2008), 11–12.

47. Bird and Crossley, *How Did Christianity Begin?*, 55; similarly, Crossley, "Against the Historical Plausibility," 181–182.

48. Bird and Crossley, *How Did Christianity Begin?*, 59–61; Crossley, "Against the Historical Plausibility," 184–185.

49. Bird and Crossley, *How Did Christianity Begin?*, 52; also Crossley, "Against the Historical Plausibility," 178.

50. Bird and Crossley, *How Did Christianity Begin?*, 54; Habermas, "Experiences of the Risen Jesus," 290.

51. For instance, Gerald O'Collins, *Interpreting Jesus* (London: Geoffrey Chapman, 1983), 126. Stephen T. Davis considers this one of the two strongest arguments for the independence of the testimony, in *Risen Indeed: Making Sense of the Resurrection* (Grand Rapids, MI: Eerdmans, 1993), 78–79.

52. Crossley seems to imply something like this ("Against the Historical Plausibility," 178). Skeptical scholar Thomas Sheehan also agrees, in *The First Coming: How the Kingdom of God became Christianity* (New York: Random House, 1986), 135, 140, 143; Marion Soards surveyed a group of representative scholars and found this to be the predominant view, in "The Question of a Premarcan Passion Narrative," in Raymond E. Brown, *The Death of the Messiah*, 2 vols. (Garden City, NY: Doubleday, 1994), vol. 2, 1492–1524.

53. O'Collins, *Interpreting Jesus*, 109. See especially Acts 13:29–31, 34–37; cf. Acts 2:29–32.

54. Habermas, "Experiences of the Risen Jesus," 292.

55. Bird and Crossley, *How Did Christianity Begin?*, 52, 55; Crossley, "Against the Historical Plausibility," 177–178, 185.

56. Bird and Crossley, *How Did Christianity Begin?*, 59; cf. Crossley, "Against the Historical Plausibility," 184–185.

57. For this question in its ancient social context, see Carolyn Osiek, "The Women at the Tomb: What are they Doing There?" *Ex Auditu* 9 (1993): especially 104.

58. Osiek, "The Women at the Tomb," 106.

59. Bird and Crossley, *How Did Christianity Begin?*," 32, especially 64; N. T. Wright, "Resurrecting Old Arguments: Responding to Four Essays," *Journal for the Study of the Historical Jesus* 3 (2005): 219–220; William Lane Craig and James Crossley, "First Rebuttal," in *"Was Jesus Bodily Raised from the Dead?"* DVD, Sheffield University, 2007.

60. Craig and Crossley, "First Rebuttal."

61. For one of several arguments for an afterlife regarding some of the rather incredible evidence in favor of near-death experiences, see Gary R. Habermas and J. P. Moreland, *Beyond Death: Exploring the Evidence for Immortality* (Wheaton, IL: Crossway, 1998), chaps. 7–9.

▨ FOR FURTHER READING

Craig, W. L. *Assessing the New Testament Evidence for the Historicity of the Resurrection of Jesus.* Lewiston, NY: Edwin Mellen, 1989.

Davis, S. T. *Risen Indeed: Making Sense of the Resurrection.* Grand Rapids, MI: Eerdmans, 1993.

Habermas, G. "Experiences of the Risen Jesus: The Foundational Historical Issue in the Early Proclamation of the Resurrection." *Dialog: A Journal of Theology*, Vol. o. 3 (Fall, 2006), pp. 288–297.

_____. "Resurrection Research from 1975 to the Present: What are Critical Scholars Saying?" *Journal for the Study of the Historical Jesus*, Vol. 3.2 (2005), pp. 135–153. *The Risen Jesus and Future Hope.* Lanham, MD: Roman and Littlefield, 2003.

Licona, M. R. *The Resurrection of Jesus: A New Historiographical Approach.* Downers Grove, IL: InterVarsity Press, 2010.

McGrew, T., and Lydia McGrew. "The Argument from Miracles: A Cumulative Case for the Resurrection of Jesus of Nazareth." In *The Blackwell Companion to Natural Theology*, ed. W. L. Craig and J. P. Moreland, 593–662. West Sussex: Wiley-Blackwell, 2009.

Wright, N. T. *The Resurrection of the Son of God.* Minneapolis: Fortress, 2003.

36 The Resurrection Probably Did Not Happen

■ JAMES G. CROSSLEY

INTRODUCTION

Should those of us who work in universities, and do not live our lives believing the supernatural intervenes in the natural world, even engage with ideas concerning the plausibility of supernatural explanations for historical change? Some of my more secular-minded colleagues in biblical studies would certainly think not and have occasionally urged me not to do so. After all, these things are not the sort of things historians typically do.[1] However, even if we leave aside uncomfortable questions about who can study what and where, there is a pragmatic reason for engaging with historical explanations that resort to the supernatural: they are common enough in biblical studies. One of the major mainstream books of the last decade was N. T. Wright, *The Resurrection of the Son of God*, which contained detailed arguments in favor of a supernatural explanation for the resurrection. Indeed, in his summary of scholarship on the resurrection in Europe and North America from 1975 to the present, Gary Habermas claims that there is "an approximate ratio of 3:1 of moderate conservative to sceptical publications."[2] These sorts of debates may not be so common in, say, discussions of seventeenth-century history, but we cannot avoid the peculiarities of the discipline of biblical studies with its not always comfortable mix of secular and confessional traditions. We might accept that Licona and van der Watt are right in defending the confessional historian and how such people can provide an interdisciplinary insight,[3] but we can equally accept the opposite: the irreligious scholar who tries to present a naturalistic explanation of the world and puts it out there for everyone to debate.

That being said, I am going to attempt to undermine some of those arguments that favor a supernatural explanation for the resurrection and, perhaps most ambitiously, suggest that various wings, including secular and evangelical, could unite behind explanations for the resurrection without ever needing to resort to the supernatural, irrespective of what they personally believe. Before we turn to such questions, a more detailed evaluation of the key texts is first required. And before we do that, a brief summary of a key issue in establishing the historicity of the resurrection may help. The Gospels certainly talk of Jesus' tomb being empty, and this is because, obviously, Jesus was raised from the dead and thus a lot of scholarly energy is spent on establishing just how early this tradition of an empty tomb was. While supernatural explanations for the resurrection of Jesus are typically based on there being an empty tomb, it does not follow, of course, that the historicity of the empty tomb story necessarily means that Jesus was bodily raised in any supernatural sense. As Dale Allison points out, any number of explanations—this-worldly or supernatural—could account for an empty tomb.[4] Showing that the empty tomb story was fictitious is a common feature of those scholarly explanations that do not believe that anything supernatural happened. While showing the empty tomb was a fiction does not necessarily mean that Jesus was not bodily raised from the dead, it would make it increasingly difficult to sustain such an argument with less and less evidence to support it. We can now develop this latter point further.

1. WAS THERE AN EMPTY TOMB? 1 CORINTHIANS 15:3–8

The earliest non-Gospel witness is Paul in 1 Corinthians. Furthermore, it is clear that Paul is working with a tradition he inherited from the earliest years after Jesus' death:

> For I handed on to you as of first importance what I in turn had received: that Christ died for our sins in accordance with the scriptures, and that he was buried, and that he was raised on the third day in accordance with the scriptures, and that he appeared to Cephas, then to the twelve. Then he appeared to more than five hundred brothers at one time, most of whom are still alive, though some have died. Then he appeared to James, then to all the apostles. Last of all, as to someone untimely born, he appeared also to me (1 Corinthians 15:3–8).

A conventional point raised by those not convinced that there was historically a physical resurrection, or by those who do not believe that a physical resurrection was a view widely held among the earliest Christians, is that this passage does not have any mention of the empty tomb and therefore this is a view that does not necessarily assume a bodily or physical resurrection. However, a number of scholars have pointed out that "raised" (*egēgertai*) typically meant raised in a bodily sense, hence "he was buried...he was (physically) raised."[5] If we assume that this strongly literal reading of 1 Corinthians 15:3–8 is correct, this would mean that Paul assumed that there was a bodily resurrection in the sense that it would have left an empty tomb. What needs to be stressed is that this means that the belief in a bodily raised Jesus was very early indeed—even as early as Paul's Damascus road experience—and that people really did believe that they had seen the risen Jesus. But on the basis of 1 Corinthians 15:3–8, this is about as far as we can push the evidence and this passage provides no evidence that anyone knew where Jesus' tomb was. Unlike the appearances, there is no eyewitness testimony to be reconstructed.

If we accept the historicity of the following passage from Acts (or variations of it), the earliest sightings of the resurrection of Jesus might have been recalled as something like this:

> Now as he was going along and approaching Damascus, suddenly a light from heaven flashed around him. He fell to the ground and heard a voice saying to him, "Saul, Saul, why do you persecute me?" He asked, "Who are you, Lord?" The reply came, "I am Jesus, whom you are persecuting. But get up and enter the city, and you will be told what you are to do." The men who were travelling with him stood speechless because they heard the voice but saw no one (Acts 9:3–7).

Continuing the assumption of the historicity of this passage for one moment, what we have here is the description of a vision and this may well be in line with the experiences of those others mentioned by Paul. Visions are common enough in different cultures and do not require a supernatural explanation. Various scholars have pointed to bereavement visions people have when relatives die as a suitable context for understanding why the earliest Christians had resurrection appearances.[6] This explanation is certainly important, but for now we need only make the point that people as individuals or in groups and in many cultures have visions and so visions of the raised Jesus hardly mean that he really was bodily resurrected in the sense that would have left behind an empty tomb or that we must accept a supernatural explanation for these visions of the raised Jesus. As Pieter Craffert rightly put it, these "culturally constructed intentional objects and phenomena are not necessarily objectively real."[7]

The context and content of a vision obviously differs from culture to culture and so it is helpful to establish the kinds of things that might have influenced the first visions of Jesus. One possible influence might have been the tradition of martyrdom in early Judaism, particularly the most famous stories of the "Maccabean martyrs" who were remembered (and remembered annually at Hanukkah) as giving up their lives in defense of Jewish law. Indeed, these martyrs were thought to have talked about being physically restored or resurrected. One early Jewish text records the following:

> And when he was at his last breath, he said, "You accursed wretch, you dismissed us from this present life, but the king of the universe will raise us up to an everlasting renewal of life, because we have died for his laws." ... "I got these (hands) from Heaven and because of his laws I disdain them, and from him I hope to get them back again" (2 Maccabees 7:9, 11).

Even if we do not accept that the historical Jesus believed he was going to be martyred in Jerusalem, it is clear that the earliest followers did believe Jesus was martyred and so the tradition of martyrs being physically restored could have influenced the context of the visions of the raised Jesus. Another important tradition influencing the resurrection stories has been suggested by Roger

Aus. Aus argues for the influence of a fusion of contradictory Moses traditions where Moses was either "translated" to heaven without dying or the soul of the dead Moses was taken to heaven.[8] Aus is suggesting that these Moses traditions influenced the writing of the Gospel accounts (which he regards as fiction), but his suggestions could also apply to the cultural influences on the content of the earliest visions of the risen Jesus.

These Moses traditions already show the problems involved in understanding any differences between a bodily raised Jesus and a more "spiritual" or "ghostly" encounter some might expect of a description of a vision. Indeed, in Mark's account of the Transfiguration (Mark 9:2–8), Moses, along with Elijah (who, recall, was believed not to have died), both appear and disappear suddenly. This is not the sort of thing a normal body does and can account for the clear possibility of the perception of similarity between a vision of something deemed physical and something more "ghostly." Indeed, as Mark's Gospel puts it in the story of the walking on water: "But when they saw him walking on the lake, they thought it was a ghost and cried out" (6:49).

What should be clear from 1 Corinthians 15:3–8 is that we can only go as far as saying that people really did believe they had visions of the risen Christ and that there are perfectly plausible cultural and psychological explanations for why. This, of course, does not disprove that God was intervening in human history, and for all I know, God may have been. However, while not wanting to downplay the cultural specifics, there is a clear case for suggesting that 1 Corinthians 15:3–8 is not evidence of anything particularly unusual in human history.

■ 2. WAS THERE AN EMPTY TOMB? MARK 16:1-8

The other crucial piece of early evidence is Mark 16:1–8. Here Mark tells us that certain women went to the tomb and wondered who would roll away the massive tombstone. A man dressed in white was present and he told the women that Jesus had risen. The man dressed in white said that the women should tell the disciples and Peter that Jesus is going ahead of them to Galilee and there they will see Jesus. The frightened women fled and told no one, for they were afraid.

These are the final verses of Mark's Gospel and there is, obviously, no narration of resurrection appearances here. As Christian scribes later added endings to Mark's Gospel, contemporary scholars sometimes speculate about an original lost ending of Mark. But even if there was a lost ending, guessing what it might have been like is hardly the most solid base for historical reconstruction so, unfortunately, we will have to turn to what we have. This also means we are left with the final verse of Mark being, "they [the women] said nothing to anyone, for they were afraid" (Mark 16:8). It is not easy to establish how literally we are to take this. Presumably the author of Mark implies that the women told someone at some time, hence the story turns up in Mark's Gospel. But when and where?

Equally, the author of Mark must also be implying that the women delayed in telling people for at least some period of time. Whatever we make of this verse, we have to accept that all we have is the first witnesses telling no one and that is it. Some scholars point to Mark 1:44, where Jesus tells the healed leper to tell no one and that he should show himself to the priest.[9] However, Mark tells us that the healed leper did tell people, which is precisely what Mark does not tell us about the women in 16:8. If anything, Mark 1:44 counts against the idea of the women telling people en route.

It may be the case that, as some have argued (myself included), the author of Mark did not know where Jesus was buried and thus has to invent a story to explain where it was. But whatever we make of Mark 16:8, we are still left with a story that has key witnesses not telling people where the tomb is or any details of their experience, at least for some time, thus making it increasingly difficult to establish who would even have known where the empty tomb was. It is important to recall that in 1 Corinthians 15:4, Paul assumed that there was an empty tomb, but, in direct contrast to reports of visions, Paul provides no eyewitnesses to the empty tomb and only mentions general handed-down tradition ("what I in turn had received: that Christ died for our sins in accordance with the scriptures, and that he was buried, and that he was raised on the third day in accordance with the scriptures and that he appeared to Cephas"). This combination of a lack of eyewitnesses and the Gospel witnesses running away and telling no one hardly forms solid foundations for the historicity of the empty tomb and to some extent undermines the idea that the tomb could have generated the resurrection stories in some way.

There is another well-established counterargument that Mark 16:1–8 does provide strong evidence for eyewitnesses to the empty tomb and it involves the idea of women as witnesses. Habermas argues that "in the Mediterranean world in general, female testimony was normally avoided wherever possible in courts of law, especially in crucial issues, and it was often disbelieved... if you're fabricating the account of the burial, then don't allow the case for the disappearance of the body to rely on female testimony. Obviously, that would invite ancient listeners to reject the story from the outset."[10] This is a very common argument, but it is not as strong as is often believed. For a start, we are not dealing with a court of law in Mark 16:1–8. Habermas's argument, like many other manifestations of this argument, can only work properly if this generalization holds for all contexts in early Judaism and early Christianity. But we know, as Habermas rightly points out, that "there were exceptions."[11] Celsus, the second-century CE opponent of Christianity, was critical of the prominent role of women in Christian history and the ministry of Jesus,[12] which suggests women could play a significant role for certain Christians at least. We also know that women such as Esther and Judith were remembered as significant figures in Jewish tradition, so could not the earliest Christians also view women as having significant roles in certain instances? We might point out that women appear to play a relatively significant role in the ministry of Jesus. Indeed, in Mark's Gospel there are women left at the cross and are clearly named for their importance: "There were also women looking on from a distance; among them were Mary Magdalene, and Mary the mother of James the younger and of Joses, and Salome. These used to follow him and provided for him when he was in Galilee; and there were many other women who had come up with him to Jerusalem" (15:40–41). Clearly, then, there were contexts where women could have been given a culturally central role in a story of the empty tomb. All it takes is for one section of earliest Christianity to have had an interest in the prominence of women for this story to have been generated. But despite all this, we might be reading too much into the story because, in narrative terms, the first known witness is the man dressed in white who, for all we know, may have provided all the authority Mark's audience required.[13]

▩ 3. STORYTELLING: MATTHEW, LUKE, AND JOHN

If Mark is not a solid foundation from which to build a historical reconstruction of the events following Jesus' death, then this raises problems in using the other Gospel narratives because Matthew and Luke were directly dependent on Mark. John may or may not have been, but John is certainly later and has a clear awareness of resurrection stories. Furthermore, Matthew, Luke, and John all develop the resurrection stories with later theological concerns in mind.

There is some evidence that Matthew was happy to invent stories about people rising from the dead. In Matthew 27:52–53 we read: "The tombs also were opened, and many bodies of the saints who had fallen asleep were raised. After his resurrection they came out of the tombs and entered the holy city and appeared to many." N. T. Wright claimed that "some stories are so odd that they may just have happened. This may be one of them, but in historical terms there is no way of finding out."[14] This approach comes close to advocating the end of historical reconstruction as we know it, but I would prefer to go along with those who use the standard historical arguments that since this story occurs in Matthew alone and since no contemporary non-Christian figures record the sightings of various dead people rising from the ground (would the Jewish historian Josephus really have neglected to record such a spectacular event?), we should see this as Matthew writing fiction.

There is more direct evidence of Matthew rewriting history in his handling of Mark. Whereas Mark has the women telling no one out of fear, Matthew has the women immediately telling the disciples:

> Then go quickly and tell his disciples, "He has been raised from the dead, and indeed he is going ahead of you to Galilee; there you will see him. This is my message for

you." So they left the tomb quickly with fear and great joy, and ran to tell his disciples. Suddenly Jesus met them and said, "Greetings!" And they came to him, took hold of his feet, and worshipped him. Then Jesus said to them, "Do not be afraid; go and tell my brothers to go to Galilee; there they will see me" (Matthew 28:7–10).

Is not the best explanation that Matthew has deliberately changed Mark to iron out the difficulty of the women telling *no one* out of fear? Furthermore, the post-Markan Gospels start adding figures present at the tomb, such as Peter (Luke 24:11–12; John 20:6–8). Is not the best explanation that the preeminent disciple, and one of the major figures of the early church, has been fictitiously placed at the empty tomb? After all, why was Peter not there in Mark?

Luke has arguably the most explicit change to Mark's story. In Mark 16:7, the man dressed in white tells the women, "go, tell his disciples and Peter, He is going ahead of you into Galilee. There you will see him, just as he told you." Luke not only has *two* such figures, but clearly rewrites the role of Galilee: "He is not here; he has risen! Remember how he told you, while he was still with you in Galilee: 'The Son of Man must be delivered into the hands of sinful men, be crucified and on the third day be raised again'" (Luke 24:6–7). According to Luke (and Luke Acts), the resurrection appearances and the ascension do not take place in Galilee, but in Jerusalem. Is this not powerful evidence that Luke is writing fictitiously in his resurrection account to suit his own Jerusalem-centered story?

There are also theological additions that look suspiciously like a rewriting of earlier traditions. For instance, John's Gospel has the following: "Thomas said to him: 'My Lord and my God!' Then Jesus told him, 'Because you have seen me, you have believed; blessed are those who have not seen and yet have believed'" (John 20:28–29). This is not in the other Gospels and, given that John 20:28–29 dramatically justifies one of the most important Christian affirmations, it is difficult to see why the other Gospel writers would have left it out if it were known. Similarly Matthew ends with the resurrected Jesus talking about a mission to Gentiles (Matthew 28:16–20). Even according to Acts the mission to Gentiles only really gets going some years after the resurrection, so it would seem that the best explanation is that Matthew has fictitiously created a story justifying the mission to Gentiles.

Collectively then we have our two earliest sources on the empty tomb having either no direct eyewitness report (Paul) or women telling no one (Mark) and nothing more. While people really did believe they had visions of the risen Jesus and that these were probably understood to be the physically raised Jesus who had left behind an empty tomb, this does not demand a supernatural explanation, as visions are common enough across different cultures and times. The narratives in Matthew, Luke, and John are of minimal use, and not only because they are based on Mark. We have a combination of "correcting" Mark's account to make sure there were other key people present at the resurrection and to justify theological beliefs and interests that are located some years after the resurrection appearances. Whether any of the earliest Christians knew where Jesus' empty tomb was, we simply do not know. That is about as far as history will take us.

▪ 4. CONCLUDING THOUGHTS AND WAYS FORWARD

Craffert has made the case for the importance of moving beyond the traditional question of "did it happen or not?" He advocates more anthropologically guided approaches to history and understanding the "conventions of discourse, the cultural dynamics, the social processes and the cultural assumptions that the subjects took for granted."[15] What this means for Craffert is that there are ethnocentric problems with "the vision-as-delusion view" that "considers the ancients to be psychologically challenged (they were fully convinced of the reality of the visions without knowing that they were hallucinations)."[16] It is true that we can be respectful by following more contemporary anthropological approaches by not simply dismissing ghosts and so on as unrealistic but acknowledging multiple cultural realities.[17] To this we would argue that the use of ancient concepts of storytelling and fiction, which are not necessarily to be equated with our concepts of truth and deceit, ought to be remembered when studying the resurrection narratives: people were happy to invent stories![18]

On one level Craffert is right: we can follow contemporary anthropological approaches by not simply dismissing ghosts or visions as unrealistic and acknowledge multiple cultural realities.[19] But I return to the introduction and the argument that biblical studies is a strange discipline in the kinds of questions asked and that this will not change any time soon. So when conservative evangelical scholars make claims about proving supernatural origins or, by analogy, when someone really does think ghosts are real and tries repeatedly to convince me, then it is unlikely that there will not be a response. It may be (as Craffert implies) ethnocentric and it may be on our own terms, but this may be unavoidable. Yet we can also point out that explaining the origins of the supernatural is something carried out in the sciences and in the humanities without having to engage with questions of objective supernatural or religious causes and by explaining things (as best as such things can be done) in terms of evolutionary and/or neurological terms. I would happily endorse Pascal Boyer's motives in his bold book *Religion Explained*, which, while explicitly taking an approach to others we find with Craffert, equally explicitly takes a thoroughly "humanistic" approach to explaining the occurrence of "religious" or supernatural phenomena.[20] Unlike E. P. Sanders, who felt he could not explain what gave rise to the resurrection experiences,[21] I find that explanations of visions, and perhaps even bereavement visions, do go some way to explaining the resurrection stories.

Finally, however, there may be a surprise compromise, where the conservative evangelical can lie down with the atheist. Whether this compromise works across the humanities and sciences, or even biblical studies as a whole, is another question, but I think this compromise can certainly work with the critical study of the resurrection. The question of whether God intervened in history in the resurrection cannot be shown on the basis of the relatively meager historical evidence we have. There are plenty of plausible this-worldly explanations for the resurrection and it seems to me that if we resort to the supernatural explanation we are—rightly or wrongly—entering a different field of understanding, namely philosophy of religion and raising questions along the lines of God's existence. Of course, if we had a much fuller range of evidence and that hypothetical time machine and that hypothetical video camera, then we might be in a position to say once and for all what really happened. But we do not. Yet it is for these reasons that I would argue that scholars from a range of perspectives, from conservative evangelical to ardent atheist, could, in theory, work together on the question of the resurrection. The conservative evangelical may believe that the resurrection really did take place while the atheist may not, but both could agree that there were people who believed that they saw the risen Jesus.[22] It is what we do then that can really contribute toward historical explanation, irrespective if one scholar believes God did it and the other Mother Nature. The question now becomes, what did these experiences do in terms of generating a new movement in Jesus' name and in the development of the ways in which the first Christians understood Jesus?

■ NOTES

1. The issues of the historian and the miraculous, with reference to the resurrection, have been discussed at length in M. R. Licona, *The Resurrection of Jesus: A New Historiographical Approach* (Downers Grove, IL: InterVarsity Press, 2009).

2. Gary R. Habermas, "Resurrection Research from 1975 to the Present: What Are Critical Scholars Saying?" *Journal for the Study of the Historical Jesus* 3 (2005): 140.

3. M. R. Licona and J. G. van der Watt, "The Adjudication of Miracles: Rethinking the Criteria of Historicity," *HTS Theological Studies* 65 (2009): 62–68.

4. D. C. Allison, *Resurrecting Jesus: The Earliest Christian Tradition and Its Interpreters* (London: Continuum, 2005), 198–375.

5. N. T. Wright, *The Resurrection of the Son of God* (London: SPCK, 2003), 317–322.

6. M. Goulder, "The Baseless Fabric of a Vision," in *Resurrection Reconsidered*, ed. G. D'Costa (Oxford: Oneworld, 1996), 48–61; G. Lüdemann, *What Really Happened to Jesus: A Historical Approach to the Resurrection* (Louisville, KY: Westminster John Knox, 1995); M. Goulder, "The Explanatory Power of Conversion-Visions," in *Jesus' Resurrection: Fact or Figment: A Debate Between William Lane Craig and Gerd Lüdemann*, ed. P. Copan and R. K. Tacelli (Downers Grove, IL: InterVarsity Press, 2000), 86–103; Allison, *Resurrecting Jesus*, P. F. Craffert, "Jesus' Resurrection in a Social-Scientific Perspective: Is There Anything New to be Said?" *Journal for the Study of the Historical Jesus* 7 (2009): 126–151.

7. Craffert, "Jesus' Resurrection," 148.

8. R. D. Aus, *The Death, Burial, and Resurrection of Jesus, and the Death, Burial, and Translation of Moses in Judaic Tradition* (Lanham, MD: University Press of America, 2008).

9. Cf. Licona, *Resurrection*, 346–348.

10. G. Habermas, "Part I: 2003 Resurrection Debate Between Antony Flew and Gary Habermas," in *Did the Resurrection Happen? A Conversation with Gary Habermas and Antony Flew*, ed. D. Baggett (Downers Grove, IL: InterVarsity Press, 2009), 29–30.

11. Habermas, "Resurrection Debate," 29.

12. Origen, *Contra Celsus* 3:10, 44.

13. Crossley, "Historical Plausibility," 184. The range of arguments and the argument of collective weight involved is the case I have made on the role of women is not properly addressed in Licona, *Resurrection*, 353–354, who is too confident in his historical evaluation that "while their involvement may have made their testimony more acceptable to some, overall it would have done more harm than good." Maybe, but this would only tell us about Mark's judgment, not the historical reliability of the tradition. Furthermore, could Mark not have made a "poor" judgment here and hence provide a good reason for Matthew, Luke, and John to change the narrative?

14. Wright, *Resurrection*, 636.

15. Craffert, "Jesus' Resurrection," 138.

16. Craffert, "Jesus' Resurrection," 145.

17. Craffert, "Jesus' Resurrection," 131.

18. See especially Crossley, "Historical Plausibility," 184; and Aus, *Death, Burial, and Resurrection of Jesus*.

19. Craffert, "Jesus' Resurrection," 131.

20. P. Boyer, *Religion Explained: The Human Instincts That Fashion Gods, Spirits and Ancestors* (London: Vintage, 2002).

21. E. P. Sanders, *The Historical Figure of Jesus* (Penguin: London, 1993), 278–280.

22. As Habermas, "Resurrection Research," 151, puts it, "it is still crucial that the nearly unanimous consent of critical scholars is that, in some sense, the early followers of Jesus thought that they had seen the risen Jesus."

▓ FOR FURTHER READING

Allison, D.C. *Resurrecting Jesus: The Earliest Christian Tradition and Its Interpreters*. London: Continuum/T&T Clark, 2005.

Aus, R.D. *The Death, Burial, and Resurrection of Jesus, and the Death, Burial, and Translation of Moses in Judaic Tradition*. Lanham: University Press of America, 2008.

Boyer, P. *Religion Explained: The Human Instincts That Fashion Gods, Spirits and Ancestors*. London: Vintage, 2002.

Craffert, P.F. "Jesus" Resurrection in a Social-Scientific Perspective: Is There Anything New to be Said?" *JSHJ* 7 (2009): 126–151.

Crossley, J.G. "Against the Historical Plausibility of the Empty Tomb Story and the Bodily Resurrection: A Response to N.T. Wright." *JSHJ* 3 (2005): 153–168.

Goulder, M. "The Baseless Fabric of a Vision." In *Resurrection Reconsidered*, edited by G. D"Costa, 48–61. Oxford: Oneworld, 1996.

Goulder, M. "The Explanatory Power of Conversion-Visions." In *Jesus" Resurrection: Fact or Figment: A Debate between William Lane Craig and Gerd Lüdemann*, edited by P. Copan and R.K. Tacelli, 86–103. Downers Grove, IL: Inter-Varsity Press, 2000.

Habermas, G. "Resurrection Research from 1975 to the Present: What are Critical Scholars Saying?" *JSHJ* 3 (2005): 135–153.

Habermas G. (with A. Flew). "Part I: 2003 Resurrection Debate between Antony Flew and Gary Habermas." In *Did the Resurrection Happen? A Conversation with Gary Habermas and Antony Flew*, edited by D. Baggett, 21–67. Downers Grove, IL: InterVarsity Press, 2009.

Licona, M.R. *The Resurrection of Jesus: A New Historiographical Approach*. Downers Grove, IL: InterVarsity Press, 2009.

Licona, M.R., and van der Watt, J.G. "The Adjudication of Miracles: Rethinking the Criteria of Historicity." *HTS* 65 (2009): 62–68.

Lüdemann, G. *What Really Happened to Jesus: A Historical Approach to the Resurrection*. Louisville: Westminster John Knox, 1995.

Sanders, E.P. *The Historical Figure of Jesus*. Penguin: London, 1993.

Wright, N.T. *The Resurrection of the Son of God*. London: SPCK, 2003.

Only One Way to God?

37 Jesus Is the Only Way to God

■ HAROLD NETLAND

1. IS THERE ONLY ONE WAY TO GOD?

Not that long ago this question would have elicited a perfunctory affirmative in much of Europe and North America. It was taken for granted in much of the West that Christianity is the one true religion and only through Jesus Christ can one be brought into a right relationship with God (allowing, of course, for disputes as to just whose particular understanding of Christianity is correct).

But times have changed. The suggestion that there is only one way to God—and especially that this is found in Christianity—is summarily dismissed by many today as intellectually and morally indefensible. Globalization has made us aware of the rich diversity of cultures and religious traditions. We are also more sensitive to the complex interconnections between peoples, cultures, and religions, and the role of religion in the upsurge in global conflicts. While globalization in some ways brings together disparate groups, it also provokes new forms of tribalism that react—sometimes violently—against the "other." Unfortunately religion can be an important contributor to such tensions. As Mark Juergensmeyer observes, "religion seems to be trying to tear the planet apart, even as other cultural forces seem to be trying to pull it together."[1] Many assume that insistence upon there being just one correct way in which to approach the divine (inevitably?) promotes prejudice and mistreatment of religious others. So the only way to avoid religious violence, we are told, is for believers to abandon the dangerous conviction that their religion alone is the only way to respond to the divine.

This is an attractive position today. The proliferation of religiously sanctioned or inspired violence is an urgent problem that must be addressed responsibly by all faith communities. But embedded within this view is a host of complex issues that need to be worked through carefully. What appears to some today as perfectly obvious may, upon further reflection, turn out to be considerably more problematic. In this brief chapter we can do no more than clarify some of the issues and suggest what might be involved in making the claim that Jesus Christ is the only way to God. It will be helpful first to get a clearer picture of what we mean by "religion" and something of the differences and disagreements among the religions.

2. RELIGIOUS DISAGREEMENTS

While our world today is deeply religious, religious commitments are manifest in strikingly different ways. Roughly 80 percent of people worldwide profess some religious affiliation.[2] In addition to the large families of Christians, Muslims, Hindus, Buddhists, and Jews there are many millions who follow indigenous religious traditions or one of the thousands of new religious movements that have emerged in the past century or so.

Religions are complex, multifaceted phenomena, and no definition is without difficulties. But Roger Schmidt helpfully defines religions as "systems of meaning embodied in a pattern of life, a community of faith, and a worldview that articulate a view of the sacred and of what ultimately matters."[3] The complexity of religious traditions is captured in Ninian Smart's suggestion that we think in terms of seven dimensions of religion—the ritual, mythological (or narrative), experiential, doctrinal, ethical, social, and material dimensions of religion.[4] It is clear, then, that religions include much more than merely beliefs or doctrines.

But beliefs are central to religion. A religious community—Shi'a Muslims in Tehran or Presbyterian Christians in Seoul—is expected to live in a certain way and to regard all of life from a particular perspective. At the heart of the worldview of a particular religious community are some basic claims about the nature of the cosmos, the religious ultimate, and the relation of humankind to this ultimate. Such beliefs are significant, for as Smart notes, "the world religions owe some of their living power to their success in presenting a total picture of reality, through a coherent system of doctrines."[5] Religious believers are expected to accept as true the authoritative teachings of their tradition and to structure their lives accordingly. Paul Griffiths states, "a religious claim...is a claim about the way things are, acceptance of or assent to which is required or strongly suggested by the fact of belonging to a particular form of religious life."[6] In other words, one cannot reject the central claims of a religious tradition and remain a member in good standing within that community.

Careful observation of actual religious beliefs and practices reveals both similarities and differences across the religions. There are significant agreements in some beliefs and values among the religions, with similarities perhaps most apparent in ethical teachings. The ethical principle behind the Golden Rule, for example, is reflected (with varying degrees of clarity) in the teachings of many religions.[7] At the same time, however, it is also clear that when we consider carefully what the religions have to say about the religious ultimate, the human predicament, and the nature of and conditions for salvation, enlightenment, and liberation, there is significant disagreement.

Now some differences are not particularly problematic. Differences in dress, food, or marriage rituals can be interesting and in themselves do not pose a problem. But what does create difficulty is the fact that the religions advance very different claims about how humankind ought to understand the nature of the cosmos, human beings, and what is religiously ultimate. It is at this point that differences turn into disagreements. For each religion regards its own assertions to be correct or superior to those of its rivals, and attainment of the desired religious goal is often directly linked to understanding and accepting these teachings.

Christians and Muslims, for example, believe that the universe was created by an eternal Creator. Buddhists deny this. Christians traditionally have insisted that Jesus Christ is the incarnate Word of God, fully God and fully man. Muslims reject this as blasphemous. While Hindus, Buddhists, and Jains all agree that there is rebirth, they disagree vigorously over whether there is an enduring, substantial person or soul that is reborn. All of the religions acknowledge that the present state of the world is not as it should be, but they disagree over the cause of this unsatisfactory state and its proper remedy. For Christians, the root cause is sin against a holy God and the cure consists of repentance and reconciliation with God through the person and work of Jesus Christ on the cross. For many Buddhists, Hindus, and Jains, in contrast, the cause lies in a fundamentally mistaken view of reality and the remedy involves overcoming such false views. But Hindus, Buddhists, and Jains disagree among themselves over the nature of this ignorance and how it is to be overcome.

Such disagreements result in differences over how we are to pattern our lives. The disagreement here is not simply over the best way to achieve the same end. Differences between Christianity and Theravada Buddhism, for example, over what one ought to do—whether one should repent of one's sins and embrace Jesus Christ as Lord and Savior or follow the Noble Eightfold Path—reflect not so much disagreement over the best *means* toward a common goal, but rather very different understandings of the *ends* that ought to be pursued. Different conceptions of the ends to be pursued are rooted in more basic disagreements over what is religiously ultimate, the nature of the problem plaguing the universe, and the proper remedy for this predicament.

3. FRAMING THE QUESTION

With this understanding of religious disagreement, let's return to the original question: Is there only one way to God? The first thing to observe is that this question makes sense only within certain religious traditions. For example, the question presupposes the reality of God. But if "God" denotes an eternal, morally pure Creator of everything apart from God that exists (as in Judaism, Christianity, and Islam), then the question will be appropriate only within theistic contexts. Furthermore, the question also presupposes that humankind, in its present state, stands at some distance from God and is in need of some sort of reconciliation with God. We need a way back to God. Again, this makes sense within theistic contexts with teachings about sin. With appropriate modifications for the respective traditions, this question can thus be acceptable to Jewish, Christian, and Islamic communities.

But the question makes little sense within nontheistic religious traditions. Daoists, certain kinds of Hindus, Buddhists, Jains, and Shintoists, among others, will reject the question for not addressing their respective concerns, for each, in different ways, denies the reality of an eternal Creator. The question, Is there only one way to God?, is frequently posed as if all religions share common assumptions about God and that they simply disagree over the proper way to God. But the disagreements are far deeper than this and are embedded in very different metaphysical assumptions. Thus while some religious traditions will embrace the question, others will reject it as misleading.

The idea that all religions do not accept some belief in God strikes many in the West as strange. In particular, the claim that Buddhism is incompatible with belief in an eternal Creator might need some defending. For it is common in the West to portray Buddhism as simply being agnostic about a Creator, leaving open the question whether the notions of the religious ultimate, as understood in Buddhism and Christianity, might actually be complementary rather than contrary. Much of the Western interreligious dialogue between Buddhists and Christians has involved a search for a common ontological reality behind Buddhist and Christian metaphysical categories.[8] This is a complicated issue, but two brief comments are in order. First, there are some traditions within Mahayana Buddhism (such as Pure Land Buddhism) that do resemble theism in some respects. But it is not at all clear that these should be understood as embracing the reality of an eternal Creator. Second, religions change over time and Buddhism is undergoing significant changes as it adapts to North American and European contexts. Some of the metaphysical assumptions of traditional Asian Buddhism are being discarded and in some ways Buddhism in the West is taking on certain similarities to Christianity. Nevertheless, Buddhists in south and east Asia traditionally have rejected the idea of an eternal Creator or God. Consider the following statements from scholars of Buddhism:

> Buddhists do not believe in the existence of God. There need be no debating about this. In practicing Buddhism one never finds talk of God, there is no role for God, and it is not difficult to find in Buddhist texts attacks on the existence of an omnipotent, all-good Creator of the universe... To portray Buddhism as agnostic... seems to me a modern strategy. In ancient times Buddhists were quite clear that they denied the existence of a personal creator God as taught in rival theistic systems.[9]
> The Buddhist is an atheist and Buddhism in both its Theravada and Mahayana forms is atheism.[10]
> The entire Buddhist worldview is based on a philosophical standpoint in which the central thought is the principle of interdependence, how all things and events come into being purely as a result of interactions between causes and conditions. Within that philosophical worldview it is almost impossible to have any room for an

atemporal, eternal, absolute truth. Nor is it possible to accommodate the concept of a divine Creation.[11]

The issue, then, is not whether the different religions provide equally effective ways to the one God, rather, given their different metaphysical commitments, the more basic question is which—if any—of the religious perspectives is correct. In this connection, Keith Yandell observes that "a religion proposes a diagnosis of a deep, crippling spiritual disease universal to non-divine sentience and offers a cure. A particular religion is true if its diagnosis is correct and its cure is efficacious."[12] If we are to take the religions seriously on their own terms we cannot avoid the question of which perspective—that is, which diagnosis of the human predicament and which prescription for the cure, along with accompanying metaphysical assumptions—is correct. It is possible that none of the religions is correct. But they cannot all be correct.

▪ 4. JESUS IS THE ONLY WAY TO GOD

Let us then reframe the original question from within an explicitly Christian context. There are at least three major assumptions underlying traditional, orthodox Christian theism. First, Christian faith teaches that everything apart from God was created by an eternal, holy God. Second, it affirms that God has revealed himself in the scriptures (the Old and New Testaments) and that the apex of God's self-revelation is in the incarnation in Jesus of Nazareth. Third, it maintains that the New Testament is a reliable witness to the teachings and deeds of Jesus Christ. Each of these claims is controversial and demands both explanation and defense, although this cannot be pursued here.[13]

Moreover, Jesus' life must be understood within the broader context of the Hebrew scriptures and Jewish monotheism. Jesus' sayings and deeds appear within a framework that took for granted the reality of the God of Abraham, Isaac, and Jacob; of human sin and rebellion against God; the need for forgiveness and reconciliation with God; and the anticipation of God's provision for salvation. The New Testament claims that it is in Jesus of Nazareth that God has provided the way to reconciliation with God. So, from within the Christian context, the question becomes, Is Jesus the only way to God?

The comprehensive witness of the New Testament is that God was present and active in Jesus of Nazareth in an utterly unique way. Jesus is not portrayed as simply one among other great religious figures. A full discussion of the New Testament data concerning Jesus is impossible here, but some major themes can be highlighted. The Letter to the Hebrews states that although in the past God spoke through the prophets, "in these last days he has spoken to us by his Son, whom he appointed the heir of all things, through whom also he created the world" (Hebrews 1:1–2). Jesus is said to be "the radiance of the glory of

God and the exact imprint of his nature" (Hebrews 1:3). The Gospel of John affirms that in Jesus Christ the eternal Word, "who was with God and who was God," became flesh and dwelt among us (John 1:1–2, 14). In Jesus all the fullness of deity dwells bodily (Colossians 1:19, 2:9). The Christological hymn in Philippians 2:5–11 ascribes to Jesus language that Isaiah uses of God (Isaiah 45:23), so that "at the name of Jesus every knee should bow, in heaven and on earth and under the earth, and every tongue confess that Jesus Christ is Lord, to the glory of God the Father" (Philippians 2:10–11). It is through Jesus' death on the cross—"the righteous for the unrighteous"—that sinful humankind can be reconciled to God (1 Peter 3:18). Jesus is the one mediator between God and humankind (1 Timothy 2:5). 2 Corinthians 5:19 claims that God was in Christ reconciling the world to himself, and there is no suggestion in the New Testament that God was also doing this equally through other religious figures and traditions. While Jesus' teachings are distinctive, it is not just his teachings that set him apart. It is who Jesus is and what he has done on behalf of humanity on the cross that distinguishes him as the one Savior for all humanity. It is because Jesus is the incarnate Word, and because of his death and resurrection, that he is said to be "the Way, the Truth and the Life," indeed the only way to God (John 14:6).

■ 5. RELIGIOUS PLURALISM

Although clearly taught in the New Testament and affirmed by the Christian church throughout the centuries, the assertion that Jesus is the only way to God has become controversial among Christians in recent years. A growing number of Christian theologians suggest that while Jesus might be the Savior for Christians, he is not necessarily the Lord and Savior for all people; there are other equally legitimate saviors for adherents of other religions. This claim is part of a broader framework for understanding the relations among the religions referred to as religious pluralism. At the heart of religious pluralism is the contention that no single religion can legitimately claim to be uniquely true and normative for all people in all cultures at all times. Thus no single religious leader is in principle authoritative or normative for all people. Religious pluralism maintains that the major religions all, in principle, offer roughly equally legitimate and effective ways of understanding and responding to the religious ultimate. Pluralists reject the idea that Jesus Christ is the only Lord and Savior for all people. In the West it has been championed in recent years by Christian theologians such as John Hick and Paul Knitter.[14]

Is religious pluralism, with its assertion that Jesus is not the only Lord and Savior and that there are many acceptable ways to the divine, an option for Christians today? I think not. There are many reasons for this, but I will briefly note three problems with this perspective.

First, an acceptable model of religious pluralism will not privilege the views of any particular religious tradition; all religions are to be roughly equally true or acceptable. What is really religiously ultimate, then, will transcend the conceptions of both theistic and nontheistic traditions. Thus pluralism is incompatible with theistic traditions that maintain that an eternal creator God exists and is the religious ultimate. If God, as understood in Christian theism, exists, then pluralism is false. If we have good reasons to believe that a creator God exists, then pluralism is untenable. Although I cannot defend the claim here, I believe that there are strong reasons for believing that God does exist.

Second, there are enormous problems confronting any attempt to formulate a coherent model of religious pluralism.[15] There are many issues here, but consider just the problem of conflicting truth claims. We saw earlier that the religions make different, and at times incompatible, claims about the nature of the religious ultimate, the human predicament, and how to overcome this predicament. A viable model of religious pluralism must provide a coherent explanation as to why, despite these basic disagreements, it is reasonable to maintain that the many religions are nevertheless equally true and effective ways of responding to the one ultimate reality. I simply do not see how this can be done.

How do pluralists deal with conflicting claims? John Hick maintains that, despite conflicting truth claims, Christians, Muslims, and Buddhists are all "in touch" with and responding appropriately to the religious ultimate—which he calls "the Real."[16] The Real transcends conceptions of religious ultimacy in the religions such as God the Holy Trinity, or Allah, or nirvana. The latter are merely penultimate symbols through which Christians, Muslims, and Buddhists relate to the ultimate reality—the Real. Hick argues that teachings about the Trinity or Allah or nirvana cannot be accepted as they are taught within the respective religions but must be reinterpreted in mythological terms. Doctrinal disagreements thus pertain to penultimate matters and, according to Hick, are not significant since they do not affect the "transformation from self-centredness to Reality-centredness."[17]

But this is simply reductionism that refuses to take seriously the claims of the various religions on their own terms. Part of the appeal of religious pluralism is the perception that it accepts the different religions just as they are, without making negative judgments about them. Pluralism seems to offer a way of avoiding the conclusion that large numbers of sincere, intelligent, and morally respectable people are simply mistaken in their religious beliefs. But although pluralism does accept the major religions as equally legitimate responses to the Real, it does so only by changing in important ways the core beliefs of Christians, Muslims, and Buddhists. No mainstream Christian, Muslim, or Buddhist would accept this reduction of what they regard as the religious ultimate to merely a penultimate, symbolic status. So if religious pluralism is correct, then traditional Christians, Buddhists, and Muslims are all mistaken in their respective claims about the religious ultimate. Thus, even with pluralism we cannot escape the conclusion that large numbers of sincere, intelligent, and morally good people are mistaken in their basic religious commitments.

Speaking of the view that all religions teach the same truth and are responding to the same divine reality, Stephen Prothero, professor of religion at Boston University (and not committed to any particular religion) astutely observes:

> This is a lovely sentiment but it is dangerous, disrespectful, and untrue. For more than a generation we have followed scholars and sages down the rabbit hole into a fantasy world in which all gods are one... The world's religious rivals do converge when it comes to ethics, but they diverge sharply on doctrine, ritual, mythology, experience and law... Faith in the unity of religions is just that—faith (perhaps even a kind of fundamentalism). And the leap that gets us there is an act of the hyperactive imagination.[18]

The third reason for rejecting religious pluralism is the fact that pluralism is incompatible with the New Testament picture of Jesus. How do pluralists understand the significance of Jesus? John Hick rejects the orthodox view of Jesus as God incarnate, fully God and fully man, in favor of a metaphorical understanding of the divine incarnation. He states, "We see in Jesus a human being extraordinarily open to God's influence and thus living to an extraordinary extent as God's agent on earth, 'incarnating' the divine purpose for human life."[19] But this does not make Jesus unique, for Hick claims that not only Jesus, but also Moses, Gautama, Confucius, Zoroaster, Socrates, Mohammed, and Nanak "have in their different ways 'incarnated' the ideal of human life in response to the one divine Reality."[20] Hick is not calling for Christians to abandon their commitments to Jesus as their Lord, but he maintains that traditional claims about Jesus Christ as the only Lord and Savior for all humankind, the unique incarnation of God, should be rejected. Jesus can be the Savior for Christians, so long as they acknowledge that adherents of other religions have their own, equally legitimate religious leaders.

Similarly, Paul Knitter calls for a reinterpretation of the Christian understanding of Jesus that rejects the idea that "Jesus is the *only* mediator of God's saving grace in history." Knitter distinguishes Jesus being *truly* a Savior from his being the *only* Savior. "As a pluralist Christian, even though I do not feel it possible or necessary to affirm that Jesus is the *only* Savior, I still experience him to be so *truly* a Savior that I feel compelled to cast my lot with him."[21]

What about the many Biblical texts that speak of the exclusivity of Jesus Christ? Knitter acknowledges that "much of what the New Testament says about Jesus is...*exclusive*, or at least *normative*."[22] But he argues that the "one and only" language should be understood as "confessional" or "love" language, and not as making ontological claims about Jesus' uniquely divine status or being the only Savior.[23] When Peter, for example, states that salvation is found in no one else, "for there is no other name... by which we must be saved" (Acts 4:12), or when Jesus is called the "one mediator between God and man" (1 Timothy 2:5), we should not understand these statements as metaphysical claims that rule out the possibility of there being other saviors. The purpose of such "love language" is to express total, personal commitment of the Christian community to Jesus and to proclaim the universal meaning and urgency of what God has revealed in Jesus. As far as the early disciples are concerned, Jesus is the one and only. But this is compatible with our recognizing today that other religious communities can also have their own, equally legitimate saviors.

Surely Knitter is correct in noting that the New Testament includes "love language" or expressions of commitment to Jesus Christ. But he draws a misleading exclusive disjunction between expressions of commitment and ontological claims. Language serves many functions simultaneously and he provides no reason for concluding that exclusive statements as found in John 3:16, 14:6 and Acts 4:12 cannot be both expressions of adoration and also statements with significant ontological implications. Christological language in the New Testament is full of ontological implications. Even if we accept John 14:6 or Acts 4:12 as expressing "love language," we must ask what it was about the nature of Jesus that evoked this unusually expressive language of love and commitment. And answering this will result in unpacking the ontological implications of the New Testament understanding of Jesus and his relation to God. The conclusion of the early followers of Jesus was that, in an admittedly mysterious and paradoxical sense, the human Jesus is to be identified with the eternal creator; Jesus is God in human flesh.

The issue, then, is whether the traditional, orthodox perspective of Jesus as God incarnate is the best way to understand the significance of Jesus. Significantly, Hick acknowledges that if the traditional view is correct, then religious pluralism is untenable.

> Traditional orthodoxy says that Jesus of Nazareth was God incarnate—that is, God the Son, the Second Person of a divine Trinity, incarnate—who became man to die for the sins of the world and who founded the church to proclaim this to the ends of the earth, so that all who sincerely take Jesus as their Lord and Savior are justified by his atoning death and will inherit eternal life. It follows from this that Christianity, alone among the world religions, was founded by God in person. God came down from heaven to earth and launched the salvific movement that came to be known as Christianity. From this premise it seems obvious that God must wish all human beings to enter this new stream of saved life, so that Christianity shall supersede all the world faiths... Christianity alone [in this view] is God's own religion, offering a fullness of life that no other tradition can provide, it is therefore divinely intended for all men and women without exception.[24]

If the traditional view is correct, then Jesus is the only way to God. Now it is not as though the first-century world was unaware of other religious figures and traditions. Early Christians were familiar with the popular religious movements of the day—the cults of Asclepius or Artemis–Diana, the "mystery religions" of Osiris and Isis, Mithras, Adonis, or Eleusis, the cult of the Roman emperor, and the many versions of Stoicism, Cynicism, and Epicureanism were also available. It was widely accepted in the ancient Mediterranean world that the same deity could be called by different names in different cultures. Historian Robert Wilken observes that "the oldest and most enduring criticism of Christianity is an appeal to religious pluralism... All the ancient critics of Christianity were united in affirming that there is no one way to the divine."[25] Had the writers of the New Testament wished to say merely that Jesus is their Lord, but that he is only one among many alternative lords and saviors, they certainly could have done so. Not only did they not do this, but they insisted that Jesus is in fact the Lord of lords (1 Corinthians 8:5–6).

■ 6. SUBSIDIARY ISSUES

We might conclude by distinguishing the claim that Jesus is the only way to God from other subsidiary issues. For example, the affirmation of Jesus as the only Savior must be distinguished from the question of the extent of salvation. While affirming that Jesus is the only Savior for all humankind, Christians have nevertheless disagreed over the question of how many people will be saved or whether salvation is limited to those who explicitly accept the Gospel of Jesus Christ in this life. A variety of perspectives on the issue have been offered by evangelicals, mainline Protestants, and Roman Catholics. The point here is simply that there is no logical connection between the claim that Jesus is the only Savior for all people and any particular view of the extent of God's salvation.

Furthermore, affirming Jesus as the only Savior does not mean that there is no truth, goodness, or beauty in other religions. The Christian faith shares some significant common beliefs and values with other religions, with some more so than others. And surely Christians can and must acknowledge that there is goodness and beauty in other religious traditions as well.

Nor should this affirmation be understood as suggesting that Christians are necessarily morally better people than followers of other religions. Sadly, Christians often do not live up to the expectations Christ places upon his disciples, and there is much in the history of Christianity for which we must be profoundly contrite.

Finally, there is nothing in the affirmation of Jesus as the only way to God that suggests that Christians should not cooperate with other religious communities to further the common good. To the contrary, given the very real tensions in our world, Christians must work humbly with leaders of the major religions to reduce conflict between religious communities and to address our many common problems. Acknowledging Jesus as the only Lord and Savior is fully compatible with a sense of the urgency of interreligious understanding and cooperation.

NOTES

1. Mark Juergensmeyer, "Introduction: Religious Ambivalence to Global Civil Society," in *Religion in Global Civil Society*, ed. Mark Juergensmeyer (New York: Oxford University Press, 2005), 3.

2. Joanne O'Brien and Martin Palmer, *The Atlas of Religion* (Berkeley: University of California Press, 2007), 14.

3. Roger Schmidt et al. *Patterns of Religion* (Belmont, CA: Wadsworth, 1999), 10.

4. Ninian Smart, *The World's Religions*, 2nd ed. (New York: Cambridge University Press, 1998), 11–22.

5. Ninian Smart, *The Religious Experience*, 5th ed. (Englewood Cliffs, NJ: Prentice-Hall, 1996), 5.

6. Paul J. Griffiths, *Problems of Religious Diversity* (Oxford: Blackwell, 2001), 21.

7. The Golden Rule is explicitly stated in the *Analects* of Confucius and is implicit in the writings of other religious traditions. See Confucius, *The Analects*, trans. D. C. Lau (London: Penguin Books, 1979), 12.2 and 15.24.

8. See, e.g., Paul F. Knitter, *Without Buddha I Could Not Be A Christian* (Oxford: Oneworld, 2009).

9. Paul Williams, *The Unexpected Way: On Converting From Buddhism to Catholicism* (Edinburgh: T&T Clark, 2002), 25.

10. K. N. Jayatilleke, *The Message of the Buddha*, ed. Ninian Smart (New York: Free Press, 1974), 105.

11. The Dalai Lama, *The Good Heart: A Buddhist Perspective on the Teachings of Jesus*, ed. Robert Kiely (Boston: Wisdom Publications, 1996) p. 82.

12. Keith Yandell, "How to Sink in Cognitive Quicksand: Nuancing Religious Pluralism," in *Contemporary Debates in Philosophy of Religion*, ed. Michael L. Peterson and Raymond J. Vanarragon (Oxford: Blackwell, 2004), 191.

13. In addition to essays in this volume, one might consult Richard Swinburne, *The Existence of God*, 2nd ed. (New York: Oxford University Press, 2004); C. Stephen Evans, *Natural Signs and Knowledge of God: A New Look at Theistic Arguments* (New York: Oxford University Press, 2010); Richard Bauckham, *Jesus and the Eyewitnesses: The Gospels as Eyewitness Testimony* (Grand Rapids, MI: Eerdmans, 2006); and Ben Witherington, *Christology of Jesus* (Minneapolis: Fortress Press, 1990).

14. See John Hick, *An Interpretation of Religion*, 2nd ed. (New Haven, CT: Yale University Press, 2004) and Paul F. Knitter, *No Other Name? A Critical Survey of Christian Attitudes Toward the World Religions* (Maryknoll, NY: Orbis, 1985).

15. The literature on pluralism is enormous. My critique can be found in Harold Netland, *Encountering Religious Pluralism* (Downers Grove: InterVarsity Press, 2001), 212–246, and "Religious Pluralism as an Explanation for Religious Diversity," in *Philosophy and the Christian Worldview*, ed. David Werther and Mark D. Linville (New York: Continuum, 2012), 25–49.

16. See Hick, *An Interpretation of Religion*, chap. 14.

17. Hick, *An Interpretation of Religion*, chap. 20.

18. Stephen Prothero, *God Is Not One* (New York: HarperOne, 2010), 3.

19. John Hick, *The Metaphor of God Incarnate: Christology in a Pluralistic Age* (Louisville, KY: Westminster John Knox, 1993), 12.

20. Hick, *The Metaphor of God Incarnate*, 96, 98.

21. Paul F. Knitter, "Five Theses on the Uniqueness of Jesus," in *The Uniqueness of Jesus: A Dialogue With Paul F. Knitter*, ed. Leonard Swidler and Paul Mojzes (Maryknoll, NY: Orbis, 1997), 7, 15 (emphasis in original).

22. Knitter, *No Other Name?*, 182.

23. Knitter, *No Other Name?*, 182–186.

24. John Hick, "A Pluralist View," in *Four Views on Salvation in a Pluralistic World*, ed. Dennis L. Okholm and Timothy R. Phillips (Grand Rapids, MI: Zondervan, 1996), 51–52.

25. Robert Wilken, *Remembering the Christian Past* (Grand Rapids, MI: Eerdmans, 1995), 27, 42.

■ FOR FURTHER READING

Chung, S. W., ed. *Christ the One and Only: A Global Affirmation of the Uniqueness of Jesus Christ* (Grand Rapids, MI: Baker Academic, 2005).

D'Costa, G., ed. *Christian Uniqueness Reconsidered: The Myth of a Pluralistic Theology of Religions* (Maryknoll, NY: Orbis, 1990).

Edwards, J. R. *Is Jesus the Only Savior?* (Grand Rapids, MI: Eerdmans, 2005).

38 There Are Many Ways to God

PAUL F. KNITTER

It is as a Christian theologian—that is, as a scholar and as a believer—that I affirm the sentence that constitutes the assigned title for this chapter: "There are many ways to God." That title is a declaration that I believe every Christian who has experienced the God revealed in Jesus Christ and who thinks carefully about what she or he has experienced will want to and will feel compelled to affirm. That is the case I would like to propose in the following reflections—that to believe in the Christian God is to believe in a God of many ways.

But there is a paradoxical ingredient in such a statement, for the universal God that I believe to be the Christian God is also the particular God who has made Godself known in and as Jesus of Nazareth. Christian theism has to be, in other words, a constant and a life-giving balancing between universality and particularity. To emphasize one at the cost of the other is to lose touch with the full reality of God—or, at least, of the God made known in Jesus. So what I'm proposing for the readers of this volume is a two-step movement that seeks to keep the two pieces of our paradox together: first, I will offer reasons why Christians are called to embrace a God of many ways, and then I would like to explore how such a universal God is the same God we encounter in the unique particularity of Jesus the Christ.

1. A UNIVERSAL GOD WHO WORKS THROUGH MANY WAYS

As I try to understand, and be faithful to, the God of Jesus as witnessed in the New Testament and reflected upon through Christian tradition, I find four qualities of that God that, if taken seriously, call us to recognize that this God reveals and communicates God's self in many ways. If we believe that our God is loving, transcendent, Trinitarian, and jealous, we will also have to believe in a God who cannot be confined to one way. Let me try to explain.

1.1 A God of love: who seeks the well-being of all

There is a line-up of New Testament "proof texts" that can establish what I believe is the clearly audible undertone running through all that the sacred pages say about the God who spoke through and as Jesus: this is a God who is "defined" simply as Love (1 John 4:8), a God who "loves the world" (John 3:16), who loves us no matter how sinful we might be (Romans 5:8), whose accepting, affirming "grace" is given unconditionally and despite all obstacles (Galatians 2:15–21; Romans

3:21–31), and who therefore wills the well-being, the flourishing, the salvation of "all human beings" (1 Timothy 2:4). Yes, this is a God who calls for justice, who calls for a change of heart, who looks for "good works." But preceding and pervading all the "commandments" of God is the first commandment that, all by itself, fulfills the entire law (Romans 13:8)—God's love that embraces us and so enables us to love. This primacy of love, this unconditionality of well-wishing on the part of God, was summarized succinctly and powerfully by Irenaeus: *Gloria Dei Vivens Homo*[1]—the glory of God and the well-being of humanity are one and the same! God is well when humans are well.

For me, such an understanding of God was summarized by my teacher, Karl Rahner, in his emphasis on the *universal salvific will of God*. Simply but powerfully stated: Christians believe in a God who wills that all men and women be saved—that is, find their fulfillment in sharing in God's life, now and in what is to come after death.

But then Rahner, systematic theologian that he was, guided his fellow believers to take two further steps:[2]

1. If God wills something, God will, given divine omnipotence, bring it about. Or, in the case of humans and their free will, God will make it possible. This means that God will make it possible for every human being to choose to be saved. Further, this implies that, in one form or another, God offers God's saving grace to every single human being. Grace, always unmerited and always connected with God's saving action in Jesus, is a universal reality. It is in this context that Rahner, indulging in the excess of Paul's claim that the abundance of grace always exceeds the abundance of sin (Romans 5:20), urges his fellow Christians to embrace a *"Heilsoptimismus"*—an optimism about how many are saved.

2. Having made this theological step, Rahner invites Christians to follow through with an anthropological step. Grace has to conform to our human nature—to the way God made us. And God made us as bodily and as social beings. Therefore, if the universal offer of God's saving grace is going to be real in our lives, it has to come through some form of social, cultural, embodied mediation. At this point, Rahner makes his famous case that the religions of the world can (not must) serve as *"Heilswege"*—ways or mediations of God's revelation and grace (mediations, Rahner adds, that are ultimately to be fulfilled in the fullest revelation in Christ). Whether it will be religion or whether it will be a particular person or movement or situation, the point that Rahner is asking us to consider is that we can expect God's saving grace to be mediated through many other ways.

Put in its most straightforward form: if we Christians truly believe that our God is a God who loves and seeks to embrace all human beings, then this God will necessarily seek many ways to make that love real in our lives.

1.2 A transcendent God: who exceeds all human comprehension

I suspect that one of the few things that all Christians—no matter what their denominational or theological colorings—would agree on is the recognition that God is a reality that no human mind can fully grasp. What was defined for Catholics back in the Fourth Lateran Council in 1215 and then reaffirmed by the First Vatican Council in 1875 is something that other Christians will recognize whether they're told to or not: that God is "incomprehensible."[3] God will always *transcend*, always be more than, what human beings can know or what God can give them to know. Or as Thomas Aquinas reminds us with his usual pithiness: God "surpasses every form that our intellect reaches."[4] This, of course, does not mean that we cannot really, truly, overwhelmingly know God's truth and God's reality. We can, and it will usually shake up and redirect our lives. But while we know enough of God's truth to ground and direct our lives, we will never be able to know *all* of God's truth. Rivaling Aquinas's pithiness, Paul Tillich tells us that divine reality is "infinitely apprehensible, yet never entirely comprehensible,"[5] as mysterious as it is real, as truly transcendent as it is truly immanent. That's why Christian mystics have spoken of God as the *notum Ignotum*—the known Unknown. In the very moment of knowing something about God, they know for sure they can never know everything about God.

Now, if this is what all Christians believe, if God for them can really be known but never fully be known, then it follows with both logical and theological necessity that there cannot be only one way to know God. Why? Because there is always more to know about God. To hold to only one way is to close oneself to knowing more of the depths of divine truth. The "more," the excess, the transcendence of the God of Jesus calls us, therefore, to be open to "more ways" to know God. There can be no "only one" or "final" truth. No one truth can say it all. If any truth says it does, it is probably an idol—a finite something that sets itself up as the everything of God.

1.3 A Trinitarian God: who includes and embraces diversity

In exploring the Christian belief in the Trinity, we're diving into deep waters—but also beautiful waters. The central Christian belief in God as triune is as complex as it is enriching. But we have to swim carefully.

So I don't want to explore the intricacies of the internal nature of the triune God—the relationship between one nature and three persons, the processions, the precise meaning of "prosopon" or "phusis" or "hypostasis." Rather, I want to recognize, and then reflect on, what I believe is at the heart of why Christians claim that the divine reality is a triune reality: they do so because they have experienced that the God whom they have known in Jesus is a profoundly *relational* God (which is another way of saying a profoundly loving God). And for relationship to be possible and real, there has to be more than one. In affirming the Trinity, Christians are affirming diversity. The always one God is also the always more-than-one God. Manyness is part of the very nature of God. Manyness, or more-than-oneness, characterizes the way God is and acts. That's the God Christians have come to know and experience in Jesus—a God who is called, and who is, Father, Word/Son, Spirit.

Christian theologians like Raimon Panikkar and S. Mark Heim draw out what they hold to be the necessary implications of Trinitarian faith in a world of religious diversity. Both of them suggest, simply but profoundly, that if Christians believe that there is diversity within God, that is, within the way God exists in God's self (what Rahner calls "the Trinity *ad intra*"), they can expect to find diversity outside of God, that is, in the way God acts and relates to the world (what Rahner calls "the Trinity *ad extra*"). In the world God acts out, as it were, God's diversity in many ways, and that means, more concretely, in many religions. Heim even goes so far as to say that anyone who believes in the Trinity has to believe in the validity of many religions: "If Trinity is real, then many of the *specific* religious claims and ends must also be real. If they were all false, then Christianity could not be true."[6]

Such a statement may be pushing the theological envelope a bit. Still, I believe the powerful, beautiful implication of Trinitarian faith remains: a God who is Trinity is a God who embraces and loves and acts through diversity—through many ways.[7]

1.4 A jealous God: who opposes the idolatry of empire

Normally when Christians (or Jews) speak about the jealousy of their God, it's taken to be an exclusion of other gods—that would mean, other ways. To draw such a quick conclusion, I would like to suggest, may be to miss the real intent of God's jealousy. What God is jealous about is not that there are many ways in which people approach and experience God; rather, divine jealousy is directed at any way that claims to take the place of God. The primary intent of divine jealousy is perhaps best captured in the Islamic *Shahada*: "There is no god but God!" God's jealousy is not saying "there is no religion but the Islamic, or Christian, or Jewish religion." Rather, in insisting that there is "no god but God," the monotheistic, Abrahamic religions are proclaiming that no object, no teaching, no social system, no government, and no religion shall take the place of God by claiming the absolute, full, final power and truth of God.

This, I suspect, is God's concern—a concern that is animated not by an anthropomorphic petty jealousy of having to be a divine "numero uno," but rather the divine jealousy is animated by the recognition, so evident in history, that every time human beings—whether individuals or nations or religions—attribute to themselves what belongs only to God, that spells trouble for other human beings. Having taken the place of God, humans are enabled and entitled to take whatever else they want. *Idolatry prepares the way for empire.* This, as contemporary scripture scholars are making clear, is what animated and aroused the Jewish prophets, especially the prophet Jesus of Nazareth: they were opposed to the empires that tried to take the place of God, whether such empires were found in the royal courts of Babylon, Jerusalem, or Rome.[8]

Here, I suggest, we come to the ethical bedrock for why we must recognize the diversity of God's ways: if Jesus and the God he embodied warned against the dangers of empire, they would also warn against the danger of only one way. I believe the historical record is quite clear: any nation or any religion or any ideology that claims to be the "only truth," or that feels it has been divinely designated as the final truth for all other truths, is open to the temptation, if not the necessity, of allowing such claims to justify or necessitate power over others. Such power is the stuff of empire and exploitation. I am not saying that claims to have "the only way" must lead to the demeaning and mistreatment of others. I am simply observing that they do.

One of the most powerful reminders of this is offered to us Christians by a Buddhist scholar, Rita Gross (she offers it also to her fellow Buddhists):

> The result of exclusive [only one] truth-claims is not religious agreement but suffering. The track record of religions that claim exclusive and universal truth for themselves is not praiseworthy or uplifting. How much empire building, how many crusades and religious wars, big and small, have gone on in the name of defending the "*one* true faith"? There seems to be a cause-and-effect link between claims of exclusive truth and suffering; or to say it more strongly, the main result of exclusive truth-claims has been suffering, not salvation.[9]

2. AFFIRMING AND HOLDING TOGETHER THE UNIVERSALITY AND THE PARTICULARITY OF THE CHRISTIAN GOD

But for Christians, as for Jews and Muslims, this universal God who acts through many ways is also and always the historical God who has acted through particular ways.

But what is particular is unique; there is no other like it, nothing else that can fully take its place. So, in what is particular and unique and unrepeatable, the universally loving God is making something known that is true and relevant for everyone. For Christians, the uniqueness and the universal relevance of the particular Jesus are embodied in the Christian claims that Jesus is Son of God and Savior for all peoples of all times.

Now, as I stated in my introduction, Christians face a challenge that has accompanied them throughout the centuries but which has come to an especially forceful focus in our days: how can we hold together the universality of a God who, by God's very nature as we have seen, acts through many ways with the particularity of a God who has acted uniquely and salvifically in Jesus of Nazareth? Or as Krister Stendahl, a quarter century ago, articulated this same challenge: "How can I sing my song to Jesus fully and with abandon without feeling it necessary to belittle the faith of others? I believe that question to be crucial for the health and vitality of Christian theology in the years ahead."[10]

With Stendahl, I do believe that Christian theology, grounded in the biblical witness and guided by the ongoing presence of the living Christ, can provide us with the resources to sing our *one* song about Jesus without denigrating the *many* songs in other religions and philosophies. I begin with the way that song is sung in the New Testament.

2.1 New Testament language is primarily confessional language

There is no doubt that many of the proclamations that the New Testament makes of Jesus also make it difficult, to say the least, to affirm a God of many ways. Indeed, there is a wall of texts that seems to confine God's saving action to only one way. The keystone, as it were, of these many "exclusive" or "one and only" texts is made up of Acts 4:12, "There is no other name under heaven given among mortals by which we must be saved," and John 14:6, "No one comes to the Father except through me."

Let me again turn to Stendahl to explore how he, as an acclaimed New Testament scholar and bishop of the Swedish Lutheran Church, could "sing" and understand these texts about one way without diminishing the divine love possibly expressed in other ways.[11] The hermeneutical lens through which he approaches these "one way" pronouncements is to understand them not as "dogmatic" or "propositional" or philosophical language intending to give us "absolute" knowledge about the nature of Jesus or the structures of the universe. Rather, these texts are to be felt and dealt with as beautiful and powerful examples of "confessional and liturgical and doxological language . . . a kind of caressing language by which we express our devotion with abandon and joy."[12]

The intent of this caressing or love language is to say something positive about Jesus and about the way he transformed the lives of his disciples and could transform the lives of others. The intent of this language was not to say something negative about other ways—about Buddha or any other religious leader or religion. Stendahl points out the obvious: "No where in these chapters (Acts 2–4) enter any questions about gentile gods, gentile cults, or gentile religion. Thus there is no way of knowing whether Luke, who wrote this, would consider this saying relevant to a discussion on Buddhism—if he knew anything about Buddhism, which is most doubtful."[13] Therefore "Acts 4:12 is not a good basis for an absolute claim in an absolute sense, but . . . it is a natural confession growing out of the faith, growing out of the experience of gratitude...Here is a confession, not a proposition. It is a witness,...not...an argument."[14]

Stendahl is therefore urging us not to discard such "one and only" confessional language but to use it as "home language"—within our own communities as "the language of prayer, worship, and doxology." It is not language to be used in our relationships with friends whose confessional or love language is directed to Muhammad or Buddha or Krishna.[15] The language that I use at a candlelight dinner at home when I tell my wife she is the most beautiful woman in the world, I would not use at a social dinner with friends and their partners.

2.2 Recognizing "many ways" does not endanger commitment to "one way"

The passages from the New Testament that sound so exclusive of other ways are really calls to what Stendahl terms "faithful particularity" to our own way.[16] They are consistent with the primary criterion for all New Testament hermeneutics: does the interpretation allow for and strengthen *discipleship*—the continued following of Jesus? The interpretation of these "one and only" passages as confessional or as "love language" still retains—indeed, it augments—the power of these texts to summon us to be faithful to the particular Jesus and his message, to live it out in our lives, and to let others know about it. But such faithful particularity, I suggest, in no way excludes, indeed it welcomes, the example and witness of "faithful particularities" in other ways.

Such a confessional interpretation of these one-and-only texts, in allowing for the possibility that God is acting in other ways that call others to their own "faithful particularity," in no way questions or diminishes the reality of what Christians know God has done in Jesus. A confessional hermeneutics of these exclusive texts in no way questions the *ontological reality* contained within the Christian claims that Jesus is Son of God and Savior of the world. This is not a psychologizing or subjectivizing of the texts. It is a reading and an appropriation of these texts that continue to proclaim that God has truly revealed God's saving power in the particular Jesus. But it allows for the possibility that God may be acting and revealing in other ways—ways that are multiple and different. In questioning the traditional understanding of "only," we are in no way questioning the traditional understanding of "truly."

So as I have tried to lay out more amply elsewhere,[17] with this confessional understanding of the particularity of Jesus, Christians still proclaim, for themselves and to the world, the universality, the decisiveness, and the indispensability of God's saving revelation in Jesus Christ:

- What God has done and revealed in Jesus is not meant only for Christians. Its power to transform, to provide humans with a vision of what the world can be like, and to save them and rescue them from the folly of their "hearts turned in on themselves," this power, Christians affirm, is meant for all peoples. It must be proclaimed and made available universally, "to the nations."

- And so the truth and the possibilities of the Gospel are meant to be decisive—to bring human beings to a turning point, to face them with the opportunity and the necessity of seeing things differently and turning things around. If one truly hears and feels the "good news" given in Christ, one's life will not, for it cannot, remain the same. It will be time to *de-cidere*—to cut loose from former ways and move in new ways.

- Therefore the confessional understanding of Jesus' particularity that I am recommending will continue to affirm the indispensability of what God has done in Jesus and the indispensability of announcing it to others. Christians continue to believe that if anyone has not heard about, understood, and appreciated the presence and power of God in Christ, something essentially important will be missing in whatever truth and grace they may already have. This is the meaning of belief in a God who works through particulars: what God has done through Jesus, the clarity and the particular contents of the Gospel message, can be found no where else.

But while affirming that the truth revealed in Christ is universally relevant, decisive, and indispensable, this confessional understanding of the Christian "song" about Jesus can respect the songs of others, for it does not make claims that the revelation given in Christ is full, or final, or unsurpassable.

- While Christians are impelled to continue preaching the universal importance of Christ, they will also feel impelled to continuously remind themselves that "the Father is greater than I" (John 14:28) and that the Spirit can come and reveal even greater things (John 16:12–13; 14:26). Christians will recognize that given the infinite mystery and incomprehensibility of the Divine, given the limitations of human finitude, no revelation delivered in human words (as all revelations are) can contain the fullness of God's truth and reality.

- And therefore, although Christians will continue to affirm the power of the Gospel to call people to the decisive finality of conversion, this finality can never be made absolute. While Christ calls all to conversion, such conversion is never complete. There is always more to come. If there is not more to come, more truth to learn, more decisions to make, then Christians are not taking the eschatological content of the Gospel seriously or faithfully.

- This means that even though the Gospel gives us a firm place to stand, and calls us to decide and take a stand, we can, and must, remain open to learning more from other ways. We can never say of Christian truth what philosophers, in their hubris, may say of their truth "*ne plus ultra*"—no more beyond this point. The universality of Christian truth cannot be unsurpassable precisely because it also recognizes the universality of other truths proclaimed through other ways. Here a distinction is necessary: in recognizing that their revelation is not unsurpassable, Christians admit that more truth can be added to what they know of God through Christ, but they cannot conceive of additional truth that would contradict what God has revealed in Christ.[18]

2.3 Jesus the way that is open to other ways

This understanding of how the "many ways" of God's presence throughout history and in other religions can be held in fruitful tension with the "one way" that God has become present in Jesus the Christ can perhaps best be summarized philosophically in the distinction between *universal* and *absolute*. Whenever the Divine acts or is discovered in human experience and history, that presence or revelation will have *universal* relevance and power. And that, certainly, is what Christians have experienced in Christ Jesus. But no revelation can be held up to be *absolute*—absolute in the sense that it is the only or the final vehicle by which the infinite mystery of God can be known. This, I am suggesting, is what Christians need to, and are able to, recognize more clearly in our present context than they have before.

More personally and more practically, what I am proposing can be lived out and embodied in Christian life if the disciples of Jesus come to experience him as "the Way that is open to other Ways."[19] We can follow and understand and be faithful to our own "one way" only if we are open to, in dialogue with, ready to learn from, and challenge "other ways." We can be faithful to Jesus only if we are open to others. I think this is a restatement of the central command that Jesus has given us—to love God by loving our neighbor. We can truly love the God we know in Jesus only if we are open to, and ready to love, the God that is known by others.

▪ NOTES

1. *Adversus Haereses*, IV.xx.7.

2. Rahner's theology of religions can be found in summary form at Karl Rahner, *Foundations of Christian Faith* (New York: Crossroads, 1982), 311–320.

3. Denzinger-Schönmetzer, *Enchiridion Symbolorum Definitionum et Declarationum* (Barcelona: Herder, 1963), nos. 428 and 1782.

4. Thomas Aquinas, *Summa contra Gentiles*, I, 14:3.

5. Tillich, *What Is Religion?* (New York: Harper-Collins, 1973), 15.

6. Heim, *The Depth of Riches: A Trinitarian Theology of Religious Ends* (Grand Rapids, MI: Eerdmans, 2000), 175, see also 168–174 and the entirety of pt. 3. Raimon Panikkar, *The Trinity and the Religious Experience of Man* (Maryknoll, NY: Orbis Books, 1973).

7. Here I have to note a rather stark difference with my friend Harold Netland who attributes the diversity of religions not to the Trinity but to the Fall: "We must not forget that the fact of religious diversity as we know it is itself an effect of the Fall and sin. If it were not for sin, there would not be this radical pluralization of religious responses to the divine." Harold Netland, "Toward an Evangelical Theology of Religions," in *Encountering Religious Pluralism: The Challenge for Christian Faith and Mission* (Downers Grove, IL: InterVarsity Press, 2001), 345.

8. Richard A. Horsley, *Jesus and Empire: The Kingdom of God and the New World Order* (Minneapolis: Fortress Press, 2003); John Dominic Crossan, *God and Empire: Jesus Against Rome, Then and Now* (New York: HarperOne, 2008); Brigitte Kahl, *Galatians Re-imagined: Reading with the Eyes of the Vanquished* (Minneapolis: Fortress Press, 2010).

9. Rita Gross, "Excuse me, but What's the Question? Isn't Religious Diversity Normal?" in *The Myth of Religious Superiority: A Multifaith Exploration*, ed. Paul F. Knitter (Maryknoll, NY: Orbis Books, 2005), 80.

10. Krister Stendahl, *Meanings: The Bible as Document and as Guide* (Philadelphia: Fortress Press, 1984), 233. In all candor and respect, I believe that the following statement of Harold Netland, representing the views of many Christians, does not allow him to sing his song about Jesus without belittling other religions: "In his mercy God has provided a way, through the atoning work of Jesus Christ on the cross, for sinful persons to be reconciled to God...No one is reconciled to God except through the cross of Jesus Christ." Netland, "Toward an Evangelical," 319.

11. The following section is adapted from a lecture given in Stockholm in October 2009 titled "Christianity and the Religions: A Zero-Sum Game? Reclaiming 'The Path Not Taken' and the Legacy of Krister Stendahl." *Journal of Ecumenical Studies.* 46 (2011) 5–21.

12. Krister Stendahl, "From God's Perspective We Are All Minorities," *Journal of Religious Pluralism* 2 (1993), http://bit.ly/hJOlGh, accessed December 29, 2010; Stendahl, *Meanings: The Bible as Document*, 239.

13. Stendahl, *Meanings: The Bible as Document*, 238; see also Krister Stendahl, "In No Other Name," in *Christian Witness and the Jewish People*, ed. Arne Sovik (Geneva: Lutheran World Federation, 1976), 49.

14. Stendahl, *Meanings: The Bible as Document*, 240. Furthermore, Stendahl judges as "just not apropos" the way Christians have used John 14:6 to denigrate and reject other religions: "It is odd that one of the few passages that are used by those who have closed the doors on a theology of religions in Christianity, should be a passage which is dealing not with the question of the periphery or the margins of exclusion, but which, on the contrary, lies at the very heart of the mystery of what came to be the Trinity: the relation between the Father and the Son." Stendahl, "From God's Perspective,"

15. Stendahl, "From God's Perspective,".

16. Krister Stendahl, "Qumran and Supersessionism—and the Road Not Taken," *Princeton Seminary Bulletin* 19 (1998): 140–141.

17. Paul F. Knitter, *The Uniqueness of Jesus: A Dialogue with Paul F. Knitter*, ed. Leonard Swidler and Paul Mojzes (Maryknoll, NY: Orbis Books, 1997), 3–16, 145–182.

18. This distinction is made with particular clarity by Roger Haight in *Jesus Symbol of God* (Maryknoll, NY: Orbis Books, 1999), 403–410.

19. John B. Cobb, Jr., "Beyond Pluralism," in *Christian Uniqueness Reconsidered: The Myth of a Pluralistic Theology of Religions*, ed. Gavin D'Costa (Maryknoll, NY: Orbis Books, 1990), 91.

▦ FOR FURTHER READING

Cornille, C. *The im-Possibility of Interreligious Dialogue*. New York: Crossroads, 2008.

Hick, J. *A Christian Theology of Religions: The Rainbow of Faith*. Louisville, KY: Westminster/ John Knox Press, 1995.

Fletcher, J. H. *Monopoly on Salvation? A Feminist Approach to Religious Pluralism*. New York: Continuum, 2004.

Knitter, P. F. *One Earth Many Religions: Multifaith Dialogue & Global Responsibility*. Maryknoll, NY: Orbis, 1995.

Sacks, J. *The Dignity of Difference: How to Avoid the Clash of Civilizations*. New York: Continuum, 2002.

Suchocki, M. H. *Divinity and Diversity: A Christian Affirmation of Religious Pluralism*. Nashville, TN: Abingdon Press, 2001.

Heaven and Hell

39 It is Reasonable to Believe in Heaven and Hell

■ JERRY L. WALLS

Whether or not it is reasonable to believe in heaven and hell is entirely a function of whether it is reasonable to believe in God, and what is reasonable to believe about him. The essence of heaven in Christian theology is a perfected relationship of love with God and other persons on a renewed and redeemed earth, a relationship that will fulfill our deepest longings for happiness and satisfaction. Hell, by contrast, is the eternal misery of persons who are excluded from this perfect relationship. If there is no God, there is no heaven and hell as so defined. And if it is not reasonable to believe in God, it is not reasonable to believe in heaven and hell so defined.

Obviously I do not have space to defend the rationality of belief in God, so I shall take that as my starting point. Of course, Keith Parsons does not share this belief, but the argument I develop shall nevertheless allow me to engage him on crucial issues. Moreover, objections to belief in heaven and hell often take the form of claims that these beliefs are incompatible with one or more of God's presumed attributes, as we shall see. So let me spell out what I shall assume about God as my starting point. I shall assume that God is maximally powerful and perfectly loving and good. Moreover, he knows everything it is possible to know. He is the creator of the world and everything in it, including human beings. We have the nature we do because God created us as we are, with our powers of reason, freedom, moral sensibilities, aspirations for happiness and meaning, and so on.

■ 1. AN ARGUMENT FOR HEAVEN

Now I want to argue that this conception of God gives us grounds for thinking it is reasonable to believe in heaven. We can spell out this argument as follows.

1. God, who is perfectly loving and good, created us as rational beings who deeply desire happiness.
2. Perfect happiness is preferable to happiness that is only partial and mixed.
3. Rational beings naturally aspire to perfect happiness.
4. As beings who are both rational and relational, our perfect happiness consists essentially in knowing and experiencing the highest form of love and relationship of which we are capable, with all that that entails.
5. The highest form of love and relationship of which we are capable is a perfectly loving relationship with God and our fellow human beings.

6. If we were perfectly happy in a loving relationship with God and our fellow human beings, we would not want this relationship to end, and our happiness would not be perfect if it did.

7. A perfectly loving and good God would not create us with deep desires and aspirations for good things that we have no reasonable chance to achieve.

8. God has the power to provide us a reasonable chance to achieve a perfectly loving relationship with himself and our fellow human beings.

9. Anything we have a reasonable chance to achieve must be something in which it is reasonable to believe.

10. Therefore it is reasonable to believe in heaven.

This argument gives us the conclusion I want with respect to heaven. But, of course, everything depends on whether the premises are true. So let us turn now to examine them in turn.

Premise 1 is fairly uncontroversial insofar as it claims that human beings have a deep desire for happiness. This claim is axiomatic for philosophers ranging from Aristotle to Pascal and seems hard to dispute by anyone acquainted with human nature and psychology. To be sure, people sometimes sabotage their own happiness, but when this is the case, we tend to think that those who do so suffer from psychological or emotional disorders of some kind that block them from achieving their own goals. Or worse, they have latched onto perverse motives that keep them from happiness. It is also important to emphasize that happiness as traditionally understood is not a superficial matter of self-serving personal pleasure, but rather a deeper kind of satisfaction typically experienced in community with other persons.

The more important aspect of premise 1 for my argument is that the ultimate explanation for this reality is that God designed us as rational creatures who naturally desire happiness. Our yearning for happiness is not merely the product of our evolutionarily advanced brains and our capacity for rational reflection and imagination. Indeed, this yearning is the sort of thing we ought to have if God created us, rather than merely a naturalistically evolved phenomenon that we happen to exhibit, for who knows what reason. On the theistic account, we aspire to happiness precisely because God designed our brains and our mental powers in such a way that we would inevitably pursue it and hope to achieve it.

Premise 2 also seems axiomatic. To disagree, I think, is to have a confused notion of perfect happiness. Perhaps one thinks that perfect happiness would be insipid or lifeless, and that imperfect happiness would be more interesting, that it would involve growth, challenges, and so on. To think this is to assume that perfection is static. But perhaps it is not, and perfect happiness is a dynamic thing that involves perpetual growth, learning, and so on. At any rate, if we prefer something to the perfect, we are likely thinking the thing we actually prefer is what is really "perfect" for us.

Perfect happiness as I am using the term is that kind and degree of happiness that would most fulfill us at our best, and thereby give us the deepest kind of satisfaction. There is considerable historical and empirical evidence that human beings aspire to this sort of happiness, so much so that it is arguable that the desire for perfect happiness is natural to our species, as premise 3 claims. This is not to say that the desire for perfect happiness has always been conceived in the same way, or that there is consensus on what such happiness would entail. But the belief in an afterlife that brings perfect happiness is widespread enough, not to mention various utopians' dreams for this life, that it is reasonable to believe we aspire to perfect happiness, however that may be conceived.

Premise 4 can also be supported by empirical evidence. That is to say, there is enormous evidence that human beings desire loving relationships and that they find fulfillment in both giving and receiving love. Again, I will not go so far as to claim that this value judgment is universal, only that it is widespread, and arguably reflects deeply rooted aspirations of the human heart. It is worth noting, incidentally, that Parsons agrees that personal relationships are fundamental to true happiness. He writes: "Hermits are very rare, and are almost always sociopaths or religious fanatics. Humans, then, are by nature gregarious. We find our personal fulfillment only in relations with other people."[1]

Critics may be dubious of this, and argue that our fascination with, and pursuit of, love and relationships is due to the fact that Western culture was shaped by Christian theology, with its claims about the love of God and the central importance of loving relationships. I would not deny this, and moreover, since I think the Christian God really exists, I think our aspirations in this regard are a clue to ultimate reality.

Premise 5 is reasonable to believe if one believes that God is himself a being of perfect love and goodness who is capable of communicating with, and relating to, rational creatures such as ourselves. It is hard to deny, moreover, that there could be a higher form of loving relationship than to love and to know one is loved by a being whose very nature is perfect in love. Furthermore, if our love for our fellow human beings was itself illumined and empowered by our relationship with a God of perfect love, it seems that love would then be the ultimate sort of human love of which we could be capable.

This brings us to premise 6. This also seems utterly obvious to me. If one were perfectly happy, what possible motive could one have for wanting such happiness to end? Perfect happiness is by its very nature the sort of happiness that would never end. Think of it this way. If we are not perfectly happy, we would prefer to be, and if our lives ended without our achieving perfect happiness, they would end with some degree of frustration. And if we were perfectly happy, it would be absurd to want such happiness to end, and if it did, then again, our lives would end in frustration. So the only way our lives will not end in frustration is if we achieve perfect happiness, which would never end.

Now we come to premise 7, which involves a moral judgment about the nature of perfect goodness. A truly good and loving God would not want his creatures to experience frustration of their deepest and best desires. Rather, he would want such desires to be fulfilled. Indeed, assuming that he has control over the sort of desires his creatures have and develop, he would not want them to develop desires for good things that could not be satisfied. For the frustration of good desires is a bad thing, and perhaps this is especially so for beings who feel such desires with deep emotion and personal poignancy.

Consider an analogy. Suppose a child was separated from his mother at birth, and was raised in a series of foster homes. He grew up not knowing whether his mother was dead or alive. Suppose, however, that his most recent foster father has learned that the boy's mother had recently been tragically killed. He does not share this fact with the boy. However, he begins telling the boy stories of children, separated from their mothers at birth, who later grow up and are reunited with their mothers and develop loving and deeply meaningful relationships with them. As he tells these stories, the boy develops a desire, which grows into a powerful yearning, to be reunited with his mother, and to know and love her.

It is obvious, I take it, that the foster father is not acting in a loving way in eliciting such desires and yearnings in the boy, and indeed, he is arguably perverse for doing so. Likewise, if God created us in such a way that we had deep yearnings for things, especially good things, that could not be satisfied, then he would not be good, and perhaps would even be perverse.

For another angle on the point, consider the view of sociobiologist E. O. Wilson. He writes: "The essence of humanity's spiritual dilemma is that we evolved genetically to accept one truth and discovered another."[2] What he means by this is that human beings evolved in such a way that we are incurably religious. Consequently we hunger for immortality and an everlasting union with God that will give our lives eternal significance. Without such hope we tend to feel lost in a meaningless universe. Unfortunately the discoveries of science have robbed us of this hope, and that is why we face the dilemma he identified. We have evolved in such a way that we have aspirations for meaning and happiness that, unfortunately, outstrip reality. We must choose between the eternal meaning religion has offered and intellectual honesty, but we cannot have both. To be intellectually honest requires that we give up the hope of immortality and everlasting union with God.

Now this is a painful dilemma that many persons in Western culture at least have been dealing with ever since the Enlightenment. It is painful for many people to give up the eternal meaning that religion offers and to lower the ceiling on their hopes. Here again is my point. A good God would not create us in such a way that we would face this painful dilemma. A good God would not create us in such a way that we had "incurable" longings for meaning and happiness that could never be satisfied. Nor would he create things in such a way that we had to choose between intellectual honesty and belief in the reality of the sort of meaning and happiness we long for. Rather, such belief would be reasonable to hold.

We are now almost home to the conclusion I seek. Premise 8 is also most reasonable to accept for anyone who believes in God in the classic theistic sense. The classic Christian idea of resurrection is surely an intelligible one and has been defended by a number of philosophers, and I will not reiterate those arguments here. Moreover, the historical evidence for the resurrection of Jesus gives us reason to believe not only that resurrection is conceptually possible, and well within the power of an omnipotent God, but that God has actually demonstrated this on the stage of world history.

Of course, more is needed than resurrection for us to achieve a perfectly loving relationship with God and our fellow human beings. A resurrected body is not enough to make us willing and able to both receive and give perfect love. For this to occur, our characters must be transformed in such a way that we heartily care for others and treat them in ways that respect them, empathize with them, and promote their true well-being. We often fail at this, of course, and that is why many of our relationships fall so miserably short of what they should be.

A God who is perfectly good and wise and understanding would know how to transform us in the ways necessary to make us into perfect lovers who could both reciprocate his love, as much as finite creatures can, as well as love their fellow creatures. The Christian story of incarnation, atonement, resurrection, and Pentecost is a scheme of salvation, the intent of which is not only to provide forgiveness of our sins, but also to reconcile us to God and empower us to relate to him as he intended us to do from the beginning. In this scheme, the Holy Spirit regenerates and morally renews sinners who repent of their sins and exercise faith and obedience. So again, Christian doctrine gives us reason not only to think that God could enable us to achieve a perfected relationship of love with himself and our fellow creatures, but that he has actually done so. Indeed, it gives us good reason to believe that God has given us more than merely a reasonable chance to accept this relationship. He has given us every opportunity to do so.

Since we have a reasonable chance to achieve this relationship, if God exists, to say the least, it is quite reasonable to believe in it, as premise 9 states. And this brings us all the way to our conclusion that it is in fact reasonable to believe in heaven.

Given the limitations of space, all I have been able to do is sketch the reasons why we can rationally take each of the premises of this argument as true. While some of the premises seem obviously true to me, others are less so, and they would remain more controversial even if we had more space to defend them at length. All I claim is that it is reasonable to believe all of the premises are true, and accordingly to take the conclusion of the argument as true.

■ 2. OBJECTIONS TO HEAVEN

Now I want to turn to consider some of Parsons' objections to heaven. One of his objections is most relevant to my argument above and, indeed, could be taken as a challenge to premise 3 of my argument. Parsons addresses this objection to Christians who argue that atheism makes our lives meaningless. If we are mortal, and our lives are of a finite duration, indeed, if they are but an infinitesimal moment in comparison to the physical universe, and we are fated to die and pass into oblivion, does this not threaten our lives with a sense of absurdity? Parsons protests that such a claim is not only arrogant, but also question begging in its assumption that a meaningful life must be everlasting. He insists that his own life is rich with meaning, and offers the following as the message we should draw from our mortality:

> You have a limited number of days, hours, and minutes. Therefore you should strive to fill each of those days, hours, and minutes with meaning. You should strive to fill them with learning and gaining wisdom, with compassion for the less fortunate, with love for friends and family, with doing a job well, with fighting against evil and obscurantism, and yes, with enjoying sex, TV, pizza and ballgames.[3]

Now I would hardly want to claim that Parsons's life is meaningless, and indeed, I am a fan of everything on his meaning-making list. All the activities and pursuits he recommends are very worthwhile and persons who take his advice will likely find both meaning and joy in their lives, especially when their teams win ballgames and the pizza is hot.

But I will go on to insist that while such a life might well be rich with meaning in many ways, it will not be as meaningful as a life of perfect happiness as I have argued for. There is no doubt that having only a short amount of time to live would charge our lives with a sense of the enormous value of every moment and encourage us to make the most of every one of them. However, it is hard to buy the claim that the shadow of death and oblivion do not undermine the happiness of such a life and make it less meaningful than it would be if that shadow could be lifted. Parsons seems to think not, and alleges that it is monumental egotism to think our lives should survive the death that will overtake the rest of the cosmos. He writes: "Surely there is something monstrously egocentric in thinking that my life is of such transcendent significance that I should be an exception to cosmic law—that my ego should survive when planets, stars, and galaxies are no more."[4]

Well, as Pascal pointed out long ago, our very greatness consists, ironically, of the fact that we are "thinking reeds" who are aware of our mortality. "But even if the universe were to crush him, man would still be nobler than his slayer, because he knows that he is dying and the advantage the universe has over him. The universe knows nothing of this."[5] And this knowledge is often accompanied by a sense of poignancy, a profound sense of loss, again, of which the universe knows nothing. Our sense of poignancy is not simply a matter of ego, but is the result of our very mental and emotional powers, of our very capacity to conceive of transcendent meaning, to imagine perfect happiness and to aspire to it.

To be aware of finitude, to find joy and meaning in life, and yet to profess to be indifferent to our finitude and the oblivion that awaits us if there is no transcendent meaning is an odd position to try to maintain. Think about the things that make Parsons' life rich in meaning. Is it not the case that the more he enjoys the things he does, and finds meaning in them, the more he must feel a deep sense of regret and loss at the thought of losing them forever? Would it not strike one as odd to hear someone say, "I dearly love my friends and family, and the satisfaction of doing a job well, and my roadster, and a great basketball game (one my team wins) and oh yes, let's not forget, great sex. But I'm totally cool with the fact that it's soon coming to a screeching halt, and I will not get to see how my grandchildren's lives turn out, and will not live to see whether my team ever overtakes UCLA in the total number of NCAA championships, and will never again drive my roadster on winding country roads at sunset with 'Jumpin' Jack Flash' playing on the radio, and never again know the intense joy of looking into the eyes of my lover."

This is not to deny that one could end his life with a sense of gratitude for such wonderful gifts, even with the recognition that he will never enjoy them again. But unless one simply became bored with such good things, and they lost their zest, the point remains that the more one takes joy and finds meaning in such things, the more he must regret losing such experiences forever. Surely if one continued to take pleasure in such things, he would prefer that they continue, and if possible, that he could continue to enjoy life as rich and meaningful.

On the Christian account, of course, that is exactly what will happen. The good things of this life do not represent the height of our joy and satisfaction, which must inevitably diminish and decline as time rolls on. Rather, they are intimations of a perfect happiness that we can only dimly perceive and hope for in this life. It cannot rationally be denied that this is an outcome greatly to be preferred and heartily to be hoped for if it is reasonable to do so.[6]

3. THE REASONS WHY HELL EXISTS

But let us turn now to consider whether it is reasonable to believe in hell. Hell is not a fundamental reality like heaven is, and its existence depends on the prior existence of heaven, just as evil depends on good for its existence. That is, evil things are not original realities like good things. Rather, evil things are always good things that have been twisted and distorted, and thereby made evil.

Recall that the essence of heaven is a perfectly loving relationship with God and other persons, along with all that that entails. It is the very nature of this good that raises the possibility of hell. Critics often contend that the idea of hell is incompatible with the belief that God is both perfectly powerful as well as perfectly loving. For such a God would want to save everyone since he is perfectly loving, and moreover, he could surely do so if he is perfectly powerful. However, what this argument fails to come to terms with is the hard reality that love cannot be coerced or manipulated or demanded or programmed as a matter of power. Rather, it must be elicited and given by one person to another as a freely offered gift, indeed, the most precious gift that can be given. This is true not only of human relationships, but also of our relationship with God.

And this is why it is reasonable to believe in hell. Since we are free beings, we may choose not to love and trust God, and thereby reject the happiness of heaven, and choose instead the misery of hell. To so choose is to reject the relationships for which we were created, the relationships that are essential for our true fulfillment and satisfaction. Keeping this in mind can help us answer Parsons' central objections to hell.

One of his objections is that the very idea of anyone choosing hell is far fetched to say the least. So it is not enough to make sense of hell to insist that it is freely chosen by those who go there. The glaring question this raises is why anyone would make such a counterintuitive and self-destructive choice. As Parsons puts it, "anyone who consciously chooses eternal punishment over eternal joy would have to be insane, and lunatics clearly need treatment, not punishment."[7]

Now it is worth noting that Parsons' basic point here is one that is also advanced by some Christian philosophers. In particular, this claim has been advanced with considerable force by Thomas Talbott, who argues that there is no intelligible motive for choosing eternal misery, so the doctrine of eternal hell is deeply incoherent at the end of the day. The misery of hell will eventually break the resistance of all sinners, and all will come finally to see that it is in their best interest to repent and return to God.

Talbott and I have debated these issues at some length, and I cannot begin to engage the issues involved in the space I have here. However, I want to argue briefly that we can make at least some sense of the idea of choosing eternal misery, difficult as that notion admittedly is. A crucial issue here is how the misery of hell is conceived. If hell is thought to involve intense physical pain, as a number of traditional theologians have maintained, then it is indeed inconceivable that anyone could choose indefinitely to remain in such misery. And indeed, Talbott sometimes talks as if hell involves such intense pain, and his case that there is no intelligible motive for choosing eternal hell is most convincing when he construes the misery of hell in these terms.[8]

However, not all theologians, including classical theologians, have interpreted the misery of hell in this fashion. An alternative picture of the misery of hell is that it is the unhappiness that naturally and inevitably results when we isolate ourselves from God and other persons, and thereby reject the love and joy for which we were created. What this shows is that we seldom, if ever, deliberately and directly choose misery, in the fashion Parsons describes. Rather, the choice of misery, like many other important choices, is typically made more indirectly. The same is true of happiness. The person who goes about trying to find happiness will often miss it. We choose happiness by choosing other things, like loving people, and doing meaningful work, and so on. In a similar way, misery is chosen by way of other decisions we make. Having made those decisions, we then perpetuate our misery by refusing to make the choices that could correct things or rectify the matter.

C. S. Lewis has famously summed up this notion with his contention that the doors of hell are locked on the inside, in contrast to the popular picture that sinners are forcibly detained there against their will. He made this point in, among other places, describing Satan's followers in Milton's *Paradise Lost*. There, he explicates the predicament of these fiends by comparing them to more mundane cases of evil that human readers can readily recognize.

> That is, each of them is like a man who has just sold his country or his friend and now knows himself to be a pariah, or like a man who has by some intolerable action of his own just quarreled irrevocably with the woman he loves. For human beings there is often an escape from this Hell, but there is never more than one—the way of humiliation, Repentance, and (where possible) restitution.[9]

This passage gives us insight into the mechanism whereby the doors of hell come to be locked on the inside. The way out is a painful one that requires humility, repentance, and restitution. So a person in this situation faces a dilemma. On the one hand, it is painful to remain in the hell of guilt and fractured relationships, but on the other hand, the alternative of rectifying and repairing things is also unpleasant, to say the least. Given this reality, it is understandable that some people may choose to remain in Hell rather than embrace the pain that will allow them to escape.

This also answers another of Parsons' objections to the doctrine of hell, namely, that the punishment of hell is disproportionate, and therefore incompatible with the claim that God is perfectly just. He writes: "It is God who decides that unrepentant sinfulness must bear the consequences of eternal pain. The obvious objection is that finite and temporal sin, no matter how gross, do not merit infinite and eternal punishment, and so hell contradicts divine justice."[10] This objection is misguided if hell is sustained by an ongoing decision to reject God and his love. It is not the case that the misery of hell is eternal simply because God visits eternal punishment on finite sin. Rather, hell goes on as long as sinners reject the love and grace of God and persist in keeping him locked out of their lives.

Still, the question remains why anyone would persist in such a choice, especially forever. Here again, I think we can get some insight into this phenomenon by considering the downward spiral and ever tightening grip evil can get on our hearts when we refuse to repent and rectify things. The longer this goes on, the more invested we become in justifying ourselves, and the more difficult it is acknowledge our sin and to make it right. Indeed, we can even come to a point where we take a certain satisfaction in our self-righteousness, a certain perverse pleasure in our resentment. Hell has its pleasures, tawdry imitations of the real thing though they are, and these "pleasures" go a long way in explaining why its doors may be locked forever.[11]

Parsons' critique of hell takes little or no account of the versions of the doctrine that emphasize the intrinsic connection between the choice to reject our true happiness and the misery that naturally results from this. As he sees it, the threat of hell is a form of intellectual terrorism. It is "Christianity's campaign of psychological warfare against the human mind."[12] In contrast to this, he urges that we go back to Aristotle, who made the case that there is an inherent relationship between virtue and happiness. Parsons writes:

> By living virtuously we sustain those vital social relations—friendship, family, community—without which life is solitary, poor, nasty, brutish, and short. Vice leads to misery. Scrooge and the Prodigal Son were made miserable by their vices.[13]

With this I fully agree, and it resonates completely with the account of heaven and hell that I defend. But again, I would insist that our highest and most vital relation is a relationship with God. This relationship is necessary, moreover, to empower us to be fully virtuous, and thereby to experience perfectly loving relationships with our fellow human beings, as well as God.

The prodigal son indeed chose his own misery by leaving his father and his family behind in the pursuit of selfish pleasure. Happily, as the story unfolds, we learn that he recognized this and returned to his father and his true happiness. That is an image of heaven. But it is conceivable that he may have been unwilling to humble himself before his father and might have remained in his misery and allowed his resentment to grow to the point that he loathed the very idea of returning home. Unfortunately that scenario is not at all hard to imagine or believe.

■ NOTES

1. Keith Parsons, "Seven Common Misconceptions About Atheism," 1998, http://www.infidels.org/library/modern/keith_parsons/misconceptions.html#motive.
2. Edward O. Wilson, "The Biological Basis of Morality," *Atlantic Monthly* (April 1998): 70.
3. Parsons, "Seven Common Misconceptions About Atheism."
4. Parsons, "Seven Common Misconceptions About Atheism."
5. Blaise Pascal, *Pensees*, trans. A. J. Krailsheimer (London: Penguin, 1966), no. 200.

6. For a more detailed argument, see Jerry L. Walls, *Heaven: The Logic of Eternal Joy* (New York: Oxford University Press, 2002), 161–200.

7. Keith Parsons, *Why I Am Not a Christian*, 2000, http://www.infidels.org/library/modern/keith_parsons/whynotchristian.html. The quotes from this document are from chap. 2: "Kreeft and Tacelli on Hell." Parsons is critiquing their defense of hell in their *Handbook of Christian Apologetics* (Downers Grove, IL: InterVarsity Press, 1994).

8. Talbott is not always consistent on this point. See our exchange in *Religious Studies* 40 (2004): 203–227. For another exchange, see *Universal Salvation: The Current Debate*, ed. Robin A. Parry and Christopher Partridge (Grand Rapids, MI: Eerdmans, 2003). See also Jerry L. Walls, *Hell: The Logic of Damnation* (Notre Dame, IN: University of Notre Dame Press, 1992), 113–138.

9. C. S. Lewis, *A Preface to Paradise Lost* (Oxford: Oxford University Press, 1942), 104–105. Lewis also made this point in *The Problem of Pain* (San Francisco: Harper, 2001), 130. He also depicts this with powerful psychological realism in his theological fantasy *The Great Divorce* (San Francisco: Harper, 2001).

10. Parsons, "Kreeft and Tacelli on Hell."

11. See C. S. Lewis, *The Great Divorce*, 25–31, 117–133.

12. Parsons, "Kreeft and Tacelli on Hell."

13. Parsons, "Seven Misconceptions About Atheism."

▦ **FOR FURTHER READING**

Buenting, J., ed. *The Problem of Hell: A Philosophical Anthology.* Burlington, VT: Ashgate, 2010.

Kvanvig, J. L. *The Problem of Hell.* New York: Oxford University Press, 1993.

Russell, J. B. *Paradise Mislaid: How We Lost Heaven and How We Can Regain It.* New York: Oxford University Press, 2006.

40 Heaven and Hell

■ KEITH PARSONS

■ 1. AN ABSURD DOCTRINE

It is not reasonable to believe the Christian doctrines of heaven and hell. Indeed, the traditional Christian doctrine of the afterlife is egregiously irrational as my friend and atheist gadfly Eddie Tabash has often demonstrated in his debates with religious philosophers and apologists. Eddie notes that according to traditional Christian doctrine Hitler would have been forgiven had he sincerely repented and earnestly sought salvation through Christ. On the other hand, Eddie's mother, an Auschwitz survivor who died a pious Jew, has gone to hell. No debater has ever successfully challenged Eddie's assertion that these are actual consequences of traditional Christian doctrine; they truly seem to be. Traditional Christian doctrine, whether Protestant, Catholic, or Orthodox, holds that all genuinely penitent believers will be forgiven and, eventually at least, be admitted into heaven. Such doctrines equally emphasize that those who knowingly and willfully reject essential Christian beliefs are destined for hell. Those Jews and Muslims who have heard the true Christian message, yet who intentionally reject that message and choose to remain faithful to their own convictions, are thereby condemned to hell. Any doctrine that clearly and undeniably has such a blatantly absurd consequence is itself blatantly absurd and so not a rational belief for anybody.[1]

Let's put the points of the above paragraph somewhat more precisely and clearly. A Christian creed is a formal and systematic statement of the doctrines of an ecclesiastical body (e.g., the Roman Catholic Church, the Southern Baptist Convention, etc.). These doctrines are the ecclesiastical body's official and definitive beliefs on every point of essential interest to the Christian faith. For instance, there will be a doctrine of the sacraments, a doctrine of atonement, a doctrine of the Trinity, and so on. For the sake of argument, I shall assume that each doctrine is expressed as a coherent body of propositions. If the propositions expressing a doctrine clearly entail a blatantly absurd consequence, then the doctrine itself must be regarded as blatantly absurd. Further, every traditional Christian creed asserts or at least assumes a doctrine of the afterlife. For instance, the Apostles' Creed speaks of "life everlasting" and Christ's descent into hell. Traditional Christian doctrines of the afterlife specify two things: (1) the nature of the afterlife—heaven, hell, purgatory, etc.—and (2) the ultimate fate of humans, that is, who goes to which of the postmortem abodes. My charge is that the doctrines of the afterlife expressed in the

traditional, historical Christian creeds clearly have the blatantly absurd consequence I have alleged, and therefore these doctrines are blatantly absurd and so
not rational beliefs for anybody.[2]

Here I will assume that "traditional" Christian doctrine endorses the following three theses about the afterlife:

1. ALL sincerely repentant believers, even if they are as bad as Hitler, who
   avail themselves of God's saving grace through Christ (perhaps by receiving the prescribed sacraments, doing the required penance, etc.) will be
   saved and (eventually, at least) be admitted into heaven.
2. ONLY those who fully accept certain essential Christian beliefs (e.g., that
   Christ was God incarnate, that he died to atone for our sins) will be saved
   and join the elect in heaven.
3. Salvation is attainable only in this life; there will be no "second chances"
   for salvation after death. Therefore those who die in a state of grace ultimately go to heaven and those who do not go to hell (we examine the idea
   of a "second chance" later on).

I do not have space here to justify from the original documents my claim that the
historic Catholic, Orthodox, and Protestant creeds would indeed endorse these
three propositions. I can only adumbrate a justification. Consider the following
fragments from the Athanasian Creed:[3]

> Whosoever will be saved, before all things it is necessary that he hold the Catholic
> Faith. Which Faith except every one do keep whole and undefiled; without doubt he
> shall perish everlastingly...
>
> Furthermore it is necessary to everlasting salvation; that he also believe faithfully
> the Incarnation of our Lord Jesus Christ...

These, at least, support thesis 2. More generally, it seems that traditional
Christianity must support thesis 2. After all, by choosing to adhere to their
distinctive beliefs, where those beliefs contradict Christian claims, Jews and
Muslims consciously and freely reject core Christian doctrines. If we say that
such unbelievers may nonetheless be saved, then we must blatantly contradict
such verses as John 14:6 and Acts 4:12 that insist there is no salvation by any
other name than Christ's and that no one comes to the Father except through
the Son. If, indeed, salvation is possible for Jews and Muslims (and in that case
how do we avoid opening heaven to Buddhists, Hindus, pagans, and atheists
also?), then the uniqueness, finality, supremacy, and authority of the Christian
revelation seem to be set aside. Christianity becomes just one path among
many. Some Christian pluralists such as John Hick are quite willing to accept
this consequence,[4] but the opening lines of the Athanasian Creed, quoted above,
express the orthodox view that you have to have Christian beliefs to be saved
(and you had better get them right).

As for thesis 1, consider what it would mean if some sinners were so vile that they could not be saved. This would entail that the saving power of grace is limited and that Christ's sacrifice on the cross was not really sufficient for the atonement of all sinners or the remission of all sins. Clearly this is unacceptable to any traditional Christian view. Finally, with respect to thesis 3, any doctrine of a "second chance" would undercut the traditional emphasis on the supreme importance of the decisions, choices, and commitments that we make in this life. It is hard to see how the possibility of postmortem salvation could be maintained without promoting some degree of insouciance or procrastination on the part of unbelievers.

The upshot seems to be that by the traditional Christian creeds it follows that Hitler could have been saved but not a Holocaust survivor who, by choice, dies an earnest and faithful adherent of Judaism. Thus the absurd consequence does follow, demonstrating the absurdity of the traditional Christian doctrine of the afterlife, and so establishing the conclusion of this chapter.

At this point it would be nice to simply write "Q.E.D." at the bottom and end the chapter, but, of course, this cannot be done. Christian apologists have labored with such tough issues for nearly two millennia and have come up with various defenses of the traditional doctrines, and some of these need to be examined. First, though, I would like to state what exactly I find most offensive and unacceptable about the traditional Christian doctrine of the afterlife and why I object to it.

The most obvious problems with the Christian view of the afterlife concern the doctrine of an eternal, punitive hell. Let's begin by being clear on one point: though many recent Christian writers have attempted to mitigate the horrors of the traditional doctrine of hell, perhaps by cooling its fires and reinterpreting hell more as a state of spiritual alienation rather than of literal physical torment, the traditional creeds still affirm the reality, eternity, and punitive nature of hell. For instance, the Greek Orthodox catechism affirms that after the final judgment:

> The condition of each individual will no more be changed, but those, who have gone into Paradise will live in Heaven eternally happy, and those who have gone into Punishment will live in Hades eternally unhappy.[5]

The Roman Catholic catechism says the following:

> The teaching of the Church affirms the existence of hell and its eternity. Immediately after death the souls of those who die in a state of mortal sin descend into hell, where they suffer the punishments of hell, "eternal fire." The chief punishment of hell is eternal separation from God, in whom alone man can possess the life and happiness for which he was created and for which he longs.[6]

The Southern Baptist Convention adopted the following on May 9, 1963, as part of a statement of Baptist Faith and Message:[7]

> God, in His own time and in His own way, will bring the world to its appropriate end. According to His promise, Jesus Christ will return personally and visibly in glory to

the earth; the dead will he raised; and Christ will judge all men in righteousness. The unrighteous will be consigned to Hell, the place of everlasting punishment.

So, who goes to heaven and who goes to hell? Different churches and denominations give somewhat different answers to these questions (a quite disturbing thought in itself), but there is one thing that all traditional creeds agree upon: certain beliefs are necessary for salvation. With certain possible exceptions (e.g., small children, the insane, the mentally impaired, and those who have never had the opportunity to hear the Christian message), those who lack certain essential beliefs cannot be saved. It follows that, even if your life is otherwise blameless, if you do not give assent to certain propositions, you are doomed to hell.[8] Unbelief per se is sufficient for damnation. In other words, hell is the penalty for disagreeing with Christians.

This, to my mind, is the most unreasonable thing about the Christian view of the afterlife, what I call the "doxastic requirement" (DR). Again, all traditional Christian creeds impose a DR, (i.e., certain beliefs are regarded as necessary for salvation). The only possible rationale for imposing a DR for salvation is that willful unbelief is morally culpable. When is it wrong to lack a belief—wrong enough to deserve eternal damnation? The only conceivable answer is that the belief is in some sense overwhelmingly obvious, so that rejection of the belief is truly perverse, a monstrously irrational defiance of what one knows to be true. For St. Paul, this is precisely what unbelief is. St. Paul famously asserts (Romans 1:20) that unbelievers are "without excuse" because God's existence is "manifest" to unbelievers yet they perversely persist in unbelief:

> Because that which may be known of God is manifest in them; for God hath shown it unto them. For the invisible things of him from the creation of the world are clearly seen, being understood by the things that are made, even his eternal power and Godhead; so that they [unbelievers] are without excuse (Romans 1:19–20).

So those who willfully reject belief are culpable because, though God has shown his existence to them, and even "his eternal power and Godhead," yet they sinfully refuse to acknowledge him. By saying that "that which may be known of God" is "manifest in them," I take Paul to mean "obvious to them." Paul even says that unbelievers know God yet fail to honor him:

> Because that, when they knew God, they glorified him not as God, neither were thankful, but became vain in their imaginations, and their foolish heart was darkened (Romans 1:21).

The problem is that any claim of obviousness inevitably comes, explicitly or implicitly, with a "to me" qualifier. It may be obvious to Paul, but it is not to me or billions of other people. Now Paul would no doubt regard our failure to see the purportedly obvious truths about God and his nature as evidence of how far into reprobation we had sunk. What do you say to someone who thinks that you are a reprobate because you do not find obvious what he does? Several rude responses suggest themselves, but I'll just politely say: "Nonsense!" The very fact that this chapter is part of a "debate" book belies Paul's claim. If God's reality and nature were as obvious as Paul claims, the whole enterprise of religious apologetics, and, indeed, of much of the philosophy of religion, would be laughably pointless. For instance, it would be highly eccentric, to say the least, to devote hundreds of hours of scholarly lucubration to devising recondite proofs for God's existence when it is already patently obvious to everyone. As for those unbelievers who persist in denying the obvious, they would seem much more in need of therapy than argument. Like flat-earthers, they would surely be impervious to logic, evidence, and argument.

On the other hand, if Christians are allowed to assert claims of obviousness, then I am too: contrary to Paul's assertion, it is obvious that the existence of God is not obvious, and further, that it is obvious there are many reasonable people who rationally and nonculpably reject some or all of Christian doctrine. Among these latter are many faithful but open-minded Jews and Muslims, who, having heard the Christian message, do not find it moving, appealing, or even sensible, and so remain devoted to their faith. Can you blame them? Doesn't it appear very likely that their beliefs seem as true to Muslims or Jews as your deepest beliefs seem to you?

Also, among the reasonable infidels are many millions of atheists and agnostics who have heard the Word and find it simply unbelievable. Let me clarify a point here, and I hope the reader will excuse the self-reference: though we have so far spoken of beliefs as chosen, it is not really the case that I *choose* not to believe the Christian message. I *cannot* believe it. Speaking personally (and apologizing in advance for the offense these comments will unavoidably give), I find the claims of Christianity to be simply fantastic, no more believable than Grimm's fairytales, Greek mythology, or Tolkien's stories of Middle Earth. I cannot, by an act of will, make myself believe that Frodo, a Hobbit of the Shire, saved us from the Dark Lord Sauron by destroying the evil ring. Neither, by an act of will, can I believe that Jesus of Nazareth, an itinerant Jewish preacher from Galilee, saved us from Satan by being nailed to a cross. To me, the one seems just as fictitious as the other. Indeed, I think it is hard for a devoted Christian—one who lives, and moves, and has his being in the faith—to even imagine how utterly incredible the Christian message can sound to an outsider.

■ 2. DEFENDERS OF HELL

Let's now turn to some of hell's defenders. The view of hell defended by *The Catholic Encyclopedia* is sternly old-fashioned, defending a sort of hell Dante would have recognized.[9] I begin by looking at some of the arguments there.

I then turn to a defense of a version of the DR by Jerry L. Walls. I end by reflecting that since the doctrine of hell is so odious, and since the purported justifications for the doctrine are so transparently thin, there must be a very strong motive behind Christianity's historic emphasis upon eternal punishment. That motivation is not hard to spot.

> Sin is an offence against the infinite authority of God, and the sinner is in some way aware of this, though but imperfectly. Accordingly there is in sin an approximation to infinite malice which deserves an eternal punishment.[10]

Response: What is "infinite malice?" Is it a conscious intention to offend the infinite authority of God? If so, then it follows that the belief that God exists is a necessary condition for being guilty of infinite malice. Apparently, on this definition, atheists cannot sin. On the other hand, it hardly seems just to deem one guilty of infinite malice when that person has no awareness that in sinning he is defying God's authority. It must be, therefore, that everyone, even the professed atheist, is to some degree aware that he is offending the infinite authority of God when he commits a sin. We are right back with St. Paul and the claim that everybody is aware of God's existence and nature, so that we are without excuse in offending him. There is no way to argue rationally with such an assertion, so I will once again dismiss it.

> The fear of hell does really deter many from sin; and thus, in as far as it is threatened by God, eternal punishment also serves for the reform of morals. But if God threatens man with the pains of hell, He must also carry out His threat if man does not heed it by avoiding sin.[11]

Response: Does the fear of hell deter people from sin? Bertrand Russell notes that Christianity's policy of "sin now, repent later" undercuts the deterrent effect:

> [Emperor of the Holy Roman Empire] Charles V, after spending the day conquering a Protestant city, felt that he had earned a little relaxation; he sent his servants out to find a virgin, and they found one of seventeen. Presumably she got syphilis, and the emperor got absolution. This is the system that is supposed to preserve men from sin.[12]

Now, some people do live in fear of hell, but it mainly seems to deter them from entertaining honest doubts (more on this below).

> Nor can it be said: the wicked will be punished, but not by any positive infliction: for either death will be the end of their existence, or, forfeiting the rich reward of the good, they will enjoy some lesser degree of happiness. These are arbitrary and vain subterfuges, unsupported by any sound reason; positive punishment is the natural recompense for sin.[13]

Response: This is the nub of the matter. The whole doctrine of hell turns on the idea that justice is retribution, that is, that it is right that evildoers be made to suffer purely because they deserve to suffer and not because the suffering serves some utilitarian purpose such as deterrence or reform.

Admittedly it was viscerally satisfying to see the top Enron executives do the "perp walk" in handcuffs, knowing that their greed and lies had destroyed many lives and livelihoods. Indeed, we need not deny that some degree of retribution might be justifiable. One of our deepest ethical intuitions is that those who do good things deserve reward and those who do bad things deserve punishment. Surely it is good that Adolf Eichmann, responsible for facilitating Hitler's program of genocide, was captured, tried, and punished, even if he never repented and even if his punishment deterred no other crimes.

On the other hand, consider that in some ways we rightly feel ourselves more enlightened than our forebears of a few centuries ago. At one time, in the most "civilized" societies, criminals were roasted over slow fires, broken on the wheel, torn apart with red-hot pincers, drawn and quartered, disemboweled, crucified, impaled, flayed, starved, thrown to wild animals, etc. Now, at least in liberal democracies, even the worst of criminals—say someone who kidnaps, tortures, rapes, and murders a small child—is spared such treatment. Why? If the doctrine of hell is right, and it is just that evildoers be subjected to atrocious torture for eternity, why should we have the least scruple about inflicting malefactors with far less severe pains? Why not go back to flaying alive, boiling in oil, etc.? I am sure that torturers have often justified their practice by noting that God does much worse. Cruel dogmas make cruel people.[14]

The fact of the matter is that we now regard some punishments as too horrendous to be inflicted upon criminals, however heinous their offense or however despicable they are. Enjoying seeing the Enron rascals do the "perp walk" is excusable; wanting to see them broken on the wheel (i.e., beaten to death with sledgehammers) is not—even if it is your 401k they destroyed. Shouldn't we expect God to have made at least as much moral progress since the Middle Ages as we think we have? The doctrine of retribution in its pure form is the old *lex talionis*, the law of an eye for an eye and a tooth for a tooth. The *lex talionis* no longer enjoys the respect it once did.[15] Even in Texas, where executions are about as common as 100 degree days in Dallas, we do not inflict on murderers the same treatment they inflict on their victims. Ax murderers are not hacked to death, but are executed by lethal injection, which is supposed to be painless. Even in Texas we are learning to distinguish justice from payback. Yet the traditional beliefs about hell retain the *lex talionis* in its full fury: "infinite malice" demands infinite retaliation. The doctrine of hell makes Texans appear more morally advanced than the God they worship.

■ 3. WHAT ABOUT A SECOND CHANCE?

But what about the DR, the requirement that certain things must be believed in order to be saved? Jerry L. Walls, my opposite number in this debate, addresses precisely the question of who is saved in his book *Heaven: The Logic of Eternal Joy*. He rejects "particularism," the view that those who die without explicit faith in Christ are lost forever.[16] Faith in Christ obviously entails certain beliefs, such as that Christ was God the Son incarnate, that he was resurrected, and that he died for our sins, and a number of other propositions. Particularists therefore hold that those who die without believing certain things are doomed to hell (and, again, particularists disturbingly differ over precisely which things must be believed). Walls also rejects the kind of pluralism espoused by John Hick in such works as *An Interpretation of Religion*. Hick holds that transcendent reality, what he calls The Real, cannot be adequately conceptualized within any religious tradition, so no such creed can claim the one "True Religion," and that it is hubris for any one religion to claim that adherence to its creed is necessary for salvation.

Walls plausibly objects to particularism on the grounds that a wise and loving God will also be a fair one, and will offer his grace equally to all, so that no accident of birth or circumstance will prevent some from having the same chance at salvation that others have. Yet, says Walls, it clearly is the case that in this life some persons have less access to the "truth about Christ" than others.[17] Walls also understandably objects that, by demanding that all religions surrender their claims of superiority or exclusivity, Hick's pluralism removes so much from traditional Christian doctrine—for example, the incarnation, the resurrection, the Trinity, atonement—that the remnant is hardly recognizable as Christianity.[18] Walls therefore presents a middle path between these two extremes, which he calls "inclusivism."

Walls's inclusivism retains the traditional Christian insistence on the truth of Christian doctrine vis-à-vis competing claims of other religions:

> The inclusivist readily admits that there are real contradictions between essential Christian doctrine and the fundamental commitments of other religions. Where this is the case, moreover, the inclusivist believes the Christian claim is true in the realist sense and rejects what is incompatible with it as false.[19]

Inclusivists oppose pluralists by holding that salvation is only through Christ, but oppose the particularist claim that salvation must come by an explicit commitment to Christ in this life.[20] How, then, could nonbelievers be saved? Walls thinks it is most likely that those who have not had a full and fair chance to learn the "truth about Christ" in this life will be given a second chance by "eschatological evangelism."[21] That is, he thinks it most plausible that after death those who die without having had the same chance at salvation as others will be given a second opportunity:

> One way to describe the optimal grace that I have argued God would give all persons is in terms of a leveling of the epistemic playing field. This would involve God giving all persons time and opportunity to see through the blind spots they may have from

social, political, cultural, or psychological factors. Then the truth would be seen with a clarity that would be optimal to elicit a positive response from free creatures.[22]

In short, those who now see through a glass darkly will then see face to face.

Walls's suggestion is an attractive one. It intimates that perhaps people like Eddie's mother in fact have "blind spots" due to social, political, cultural, or psychological factors and will get a chance after death to learn the "truth about Christ" (what an Auschwitz survivor would think if she goes to heaven and meets Hitler there is another question). In fact, Walls's argument partially supports mine. I think it is fair to say that the traditional Christian view of the afterlife, which I have so far been criticizing in this chapter, has been largely particularist, and that inclusivism has been very much a minority view. For instance, the Roman Catholic catechism quoted earlier says that immediately after death, those who die in mortal sin go directly to punishment in hell (section 1035). There is no explicit mention of a postmortem "second chance" in any of the traditional creeds. So, insofar as particularism has been an aspect of the traditional Christian view, Walls's critique supports mine.

Still, the suggestion of "eschatological evangelism" raises far more questions than it answers. Indeed, without some sort of idea of what this postmortem proselytizing would be like, it is very hard to say whether it could do what Walls wants, that is, provide unbelieving souls with a full and fair hearing of the "truth" without abrogating their freedom to accept or reject the proffered salvation. If, after death, I found myself in the presence of angelic beings who earnestly appealed to me to accept Christian tenets (if this is the scenario Walls has in mind), I would immediately conclude (a) that the atheistic/naturalistic convictions I had maintained during my life were patently wrong, and (b) that I had better get with the program. Would I still have the freedom to reject the angelic message? Doesn't God have to maintain some degree of "hiddenness" so as not to abridge human freedom? I think I would be pretty overwhelmed in the imagined situation. If Walls thinks it would not be like this, we need to hear another scenario.

Other questions abound: If God could give us a full and fair understanding of the Gospel in the afterlife, why cannot he do it in this life? Why cannot everyone have the advantage, say, of the visual and tactile evidence given to the doubting Thomas? Why doesn't the fact that God does not give everyone equal grace in this life count against the claim that he will do so in the next life? Is the God of the Bible consistently merciful or fair? Isn't the whole point of the Book of Job that God is not fair—and who are we to question? What about the forty-two children that were mauled by she-bears in 2 Kings 2 because they mocked the prophet Elisha? Were they treated fairly? Were the infants of Amalek treated fairly when they were murdered on God's orders (1 Samuel 15:3)? What about all the innocent children, infants, and mentally impaired persons drowned in Noah's flood? It seems to me that an unbiased reading of the Bible does not indicate that fairness is one of God's salient traits. If God is fair after all, then will every unbeliever get a second chance? Why not? Surely almost every unbeliever could appeal to political, social, cultural, or psychological factors to account for his unbelief. Are "blind spots" therefore like excuses—everybody has one? On the other hand, if unbelievers think that they might get a second chance after death, will this not discourage them from taking Christian claims as seriously as they should, that is, will it not encourage some degree of apathy or procrastination?

Finally, Walls's view still entails that a clear-eyed, fully informed rejection of Christianity, either in this life or the next, cannot be morally excusable. Those who reject the "truth about Christ" in this life must do so because of culpable intransigence or because they are nonculpably afflicted with "blind spots" due to political, social, cultural, or psychological factors. On Walls's view there still can be no such thing as someone who fairly and fully, and without "blind spots," considers the claims of Christianity and reasonably denies them. Such open-eyed repudiation can only be due to "concupiscence and wickedness of heart."[23] Again, perhaps it is very hard for faithful Christians to appreciate the extent to which such a view strikes thoughtful unbelievers as astonishing arrogance.[24] To us it seems as offensive as accusations made by the "new atheists" like Sam Harris or Christopher Hitchens to the effect that Christians are all fools or knaves.

4. WHY HELL?

We, see, then, that the defenses of hell are extremely dubious or at least leave us with far more questions than we started with. When very smart people say very strange things, and when very nice people, who probably would not torture a fly, defend eternal punishment, something odd is going on. Why has the Christian church insisted on the doctrine of hell and demanded vast labors from its most articulate defenders in attempting, vainly, to justify the doctrine? The answer is not hard to spot. Hell is the ultimate *argumentum ad baculum*: Do what we say, indeed, think what we think, or suffer consequences too horrible to contemplate (the Orwellian idea that thoughts can and should be controlled was not an invention of twentieth-century totalitarianism, but a creation of the Christian church). What would the history of Christianity have been without the doctrine of hell? Claiming to be able to impose an unsurpassable sanction is the cleverest propaganda tool ever devised. Nothing else could so effectively squelch doubt and dissent. Indeed, there are many persons today who confess that they cannot entertain honest doubts without catching a whiff of brimstone.[25]

In their *Handbook of Christian Apologetics*, Peter Kreeft and Ronald K. Tacelli demand that we accept Christianity and the doctrine of an eternal punitive hell, or reject hell and Christianity too.[26] I end by recommending rejection of the doctrine of hell as irrational and morally opprobrious. If this entails the rejection of Christianity as well, so be it.

■ NOTES

1. Somebody will inevitably ask, "Well, what's so absurd about Hitler going to heaven and his pious Jewish victims going to hell?" The only possible answer is the one the wise philosopher Louis "Satchmo" Armstrong gave when asked to explain what jazz is: "Man, if you gotta ask, you ain't never gonna know."

2. Actually, the traditional doctrine of the afterlife is absurd in many ways. Naturally, some of the most notorious absurdities involve hell. One of the most odious ideas is that the saved in heaven will take pleasure in the torments of the damned. A selection of quotes from noted Christian leaders on this topic can be found via the Internet at http://www.tentmaker.org/Quotes/hell-fire.htm.

3. Athanasian Creed, http://www.ccel.org/creeds/athanasian.creed.html.

4. John Hick, *An Interpretation of Religion*, 2nd ed. (New Haven, CT: Yale University Press, 2004).

5. Greek Orthodox Catechism, http://www.bible.ca/cr-Orthodox.htm.

6. Roman Catholic Catechism, (section 1035, http://www.scborromeo.org/ccc/p1s1c2a3.htm#I

7. Baptist Faith and Message, 1963, http://www.baptiststart.com/print/1963_baptist_faith_message.html.

8. There is, of course, some disagreement among the churches concerning which beliefs are essential for salvation. For instance, I once heard a televised sermon by the late Reverend Jerry Falwell in which he pronounced authoritatively that anyone who accepts biological evolution, and thereby rejects the six-day creation spoken of in Genesis, is bound for hellfire. Pope John Paul II, on the other hand, said that evolution is "more than a theory," that is, it is a scientific fact. Clearly it cannot be essential to Catholic faith to deny evolution. So who is right? Are Catholics who, on the Pope's authority, freely accept the reality of evolution doomed to an eternity in hell?

9. *The Catholic Encyclopedia*, "Hell," http://www.newadvent.org/cathen/.

10. *The Catholic Encyclopedia*, 6.

11. *The Catholic Encyclopedia*, 6.

12. Bertrand Russell, "The Value of Free Thought," in *Bertrand Russell on God and Religion*, ed. A. Seckel (Amherst, NY: Prometheus, 1986), 245.

13. *The Catholic Encyclopedia*, 4.

14. As this was being written there was a story in the news about a 42-year-old Iranian woman who had been convicted of adultery and sentenced to be stoned to death. The rest of the world has reacted in shock and outrage. However, again, a defender of the traditional doctrine of hell would have to ask why the outrage. If adultery is a sin of sufficient magnitude to deserve eternal punishment in hell, and all traditional creeds hold that it is, then what is the objection if the civil authority punishes it by stoning, a punishment literally infinitely milder than eternal damnation?

15. Perhaps the wisest comment ever on the *lex talionis* was uttered by the impoverished milkman Tevye in *Fiddler on the Roof*. His response to the demand of an eye for an eye and a tooth for a tooth was "Yes, and at that rate the world will soon be blind and toothless."

16. Jerry L. Walls, *Heaven: The Logic of Eternal Joy* (Notre Dame, IN: Notre Dame University Press, 1992), 68.

17. Walls, *Heaven: The Logic of Eternal Joy*, 66.

18. Walls, *Heaven: The Logic of Eternal Joy*, 77.

19. Walls, *Heaven: The Logic of Eternal Joy*, 80.
20. Walls, *Heaven: The Logic of Eternal Joy*, 80.
21. Walls, *Heaven: The Logic of Eternal Joy*, 82.
22. Walls *Heaven: The Logic of Eternal Joy*, 87.
23. Walls, *Heaven: The Logic of Eternal Joy*, 87.
24. Unbelievers, after all, have recourse to a vast literature criticizing Christian claims. The Secular Web Library contains many historical and contemporary critiques. My *Why I am not a Christian* is available there. I think that I have the right to expect that my arguments there first be refuted by Professor Walls or any Christian who attributes unbelief to "concupiscence and wickedness of heart." An excellent recent anthology addressing the claims of Christian apologists is *The Christian Delusion*, ed. John Loftus (Amherst, NY: Prometheus, 2009). See also *The End of Christianity*, ed. John Loftus (Amherst, NY: Prometheus, 2011).
25. Indeed, there are many people who will attest to the terror and trauma the fear of hell has caused them. See http://www.tentmaker.org/articles/hell_terrorizes.htm.
26. Peter Kreeft and Ronald K. Tacelli, *Handbook of Christian Apologetics* (Downers Grove, IL: InterVarsity, 2004), 285.

▨ REFERENCES

The Athanasian Creed. http://www.ccel.org/creeds/athanasian.creed.html
Baptist Faith and Message, 1963:
http://www.baptiststart.com/print/1963_baptist_faith_message.html
The Catholic Encyclopedia. "Hell." http://www.newadvent.org/cathen/
The Greek Orthodox Creed: http://www.bible.ca/cr-Orthodox.htm
Hick, J. (2004) *An Interpretation of Religion*, 2nd Edition. New Haven: Yale University Press.
Kreeft, P. and Tacelli, R.K. (1994). *Handbook of Christian Apologetics*. Downer's Grove, IL: InterVarsity.
Roman Catholic Catechism: http://www.scborromeo.org/ccc/p1s1c2a3.htm#I
Russell, B. "The Value of Free Thought," in Seckel, A., ed. (1986). *Bertrand Russell on God and Religion*. Amherst, NY: Prometheus Books
Walls, J. L. (2002). *Heaven: The Logic of Eternal Joy*. Oxford: Oxford University Press.

▨ FOR FURTHER READING

Alighieri, D. *The Inferno*, translated by John Ciardi. New York: Signet Classic, 2001.
Bernstein, A. E. *The Formation of Hell: Death and Retribution in the Ancient and Early Christian Worlds*. Ithaca, NY: Cornell University Press, 1993.
Edwards, J. "Sinners in the Hands of an Angry God." http://www.apuritansmind.com/jona-thanedwards/JonathanEdwards-Sermons.htm.
Johnson, P. *A History of Christianity*. New York: Atheneum, 1976.
Walls, J. L. *Hell: The Logic of Damnation*. Notre Dame, IN: Notre Dame University Press, 1992.

■ INDEX

CPSIA information can be obtained
at www.ICGtesting.com
Printed in the USA
BVHW030512070121
596801BV00005B/23